October 15–19, 2012
Memphis, Tennessee, USA

**Association for
Computing Machinery**

Advancing Computing as a Science & Profession

SIGUCCS'12

ACM Proceedings of the

SIGUCCS Annual Conference

Sponsored by:
ACM SIGUCCS

Supported by:
*lynda.com, SchoolDude.com, Mozy, Emergent, Cherwell Software,
Computer Lab Solutions, TaskStream, HDI*

Association for Computing Machinery

Advancing Computing as a Science & Profession

The Association for Computing Machinery
2 Penn Plaza, Suite 701
New York, New York 10121-0701

Notice to Past Authors of ACM-Published Articles
ACM intends to create a complete electronic archive of all articles and/or other material previously published by ACM. If you have written a work that has been previously published by ACM in any journal or conference proceedings prior to 1978, or any SIG Newsletter at any time, and you do NOT want this work to appear in the ACM Digital Library, please inform permissions@acm.org, stating the title of the work, the author(s), and where and when published.

ISBN: 978-1-4503-1494-7 (Digital)

ISBN: 978-1-4503-1925-6 (Print)

Additional copies may be ordered prepaid from:

ACM Order Department
PO Box 30777
New York, NY 10087-0777, USA

Phone: 1-800-342-6626 (USA and Canada)
+1-212-626-0500 (Global)
Fax: +1-212-944-1318
E-mail: acmhelp@acm.org
Hours of Operation: 8:30 am – 4:30 pm ET

Printed in the USA

A Message from the SIGUCCS 2012 Conference Chair

With great pleasure I welcome you to the 40th annual ACM SIGUCCS 2012 Management Symposium and Service & Support Conference. The theme of this year's conference, "IT: All Shook Up," brings to mind myriad images. The very words in this two-part title form a contradiction in terms. On either side of the punctuation mark, we hear the contrast of hot-blooded mid-50's musical Americana with the sound of cold metallic gadgets transferring bits of virtual information. A long gaze from vinyl media to social media tells us just how far we've come in the last half-century. Our worlds are constantly being upended by changes - in educational practices, innovations, and budgetary pressures. We are indeed IT, all shook up.

Following this theme, it's hard to be in Memphis and not think about the rich musical history and the innovations that are centered in this diverse Mississippi river town. It's the home of jazz, blues, soul, and of big changes in the way we do business. Thus, it's a fine place for us to convene to talk about soul, innovations, and IT. As you share and commiserate with your colleagues, remember that YOU are the visionary leaders. You have made this happen. And like making music, remember that improvisation is important, and also that riffing with the happening sound may be the best kind of leadership.

Putting together the SIGUCCS 2012 Conference was a team effort. I want to extend special thanks to the SIGUCCS planning team, who worked very hard for more than a year to make this happen. Thanks to all the presenters, who are providing the rich content of this conference. In addition, we applaud the entire chorus of volunteers. Your orchestrated effort from June 2011 to now has brought this conference to life.

And thanks to you, the people of SIGUCCS. We hope that you will find this program interesting, inspiring, and thought-provoking, and that the conference will provide you with a valuable opportunity to share ideas with other professionals in university IT management and support. We hope you learn, make and renew friendships, enhance your careers, and enjoy.

Carol Rhodes
SIGUCCS 2012 General Chair

A Message from the SIGUCCS 2012 Service & Support Program Chairs

We are delighted to welcome you to the 40th annual ACM SIGUCCS 2012 Conference in the heart of "Blues City" Memphis, Tennessee. This magnificent city embodies the spirit of the conference theme, *IT: All Shook Up*.

The second annual combined conference brings together managers and support personnel who are enthused with keeping up with new technologies, procedures and insights. The sharing of information and exchange of ideas in Information Technology is a most valuable asset we have to enhance our educational institutions and careers. We welcome your participation!

We are thrilled with the variety of topics secured for this year's conference and appreciate each and every one of you for your contribution of time and willingness to share your expertise and experiences. We look forward to many lively and informed presentations over the next few days that will enhance your technical, leadership and client services skills. Our speakers and keynotes will undoubtedly shake up and inspire new thoughts and ideas for you to take home and implement in your ever-evolving dynamic world of IT.

A heartfelt, *Thank You, Thank You Very Much* to the keynotes, authors and presenters, track and session chairs, readers and reviewers who have worked so hard to make this conference happen. We are delighted to have worked along side a group of talented and dedicated conference committee members from various institutions across North America to help in the planning and organizing of the ACM SIGUCCS 2012 Conference. We encourage you to plan to present a paper at the upcoming conference or consider joining the organizing committee as you will experience growth both as an individual and as a member within the larger SIGUCCS community.

We sincerely hope that you find the program stimulating and encounter renewed insights and ideas at this conference, that you depart feeling motivated and energized, and that you return safely home with an abundance of new friends and fresh perspectives to share with your colleagues and those we serve to achieve the best use of technology.

Finally, when back home, remember to thank your bosses for allowing you to take part in SIGUCCS 2012. Enjoy your stay in Memphis!

Gordana Brouilette
SIGUCCS 2012 Service & Support Co-Chair

Cindy Stewart
SIGUCCS 2012 Service & Support Co-Chair

A Message from the SIGUCCS Chair

Welcome to the 2012 Annual ACM SIGUCCS Conference in Memphis Tennessee. On behalf of the SIGUCCS Executive Committee, I want to thank Carol Rhodes, Conference Chair, and her entire committee for their tireless work to shake us all up, and to keep us thinking and discussing the changes that are happening in higher education in general, and in IT organizations more specifically.

SIGUCCS, the Special Interest Group for University and College Computing Services, is one of ACM's 37 special interest groups. Our annual conference is one of the foremost professional development opportunities for IT professionals in higher education. Beyond the annual conference, SIGUCCS also offers webinars, an online LinkedIn community, a member newsletter and we are proud to announce at this conference a new mentoring opportunity. I encourage you all to maintain your SIGUCCS membership and take advantage of the year-round benefits of SIGUCCS!

My colleagues and I on the SIGUCCS Executive Committee, the group elected every three years to guide SIGUCCS' efforts, are continually exploring ways that we can help our membership to continue to grow in their profession. Please talk with any of us to give your ideas of how you'd like to see the SIGUCCS organization progress.

But what I love most about SIGUCCS are the people—peers, colleagues, friends and partners in crime, I have met them all during my years in SIGUCCS. SIGUCCS members are a passionate group who want to share their ideas, learn new skills and develop a community dedicated to supporting each other in our professional endeavors. Please continue to contribute your ideas and experience to the SIGUCCS listservs and consider becoming more involved by volunteering for a future SIGUCCS conference. We need you in order to keep SIGUCCS alive and well!

While you are in Memphis, surrounded by the beautiful noise from Beale Street, networking and learning, also remember to have some fun! I highly recommend the barbeque—it is delicious! And hopefully you will have a chance to make a pilgrimage to Graceland, home of the King. And when you go home, be sure to take some of the ideas that you learn in Memphis back to your institution to continue shaking things up.

Have a great conference!

Kelly Wainwright
Chair, SIGUCCS

A Message from the
SIGUCCS 2012 Management Symposium Chair

Welcome to Memphis, Tennessee, for the 40th Annual SIGUCCS Management Symposium. As many of you know, this is the second year of the combined SIGUCCS conference. The Management Symposium was typically held in the spring and the Service and Support conference in the fall. Last year's first combined conference (in San Diego) was a huge success and really set the bar high for future conference committees. This year, we promise you a great experience at both the Management Symposium and the Service and Support conference and feel confident you will come away with many new ideas, solid networking opportunities as well as an overall good time.

We have an excellent program in store for you. Sue Workman, Associate Vice President for Client Services and Support at Indiana University will open the Symposium (Monday) by discussing a topic that is a daily struggle for most of us – implementing change through the effective collaboration of groups within higher education. The opening keynote will transition into break out sessions that are made up of three tracks: Leadership, Partnerships and Professional Development; Resource Planning and Fiscal Management; and Technology Management. The break out sessions in the Management Symposium are designed to be "Facilitated Discussions" whereas the presenter will present an idea or topic and leave a significant amount of time for discussion with/among the audience. Similar to last year, on Tuesday, the program committee will be leading a Plenary session entitled "Current Topics Exchange" where attendees will have the opportunity to move from table to table (every 20 minutes) to discuss popular IT topics that have an impact on higher education. Each table will have a moderator that will guide you through a discussion with your peers about problems, successes and failures relating to the table topic. On Wednesday, the Management Symposium will transition to the Service and Support Conference with a Joint Plenary delivered by Jim Sevier from Convergence Readiness Incorporated.

I would like to extend a special thanks to the Management Symposium Program Committee: Cindy Dooling, Pima Community College, Jenn Stewart, Penn State University, and Tim Foley, Lehigh University, for their hard work and commitment to the development of an outstanding program. We feel the diversity of the topics; keynotes and BOFs as well as the networking opportunities available at the Management Symposium will interest and excite you. So plan on becoming engaged, involved and informed as you participate in the 40th Annual SIGUCCS Management Symposium.

Gale Fritsche
SIGUCCS 2012 Management Symposium Program Chair

Table of Contents

Session 4

Session 5

Session 6

Session 7

Session 8

Session 9

Session 10

Session 11

Author Index

2012 SIGUCCS Fall Conference Organization

General Chair: *Carol Rhodes (Indiana University, USA)*

Program Chairs: *Gordana Brouilette (University of Alberta, Canada)*
Gale Fritsche (Lehigh University, USA)
Cindy Stewart (University of Alberta, Canada)

Conference Liaison: *Parrish Nnambi (University of California San Diego, USA)*

Conference Treasurer: *Allan Chen (Menlo College, USA)*

Communication Awards Chair: *Trevor Murphy (Williams College, USA)*

Workshops Chair: *Beth Rugg (Ithaca College, USA)*

Conference Registrar: *Melissa Bauer (Baldwin Wallace College, USA)*

Volunteer Coordinator: *Beth Rugg (Ithaca College, USA)*

Social Networking Chair: *Laurie Fox (State University of New York Geneseo, USA)*

Publicity Coordinator: *Gail Rankin (Salem State, USA)*

First Timer's Chair: *Keniesha Etheridge (The Citadel, USA)*

Vendor Coordinator: *Scott Trimmer (Findlay University, USA)*

Webmaster: *Jim Yucha (Virginia Commonwealth University, USA)*

Publications Designer: *Jacquelynn Hongosh (Oberlin College & Conservatory, USA)*

Evaluations Chair: *Janice Tulloss (University of North Carolina, Greensboro, USA)*

Session Chair Coordinator: *Leila Shahbender (Princeton University, USA)*

Photography Chair: *Karl Owens (University of Oregon, USA)*

Birds of a Feather Coordinator: *David Weiss (Nazareth College, USA)*

Newsletter Chair: *Karen McRitchie (Grinnell College, USA)*

Local Arrangements Coordinators: *Ann Harbor (Memphis University, USA)*
Robert Jackson (Memphis University, USA)

Program Committee: **Track Chairs:**

Management Symposium
Cindy Dooling (Pima County Community College, USA)
Tim Foley (Lehigh University, USA)
Jennifer Stewart (Penn State University, USA)

Service & Support:
Vijay Anand (Southeast Missouri State University, USA)
Michael Cooper (West Virginia University, USA)
Laurie Fox State (University of New York Geneseo, USA)
Kelly Hughes (Lander University, USA)
Trevor Murphy (Williams College, USA)
Carol Sobczak (University of Maine, USA)
Jean Tagliamonte (Vassar College, USA)
Janice Tulloss (University of Northern Carolina at Greensboro, USA)

Additional reviewers: *Blake Adams (University of West Georgia, USA)*
Ben Arnold (University of Northern Iowa, USA)
Lisa Brown (University of Rochester, USA)
Kristen Dietiker (University of Washington, USA)
Kathy Fletcher (West Virginia University, USA)
Laurie Fox (State University of New York Geneseo, USA)
Ken Gilliland (University of Western Ontario, USA)
Cindy Guerazzi (University of Delaware, USA)
Robert Haring-Smith (West Virginia University, USA)
Susan Kerr (Georgia Gwinnett College, USA)
Kathy Kral (University of West Georgia, USA)
Scott Saluga (Oberlin College & Conservatory, USA)

SIGUCCS 2012 Sponsor & Supporters

Sponsor:

SIGUCCS

Gold Level Supporters:

lynda.com
You can learn it.™

SCHOOL
DUDE
.com.

::mozy®

emergent™

CHERWELL
SOFTWARE™

Silver Level Supporter:

Computer Lab Solutions

Bronze Level Supporters:

TaskStream
Advancing Educational Excellence

HDI.
The IT Service & Technical
Support Community

Logos: The Power of the Word in IT Support

Christopher H. King
NC State University
Box 7109 – NCSU
Raleigh, NC 27695-7109
(919) 515-5431

chking@ncsu.edu

ABSTRACT
Too many people focus on the "technical" part of "technical support." This means that we have support staff who are highly trained in software, hardware, specs and certs, who can give highly detailed descriptions of problems and resolutions, both in writing and in person. What gets lost, however, is the focus on the communication itself, and how their words and phrases are perceived by the end-users themselves. This paper/presentation will focus on the importance of "soft skills," namely how phrasing, intonation, levity (or lack thereof), and simple choice of words can make the difference when announcing interruptions, documenting changes, and generally supporting customers.

This paper and presentation will be useful to people directly interacting with end-users, either in technical support, documentation, or training.

Categories and Subject Descriptors
H.5.2 [**User Interfaces**]: Style guides, Theory and methods, Training, help, and documentation

General Terms
Design, Documentation, Human Factors, Standardization.

Keywords
Communication, Written Communication, Training, Technical Support, Incident Management, Problem Management, End-User Support

1. INTRODUCTION
"If you want to build a ship, don't drum up people together to collect wood and don't assign them tasks and work, but rather teach them to long for the endless immensity of the sea." -- Unknown (attributed to Antoine de Saint-Exupery)

As a manager in technical support, people often seem shocked when I say that I have an English degree. The general assumption is that IT people all have computer science degrees, but that is silly for several reasons. First off, we are still at the point where career IT staff began their duties before there was really a

hardcore need for generalized computing support. As a result, many people were given desktop support duties as part of their "real" jobs in fields like science, marketing, livestock management, or whatever the business did as its business. A second reason is that there are plenty of degrees out there that specifically deal with IT support these days. Certifications in Help Desk Management, sometimes coupled with Management or Business degrees, are all over the place, and provide options for people who do not want to go into too technical a degree program. Lastly, as E. W. Dijkstra famously said, "Computer Science is no more about computers than astronomy is about telescopes." Computer Science degree programs teach the logic of how computers (and their operating systems) are built, and the understanding of how to best utilize and optimize their functionality. They don't teach students how to help someone use mail merge, or how to explain why a server outage in Oregon is affecting mail operations in North Carolina. In my personal (albeit heavily-biased) opinion, there is no better source for support than the font from which the need for support flows -- the non-technical end-user. As a former end-user (or at least someone without a formal education in technology), an English major (or historian, or soldier, or ditch digger) has much more experience with the frustrations involved in daily computer use, which translates into a better overall experience for the caller and the support staff when handling incident reports. That background allows a viewpoint that can be rare in this field, and gives the support professional the ability to see problems as impacts on productivity, as opposed to blips on uptime charts.

How does this outlook enable support staff to resolve issues as they arise? It doesn't. What it does do is enable the support staff to better communicate technical issues, both planned and unplanned, by putting them into the proper perspective and in their correct places of importance, relevance, and scope.

2. DELIVERY MECHANISMS
"You will forgive me for not telling you that instruments with which you work are miraculous, that your responsibility is unprecedented or that your aspirations are frequently frustrated. It is not necessary to remind you that the fact that your voice is amplified to the degree where it reaches from one end of the country to the other does not confer upon you greater wisdom or understanding than you possessed when your voice reached only from one end of the bar to the other." (Murrow)

In some respects, how a message is delivered is more important than the message itself. Some messages sacrifice immediacy for duration, while others opt to be ephemeral in favor of prompt

1

delivery. There are four primary categories for delivery mecahnisms:

Print: "Warning: Fire Hazard"
Verbal (or Two-Way): "Let's talk about fire safety"
Broadcast: "FIRE!!!"
Dynamic (online/streaming): "Let's track the fire's progress on Google Maps"

Each method of delivery has its uses, its strengths, and its weaknesses.

2.1   Static (print)

"I used to hate writing assignments, but now I enjoy them. I realized that the purpose of writing is to inflate weak ideas, obscure poor reasoning, and inhibit clarity. With a little practice, writing can be an intimidating and impenetrable fog!" (Watterson)

Printed materials are the tried and true default for information dissemination. Whether in the form of flyers, brochures, newsletters, or pens at a trade show, printed materials aren't bound by technology (no servers to go down), time (how many of us still have pens from SIGUCCS 2008?), or display issues (have wall, will travel).

Print is a good medium for long-term permanent information that you want displayed in a broad range of places. Advertising is a great example of this -- printing your organization's contact information on a magnet or flyer ensures that your customers can reference that information easily when necessary. Announcing a meeting across your campus is much easier if you can capture your audience by putting flyers in conference rooms, parking decks, and even bathroom stalls. (Laugh all you want, but name another place where your audience is immobile, undistracted, and wanting to focus on anything but their surroundings.) Reference material is also a good thing to have printed, especially for one-time events. When NC State University was rolling out its new email system, we printed "cheat sheets" for everyone for initial access, since emailing that same information would have been counterproductive (and rude) since the target audience would not be able to access their email.

These qualities that make print so useful are also some of its negatives. Until the printing industry catches up to *The Daily Prophet*, once something is printed one way, it stays that way forever. If your organization changes names, or you move to a different building, or you reschedule a meeting location, your print media cannot be updated apart from physical replacement -- a very difficult task if you didn't keep track of all of those "Save the Date" magnets and door hangers.

2.2   Verbal (or Two-Way)

*"For God's sake, let us sit upon the ground
And tell sad stories of the death of kings;"* (*Richard II*, Act 3 Sc. 2)

Printed material may be the default way to communicate, but actual interactive communication was the first. Never underestimate the importance of being able to relay information to someone (or a group of someones) and then tailor that information

based on their response. Static delivery methods like flyers don't take into account the differences (vast or subtle) between various members of your audience, and were often crafted in a closed group based on the assumptions of those group members alone. Concepts that are taken for granted by the support staff might be unheard of to the end-user, or confusing, or worse, misinterpreted. Without feedback to these sentiments, users quickly make assumptions based on their bad information, and the issue escalates. This leads to FUD -- fear, uncertainty and doubt, which can cause problems far above whatever the original incident would have produced.

An interactive session can be done in many ways. The most common is a call center, where users get into contact with support professionals for information. "Contact" can be via telephone, instant message, or even email and blogs. Classroom lectures and short courses are also interactive, although by their nature there is already a format involved that can only change slightly given input from the class. If an incident requires interactivity, but no permanent solution is convenient, don't underestimate the idea of disposable drop-ins. Get a table, two chairs, and some publicity, and an impromptu service desk can be set up in the midst of fall move-in weekend, new employee orientation, or the rollout of a new service.

The soft side of interactivity should not be overlooked. People are comforted by hearing another human speak directly to them -- it's in our DNA. That comfort is reflected in the positive response to the message itself as well as the higher likelihood that your audience members will respond to the message, offer feedback, and request clarity. Even Belshazzar needed more than the writing on the wall to convince him of his problems -- it was *how* the words were written that upset him, and it took Daniel's words of warning in person to convey the importance of the message.# At the heart of it, we communicate with our audience to engender a relationship, and broadsides to their inboxes are not always the best way to do so.

2.3   Broadcast

"Nothing travels faster than the speed of light with the possible exception of bad news, which obeys its own special laws." (Adams)

Sometimes, however, there arises the need to get information out as quickly and broadly as possible. These messages are usually short, direct, and widespread in impact. Most often, this is because of an unforeseen event, possibly an emergency or threat to more than just network stability, but broadcasts can also be useful for communicating simple message to the masses.

Broadcast messages can occur via mailing lists, voicemail trees, or even a campus loudspeaker. They offer the luxury of getting your message out to as many people as possible by the most direct method. If your audience knows that these messages are important, then they will pay attention when they arrive, and act accordingly. By their widespread target audience, broadcasts also ensure delivery secondhand -- although one person may not have checked their voicemail, someone else in the office did, and spread the word internally.

One of this method's benefits is also its downfall. Since broadcast systems tend to be simple (and therefore easier to implement in a hurry), the folks who can fire these spam cannons tend to see them as more all-purpose weapons. The more often tools like these are used, the less-effective they become simply by audience indifference. If "emergency" messages are sent every three days, and mostly consist of infomercials for the new employee survey, the audience will ignore them (and even mark them as spam), and then complain later when they didn't get the information they did need. Think about "Peter and the Wolf" -- abusing the emergency broadcast system didn't turn out so well for Peter, and your organization will fare no better.

2.4   Dynamic (online)
"Instant gratification takes too long." (Fisher)

Ah, the Internet. Never before in human history has a technology allowed mankind to project its thoughts across the planet in an instant. For good or for ill, the wide reach of digital communications has changed nearly every aspect of our existence. Fortunately, that reach is not without restrictions, and the means to broadcast also allow for the updating, changing, or revocation of those thoughts.

Dynamic online media is most often used for stable communication needs such as documentation, corporate information, and long-term scheduling and planning. Its nature allows for changes to occur when necessary -- when your university gets a new sports title, logo, or even chancellor, updating your information is only a few saves away.

Campus television is also an example of dynamic media. As streaming sites and media pull viewers away from our campus cable services, this method is less pervasive in residence halls, but you still control the digital signage in lounges, academic buildings, and eating establishments. Most might think of it as just background noise, but when that noise changes, people will take notice.

3. CHOICE OF WORDS
"Think of the fellow in the play that calls out 'My kingdom for a horse' -- it would not have been poetry at all, had he said sheep." (O'Brian)

Choosing a method (or multiple methods) of delivery for your message is only the beginning. An envelope is only as useful as the letter inside, and the content of that letter can have a huge impact on how that message is received, understood, and ultimately acted upon. Specifically, the use of certain words or sentiments versus others can have a profound effect on your audience, based on the situation, sentiment, and the composition of the audience itself.

3.1   Know Your Audience
"Talk sense to a fool, and he calls you foolish." (Euripides)

It cannot be stressed enough that communication to an audience should have as its primary architectural guide the audience itself. At its basest level, your communication should be understandable to its target audience -- if your audience is in Barcelona, you will want your message sent out in English, Spanish, and possibly Catalan. And while knowing the audience's base language is important, knowing their level of understanding is equally necessary.

Technical knowledge, as has been mentioned previously, isn't necessary to be an end-user. Most users go through their careers happily and competently using technology without understanding any of the infrastructure responsible for making that technology possible or useful. Just as knowledge of the IMAP protocol isn't necessary to use Thunderbird, hearing that there is an issue with an IMAP server may not necessarily be the right type of information to let someone know that their email is unavailable.

On the flip side, if you're sending out a notification to your system administrators, not only will you want to mention the IMAP server, but you will also want to say whether it is an issue with the network, storage, certificate, or whatever is causing (to the non-technical end-user) Thunderbird to fail. These consumers need specifics, so that they can assess impact, scope, and criticality.

However, keep in mind that your system administrators are email users as well. Occasionally, it is useful to send out both types of information, and let the users decide which is pertinent to them. This can lead to confusion, though, so a certain amount of experimentation should be done first. At NC State, we have a system outage site (sysnews.ncsu.edu) that contains both "public" and "technical" details in each post. It works well for the most part, but requires constant badgering to ensure that both areas get equal consideration when filling out incident reports.

3.2   Negatives are a no-no
"No man ever listened himself out of a job." – Attributed to Calvin Coolidge

In some cases, a message has no choice but to be negative. When a service is down, it is unavailable, and users will have to be told "no," either by the service desk or by an error message. When dealing with general support, however, there are many ways of saying "no" without actually using negative words.

Using words (or contractions) like "no," "can't," or "won't" puts people on the defensive. As I am fond of telling my staff, people never call the Help Desk in a good mood. They are always in need of something: information, resources, or most commonly, assistance with a problem. Their work has been interrupted, deadlines loom, and these things put people on edge. They reach out to their support staff for help, hoping that their problems can be resolved. When they are told "no," there is usually nowhere else for them to turn, and that will escalate quickly.

Instead of saying "no" as a final answer, or the dreaded "we don't support that," offer alternative solutions. In the discussion on proper communications, it is good to remember that your users rarely say what they mean. Listen to their questions, translate that into what their actual problem could be, and give them other ways to resolve their problem. When a user says "Give me admin rights for my employee's account," and that is not common practice, don't just say "no." Find out *why* they need those rights. If it turns out that they need old emails for a project, instead get them information on your email retention service, or tell them that your legal department has access for litigation holds. By taking some time for basic troubleshooting, you can turn a negative situation into one with potential, making everyone's day better.

3

3.3 Acronyms? Abbreviations! And Bears! (Oh my!)

"I can't understand it. I can't even understand the people who can understand it." -- Attributed to Queen Juliana, of the Netherlands

Regardless of the level of understanding of your users or your support professionals, they will likely speak two different languages when it comes to campus operations. As people become familiar with their areas of expertise, they use abbreviations, nicknames, and acronyms to expedite their daily routines. The issues arise when they try to talk to people outside of their professional community. The best example of this is the military. The military uses as many abbreviations as articles in its daily verbiage, and it makes perfect sense to its initiates while, at the same time, completely obfuscating its message to those not in uniform.

The same idea applies to technical communications. When discussing a service, resource, or location, try and use fully-qualified names whenever possible. It may be easier to say VM when talking about your virtual machines, but if your university also has a veterinary medicine program, confusion can arise. In lengthy missives, such as documentation, announcements, or training, abbreviations are fine once those abbreviations have been defined (most often the first time that the abbreviation is used). Another useful practice is to have a well-known and available glossary of terms. This allows not only for translation of shortened terms, but also a more lengthy definition of the service itself and what it does. If this documentation is online, then linking the acronym or abbreviation to an online glossary will make it even easier and more seamless for your audience to translate for themselves.

4. MESSAGE CONSTRUCTION

"'Crap,'I said. I'm quite eloquent in times of crisis." (Butcher)

With your delivery method(s) chosen, and your words narrowed down, it's now time to make the message itself. Message construction has a huge impact on how well the message is received – at times, even before the message itself is even read (or heard). Unless it is absolutely necessary, think through your message before posting/sending/screaming it, to ensure that you will get the most out of it.

4.1 Don't be succinct when being short will do

"The great enemy of clear language is insincerity. When there is a gap between one's real and one's declared aims, one turns as it were instinctively to long words and exhausted idioms, like a cuttlefish spurting out ink." (Orwell)

If you've read this far into this paper, you may be astonished to find its author championing brevity in writing. However, the most important aspect of a message is its ultimate delivery – if your audience doesn't get the information, then all of your work has been for nothing.

One contribution to this is the size of the message itself. If your users see a quick summary of an issue, they are much more likely to take the time to read or process it than if it's preceded by a lot of fluff or flowery language. If it takes you paragraphs of prose to explain a simple (but important) concept, you will fall victim to the Internet meme that says it all: tl;dr[1]. Instead, make sure that your message is only as long as it needs to be. For emergencies, that may only be a sentence or two. For technical documentation or meeting announcements, that might be longer, but you still run the risk of boring your audience into indifference if you don't stick to your subject matter and keep your wording tight.

This also applies to the words that you choose. Words that look great on paper may not come out of someone's mouth or speaker with the same intention as a smaller or more concise word, and may take the audience in a different direction. For example, if you are announcing an outage affecting a service at your College of Veterinary Medicine, it does not pay to keep saying "College of Veterinary Medicine" when "vet school" or "CVM" would suffice after the first mention, and could end up being tedious if repeated. In some cases, this is not as easily avoided, but can be worked around. If your vet school has a sponsor that likes their name in all press releases, try to avoid a repeat mention of the organization or facility, and instead focus on the customers and the issue themselves.

Which is more appealing?

"The Victory Gin Park at Pequod Fishing Stadium is experiencing a network outage. Personnel visiting the Victory Gin Park at Pequod Fishing Stadium will be unable to access the network until repairs can be performed. Please visit the Victory Gin Park at Pequod Fishing Stadium website for more information."

"There is a network outage at the Victory Gin Park at Pequod Fishing Stadium. On-site personnel will be unable to access the network until repairs are made, and more information will be posted as it becomes available."

4.2 Focus on the effect, not what's affecting it

"When life gives you lemons, don't make lemonade. Make life take the lemons back! Get mad! I don't want your damn lemons, what am I supposed to do with these? Demand to see life's manager! Make life rue the day it thought it could give Cave Johnson lemons! Do you know who I am? I'm the man who's gonna burn your house down! With the lemons! I'm gonna get my engineers to invent a combustible lemon that burns your house down!" (Portal 2)

A common misconception in technical communication is the assumption that users understand the relationship between a server and its corresponding service. To an IT professional dealing with this association on a regular basis, it makes perfect sense that "a database issue on server authsmtp-foo" would affect outgoing

---

[1] Too long; didn't read. http://knowyourmeme.com/memes/tldr

email. To all of the regular humans out there who are trying to send newsletters or updates, there is nothing in the previous sentence to imply that email is affected at all. In their mind, it is a completely separate relationship on which they are focusing – "If I can RECEIVE email, why can't I SEND it?"

Because of this disconnect, it is important for communications to focus on what's wrong as opposed to what's down. If a planned server upgrade in the future will affect networked file storage, phrase your communication to not only highlight that, but to focus on that as the main thrust of the message:

Bad:

Subject: Database server upgrade

OIT is planning to upgrade the database server authsmtp-foo on Sunday. Service will be restored as soon as possible.

Better:

Subject: Outgoing email outage

OIT will be upgrading the database server (authsmtp-foo) that manages email sent outside of the company. During this outage, campus users will be unable to send email. However, any messages that are sent will be stored in your Exchange outbox, and will be sent after service has been restored.

Notice as well that even the title of the message reflects the users impact, as opposed to the backend server that is actually being affected. Phrasing communications like this will ensure that your audience pays attention when the communication comes to their inbox.

This is also important if you are announcing a discontinuation of service. The unfortunate phrase "end of life" strikes many folks the wrong way, so be sure to highlight whatever service (if any) is slated to replace the recently deceased product. "GroupWise email and calendaring to be turned off November 30" might cause a riot, whereas "Introducing new and awesome Google Apps, with Email, Calendaring, and Chocolate Puppies" will show your users the reasoning behind the replacement.

4.3   Don't hide problems that are obviously problems

"The truth does not change according to our ability to stomach it." -- Flannery O'Connor

Stuff goes wrong. Services fail, certificates expire, and squirrels sacrifice themselves to short out power transformers.[2] When things go wrong, and service is affected, it is important to announce that to your customers. Contrary to popular belief,

---

[2] This happened at NC State often enough that papers were written on prevention:
http://etd.lib.ncsu.edu/publications/bitstream/1840.2/643/1/cho w_1995_ieee_transactions_power_del..

customers do notice problems, and throwing something shiny in the opposite direction will not distract your users for long before they come back to the reason for their anger. It is NEVER a good idea to turtle in and fix a problem without announcing it to your customer base, and it is even worse to not announce fault afterwards. Many organizations have an after-action process to determine a root cause in a situation, and oftentimes that report is published. If your organization does not have such a process, create one through your emergency announcement system. Own up to the mistake (whether it was preventable or not), and your audience will understand. Everyone is only human (even faculty members), and they will understand occasional mistakes. If those mistakes are so common that secrecy is required to ensure security, then perhaps a more broadly-enforced doctrine for quality is necessary.

One side-effect to hiding problems is its impact on your front-line support infrastructure. An outage on a system means that customers will call in to get updates, and that can cause stress in the call centers and service management systems that track incoming tickets. If the call center can refer people to a common announcement site or, even better, record a "Message Of The Day" to play for callers in a waiting queue, then it will inform the users while, at the same time, rescuing what remains of the sanity of the first-tier support staff.

5. SUMMARY

"In the beginning was the Word, and the Word was with God, and the Word was God." (1 John 1:1, KJV)

Words have power. When early Christians were describing Creation and God Himself, they did so via the concept of "logos", or the Word. Creation occurred when God spoke -- the first example of the power of communication.

In case this message was not highlighted enough, it will be repeated:

Communication is really darn important.

Whether you are documenting a new process, announcing changes to a current process, or warning about issues affecting your audience, how you communicate is just as important, if not more, than what you are trying to communicate. By choosing your delivery mechanism, words, and message construction, you can help to ensure that the right people get the right information at the right time and in the right amounts.

Do not, however, fall into the trap of exclusive choice. Just because one method makes the most sense does not mean that it makes all of the sense. As a former anthropology professor once highlighted, our ancestors didn't just wake up one Thursday and decide to switch from hunting to gathering. There was a time of overlap where both worked for different reasons in different situations. The same can apply to communications – try out as many as you like, and let user reaction over time dictate how your messages will be received in the future.

And when you're screening applications for your next employee, give the English major a shot. Your customers will thank you for it.

6. ACKNOWLEDGMENTS

Special thanks to John Martin at NC State University for his assistance with this paper.

7. REFERENCES

[1] Murrow, Edward R. (1958, 15 October). Speech to the Radio and Television News Directors Association (RTNDA) convention, Chicago, IL.

[2] Watterson, Bill. Homicidal Psycho Jungle Cat. Andrew McMeel Publishing. Kansas City, MO. 1994.

[3] Adams, Douglas. Mostly Harmless. Del Rey Publishing. 2000.

[4] Fisher, Carrie. Postcards From The Edge. Simon and Schuster. New York. 1987.

[5] O'Brian, Patrick. The Ionian Mission. W. W. Norton and Company. New York. 1992.

[6] Euripides. Bacchæ l. 480

[7] Butcher, Jim. Storm Front (The Dresden Files, Book 1). Penguin Group. Kindle Edition. 2000.

[8] Orwell, George. "Politics and the English Language," The Complete Works of George Orwell, http://www.george-orwell.org/Politics_and_the_English_Language/0.html, Accessed 11 June 2012.

[9] "Portal 2", vers. 2.0.0.1 (24 October 2011). Valve Computing. Accessed 1 June 2012.

Partnership Between Center for Online Learning (COL) and Office of Information Technology – User Support Services (OIT-USS)

Jahed M. Sukhun
Portland State University
1825 SW Broadway
Portland, OR 97201
(503) 725-3323
sukhunj@pdx.edu

Mark Terui
Portland State University
1825 SW Broadway
Portland, OR 97201
(503) 725-5020
mterui@pdx.edu

ABSTRACT

How did Portland State University (PSU) achieve success with limited resources when it comes to LMS support? Portland State University implemented Desire2Learn (D2L) in the summer of 2010. There are currently 1,340 activated courses, with an average of 17,670 unique student accounts and about 3,423 unique faculty and teacher assistant log ins. Historically LMS support was provided by the Center for Online Learning (COL) and Center for Academic Excellence (CAE) and the Help Desk. These three units were in three different buildings. These units reported to three different management structures. This proved to be very confusing and frustrating to the users.

Categories and Subject Descriptors

A.m General Literature: MISCELLANEOUS

General Terms

- Management

Keywords

Customer support, faculty support, staffing, Help, training, collaboration, Learning Management System (LMS).

1. INTRODUCTION

Portland State University is the largest university in Oregon with 30,000 students enrolled and 4,000 faculty and staff serving the students. In 2008, PSU sought to find a new LMS (Learning Management System) to replace the current Blackboard system (actually a WebCT system that had been bought out by Blackboard). PSU invited three vendors, Moodle, Blackboard, and Desire2Learn, to participate in this process. After considerable research and several presentations & demonstrations by the three vendors to faculty & student focus groups, PSU decided on implementing Desire2Learn as its next LMS system.

PSU started the conversion from Blackboard to D2L in the summer of 2010. During this summer term, a group of instructors volunteered to use the D2L platform with their courses as a trial run of the system.

There were a total of 30 courses (a mixture of fully online, hybrid, and web-enhanced courses) that used the new LMS. During the fall of 2010, we had another pilot of 138 courses offered on the D2L system. In the winter term of 2011, we moved all of the fully online and hybrid courses (347) that were offered that term, onto the D2L system. In the spring term of 2011, we discontinued the Blackboard system and all courses that wanted to use an LMS were offered on D2L. See Figure 1 for a comparison of the number of courses offered on the D2L system during the first two years.

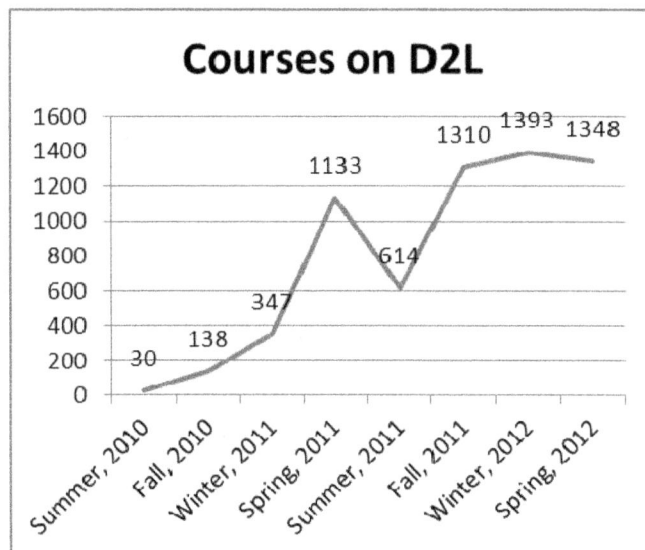

Figure 1. Courses offered on D2L during the first two years

2. THE BODY OF THE PAPER

During the spring term of 2012, we have 5,272 instructors & TAs and nearly 15,000 students actively using D2L. Each year we are seeing an increase in use of the LMS, which is creating an increased demand for support for our faculty and students. When we started the D2L conversion project, we initiated a mandatory training workshop on D2L for our faculty who were planning to use the LMS to introduce them to the basic tools this system provided. However, our faculty didn't like this "required" option and this was quickly changed to "optional" participation. We also started with a fully online version of our D2L workshop that was moderated by three of our faculty members, who were early adopters of the system, and was "held" over a period of 5 weeks. We offered 13 of these online workshops with an average of 30 "students" in each session. While some of the faculty enjoyed the freedom an online course provided and the interaction of online discussions with other faculty, many of them missed the "human touch" and the opportunity for real-time interaction with the instructor. However, this online workshop not only allowed the faculty to see how D2L functioned from a student's perspective, it also introduced many of them to the facets of designing an online course. After 6 months, we discontinued the online workshop (due to organizational changes). Currently, we are offering face-to-face, 2-hour workshops on the basic tools of D2L and face-to-face, 2-hour workshops on design principles for online courses.

At the time that the D2L implementation project started, PSU had two different teams of instructional designers that were providing the majority of the support for the LMS. One team started in the School of Extended Studies where most of the fully online courses are located. The second team was under the Center for Academic Excellence and provided most of the support for hybrid and traditional classes that used the LMS. These two teams have since been combined into a new unit called the Center for Online Learning (COL). COL assists faculty in the design & development of their course using principles of learning design to create a good experience for both the faculty and the student.

In the summer of 2011 the first collaboration between COL, and the Office of Information Technology (OIT) – User Support Services (USS) was established to take care of the faculty and students need when it came to supporting D2L, and any online learning tools such as Blackboard Collaborate and Echo 360. The User Support Services Helpdesk at Portland State University is the first stop for Faculty, Staff, and Students needing assistance with PSU technology resources. Helpdesk technicians are available to support and troubleshoot accounts and network connectivity for students, and provide in-depth hardware and software support for staff and faculty members. The Help Desk is the tier one support, and any issues that can't be resolved by them, they escalate to tier two and three. USS consists of the following groups:

Help Desk (Support all faculty staff and students. They average 800 calls a week)

IDSC lab supports faculty, staff and graduate students

Labs and classroom team (responsible for 1000 computers in the general access labs)

Desktop support and projects team (responsible for 4000 computers on campus)

In order to perform this partnership, both COL and OIT-USS identified a specialized lab that has already been serving faculty for several years. The Instructional Development Support Center (IDSC) is a robust multimedia computing lab open specifically to faculty, graduate students, and staff at PSU. The lab provides a unique environment for users to develop multimedia products that enhance pedagogy and research. The IDSC staff (one full time employee and 10 students) are well trained and eager to assist faculty in this sense with traditional teaching media and emerging technologies.

This lab houses state-of-the-art multimedia hardware and software on both the Macintosh and Windows platforms. Additionally, the IDSC has specialty color, B&W multifunction and wide-format printers to help faculty in their course development, and research. The range of resources and services includes digital video and audio production, image manipulation, interactive multimedia development, desktop publishing, graphic design, web development, media archiving, OCR, PDF development, large and standard format color printing, and DVD authoring.

The IDSC lab is already under OIT-USS. There was no need to create another area for support, nor did we require any extra financial resources. In addition, this lab is adjacent to the Help Desk, which made it perfect for our faculty and graduate students in that they can come to a central location for support.

In order to facilitate this collaboration and provide the best support for our faculty with D2L, a new process had to be implemented. Our staff (students and regular employees) had to be trained to support this new application. Phone numbers and web sites had to be changed, and course designers were added to the IDSC lab. Training of our support staff was provided by our internal experts, which consisted of Instructional designers and the D2L system administrator. They provided face-to-face instructional workshops; online documentation and internal FAQ WIKI sites are also available for them

Through this agreement, multiple levels of staff are supporting faculty and students with D2L in innovative ways such as:

2.1) Utilizing student employees.

Due to limited resources, OIT-USS puts a heavy emphasis on using student labor to provide support to our customers. Currently Tier One support is available at the Help Desk for general support including D2L. All of the students working at the Help Desk go through basic training on D2L and are able to answer questions on how to log into the system, finding their courses, using the basic tools of D2L (such as Discussions, Quizzes, Dropbox, D2L mail, etc.). If the Help Desk is not able to provide support, the customer is then referred to the IDSC lab staff (next door), which is Tier Two support. Tier Two support went through more rigorous training on how to use the different tools in D2L and are more familiar with application and are able to spend more time with the customer. The IDSC lab staff are also trained on developing D2L courses from an instructor's perspective.

2.2) Using full time Help Desk staff to aid in the support of this product.

When students are not able to help the user or they are busy with other users, full time staff are available to provide additional support. This includes the D2L & Blackboard Collaborate system administrator and is considered as Tier Three support.

2.3) Having a full time instructional designer housed in the IDSC to help faculty in their course design, troubleshoot issues and to help explain the different tools available for the users.

Course designers (CD) are a crucial part of this partnership. Faculty can make appointments with the CD to get more advanced support. Some of this support is:

- Course design

- Using online grade books

- Developing and using online quizzes and exams

- Training and advanced-function support with instructional application of technology

2.4) Creating multiple workshops to provide faculty with the tools & ideas needed to integrate technology in their classes.

3. STATISTICS

Currently the Help Desk and the IDSC lab are open 8AM-7PM Monday-Friday and 10AM-4PM on Saturdays. In addition to that, PSU has an after hour telephone support provided by an external vendor (this might change in the future). During business hours we receive walk-in customers, email and telephone calls.

On a weekly basis, our average ticket intake is as follows (see Figure 2):

- Tier One – Help Desk: 21

- Tier Two – IDSC: 3

- Tier Three – Course Designer and Staff Technical Support: 21

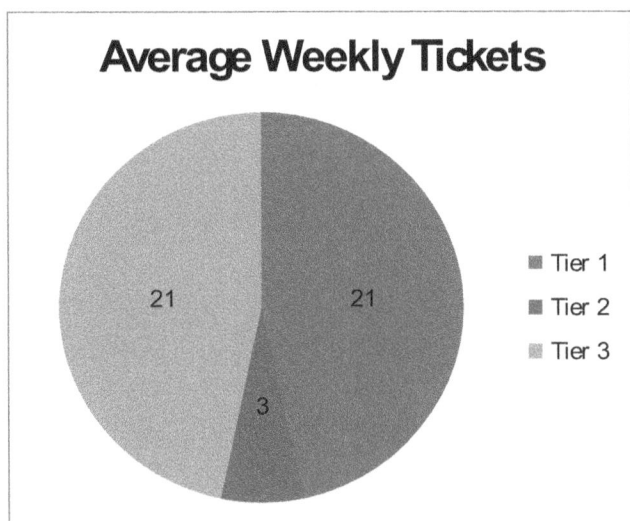

Figure 2. Average Weekly Help Request Tickets

4. ISSUES

- Improved tracking of the type of courses using D2L: fully online, hybrid, web-enhanced.
  Currently, we can extrapolate this information if we use Banner (Banner is PSU's enterprise student information system) to identify fully online and hybrid courses, then get a list of the active D2L course shells, and compare the two lists (see Figure 3 for an example). But D2L, by itself, does not have any method for determining whether a course shell is fully online, hybrid, or web-enhanced.

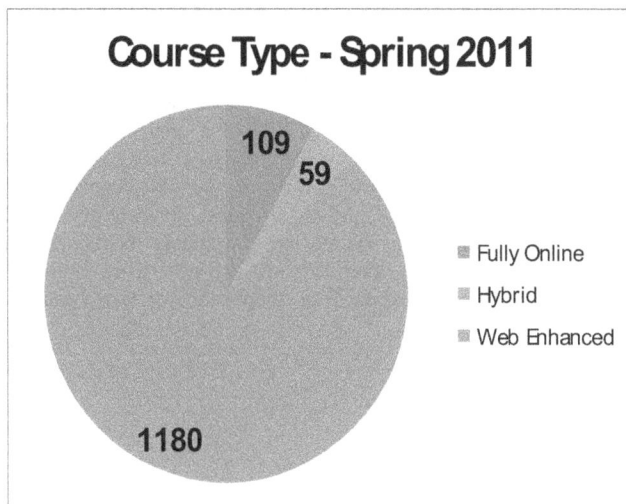

Figure 3. Example of the distribution of the different types of courses using D2L for a single term.

- Developing a method for measuring user satisfaction (instructors, students) of the D2L.
  We plan to develop in the near future, a survey for our instructors and a survey for our students on the usability of D2L.

- Adapting to organizational changes.
  There have been a number of changes of the PSU organization on both the academic side (e.g. Center for Online Learning) and the administrative side (OIT). Each change has affected our support structure in different ways, but the end result is always a disruption to our faculty & students and they must adjust to the changes.

- Distributed and "silo" academic/instructional technology support.
  There are many different individuals around the university that currently provide technology support. Some of them have been hired by a particular program (e.g. School of Business or the department of Criminology and Criminal Justice). This can result in different levels of support and/or inconsistent application and design of D2L courses.

- Increased faculty training on D2L and other instructional technology.

- Establishing policies on developing fully online & hybrid courses.
  PSU does not currently have any policies on how a fully online or hybrid course can be created and added to the university's curriculum.

- Establishing quality control standards and processes for evaluating all instructional materials available online.

- Provide more training for student employees and full time support at the Help Desk and the IDSC lab on instructional technology.

- Increasing the online documentation of D2L available for faculty and students.

5. BENEFITS OF THIS PARTNERSHIP

5.1) Cross training between COL and OIT-USS

Generally, technical support personnel are trained on how a technology works, but do not usually learn about the instructional applications of that technology. On the opposite side, course designers learn about how to apply a technology to an instructional environment, but they do not know how a technology support unit processes requests for help and trouble-shooting issues. This partnership has helped both sides gain insight on what each other does and can now share information with each other that improves the support of faculty and students.

5.2) Bridging communication between COL and OIT-USS

In the past, PSU has not had an on-going process for communicating the technical needs of academic units and associating them with the resources available from OIT (which is an administrative unit). Usually the communication between academic and administrative units is handled through a project team, but once a project is completed, the team is dissolved. This has resulted in problems with day-to-day support when faculty and students have not known who they should contact for help.

5.3) Increasing the understanding of what each unit is doing, long tem projects, policies, process of work, etc.

Having a course designer physically located and working with OIT-USS has created a liaison between the academic and administrative units that helps keep both sides informed about current issues and future events.

Introduction and Experience with the Primary Mail Services Based on their Names for Students

Naomi Fujimura
Kyushu University
4-9-1, Shiobaru, Minami-ku
Fukuoka Japan
+81 92 553 4434

fujimura.naomi.274@m.kyushu-u.ac.jp

Yoshiaki Kasahara
Kyushu University
6-10-1, Hakozaki, Higashi-ku
Fukuoka Japan
+81 92 642 2297

kasahara@nc.kyushu-u.ac.jp

Tadatsugu Togawa
Kyushu University
6-10-1, Hakozaki, Higashi-ku
Fukuoka Japan
+81 92 642 2202

togawa@cc.kyushu-u.ac.jp

Eisuke Ito
Kyushu University
6-10-1, Hakozaki, Higashi-ku
Fukuoka Japan
+81 92 642 4037

Ito.eisuke.523@m.kyushu-u.ac.jp

ABSTRACT

Kyushu University provided mail service based on student IDs such as "1AB10123X" to the university students for many years. Using this model, we had problems communicating with the students who graduated from the University and enrolled in the graduate school. The students received new mail addresses based on their new student IDs such as "2AB12789Y". Faculty members were forced to change the student mail addresses in the mailing lists and in their mail client address book. Furthermore, students were forced to notify the e-mail address change to all of their existing contacts.

We introduced a new mail system to provide addresses based on the student name, as well as student ID in April 2011. The new naming convention uses the following format: "lastname.firstname.999" where "999" is a random number of 3 digits. Students can select some combination patterns of their first and last names for Japanese. We also consider the middle names for foreign students.

In the system implementation, we did not have the formal information of alphabetical names for students. We generated alphabetical names from Japanese Katakana names. It is not easy for us to get the appropriate name in this manner. We implemented a confirmation stage of the alphabetical name at first use, and then students can select their mail addresses for their convenience. We paid much attention to the user interface in the system.

Since April 2011, the number of users who use the mail address based on their own name has been increasing gradually. This paper will detail the usage status of the new system.

Categories and Subject Descriptors

H.4.3 [**Information Systems Applications**]: Communication Applications – Electronic mail

General Terms

Management, Design, Economics, Reliability, Security, Human Factors.

Keywords

ID base mail address, Name based mail address, University mail service.

1. INTRODUCTION

We started the mail service (Kyushu University Primary Mail Service) for all staff members as the most important communication infrastructure in Kyushu University [1]. The primary purpose is not only to use e-mail in daily work, but also to utilize it as a notification tools in the event of natural disaster, calamity, and/or pandemic. We also provided the mail service for all students as a part of the ICT (Information and Communication Technology) learning environment. The space for a user was limited to 30MB and the mail address was based on student ID such as "1AB10123X". As a result, it was not convenient for students in daily use. We improved the space limit to 300MB and provided a file sharing system for students in June 2011 [2].

Students had some problems using their university primary mail service. When students graduate from the university, and subsequently go on to the graduate school, they receive a new mail address based on a new student IDs such as "2AB12789Y". Faculty members are forced to change the mail address in their mailing lists and address books in their mail client software. Students are forced to notify all their contacts of the mail address change.

We introduced a new mail system to provide mail address based on the student's names as well as the student IDs in April 2011. The primary purpose is to provide the student life long e-mail address instead of the student ID base e-mail address for the student in Kyushu University. The new naming convention uses the following format: "lastname.firstname.999" where "999" is a random number of 3 digits. Students can select some combination patterns of their first and last names for Japanese students. We also considered the middle names for foreign students.

In the system implementation, we did not have the formal information of the alphabetical names for students. We generated alphabetical names from Japanese Katakana names. It was not easy for us to get the appropriate names in that manner. We implemented the confirmation stage of the alphabetical name when a student logs in at the first time, and then students can select the mail address. We paid much attention to the user interface in the system.

We have been operating the system since April 2011. The number of student users, who use the e-mail addresses based on their own names, has been increasing gradually. We will report the detail and usage status within the system in this paper.

2. OUTLINE OF OLD E-MAIL SERVICE FOR STUDENTS

2.1 System Configuration and Service

Figure 1 shows the system configuration for student mail service before April 2011 Table 1 shows the detail of the mail service during that time.

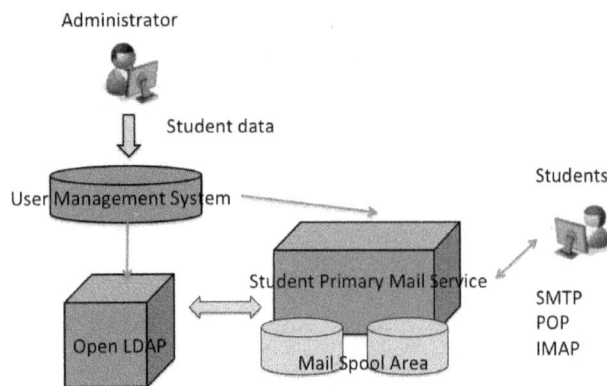

Figure 1. System Configuration before 2010

Table 1 Detail of the Old Mail Service

Item		Detail
Users		All students including non-regular students
Space for spool		30MB/user
Keep period		Unlimited
Size limit for a mail		10MB/mail
Authentication ID		Student ID (9 or 8 digits)
Send Protocol	SMTP	465（TLS）
Receive Protocol	POP	995 (SSL) / 110 (TLS)
	IMAP	993 (SSL)/143 (TLS)

2.2 Mail Address

Students use their student IDs and passwords to use student primary mail service. The mail address is based on student IDs. A student ID contains attribute information about the department the student belongs to, entering year, and student type (e.g. undergraduate, graduate). Therefore, a student ID usually changes when the student graduates from an undergraduate school and enter a graduate school. As a result, the e-mail address also changes from an undergraduate school to a graduate school as shown in Figure 2. The change is more serious when a student moves to another department in the undergraduate school. We also would like to respect the students' individuality by integrating their name into the e-mail address.

Status of student	Students' ID	e-mail address
Under graduate	1AB08012X	1AB08012X@s.kyushu-u.ac.jp

Status of student	Students' ID	e-mail address
Graduate	2AB12345Y	2AB12789Y@s.kyushu-u.ac.jp

Figure 2. E-mail address from undergraduate to graduate school

3. MAIL ADDRESS BASED ON NAME

3.1 Basic Policy

In order to solve the problems described above, we established the new e-mail address policy based on names and implemented the new system to make the new e-mail address available. We also realized the following two improvements:

· Students can select their e-mail addresses from the various combination patterns of first names and last names. They can always change the combination patterns when they desire to change them. It helps students manage spam e-mails.

· Some patterns of e-mail addresses contain the initial of first and last names. It helps some students, especially foreign students, avoid long e-mail addresses.

3.2 System Configuration

Figure 3 shows the system configuration to realize the new mail address policy. The school affair system provides the information about students' names to the setting system for name based e-mail addresses. Students are expected to confirm their names with the web interface in the setting system for the name based mail addresses.

3.3 Implementation

Our Approach is to assign a name based e-mail address to the student ID based e-mail address. The setting system prepares a map file between a student ID and the name based e-mail address for each student as shown in Figure 4. The map file is transferred to the student primary mail server. The map file is compared with the previous map file every five minutes. If the map file is different from the previous map file, it replaces the alias file with a new map file, and the "newaliases" command is executed. As a result, a mail to name based mail address is forwarded to the student ID address.

When a student has changed his or her name based mail address, two lines are generated in the alias file as shown in Figure 4. A mail to new and old mail address is forwarded to the corresponding student ID. After about three months (exactly one hundred days), the alias line for the old mail address is deleted.

When a student graduates from an undergraduate school and enters a graduate school, the student ID changes. We adopt a unique key number to link old and new student ID in our system. After a student has entered a graduate school, his or her old ID is invalidated and his or her mail to the name based address will be forwarded to the new ID in the graduate school. Students, who enter the graduate school, are supposed to change the setting to send and receive mails when they enter graduate school. We could not change the mechanism to deliver mails to unique numbers adopted for unique key because it requires a huge modification in the current mail system.

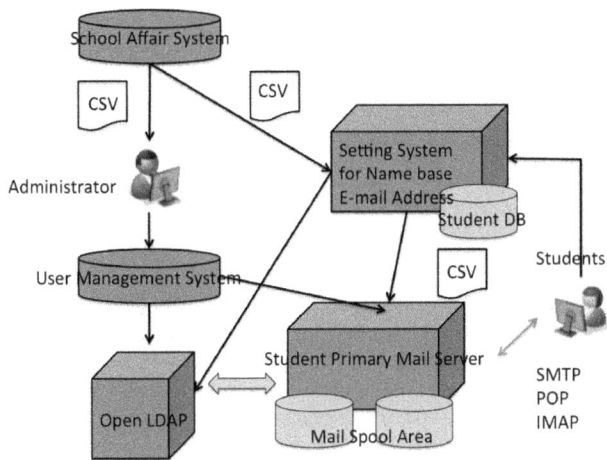

Figure 3. System configuration of the new system

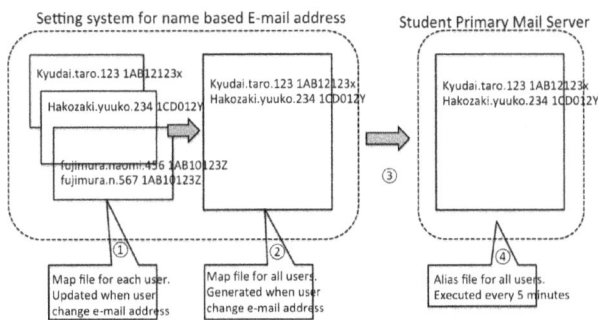

Figure 4 Adaptation of alphabetical name and mail address

Table 2 Result of users in generation method

No.	Category	Data characteristics	Method
(a)	Foreign students	In many Korean and Chinese students, the order is last and first name	Divide into last, first, and middle name
(b)	Students except (a)	Almost Japanese, the order is last and first name	Divide into last, first, and middle name
(C)	New comer	First and last name because the input field is one area	Divide into first and last name or first, middle, and last name

3.4 Generation of Alphabetical Name

In order to prepare alphabetical name based mail address, it is necessary for us to get the information about alphabetical names of students. However, we did not have the necessary information. We could get alphabetical names for some foreign students from the database of foreign affairs. We decided to prepare a new field to describe alphabetical name in the paper form - which students must fill to enter university- for new students beginning 2010. Table 2 shows the category of users in generation method. Table 3 shows the number of students in three categories.

Table 3 Method and the numbers to divide Japanese Katakana to Alphabetical name

	Category	Number	Generation method
(a)	Foreign students	1,978	Alphabetical name from the database of foreign affairs
(b)	Students except (a)	16,658	Convert from Japanese Katakana which are contained in user management system
(C)	New comer	2,917	New field is prepared to get alphabetical name, but took much time

We generated the alphabetical names from Japanese Katakana name for Japanese students. It is not easy to generate them because some pronunciations have several representations such as "chi" and "ti", "shi" and "si". In other cases, the representation changes according to one's preference such as "ota", "oota", and "ohta". Additionally, "KIYUU" should be converted to be "KYU", KIYO" to "KYO", "RIYU" to "RYU" in some cases. We assume the popular representation for such cases in our system, and the system shows the candidate considered most popular to make students confirm their alphabetical names.

The Japanese Katakana name is contained in one field without any separation for first, last, and middle name in various orders. We have to divide and distinguish them into first, last, and middle name separately.

The email address consists of first name, last name, middle name, and 3 random digits to avoid generating the completely same address for different people with the same name. Table 4 shows the various address patterns that we provide.

Table 4 Mail address pattern

	User without middle name	User with middle name
	5 pattern	13 pattern
1	No name based address	No name based address
2	Last. First. 3 digits	Last. First. 3 digits
3	Last. Initial of first. 3 digits	Last. Initial of first. 3 digits
4	First. Last. 3 digits	First. Last. 3 digits
5	Initial of first. Last. 3 digits	Initial of first. Last. 3 digits
6	-	Last, First, 3 digits
7	-	Last, First. Initial of middle. 3 digits
8	-	First. Middle. Last. 3 digits
9	-	First. Initial of middle. Last. 3 digits
10	-	Last. Initial of middle. 3 digits
11	-	Last. Initial of middle. First. 3 digits
12	-	First. Last. Middle. 3 digits
13	-	First. Last. Initial of middle. 3 digits

3.5 User Operation in Our System

3.5.1 Confirmation of alphabetical name

We prepared alphabetical names for all students with various methods. Students are expected to check and confirm their alphabetical name at the first time they log in. They can correct their alphabetical name only at that time. The alphabetical name is very important because it will be used in the English certificate for foreign students when they graduate from school.

3.5.2 Selection of e-mail address

After the confirmation of their alphabetical name, students can select their e-mail address from various patterns as shown in Table 4. They can change the pattern of their e-mail address when they desire to address spam mail and other concerns. When a student changes the e-mail address, e-mails to the old address will be delivered to the new address for one hundred days (if desired), then the forwarding will stop. If the student changes the e-mail address again in less than one hundred days, only the last mail address before the newest one is valid and forwarded to the newest mail address. They can select "no forwarding" to avoid spam mails.

4. NEW SYSTEM

We started the temporary service of the name based e-mail address on April 1st in 2011. Initially, we did not announce the new service extensively. We announced the new service only in a web announcement page on June 8th, 2011. Later, we announced about the name based mail address to all students via email directly on July 11th. The number of users has been increasing since that time.

We changed our operation policy in March 2012. We decided to provide the name based mail addresses for new students in the beginning of the first day of new semester. We prepared alphabetical names before April 8th (the beginning day of classes) to make them available for new students. Some teachers taught the availability of name based mail addresses in the class this year. The number of users is increasing dramatically after April 2012 as shown in Figure 5.

Table 5 shows the detailed number of users who confirmed their alphabetical names (upper line in Figure) and name based mail addresses (lower line).

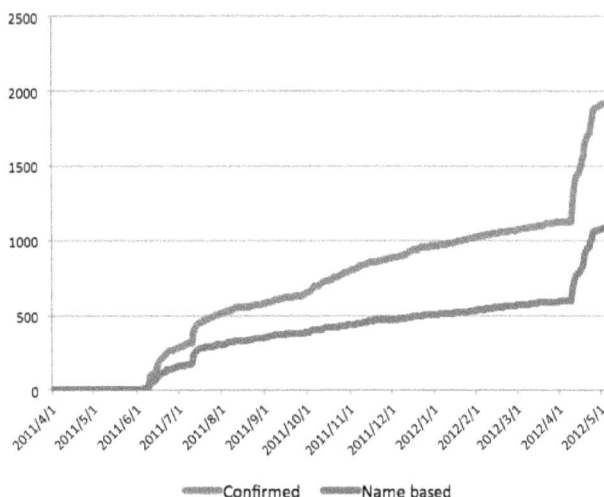

Figure 5. History of new service users

5. ISSUES

We have a couple of problems relating to our new e-mail system now. One is that from the viewpoint of users. Another is that comes from our operation.

Table 5. Number of users

Category	Number	Ratio
Student primary mail account	19,506	–
Confirmed alphabetical name	2034	10.4%
User of name base e-mail address	1124	5.7%

(2012/05/21)

The name based e-mail address is now available during the student life in Kyushu University, but mail is delivered to the spool area assigned to each student ID. Therefore, when a student gets a new ID for graduate school, mail is delivered to a new spool area assigned to a new ID. This means that students are forced to change the mail client setting when they get new student IDs. In order to solve the problem, the spool area should be assigned to the space assigned to the unique ID that won't be changed during the student life. We are going to establish a new student database including unique ID during the student life.

It is not easy for us to get the information of student alphabetical name timely manner. It is not a technical problem. It is a problem with the application form to enter the university. It takes too much time to input the name information on the database in referring papers. We expect to begin the name based mail address as early as possible for students comers in April, however, it will be difficult because we have to change the entire official procedure from the entrance examination to the entrance ceremony. It seems very difficult to realize it so far.

6. CONCLUSION

Students have been using e-mail addresses based on their student IDs at Kyushu University for a long time. It caused communication problems for students, teachers, and staff members to, especially following the transition to graduate school. We can get some attribute information of a student from his/her ID, but we can't get his/her name. We should respect the students' individuality by integrating their name into the e-mail address. Therefore, we decided to provide mail addresses based on their names. The number of users using name based mail addresses has increased rapidly. Students seem to welcome new name based e-mail address service. Many universities have outsourced the mail facility recently, but we have strong intention to implement and maintain our own mail system for safety and security purposes.

7. ACKNOWLEDGMENTS

Our thanks to all students who are using our new service and staff members of our working group to develop and maintain our new mail system in Information Infrastructure Initiative in Kyushu University.

8. REFERENCES

[1] Naomi Fujimura, Keisuke Masuoka, and Yoshinori Masaki. 2010. Experiences with Individual Receipt Confirmation System and the University Primary Mail Service. In Proceedings of SIGUCCS 2010 (Norfolk, VA, October 24 – 27 2010), pp.65 - 70.

[2] Naomi Fujimura and Zen'ichi Hirayama. 2011. Comparison of the Usage and Experience of a File Sharing System with Different Operation Policy. In Proceedings of the SIGUCCS 2011 (San Diego, CA, November 12 - 19, 2011), pp.131-134.

Evaluating IT Service Quality Using SERVQUAL

Janice El-Bayoumi
University of New Brunswick
PO Box 4400
Fredericton, NB E3B 5A3 Canada
(506) 453-3551
janice.el-bayoumi@unb.ca

ABSTRACT

What is the quality of our services? Increasingly organizations are finding that delivering quality service is a requirement for success. Understanding and measuring service quality can pose a significant challenge in a conceptual area that has few physical attributes to measure, and in which the perception and meaning of quality will vary from person to person. Service quality information is important in IT planning, enabling universities to target and prioritize areas for service improvement. Information Technology Services (ITS) at the University of New Brunswick adopted the SERVQUAL approach to evaluate our IT service quality. This approach, based on the customer's perspective, assesses five dimensions of quality: assurance, reliability, responsiveness, empathy and the tangible aspects. This case study will provide an overview of the SERVQUAL methodology and ITS's implementation. Through survey design and question development the methodology was adapted to minimize survey length, produce actionable results and enable iterative improvement.

Categories and Subject Descriptors

K.6.0 [Computing Milieux]: Management of Computing and Information Systems - General

General Terms

Management, Measurement, Performance.

Keywords

Survey, Service, Customer Service, Planning, Quality Assurance, Reliability, Responsiveness, Assurance, Empathy, Tangible.

1. INTRODUCTION

The University of New Brunswick, UNB, was established in 1785. It is a comprehensive university with two main campuses located about 120 kilometers apart. UNB also has smaller campuses located within the province and at various locations around the world. UNB has an enrollment of over 11,000 undergraduate and graduate students and offer degrees in more than 60 disciplines and continuing education in a variety of fields.

The ITS department is responsible for the information, technology, and communications (ITC) enterprise strategy as well as the delivery of many enterprise and Fredericton-campus-specific ITC services. Among early accomplishments, UNB was the first Canadian university to have a web site and to provide email accounts for all students. UNB runs a quality assurance (QA) program for academic and administrative units. This program coordinates the external review of departments on a seven-year cycle. ITS was recently added in to the cycle with the QA review to be completed by the end of 2012. The QA review includes a self-assessment component in which the department being reviewed evaluates the quality of services they provide. This evaluation must have rationale behind it. In the past ITS has not systematically evaluated its services, although some targeted evaluations have taken place. With the QA review as one driver, ITS decided to survey the UNB community to inform the self-assessment component of the QA review. An additional driver for the survey was a changing ITS culture. This change included a move to an iterative approach to service improvement. The survey mechanism would be used to track changes. This precedent was already established in the UNB library world which uses the LibQUAL+® [1] survey on a three year cycle to evaluate their services. ITS will adopt this best practice as a basis for iterative service improvement. The survey used by ITS and the LibQUAL+® survey are based on the same methodology. The survey undertaken at the time of writing this article is the first comprehensive survey of services completed by the department. For many services the survey results will provide an initial benchmark of the service quality.

2. SURVEY DEVELOPMENT

A number of challenges needed to be addressed in creating the survey. A methodology needed to be selected that was known to be valid. In a university environment in particular, the validity of any methodology is more apt to be questioned. This methodology needed to be easily understood by a person with little survey expertise. This person would be responsible for all aspects of the survey, from question creation to results presentation. Another challenge was the large number of services provided by ITS which needed evaluation, the challenge being how to get people to take the survey without abandoning it due to length. In addition, some services were campus specific, adding an additional level of complexity. Many students are also exhausted by the number of surveys they are asked to participate in, and getting faculty and staff participation can be difficult. A long survey would have little take-up. It was also important to us that the results of the survey would be actionable. This requirement needed to be incorporated into the survey design. We had our usability expert and accessibility expert review the first survey to ensure it was as usable and accessible as possible. The suggested changes were carried forward to all other surveys.

2.1 Methodology

An industry standard methodology was selected. The survey methodology (SERVQUAL) was obtained from an ISACA Journal article[2]. ISACA [3] is an independent, nonprofit, global association, engaging in the development, adoption and use of globally accepted, industry-leading knowledge and practices for information systems. SERVQUAL measures service quality from a customer perspective because quality means different things to different people. Service quality is defined as the difference between the customer's expectation of service excellence and the perception of the actual service they received. Five dimensions of service quality are considered:

1. The assurance dimension considers the ability of the employees to inspire trust and confidence. This dimension is the most important to people.
2. The reliability dimension considers the service dependability and accuracy.
3. The responsive dimension considers helpfulness and reaction time to customer need.
4. The empathy dimension considers the extent to which caring, individualized service is given.
5. The tangible dimension considers the physical aspects of the services such as facilities, equipment and staff appearance.

In the methodology, participants are asked to rate their expectation of an excellent service and their perception of the delivered service. In our implementation, we discovered that participants always rated their expectation very high. To obtain more meaningful results we rephrased the expectation question asking participants to rank the importance of various aspects of excellent service instead. A 1-7 scale was used.

2.2 Development Principles

To be thorough and accountable, keep the survey as short as possible and ensure all results have a reasonable potential for action some development principles were established.

2.2.1 Thoroughness and accountability

- Survey **all** quality **dimensions**. To ensure evaluation thoroughness, all quality dimensions would be represented in the questions for each service. This was achieved in almost every case. We chose to weigh all quality dimensions equally.
- **Transparency** of survey **results'** distribution and use. We ended up administering a number of surveys. In each case we included statements within the survey on how survey results would be used and a target date by which they would be distributed. Results transparency is important to maintaining a unit's reputation and accountability.

The survey introduction and close supported these principles by describing the survey methodology, why surveys were being done and how and by when survey results would be made available.

Sample survey introduction:
Welcome to Information Technology Service's (ITS) and Information Services and Systems (ISS) survey on the quality of the general IT services provide for UNB faculty and staff. This survey is part of on-going efforts to deliver high quality services. We appreciate your taking the time to help us improve the quality of services you use.

For each service, you will be asked to rate the importance you give to various aspects of an excellent service and then your experience with the service you have received. Depending on how you rate each statement, you will be given the opportunity to provide specific suggestions on how we can improve.

Please provide input only on services you have experience with. All responses are anonymous.

It will take about 10 - 30 minutes to complete the survey depending on the number of services you have experience with.

What is service quality? Of course it is different for each person! *(This section had to be clicked on to be viewed)*

This survey defines quality as the difference between your expectation of an excellent service and the perception of the service provided by ITS. Five dimensions of quality are considered:

- The tangible dimension considers the physical aspects of the services such as facilities, equipment and staff appearance.
- The responsive dimension considers helpfulness and reaction time to customer need.
- The reliability dimension considers the service dependability and accuracy.
- The assurance dimension considers the ability of the employees to inspire trust and confidence.
- The empathy dimension considers the extent to which caring, individualized service is given.

Sample survey close:
ITS and ISS will use survey results for 2 purposes:

1. To inform the ITS and ISS strategic plans by enabling each department to target quality improvement that maximize value to faculty and staff.
2. To inform the ITS and ISS self-evaluations which are a required component of UNB's Quality Assurance Program for non-Academic Service and Support Units. Both departments are participating in the program this year. The self-evaluations are provided to the Quality Assurance Review Committee for consideration as part of the review process.

Survey results will be posted on the ITS website within 2 months of survey close and an announcement will be made in eDaily and eNews.

2.2.2 Actionable results

- Each **service** has an **owner**. For each service a person is assigned to be accountable for final question authorization and for service results. Typically, the owner is the Manager of one of the functional teams within ITS. The owner often assigns a subject matter expert to help in the first draft of question development.
- Potential **action known**. To achieve this during question development, the manager must have in mind a course of action that could be taken in the event of a poor evaluation. To ensure service owners stay on track with this principle it is beneficial, during question development, to periodically verify what that corrective action would be. It does NOT mean that all services components with poor evaluations WILL be improved. The decision on which issues to address would be

based on how easy improvement is, the staff resources required and strategic importance.

- Participants would be able to provide **comments**. For all components of a service in which the expectation was rated 2 steps higher than the perception, the participant would be given the opportunity to provide specific input. This allows for input only in cases of very poor quality and helps service owners target improvements.

2.2.3 Minimize survey length

- Use as few questions as possible per service. The ISACA article posed 22 questions per service, spread across the five dimensions. Our surveys used targeted questions in order to shorten survey length. A minimum of five questions per service was developed (one for each dimension) with a maximum of 10 questions. This allowed some flexibility to target particular service components. Most services ended up with about seven questions.
- Don't make people see questions on services they don't use. To achieve this we prefaced each question set with a question asking if the person had experience with the service. If the answer was no, then the question set was skipped.
- Use **targeted audiences** when possible. Look at the services you will be surveying. Can you target some services to particular people? We managed to reduce the size of our general survey of faculty and staff services from thirty five services down to fifteen using this principle. An example is the project services we provide. This survey evaluated five services areas provided by ITS: Portfolio Management, Project Management, Business Process Analysis, Software Development, and Website Transition. We knew who had submitted to our Portfolio Management System and who had participated in our projects and thus were able to create a specific survey targeted only to this audience. In the end to evaluate all our services we ended up with eight different surveys. Two were general surveys (Student, Faculty/Staff audiences) and six were targeted to specific, narrowly defined audiences.
- **Service granularity.** When selecting services to survey it is important to consider how granular you want to get. Our initial list was quite high-level and omitted many services. We looked at each staff member to make sure his or her work was represented somehow in the surveys. Later, we found we had gotten too granular. Screens we used to determine granularity were: the number of people using the service (if it was small we didn't ask) and whether it can be combined with a similar service by consolidating two service question sets.

2.3 Question Development

Questions were developed to be actionable; to evaluate the five dimensions of each service (Reliability, Responsiveness, Assurance, Empathy, Tangible); to take into account the current knowledge about writing for the web (short, concise, appropriate grade level); and to be consistent both in wording throughout the survey and in order of presentation (we started with the tangible dimension). The ISACA ServQual articles gave examples of questions for each dimension which were very helpful in development. For example, in the assurance dimension, on the perception part of the survey:

Article suggestions:

- The behavior of employees in the SAS 70 audit firms instills confidence in you.

- You feel safe in your transactions with the SAS 70 audit firm.
- Employees at the SAS 70 audit firm are consistently courteous to you.
- Employees at the SAS 70 audit firm have the knowledge to answer your questions.

Our application in five service areas:

- Business Analyst Service: I am confident that the business analysts helping me recognized the private aspects of my business information and treated it accordingly.
- On-site Technical Support Service: When my computer was being worked on I was confident that my computer data and office possessions were safe and secure.
- ITS communication: I feel confident the IT information provided on each topic is complete.
- Computer Lab Services: When using general computer labs I feel my work, identity and access will not be affected by hackers and malicious software.
- Project Management Services: Project Managers know how to recognize project issues and get them resolved.

A work flow was developed to ensure that the question met the required development principles, were grammatically correct and typo free, and were authorized. The work flow was as follows:

1. Survey leader: Develop draft question set (expectation and perceptions) in conjunction with assigned content expert.
2. Survey leader: Review draft, make any adjustment and get authorization from service owner.
3. Survey leader: Upon completion of all questions in the survey, do a horizontal review of all question sets for consistency in order and wording. This work was sometimes assigned to an assistant.
4. Communications Manager: Review all question sets for grammar, typos, web writing and proper communication.
5. Assistant: Input questions into survey tool (we used LimeSurvey [4]).
6. Survey leader: Activate survey and ask service owners to do a last check of the questions related to their surveys for all aspects from content to survey function.
7. Assistant: Input any changes.
8. Survey leader: Ask a few people outside the department to take the survey as a pilot run and provide any suggestions for improvement.
9. Assistant: Input any changes.

At this point the survey would be closed until it was officially launched. We found that every step in this workflow yielded improvements, either an improved formulation of a question, removal of a question that ended up of little value or catching of typos. An example of a change we made based on input from a pilot run was to depersonalize questions as much as possible. For example instead of asking: "The employee providing on-site technical support responded to my support requests promptly" use "My support requests were responded to promptly." The input was that people often knew their technician and did not want to provide any negative input. The reworded version of the question elicits the same evaluation, but seems less personal. It was definitely the case that the more eyes on any survey before launch the better. Even with all these reviews mistakes were found after surveys were launched.

This is an example of a service question set for the Server Hosting service we provide.

Question: ITS hosts a server for me.

Yes or No were the possible responses. This question was mandatory. If "NO" was selected, the question set was skipped. The question must be clear enough to enable survey participants to identify whether they should answer yes or no.

Service: Server Hosting – Expectations Component of Question Set

Comment: Expectations set the benchmark against which Perceptions are compared. Each Expectation question has a corresponding Perception question. Each question is rated on a scale of 1-7. A "No Answer" response is also available.

Not Important						Very Important
1	2	3	4	5	6	7

Opening sentence: Some University IT departments host servers for researchers and for specific departmental services. How do you rate the importance of various aspects of excellent server hosting services?

1. Written communication about hosting services is professional. (Tangible dimension)
2. Hosted servers are always available. (Reliable dimension)
3. Requests for information about or issues related to server hosting are responded to promptly. (Responsive dimension)
4. Clients are told exactly what services will be provided as part of the hosting service. (Responsive dimension)
5. Costs for hosting servers are appropriate to the services delivered. (Assurance dimension)
6. Employees managing hosted servers are knowledgeable. (Assurance dimension)
7. Server hosting is done in a safe and secure physical environment. (Assurance dimension)
8. Hosted servers are configured to industry standards for a safe and secure operating system environment. (Assurance dimension)
9. Departments providing server hosting services have an effective way to address exceptions to standard hosting options. (Empathy dimension)
10. Departments providing server hosting services understand the hosting needs of the university. (Empathy dimension)

Service: Server hosting – Perceptions Component of Question Set

Comment: This question set evaluates the service the participant has received. If a perception question is evaluated at more than 2 below the corresponding expectation question a comment box

appears asking how the service could be improved. Each question is rated on a scale of 1-7. A "No Answer" response is also available.

Strongly Disagree						Strongly Agree
1	2	3	4	5	6	7

Opening sentence: ITS hosts servers for research and to meet specific departmental needs. To what extent do you agree or disagree with the following statements regarding your experience with the server hosting service you have received?

1. Written communication from employees providing server hosting services for me was professional. (Tangible dimension)
2. The servers hosted for me are always available. (Reliable dimension)
3. My requests for server hosting consultation and issues around implementation and operations are responded to promptly. (Responsive dimension)
4. I was told exactly what services will be provided as part of ITS's hosting service. (Responsive dimension)
5. I feel confident that the costs for hosting servers are appropriate for the services I receive. (Assurance dimension)
6. I feel confident that the employees advising me on and providing hosting services are knowledgeable. (Assurance dimension)
7. I feel confident that my hosted servers are housed in a safe and secure physical environment. (Assurance dimension)
8. I feel confident that my hosted servers are configured to industry standards for a safe and secure operating system environment. (Assurance dimension)
9. ITS was able to effectively address any exceptions I have had to standard hosting options. (Empathy dimension)
10. I am satisfied by the server hosting services offered by ITS. (Empathy dimension)

3. RUNNING THE SURVEY

Prior to running each survey a communication plan was developed. Once the survey was launched response was monitored. A number of activities needed to take place before the survey could be closed.

3.1 Communication Plan

For each survey audience a communication plan was developed. This plan contained: the communication channels; activities related to each channel; position responsible for each activity and when it was to be done; key messages and a target number of responses. The response rate was determined by using the Sample Size Calculator available on The Survey System [5] website. This Sample Size Calculator is presented as a public service of Creative Research Systems survey software. It can be used to determine how many people you need to participate in a survey in order to get results that reflect the target population.

An abbreviated example of a typical communication plan looks like this:

Survey Audience: Faculty and staff

Target Response Rate: 100 completed surveys

Channels: ITS Website, email, ITS blog, Twitter and Facebook, eNewsletters, myUNB Portal, Inside UNB web page

Key Messages:

- Feedback is important to identify areas for improvement
- Results and improvement progress will be posted on the ITS website
- Needed for UNB Quality Assurance program

Activities:

Who	Channels & Activity	Date	Purpose	Who
Faculty Staff	Posting - eNewsletter, ITS blog, on Twitter and Facebook Ad blocks on Inside UNB and ITS websites	Launch date eNewsletters will be reposted every Monday until survey close	General awareness Promotion	Comms Manager
Deans Directors	Request to encourage departmental staff to participate - Email	3 days after launch	Targeted promotion to dept. staff	Assoc VP-ITS
Faculty Staff	Inadequate response repost to eDaily, eNews	3 days before survey close if target response not reached.	Reach response rate target	Comms Manager

3.2 Monitoring

Each survey was monitored regularly for response rate. The purpose of the monitoring was to be able to assess the progress toward target response rates. In some cases it was necessary to do additional promotion and the monitoring provided the lead time to put the communication in place.

3.3 Survey Close

A number of activities took place once it was determined that the survey could be closed. First the results and questions were downloaded and then the results and question codes were downloaded. These are combined and used in results analysis. A single question set is analyzed as a test case to ensure no errors occurred during the downloads. Finally, the survey, including its structure, is downloaded, ready to be uploaded for future use. The survey can then be closed.

4. SURVEY RESULTS

Survey results were presented in two different ways in order to address the needs of different audience groups. The first audience group was service owners and their staff. Results for this group needed to provide the level of detail for understanding and to enable prioritization of actions. The second audience—UNB senior administrators, the UNB community and the external Quality Assurance Review examiners—needed to be able to review results at a high level, only looking at detail as required.

4.1 Results for Service Owners

Survey results were presented to service owners in the following way:

1. Comments were separated by campus, service category and service question. Survey results were placed on our departmental shared folder for ease of distribution. In a few cases personal comments were made regarding specific staff members. As a result comments were previewed to ensure that they did not contain sensitive information before being placed in shared folders. Performance management was NOT identified as a use of results. Responses to the survey were anonymous, and comments could not be validated. Service comments that contained personal comments were shared only with the appropriate manager.

2. Detailed results were presented in an Excel workbook The workbook contained:

   a. Question set for each service. For each question set a detailed analysis showing the number of responses for each quality level was created. Quality levels are based on the difference between the expectation and perception of each question set that was asked about the service. This is displayed as a histogram. The histogram represented the number of responses at each quality level. For example, in Figure 1, 143 is the number of responses in which the expectation of service desired is the same as the perception of service received (shown as "Meets" on the graph).

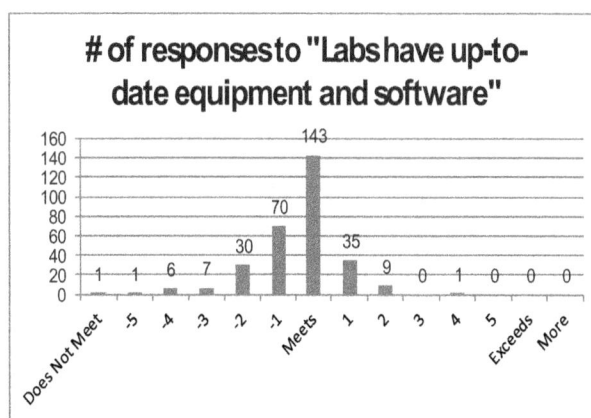

Figure 1 Histogram of responses based on quality

   b. Analysis of results of perceptions-only responses. It was our thinking that there is a tendency of survey participants to mark all questions in the expectations questions as high as possible. To counter this, we wanted service owners to see how survey participants ranked services without comparison to the "ideal" as represented in the expectations questions. We felt this would be helpful in interpreting the results and give a better understanding. Figure 2 shows this graph.

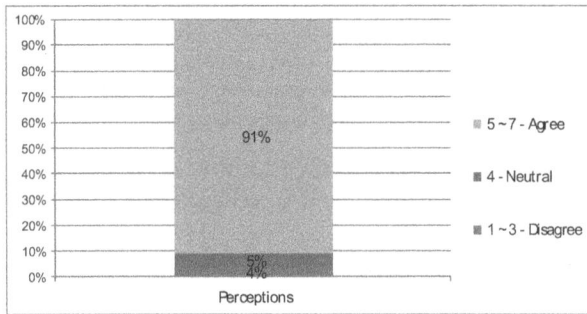

Figure 2 Graph of perception results

c. Satisfactory, Potential for Improvement and Key Areas for Quality Improvement. To put a consistent structure around the results we broke them out into three categories: Satisfactory (quality), Potential for Improvement (in quality) and Key Areas for Improvements. Satisfactory and Potential for Improvement response percentages were captured in a service roll-up graph.

   • Satisfactory quality was defined as when perceptions are close to (within 1 step), equal to or above expectations (--1 through +6 on question set graph).

   • Potential for improvement was defined as when perceptions are 2 steps or more (-2 through -6 on question set graph) lower than expectations.

   • Key area for quality improvement was defined as 25% or more of respondents must have given an evaluation in the potential for improvement category. This information helps service managers focus on problem areas and produces a manageable number of potential improvements to review.

   • The Satisfactory and Potential for Improvement response percentages were captured in a service roll-up graph. Knowing this information helps service managers key in on problem areas.

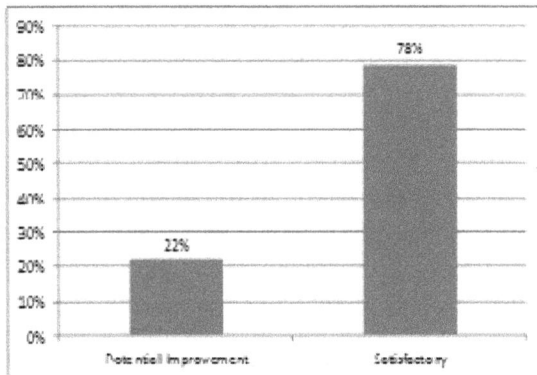

Figure 3 Roll-up graph of all service components

d. When possible, the number of people surveyed was included in the results. The more responses, the more reliable the results. In most cases, this is pretty straightforward information, but in the case of students it can be difficult. For example, UNB has about 11,000 full-time equivalent students, but about 25,000 individuals. These can be on-campus, off-campus, taking one course or many. Many questions were only applicable to a subset of students whose numbers cannot be estimated very accurately.

e. Service roll-up. The service roll-up represents percentages of RESPONSES (not people). The service rollup compiles the quality results of all the questions in a single service question set. Figure 3 shows an example of this graph.

4.2 Results for the UNB Community

There were several challenges in presenting survey results for the UNB community. One was to present it at the right level. High-level views would interest most people. However, some people would be interested in more detail. Our commitment to transparency required that both services with satisfactory quality and those with areas for potential improvement needed to be presented. Another challenge was the large number of services which were surveyed. To cover all our services we ran eight surveys to evaluate fifty three services each with multiple components. Some services were also separated out by campus. To meet the challenges we posted our survey results on the ITS website to allow for easy access and wide distribution. A menu selection for each survey allows viewers to more easily find the survey results they were interested in. High-level results were provided as well as the functionality to obtain more detail. The following general information, which applied to all surveys, was provided:

   • A description of Service Quality along with the information on the methodology and where it was obtained.
   • A description on how to interpret the survey results that were presented.

Figure 4 shows what the survey results homepage looks like.

Figure 4 Survey results home page

Survey results were displayed as bars tracking percentage of responses in the satisfactory, and potential for improvement areas.

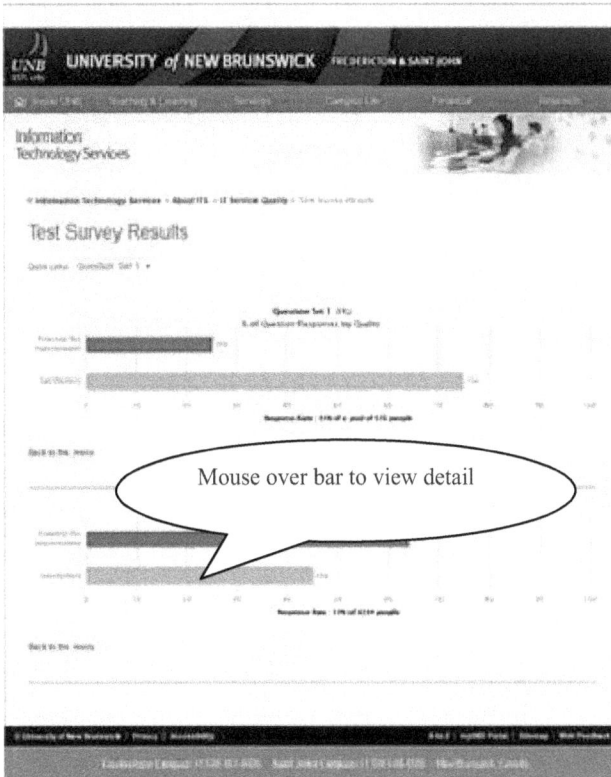

Figure 5 Web display of survey results

A drop-down menu allows viewers to easily select the service they are interested in. Positioning the mouse over the graphic bars displays detailed information. Figure 5 shows this layout.

5. CONCLUSION

The benefit in finding out the quality of your services is not in the knowing – but in the actions that follow. Results provide management with the information needed to identify and prioritize improvements leading to a more responsive and successful department. Running the survey every three years, according to best practice, will help us to track and publicize improvements as well as identify areas of slippage. While the initial effort to develop, launch and analyze survey results took several months, it is anticipated that service quality evaluations will take much less time now that the survey structure and questions are in place, analysis of results has been largely automated and decisions related to transparency have been completed. However, as with most activities, we expect to improve our service evaluations over time by applying iterative improvement based on lessons learned from each survey season.

6. ACKNOWLEDGMENTS

Thanks to Bobby Jones and Tracy Allen for editing and suggestions. Thanks to Melissa Hannah for communications plan.

7. REFERENCES

[1] LibQUAL+®. http://www.libqual.org/

[2] ISACA http://www.isaca.org/

[3] Bell, Thomas J., and Smith, Thomas. The Assimilation of Marketing's Service Quality Principles and the IT Auditing Process. In ISACA Journal. Volume 4, 2011.

[4] LimeSurvey website. http://www.limesurvey.org

[5] The Survey System website. http://www.surveysystem.com

Yes You Can: Offer a Comprehensive Set of Technologies to Enhance Teaching and Learning

Apurva Mehta
University of Massachusetts Boston
100 Morrissey Blvd
Boston, MA 02125
617-287-5952

apurva.mehta@umb.edu

ABSTRACT

The wide array of educational technologies available today has evolved substantially in the past few years. Tools which had been released just a few years back, are now more feature rich, easier to use, are able to integrate into campus portals. More importantly the systems have become more affordable – in that most are now hosted in the cloud, not needing developers and technical staff to maintain; thereby allowing instructional designers, media and content specialists to concentrate their work on assisting faculty to use these technologies.

UMass Boston has over the past 4 years, has taken advantage of these developments and is able to offer the community a wide variety of options for engaging students. The presentation will show how a public university like UMass Boston has been able to offer a wide variety of systems, extended hours support, Wiki's, Blogs, classroom capture systems, iTunes U, personal response systems and other services with a small staff and limited budgets. Offering wide choices allows faculty to teach with tools that suit their teaching styles, but more importantly allows students who become aware of these tools to demand that their faculty adopt them, because the way students learn today has changed dramatically. It is our obligation to meet their learning needs.

Categories and Subject Descriptors

K.6.3 [Management of Computing and Information Systems]: Software Management – software selection

General Terms

Management, Reliability, Human Factors, Standardization

Keywords

Instructional Technology, Support, Wiki, Blog, Lecture Capture, iTunes, Personal Response System, Open Courseware, Budget, Teaching, Learning

1. INTRODUCTION

The University of Massachusetts Boston is nationally recognized as a model of excellence for urban public universities. The scenic waterfront campus is located next to the John F. Kennedy Library and the soon to be built Edward M Kennedy institute and is within short distance from downtown Boston. UMass Boston is the second largest campus in the UMass system with a student population of just over 16,000, 75% of which are undergraduates. A commuter campus has a very diverse student body with about 40% belonging to a minority group. The university employs over 800 full and part-time faculty allowing a faculty to student ratio of 16:1

The Informational technology (IT) and the library are independent divisions that report to the Provost. The two divisions do work closely together as most of the services are located in the same building. Projects as surveys, technology conferences, workshops and liaison program bring the librarians and educational technology staff working together. The educational technology department is one of three departments within IT and is responsible for instructional support, classroom technology, computer labs, media and training. With a staff of 35 motivated team members the department supports the over 800 faculty, a rapidly growing online program and over 16,000 students.

In 2007 when I assumed responsibility of the educational technology department, the only product we supported that faculty could use to manage their course and enhance teaching was Blackboard Vista, formerly WebCT. Having been put through two migrations within a similar period, the faculty was frustrated as the newer learning management systems are more complex to use, because they offer more features and some of the earlier systems were much simpler to use. In many cases faculty were just interested in putting up their syllabus and a few readings and the question to ask is whether we need a full LMS to accomplish this? So faculty were creating their own websites hosted across various ISP, hence not under UMass Boston's branding umbrella, clearly not something a world class university would like to do. Clearly a problem we had to solve.

In 2002 UMass Boston became a member of UMass Online whose role was to host the learning management system. Our instructional designers provide direct support to our faculty. Having this system hosted by an external entity, allowed us to concentrate on putting systems together to truly enhance teaching and learning.

2. BUILDING OUR TEACHING PORTFOLIO

2.1 Collaboration with the Library and Wikis

While faculty at UMass Boston were adapting to Blackboard Vista, the library began to use Wiki's as a way to organize library resources that faculty might use in their teachings. The librarians and the instructional designers worked together to embed access to the library resources within the LMS. As more and more faculty started using Wiki's it quickly became apparent that this tool had merit as faculty found the system flexible and easy to use and students adapted to it easily as well. There was no need for us to employ resources to support such a service as was being done to support Blackboard Vista. Thus began the search for a Wiki service that we could support. The first place we looked was at our sister schools and we found UMass Lowell using 'Wikispaces'. A short 40 minute ride and we were at the Lowell campus meeting the faculty and staff that support the Wiki application. In about an hour after the visit I decided that Wikispaces it is. Why?

1. The system was being used by the library and the faculty and students were familiar with the application.

2. Wikispaces offered unlimited Wiki's for a fixed reasonable price – $6,000 a year.

3. The system offered a way for us to authenticate our faculty & students against our Active Directory.

4. The system is hosted in the 'cloud'. This allows our staff to concentrate our efforts on supporting the application.

5. We had a very large department that had committed to using Wikis. The English department was using a home-grown, locally hosted wiki like system whose main feature was to permit students and faculty to review each others submissions and comment on it. Our Faculty Liaison person is a retired English Faculty and she helped implement this service for the department.

6. The librarians were using the system to organize reading and research material that faculty might use in their courses.

We rolled out Wikispaces in 2009 and today we have over 400 courses that use this system. What did faculty like about the system? They like the simplicity of using the system. It was extremely easy for them to upload their syllabi and readings and some of them even used the system for discussions.

Because we were in the midst of rolling out Blackboard Vista we had a graduate student in the instructional design program and a faculty liaison, market and support the system. In the first year we had our staff offer training / workshops but once we had a few faculty on-board using Wikis we asked them to present workshops on how they use the system. This method worked very well and we were extremely pleased when our Dean of Science and Math used Wikis as the platform for his *Freshmen Success Community* project. The goal of the project was to enhance the experience and academic success for the new freshmen entering the college of Science and Math. The Wiki tool was used to organize the entire project. It contained the Syllabus, the Assignments, and the 5 cohorts of students, each of which used the wiki to submit their assignments and track their progress. We had the Dean be our keynote speaker at our annual educational technology conference (http://umbmedia.wordpress.com/)[1] [2]

At our 2009 technology conference we had 3 faculty along with our wiki administrator talk about how the faculty were using Wiki's in lieu of Blackboard. There was considerable feedback I received from faculty telling me that they were not satisfied with Blackboard and that it was difficult to use. All the faculty really wanted was a place to post their syllabus, readings and the occasional posting for discussion. The faculty were not interested in the grading and other modules available in Blackboard. Our initial goal of offering Wikis was to having a stepping stone that faculty could use to eventually migrate their courses onto Blackboard. Overtime we have found most faculty who adopted Wikis have stayed with the platform, unless they have decided to use some of the advanced features, such as SafeAssign, grading, discussions, etc.

You can learn more about our Wikispaces roll-out by visiting - http://www.wikispaces.umb.edu/

2.2 The Adoption of Blogs

Our next step was to invest in a Blog system. This was based on requests we received from two very different constituents – university staff and faculty. The university administration wanted a system which they could use as a way of getting the UMass Boston message out to prospective students, and the community in general. The new and often younger faculty that we were hiring were asking for a Blog system they could use in their course and also as a way of collaborating and sharing their work with members of other universities. Based on this we used the same method of selecting a system as we did with Wiki's. We looked around and found another sister school – UMass Amherst that had rolled out a Blog service. After learning more about their system, we decided to replicate their setup. We invested in a server, hired a developer to roll out the system along with a few templates that we had selected. After trying to roll out this service for well over a year and investing a significant amount of money, we realized that the system was not going to fly, mainly because once our contract with the developer expired; we knew we would be unable to maintain the server and the WordPress updates. Many of the add-ons would not work properly with our templates and this caused much confusion and frustration with our faculty and administration. Each update of WordPress that we applied would break something else. Hence we started looking for another solution....one that is hosted and managed in the cloud, offers single sign-on and unlimited blogs. We found all this in one vendor – eduBlogs.com and after negotiating a contract decided to roll out this service. This has worked very well.

Although a majority of the blogs on our system is created by administration (admissions) the academic side of the house is just as popular, with college programs, research institutes and faculty using the blog as a way to reach out and document their work. The admissions office uses this free format to get students to share their experience, maybe as a freshman or as a transfer student. [3]

The research institutes at UMass Boston have also adopted this platform and have documented their work and findings on this platform. Student researchers are using blogs as a way of building their portfolio.

Our University Advancement office is also a client and one that started just a few months ago. However, probably one of our most popular and long running blogs is our "Venture

Development Center" which has been using the blogs to promote their center.

The faculty adoption of the system has been slow mainly because we have had problems with our initial rollout (hosted and supported in-house) and hence we never got around to marketing the service. Now that we have a dependable (hosted and supported in the cloud) system we are able to begin marketing the system.

Today we have over 722 blogs; 320 being used by students, 36 by departments, 38 by Institutes/Clubs and Centers, and 23 class blogs. Although the number of class blogs is relatively small we feel that in a short time we have been able to market this service across the university and adoption will continue to grow. The number of blog posts for Spring 2012 is 172 a 200% increase for the same time last year (Spring 2011).

The system is hosted in Australia – yes, the world is indeed flat! [4] And they offer everything we needed. Our only issue was technical support…the time difference made it difficult for us to get just-in-time support. Our faculty and administration are truly happy. As you can see, we tried the in-house method of hosting and supporting Blogs but eventually settled for a hosted cloud based solution.

2.3 Classroom Capture & iTunes U

With mobile technology becoming mainstream and with most students equipped with an iPod we quickly learned that one way of getting information into the hands of students was to capture the classroom content and push it out via iTunes U or have it hosted on the web, so students can gain access to the classroom lectures. After doing our research and with a very tight budget in 2010 we selected and decided to deploy "Camtasia Relay" as our classroom capture system and to have the recordings hosted at "Screencast.com" – also a Tech Smith product. For a fixed price we got unlimited licenses and because we were not sure whether faculty would embrace this system we invested in the base system which allows for one recording to be processed at a time. We worked very closely with our 'Classroom Technology' team as it is very important that faculty get assistance with this technology if needed. As the popularity of this service grew, we upgraded our license so we could processes 2-5 recordings concurrently. This allowed faculty to have access to their recordings in a more timely manner. Recordings were posted on Screencast.com and in the last year we have started to move content over to iTunes U if the faculty gave us permission. The system Camtasia Relay has grown very nicely over the last 3 years allowing for captioning on the fly which helps students with disabilities. There are a number of nicer systems on the market, offering features that would make accessing data easier, integrating with LMS systems; however each of them are much more expensive. I am optimistic that Tech Smith--makers of Camtasia Relay will get there, and investing in a system that is beginning to grow will allow us to reap the benefits in the coming years at a fraction of the cost. However most importantly I would like to see Tech Smith offer Relay as a cloud based service. This will allow us to move away from managing the server. The one thing that I do not like is every-time the server software is upgraded, the client software must also be upgraded…the client and server must be in sync.

I would like to share with you how one our Biology professors teaching a 300 level course has decided to record his lectures with Relay and he presented his findings at our workshops and the conference. The professor was recording his lectures – audio only,

but then decided to use Relay. Because the subject Biology has many charts, diagrams the importance to introduce a format that allows students to review lecture content was very important. Students have told the professor that they have a better comprehension of the material because they can replay the lecture. The students also listed to the content while commuting or when studying in their room. Students did not like the faculty saying "Over here you can see this" because its not something they can "see"…hence faculty have to make minor tweaks.[5] ESL students said that the recordings helped them get a better grasp of the material. Hearing impaired students also benefited and today his students "demand" that the lectures be recorded. In Spring 2011 the same faculty member used the updated version of Relay to caption his recordings. The error rate was quite high, which may have been because of the technical terms; so we decided to not continue down this road.

By and large we have noticed that the Science and Nursing faculty have adopted this technology.

In 2009 we signed an agreement with Apple to offer iTunes U as a learning tool. I first saw a demo of this product at Educause and learned how Duke and other universities were using this tool. It was nice to see an easy to use platform that our students can use to hear lectures or access classroom material. Although we only offer the "public" site of iTunes U to our students, many faculty have adopted to use this service to post their classroom content. The service has become quite popular with over 40,000 downloads taking place every month. Best of all iTunes U is free.

2.4 OpenCourseWare (http://ocw.umb.edu)

An open source system that was developed at MIT and deployed at several universities across the world, allows universities to make available courses that anyone can take. Although this may not be seen as an important teaching tool for students enrolled in our university, it is an important marketing tool. Many faculty have elected to post their courses on this platform to attract a wider audience to enroll in either online or face2face courses.

Today we offer courses in over 17 subject area and 45 courses….ranging from Biology to Psychology, with EEOS (11), Early Education (6), History and Chemistry with four each as the more popular subjects. The concept behind OCW, is that it is the responsibility of the student to download and access all the information that a faculty would use to teach the face2face or online course. Content that faculty make available are – syllabus, readings, lecture notes, images, exams, etc.

The cost of the system is zero; however we did have to invest in a server; although a virtual server would also be able to handle the load. Support for this system, like other open-source systems is based on the kindness of the community.

2.5 Personal Response System

Whether you look at Personal response Systems (PRS) as an instructional tool or a classroom technology tool, it is an essential service that engages students. This tool is especially useful for classes that have large enrollments; where numbers are greater than 35. The initial investment to deploy this service is minimal. We purchased a couple of base units and about 40 clickers which we loaned out to faculty. We selected the iClicker system because a couple of science faculty were already using the system and when they heard that we were looking to deploy this service they strongly recommended that we select the iClicker system.

After doing some research we found the iClicker system to be widely used. This satisfied the team here and we worked with the vendor who offered free training when we purchased the base units. We worked with the faculty who were using the system to offer workshops so other faculty would adopt the system.

In 2007 we hosted an annual "Educational Technology" conference as a way to promote the use of technology by faculty. In our very first year we invited two science faculty teaching large classes –100+ students - one teaching Biology and another Chemistry. Both faculty used the system in the similar fashion. I had the opportunity to sit in one of the Biology classes and witness first-hand how the system was being used. The faculty member would ask the students a couple of questions on topics he covered in his previous lecture. This would allow him to gauge whether the students were grasping the concept. This initial interaction is recorded as part of attendance as well as grades. During the course of the class the faculty will use the PRS to ask questions and one final set of questions at the end of the class. This allows the faculty to (a) keep the students engaged plus (b) gauge if the content is getting to the students. If not, the faculty member can go over topics that students may have difficulty with.

We also had an EEOS faculty member be our keynote speaker at our 3rd annual ed tech conference where he spoke about how he uses the iClickers to engage his students. His classes have about 200 students. He begins his class by using media to engage students to introduce and reinforce concepts. He then uses iClickers during the class for formative assessment.

Once the demand by faculty to use clickers began to increase started installing the base units in all large classrooms and today we have about 35 units installed. As more and more faculty use this system, students are able to use the clicker for multiple classes. The main complaint we hear from students is that the unit is fairly expensive. This service is supported by a part-time instructional designer in conjunction with our classroom technology team. Support has been minimum and because of the number of clickers that our bookstore sells we are able to get a free base unit for every 75 clickers.

With the introduction of Web clickers we are in the midst of piloting this new system. So far the feedback has not been positive and that may have been because wireless access may not have been prevalent and reliable. However as this changes, our goal would be to migrate to a system that does eventually need a clicker unit, instead the student would use their smartphone.

3. WHAT'S ON THE HORIZON?

So what is in store for all of us? As with anything, with time technology continues to move forward and it is our obligation to stay in tune with it so that each new generation entering higher-ed, have the opportunity to use these to stay engaged with learning. Some of technologies we are about to roll out or are thinking about:

a. Voicethread – if you visit their website (https://voicethread.com/) you will see their tag line – "*Conversations in the Cloud*'. This says it all....and that is where we would like to be. With an app for the iPad Voicethread allows faculty and students to collaborate through video and audio without the need for installing any software on the system. Our modern languages department has been piloting this system for the past year and we have been so happy with the results that we have committed to purchasing a site license in FY 13.

b. iPad in the Classroom – the iPad has become the fastest selling device and is making major inroads into college campuses. Apple has taken this vertical market very seriously and has developed programs to meet the needs of faculty and students. This allows universities to manage the deployment of iPads and apps. [6]

c. eTextBook – integration with LMS – The publishing industry is undergoing a revolution. As printed text books get more and more expensive colleges and university are looking at ways to reduce the burden of textbooks. One option is for students and faculty to adopt etextBooks, which tend to save between 20 and 40% off the cost of a printed book. Besides the cost advantages, etextBooks add interactive learning modules which enhances learning. Major learning management systems have built interfaces that allow eTextBook chapters and interactive modules to integrate seamlessly with their systems. This allows faculty to take advantage of all the features of eTextBooks. [7]

d. Just-In-Time Training – there is nothing more frustrating than not knowing how to do something, especially when it is needed the most. There is a very interesting product that our instructional designers have found – Atomic Learning which has short, and I mean very short videos on a wide variety of topics. These clips are even shorter than the Khan Academy ones.

So as you can see, the horizon does look bright and I am sure there will be many promising systems and applications that will rise to the surface which will make teaching and learning exciting, especially in the mobile marketplace. Some of the high schools use interesting technology and because most of them are on tight budgets, that might be a good place to look.

4. CONCLUSION

As you can see we have been able to deploy a wide variety of tools and services, most at very reasonable costs. This is really due to the fact that we have elected to go with systems that are hosted in the cloud and are not premier system. What I mean here is that the system we select tend to offer 80% of the services that a premier system would offer, but the price if often significantly less. Here are some of the features or criteria we look at prior to selecting a system:

a. Is the system hosted in the cloud? This reduces hardware costs and more importantly the time and money spent on supporting the system.

b. Does the vendor offer unlimited licenses, storage and support? If you want a product to be successful, it is important that you invest in an unlimited license, it one less hurdle to jump through. It will help you market the service.

c. Don't ignore free, open systems. Yes, such systems do require "people" time to support, but consider the trade-off. iTunes U, Opencourseware are two good examples. It will propel the image of your institution.

d. Invest heavily in 'people' – Instructional Designers, Classroom Technology Support, Media Specialists. No amount of technology will work without motivated and skilled staff. The staff should be willing to learn new technologies and more importantly willing to change with the times.

e. Its best to avoid developing your own systems, unless of course you have the money and the people to nurture and sustain it.

f. Use graduate students for more complex systems and under-graduate students for repetitive tasks. Graduate students can be a great asset in rolling out a new service. We hire a couple of students each year from our instructional design program and tend to be very motivated and eager to learn new skills. Remember to pair them up with a full-time team member, because you do not want to lose the skill sets once they graduate.

g. Learn how other area universities have deployed a service or a system. Rather than trying to reinvent the wheel or spend valuable time researching the landscape, its best to see what your peer institutions are doing. Pay them a visit and talk with their staff about what they liked and disliked about the system.

Figure 1: List of eLearning Tools Available

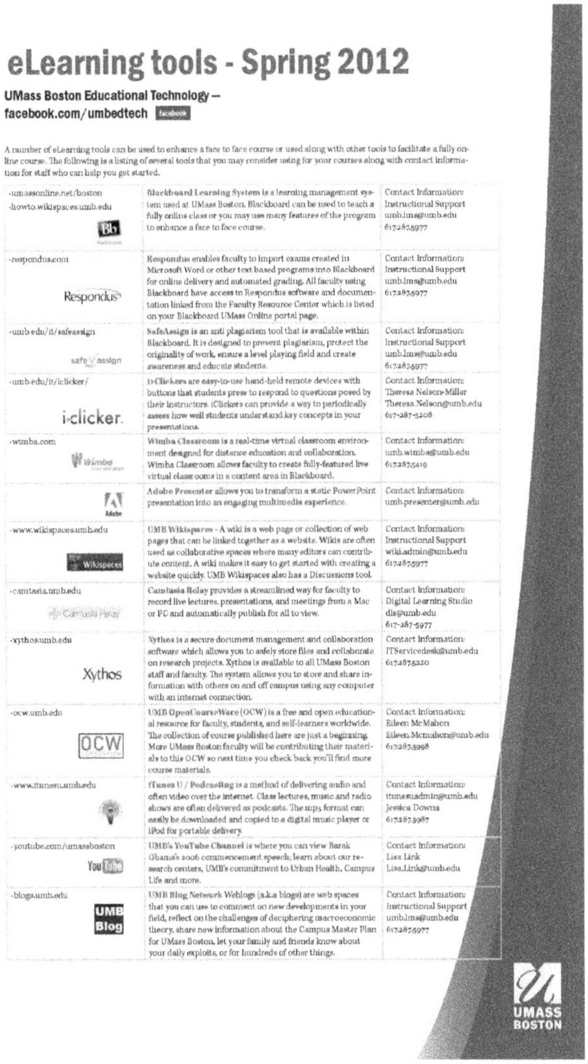

eLearning tools - Spring 2012

Table 1. Overview of Services & Systems

Product / Service	Features	Cost
Wikispaces (www.wikispaces.umb.edu)	Unlimited Hosted in the Cloud Ease of Use Single Sign-On	$6,000
Blogs (blogs.umb.edu)	Unlimited Hosted in the Cloud Variety of Templates University Wide (Faculty & Administration) Single Sign-On	$6,000
iClickers (http://www.umb.edu/it/getting_services/instructional_support/iclicker/)	Easy to Use Nearly Free (small initial investment) Promising Future (Web Clickers)	$0
Itunes U	Universal Source Ease of Use – Students Hosted by Apple	$0
Open Course Ware (ocw.umb.edu)	Course Content Available to the World University Image / Marketing Tool Based on Open Source – Needs TLC	$0
Classroom Capture – (http://class-capture.wikispaces.umb.edu/Welcome	Unlimited Licenses Simple to Use	$6,500 – one time $1,500 annually

5. ACKNOWLEDGMENTS

I would like to thank and recognize Dr. Anne S. Agee, Vice Provost for Information Technology and CIO for UMass Boston for her leadership and guidance. She has allowed me the freedom to experiment and explore various learning technologies and supported each endeavor with enthusiasm and guided me along the way in each of my projects. I would also like to thank the staff in the Instructional Support team, especially Mark Lewis (Manager), Mary Simone (Classroom Capture & Voicethread) Eileen McMahon (Blogs & OCW), Jessica Downa (iTunes) Christian de Torres (Wiki), Theresa Nelson-Miller (iCLickers), the Dean of Libraries Dr. Daniel Ortiz and the SIGUCCS support team especially Trevor Murphy.

6. REFERENCES

[1]   Dean Grosovsky, A. – Freshman Success Community Project - http://intrd187s-f11-grosovsky.wikispaces.umb.edu/

[2]   Educational Technology Newsletter Website - http://umbedtech.wordpress.com/category/wikis/

[3]   Blogs Website – Transfer Students - http://blogs.umb.edu/transferadmissions/

[4]   Friedman Thomas L., The World is Flat.

[5]   Educational Technology Conference 2011. Prof. Ackerman "Camtasia Relay and Beyond" - http://www.screencast.com/t/56qpA41MTRFR

[6]   Apple Website - http://www.apple.com/education/ipad/

[7]   Rickman Jon T, Holzen Roger V, Klute Paul G. and Tobin Teri - A Campus-Wide E-Textbook Initiative – Educase Webiste - http://www.educause.edu/ero/article/campus-wide-e-textbook-initiative

A Little "More" Conversation and Practice: Training Student Technology Trainers

Christine L. Vucinich
Technical Education & Outreach Coordinator
Duke University - Office of Information Technology
334 Blackwell Street, Suite 1100
Durham, NC 27701
(919) 613-3782
clv4@duke.edu

ABSTRACT
This paper outlines the processes and best practices implemented to train Duke's Office of Information Technology (OIT) student technology trainers on technical topics and to help them become comfortable in the classroom (public speaking, handling questions, etc.).

Categories and Subject Descriptors
K.6.1 [**Management of Computing and Information Systems**]: Project and People Management – *training*.

General Terms
Performance, Standardization.

Keywords
Duke University, train-the-trainer, IT Training, student technology trainers, Panopto

1. INTRODUCTION
The Office of Information Technology Training program (OIT Training) is within the Academic Services department of Duke University's Central IT Office. OIT Training provides technology training opportunities to support the academic needs of Duke students, staff, and faculty. The program includes pre-scheduled instructor-led training seminars (free technology seminars), brown bag lunch sessions (Learn IT @ Lunch), and just-time-time training opportunities (OnDemand Training) for Duke-specific tools and academic needs. [1]

OIT Training has one full time staff member, Christine Vucinich, who coordinates the overall training program and also teaches seminars and supervises the student trainers. Trainers for the program include full-time staff training partners who lend their expertise by training on various topics (such as Security, Scalable Computing, Qualtrics, SharePoint) as well as undergraduate student technology trainers who teach a variety of free technology seminars including WordPress, iMovie, Photoshop, PowerPoint and more. Throughout the academic year, the student technology trainers teach a variety of pre-scheduled technology seminars and OnDemand sessions to meet a small group and academic needs.

2. STUDENT TECHNOLOGY TRAINERS
The student technology trainers are part of the overall Student Workers Assisting with Technology (SWAT) Program. In addition to the OIT Training program, students work in other areas including the Link Service Desk, Community Outreach, the Multimedia Project Studios and OIT's News & Information Office. The job description and application for the student technology trainers are both available on Duke's OIT Website. [2] Each year, our staff consists of five to seven student technology trainers. The number of students we hire depends on the number of student trainers we retain each year.

2.1 Interview process
Students are initially interviewed by Erin Nettifee, Duke's Coordinator of Academic Support, who manages the overall SWAT program. Based on the students' submitted applications and interests indicated on their online applications, she gauges the area(s) where each student would be a good fit. Students sometimes work in multiple areas of the SWAT program. She uses this application process and initial interview to weed out students who would not be a good fit for OIT.

Students are invited to come back for a training interview when they show an interest in the training program, have experience conducting presentations or assisting others in a 1-1 or small group setting, and have some technical knowledge.

For the training interview, the student is interviewed by the training coordinator and the training student supervisor. The interview consists of a series of formal questions to get more information about why the student is interested in OIT Training, their strengths and weaknesses, the technology they would be comfortable teaching and prior presentation experience. The interview concludes with a required five minute training demo on a technology topic of their choice.

We use this interview to get a feel for their communication and presentation skills as well as to give them an overall sense of our program and our program culture—which is to provide ongoing and constructive feedback to one another.

3. NEW HIRE ORIENTATION
Once the student technology trainer is hired, new hire orientation begins. Orientation consists of attending an initial SWAT orientation, completing a new hire checklist housed on a Wiki, meeting with the student supervisors, and conducting demo sessions.

3.1 SWAT Orientation

Every student hired into the SWAT program goes through a SWAT Orientation with Duke's Coordinator of Academic Support, who oversees the SWAT program. The orientation consists of information that applies to all of our staff: policies/procedures, scheduling, dress code, expectations, and customer service.

3.2 New Hire Checklist

To learn the specifics of the training program, students are required during their training preparation hours to go through a new hire checklist. The checklist for new student trainers includes items that we want each student to do including submitting a photo and writing a bio for our training website staff profile page, accessing the registration system, accessing lynda.com online training tutorials, and reviewing existing materials and trainers' outlines. We update this checklist as needed.

This checklist has an estimated due date for each activity and takes approximately the entire semester to complete. The training coordinator and student supervisor checks in periodically with the new student trainer to see where they are in the process and to see if they have questions.

Task to complete	Due Date?	Date Completed	Notes
Submit all employee paperwork to Erin	before your first day		This must be completed before you start working, to make sure we can pay you for your training hours.
Fill out your first timecard	by end of first week or first payroll deadline.		
Review OIT Training Website	by end of first week.		Let Christine or Training Student Supervisor know if you have questions.
Read Training Section of this wiki	Before meeting with Christine and/or Training Student Supervisor.		Pay special attention to Trainer & Train-the-Trainer information.
Meet with Student Supervisor.	by end of second week.		Tour OIT Training Lab (133 Soc. Psych), review Wiki information (any questions?), Review Registration System, Review Schedule, Discuss Professional Development, Create schedule/assign dates to tasks below.
Access the Training Registration System.	by end of second week.		Register for a seminar (public side); interact with Admin. Interface- If you don't have access, let Christine know.
Create your Training Website Staff Profile	by end of second week		Email Christine a picture and bio to post.
Attend/observe 2 technology seminars	tbd		Discuss with Christine and/or Student Supervisor which sessions you should attend.
Access lynda.com tutorials	by end of second week.		View tutorials of your choice. Coordinate with Christine and/or Training Student Supervisor on the topics and length of time you should dedicate.

Figure 1. A screen capture of the new hire checklist on our SWAT wiki space.

3.3 Initial Student Supervisor Meeting

When a student technology trainer is hired, they are required to meet with the student supervisor during his or her first two weeks.

This 1-1 meeting consists of a tour of labs where we commonly teach training sessions, review of our Wiki space including train-the-trainer information (e.g. preparing for a seminar, question handling, etc.), a tour of the registration system, available OIT resources and reviewing any questions s/he may have. They also look at the existing seminar schedule to see which seminars s/he can attend. While new student trainers are required to attend at least two seminars their first semester, we encourage all student trainers to attend as many seminars as possible so they will get an overall sense of our offerings as well as the variety of training techniques as they develop their own style. It's also beneficial to have a second person in the room to help with session set up and to assist the participants.

The 1-1 meeting sets the stages for the ongoing relationship that the supervisor will have with all of the student trainers throughout their employment in OIT Training.

Figure 2. Boris Lau, Student Supervisor (2009 – 2012) mentoring new student trainer, Kevin Hu.

3.4 Conducting "Demo" Sessions

As part of the new hire checklist, student hires are required to give a demo session of a topic. We will work with the student trainers to determine the topic. This is typically one of our core topics (topics that each student trainer is expected to know and be comfortable with). This list has evolved depending on the most requested technology. The core topics are currently Duke's WordPress, iMovie and Sakai Project Sites.

Demoing a session includes teaching in front of an audience of peers. These sessions are typically 20 to 30 minutes and are a part of an existing staff meeting time, when possible. For many of the demo sessions, we use DukeCapture (which is the tool Panopto branded at Duke) to record these sessions. [3] We record their voice and screen.

Figure 3. A screen capture from student trainer Tim Yoon's demo presentation when developing a new seminar.

When the student has completed his or her demo, all of the staff present will give feedback in round-robin fashion. We give oral feedback on what worked well in addition to areas that need improvement.

Student trainers are then encouraged to review their own sessions during their training prep hours as part of a self-evaluation process. They are encouraged to look at their sequencing of content, clarity and pacing.

It is important to note that trainers are required to do demo sessions for new seminars they are developing or for existing seminars that are already developed but they are new to teaching.

We have also invited other full time staff to participate in demo sessions. For example, consultants from Duke's Career Center participated in demo sessions and provided feedback on two seminars that we developed with their input: "Designing your Resume for Internships & Beyond" and "Navigating Excel for Consulting & Finance Internships."

Over the past two years, the student trainers also conducted presentations for Blue Devil Days, a welcoming event for admitted students and their families. It was key for the student trainers to review the presentation and script many times before presenting their first live session.

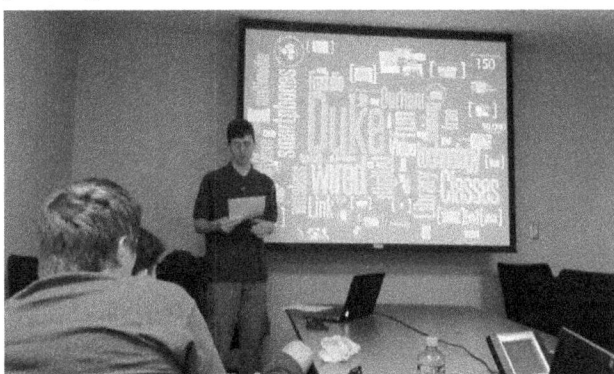

Figure 4. Patrick Royal demoing a "Technology @ Duke" presentation for Blue Devil Days.

4. "LIVE" TRAINING SESSIONS

We require new trainers to use the first semester as a learning/growing period. As mentioned earlier, new trainers spend their time reviewing existing materials, attending seminars, and preparing for their first live seminar by conducting a demo. We schedule them for their first seminar once we feel they are ready. We don't want to send them into "battle", so to speak, too early where they may get poor evaluations and feel defeated and we don't want to wait too long where they don't feel like they are contributing to the program.

Figure 5. Ryan Lipes teaching a free technology seminar.

4.1 Evaluations

Whether a veteran or a new trainer, evaluations play an important role in customizing the experiences to best meet the needs of each trainer. Evaluations take place after each session throughout the year through online post seminar evaluations. We also give just-in-time feedback as well as conduct end of semester reviews.

4.1.1 Online Post Seminar Evaluation

After each seminar, the trainer updates our online registration system to indicate who attended the session and who did not. The next day, evaluation forms are automatically sent to all of the attendees. Our evaluation form was developed in Qualtrics, an online survey tool being used at Duke. Questions include effectiveness of the seminar, seminar handout, and the overall presentation. We also ask for the best features of the seminar and areas of improvement.

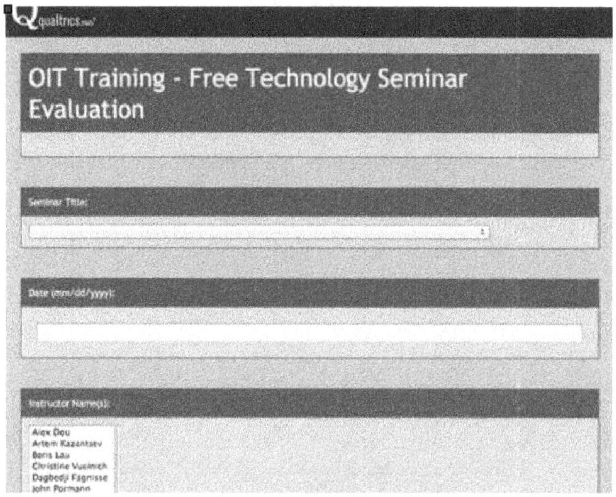

Figure 6. OIT Training online post seminar evaluation form.

While the response rate for our online evaluations is very low, we do get some valuable information. The training coordinator shares a summary of the information via email - specifically highlighting what worked well, areas for improvement, as well as, some suggestions for improving their session. The student trainers are also encouraged to self-reflect after each seminar: what worked well, what didn't and which examples did you use/stories did you tell that resonated with the participants and which did not.

4.1.2 Just-in-time Feedback

Throughout the semester, the training coordinator and student supervisor sit in on various live seminars. While we typically let the student trainers know which session(s) we plan to attend, we will sometimes pop in on a session to spot check or just say hello. This has helped build a relationship among the staff, create a team environment and provide an opportunity for just-in-time questions and peer mentoring.

4.1.3 End of Semester Reviews

At the end of the semester, every SWAT student participates in an end of the semester review. This is an opportunity for the student staff to formally sit down with both their supervisor(s) and the SWAT coordinator to give them feedback, solicit feedback on the program and how we are doing. Each session is approximately 20 to 30 minutes. Each staff member is required to bring copies of a completed self-evaluation form to this meeting. Questions include: what is your greatest strength, what area(s) have you shown improvement, and what areas do you need to improve? This self-evaluation form facilitates this two-way conversation.

5. STANDARD DOCUMENATION

Over the past two years, we have created standard documentation for each of the free technology seminars. This has allowed us to provide better consistency from trainer to trainer as well as to offer a good resource for our participants during and after the seminar.

5.1 Handouts

Handouts are developed in a standard Microsoft Word template. The handouts are available online on the OIT Training Website in PDF format. [4]

5.2 Trainer's Guides

For each seminar, we also created a trainer's guide (a.k.a. seminar outline). The guide includes the seminar description, materials/preparation tips as well as step-by-step outline of what is covered in the seminar. Trainers were encouraged to include any tips or examples that would be helpful to anyone teaching the seminar. Guides are now required for each new seminar that is developed.

Currently, we are working on creating a run-through of each of the core topics with DukeCapture. This recording is for internal purposes to walk another trainer through a seminar. This recording will also help with consistency and serve as intuitional memory once the student trainer is no longer employed with us.

Figure 7. DukeCapture recording of a core topic.

6. TRAIN THE TRAINER ACTIVITIES

In addition to learning the technical skills required to train a specific topic, the student trainers also need to pay attention to the soft skills to complement the technical skills including handling questions, preparing for a session, and interacting with participants.

6.1 Discussions

As part of our trainer staff meetings, we have formal discussions on training topics. Also outside of our meetings, we informally talk about our training sessions and experiences – what worked and what didn't as well as situations that arose and asking for feedback.

6.2 Fun Activities

At the end of the spring 2012 semester, the student trainers were divided into teams and asked to put together "How *Not* to Train" videos which were viewed during the annual end-of-semester meeting. This activity served multiple purposes: team building, becoming more familiar with video equipment and iMovie for editing, and having fun with the content (e.g. what happens when you don't prepare for a seminar.)

7. PROFESSIONAL DEVELOPMENT

All students are encouraged to take advantage of professional development opportunities. This includes sitting in other students training sessions, using the online resources as they develop new seminars and attending OIT sponsored guest presentations that are organized throughout the year. Guest speakers throughout the university have conducted sessions on Good Presentation Skills, the Duke Network, IT Security and Copyright/Fair Use.

We will pay each student two hours per semester to participate in a professional development opportunity of their choice as long as their supervisor approves it. This may be attending an in-person session on campus or viewing an online training session. Though many of the SWAT students do not take us up on this option, those who do find it to be very valuable. Recently, one of our student trainers indicated that it is often more valuable to see someone else present than the actual content of what they are presenting about.

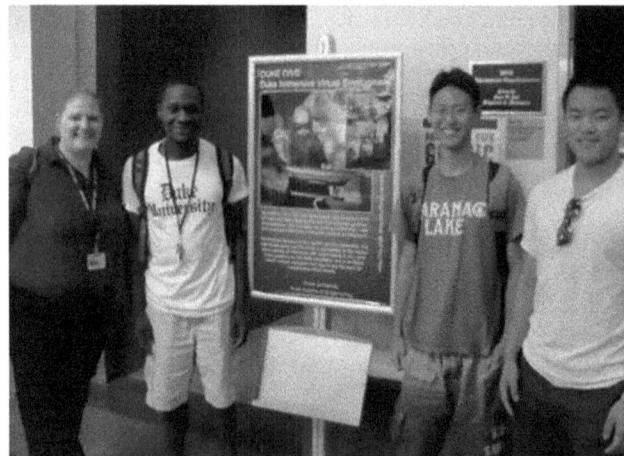

Figure 8. Christine Vucinich (Training Coordinator) with Student Trainers: Dagbedji Fagnisse, Tim Yoon and Alex Dou as they toured The Duke Immersive Virtual Environment (DiVE).

8. NEXT STEPS

As we continue to develop our train-the-trainer program, we will create a self-evaluation form that can be used after each training session and add specific lynda.com tutorials to the new hire checklist for each of the core topics. We will also explore discussing more train-the-trainer topics outside of meetings via an online community.

9. CONCLUSION

This paper discussed how we formalized a train-the-trainer program as part of the OIT Training student trainer program and how mentoring, evaluation, and professional development opportunities play an important part in customizing the experience to best meet the needs of each student technology trainer.

Since we implemented a more formal train-the-trainer program in addition to some of our other changes (developing team building opportunities, adding a set schedule, and having more regular meetings), we have seen improved staff retention. Also, we have seen improved confidence, morale and pride in work.

10. ACKNOWLEDGMENTS

Thank you to everyone at Duke University who has helped the training program grow over the past three years especially Boris

Lau, Student Supervisor, for his ongoing support & dedication to the OIT Training program. Also, thank you to the current student trainers: Alex Dou, Dagbedji Fagnisse, Kevin Hu, Ryan Lipes, Patrick Royal and Tim Yoon as well as Erin Nettifee, Duke's Coordinator of Academic Support, for her overall coordination efforts and support of the student trainer program.

11. REFERENCES

[1] OIT Training Website:
http://oit.duke.edu/training

[2] OIT SWAT Website:
http://oit.duke.edu/help/swat/join.php

[3] DukeCapture – Panopto Information:
http://oit.duke.edu/vvw/web_multimedia/multimedia/dukecapture

[4] OIT Training Free Technology Seminar Handouts:
http://oit.duke.edu/comp-print/training/free-seminars/handouts.php

Creating a Repeatable Framework for Campus Communication

Blake Adams
University of West Georgia
1601 Maple Street
Carrollton, GA 30118
(678) 839-5000

badams@westga.edu

Kathy Kral
University of West Georgia
1601 Maple Street
Carrollton, GA 30118
(678) 839-5000

kkral@westga.edu

ABSTRACT

IT Services are provided to campuses in a variety of different environments. Failure to keep customers aware of the status of major enterprise level services can quickly generate a variety of problems: an overburdened help desk, longer hold times, erratic communication within IT, and customer dissatisfaction. In this paper we explore the approach the West Georgia took to develop a communication strategy to mitigate challenges by enhancing how IT positions itself to manage customer expectations through informed, constant, proactive updates using multiple channels. The result was a step-by-step, phased framework approach. By approaching the implementation in phases, the school worked in manageable steps with clearly defined objectives for each phase. Each step is solution-independent and can be implemented using the best-fit approach for any school. We believe this model holds great value, not only in its ability to improve customer relationships, but also in its ability to be adapted to fit any organization, based upon need.

Categories and Subject Descriptors

H.1.1 [**Systems and Information Theory**] *General systems theory, Information theory, Value of information.*

General Terms

Management, Documentation, Design, Standardization

Keywords

Communication, Information Distribution.

1. THE UNIVERSITY OF WEST GEORGIA

The University of West Georgia is a 645-acre campus located in Carrollton Georgia. It is a mid-sized college serving approximately 11,600 pursuing undergraduate and graduate degrees[1]. A centralized IT support team of approximately 60 full time staff members and several student assistants are responsible for the technical support and delivery of services to both the student population and a faculty/staff population of approximately 1000.

2. HISTORY OF SUPPORT

During the history of the school the model of IT support has shifted from centralized to decentralized and back to centralized. The most recent shift from decentralized to centralized support occurred in 2008 and communication was one of the major issues the reorganization was intended to address. The current model for support places User Services (The Service Desk, Desktop Support, Classroom Support, Special Event Support, and Web Support), Infrastructure Services (System Administration, Network Support, Operations, and Telecommunications), and Software Development Services (Business Applications and Student Applications) under three directors all reporting to the Chief Information Officer. This allows the majority of IT support services to be housed under the same office and facilitates communication between support groups.

2.1 Technical Support

West Georgia is not unique in its challenge to support a variety of technical services with technical scopes that stretch from simple to highly complex. Likewise, the IT group must support a variety of services that can serve as few as one, or as many as the entire campus (enterprise level services).

2.2 Communication

Communication between IT and the campus has been an ongoing challenge for some time. Historically, word-of-mouth and e-mail communication was enough to meet the needs of the campus, but as the campus grows, the systems become more complex, and the services trend towards enterprise level, the complexity of communication explodes.

3. OUR CHALLENGE

As the number and complexity of enterprise services continue to grow, so grows the pressure to communicae vital information about these services. Failure to keep customers aware of the status of major enterprise level services can quickly generate a variety of problems: an overburdened help desk, longer customer hold times, erratic communication within IT, and general customer dissatisfaction. This can ultimately lead to a loss of trust between IT support and the customer base. As the provider of IT services, it was our responsibility to examine how we could improve communication between groups within IT, and between IT and our customer base.

4. COMMUNICATION ELEMENTS

The first step in finding direction to resolve our challenge was to examine all elements of communication – both internal and external – and determine how we could leverage tools we already have in place (or could easily develop) to improve the communication experience for our customer.

4.1 Delivery Format

UWG's reliance on e-mail was too high. Our customers receive hundreds of emails on a daily basis. The odds of them noticing an important message regarding a service outage from IT were slim. Worse yet, if the IT service down was e-mail, there was no way to notify the customer that the campus email was down. Our customers leverage multiple channels of communication – it is our responsibility to tap into those channels and deliver the information they need in a format they find usable. This includes creating a dynamic website that communicates relevant information about services, providing communication updates via social media elements such as Facebook[2] and Twitter[3], providing updates that are readable by an RSS reader, and creating an easy way for customers to quickly get major announcements and updates by calling the service desk without tying up a customer support agent.

4.2 Message Content

The content of any announcement should be relevant, and clearly define who is going to be affected and for how long. In every case, at least one customer will be interested in the technical details of a service outage, so these details should be communicated as well, but positioned at the end of a message to avoid confusion.

4.3 Message Format

The format of a message is equally as important as the content. It's critical that customers know what to expect to see when they receive an announcement and that the customer sees the information the same way for every event. In formatting our messages UWG felt it was important to deliver a meaningful title, followed by who is affected, what it means to the user, a time frame, and why the event occurred. Finally the message concludes with "Further Details" – a section provided for high end users that want to know more about the technical side of the event.

4.4 Tools

A large variety of tools are necessary to make the communication framework successful. Chief among these is the development of a dynamic web accessible status page with branded services that are easily identifiable by the customer. Equally important is the development of a "Service Interruption Message" (SIM) that can be accessed by calling the support center. Working through the phases of the framework will lead to more complicated tool integration like methods for pushing announcements to social media and development of RSS content. Ultimately the model explores the integration of mobile application technology and mission critical text messaging. Never the less, the most crucial tools to successfully implement the framework is a dedicated staff committed to ensuring quality communication to the customer throughout a service interruption.

4.5 Agreements

It is important that the ground rules of how communication will flow are clear to all parties involved, typically this will be the service providers, the service owner (sometimes the same as the service provider), the Service Desk, and the customers. Agreements and guidelines should be written, agreed upon, and held accountable to. This includes operating level agreements (OLAs) between internal IT groups and the Service Desk regarding how communication will flow between parties, agreements with 3rd party vendors to underpin support, and agreements with the customer regarding how and how often they can expect communication during a service outage.

5. THE FRAMEWORK

The framework was developed during a joint session between customer service leadership within the University System of Georgia's IT support center[5] and the University of West Georgia.

Over a four-year period of time, the Information Technology Services Customer Service group for the University System of Georgia implemented several controls and tools to develop top tier customer communication. Working with West Georgia, the two groups were able to isolate each component of their communication structure and develop it into a model framework that could conceivably be used by any organization interested in enhancing and standardizing communication. These elements were slotted into 4 separate progressive phases to allow users of the framework to work on the plan in segmented but effective units. The elements are described in the phases below.

5.1 Phase I – Building the Foundation

The first phase of the framework focuses on establishing a single source for consistent information, as well as techniques for driving customers to that location. In order for the framework to be successful, the information contained on this page must be relevant, timely, and easy to read for the layperson.

5.1.1 The Status Page

This is the absolute backbone of the communication framework. Everything done within the framework will have to be able to tie back to the status page. The status page is nothing more than a very readable page listing all enterprise level services as well as color-coding indicating their status. The services should be in one of three states:

5.1.1.1 Green

When a service is in a green state, the message being sent to the user is that everything is working just as it should.

5.1.1.2 Yellow

When a service is in a yellow state, the message being sent to the user is that the service has been slowed or stopped altogether for parts of the campus.

5.1.1.3 Red

When a service is in a red state, the message being sent to the user is that the service is completely unavailable campus wide.

5.1.2 Service Branding

IT departments on campuses around the world all support some number of IT services used by the entire campus, and most of the time IT and the customer call them something different. In some cases it may be a difference as subtle as calling "e-mail" "wolf-mail." For the status page, these services must be identified and branded on the status page in the terms the customer would use. Common examples include e-mail, wireless, print services, and telecom (phones).

5.1.3 Informal Internal Communication OLA

Moving to a status page format to enhance external communications may place an additional burden on service owners. The owners will now be responsible for communicating with the Service Desk (or designated party) on a consistent basis from the beginning to the end of a service interruption. To reduce friction, we recommend an informal internal communication operating level agreement. This OLA doesn't need to be a well written document with clear delineation of who does what when, typically this works better as a face-to-face conversation, a handshake agreement, and the willingness on behalf of the status page owner to work with the service owners when information is not being communicated.

5.1.4 Calendar of Maintenance
A calendar of maintenance is an excellent supplement to any status page, as it provides users with a single place to go look for planned outages. Even with the calendar of maintenance, we recommend making a scheduled maintenance announcement at least a week before the event occurs.

5.1.5 Service Interruption Message
The Service Interruption Message (SIM) acts as a pointer for users who prefer to contact IT via phone. By crafting a standard SIM and making it reasonable easy for a caller to access (e.g. "for known issues – press 2") the customer can often get the information they need without ever encumbering a member of the Service Desk or support staff.

5.1.6 Defined ownership of Status Page and SIM updates
While the authors feel the ownership of the Status Page and SIM belongs with the Service Desk, it is up to the user of the model to make that decision. It is important to understand who is responsible for updating the status page and the SIM.

5.1.7 Defined announcement types
Once the status page has been populated with enterprise services, announcement types should be defined and standardized to provide the customer with a consistent experience. We find the five following announcement types to be adequate:

5.1.7.1 Initial
An initial announcement occurs when a service interruption is first noticed; this may be initiated by the service owner or the service desk, depending on who notes the interruption first. In either case, the service owner should be made aware of it and is responsible for all communication back to the status page owner until the service is restored.

5.1.7.2 Update
An update announcement is typically initiated by the service owner and is used when significant progress has been made on the interruption.

5.1.7.3 Resolved
A resolved announcement can only be initiated by the service owner and indicates that the service has been fully restored. At this point the service is put back in to "green" status.

5.1.7.4 Scheduled
A scheduled announcement is made to notify the campus of an upcoming planned service outage due to maintenance etc.

5.1.7.5 Post Action
A post action announcement should be used in the event that an outage occurs and is restored before any other announcement can be made. These types of announcements are the exception, not the rule, and usually occur during weekends or odd hours.

5.1.8 Defined announcement frequency
When developing the communication strategy, the status page owner and service owners must come to an agreement on how often customers can expect to receive announcements during a service outage. In the worst case scenario, we recommend this not exceed eight business hours. Typically, customers expect updates on services outages at least every two hours.

5.1.9 Service Level Guidelines – Communication
Before establishing any sort of service level guidelines or agreements with customers for the individual services listed on the status page, a communication based service level guideline (SLG) should be developed to encompass the entire campus communication project. This SLG should, in as simple terms as possible, clearly communicate to the customer: "This is how you can communicate with us, this is how we will communicate with you."

5.1.10 Value Touch Points defined and marketed
Once you've completed all components of Phase I, it's time to clearly define the "value add" that this project is bringing to the customer, then go live and market the value add to the customers. This is the only step repeated throughout the model.

5.2 Phase II – Integrated Communications
Phase II of the Framework focuses on delivery of the message to the customers in the format of their preference. It also emphasizes formalizing definitions and process to ensure everyone within the IT organization understands the role he or she plays and what to do when a service interruption occurs.

5.2.1 Formal OLA for communication
The informal handshake agreement from Phase I is ready to be formalized and documented in Phase II. This OLA should clearly define how handoff, response, and ownership through resolution are handled during a service interruption. This is a high stakes document with several players, so it's best to take time and make sure everyone is on the same page.

5.2.2 Social Media Integration
Once the campus has had time to get accustomed to the status page, it's time to start allowing them to harvest the information in the format that makes them most comfortable. This occurs during social media integration. The idea is to provide as many access points as reasonable to allow customers get updates from the status page. At West Georgia we have integrated Facebook, Twitter, and RSS feeds. If your school uses other social media regularly (e.g. Yammer) it's highly recommended that you build that integration in as well.

5.2.3 Web Accessible Customer Self Service (based on ability to deliver)
This component has an ambiguous definition to the extent that during Phase II your school should be integrating the level of customer self-service is a reasonably able to deliver. It can be as minor as a static set of frequently asked questions, or as intricate as single sign-on self-service with the ability to check the status of individual as well as enterprise wide incidents.

5.2.4 Global Incident Communication
Again, this is a somewhat ambiguous component. Based on the ability of the school to deliver such a service, the ability to auto subscribe to a specific incident and be automatically notified once the issue has been resolved is ideal.

5.2.5 Formal Service Level Guidelines
This is in reference to the services branded and placed on the status page in Phase I. This will be a time consuming process depending on how many services are represented on the status page. The recommended approach is to create a standard Service Level Guideline template. Each service can then be worked through the template and customized to best suit the organization's ability to deliver the service while meeting customer expectations. The Service Level Guideline must be agreed upon with, and adhered to by the service owner.

5.2.6 Value Touch-Points defined and marketed
Repeat the process from Phase I, taking in to account the newly added value from Phase II.

5.3 Phase III-Unified Communication
Phase III of the frame work focuses on behind the scene work that ensures clean delivery of services via 3rd party agreements and agility of the service desk to spot service interruptions when provided with the proper tools.

5.3.1 Service Desk monitoring of Mission Critical Services.
By Phase III, the communication centering on the status page (and all associated processes) should be routine. In Phase III, where appropriate, the Service Desk (or status page owner) should be equipped with the appropriate tools to monitor mission critical services. For example, a monitoring tool to indicate the loss of networking to one or more buildings or locations. This enables the status page owner to quickly generate an initial announcement indicating awareness of the interruption. This post can be quickly follow up with an update by the associated service owner with additional information.

5.3.2 Mission Critical Emergency Text Messaging
Several universities have implemented emergency text messaging systems, often though the campus police or IT. If this sort of service is available, it serves as a good way to communicate mission critical emergencies to subscribers of the service in a timely manner, even if the message is little more than "service X is down campus wide, please visit our status page for further details."

5.3.3 Standardized communication procedures.
By Phase III, this should be nearly complete, however an audit of your campus communication plan should quickly identify any areas where communication procedures are undocumented, unclear, or (where possible) not in a template format.

5.3.4 Complete and Current 3rd Party agreement catalog.
Examine all 3rd party agreements within the IT department that underpin delivery of services on the status page. Ensure that all agreements are in order, and allow the department to meet the promises of the SLGs. Make sure these agreements are up to date, and easy to access.

5.3.5 Value Touch Points Defined and Marketed
Repeat the process from Phase II, taking in to account the newly added value from Phase III.

5.4 Phase IV – Preparing for the Future
It's difficult to put a framework together than can account for the continuous growth of technology. When this framework was developed, Phase IV was created as a placeholder for ideas and projects that most universities are not ready to tackle yet, but could become more achievable in the future. Phase IV should not be considered static, rather it should be looked at as a holding ground for new ideas.

5.4.1 Mobile Application Development
If your campus is currently active in the mobile application market, consider including service status update components within your mobile application suite.

5.4.2 Knowledge Level Management
This speaks to an extension of customer self-service. Consider creating a space for extended, advanced, or specialized FAQs.

5.4.3 Crowdsourcing
Often application driven, crowdsourcing is heavily dependent on the IT department's ability to monitor the content, and the campus' willingness to contribute information in the best interest of the campus community. Implemented properly, crowdsourcing can be an excellent tool to reduce impact on IT.

6. IMPLEMENTATION
No matter how well you think you understand the material, and no matter how much support you believe you will (or won't) have, implementing this framework is a marathon, not a sprint, that's one of the reasons why it was broken up into multiple phases. An effort aimed at implementing all of the elements simultaneously would face a strong uphill battle. The framework needs a champion, and that champion needs more than one coworker helping to push the project forward.

6.1 West Georgia – Phase I
West Georgia began implementing Phase I in the summer of 2011. Identifying and Branding the enterprise level services provided by IT as something the customer base would recognize and understand was one of the most challenging tasks. Equally challenging was the development of the Service Level Guidelines for Communication. The greatest challenge of the SLG was writing it in terms that would be clear to both providers and users of the status page. The informal communication OLA was also challenging because while the concept and process is easy to explain to service owners, achieving participation and buy-in when an outage occurs can be a challenge. Once all components were completed the value touch points were defined in marketed via e-mail, campus announcements, and paper flyers delivered to all faculty/staff service users.

6.2 West Georgia – Phase II
West Georgia Began Work on Phase II of the Framework in the Spring of 2012. The majority of components have been developed and we are on track to define new value touch points and market them at the beginning of the Fall 2012 semester.

7. FUTURE

Results of our work will be discussed in the following paragraph, but based on results to this point West Georgia will place a stronger emphasis on marketing of communication tools in the Fall of 2012. Our goal is to increase Twitter and Facebook followers by 20% and unique visits to the status page by 10%.

8. RESULTS

West Georgia implemented the service interruption message on the call center line and the service status web page as Phase I of the framework in the summer of 2011. The new services were marketed to the campus using direct e-mail, campus announcements, and printed marketing materials. Changes in internal communication were discussed with each service owner, and presented at departmental meetings. The Chief Information Officer all announced the implementation of Phase I during a presidential cabinet meeting days before launch.

A review of the analytics for status.westga.edu reflects a notable increase in hits during a service outage when compared to days without service interruptions.

9. CONCLUSION

Communication during service outages is a challenge for any IT organization. Often the same staff who are working diligently to resolve the issue are the same staff who are expected to provide the status updates. The Service Desk depends on those status updates to provide timely information to the campus. When that communication flow breaks down, all parties involved suffer. West Georgia, working in conjunction with the USG, developed the communication framework to address these issues using a phased approach. The phased approach allowed us to define goals that we could reasonably achieve, and realize improvements at every phase. We now have a functioning status page, and also make updates available via Facebook, Twitter, and RSS. We communicate using a standardized message format, and are working toward identification of a monitoring system. All of these improvements increased IT's visibility and creditability to the campus, and are helping us solve the communication challenge.

10. ACKNOWLEDGMENTS

Our thanks to Dave Disney and the IT Customer Service Center at the USG Board of Regents.

11. REFERENCES

[1] The University of West Georgia. http://www.westga.edu.

[2] Facebook. http://www.facebook.com.

[3] Twitter. http://www.twitter.com.

[4] Yammer. http://www.yammer.com.

[5] The University System of Georgia. http://www.usg.edu.

Building a Sustainable Mobile Device Strategy to Meet the Needs of Various Stakeholder Groups

Robin Honken
Director, Development and
Web Support Services
Winona State University
Somsen Hall 208
507-457-2251

rhonken@winona.edu

Kenneth Janz
Associate Vice President /
Chief Information Officer
Winona State University
Somsen Hall 111
507- 457-2299

kjanz@winona.edu

Zach Boudreau
Web Master
Winona State University
Somsen Hall 208
507- 457-2932

zboudreau@winona.edu

John Yearous
Developer
Winona State University
Somsen Hall 108
507- 457-2563

jyearous@winona.edu

ABSTRACT

With the number of students owning smart phones increasing to over fifty percent in 2010 at Winona State University, Information Technology Services collaborated with University Marketing and Communications to develop Winona State Mobile http://www.winona.edu/it/winonastatemobile.asp. This paper details the initial development efforts to the mobile development strategy that allowed for Winona State Mobile to be accessed from most mobile devices, and prepare the way for future mobile development efforts.

The initial WSU Mobile application was developed with the following features: campus map, WSU bus tracker, virtual tour, WSU news, Faculty and staff directory, and the academic calendar. During the construction of this first application the programming team changed the development strategy along the way, resulting in our most recent version being quite different than the initial release. In addition, while working on an update to WSU Mobile, the mobile development team was also working with the Winona Historical Society on a virtual walking tour of some historical buildings in downtown Winona. Both of these efforts have helped shape the way we approach mobile development. This paper will provide an account of these development efforts, reasons for the change in strategy, and a demonstration the end products. Finally, this paper will discuss our most recent effort, which will be available in the summer 2012: The Winona State University Augmented Reality Tree Tour.

We are confident that our current applications have been very successful based on qualitative as well as quantitative data. We have had well over 50,000 hits on WSU Mobile since October 2011. The bus-tracking application alone has had almost 30,000 hits during that same time frame. Our team would like to share the knowledge we've gained with other institutions looking to increase their visibility among prospective students, and provide pertinent information to current students in a medium that is easily and quickly accessible to them.

Categories and Subject Descriptors
D.2.2 [**Software Engineering**]: Design Tools and Techniques

General Terms
Management, Documentation, Performance, Design, Reliability, Experimentation, Security, Human Factors.

Keywords
Mobile devices, application development, software engineering, programming environments, user interface design.

1. INTRODUCTION

Information technology is revolutionizing the classroom and the workplace. The kind of tools and devices used to facilitate the use of information technology is changing.[1] Students in greater numbers are starting to access information and campus technology resources via mobile devices.[2] Institutions of higher education are continuing to look for ways to meet the needs of students using these smaller devices.[3], [4], [5], [6], [7] Yet as with most change in an organization the unit that supports the sustainable technology is besieged with how best to support this transformation.[8] This change is not occurring just in higher education but in K-12 as well.[9]

This change has been seen in survey data collected from students at Winona State University. Students now expect to be able to access institutional data via smart phones and other mobile devices. With this data Winona State University, Information Technology Services collaborated with University Marketing and Communications to develop Winona State Mobile, http://www.winona.edu/it/winonastatemobile.asp. Based on data collected from students the initial WSU Mobile application was developed with the following features: campus map, WSU bus tracker, virtual tour, WSU news, Faculty and staff directory, and the academic calendar.

This paper will discuss the organization of information technology to help facilitate the changing ways students are accessing information technology, the history of Winona State University mobile development, current trends in mobile development, growth of Stories and Structure, and Campus of Trees a new augmented reality application developed for mobile devices. The paper will close with a synopsis of lessons learned.

2. INSTITUTIONAL BACKGROUND

Winona State University (mid-sized university located in southeast Minnesota of 9,000 students) IT support is provided by Information Technology Services (ITS) which is organized into four units: User Services, Development and Web Support

Services, Infrastructure Services, and Teaching, Learning, and Technology Services. The ITS leadership team consists of the Chief Information Officer and the Directors of User Services, Development and Web Support Services, Infrastructure Service, and Teaching, Learning, and Technology Services. All of the activities described in this article took place within the Development and Web Support Services unit.

Winona State has traditionally been a leader in the area of technology. [10], [11] During the fall of 2000, Winona State implemented a mandatory laptop program (now called Digital Life and Learning) for all incoming students. Since that time, the University has worked to support this program through enhanced infrastructure, development and teaching and learning.

3. HISTORY OF MOBILE DEVELOPMENT AT WINONA STATE

In 2008, Winona State started a web redesign project that included a complete overhaul of the university public website, as well as the creation of audience-driven webpages for current students, faculty and staff. The site went live early 2010, (http://www.winona.edu/). With significant improvements in design, navigation and functionality of the website for all Winona State audiences, and the increase in mobile device usage, it became apparent that the university needed to start thinking about making key functionality available from mobile devices, such as the iPhone. See figure 1.

Figure 1. QR Codes and Initial Advertisement for WSU Mobile

The web development team was able to find a student that was a seasoned objective-C developer, this allowed **WSU Mobile** for the iPhone, iPod Touch and iPad to be created.. The web team, comprised of University Marketing/Communications and IT staff, used data from marketing studies done when building the new website to help dictate which functionality should be accessible from a mobile device primarily for prospective and current students. In addition to some basic features, such as a campus map, virtual tour, news, faculty/staff directory and academic calendar, Winona State's Webmaster, Zach Boudreau, also thought WSU Mobile should include some innovative

functionality like a bus tracking application, http://www.winona.edu/transportation/bustracker.asp.

At the same time WSU Mobile was being developed, Winona State started surveying incoming freshmen and current students to determine if they owned a smart phone, and if so, what kind. The results showed that that over 50 percent of the students owned a smart phone, and of those 47 percent owned an android device, while only 39 percent owned an iPhone. With WSU Mobile only accessible from iOS devices and the objective-C student developer graduating, we knew we needed to rethink our development strategy. Winona State's Webmaster and another application developer, John Yearous, were tasked with developing WSU Mobile so that it was accessible from both iOS and android devices.

4. DEVELOPING FOR MOBILE

The need to provide an Android version of WSU Mobile, and the lack of native iOS and Android platform developers forced the Department of Web and Development Services to step back and look at the mobile application development strategy and process.

The mobile application needed to provide a core set of functionality. It had to be easy to maintain, as development time was already stretched thin. It also needed to leverage existing developer skill sets.

We conducted a thorough review of the desired functionality of the Mobile application and determined that it was not necessary to access specialized hardware available on the phone. File upload of any kind was not required by the application. The review also revealed that much of the data required by the mobile app was already available elsewhere on the WSU public site. Lastly, data required by the application changed frequently and would need an Internet connection to access.

These facts led us to the idea of developing the mobile application as a pure web application, using HTML5 and CSS3. This approach presented the following advantages:

- Existing data could be made available to the application via web services/atom/rss and repackaged inside of a mobile-friendly UI using XSLT.

- Multiple developers within the web team had the ability to maintain the application.

- The application would be single-source.

- The application would be device-agnostic with no specific device-detection required to be developed (by us), only res and orientation detection.

- The application could be made available directly by accessing a unique url, http://www.winona.edu/m.

- To satisfy the portion of the population predisposed to location application via "app stores" the web application could also be packaged within an Android Webview and an iOS UIWebview for delivery through the Android Marketplace and the Apple App Store.

- The app store versions could be updated without requiring resubmission

The following flowchart illustrated the criteria used to determine the type of application we needed to develop (Native vs. Web). See figure 2.

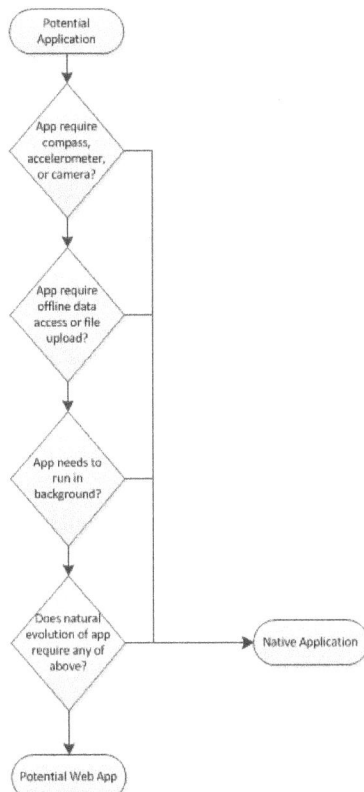

Figure 2. Mobile Web Decision Making Flowchart

5. WSU MOBILE APPLICATION

WSU Mobile was developed using a simple, lightweight, and predictably standard HTML5-based user interface. CSS3 media queries were implemented to impart slight formatting changes for different screen resolutions and devoice orientation changes. JQuery is used on the home screen to deliver higher-resolutions icons for those devices, which support them. See figure 3 for landing page of the Winona State University Mobile Application.

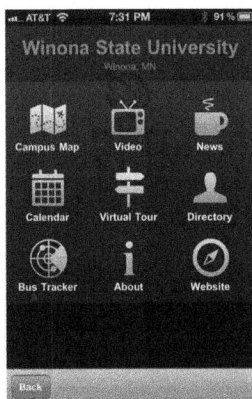

Figure 3. Landing Page of the Winona State University Mobile Application

5.1 Campus Map

The WSU Mobile Campus Map employs the Google Maps V3 API, targeted toward mobile development. It is mobile and touch-ready. Building locations were imparted to the map by using a Microsoft beta application, MapCruncher [13], to map coordinates on our existing print version of WSU's campus map to actual GPS coordinates. MapCruncher uses this information to create Bing Maps tiles at 12 different zoom levels. These tiles are programmatically converted to conform to the Google Maps naming structure at display-time, and overlayed on top of the Google map of Campus. See figure 4 for the screen capture of the campus map.

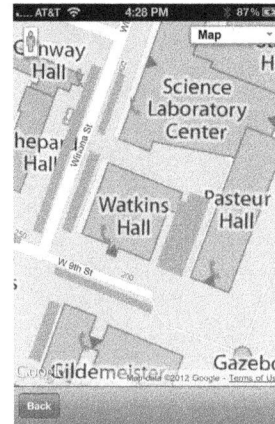

Figure 4. Winona State University Mobile Application Campus Map

5.2 Video

WSU has a YouTube account that is actively maintained and managed by the University Communications office. [12] The application parses the YouTube RSS feed and displays the video thumbnails and description formatted within the mobile application using XSLT. When a video is clicked, YouTube does the device detection "heavy lifting" required to display the video in the proper format and bitrate. See figure 5 for the screen capture of the integrated campus video page.

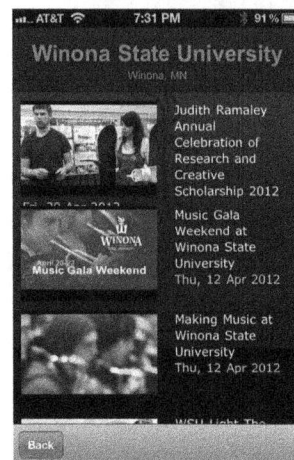

Figure 5. Integrated Campus Video Page

5.3 News

Winona State's news is maintained by University Communications within a SharePoint list. An RSS feed was generated from the SharePoint list, is parsed, and redisplayed within the mobile application using XSLT. See figure 6 for an example of the Winona State University Mobile Application news page.

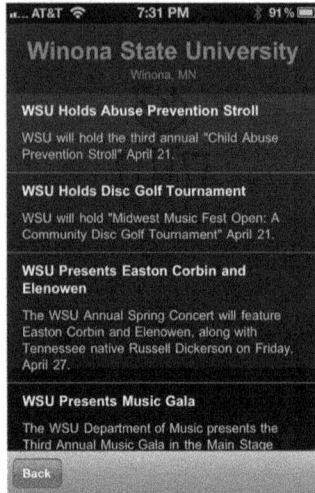

Figure 6. Winona State University Mobile Application News Page.

5.4 Academic Calendar

Winona State's academic calendar is managed using Google Calendar. An ATOM feed was generated from the Google calendar applications, parsed, and redisplayed within the mobile application using XSLT. See figure 7 for an example of the academic calendar.

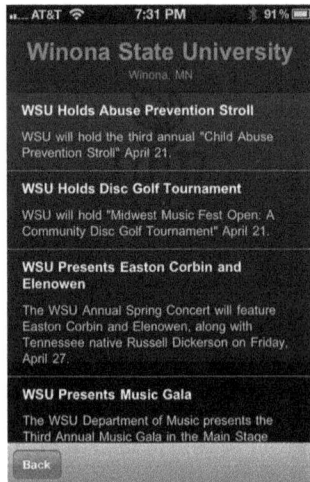

Figure 7. Academic Calendar

5.5 Virtual Tour

The WSU virtual tour presented some different challenges, mainly the expectation of the smart phone user to use swiping gestures to page through images. JQuery was used to provide the swiping experience, and images are displayed using API calls to a Flickr Gallery maintained by university communications. Figures 8 and 9 are screen captures of the virtual tour.

Figure 8. Virtual Tour

Figure 9. Virtual Tour - Library

5.6 Faculty/Staff Directory

The WSU phone directory is a function of SharePoint search services. A .NET web service was created that can search against the existing directory data. The web service response for both the initial search results and the selected person results are parsed and displayed with the mobile application using XSLT. See figure 10.

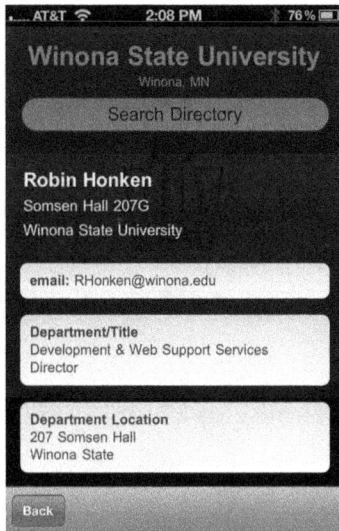

Figure 10. Campus Directory - Results

5.7 Bus Tracker

GPS devices on each bus generate the data for the bus tracking application. The devices post their current position data and timestamp to a database, using a web service, whenever the position of the bus changes by greater than a threshold amount. The Mobile application queries the database using the same web service, and plots this data onto a Google Map using V3 of the Google Maps API. See figure 11.

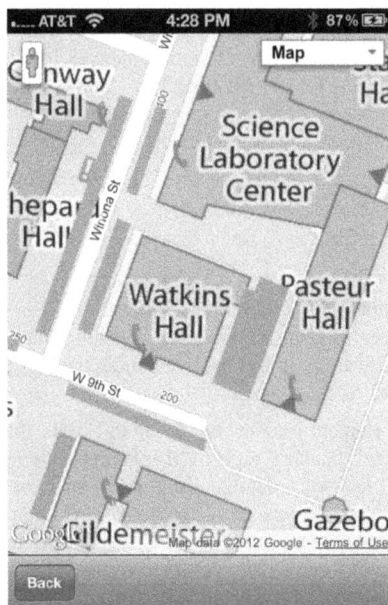

Figure 11. Bus Tracking Application

5.8 Lessons Learned

Geolocation works very well in web apps. The javascript Geolocation API provides a way for mobile web applications to access current location from the phone's GPS hardware; one of the most frequently used components in mobile application development. Great mobile UI tools exist. Frameworks such as

Sencha Touch and jQuery Mobile provide beneficial, built-in device detection and mobile UI enhancements. Using HTML5 and CSS classes, jQuery renders the UI predictably and consistently across multiple operating systems and screen dimensions. Resolution Detection is the most important asset for device targeting. CSS3 media queries, powerful UI tools, provide the means to target designs to devices of varying device dimensions and resolutions. The need for file upload, specialized hardware such as the compass or accelerometer, and offline or background data access are limiting factors for mobile web application development. In most cases, applications that require the use of these functions will need to be developed natively.

Web apps unify the development process and provide for seamless updates. HTML5/CSS3 web apps can be developed once and deployed once. Alternatively or additionally, they may be wrapped inside of an iOS or Android web view and deployed to individual application stores and marketplaces. In both cases, updates become transparent and don't require resubmission or approval. The gap between native app functionality and web app functionality has narrowed significantly. Although there are often functional and performance-based reasons to develop natively, new tools available to the web developer make a significant number of apps, previously developed natively, eligible to be developed as web applications.

6. STORIES IN STRUCTURES

At the same time WSU Mobile was being re-developed, another development effort was underway, called *Stories in Structure*. *Stories in Structure* is a mobile, historic architecture tour application created by Winona360.org, a community driven news website, Winona State University and the Winona County Historical Society. Students and staff members from those organizations developed the application during the 2010-2011 academic year. See figure 12.

▲ Scan the code with your smartphone
QR code scanner application and
Learn More about Winona's Architecture!
www.winonamntours.org

Figure 12. QR Code and Initial Advertisement for Stories and Structures

Stories in Structure guides participants in the exploration of downtown Winona's most historic buildings and allows you to interact directly with Winona's architecture using your smartphone's built-in GPS. The application marks your location on a map and guides you to one of five destinations. Once at your destination, you can interact with your surroundings by reviewing the history of your destination, viewing videos of its key moments, and comparing historical photos with your modern day surroundings. *Stories in Structure* was partially financed by the Minnesota Historical Society with funds from the Minnesota Arts & Cultural Heritage fund. Figure 13 is the splash screen of Stories and Structures.

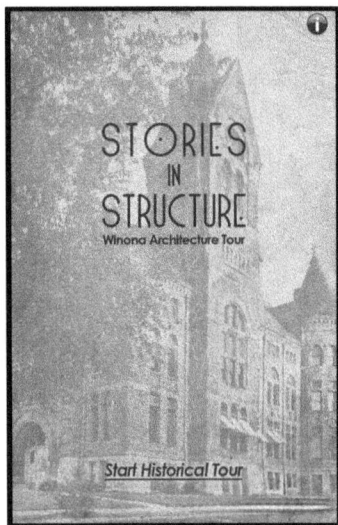

Figure 13. Splash Screen, Stories and Structures

6.1 What Technology Was Used?

The core functionality of Stories in Structure was developed around four major pieces of technology: Tap-Tours, Google Maps, HTML5 and Smartphones. See Figure 14 for menu structure of Stories and Structures.

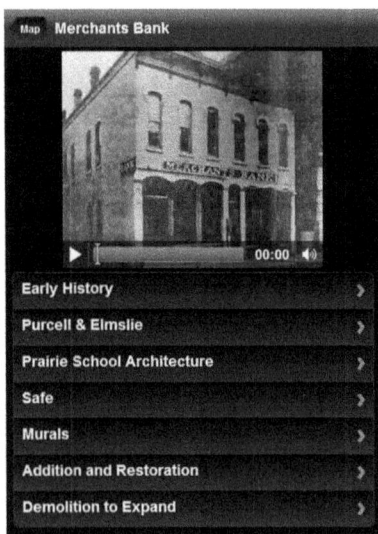

Figure 14. Menu Organization for Stories and Structures

Tap-Tours is an open source tool, built upon the popular content management system, Drupal, which allows users to easily create tours geared for museum settings. TAP enables users to create tour stops and associate with those stops audio, video, images, and content.

Next, from the Google Maps family of products, 3 features were employed: Google Maps JavaScript API v3, Google Direction Services, and Google Chart Tools. The Javascript API v3 allows developers to easily embed Google Maps into their web pages. This tool was designed to run faster and leaner, specifically with mobile devices in mind. Google's Direction Services was used to calculate directions and distance from the user's current location to their intended destination, a pre-selected historic landmark. Finally, Google Chart Tools was used to create custom map icons denoting Winona's historic landmarks. See figure 15.

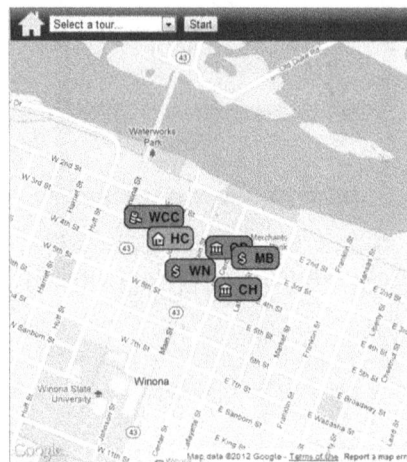

Figure 15. Map Used for Stories and Structures

HTML5, or the fifth revision of HTML, was utilized to specifically take advantage of two new features, namely the Geolocation API and the <video> tag. Geolocation provides location information for the device, such as latitude and longitude. Common sources of location information include GPS and location inferred from network signals such as IP address, RFID, Wi-Fi, and GSM/CDMA cell IDs. The Geolocation API enables developers to access a client's geographical location information via a set of common JavaScript objects.

```
navigator.geolocation.getCurrentPosition(function (position) {
    alert(position.coords.latitude);
    alert(position.coords.longitude);
});
```

It should be noted that while the Geolocation API is published by the W3C under its own specification and not a part of the W3C HTML5 specification, it is considered under the HTML5 umbrella of features and APIs.

The <video> element is a new tag added to HTML that is intended to become the standard way of displaying video on the web without the use of plugins such as Flash or Silverlight. Unfortunately, browser makers have not agreed upon which video format is best so it is currently best practice to provide video content in one of three widely accepted formats: MP4/H.264, Ogg Theora, and WebM/VP8. Fortunately, there are several free tools which enable developers to easily convert between these formats. In the end it is quite easy to create your video content in one format, convert it to another, and mark up your web page to let the browser decide which format is best to display. See figure 16.

```
<video controls>
    <source src="movie.mp4" />
    <source src="movie.webm" type='video/webm; codecs="vp8, vorbis"' />
    <source src="movie.ogv" type='video/ogg; codecs="theora, vorbis"' />
</video>
```

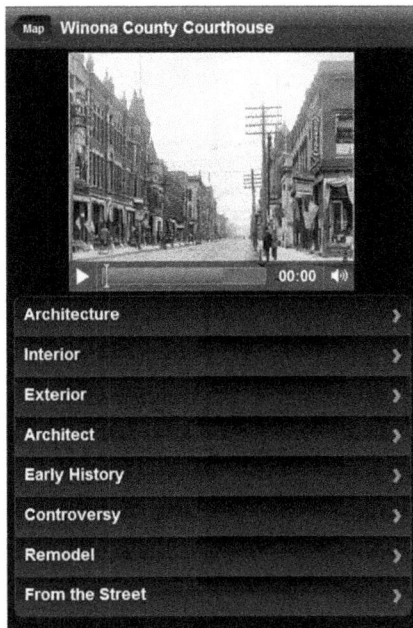

Figure 16. Video Integration

Finally, Smartphones were the last piece of technology used in the creation of this application. A smartphone is defined as a mobile device, that in addition to performing basic phone functions like voice calls and texting, runs an operating systems (e.g. Android, iOS, etc.), has internet and email access, supports advanced digital functions like GPS, music, video, gaming, and provides a standard interface and platform for developers to code against. Utilizing the smartphone was the key piece of technology used in this project because of its ability to couple geolocation in the browser with the phone's built-in GPS. This marriage enabled an interactive web-application to be created.

6.2 What We Learned

The decision to create your application as a native application or a mobile web application is not one to be taken lightly. There are many factors to consider. In order to properly make this decision, it is important to understand the strengths and weaknesses of each environment, as well as take into account the strengths and weaknesses of your developers.

Native applications have an inherent strength with the user over web applications in that they have history on their side. The culture surrounding smartphones has included applications since the very beginning. One only need think of the marketing slogan made famous by Apple, "We have an app for that," to see how entrenched native applications are in smartphone culture as compared to web applications. Users typically turn to applications to do things on their phones and will use the web for its core strength of consuming information. Despite this, mobile web applications are evolving in their abilities and are become more like native applications every day.

Developing native applications give the developer greater access to and control over the phone's hardware as exposed through the operating system's APIs. This means direct control over hardware such as GPS, compass, accelerometer, and etc. While there are

some exciting new tools that give browsers similar access and control, they are still young and not fully matured. Thus mobile browsers have less control compared to their native counterparts.

In a similar sense native applications give the developer a more robust set of tools to debug and troubleshoot their applications. While this aspect does not directly impact the end-user, it is significant for the developer. To be frank, debugging mobile web applications is a royal pain in the ass as compared to debugging native applications. Normally a web developer can utilize built in debugging tools found in modern web browsers to understand what's going on, but in the mobile browser just viewing the HTML source of an application is an arduous, convoluted process. Then to actually debug an application, developers have to choose between low-tech, "old school" methods such as, alert or print statements or complex remote debugging clients and bulky debugging frameworks. Like so much associated with the web, things are improving, but the latest attempts at solving this problem are still in their infancy.

Now all of this is not to say mobile web application development is the economy model of smartphone application development, the YUGO compared to the BMW. Mobile web application does have its areas where it is more luxurious and powerful.

One area where developing for the web is more powerful is its use of a more ubiquitous set of skills, such as HTML, JavaScript, and CSS. These common languages are well established and as a result this maturity makes coding for multiple platforms much easier. In contrast, smartphones are a cluttered landscape, with many different operating systems and devices. Thus reaching each device necessitates knowing many different programming languages and the environments they operate in. This can lead to an expensive cost of entry for a developer to become proficient in programming for each platform.

Furthermore, different platforms can require specific environments to program in. For example, developing for the iPhone can only be done on a Mac using Apple's XCode IDE and the Objective-C programming language. Developing for Android does provide more flexibility in environments and IDEs using the Java programming language, but its flexibility still pales in comparison to the universal nature of web languages. Thus, compared to the core web languages of HTML, JavaScript, and CSS, it's hard for native applications to compete against the platform agnostic nature of the web.

In conclusion, deciding between native application development and mobile web development must be weighed carefully. At Winona State we decided that it was best to leverage the strengths of our team and develop mobile web applications. We already had the experience and skills necessary to create these types of applications and determined that going this route would be the most efficient use of our resources.

6.3 What's Next?

Recently Winona State embarked upon a new project to highlight a unique feature of our campus, its trees. With almost 40 different species of trees found on campus, Winona State reflects the unique ecology of southeastern Minnesota.

Utilizing information from the book, *Campus of Trees: Winona State University,* authored by senior groundskeeper Bill Meyer (ret.) and Associate Professor Tom Grier, WSU is creating a mobile web application that will augment reality with information about our trees. Our goal is to provide another experience for users to interact with their environment and become further engaged, through the use of technology, in the community.

The application is exploring the use of several promising new tools, which we believe will leverage the strengths of both native and mobile web applications.

One tool being utilized is PhoneGap. In this framework, developers create applications with HTML, JavaScript, and CSS then build them into native applications for the major smartphone platforms. This technique has the advantage of enabling developers to develop once and deploy everywhere.

Another tool being explored is jQuery Mobile, which is a mobile-optimized web framework for smartphones and tablets. This framework provides an HTML5-based user interface that is optimized for the mobile web and built upon the already wildly popular jQuery JavaScript framework.

By combine these two tools, our goal is to create a web-based application that not only showcases our trees but also leverages Winona State's core strengths of web development and a smartphone's hardware.

7. CONCLUSIONS

As the number of students with smaller mobile devices continues to increase, Winona State's mobile development efforts will continue to evolve. WSU Mobile was developed initially for the iPhone, iPod and iPad, but with an increasing number of students owning Android phones, it was evident the platform needed to be expanded. This allowed the team to rethink the idea of developing native mobile applications, and led to version 2.0 of WSU Mobile. This application was developed as a pure web application using HTML5 and CSS3. This allowed the application to be made available by accessing www.winona.edu/m, but could also be packaged within an Android and iOS webview to be available for download from the Android Marketplace and Apple App Store.

Other development efforts, such as Stories in Structure, allowed the team to evaluate and use tools such as Drupa's Tap Tour to make the development process more efficient. The current mobile development effort, The Campus of Trees Tour, has allowed us to further evolve our development approach to allow for an augmented reality tour. We have focused our efforts on marketing and communication to current and prospective students and other external audiences. We anticipate that as we continue to develop for mobile platforms, we will move towards providing mobile support for teaching and learning in a higher educational environment.

8. REFERENCES

[1] Rainie, L. (2012, January 23) *Tablet Ownership Nearly Double Over Holiday Gift-Giving Period.* Pew Internet and American Life Program. http://libraries.pewinternet.org/2012/01/23/tablet-and-e-book-reader-ownership-nearly-double-over-the-holiday-gift-giving-period/

[2] Dahlstrom, E., Grunwald, P., de Boor, T., & Vockley, M. (2011) *ECAR National Study of Students and Information Technology in Higher Education, 2011.* EDUCUASE Center for Applied Research. http://www.educause.edu/2011StudentStudy

[3] Gagnon, D. (2010) Mobile *Learning Environments.* EDUCAUSE Quarterly 33 (3).

[4] EDUCAUSE Learning Initiative (2010) *7 Things You Should Know About… Mobile Apps for Learning.* EDUCAUSE. http://net.educause.edu/ir/library/pdf/ELI7060.pdf

[5] Liestol, G. (2011) *Learning Through Situated Simulations: Exploring Mobile Augmented Reality.* EDUCAUSE Center for Applied Research Bulletin. http://net.educause.edu/ir/library/pdf/ERB1101.pdf

[6] Dobbin, G. (2011) *Mobile IT in Higher Education, 2011.* EDUCAUSE Center for Applied Research Bulletin. http://net.educause.edu/ir/library/pdf/ers1104/ERS1104W.pdf

[7] Siegfried, B. (2011) Enhanced *Student Technology Support with Cross-Platform Mobile Apps.* One Team, One Mission, 39th Annual ACM SIGUCCS 2011. ACM Press, New York.

[8] Christensen, C. (2002) *The Innovators's Dilemma.* Harper Business, New York.

[9] Dunn, J. (2011, December 12) *10 Schools Encouraging Smartphones in the Classroom.* Edudemic. http://edudemic.com/2011/12/smartphones-in-classrooms/

[10] Winona State University (2010) Winona State University Technology Master Plan. http://www.winona.edu/it/Media/WSU_Tech_Master_Plan_-_Final.pdf

[11] Winona State University (2011, June 30) Winona State University Information Technology Services FY11 Year-End Report. http://www.winona.edu/it/Media/WSU-ITS-FY11-End_of_Year_Report.pdf

[12] Winona State University YouTube site. (2012) http://www.youtube.com/user/WinonaU

[13] Mapcruncher for Virtual Earth. (2012) http://research.microsoft.com/en-us/um/redmond/projects/mapcruncher/

Practical Uses of Cloud Computing Services in a Japanese University of the Arts against Aftermath of the 2011 Tohoku Earthquake

Hiroki Kashiwazaki[*]
Art Media Center, Tokyo University of the Arts
12-8 Ueno Park, Taito
Tokyo, Japan
reo@noc.geidai.ac.jp

ABSTRACT

Tokyo University of the Arts, which is one of the National Universities of the Arts in Japan, was also affected by the 2011 Tohoku earthquake. Many stored art items in our museums were destroyed and many events were postponed or cancelled. The Art Media Center, which manages the campus networks and the IT policies, used cloud computing services to overcome these disabilities. For instance, we used the movie streaming service "Ustream" to deliver a movie by the president of our university to substitute for our canceled graduation and entrance ceremony. We also used the cloud backup storage service " Dropbox Teams" for disaster recovery. By cooperating with other universities, we established a committee called "RICC" to promote the activities of cloud computing and we are now constructing an experimental wide area distributed private inter-cloud computer network. Through explanation of these projects, we will detail for sustainable administration on a University of the Arts in Japan.

Categories and Subject Descriptors

K.6.4 [**Management Of Computing And Information Systems**]: System Management—*Centralization / decentralization*

General Terms

Management

Keywords

Cloud Computing, Campus Network Administration, IT utilization

---

[*]http://rgb.geidai.ac.jp

1. INTRODUCTION

The 2011 Tohoku earthquake, also known as the 3.11 Earthquake, was a magnitude 9.0 Mw undersea megathrust earthquake off the coast of Japan that occurred at 14:46 (JST) on Friday, 11 March 2011. It was the most powerful known earthquake ever to have hit Japan, and one of the five most powerful earthquakes in the world since modern record keeping began in 1900. Over fifteen thousand deaths, about twenty seven thousand injured, and over three thousand people missing were confirmed on 12 March 2012 by the Japanese National Police Agency. About 120 thousand buildings totally collapsed, with a further 254 thousand buildings 'half collapsed', and another approximately 700 thousand buildings partially damaged. The main earthquake was preceded by a number of large foreshocks, with hundreds of aftershocks reported. Several nuclear and conventional power plants went offline after the earthquake. Multiple rolling blackouts were required in many areas to help meet the electricity shortage. Major disaster management headquarters required national universities to either stop using using or reduce the use of daytime lights, heaters and coolers, air conditionings and elevators. Tokyo University of the Arts, one of the oldest national universities of the arts in Japan, is located in Tokyo, Ibaraki, Kanagawa, and Nara. There are about 330 permanent professors and officers, 1,100 visiting lecturers and 3,320 students in this university. The Ibaraki facility called Toride school site was the most damaged facility which is about 350 km (215.6 miles) from the earthquake center. There is a university museum in Toride school site that stores a lot of graduation products and donated art objects. The graduation ceremony was scheduled to be held on 25 March 2011 and the entrance ceremony would be held on 5 April 2011. Because of the effect of the earthquake and concern for the safety of students and their families, both ceremonies were canceled. Many concerts related to our university were also canceled or postponed. For example, programs of a music festival called La Folle Journée au JAPON which had been held in Tokyo every May since 2005 were changed because concert halls and theatres were unavailable and some musicians rejected coming to Japan.

In the university, I belong to the Art Media Center (AMC) that provides the Internet connectivity, campus area network services, digital environments (including computers, printers and audio mixers), and the policy decisions for information technologies use around the university. From my arrival in January 2010, I have pushed ahead with campus informatization, in particular virtualization of campus information systems to save energy and physical spaces. Fortunately, this promotion of virtualization helped us recover in aftermath of the earthquake. I have also been researching the operation of inter-cloud computing which intends to make a huge cloud computing environment by inter-connecting different cloud services which are widely distributed. To promote this research activity, I set up a committee called "RICC" (Regional Inter-Cloud Committee) under a committee of JSPS (Japan Society for the Promotion of Science). The JSPS is a Japanese independent administrative institution and plays a pivotal role in the administration of a wide spectrum of Japan's scientific and academic programs. By using this environment and many public cloud services, we achieved various sustainable services with minimal costs. In this paper, we will show practical uses of cloud computing services for disaster recovery, promotion of inter-cloud networks and as well as our future prospects.

2. ISSUES

There were three representative issues to be solved at our university with limited human resources and a small budget. Especially after the earthquake, the majority of the university budget went to the repair and maintenance of facilities. The detail of the issues and simple cost estimation without cloud computing services are shown below.

2.1 movie streaming

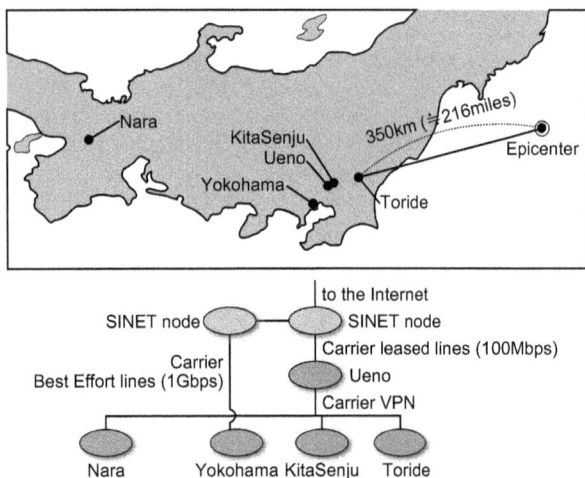

Figure 1: Geographical Positions of the School Sites and their network topology

As previously described, to protect safety of students and their families, the graduation ceremony and the entrance ceremony couldn't help being cancelled. But our university administration hoped to deliver a message from the president to the graduates and the new students after the tragic disaster all the more. Although AMC had QuickTime Streaming Server with Apple Xserve Systems, the system was several years old and we couldn't use it for movie streaming. In addition, the server couldn't serve a high quality of the movie to a large number of clients. Above all, our university has 100 Mbps leased line service with a network carrier to the nearby SINET node (Fig.1). SINET is an infor-

mation and communication network connecting universities and research institutions throughout Japan via nationwide connection points (node). If we provided 512 Kbps H.264 movie, which is a well-rounded high quality movie similar to those in YouTube, only about 200 users could watch at a time. We couldn't estimate if this number of users was sufficient or not enough. Furthermore, if we had arranged to make a contract of 1 Gbps leased line service, it would have cost about 80,000 dollars per year by using a metro ethernet. Using HTTP Live Streaming server to distribute the movie for 200 !A 2000 users at a time, we estimated that it would cost 7,000 !A 100,000 dollars, including cheap mac minis and load-balanced switches. When we prepared a movie streaming system inside the university to deliver quality video to an unpredictable number of audiences, we needed a huge amount of money and human resources. And the things that can be said with certainly is that the system would be rarely used after the events.

2.2 backup copy of files

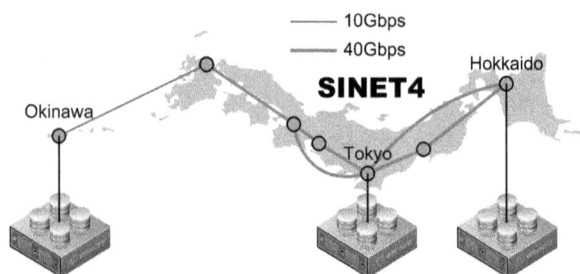

Figure 2: The Construction of Backup Copies System and its Replications for Disaster Recovery

As is well known, the earthquake caused a major tsunami that brought destruction along the Pacific coastline of Japan's northern islands and resulted in the loss of thousands of lives and devastated entire towns. In many local governments, information systems and client computers of city halls and hospitals were under the water and data such as residential information and patients' chart were totally lost. Unfortunately in many cases, they didn't have any copies or they had copies but in nearby cities so original and the copies were both lost. This made most of the Japanese population understand the importance of making backup copies and the significance of the disaster recovery (DR). But making backup copies with high frequency makes the costs of backup system higher and ease of performing restores lower. Backup client software with higher ease of use often cost more. To save on the total size of backup copies, data deduplication for eliminating coarse-grained redundant data is useful. But storage system with data deduplication also often cost more. To achieving adequate disaster recovery, backup copies should be stored in several distant places with a low probability of earthquake if possible. If we used data centers at Okinawa prefecture and Hokkaido prefecture, which are to the south and the north ends of Japan, and where there have been few strong earthquake in the past, the cost to use a server rack will be about one thousand dollars per year (Fig.2). We must place the storage systems inside the university and data centers. Using high quality EMC storage systems, we estimated that it would cost over 1 million dollars to provide to provide 200 officers each 50 GB of backup copies space. Because disk drive cost per bit comes down drastically every year, it doesn't make business sense to devote a huge budget to storage, especially in backup storage systems that don't need very high I/O performance.

2.3 Virtualization System

From early 2010, I constructed a virtualization system for campus IT systems with small start. By using VMware ESXi on only one relatively cheap server, we tried to migrate a physical machine to virtual machine environment. Though the trial was successful, some challenges were found in this single server environment. The challenges are:

- difficulty of system maintenance (e.g. applying patches, system upgrading, trouble recoverying, et.al).

- no redundancy, no availability with only one server.

- the necessity of data stores (FC or iSCSI connected storage) for achieving high availability.

- anxiety about I/O performance (especially in using cheap iSCSI storage like NAS for SOHO use).

- the necessity of measurements for existing physical servers (capacity assessment for computing resource).

- the need for uninterruptible power supply.

At the time, there were about ten IT systems inside the campus. The systems are shown below.

- Groupware System

- Supporting System for Making Government Documents

- Web-DB System for Research Achievements

- Web-DB System for Stored Items in the Museum.

- Web-DB System for Rare Old Books in the Library.

- Finance and Accounting System

- Personnel System

- Fraternal Insurance System

- Library Information System

- Alive Monitoring and Network Measuring System

I assessed the servers including the applications with help from VMware. We found that two relatively high performance servers could support all of our IT systems. The detail spec of the high performance server is dual Xeon X5670 2.93 GHz CPU (6 cores) with 36 GB of memory. Virtual machine hypervisor (vSphere) was installed on this server. Our original cheaper server that we tested ESXi on was used as the vCenter server. Even though we had done an assessment, the I/O performance for our whole IT systems was unknown. So I tentatively purchased two cheap NASs that used iSCSI. One NAS is used as data store for VM and the other is used as backup storage using VDR (VMware Data Recovery). Eventually, after two years, the storage system was upgraded and the GbE L2 switch was replaced with 10GbE (Fig.3).

But as is the case with a single backup system, virtualization system on the single site is weak defense against disaster. It is also necessarry for high availability to use VDR to a remote site and wide-area global migration.

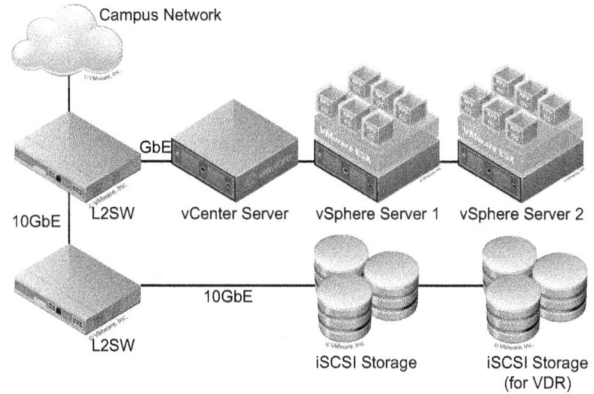

Figure 3: The Construction of Virtualization System inside the University

3. SOLUTIONS

To solve these issues, we utilized public / private cloud computing services.

3.1 Ustream

Figure 4: Distribution of ceremony message from the president by using Ustream.

Instead of getting big streaming system and network line, we decided to use Ustream [7] to distribute the movie for the graduation ceremonies. Ustream is a network made up of various channels that provides a platform for live video streaming of events online. Watershed [8] is a similar network that is pay-as-you-go version of Ustream. This movie distribution was an experimental trial, so we choose Ustream, because of free service. The movies were messages from the president for graduates and new students. The speech and live art performance (action painting) by the president was recorded as 720p quality 10 minutes movies by HD camera before the ceremonies. Then we translated these movies to adequate video format for Ustream, uploaded to the Ustream site and checked to make sure the movies were viewable. By using Twitter and official websites, these streaming events were widely announced. At the scheduled time, the events turned to be viewable. This streaming was accessible by everyone for three days and each streaming (graduation and entrance message) was watched by over ten thousand persons.

3.2 Dropbox for Teams

To provide a backup solution to 200 officers with high usability, we needed a product that had a quality user interface. We also wanted an unlimited number of copies of the backup files, and backup copies are added when files are made, altered and deleted. Periodic copies such as volume shadow copy with Microsoft Windows Server may confuse users because history is added whether files are altered or not. Additionally, file sharing with several persons or in groups is useful for these officers. For to meet these needs, we chose the Dropbox for Teams [4] as the backup copies system. Dropbox [3] is a web-based file hosting service. Dropbox uses networked storage to enable users to store and share files and folders with others. Dropbox for Teams is focused towards businesses and collaborative teams and provides administrative control. By using this service, the backup system for 200 officers and 50 GB backup spaces per officer cost 45 thousand dollars per year. This is cheaper than 5 years use of EMC storage with clients license fee. On the other hand, by putting backups outside the university, there was concern about the flow of restricted information. To deal with this issue, a hybrid operation with both public cloud storage service and inside storage for restricted information is possible.

3.3 Hokkaido University Academic Cloud

From 1st November 2011, Hokkaido University, which is located on Hokkaido prefecture and one of the most influential academic organizations in advanced IT technology in Japan, has provided a IaaS (Infrastructure as a Service) solution called "Hokkaido University Academic Cloud" for researchers and business users [6]. This system is using CloudStack [2] and the Citric XenServer hypervisor [1]. Hardware is constructed of 114 nodes of HITACHI Blade Server BS2000. One node has 4 processors with 2.4 GHz, 10 cores and 128 GB memory. The total peak performance of this cloud system reaches 40 Tflop/s. Hokkaido University Information Initiative Center accepts the submission of collaborative research proposals. If the proposal is accepted, over one thousand dollars of research budget for only usage fee of super computer and this cloud computer is offered. In comparison, a commercial solution of IaaS, with 11 VMs with 10 cores and 5 TB of storage would cost one thousand dollars for three months of use. By using VMs, I constructed a 40 TB single volume iSCSI storage target and OpenVPN [5] Server. The virtualization environments of our university are connected to the Hokkaido University Academic Cloud via this OpenVPN service and use the academic cloud as VM data store and VDR target. By using this environment, our virtualization environment can copy their backups to remote site, and if VMware hypervisor can be installed in Hokkaido University Academic Cloud, VMs can migrate from out University to Hokkaido University.

Figure 5: Remote Virtualized Data Recovery System by using Hokkaido University Academic Cloud.

In parallel, I set up the committee called "RICC" (Regional Inter-Cloud Committee) under a committee of JSPS. The objective of RICC is to inter-connect a number of academic, (local) government, and commercial cloud services and to build a robust cloud computing environment around a wide-area. At the present day, there are ten nodes associated with the project. The northern edge node is the Kitami Institute of Technology and southern edge node is Ryukyu University, which are separated by about 3,000 km.

4. CONCLUSION

I show the aftermath of the 2011 Tohoku earthquake on Tokyo University of the Arts and demonstrate disaster recovery solutions by practical uses of cloud computing services. By not only using commercial services, but also utilizing collaborative research, I demonstrate the possibility of high quality, high availability IT services such as disaster recovery. Raising quality and achieving a sustainable system is future work.

5. ACKNOWLEDGMENTS

The work is mainly supported by the collaborative research program 2011 and 2012, information initiative center, Hokkaido University, Sapporo, Japan. It is also partly supported by the collaborative research program 2012, National Institute of Informatics. Thanks also to the Joint Usage/Research Center for Interdisciplinary Large-scale Information Infrastructures (JHPCN).

6. REFERENCES

[1] http://www.citrix.com/English/ps2/products/product.asp?contentID=683148.
[2] http://www.cloudstack.org.
[3] https://www.dropbox.com.
[4] https://www.dropbox.com/teams.
[5] http://openvpn.net.
[6] http://www.reuters.com/article/2011/05/25/idUS10030+25-May-2011+BW20110525.
[7] http://www.ustream.tv.
[8] https://watershed.ustream.tv.

The Illusion of One Hundred Percent Uptime

Jeremy Kim
Wharton Computing, University of Pennsylvania
3733 Vance Hall
Philadelphia, PA 19105
(215) 898-2601

kimj3@wharton.upenn.edu

James Denk
Wharton Computing, University of Pennsylvania
3733 Vance Hall
Philadelphia, PA 19105
(215) 817-8153

jdenk@wharton.upenn.edu

Abstract

In demanding academic environments students expect 100% uptime. It is rarely the case when dealing with school technology including Macs, PCs, printers, servers, complex networks and numerous peripherals that everything will be working correctly. Given our customers desired reliability how do we meet their expectations?

We make use of a variety of software packages to identify potential problems before they impact students. These software packages focus on security state, application status, network connectivity and usage patterns. Through a combination of hot-swappable hardware, checklists, scheduled inspections and results from our monitoring software our dedicated staff is able to minimize perceived system downtime.

Our student support and student experience staff gather regular feedback from the student body. This feedback coupled with our monitoring software and a student satisfaction survey is able to gauge our results.

It is not possible to provide 100% uptime but by our constant monitoring and quick response we are able to give that illusion. To achieve this it is important to define your institutional goals and make sure you have the infrastructure in place which meets your unique needs.

Categories and Subject Descriptors

C.5.3 [**Computer System Implementation**]: Microcomputers – *Microprocessors, Personal Computers, Portable Devices, Workstations.*

K.3.1 [**Computers and Education**]: Computer Uses in Education – *Collaborative Learning, Computer-assisted Instruction (CAI), Computer-managed instruction (CMI), Distance Learning.*

General Terms

Performance, Design, Reliability, Verification.

Keywords

Classroom, Computer Lab, KACE, Monitoring, Virtualization, University of Pennsylvania, VMWare, Wharton

1. INTRODUCTION

In the Wharton Computing environment we work to present the illusion of 100% uptime. Throughout the year students are consistently using our computers and printers for their studies. To provide them with the best experience we use various software to consistently monitor our environment and resolve issues before they interfere with student productivity. At the same time we conduct semiannual survey to get feedback from our students and make necessary improvements.

2. Background

Established in 1881, the Wharton School at the University of Pennsylvania is the world's first collegiate business school. There are more than 5,000 undergraduate, MBA, executive MBA and doctoral students. The University of Pennsylvania's population of 24,832 full and part-time students may also take classes while not actively enrolled in a Wharton program. Our customer base is principally the student body, but we also provide services to faculty, staff and special events in our facilities.

The labs group is a subdivision of Public Technology, which is in turn a division of Wharton Computing. Principal support by the labs group is offered by three full time staff members and a part time staff member under the supervision of an IT Director.

3. WHARTON ENVIRONMENT

3.1 Services

Public Computing is responsible for the physical computing environment, the virtual computing environment as well as printing. These services are provided for the student-facing and instructional spaces at the Wharton School.

3.1.1 Physical Computing Environment

At Wharton we have a number of different physical spaces that come under the responsibilities of the Public Computing group. These spaces include classrooms, computer labs, email bar computers, group study rooms, group workstations and Skype stations.

Classrooms are locations that have a dedicated computer with the public computing build as well as additional software so that instructors can manage the physical infrastructure of the classroom. These computers are responsible for providing a reliable and responsive default configuration. Classrooms are the portals through which lighting, projector settings and other classroom electronic configuration options are selected.

Our computer labs are instructional spaces where students have access to a computer and in which there is also a classroom computer for the instructor. When not scheduled for an event these spaces are available for ad hoc student use. These computers have the standard public computing build and occasional one-off customizations to meet instructional requirements.

Email bar kiosks are iMacs configured with a locked down environment for students to be able to access the web, and their network file space. These computers are principally for quick communications and printing. They are installed without chairs at a height comfortable for standing.

Group study room computers are individual machines available in rooms that the students may reserve. These locations have our standard public computing build coupled with dual displays on adjustable arms. This configuration was designed to facilitate collaborative work in larger student groups.

Group workstations are computers available in public areas for student use. These computers have the public computing build and are often used to work alone with one to two other people.

Skype stations are PCs locked down to allow video conferencing. These are installed in locations that used to house public phones for students. These computers have a custom windows build to limit their functionality to Skype usage.

3.1.2 Virtual Computing Environment

In addition to our physical space we have virtual computing offerings. These offerings include a virtual computer lab for student use, a dedicated GIS build for ArcGIS programs, and in some places are coupled with zero clients as replacements for physical computers.

The virtual computing lab offers access to the public computing build from student computers utilizing the VMWare View [12] infrastructure. This is accessible to our students both on and off campus.

Our virtual GIS lab uses a custom build to provide access to ArcGIS software. These machines are given access to greater virtual resources than the standard virtual lab. The virtual GIS lab allows us to give access to a custom build for instructional needs without having to dedicate physical space for a relatively small subset of students.

In some of our physical spaces we have implemented zero clients. These devices connect to our virtual infrastructure in place of traditional desktop computers. Samsung NC240 zero clients [8] are used as test machines in some of our spaces with little demand for hardware performance. They are also used in satellite locations that we do not control directly.

The virtual environment has the auxiliary benefit of being a wonderful testing area. We can create VMs for internal use or when we are ready we can entitle other users to make use of these test builds.

3.1.3 Printing

We offer managed printing on any of our physical or virtual computers, physical or virtual, that receive the public computing build. Additionally we allow printing from email bar kiosks and student devices. This service comes with variable printing allotments depending on the student enrollment type with a fallback to central University of Pennsylvania PennCash funds.

3.2 Applications

3.2.1 Real-Time Information

We use Computer Lab Solution's LabStats [5] product to check the network connectivity of our computers. An agent will be installed on the client computer which will respond back to the Labstats server with the power status and who is currently logged on. All this information will be displayed in a web-based graphical interface. In this way we are getting real-time data that allows us to quickly see which computers might have problems. Our policy is to have all computers turned on at all times so it can be ready for use. If we see a computer that is turned off we will do a physical inspection of the computer. It might actually be that someone had turned off the computer but if it is on and we experience any issues we swap out the computer as soon as possible. In this way the computer will always be on and at top performance condition for customer use. Another service Labstats provides is that it allows us to provide information on computer availability on our digital signage so that students can know which lab will have the most computers available.

HP WebJet Admin [4] is used to monitor status of the physical printers. It will show us the level of ink, level of paper, report product life cycle and report any jams. By monitoring this system we are able to refill paper level and replace ink cartridges before it runs out. As for paper jams WebJet Admin also notifies us, giving us the capability to be onsite and assist our customers when the jam occurs.

We have centralized event logs being gathered to one server. In this way we can monitor certain events we're looking for in our environment and go to a central point to check the logs. As a result if we're seeing any strange behavior we can look for an event log associated with the behavior and quickly tell if it has occurred on any other computers. This real-time data will allows us to quickly tell which computers are showing programmatic behavior and remove it from our environment.

Another package we use is KACE 1000 [3] server appliance. KACE manages computer inventory, software inventory, security updates and third party installations. This allows all deployed computers to have the most recent security patches and all the required software installed. When Flash, Java, Adobe Reader, etc. roll out their updates we use KACE to schedule these updates to be rolled out sometime between midnight and 5AM. The updates are done in the background without any user interaction during low-usage times. In the process of deploying new computers with an older image KACE will check to see if it has the most recent updates and if not it will update it early morning or can force the update up front. KACE also checks for third party software that might be missing and deploys that as well. In this way students will always be using the most secure configuration and will not experience any software missing on the computers. The software inventory also lets us the see what software and what versions of it are installed on our computers so that we can make sure they're all up to date. The KACE inventory also allows us to provide other departments what version of certain software installed on our machines. KACE gives us the capability for enabling interactive remote desktop support in a secure way. KACE uses UltraVNC [9] to supply this connectivity but currently we're only using this in the classroom environment. This capability allows us to fix any sudden issues professors might have in the classrooms with least interference. Examining this experience will allow us to determine if remote desktop support will be rolled out to the labs.

In all these applications the purpose is to provide real-time data. In order to provide the high level of support we shoot for we need to know before the students do if there is a problem with a computer or a printer. Labstats, HP WebJet Admin, Event logs and KACE forms a powerful combination to do this. It either shows if a computer has network connectivity, the power status, inventory of software and its versions and event logs we are monitoring. In the printer aspect it will show printers running out of toner, paper and paper jams. Working together all these software can provide a wealth of real-time information to provide an illusion of one hundred percent uptime.

3.2.2 Base-Line Configuration

For initial Operating System build we are using the Microsoft Deployment Toolkit (MDT)[6] to automate the build process. This toolkit allows for replacing items involved in the build on a modular level. While we employ KACE for thin style deployment technology, MDT allows us to provision a thick image upfront, which is of value for varied requirements involved when deploying in physical and virtual spaces.

As for OS deployment we're using Windows Deployment Services [10]. Previously we had used Ghost Imaging but Windows Deployment gave us few more options that allowed us improve our service. One was being able to reimage on site. Currently we have pxe boot enabled on the WDS and it will only initiate if F12 is selected during bootup. In the Ghost setup we had to create its own LAN network and reimage machines. WDS gives us the capability to reimage without creating another network as well as not having to physically move the computer to Ghost reimaging area. WDS also gives the capability to multicast imaging by computer name so if a computer connects to WDS and its set to be part of the multicast it will join the multicast session. WDS has improved the time it takes to reimage a machine and get ready for deployment. It has also improved the capability and timeframe to reimage a lab. From here KACE takes over and updates any necessary patches and third party applications.

Microsoft's Group Policy is another component used to manage our computers. We use group policy to manage security, control applications, map share drives and deploy printers. Security settings include firewall configuration to lockdown ports or only allow connections from certain subnets. Other management settings are mapping the shared network drive called MyWhartonDrive for students. Group Policy also manages how Internet Explorer will behave if a student or a professor logs in. All this allows us to manage computers being added to our environment and to make sure they behave in a certain standard expected by our users.

Our email bar kiosks are iMacs that are managed through a combination of KACE, Apple Remote Desktop [1], and Workgroup Manager [2] coupled with MCX policies. KACE, in parity with the PC management model, is used to push updated and applications out to our iMacs after deployment, It is also our principal inventory and reporting tool. Apple Remote Desktop is used for pushing files, making live changes in the background, and for the execution of shell scripts. It is also used to remote into the kiosks and confirm their status when necessary. Workgroup manager is used to maintain MCX policies on the computers, controlling the degree to which they are locked down and the default preferences for applications. It is also used for configuring the printers for student use.

In the case of MDT, WDS, KACE, GPO, Apple Remote Desktop and Workgroup Manager it allows our computers to meet certain standard of expectation. Then KACE will update the computer to working order by updating OS and third party software. This is crucial in keeping our environment up hundred percent. Different from the real time information data, base-line configuration will

allow us to put in place preventive measures like making sure all the software are present and up to date so students don't end up using a computer that does not meet their expectation.

3.2.3 Wharton Printing Management

Our printing environment is managed by Pharos [7]. We have a basic charging setup with a variable initial allotment for students and then a funding beyond that comes from our central campus Penncard system. Student release jobs at the printers using their student IDs. Printing can happen from computers we manage, both Macs and PCs or from the students own devices. This leads to a complex printing environment. We have a clustered windows print server as our primary printing node for printing from our computers. A supplemental print server is responsible for receiving jobs from students and has a more open security model so it can be printed to from on or off campus. We couple the pharos monitoring with windows event logging for reporting redundancy.

Our fleet of printers is made up of a combination of HP and Xerox black and white, multifunction printer/copiers, color printers, and high-speed production level printers.

Our printing system supports over 7 million pages annually with peak highs of over 33,800 sheets daily and sometimes more than 10,000 sheets an hour. We couple this with real time performance monitor both through internal OS tools and utilizing VMWare's vSphere[12] monitoring for the virtual print servers. We utilize data pulled from the Windows Event Logs and Pharos Database to do trend analysis and to identify times when additional support or resources may need to be provided to address student printing requirements.

By using these monitoring tools and identifying trends we are able to create a printing environment that supports the illusion of one hundred percent uptime. These trends will allows us to see when high volume of printing will occur so we can have more staff at hand to refill paper trays. Or what time of the day experiences heavy printing volume so we can have more staff walking around.

3.3 Procedures

There are several procedures that we deal with in the Wharton environment. One is doing regular checkups of the printers and computers every morning. The first thing one of our staff member does is to check the paper levels on our printers and deal with any needs the printers might have like changing ink cartridges or fuser. At the same time this staff will check Labstats and make a list of offline computers. With this list he will check on these computers. Any computers showing any issues will be swapped out with a spare. All this is done before most of the students are on campus allowing us to enforce our policy of 100% uptime. We also have routine scheduled checkups of printers during the day. It is usually scheduled for between classes where there are large volumes of student printing. In this way we can assist students that might have issues printing and resolve it when the issue occurs.

Dealing with procedure on new images or checking out our image before an event we provide virtualized PC through VMWare View. Staff and professors have access to our virtual lab computers that is the same build as the image in our labs. This allows an opportunity for people wanting to use our computers for an event or a class to make sure they are getting what they expected before the actual date of the event. In this way they can see if a video might work, if a software package is available or if a simulation on the web will work. This puts the initial troubleshooting in the hands of the user and prevents unexpected surprises on the day of the event.

Creating a master image for our labs is done once every semester. VMWare View comes in handy because it allows staff and faculty to check our new master image before being released and provide us with any feedback. After a new image is rolled out and before another master image is created there might be new updates and new third party software installed on our machines. As a result it is our procedure to install KACE agent on all new images deployed. In this way the KACE agent will update the computer with the newest updates and install any third party software that might have been installed after the master image was created. This allows us to make sure the computer meets security standards and has all the necessary software. It also benefits us by allowing us to create fewer master images.

Procedures are in a way combination of real time information and base-line configuration. They allow us to get real time information on what students are experiencing when we perform routine checkups of our environment. These procedures enable our customers the opportunity to perform tests on our image. Their feedback helps us to keep our base-line configuration image configured for optimal use. In this way all these procedures contribute to the illusion of one hundred percent uptime.

3.4 Information Gathering

Wharton conducts semiannual surveys to receive student feedback about our environment. From these feedbacks we make necessary changes to our environment. Since a lot of these changes were from direct suggestions from the student body it has a high satisfaction level to students. It also affirms our students that their suggestions matter. At the same time since we're making changes to meet student needs it improves our service as a whole.

Throughout the year we hold Student Experience Support tables where students are encouraged to come and get some snacks while we talk to them about their experience with technology at Wharton. Again this is very valuable for us as it is a direct feedback and good measurement of our service to students. It allows us to see problems we might not have notice or expected.

Surveys allow us to improve our base-line configuration by allowing direct input from our students to improve our technology environment. While Support table allows us to gather any real time information on problem we might not have seen through our data and allows us to quickly pin point problems and fix it. In this way we continue to strive to create an illusion of one hundred percent uptime.

4. CONCLUSION

In providing an illusion of one hundred percent uptime we strive to create redundancies of all the important services we provide. In this environment we strive to never have a student suffer from the same problem twice, nor to have more than one student be impacted by a preventable problem.

Be it KACE, Pharos, the VMWare View environment, or other infrastructure components we believe downtime of services can cause great disturbance to our customers. With this vision in mind we have in place monitoring and engage in constant review of our response procedures. Externally we rely upon the Student Experience table and our semiannual surveys to gauge our success in the eyes of our primary customers, the students.

The illusion of one hundred percent uptime is less a technical matter and more a matter of perception. We are working to decrease login times at the computers and adding additional staff to decrease response times. At the same time we're evaluating methods to detect problems faster and to make it easier for students to report them. In the end, you can't tally your system uptime to determine the success of your services, it is defined entirely by the perception of your customers.

5. ACKNOWLEDGEMENTS

Our thanks to David Siedell, Senior Director for Public Technology for his support in allowing offering the level of service we provide. Thanks also to Antonio Vivas, IT Director for Public Computing for his support and funding of our conference travel.

6. REFERENCES

[1] Apple Remote Desktop
http://www.apple.com/remotedesktop/

[2] Apple Workgroup Manager
http://support.apple.com/kb/HT5050

[3] Dell KACE
http://www.kace.com/

[4] HP WebJet Admin
http://h20331.www2.hp.com/hpsub/cache/332262-0-0-225-121.html

[5] LabStats
http://www.computerlabsolutions.com/

[6] Microsoft Deployment Toolkit
http://technet.microsoft.com/en-us/solutionaccelerators/dd407791.aspx

[7] Samsung NC240
http://m.samsung.com/au/consumer/tvav/professionallfddisplays/viewall/LF24PPBCB/XY

[8] UltraVNC
http://www.uvnc.com/

[9] Pharos Uniprint
http://www.pharos.com/uniprint

[10] Windows Deployment Services
http://technet.microsoft.com/en-us/library/cc771670(v=ws.10).aspx

[11] VMware View
http://www.vmware.com/products/view/overview.html

[12] VMWare vSphere
http://www.vmware.com/products/vsphere/mid-size-and-enterprise-business/overview.html

Shaking Up Traditional Training With lynda.com

Courtney Bentley
Lafayette College
109 Skillman Library
Easton, PA 18042
610-330-5504
bentleyc@lafayette.edu

Kathryn Fletcher
West Virginia University
OIT, PO Box 6501
Morgantown, WV 26506
304-293-8769
kathy.fletcher@mail.wvu.edu

Chad Fust
Vassar College
124 Raymond Ave, Box 13
Poughkeepsie, NY 12604
845-437-7545
chfust@vassar.edu

Rebecca Klein
Valparaiso University
1410 Chapel Dr, CLIR 171
Valparaiso, IN 46383
219-464-5986
becky.klein@valpo.edu

Carol Rhodes
Indiana University
IT Training
Bloomington, IN 47405
812-856-2007
csrhodes@indiana.edu

Cynthia Sanders
Oberlin College
148 West College St.
Oberlin, OH 44074
440-775-8197
Cindy.Sanders@oberlin.edu

Karen Sirman
Louisiana State University
ITS 103 Frey Comp Svc Ctr
Baton Rouge, LA 70803
225-578-1914
karen@lsu.edu

Elizabeth Wagnon
Texas A&M University
CIS Department, MS 3142
College Station, TX 77843
979-458-1623
eheilman@exchange.tamu.edu

ABSTRACT

Supporting the diverse technology training needs on campus while resources continue to dwindle is a challenge many of us continue to tackle. Institutions from small liberal arts campuses to large research universities are providing individualized training and application support 24/7 by subscribing to the lynda.com Online Training Library(r) and marketing the service to various combinations of faculty, staff and students.

As a supplemental service on most of our campuses, lynda.com has allowed us to extend support to those unable to attend live lab-based training, those who want advanced level training, those who want training on specialized applications, and those who want to learn applications that are not in high demand. The service also provides cost effective professional development opportunities for everyone on campus, from our own trainers and technology staff who are developing new workshops, learning new software versions or picking up new areas of expertise from project management to programming, to administrative and support staff who are trying to improve their skills in an ever-tighter economic environment.

On this panel discussion, you will hear about different licensing approaches, ways of raising awareness about lynda.com on our campuses, lessons learned through implementation, reporting capabilities, and advice we would give for other campuses looking to offer this service.

Categories and Subject Descriptors

K.3.1 [**Computers and Education**]: Computers Uses in Education – *Computer-managed instruction (CMI)*.

General Terms

Management, Performance.

Keywords

online training.

1. Indiana University

Indiana University is a multi-campus public university with a combined student body of more than 100,000 students, including approximately 42,000 students enrolled at the Indiana University Bloomington campus and approximately 37,000 students enrolled at the Indiana University-Purdue University Indianapolis (IUPUI) campus. In addition to these two core campuses, IU includes six smaller campuses and three centers/extensions spread throughout Indiana.

Because of the wide dissimilarities in campus size, the training units on each campus differ greatly in human and financial resources. To address these inequalities and more evenly distribute resources and knowledge across the state, IU's IT division (University Information Technology Services) recently combined the units from all campuses into one centralized IT division. Leveraging lynda.com statewide is one strategy which enables IU to equitably distribute IT training to the entire IU community.

Even IU's strongest IT Training units—the Bloomington and Indianapolis campuses—have been stretching resources in an attempt to continue to develop and update face-to-face and online training materials in leading technologies. Thus, offering lynda.com is the best online solution currently available to allow the entire IU community to keep up with myriad technologies-- as needed, on a 24/7 basis.

2. Lafayette College

Lafayette College is a private, residential campus of just over 2300 students and 200 full-time faculty focusing on the liberal arts and engineering. Because of the campus' focus on interdisciplinarity, professors are encouraged to work with students from vastly different disciplines on a regular basis to solve real problems. This sometimes means engineering students are working with photographers and both need extensive

Photoshop training or neurobiology students are working with musicians and need help with GarageBand or Logic Pro. While exciting work, these training demands can become overwhelming for a small campus.

Information Technology Services currently employs 29 full-time staff and is comprised of five units—Administrative Information Systems (AIS), Instructional Technology, Network and Systems, User Services, and Web Application Development—and is overseen by the Associate Vice President and Chief Information Officer. While the User Services group provides helpdesk support and some deskside assistance and training, group technology training and documentation is developed primarily by three instructional technologists.

A majority of group technology sessions are customized for academic courses or administrative units, or when new systems or new versions of applications are introduced. These sessions are generally well attended because there is added motivation or incentive, but once a saturation level is achieved for a particular topic, attendance dwindles, and we turn more to one-on-one training to meet the specific needs of a person working on a particular project. While highly time intensive, this just-in-time model is effective in meeting the needs of the campus.

As our success has grown in supporting the diverse training needs of the campus, more demand has been placed on our time so adopting the lyndaCampus solution helps us augment our staff time and expertise. In addition to meeting the just-in-time training expectations, lyndaCampus has allowed us to provide support for applications we would not usually staff for—AutoCAD, Python, Blender. And it also provides more in-depth information on applications we do support but have varying levels of use across campus.

All students, faculty and staff with a valid network account are covered in our lyndaCampus license although only around 11% have logged in. We use Shibboleth authentication to the service, and the first time a user accesses the service, their account is created and we release the user's first and last name in addition to their campus email address and primary affiliation of faculty/staff or student. Passing this affiliation information allows us to review usage reports in a more meaningful way to better understand where these populations are focusing their training time.

Communicating the availability of the service to campus, and promoting its usage has been and continues to remain a focus of our attention. During group training sessions, we usually take a few minutes to demo features of the site and show the group how to locate additional information on the topic we're covering so they can refresh their skills later or dig more deeply into topics. A few faculty have begun to assign certain segments for students to review outside of class, and many more suggest segments to students who may be struggling or interested in taking their skills further. We also pursued more broad marketing through a variety of channels including:

- a series of 30-minute introduction sessions so people could meet lynda.com and the training she could offer.
- dedicated open lab times in our technology consulting center when staff can get out of their offices and focus on completing lynda.com training.
- posters in residence halls, academic buildings and computer labs, and bookmarks available in the libraries and labs..

- lynda pencils with a information card attached to faculty and staff.
- a drawing once a month for the first six months to award a lynda mug to one student and one faculty or staff member who had used the service that month.
- monthly news item on the ITS web site listing the winners of the drawing in addition to the top five viewed sites that month, five new courses added to lynda.com that we thought would be of interest to the campus, and information on how to get started.

In addition to continuing many of the things above, future plans for increasing visibility and use include:

- hosting an information table in the student center one day during the semester to attract student interest and demonstrate the iPad application.
- publicly recognizing staff who have received lynda.com certificates of completion.
- work with Human Resources to help promote the service as a professional development opportunity.

Our goal is to continue marketing the service so it becomes one of the campus resources that comes immediately to mind when training and support needs arise.

3. Louisiana State University

LSU is located in Baton Rouge, Louisiana and is the flagship university for the state of Louisiana. LSU's enrollment for Fall 2011 was 29,000 students, both graduate and undergraduate students. LSU is comprised of 14 academic colleges and approximately 70 administrative departments. LSU is home to approximately 5,000 faculty and staff. LSU is an agricultural and land grant institution and serves the entire state in many capacities.

Training at LSU is managed by three main departments:

ITS Information Technology Services manages information technology training for users.

HRM Human Resources Management manages LSU HR and soft skills training.

CCT Center for Computation and Technologies manages research computing training.

The focus of this paper is the information technology training provided by Information Technology Services (ITS). ITS employs 178 staff members. There is one Manager for IT Training who reports to the User Support Director; however, employees from the Faculty Technology Center and User Support teach workshops as needed. In addition, students employed in the START program (hands-on technology workshops for students) teach workshops and conduct one-on-one software consultations (http://www.lsu.edu/start)

In February 2011, LSU began a limited pilot program with Lynda.com training to supplement hands-on IT workshops for campus. The pilot allowed a limited number (up to 5,000) of LSU students, faculty, and staff to take any of the courses in the Lynda course library. In March of 2012, LSU implemented the Lynda Campus model for online user training. Any student, faculty, and staff can now take the Lynda video courses, track their own progress and receive completion certificates. LSU ITS created a portal called **mySTART powered by Lynda.com** for users to login using their lsu.edu ID.

Marketing of Lynda Campus for this year has just begun. We make the campus aware of this valuable resource via:

- announcements at campus meetings, such as Staff Senate or Campus Communicators
- through newsletters, such as the campus IT Wire
- through graphics on web pages and portals, such as myLSU and the GROK knowledge base
- through meetings with LSU IT students
- via the Spring technology fair, TechPawLooza 2012
- through articles in the Faculty Senate newsletter
- through the START program (students teaching students) as a complement to the workshops
- through Facebook and other social media

Our pilot program was very successful and the faculty who utilize in their classrooms many of the Adobe products, web design products, and multimedia use this as a training medium for their classes. The Communication Across the Curriculum (CXC) department uses it heavily for instruction of faculty who teach communications intensive courses.

Throughout the pilot program and over the last few months with Lynda Campus, we have learned that, while licensing is a bear—getting all the i's dotted and the t's crossed for Purchasing—the hardest part is always the marketing and awareness. While faculty are utilizing Lynda Campus to teach their students software, not many staff have used the resources. The most prevalent departments to use Lynda Campus are the Mass Communications, Art and Design, and Business colleges. However, we still have a long way to go to promote this resource to campus. Still, it is an invaluable tool for training large amounts of students, faculty, and staff with very limited resources.

4. Oberlin College

Oberlin College is a small, private, liberal arts college and conservatory of music, located in Oberlin, Ohio, 35 miles southwest of Cleveland. Student enrollment is 2800, with 2200 enrolled in the College of Arts & Sciences, and 600 in the Conservatory. 175 students are double-degree majors. Faculty and staff number 900.

In the past, the Center for Information Technology (CIT) provided "short courses" in a classroom setting. These classes provided training on computer and other Information Technology (IT) resources, such as the College's email program, Word, Excel, FileMaker Pro, and so forth. After some number of years being well-attended, as users became more accustomed to these programs, attendance dwindled to the point where it no longer was effective or efficient to offer training in this manner.

In recent years, CIT has offered short training classes when new resources have been introduced. For example, when we moved our email system to the Google environment, we offered morning and afternoon training sessions for several weeks. These were well- attended. It became apparent to us that "just-in-time" training provided the best benefit, and was most desired, by our constituents. Thus, whenever we offer something new or unique, we schedule a few sessions to meet the needs of those who prefer a dedicated classroom environment. We continue to find these to be sparsely attended. In addition to this mechanism, over the past several years, CIT has offered one-on-one training, wherein we will visit a constituent in her/his office to provide up to an hour of dedicated training on a topic of her/his choice, or the client will come to the office of the CIT trainer for their one-on-one training session. Our trainer is one staff person, our Help Desk Manager, who is assigned many other duties as well. We do not have a dedicated training group.

At Oberlin College, we have several unions comprised of administrative assistants, security personnel, dining services personnel, tradespeople (carpenters, electricians), etc. The Oberlin College Office and Professional Employees (OCOPE) union (the administrative assistants' union) have a section in their contract stating that the College will provide funding for job-related training, primarily in computing. Thus, the Human Resources Department has contracted with external trainers to provide the training desired, as established by a training committee made up of HR staff and OCOPE members. The training has mainly consisted of classes in Word, Excel, and FileMaker Pro, plus classes such as "Dealing with Difficult People".

Thus, in recent years, both CIT and the HR Department have provided some means for training in IT. These mechanisms have not been wide-ranging in their reach or their subject matter. We did investigate online courses in the past, but did not believe they would be cost effective or well-used.

With lynda.com, we finally saw a product that provided a wide range of courses, designed in a manner wherein a user could easily address the specific topic they needed to learn more about, i.e., the user could acquire "just-in-time" training. Thus, a person wanting to learn about merging in Word could specifically address that aspect, without having to take an entire course on Word. After we learned more and more about the product from the lynda.com, we acquired a demo. The demo led us to conclude that this was a product that could fill a huge need on campus.

Thus, in the summer of 2011, we decided to procure a 1-year unlimited license to LyndaCampus. We wanted the courses to be available to everyone, whenever they needed or wanted to view them. We configured the system to allow any user on the campus network to have access. This also allows clients using VPN from off-campus locations to have access.

We then worked hard to market the product. We very much wanted to have data in this first year that would support procurement of the product in future years. The following are some of the processes we used to market this online learning system:

- campus-wide email messages to all constituents - faculty, staff, and students (once in the fall, once in the spring)
- posted info on the CIT website
- posted "how-to" information on the CIT Wiki
- placed an article in our online IT newsletter
- posed info on our Client Services Facebook page
- worked with our Office of Communications to provide an article in our internal college-wide newsletter, "The Source".
- worked with lynda.com marketing personnel to acquire posters and other marketing material and then placed posters throughout the campus
- offered short classroom sessions on how to use lynda.com

At present, we are working with lynda.com to customize our lynda.com login page with Oberlin College images/logos.

We were very encouraged in the beginning with the number of people who sent appreciative email responses, and the number who quickly created accounts. That has tapered off, though, and we have wondered if the numbers warrant continuing with the product, at least in the unlimited way we have licensed it. However, we are yet encouraged by those who do use it, as they express extreme satisfaction with it. This has made us work harder on marketing the product more, since we believe the more people use it, the more they will want to do so. The biggest deterrent to increased usage seems to be the time commitment, and we are also working with HR to determine if this will meet some of their needs in providing training to OCOPE members, and others.

5. Texas A&M University

Texas A&M University (TAMU) opened in 1876 as Texas' first public institution of higher learning. Texas A&M University is a research-intensive flagship university with Fall 2011 enrollment at a record 49,961 of which 8,254 were entering freshmen and 9,500+ graduate students studying in more than 120 undergraduate and 240 graduate degree programs in ten colleges.

The Computing and Information Services (CIS) at TAMU provides information technology resources, facilities and support to help the students, faculty and staff of Texas A&M University achieve their learning, teaching and research goals. CIS consists of 7 different divisions: Help Desk Central, Infrastructure Systems and Services, Networking and Information Security, Open Access Labs, Information Technology Solutions and Support, Supercomputing and Business Services. I am the Training Director of the Open Access Labs (OAL). OAL provides computing and printing access to the students, faculty and staff across campus. Many of our facilities are available 24 hours per day in numerous locations across campus. A wide array of software, specialty printing and plotting, graphic production equipment, computerized teaching classrooms, group study areas, remote printing access, home-drive space, personal webpage access and off campus access (virtual lab) are just a few of the services OAL provides.

With more than 2000 computers supported in 30+ locations, OAL employs 25 full time staff, and approximately 150 student workers. It is my job to see that those people can do their job! Historically I maintained a staff of 4 Graduate Assistants who taught customized training on the major software packages installed in our labs (Office, Adobe, Autodesk, etc.) as well as much of the specialty equipment and applications. The classes were tailored to the lab environment rather than "off the shelf" business directed training. Training was mandatory for all student workers to attend...everyone had to attend a training class each semester that met once a week for eight to ten weeks each semester. We usually offer 8 different topics taught twice each week for a total of 16 classes per week. Doing the math, that's approximately 9 attendees in each class but it seldom worked out that way. Each semester for the past 10 years we encountered the same difficulties:

1. How do ensure the student workers who need or want to take a particular class are available at the time the class is offered? How do you ensure workers are not repeating the same class because it's the only class available when their schedule allows? Remember training is mandatory...

2. How do you compete with 6000 faculty who also need/want the same computerized classrooms we need?

3. How do you encourage retention of material learned over time if not used frequently?

Our solution was to try lynda.com. For a one year period of time we are committed to using lynda.com in place of our instructor-led training, supplemented with our own exercise files and assessments. Talk about a stretch! We went from being in the teaching business to spending an entire semester writing exercises and assessments to directly match the videos for 20 different classes (many of which incorporate multiple videos such as the Advanced Photoshop CS5 class made up of Creative Compositing and Creative Effects videos). We used our existing "Training Tracks" and created a curriculum for each track: MS Office, Video Production, Graphics, Web Development and Cad. This summer we test our new training plan on a select group of student leaders with the intention of going "live" in the fall.

We purchased 60 seats of Lynda Pro for 120-150 student workers. That was the breaking point for a substantial discount per seat. We can add seats at any time. The administrator (me!) or one of my sub administrators will move workers in and out of seats as they register for a class. Each class has an estimated number of hours to complete the course (assessment included). We pay our employees to take training but set the limit on how much time they can take to complete the course, both in time paid and in the length of time they can occupy the seat. Subject matter training is now optional for student employees. However, pay increases, title changes, leadership, etc. is based on a worker's value to the department rather than tenure (a change to go along with the changes in training). If a student worker wishes to not work towards proficiency on one or more of our Training Tracks, they can continue to work in the printrooms at the same pay rate they were hired at. The potential is unlimited...they can take as many classes as they want and are approved to take (depending on the training budget).

Keep in mind that this is all in speculation. So far the seats have been occupied by our full time staff (to use freely until we begin testing) and my training staff. There has been no moving in and out of seats, no quality checks, no testing of "the plan". There are many decisions yet to come on how to manage the workers legitimately working to complete the classes. Where do they work (on their own or in a lab environment)? Are they monitored? Do we ask them to work on classes while already at work during slow times?

My part of this paper will be about the buildup to incorporating lynda.com into our department at TAMU. Hopefully at the panel in Memphis I will have wonderful results to report!

6. Valparaiso University

Valparaiso University is a private, coed, four-year residential Lutheran institution located in northwest Indiana on a single campus. Information Technology (IT) serves approximately 2,800 undergraduates, 1100 Grad School and School of Law students, 480 faculty and 630 staff members, as well as Valparaiso University retirees and community members. This is a total customer base of more than 5,000. IT currently has 33 FTEs divided into five units plus an administrative group:

Support Services, Instructional Technology Services, Systems Administration, Management Information Systems, and Networking & Telecommunications. Within the Support Services group are the Help Desk, Tech Support, classroom support, OneCard Services, Client Services, and training.

Only one IT staff member is in the official capacity of departmental Trainer. Historically, most training classes offered tended to focus on the campus email system and the Microsoft Office suite. Sessions are open to all faculty, staff, and students. Requests have frequently been made to offer additional courses that are more in-depth or that cover other systems on campus. However, attendance is often low, with many people indicating difficulty in making time to attend a session in their busy schedules. Class development has been challenging since actual attendance rates are unknown. In the last few years, the number of one-on-one sessions offered has increased because it is more convenient for the user. This is inefficient, however, and limits IT's ability to offer a wider range of training classes. We utilized Element K in the past, but found it wasn't used very heavily, and the course listings were frequently out-of-date, with newer technologies being slow to join the list. We will be implementing the Microsoft IT Academy on campus to offer certification opportunities. Access will first be available to IT staff as well as students in the Masters of Science in Information Technology program; it will be rolled out to other constituents as we move forward.

Several other departments on campus also offer various training opportunities to constituents on campus. IT's Instructional Design and Faculty Consulting group (within Instructional Technology Services) works with faculty on matters relating to delivery of course materials, syllabus design, and more. Workshops and one-on-one sessions are offered to faculty to train them on using the Blackboard Learn™ system. IT's Help Desk offers training to student employees who work at the Help Desk so they can do their job more effectively. Students are paid for the time they spend attending technology training classes. The Human Resource Services department on campus offers employee development opportunities, and has been seeking ways to expand their offerings, including necessary job skills that are more technical in nature. The Teaching Resource Center seeks to help faculty discover tools and resources that will help them to be more effective in the classroom, whether the necessary skills are technical or professional in nature. The Academic Success Center helps students find the resources they need to be successful students, whether it is tutoring in a specific subject, or general skills to be better at studying, time management, and more.

At the EDUCAUSE 2010 conference, the Director of IT Support Services heard a presentation by Penn State University about their use of the lynda.com Online Training Library®. Bringing this service to Valpo would be a way to broaden our training course offerings while offering more convenience to end users. After some conversations between PSU staff and Valpo staff, we arranged a trial of lynda.com for the entire campus. Feedback received from the trial was extremely positive, with people impressed at the catalog of courses, the quality of instruction, and the convenience of watching the videos anytime, anywhere. A proposal was sent to university administration asking to proceed with a lyndaCampus agreement. It was approved, and our license began on July 1, 2011.

The lyndaCampus agreement gives us the ability to offer every person a personal Premiere account on lynda.com and access is restricted based on IP range. Users on campus can easily access the site at any time; if a user is off-campus, they first go through our EZProxy system to obtain a Valpo IP address and then proceed to the lynda.com login page. We will be investigating Active Directory authentication, as we are about to convert from Novell NetWare servers to Microsoft Windows servers with Active Directory.

To spread the word on campus about the lynda.com trial, we formed an implementation team that worked hard to market the service. The team consisted of faculty, staff, and one student and primarily represented IT and HR. We held "Meet & Greet" sessions with refreshments and targeted specific audiences to bring them over to see a preview of the site, learn how it works, and find out benefits of using it. We also created a section on our website with information about how to login, common questions, and testimonials. We sent out several mass email messages in conjunction with the marketing department on campus. In addition, we created digital posters for our digital signage system, table toppers to place in the dining hall on campus and computer labs, hung lynda.com posters in strategic areas on campus, and wrote announcements for the campus e-newsletter.

Since the official launch on July 1, we have found that the most difficult part of maintaining the service is marketing it to campus to encourage usage. We are currently using less than 20% of the accounts we are paying for via the lyndaCampus agreement, and we want usage to get much higher. Feedback about the service is excellent and users really like the convenience and breadth of courses available. We have formed an ongoing team to help continue marketing the service on campus. Representation on this group includes faculty and staff from many areas: Human Resource Services, Academic Success Center, Teaching Resource Center, IT, and Integrated Marketing and Communication. In my position as Manager of Client Services, I will partner with other departments who benefit from using the service in their areas, such as the Career Center, the academic Department of Communication, and the IT Help Desk.

Having the lynda.com service has provided an invaluable benefit over the past six months, as our campus has recently switched from a Novell GroupWise system to Google Apps for Education. We were able to leverage the lynda.com courses on Gmail, Google Calendar, and Google Docs to supplement our training offerings. It was very attractive to our user base to have the option of attending a classroom session with live people to provide assistance and ask questions, as well as the "anytime, anywhere" convenience of the lynda.com Online Training Library® courses.

7. Vassar College

Vassar College is a highly selective, residential, coeducational liberal arts college located 75 miles north of New York City in Poughkeepsie, New York. Over 290 faculty members offer 51 degrees to an undergraduate student body of 2,400. Total employees number about 800.

Vassar Computing and Information Services (CIS) employs 42 professionals who provide services ranging from network administration and audio/visual support to custom programming and end-user consulting. As the Technology Training Coordinator, my role is to guide and support technology training campus-wide, not only for administrators, but also for students, faculty, and emeritus. While some specialized software training occurs within the various programs and departments, most formalized technology training is conducted by me, our user services consultants, or our academic computing consultants.

When I began working at Vassar, the position was part-time, and much of the technology training was offered in a walk-in format out of necessity; I could not always meet on the days and times that the learners preferred. This format was less than ideal. Many of the calls and emails I fielded required an urgent response, and often people would simply not be able to attend any of the scheduled open sessions due to scheduling conflicts. When my position became full-time, I found myself handling most training needs in a one-on-one just-in-time manner.

But no matter how much time I spent learning and reading about new software, I could not hope to become an expert on all of it, and many users wanted broader and deeper training that they could tackle on their own time. One supplement we offered was an e-learning site called Element K. While Element K's materials covered a fair number of software titles, they were not updated quickly as new upgrades appeared. The courses also tended to be fairly cursory, and advanced users often had few choices for learning about the more complex software features. CIS staff also found the user licensing system to be obscure and confusing. We decided to search for an alternative to Element K.

After a relatively brief search, our research group settled on lynda.com as the best option to research in depth. After a short trial, we purchased a 10-user license which we used mostly within CIS. During this period, if a user asked for training in a program that our staff was not well versed in, we would suggest that they try a lynda.com course for a week or two. Though managing the accounts took some time and effort, I found the lynda.com system much easier to use and understand than Element K's. After four or five months of testing, and with generally positive feedback from CIS employees and users, we decided to purchase a campus-wide license.

Our formal rollout of lynda.com has been slow and uneven. We sent out a number of campus-wide emails announcing access to lynda.com, and we display prominent banners on the training section of the CIS website. There has not been a concerted awareness campaign, but there is a good opportunity this summer and fall to ramp up such an initiative. Our campus is transitioning to Google Apps for Education, and with this change will come a huge demand for training. We plan to heavily push self-paced training on lynda.com.

For users who know what they want to learn and are interested in a longer learning process, we suggest that they explore the self-paced courses. Many users have responded positively, as they can watch a short video or two at various points in their workday. The depth of the lynda.com library (with multiple tiers of courses) allows even advanced users to hone their skills.

8. West Virginia University

West Virginia University (WVU) is the state's public land-grant institution located in Morgantown WV with small divisional campuses throughout the state. In fall 2011, WVU had more than 29,600 students and more than 5,600 full-time employees. The Office of Information Technology (OIT) provides both systems and end-user support for all WVU campuses. Several

units on campus employ their own technology staff and maintain their own networks to supplement OIT resources.

The OIT Application Support and Training unit (7 employees including the director) conducts online and hands-on workshops for all faculty, staff, and students. Less than 2 FTE is dedicated to training; the rest of the time, our unit works on information technology projects and serves as application administrators and third-tier help desk support.

OIT purchased a 10 seat license for lyndaPro from lynda.com in 2006 to provide professional development for its own staff; each of the ten accounts was assigned to a particular employee for the year. At the end of the year, we realized that this model did not make best use of the lynda.com resource; only three of the accounts had more than a few hours of access. In August 2007, the Application Support and Training unit took over management of the OIT licenses and switched to a "lending library" model for access, activating an account for two weeks for any current WVU employee or student.

Employees and students complete an online form to request access to a loaner account. The account administrator manually sets up individual accounts in each requestor's name which allows for detailed reporting, individual learning histories, and certificates. An individual can continue using an account past the loan expiration date until we need the seat for someone else. Individuals can check out their accounts multiple times. We track requests including demographic data along with waitlists in an Excel worksheet and use this data to supplement lynda.com reports. Waitlisted individuals currently get access within one week. If our waitlists increase, we intend to purchase additional seats to meet the demand.

Three other departments on campus manage their own lyndaPro licenses, each with 5 seats plus a free administrator account. Some departments on campus share a single lynda.com subscription or purchase a subscription for one or more of their employees. WVU's Health Sciences Center purchased online tutorials from Atomic Learning with access restricted to their employees and students via their in-house portal.

Since OIT only has 10 lyndaPro seats, we have not gone to extraordinary measures to market this service. We list our lynda.com "lending library" as a service on the OIT training web page. We announce the service in campus meetings, in monthly training email newsletters, in training workshops, and in workshop handouts. We email information about this training option to those who cancel workshop registrations and to those who request training we are unable to provide.

We analyzed our current usage data and are not convinced WVU would benefit at this time from an expensive campus-wide license, though the vendor pushes lyndaCampus on a regular basis. Based on a recent survey, several of our regular users would appreciate easy long-term access to accounts that their own departments did not have to pay for; however the funding for a campus license has to come from somewhere.

We plan to renew our current lyndaPro license in August, budget permitting. We find this resource to be useful for OIT staff development and for our trainers as they develop and update their instructor-led workshops. Our lyndaPro lending library allows us to offer a training alternative for those:

- whose schedules preclude workshop attendance

- who need to learn a new skill right now instead of waiting for the next workshop
- who cannot come to the Morgantown campus
- who desire advanced training
- who need a quick review of a specific topic
- who desire training on topics we do not support.

9. Summary

All eight of the colleges and universities represented on this panel found our way to lynda.com through different paths. Our campus licensing schemes vary from each other and might change over time. However, the consensus of the group is that offering access to lynda.com tutorials as an alternative or supplement to instructor-led training provides an essential service that benefits our campus clients.

Student Hiring: Why Not Make It An Event?

Ashley Weese
195 Durham Center
Ames, IA 50011
1.515.294.7313

aweese@iastate.edu

ABSTRACT

Managing student employees is like raising a family. Like most parents, seeing their child grow and move away to school is hard. One of the more difficult things about managing students is when you watch the employee, who you've seen change from student to adult, leave or graduate. For the ITS group at Iowa State University, this happens each semester.

This spring we needed to fill twenty positions to be fully staffed for the fall. Before going through a number of applicants and interviews, we decided to take a different approach to the hiring process, so we made an event out of it. We offered a mass interview process and had twenty applicants respond. Once applicants arrived, we explained that they would be interviewing each other, based on the guidelines we had created, for a set amount of time. Then we divided them into small groups and put a current employee in each group that took notes on interactions and responses.

The applicants who felt comfortable meeting new people and were able to carry a friendly conversation excelled. They were able to see potential peers and get a jumpstart on building work relationships. We found this form of hiring to be successful and extended an offer to about 50% of the applicants. We also found a few applicants that most likely would have been hired through the "normal" interview process, but did not blend well during the interview event, causing them to be taken out of the applicant pool.

Categories and Subject Descriptors

K.6.1 [**Management of Computing and Information Systems**]: Project and People Management – *Staffing*.

General Terms

Management, Human Factors.

Keywords

Management, Student Staff, Hiring, Team Hiring, Customer Service, Technical, Interview.

1. INTRODUCTION

Iowa State University, located in Ames, Iowa is a comprehensive research university with nearly 30,000 students and 6,000 faculty and staff members [1]. ISU has been recognized as a place of beginnings; whether it be the first electronic computer that was created on the campus by John Vincent Atanasoff, Carrie Chatman Catt's leadership role involving women's right to vote, or George Washington Carver's numerous inventions that lead to the discovery of peanut butter.

Information Technology Services (ITS) is infused into all aspects of everyday life at ISU. ITS maintains both the wired and wireless network across campus, manages and supports a University-wide web portal, Exchange 2010 for faculty and staff, CyMail, a partnership between Iowa State and Google Apps for Education for students, as well as other classroom learning technologies, including Blackboard Learn. The department is responsible for leading and ensuring that Iowa State's information technologies support the university's mission to excel at teaching and learning, research and creative endeavors, outreach, and university leadership. [2]

The Solution Center houses the two support realms within ITS. It includes an employee side, known as Employee Technical Services, where it employs twelve full time staff members who answer questions from supported users that pay for support and acts as the single point of contact for account management troubles. Then, there is Student Technical Services, which is the single point of contact for students as well as faculty and staff who do not pay for support. STS, often times referred to as the Solution Center in general, is open an extended number of hours and staffed seven days a week with up to 60 part time student employees. We have several different positions within STS which includes a technical path and a customer service only path. The technical support path includes students answering phones, emails, working with customers in person on appointments and removing viruses from computers. The customer service only path, known as "concierge" consists of students working as the face of the Solution Center. These students are the first contact when a customer walks in the door. They assist with general questions about accounts, advise customers on where to get specific support, and help answer basic questions. The STS side is managed by one full time employee everyday with five "shift managers" who normally work on the ETS side, but manage, on average, one day a week, or one weekend every six weeks.

2. PREVIOUS HIRING PROCESS

For the past five years, the Solution Center has hired based on a three step interviewing process. We asked students who were interested in working at the Solution Center to fill out our application form online. We then reviewed applications, determined if they would be better suited for the technical track or customer service track and sent an email describing the two jobs. Those who were interested in the technical track were asked to log into our Blackboard Learn session and go through a pre-test. The test covered questions like network troubleshooting, account management as well as software offered by ISU. If the candidate took the time to take the test and passed (80% or higher) we moved them into the second phase, the phone interview. We had them call and act as if they were the technician, asked that they use their computer resources and we posed as customers. We asked questions involving ISU, technical issues as well as what services were offered through ITS. From this, we were able to see if the candidate was quick on their feet, had decent phone skills, and exuded confidence while on the phone. If the applicant was successful, we offered them an in person interview. If the applicant was more interested in the customer service track, we moved them directly into the third phase, the in person interview. While the three-step phase was time and labor intensive, we were getting successful candidates. We felt that these steps worked fine for hiring one or two people, we were getting ready to hire fifteen new students. We needed to streamline the process.

3. HIRING OBSTACLES

Some of the obstacles that the Solution Center faces are common among other universities as well. We face departments that pay better for easier jobs and house potential employees who know a lot about technology but are not great with people. Then, there's graduation...you can hire some outstanding students, train them, watch them grow, and then they leave the nest. It's amazing to see students mold into adults and take jobs with fortune 500 companies, but it's still bittersweet. You have to fill that open position, or twelve, depending on how many students graduated that semester.

4. GOALS

Each semester we have a number of students leave due to graduation, study abroad and/or Co-Ops. As with every semester, we needed to fill those roles in order to provide the same service and support. In the past, we found ourselves going through the hiring process and asking the same three questions while reviewing the candidates: Can they do the job? Are they willing to do the job? Would they fit in? We wanted to make sure all the new applicants also met the goals we had put in place. We were looking for students who had customer service experience and enjoyed technology. We needed them to be humble, have manners, be willing to learn new technology in an always changing realm, and go above and beyond to provide the level of support our customers had come to expect.

5. THE IDEA

Since we needed to hire so many people and didn't want to go through hours and hours of interviews and applicants, we were looking for new ideas when we recalled a previous blog post by Seth Godin [3]. In this post, he spoke about an alternative MBA program he was offering and that he had hundreds of candidates and only a few seats were available. He decided to fly out 27 finalists to New York and have them all meet each other during a cocktail party. He asked each finalist to interview as many others as they could, take notes, and at the end of the party, he took each one aside and asked them who they would like to work with. The results were fascinating. He realized after speaking to each finalist that the same names kept coming up, and after reviewing, he would have chosen the same finalist as well. We realized that we could use this same concept for a hiring event, minus the cocktails.

6. THE PLAN

We had the idea, now we needed to implement a plan. We needed to figure out how to reach out to potential applicants and how we could have a successful event and learn about each applicant at the same time. We realized that in order to have the event run smoothly, we needed to plan, document and expect the unexpected. We decided that once the applicants applied, we'd send them an email describing the event. We offered dinner, as we all know, the best way to each college student's heart is through pizza. We also saw this as an opportunity for them to get to know each other before the interview process started. We needed to create a specific outline describing a timeline of the event so the applicants as well as the staff stayed on track and it didn't get too long, rules of what they could not say, as most of them had not been on the interviewee side of an interview and a list of questions they were required to answer to each staff member by the end of the night. Then, we realized we were going to give them all the information about the event, but hadn't even thought of how to describe ITS, the Solution Center or the jobs they were applying for, so we created a PowerPoint presentation as well. We asked a fellow co-worker and peer from a different section of ITS to emcee the event. This way, we could focus our attention on what discussions were going on and not how much time we had left. A current employee was asked to sit in on the hiring event and take notes on interactions. They would provide guidance, if needed, and review candidates after the event ended.

6.1 COMMUNICATION

The first step in hiring is always communication. Spreading the word about the Solution Center hiring had always been a toss-up. In the past, we had done the social networking route, using the ITS Facebook account as well as the ITS twitter account, posted job announcements on our website, posted on the student job board and asked current employees to let all their friends know. This gave us a number of good candidates, but we needed more. So, we chose to send a mass mailing out to all current undergraduate students in the Management Information Systems (MIS) undergraduate program. We made sure to give them a description of each job, what type of candidates we were looking for, and how it would benefit them to obtain experience and help them in their future.

6.2 THE ROOM LAYOUT

We reserved a room in advance that's location was easy to find and was directly down the hallway from the Solution Center. We arranged the room (see Figure 1) to look inviting, but still practical and open. We needed space for the applicants to mingle, eat pizza, watch a PowerPoint presentation, answer the specific, required questions to each staff member and of course, interview each other. Since we had twenty applicants, we placed four seats at each table for them and one staff member on the end.

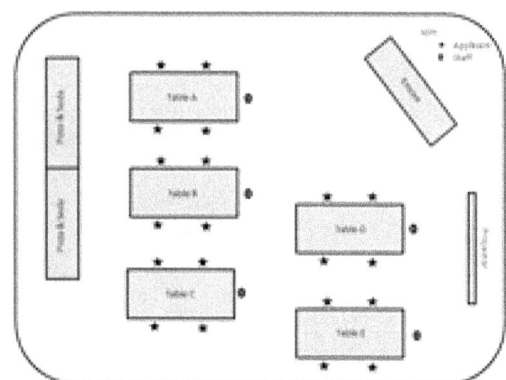

Figure 1. The Room Layout

6.3 TIMELINE

We needed to make sure everyone stayed on topic, make sure everyone got a chance to meet each other and each person had time to take notes, we created a timeline of events. From what we saw, the candidates took it upon themselves to make introductions and get to know others as they ate pizza. We felt we didn't need to do an ice breaker.

Table 1. Timeline of events

Start	Topic	Duration
5:00 PM	Students Arrive/Eat Pizza/Mingle	20 minutes
5:20 PM	Staff Introductions are Made	20 minutes
5:40 PM	Round 1 of Interviewing	20 minutes
6:00 PM	Free Time	20 minutes
6:20 PM	Round 2 of Interviewing	20 minutes
6:40 PM	Free Time	20 minutes
7:00 PM	Round 3 of Interviewing	20 minutes
7:20 PM	Free Time	20 minutes
7:40 PM	Conclusion	20 minutes

6.4 THE INTERVIEW PROCESS

Since we had five tables with room for four different applicants each, we assigned groups randomly to each table for a twenty minute time period in hopes that each person would get five minutes of time to answer questions. After the twenty minutes, we gave them twenty minutes to wrap up any questions they had for each other, take notes on if they could do the job, would they do the job and if they would fit in. During this time the candidates were asked to find a staff member to answer the required questions, such as:

- Why you are interested in this position and what do you hope to get out of the job?

- Give me an example of a situation where you've had problems dealing with someone. What was the situation and how you handled it?

-
- What part about this job do you suspect that you are least qualified? What part about this job do you suspect that you are most qualified?

- Tell me about a current technology that you find interesting. What about it do you find interesting? How have you explored it?

- What resources do you use for troubleshooting problems you have with a computer?

- What role do you generally assume in a team environment? Why?

6.5 THE APPLICANT PACKET

Each applicant was given a packet of information about the event, rules, a candidate list, feedback cards about themselves and their top three choices of whom they would like to work with, and scratch paper.

6.5.1 The Interview Outline

An interview outline was created to help ease the applicants into the interviewing process by explaining the job and how the event would work. The information given in the outline included:

- An introduction of our emcee and staff

- Details about the ITS organization

- What we do and the tools we use

- What the job entails

- The interview process

- The questions we wanted them to keep in mind when interviewing others

- Required questions they needed to answer to each current employee

- Timeline of events

6.5.2 The Interview Rules

Because the applicant is acting as an interviewer on behalf of IT Service, they were told they must obey the University rules for interviews. In particular, the topics listed below were topics they were not allowed to broach and questions they could not ask. They were asked if they have ANY hesitation, to ask the current employee at the table first.

- Last Name – you cannot ask the maiden name of an applicant and in this setting you may not ask any last name or other personally identifiable information.

- Birthplace or Residence – person's permanent residence or place of origin

- Creed or Religion – religious affiliations, churches, or religious holidays

- Race or Color – do not record the person race, color of hair, skin, eyes, etc.

- Photographs – you many not photograph the applicants

- Citizenship – any inquiries into whether the applicant is or intends to become a US citizen

- National Origin and Ancestry – lineage, ancestry, national origin, descent, parentage, or nationality of a spouse

- Language – applicant's mother tongue, or commonly used language (you are allowed to discern if the applicant can speak and write fluently)

- Relatives – you many not ask any questions about an applicant's family

- Military Service – these will be handled by staff

- Organizations – religious, social organizations, political, labor unions. You may inquire as to any professional organizations related to web/programming.
- References – these will be handled by staff
- Sex and Family – gender should not be considered, nor marital status, dependents, children, or sexual preference
- Arrest Record – these will be handled by staff
- Height and Weight – you may not ask the persons height or weight
- Mental and Physical Disabilities – any mental or physical disabilities, or how many days absent due to illness
- Age – inquiries into the age or date of birth

6.5.3 Applicant Feedback Cards

The applicant feedback cards were used to gauge the both the applicant and who they would recommend be hired. They were asked to fill the card out for their top three candidate choices. The first card included a list of questions the applicant was required to answer about themselves (see figure 2).

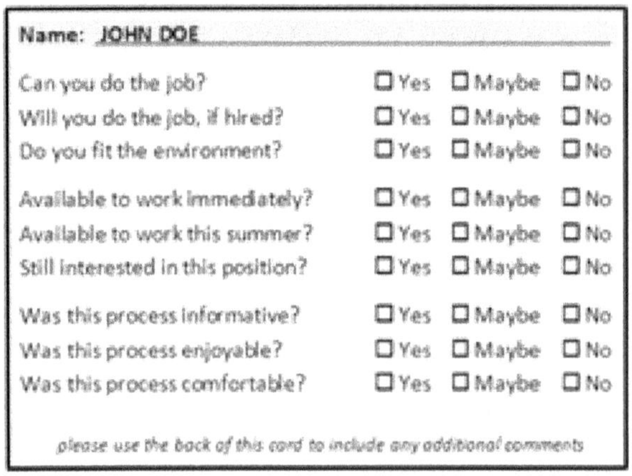

Name: JOHN DOE

Can you do the job?	☐ Yes	☐ Maybe	☐ No
Will you do the job, if hired?	☐ Yes	☐ Maybe	☐ No
Do you fit the environment?	☐ Yes	☐ Maybe	☐ No
Available to work immediately?	☐ Yes	☐ Maybe	☐ No
Available to work this summer?	☐ Yes	☐ Maybe	☐ No
Still interested in this position?	☐ Yes	☐ Maybe	☐ No
Was this process informative?	☐ Yes	☐ Maybe	☐ No
Was this process enjoyable?	☐ Yes	☐ Maybe	☐ No
Was this process comfortable?	☐ Yes	☐ Maybe	☐ No

please use the back of this card to include any additional comments

Figure 2. Applicant Response Card

The other three cards were reserved for their hiring recommendations (see figure 3).

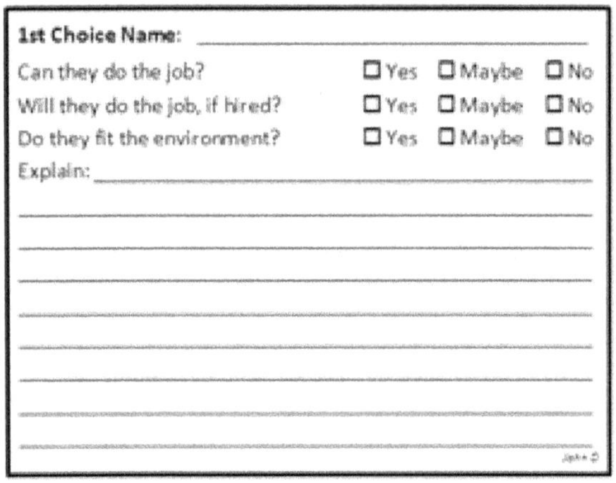

1st Choice Name: __________

Can they do the job?	☐ Yes	☐ Maybe	☐ No
Will they do the job, if hired?	☐ Yes	☐ Maybe	☐ No
Do they fit the environment?	☐ Yes	☐ Maybe	☐ No

Explain: __________

Figure 3. Applicant Recommendations

7. RESULTS

As students started showing up and speaking to one another, we realized how magnificent some of the candidates actually were. They stayed on task when we asked them to start interviewing each other, made sure not to ask any questions that were not allowed, answered the specific questions to each current staff member, and took diligent notes. At the end of the night, we asked them to fill out the applicant feedback cards and no one objected. Most of them said that they enjoyed the event more than an actual interview and said they felt very comfortable in the environment. Just like Seth Godin's results [3], we realized that the same names kept coming up as to each applicant recommended for hire.

We noticed that some of the candidates who would have normally gotten through the old hiring process and most likely hired, were not hired in this situation. Some of the applicants found it hard to meet the requirements laid before them, such as answering each staff members question or mingle with the other candidates. We were thankful that we saw this before we hired them, as they showed that they would not have fit into our environment. There were two candidates who, based on what the six staff members saw, could not firmly decide if we should hire them or not. At the end of the night, we decided to offer an in person interview to those candidates. Eventually, we decided against hiring them. We could see that they would fit into the group, but lacked the skills needed to be successful.

8. DIALOGUE

Below is an example of the type of conversations and interview questions the candidates were asking each other. These were taken directly out of conversation. The only changes made were the names of candidates.

Candidate 1: Hi, I'm Oliver. What's your name?
Candidate 2: Hi Oliver, I'm James. What's your major?
Candidate 1: Management Information Systems -- Yours?
Candidate 2: I'm a freshman in Electrical Engineering. Do you have any experience with IT?
Candidate 1: I haven't had much formal experience with IT, but I'm the "go to" guy for people in my family.
Candidate 2: What are you looking to get out of this job?
Candidate 1: To learn technical knowledge that will be useful moving forward into my life along with gaining technical and customer service experience. How about you?
Candidate 2: Same. I am looking to learn more about computers and increase my tech skills.
Candidate 1: What is your favorite thing about technology?
Candidate 2: Technology is constantly changing and there is always something new to learn about. Have you ever worked in an IT position before?
Candidate 1: I was part of my High School's computer club where we worked on all of the computers in the school. Never got paid for it but we did lots if IT related things. So, what are some of your interests?
Candidate 2: I'm interested in networking, how so much can be accomplished by connecting different devices together. I'm also interested in getting more involved with the hardware aspects. What would you say is your strongest area of IT?
Candidate 1: Definitely the hardware side of things. I have been taking computers apart and putting them back together for a few years now.

9. CONCLUSION

Based on the feedback we got, the number of willing applicants and the type of applicants actually hired, I would recommend this process to not only university related interviewees, but to all hiring managers looking for specific candidates that need to work together in a team environment. We ended up hiring ten of the twenty applicants and all have going through training and been more successful than any hires before. They came into the job with a sense of teamwork and had already bonded with each other to create outstanding synergy. When it comes to hire multiple students again, the Solution Center will have another hiring event. It was fun, interesting and provided us with employees who are excelling already.

10. ACKNOWLEDGMENTS

Our thanks to Seth Godin for sharing a simple idea and allowing us to mold it into a successful event.

11. REFERENCES

[1] Iowa State University. "ISU Fact Book 2011-2012." Last modified February 2012. http://www.ir.iastate.edu/FB12/PDF/FB2012ALL.pdf

[2] Iowa State University. "About the Office of the CIO." Accessed May 1, 2012. http://www.cio.iastate.edu/about/

[3] Seth Godin's Blog. http://sethgodin.typepad.com/seths_blog/2009/06/learning-from-the-mba-program.html

A Case Study of a Phased Approach Methodology for Application Development and Implementation

Meri Williams
University of Memphis
001 Wilder Tower
Memphis, TN 38152
901-678-3809

mkwillim@memphis.edu

Robert Jackson
University of Memphis
001 Wilder Tower
Memphis, TN 38152
901-678-5103

rjax@memphis.edu

ABSTRACT

The Academic Affairs faculty evaluation process was once a paper-based process used by colleges and schools at the University of Memphis (UofM). The College of Arts and Sciences (CAS) developed an online alternative to the paper evaluation process and used it successfully for multiple years. As the electronic evaluation process gained cultural acceptance within the college, Academic Affairs sought a way to provide this enhancement throughout the academy. Academic Affairs Technology (AATECH) was charged with scaling the original application, providing training, and implementing the application for use in all colleges and schools. A phased approach was selected for this project implementation. Initial phases included: phase 1 (scaling the application), phase 2 (reports and major improvements), and phase 3 (annual maintenance). This paper will provide a brief history of the faculty evaluation system, the phased approach used to implement a web-based system, where we are now and lessons learned.

Categories and Subject Descriptors

K.6.1 [**Project and People Management**]: Systems analysis and design.

General Terms

Management, Measurement, Documentation, Performance, Design, Reliability, Human Factors, Standardization, Verification.

Keywords

Implementation, communication, faculty evaluation.

1. INTRODUCTION

The UofM Academic Affairs Division uses a paper-based instrument for the evaluation of faculty. This instrument is the basis for a variety of evaluation procedures used in the colleges on campus. In support of the university's commitment to business process improvement, a project was undertaken to transform the paper-based system to an electronic web-based system. This paper will provide a brief history of the paper-based faculty evaluation system, the phased approach used to implement the web-based system, where we are now and lessons learned.

2. HISTORY OF THE FACULTY EVALUATION SYSTEM

Faculty evaluations were performed using a paper-based standard throughout the university. The form was made available via an MS-Word document on the Academic Affairs Division website. The form contained fields for identifying the faculty, department, and rank. Spaces were provided to allow narratives in the following activities: teaching, advising/mentoring, scholarship/creative activities, external support, outreach, and service. Sections of the form were provided for narrative from the department chair, the chair's overall rating of the faculty member (exceptional, very good, good, improvement needed, or failure to meet responsibilities), faculty response to the evaluation, and dean's comments on the evaluation. Signature spaces were allocated for each participant in the process. It was the responsibility of colleges to complete the form.

CAS developed an electronic faculty evaluation instrument based on the Academic Affairs Division evaluation form. CAS has utilized this instrument successfully since implementation in 2008. The process implemented by CAS was based on a top-down model (Figure 1).

In light of the university's commitment to continual process improvement, the desire from Academic Affairs leadership was to scale and implement the CAS instrument throughout the division. This would allow all deans, chairs and faculty to utilize a web-based system and it would also provide a mechanism for identifying participation rates at the college level.

3. SELECTION OF PHASED APPROACH

Initial discussions with Academic Affairs Division leadership and CAS representatives occurred in January and February of 2011. By the end of February, 2011 the project scope had been defined to include only scaling the existing top-down evaluation approach used by CAS and development of some basic reporting. Buy-in for the new system implementation was obtained from other deans through CAS system demonstrations at leadership meetings. The implementation date was set for January, 2012.

When the decision was announced that the CAS standard would be adopted, some technical groups on campus took initiative and requested copies of source code, allocated server resources, etc., and began to customize code to meet their individual college needs. However, an enterprise solution was desired to allow an overview of college performance at the Academic Affairs Division level.

Faculty Evaluation
(by chair or director)

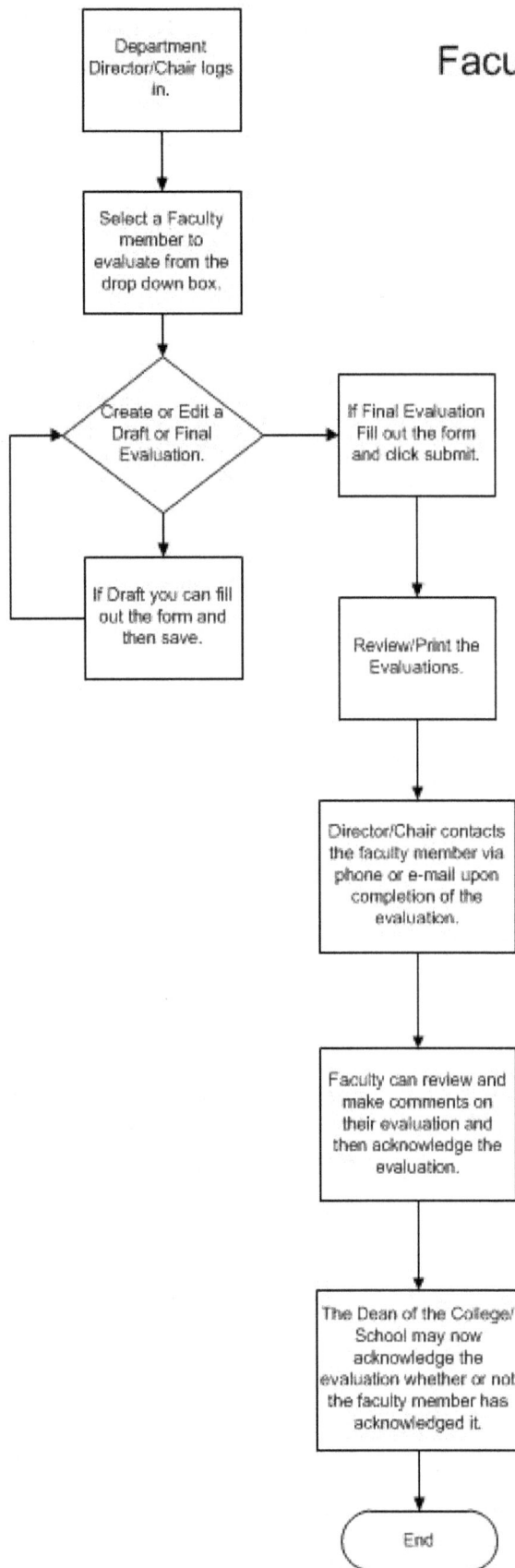

```
┌─────────────────┐
│   Department    │
│ Director/Chair  │
│   logs in.      │
└────────┬────────┘
         │
         ▼
┌─────────────────┐
│ Select a Faculty│
│   member to     │
│ evaluate from   │
│ the drop down   │
│     box.        │
└────────┬────────┘
         │
         ▼
```

Create or Edit a Draft or Final Evaluation.

If Final Evaluation Fill out the form and click submit.

If Draft you can fill out the form and then save.

Review/Print the Evaluations.

Director/Chair contacts the faculty member via phone or e-mail upon completion of the evaluation.

Faculty can review and make comments on their evaluation and then acknowledge the evaluation.

The Dean of the College/ School may now acknowledge the evaluation whether or not the faculty member has acknowledged it.

End

Business Rules:
1. Once Final draft is submitted, the chair/director cannot modify the evaluation.
2. Faculty can acknowledge evaluation without agreeing to evaluation.

Figure 1. Process flow for CAS evaluation system

Several factors contributed to the decision to select a phased approach for implementing this project: availability of staff, implementation timeframe, and the magnitude of training stakeholders in the new process.

The unit charged with developing the application, Academic Affairs Technology (AATECH), consisted of one full-time equivalent position dedicated to web development and the availability of that employee was limited. AATECH was in the midst of developing and maintaining applications for other departments so 100% of the developer's time could not be devoted to the project in the beginning. Additionally, due to other project commitments that were already on the AATECH calendar, periods of time were identified that would further limit the developer's availability for the project.

When the project was assigned to the developer in February, 2011 only ten months (less time previously committed for other projects) remained to meet with CAS to evaluate the current system, write a new system, and develop new documentation.

Due to the complexity of developing the new system and anticipation of disruption to college cultures that this implementation would bring, a phased approach was selected. Three major phases were identified: phase 1 to scale the existing CAS application for use at the university level, phase 2 for major enhancements, and phase 3 for continual improvements.

3.1 Phase 1

Phase 1 included scaling the current application used by CAS to an application that could be used throughout the academy.

AATECH met with the CAS web developer for demonstrations of the CAS system. CAS provided hardcopies of system screenshots and access to a test system so that AATECH could review the user interface. Additional meetings, phone calls, and email exchanges occurred to clarify AATECH questions about the system. CAS also provided copies of source code, assumptions about business process rules, and database design for the existing system. This collaborative exchange of information between CAS and AATECH was critical in helping to identify changes necessary (both program logic and database design) to scale the application from a specific college to the university. Also, having this information was very helpful when AATECH encountered design questions and wondered, "How did CAS do it?"

AATECH began reviewing the CAS code to establish a timeline for the project. Considering the amount of time that would be required to scale the application to the university and add some enhancements, AATECH decided to write a new system from scratch and use the existing code and database design as guides. Coding began once the new database design was complete.

AATECH struggled to control scope creep. The phase 1 implementation was to be a basic replication of the existing system used by CAS. A key component of the system is a control center dashboard (Figure 2).

However, some of the existing features were given a low priority during phase 1 in order to meet timelines. AATECH met with Academic Affairs and CAS leadership to discuss project timelines and prioritization of features. The group decided that the reports and the ability of faculty to evaluate chairs would be implemented in a later version.

As word began to spread that a new faculty online evaluation system was being developed, it was discovered that the paper-based standard evaluation form was not being utilized the same by all colleges. For example, some colleges utilized a peer evaluation system whereby the solicited feedback was compiled onto the faculty evaluation form. This discovery required discussions to confirm whether the project should move forward. The decision was to move forward yet provide latitude for departments that needed time to adopt the new system. This would have later implications.

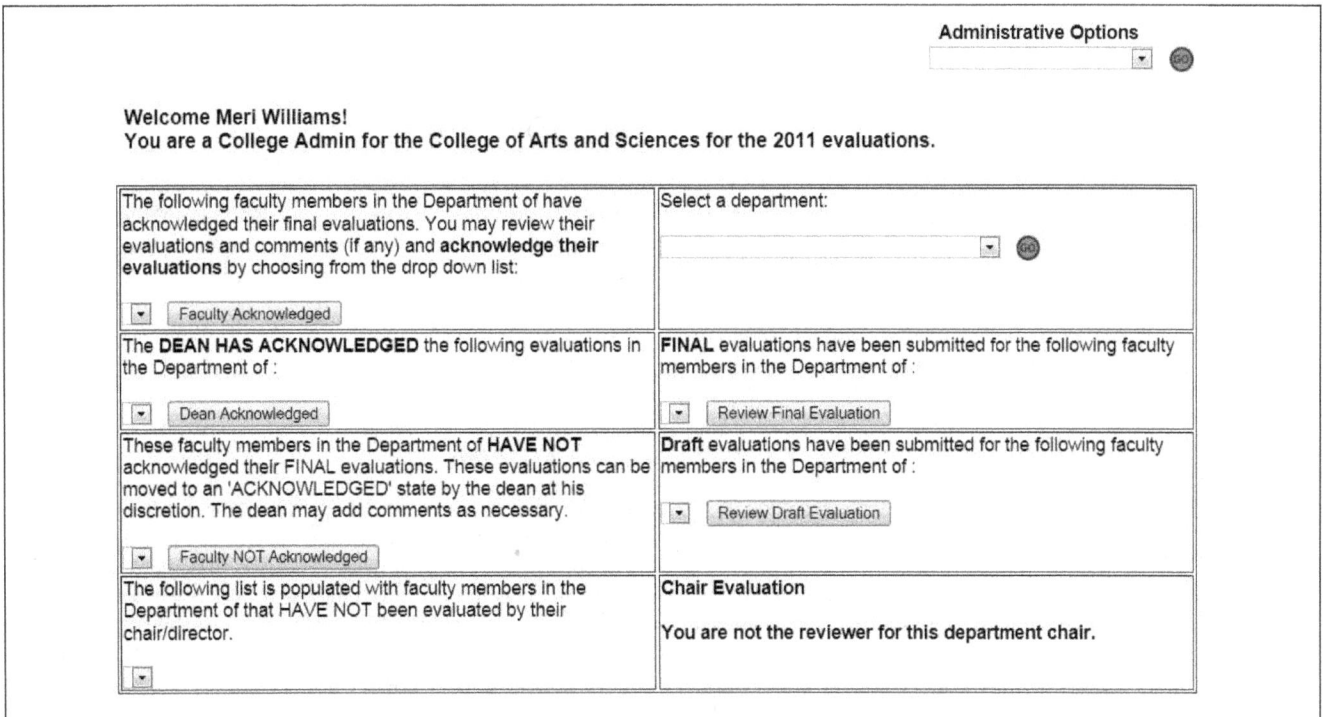

Figure 2: Control center dashboard

College Status Report

Reporting Date: 05/04/2012

	Total Faculty	Not Started	Draft Status	Final Status	Faculty Acknowledged	Dean Acknowledged
Cecil C. Humphreys School of Law	23	23	0.00%	0.00%	0.00%	0.00%
College of Arts and Sciences	359	42	0.00%	88.30%	77.99%	0.00%
College of Communication and Fine Arts	125	119	0.80%	4.00%	2.40%	0.00%
College of Education, Health and Human Sciences	123	7	0.00%	94.31%	87.80%	86.18%
Fogelman College of Business & Economics	105	105	0.00%	0.00%	0.00%	0.00%
Herff College of Engineering	53	14	0.00%	73.58%	43.40%	0.00%
Loewenberg School of Nursing	43	3	0.00%	93.02%	93.02%	93.02%
McWherter Library	19	19	0.00%	0.00%	0.00%	0.00%
School of Communication Sciences and Disorders	23	5	17.39%	60.87%	52.17%	47.83%
School of Public Health	0	0	0%	0%	0%	0%
University College	9	5	0.00%	44.44%	0.00%	0.00%

Figure 3. Status report showing completion rates by college

Colleges were given a great deal of flexibility in determining whether to adopt the system in year one. This resulted in partial adoption at both the college level and the departmental level within colleges (Figure 3).

As the implementation date neared, several issues were discovered.

A critical factor in the success of the system was accurate information about faculty and department reporting structures. The ability to import data to correct information or to include missing information was built into the system. However, a bug was discovered that allowed users to inadvertently import faculty from all colleges, not just theirs. Luckily, this did not affect individuals with evaluations already in progress.

When the project launched, demonstration meetings were scheduled with various stakeholders throughout the university. While CAS adapted to the new system with ease, other colleges had a more difficult time. CAS easily adapted to the new system because it was similar to the system they had previously used. The interface was very similar to the CAS version and the top-down evaluation process of chairs evaluating faculty remained unchanged. However, other colleges experienced difficulty adapting the system into their culture. For example, several department chairs from other colleges desired that faculty should initiate the evaluation process instead of department chairs. It became evident at this point that basic underlying assumptions in the CAS instrument (i.e., top-down evaluation process) posed challenges with other colleges.

Some of the modification requests struck at the very core of the application's design and, therefore, could not be implemented in Phase 1. As a result, some colleges and departments chose to continue using the paper-based form and review the online system at a later date. Other colleges used a hybrid approach by completing the paper-based form and then having administrative associates key the information into the new web-based system.

3.2 Phase 2

Phase 2 will include major improvements required before the next evaluation cycle begins. These improvements include feedback from deans, chairs and faculty submitted via email, reporting, and major design changes.

3.2.1 Feedback

The user interfaces and business rules from the CAS system were carried forward into the new system with very few changes. One major business rule from the CAS system that was included in the new system was that college leadership would notify stakeholders when it was time to perform various evaluation activities. For example, department chairs would be notified to complete evaluations by a certain date and then faculty would be given access to review the evaluations by another certain date. This structured approach was not a good fit for all college cultures, however, and AATECH received feedback from participants requesting that email notifications be sent when an evaluation was ready for review. This was a common request from deans, chairs, and faculty.

3.2.2 Reporting

As previously mentioned, much of the reporting functionality was placed at a lower priority in order to meet the project implementation timeline. Although some basic overview reporting has been created, additional reporting has been requested. Requests included percent complete by college and department and score by professorial ranks (i.e., instructor, assistant professor, associate professor, and professor). At the time of this writing, priority for these two reports was increased and the reports are in production.

AATECH plans to expand the current faculty user interface to allow viewing of previous evaluations. This will provide faculty, especially tenure and promotion candidates, the ability to retrieve and maintain hardcopies of their finalized evaluations. To accommodate interdisciplinary faculty who may move from various departments or colleges, the system will track evaluations by year, college, and department.

3.2.3 Major design changes
A major change that will require further discussion involves allowing faculty members to initiate their evaluation. This poses a real challenge because it is not clear whether that paradigm will meet the needs of all colleges. AATECH has had internal discussions on the possibility of allowing such a feature to be enabled at the college level. However, it is not currently clear whether such an option would be more suited at the college level or the department level. This adds additional complexity to the design of the application and may require a major rewrite of substantial portions of the code. This issue may be pushed to phase 3 as stakeholders and leadership teams navigate college and department cultures.

3.3 Phase 3
Phase 3 will include annual maintenance and continual improvements. AATECH implements applications with the expectation that enhancements will be implemented on an annual schedule. This method has historically worked well for AATECH customers because it provides a predictable timetable by which a small set of "features" can be implemented on an annual basis. Typically, AATECH meets with customers to obtain a prioritized list of "features" that are desired. The amount of work required to implement the desired "features" is discussed and the final list of "features" to be implemented is agreed upon. This approach also allows AATECH to allocate resources for other projects and is helpful in avoiding last-minute ad hoc change requests. Phase 3 enhancements may include user interface modifications, reporting modifications, and system enhancements.

3.3.1 User interface modifications
Reaction to the dashboard used by deans and department chairs has been mixed. The dashboard may evolve over time to accommodate the needs of other colleges and departments. AATECH also anticipates change requests for phase 2 roll-outs (e.g., the new faculty dashboard that allows viewing of previous evaluations).

3.3.2 Reporting modifications
The ability to analyze the performance of faculty is a desire of some administrators although the specifications for these reports have not yet been gathered. Though the existing reports provide an overview of performance at the various professorial ranks, integration with other existing systems may be beneficial. One such modification could include integrating the faculty evaluation system with the Student Evaluation of Teaching Effectiveness (SETE) scores for faculty. SETEs are completed by students in course sections each semester. It may be desired at some point to integrate a summary of SETE information or a link to allow easy retrieval of SETE information when the department chair is completing an evaluation. From an analysis perspective, it may be desired at some point to perform a comparison of faculty evaluations versus SETE scores.

3.3.3 System enhancements
As with many systems, there is a degree of system administration that must occur "in the background" to ensure systems work smoothly or continue to work at all. For example, upgrades to the server, application programming language, or database require testing to ensure functionality is maintained. In some cases, new functionality may be introduced or existing functionality improved by implementing these sorts of system updates.

Additionally, AATECH recognizes that ongoing maintenance will include cosmetic touch-ups, the inevitable bug report, and the "How did we miss that??!!!" moment. AATECH realizes that testing is just that and the real test occurs when the system is made available to end-users.

4. WHERE WE ARE NOW
Phase 1 is complete and AATECH has identified a list of modifications for future development. At the time of this writing, 7 of 11 colleges participated in phase 1. One college failed to participate at any level. Three colleges imported faculty but failed to start the evaluation process. Phase 2 is in progress and enhancements are being made for next year's cycle. Meetings are planned to review the requested modifications identified from phase 1. Some reports have been created to give the administrators (Provost, College or School Dean and College Administrators) information about how the colleges are progressing and faculty scores. The College Status Report indicates the completion rate for an individual college (Figure 3).The Scores by Rank report indicates the scores received by faculty ranks within departments (Figure 4). The implementation of the online faculty evaluation system at the enterprise level was a success but challenges still remain.

5. LESSONS LEARNED
A critical success factor in many projects is buy-in from end-users. This project was initiated with the understanding that deans had agreed to implement the CAS evaluation instrument. However, some deans and department chairs seemed unaware of the process changes that would be required at the departmental level to use the new system. This indicates a potential breakdown in communication which brought about confusion and contention.

Single system feasibility may not be ideal in an environment where colleges operate with a high degree of independence and perform their tasks in a unique way. Even within colleges, some departments exert a high degree of autonomy so culture at the university, college, and department levels must be considered.

Users will shape the system to meet their needs. For example, colleges that use a paper-based peer evaluation system did not fully leverage the benefits of the new system. Instead, those colleges continued to utilize the paper-based peer evaluation system they constructed and then assigned the task of inputting all the needed data into the new online evaluation system. In this particular instance, inefficiency seems to have been created.

Allowing flexibility for colleges and departments to "try out" the system, rather than forcing adoption in phase 1, provided an opportunity for feedback and laid the groundwork for later adoption as new features are implemented. Providing this degree of flexibility fit nicely with the phased approach for this project implementation.

The phased approach seemed to work well for AATECH in scheduling project milestones and allocating resources. Future projects could be improved by including information about the phased approach in meetings and communications with stakeholders. Including such information about the phased

Scores by Rank for Herff College of Engineering

Reporting Date: 05/04/2012

	1				2				3				4				5				6			
	Assistant Professor	Associate Professor	Instructor	Professor	Assistant Professor	Associate Professor	Instructor	Professor	Assistant Professor	Associate Professor	Instructor	Professor	Assistant Professor	Associate Professor	Instructor	Professor	Assistant Professor	Associate Professor	Instructor	Professor	Assistant Professor	Associate Professor	Instructor	Professor
Biomedical Engineering	0	0	0	0	0	0	0	0	0	0	0	0	1	1	0	1	1	0	0	3	0	0	0	0
Civil Engineering	0	0	0	0	0	0	0	0	0	0	0	0	0	0	0	2	1	2	0	1	0	0	0	0
Electrical and Computer Engineering	0	0	0	0	0	0	0	0	0	0	0	0	3	4	1	0	0	0	0	0	0	0	0	0
Mechanical Engineering	0	0	0	0	0	0	0	0	0	0	0	0	1	4	0	4	0	0	0	0	0	0	0	0
Engineering Technology	0	0	0	0	0	0	0	0	0	0	0	0	2	3	0	0	1	0	0	0	0	0	0	0

Figure 4. Report showing scores by professorial rank

approach might help to reassure stakeholders and allay concerns about when specific enhancements will be implemented.

6. CONCLUSION

This paper covered the evolution of the online faculty evaluation process, the phased approach utilized to implement it, where we are now and lessons learned.

The implementation of the online faculty evaluation process included several challenges including scaling an existing college application to the enterprise level, overcoming assumptions and misunderstandings about what a "standard" implies, and managing user expectations. One serious drawback of using the phased approach was that unanticipated modifications were desired before the originally-planned phases were complete thereby complicating and throwing into question development of later phases. However, the use of the phased implementation allowed AATECH to meet the project timeline with existing human resources while also balancing demands of other projects. It also provided an opportunity to implement changes as gradually as possible while identifying the need for future modifications.

7. ACKNOWLEGMENTS

The authors would like to thank the following people: Ann Harbor, Provost Office, for being our liaison to the colleges and deans; Melissa Buchner, College of Arts and Sciences, for helping us with testing during phase 1; and Debra Turner, College of Arts and Sciences, for providing the CAS demonstrations, source code, and database design that gave us a great starting point.

The authors also acknowledge the contributions of the reviewers whose feedback helped identify improvements for this paper.

The Science of Computer Allocations

Jean Tagliamonte
Vassar College
124 Raymond Avenue
Poughkeepsie, NY 12604
845-437-7743
jetagliamonte@vassar.edu

Jean Ross
Vassar College
124 Raymond Avenue
Poughkeepsie, NY 12604
845-437-7716
jyross@vassar.edu

ABSTRACT

Computing and Information Services at Vassar College replaces and refreshes all college-owned computer hardware on a 4-year replacement cycle. Roughly 25% of all campus computers, including those in classrooms and labs, are replaced during the summer of each year (June, July, and August). All regular employees and tenure/tenure-track faculty receive new computers with up-to-date operating systems.

A team of approximately 10 employees from our User Services group comprises the Allocations Team.

A team member visits each scheduled office to ensure the process is as efficient as possible with minimal disruption to the department's workflow. We provide detailed documentation to all techs so that everyone is on the same page and we leave the users with a wealth of resources and available training options to make them comfortable with their new computing environment.

Our User Services group has worked to perfect this process year after year. Read further to learn more about the consultation plan, imaging process, asset tracking, documentation, recycle procedure and of course, good spirits and teamwork that makes our Allocations machine tick.

Categories and Subject Descriptors

K. Computing Milieux
K.6 Management of Computing and Information Systems
K.6.2 Installation Management

General Terms

Reliability, Documentation, Performance, Standardization, Human Factors, Economics

Keywords

Documentation, Communications, Hardware, Software, Mac, PC, Resources, Support, Process, Allocation, Deployment

1. INTRODUCTION

There are approximately 2000 Vassar-owned computers on campus. In an effort to keep up with new hardware and software innovations, a campus IT department must have a scalable and sustainable update process. Replacing computers before they break or become out-of-date can be overwhelming. Computing and Information Services at Vassar College employs a 4-year

hardware replacement cycle during which we update all of the computers on campus. To keep this project manageable, we process roughly 25% (400-500 computers) of the Vassar-owned computers every summer so that over 4 years, all of the computers on campus have been replaced with the exception of a few departments and specialty labs that are replaced on a 2-year cycle. This ensures that all departments and public spaces are able to work with up-to-date software and a very low percentage of hardware failure, which results in cost savings and fewer employee hours dedicated to repair and rescue. Also during the summer we refresh the technology in half of the campus smart classrooms (45 classrooms) to ensure faculty and students have the latest in available technology. The entire Allocations process is overseen by the Director of User Services but it is the seamless collaboration and independent thinking of the various team members that make the process run as smoothly as it does.

2. ALLOCATIONS TIMELINE

- Allocations Team Kick-Off
- Initial Communication
- Pre-Allocations Survey
- Department Interviews
- Scheduling
- Updating Assets
- Hardware Bake-Off
- Ordering
- Instructions
- Finalizing the Image
- Inventory / Imaging
- Hardware Prep
- Allocations
- Remove / Recycle / Re-Image
- Debrief
- Follow-Up

2.1 Allocations Team Kick-Off:

In early March, the Allocations team meets to review the academic and administrative departments whose computers are scheduled for replacement in the current allocation cycle year. During this meeting, the team reviews the department names and employees for accuracy and assigns a liaison or allocations team leader for each department. Depending on the size of the department, each of the 6 liaisons is assigned approximately 2-3 departments. The liaison then schedules time to meet with each department and conducts a pre-allocations interview. We also review the initial communications that we will send to the department and determine any other supplies we need to start gathering such as firewire cables, external hard drives, monitor cables, asset tags, computer labels and, of course, team t-shirts.

2.2 Initial Communication:

An email is sent to the entire campus outlining the departments scheduled for allocations. In this communication we summarize the process and ask anyone who has any out-of-cycle requests to submit a request form. We also use this as an opportunity to make sure no department has slipped through the cracks due to reorganization or name change. The 2012 communication is shown. (Figure 1)

2.3 Pre-Allocations Survey:

We create a survey using our ticket and asset-tracking system. The system allows us to send the survey to just the employees scheduled to receive new hardware. The survey asks that they alert us to any special software or hardware needs they have in their offices. We use this survey to prepare for any special concerns a user or department may have, such as external scientific instruments and peripherals, non-site licensed software, unique printing needs such as graphing printers or plotters, etc.

2.4 Department Interviews:

The liaisons meet with either the department chair or office manager to determine specific hardware needs for each employee in the department. We have interview guidelines for each liaison to follow. An example is shown. (Figure 2)

2.5 Scheduling:

After the liaisons have met with the departments, each department is added to the schedule starting the last week of May and continuing into early July. We must accommodate building renovations or office relocations. We attempt to be sensitive to the schedules of the department employees but sometimes we ask them to leave their computers behind and we allocate in their absence.

2.6 Updating Assets:

Each liaison is responsible for updating the asset database, which is a part of our ticket management system, to reflect the needs of that department. The assets are defined as either Mac Desktop, Mac Laptop, PC Desktop, PC Laptop, Mac Mini, Ultrabook or iPad. We assign an asset for each employee scheduled to receive new hardware. These numbers are essential when negotiating with our vendors.

2.7 Hardware Bake-Off:

We invite our user community to help us make the decision when it comes to the PC laptops and desktops. We choose the models of desktops and laptops from the top 3 manufacturers to determine what model we want the community to evaluate. Employees are encouraged to come to a room that we have set up with the available hardware and use the different computers we are considering, filling out an evaluation form with comments and choosing the one they like best. One vendor will be chosen for all the PCs on campus with the exception of special needs that arose during pre-allocations interviews. A sample of the Bake-Off Survey is shown. (Figure 3).

2.8 Ordering:

Using the asset database for the final count, our director contacts the vendors to negotiate best prices. Each year Apple makes new product announcements and we attempt to time our ordering with that announcement if possible, so users are getting the newest models available.

Dear Members of the Vassar Community,

We are pleased to announce the start of the Allocations cycle is upon us. The following departments are scheduled to receive new computers this summer:

2012 (Cycle Year 4)

- *Benefits*
- *Biology*
- *Bookstore*
- *Chemistry*
- *CIS*
- *Computer Science*
- *Classrooms*
- *Controller*
- *Drama*
- *Ecological Preserve & Field Station*
- *Field Work*
- *Fieldwork Tablets (GIS)*
- *Film*
- *Financial Aid & Student Employment*
- *Food Services*
- *Human Resources*
- *Library (except Reference)*
- *Library Electronic Classroom*
- *Payroll*
- *Post Office*
- *Purchasing*
- *Student Accounts (Bursar & Cashier)*
- *Teaching and Learning Center*

Clicking on your department's name will display contact information for your Allocations representative. Your representative will be visiting your department within the next few weeks. If your department is not on this list and you would like to see when your department is scheduled for Allocations, you can visit our website to see the cycle years.

We will also be upgrading various labs, public spaces and classrooms around campus. If you would like to know more about Allocations, visit our website at computing.vassar.edu/allocations/

This year's Allocation will include the latest version of the Mac and Windows operating systems, which are OS X Lion and Windows 7, respectively. Click here to review the complete list of software that will be included on the computers.

Hardware specs are still being considered but you may click here to see the minimum hardware specifications for this year's allocations computers.

Out of Cycle Requests:

If you are not due for a new Allocation this year but believe that you are in dire need of either an upgrade or replacement, we ask that you make that request by submitting this form on or before May 18, 2012. Your request will then be vetted with your Senior Officer. Please be aware that these requests should only be for serious hardware malfunctions or if the computer is incapable of meeting the needs your work demands. Each request will be evaluated and your request will be approved if deemed necessary. Approved requests may be handled with a new computer, hardware upgrade to your current computer or a better, used computer, if there is one available. Click here for the 2012 Out-Of-Cycle Request Form.

The Allocations web site, computing.vassar.edu/allocation scontains the cycle years, computer choices, frequently asked questions (FAQ's), and the comprehensive list of the software that will be pre-installed on all new computers. Please visit!

NOTE: Please let us know if your department name doesn't appear as you expect in the list above so that we may update our records. If you have any questions, please contact the Computer Allocations Team at allocations@vassar.edu.

Thank you,

Vassar Computing & Information Services

Figure 1

2.9 Instructions

The imaging team leader and the communications coordinator collaborate on the instructions that will be used by the team members in field. There are two sets of instructions; one for Mac and one for PC. The instructions outline the process of taking note of the user's printers and settings, migrating the user's data, recording the assets in our asset management system and configuring the user's new computer post migration. The instructions are very detailed so that any team member could take over where another left off.

2012 Cycle Year 4
Pre-Allocations Interview

- *Mention Survey: We sent your department the Pre-Allocations Survey asking a number of questions. How would you like me to connect with the people in your department to find out what type of computer they'd like?*

- *Process Overview: If you are a regular employee (administrator, staff, or tenure / tenure-track faculty) and currently have a computer assigned to you, it will be replaced with a new computer. If you are a temporary employee, or a non-tenure track faculty member, your software will be refreshed and your computer will be evaluated and replaced with a recycled computer if deemed necessary.*

- *Printers: CIS supports only your Departmental printers. Local / desktop printers will be reconnected to your new system and driver installed if it is a supported device. If the device is not supported on the new operating system it is the responsibility of each department to replace local / desktop printers if deemed necessary.*

- *Software: The new computer will have the latest versions of all the software we site license for the campus. We do not have a site license for any Adobe software (Photoshop, Illustrator, InDesign, Dreamweaver, AfterEffects, Acrobat Pro). A complete list of software that comes on the computer is available on our website at http://computing.vassar.edu/allocations/software.html*

- *Special Software: If anyone has any special software to install, they should have the software and serial numbers available at the time of Allocations. We'd like to have a list of who has what software and what version of the software so we know if it will work on the new operating system.*

    - *Our policy on software: If you can't supply the software and serial number we can't reinstall the software. If the software no longer works because of the new Operating System on your computer, we will replace it. That is why it is better if we know what software and versions individuals have as soon as possible.*

- *New Operating Systems: All new Macs will have Mac OS 10.7 (Lion) and all new PCs will have Windows 7. Training will be available and we highly encourage you to set up a group training session for your entire department. Contact training@vassar.edu*

- *Hardware Covered in Allocations: Any hardware purchased outside of Allocations, including but not limited to hardware purchased using grant funds, start-up funds and department budgets will not be replaced by the allocations cycle.*

- *Please direct all questions about Allocations to allocations@vassar.edu*

Figure 2

2.10 Finalizing The Image:

After evaluating the results of the interviews conducted by the department liaisons, the imaging team determines the software that will be on the final images for all the allocated computers. The image includes the OS, browser, plug-ins, printer drivers and all site-licensed software. All of the images are kept on an imaging server that can be accessed by authorized personnel from anywhere on campus. This technology has made imaging computers on campus much more efficient than it has been in years past.

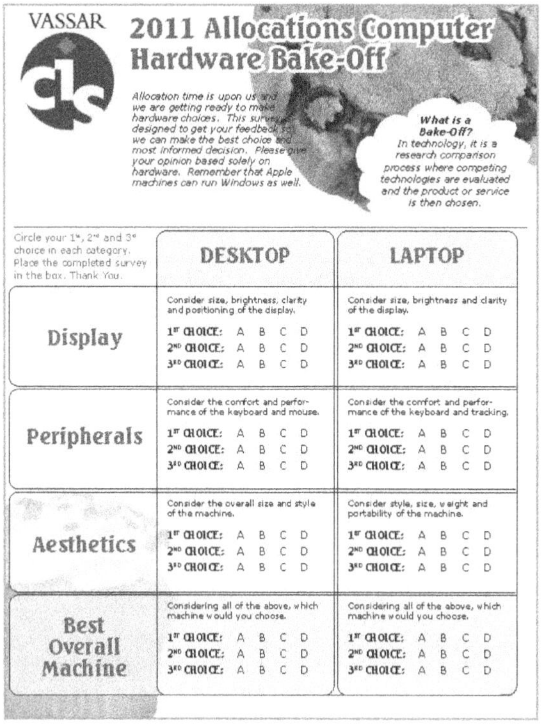

Figure 3

2.11   Inventory/Imaging:

When the new hardware arrives on campus, the imaging team inventories, unboxes, images, places asset tags on and re-packages the computers. The re-packaged hardware is labeled and ready to be moved into the Allocations van for deployment.

2.12   Hardware Prep:

The department liaison gives computer breakdown to the imaging team a few days before a scheduled allocation, for example: 30 Mac Desktops, 10 Mac Laptops, 3 PC Desktops, 2 PC Laptops. The morning of the department allocation the team and student employees go to the allocation room and load imaged computers into the van

2.13   Allocations:

The liaison directs the operation for the day or days set aside for each department. A team member is assigned to an employee or lab computer. The team member immediately begins consulting with the employee (if he or she is there) and recording the user's settings and printers. New, imaged computers are delivered and unboxed by the student employees to each location. The team member consults the instructions to begin the allocation process. For Mac to Mac transfers we use Apple's built-in Migration Assistant. For Windows transfers we use either a customized batch file or Microsoft's Easy Transfer to copy the data to an external hard drive. Mac-to-Windows or Windows-to-Mac transfers are assigned to subject matter experts only. This process is repeated until all of the department's computers have been allocated. Some departments only take a few days. Some can take a full week. The team member leaves behind an information card with references for training and support. The old computer and the box it is packed in are labeled with the user's information. The old computers are then returned to the locked allocation room.

2.14 Remove / Recycle / Re-Image:

The student employees are instrumental in removing the old computers and returning them to the allocation room where they await their fates. They will either be wiped and re-imaged for reuse or retired. The user's data is kept for a period of 30 days, mostly for the employee's peace of mind. Computers that will be re-allocated into the field will be wiped of data using a 7-pass secure process and re-imaged for deployment as either an adjunct or student employee computer. Computers that are deemed too old for field use but are still operable are wiped and re-imaged for sale. Computers that will be retired will have their hard drives destroyed and de-gaussed before being properly disposed of. A sample of the computer labels is shown. (Figure 4).

2.15 Debrief:

At the end of each department allocation, the team reconvenes to ensure we are all on the same page. During this time, the instructions are often updated and refined, unique scenarios are outlined and we review if that department will need to be revisited for deployment of any recycled computers or to allocate any employee who was abroad with their laptop.

2.16 Follow-Up:

Most of the help desk tickets that follow a department's allocation, will be addressed with training, as we have often rolled out a new operating system, Office suite, etc. The department liaisons coordinate any additional assistance the users in their departments may need after receiving their new computers.

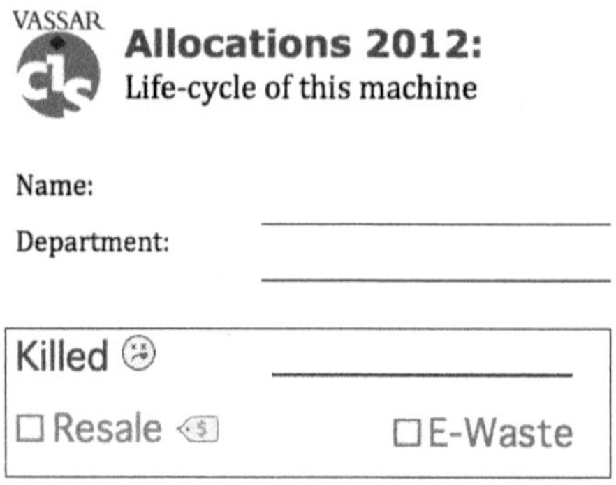

Figure 4

3. CONCLUSION

In conclusion, we have found that the method we use for the allocation of new hardware on our campus is extremely efficient and improves with each passing year. We feel that the pre-emptive replacement of out-of-date hardware greatly reduces our number of break-fix appointments and repair hours, resulting in cost-savings, less data loss and a better level of user satisfaction.

Why Virtual Desktop at CCRI?
Finding Sustainability for Desktop Support

Stephen A. Vieira
The Community College of Rhode Island
400 East Avenue
Warwick, RI 02886
011 401-825-2004

savieira@ccri.edu

ABSTRACT

There is an ever-increasing demand being placed on desktop resources to get the desktop replacement cycle and imaging of computers complete for the start of classes. Time is constantly being whittled from the larger windows of opportunity that used to exist. So now there is a need to be more efficient with less time consumed and it is becoming unsustainable. There must be a way to reduce the time needed and enable more success at the desktop support   level.
CCRI is implementing a virtual desktop initiative that will satisfy several requirements of the growing demand being placed on the desktop support staff. Doing away with the annual replacement of "old" technology and finding a means of deploying new software without delay are two main focal points of the virtual desktop. With over 3000 computers and 800 laptops on the four campuses, a staff that is not going to get any larger, will find it simpler to virtualize applications and get it to students, faculty and staff faster without having to worry about downtime or long sessions of testing.

Additionally, the virtual desktop allows the software to be delivered to the user anytime, anywhere thus eliminating the need for seat-dependent or classroom-dependent copies of software. Concentration can now be placed on getting the right tools to the right people rather than trying to figure out how to load endless software requested on particular classroom computers. Virtual desktop gets the desktop staff out of the business of replacing hard drives, power supplies and tackling virus or malware from desk to desk.

Categories and Subject Descriptors

K.6 [MANAGEMENT OF COMPUTING AND INFORMATION SYSTEMS]: Installation Management, Software Management, System Management, Security and Protection

General Terms

Management, Performance, Design, Economics, Reliability, Experimentation, Security, Human Factors, Standardization

Keywords

Virtualization, infrastructure as a service, desktop deployment, centralized management

1. The Community College of Rhode Island

As the only community college in Rhode Island and the largest in New England, CCRI annually serves 18,000 students, 1500 faculty and staff and over 57,000 alumni. With four campuses (Warwick, Lincoln, Providence and Liston) and two satellites (Westerly and DownCity Providence), the Department of Information Technology staff of forty people, only eight of whom support desktop computing regularly on the various campuses, is constantly challenged with providing quality support for the growing number of desktop and laptop computer users sponsored by the college.

Demand for services continues to grow exponentially, user expectations increase and the new "bring your own device" consumerization of IT layers additional support responsibilities on an already overtaxed team. The virtual desktop solution provides needed relief for all the various elements making desktop support problematic. Altering the daily workflow through virtualization enables staff to provide the level of customer service they were hired to do. Getting them out of the repair, replace and react business affords them the opportunity to be proactive, get to know their customer base more fully and to improve the manner in which technology is used. It has the potential to raise the level of sophistication of students, faculty and staff without increasing the workload.

2. Desktop Support – A History

Like most IT shops, the staff at CCRI were accustomed to delivering hardware and software support where needed. This obviously meant maintaining multiple operating systems, applications, peripherals, and the technical knowledge to answer most questions in a fairly rapid fashion. With the continuing economic trials facing the state and nation, higher education funding shrinks, courses offered swell in number and scheduling upgrades of hardware and software in classrooms and labs becomes difficult to schedule. The facts were clear; the number of staff to do the work was not going to grow and the amount of work to be done was not going to decrease.

2.1 Academic Computing Labs

The four Academic Computing Labs, each located at one of the four primary campuses, is the primary location of student-supported computer and the software needed for completing course assignments. Interruptions in service in these heavily-used facilities are extremely sensitive and problematic to schedule. Every semester, new faculty requests, technology-supplied upgrades and improved capabilities demanded a new image to be built.

The desktop support staff would spend weeks testing and re-testing combinations of software and configurations to enable them to work together in a cohesive manner. Each computing lab would have its own set of applications that had to be part of the campus-specific image based upon courses taught only on those campuses. Four large pools loaded through the network overnight using imaging tools that tested the bandwidth and often had errors which resulted in several restarts.

With the time-sensitive nature of the installs, the expectations of students and faculty to have the software available at the start of classes and the ever-changing image content, the task became almost impossible to accomplish. Stress, overtime and multiple attempts at the delivery of the new image became the code words for desktop image upgrading the computing labs.

2.2 Classroom and Content-Specific Labs

The classroom and content-specific labs had their own set of challenges. Due to limited licensing capabilities for certain software, specific courses using those applications and taught only at particular campuses had to be part of the image developed per classroom. Courses were scheduled into classrooms based upon the software present there and if a problem developed in any classroom, the image resident there had to be moved to a comparable facility to continue to offer the course.

At one point the use of key server management tools enabled some of the burden of software licensing being equated with specific classrooms to be minimized but not as it reflected the individual differences in those topics taught specifically at a particular campus. This was also loaded through the network per scheduled downtime in each classroom and overnight resulting in the same type of performance hits and success rate.

2.3 Faculty and Staff Office Support

Finally a base image was offered to all faculty and staff utilizing desktop or laptop computers at the college. Individual differences were distributed on demand dependent on the needs of a department or instructor. Providing as much detail and configuration as possible in the base image helped minimize the number of unique and supported images.

These loads were scheduled with faculty over a long period of time during the semester when agreement on a timeframe was found. Time-consuming and sometimes extremely difficult to satisfy, each of these installs provided its own set of challenges. Once again limited software licensing, course-specific software and individual departmental needs dictated the speed with which these could be accomplished.

3. The Basis for Virtual Desktops

Today everyone is asked to do more with less. The increasing demand upon the desktop support personnel and the dwindling pockets of time to accomplish what had to be done was evident. Strains on resources, techniques and strategies that didn't work well and the resulting inadequate delivery of desktop replacements, software images and basic services to the students, faculty and staff at the college dictated a change.

There had to be a way to become more efficient with time and personnel and to effectively handle the various problems inherent in what we were doing. The exceptional performance of server management using virtualization and the reliability of those systems led to discussions of using virtual desktops as a means of relieving the pressure and eliminating several of the roadblocks that desktop support faced.

The reality was that desktop support had focused on bringing broken machines back from the dead and not on discovering new tools or ways in which they could be used. Desktop and laptop computer users were supporting themselves in regard to using software and the number of trouble tickets handled clearly indicated that it wasn't about the user. IT wasn't supporting the user of the desktop but instead the computer that was on the desktop. To improve customer service and deliver better support, this paradigm had to change and the only way to change it was to substitute the need for hardware fixes with the ability to apply user fixes. Solving the problems that the user had required extending the knowledge base to them and eliminating the break fix endless loop that existed.

4. Benefits of Virtual Desktops

There are several benefits inherent to virtual desktop that have immediate impact on the IT efforts at CCRI. Each of these will be discussed in detail but it is important to point out that none of the essential requirements for customer service and satisfaction were sacrificed. The ease of deployment as a result of the opportunities to break down the large images into a base image with multiple virtual applications immediately reaped benefits. Additionally the multiple images that were campus-specific and classroom-specific also disappeared. At the time of implementation, the college is entertaining a new written information security policy which also plays a part in the utilization of virtual desktops. Additionally the future consumerization of IT and the BYOD capabilities that will be supported further enhance the service options for desktop support and the departments other divisions.

4.1 Centralized Operating System Management

Having a centralized facility in which to apply real-time security patches and upgrades to the various operating systems is truly an enhancement. From a virtual desktop arena, IT can offer different users the operating systems of their choice. In one instance where someone is particularly familiar with Windows Vista, and the campus is migrating to Windows 7, a virtual desktop could be provided for those not ready for the move. Additionally, multiple operating systems could be offered to a single virtual desktop user in the event that they had the need.

In the past, central distribution of patches would work based upon the response that the endpoint user selected. If patches were to be loaded and a user refused the upgrade, these systems throughout campus would be vulnerable. With central management of operating systems, each of the updates can be handled immediately after testing for their effect on the existing environment and when a user logs in, they would get those updates without asking.

Another consideration is the migration of operating systems to a new version when it concerns those classes that must offer the most current to be competitive. Whenever Microsoft moved to another version of Windows in the past, there was always concern for those courses that had to offer the latest and how IT responded while ensuring no negative impact on those who did not desire that in their classrooms. With virtual desktops, each faculty member can be served what they desire, maintaining competitive advantage sponsoring all of what faculty members need.

While the virtual desktop environment is attractive, the concern for redundancy and high availability becomes even more important. As the college moves to more and more virtual desktops, the issue of having a central site for all centralized management of this utility must be considered. The virtual system is meant to provide failover and reliable service but should the primary data center go offline, unlike in the personal computer world, all virtual desktop computer activity goes down with it. This results in appropriating an alternate location where power outages and primary data center interruptions do not forgo desktop virtualization at other campuses. Planning a secondary site could be considered as a portion of business continuity and as a result long-term disaster recovery planning as well. Having virtual desktops simply points out the need for this facility to being on the list of cataloged services offered and to be replicated

4.2 Centralized Management of Version Control

There are many course-elated and publisher-offered software packages used in the various computer-enhanced classrooms and labs. Each semester, IT is sure to get many requests for ensuring that the latest versions are available for instruction and study. Not all the deliveries of these upgrades work on a timeline that fits the academic calendar. In the past, when a new software delivery was made, the desktop support personnel scrambled to include it in the image and ensure that it was compatible with all the other packages. Timeliness of this effort was always critical and difficult to satisfy.

With virtual desktops, the new software can be virtualized and included in the applications offered. It can be done as quickly as having someone log off, install the new version, and have them log in to start using it. This immediacy is structured around the fact that all virtual applications are wrapped with the necessary libraries and operating systems elements that make it possible to function without utilizing the operating system. Examples that can be shown to demonstrate this is the capability to run multiple versions of Internet Explorer all at the same time without experiencing system failure.

Now faculty members can have confidence that their required software can be released to their course and students without having an impact on the remainder of their coursework. The desktop support person does not have to utilize valuable bandwidth or countless hours testing to ensure that compatibility can be reached. The rapid deployment aspects of virtual desktop automatically deliver better service to the students and faculty.

4.3 Ensuring the User Experience

When a virtual desktop is issued to a user, the desktop support group must spend some time with the individual discovering the various ways in which the desktop is used and appears. By taking the time to tailor the individual virtual desktop to each user, the user experience is preserved and the virtual desktop is embraced without concern. Using profile management for each user, the shortcuts, colors, styles and anything else that the user has chosen

to designate for their individual personal computer can be duplicated in exactly the same manner on any computer in which they log in anywhere.

From a student support standpoint, profiles can be maintained semester by semester in order to allow them to choose favorites, accessibility settings or other select items that also can follow them from seat to seat, even at home. Requiring a minimal amount of storage per person, these profile enhancements make the virtual desktop environment tailored despite being able to be replaced in a moment should a problem occur.

Another added feature is the elimination of "blue screens of death" or virus/malware infection on devices. If someone has such a thing, a simple load of a new virtual desktop gets them back to work in a few minutes. While this group of activities would result in multiple trouble tickets and engage desktop support in site visits and hours of clean up on occasion, this is no longer a responsibility that requires extensive time spent with a particular computer.

4.4 Reduced Cost in Purchasing Desktop Computers

With three thousand desktop computers and eight hundred laptops, the task of replacing these devices on a regularly scheduled basis is cost prohibitive. With a normal three to five year life span before recycling computers, between 700 and 1000 machines would be part of the evergreen process. One consideration in desktop replacement is the ultimate reason for doing this. In the past, the two primary justifications for upgrading a user's computer would be either inability to provide the resources needed on the existing device or the machine being too costly to run due to repairs required or other aging issues.

Today, most computers at CCRI are replaced due to requirements of the operating systems under which they run. The amount of actual computing resources consumed by the average user is minimal when considering the devices purchased. Due to the additional memory and processing speeds required by the operating system and base packages, the computer recycling program becomes a means of keeping up with the latest technology rather than providing new and improved capabilities for the average user. With desktop virtualization, there are several approaches that can be taken to alleviate this annual expense.

A simple approach is to remove the hard drive from existing computers and utilize the centralized virtual desktop system for login, storage and processing power. When looking at the beginning costs of entering into a desktop virtualization engagement, this option needs to be considered to avoid the initial costs of thin or zero clients. While the goal would be to remove the desktop computer completely and enable more mobility for students, faculty and staff, the early cists of deployment can be minimized by utilizing this method.

A second approach can be to begin replacing lab and classroom computers with thin or zero clients which have no moving parts, and are more of a pass through device which simply fosters the network connection to the virtualization central system. There are a variety of clients that can be purchased but those that should be considered first are those supporting PC over IP. This technology offers the fastest speed with the least hit on the central desktop virtualization system. Thin or zero clients are relatively inexpensive when considering the cost of desktop or laptop computers and offer all the functionality at a fraction of the cost. A modest annual investment in this technology rids the desktop support staffs from replacing power supplies, hard drives or network cards that increasingly fail with age.

While there are licensing costs for virtual desktop seats, they can be worked into a progressive project to drive down the replacement cycle costs while moving toward the virtual solution.

4.5 Rapid Client Deployment

The greatest benefit for desktop support personnel is the ease with which applications can be virtualized and offered to students, faculty and staff in a timely manner. Using any of the application virtualization tools, those individual software packages can be wrapped in their own set of libraries and operating system utilities to have them operate in their own virtual system. Virtualizing applications is simple and once tested can be offered to users as just another shortcut on the desktop.

Any time a software package is updated or patched, the new version, once tested, can be offered immediately to users by simply exercising the logoff/login procedure. Due to the granular capabilities of the system, and through the active directory, individuals can be granted access while maintaining older versions for other groups. That means that one course could be using the latest version of an application while another course could be potentially using an earlier version in keeping with their textbook. This flexibility was never an option in the past.

The loading of the base image, due to its new design supporting the virtual applications, becomes faster and simpler because its size does not tax the network and the success rate is higher for loading on the initial attempt. Everything not in the base image becomes a virtual application except where a software package is not a good candidate for virtualization. Some software requiring lots of processing power might be deemed not to be virtualized at this time and so might be loaded into the base image. The immediate benefit is the introduction of a single base image for all campuses with virtual applications delivered to students and faculty based upon their coursework requirements.

What used to take weeks and was always a stressful activity based upon time and availability has now become a standard operating procedure and more customer-oriented. Last minute changes and after the commencement of classes emergencies are now treated simply as a virtual load of software for a particular group of users. Automated provisioning opportunities through active directory group policies reflected in on demand availability.

4.6 Reduction in Operating Expenses

The most significant cost savings has to be the efficiency and effectiveness of the desktop support staff. No longer are they in the business of replacing hard drives, power supplies and network cards and cleaning up computers from malware and virus attacks becomes a thing of the past. They are now employed working with users on a face-to-face basis helping them to become more effective users of the computing resources.

Freeing up the staff to provide more outreach and training on best practices, new to the team, is a goal that is slowly being incorporated into their functional roles. Desktop support transitions from being a person supporting the computer to an aide for each individual user of the computers on campus. It evolves the service element from hardware support to software support

impacting each user's actual ability to get their jobs done more effectively and efficiently.

Statistics show that for every dollar spent on acquiring computers, three dollars are spent on supporting them. From managing operating system images and applications to supporting the multitude of endpoint devices, the IT staff is forced to supply "just in time" or proactive service levels that cannot be sustained. Everything in technology screams change and Boyle's Law has been proven repeatedly to have underestimated the pace at which these changes occur. Automating desktop and application management and applying increased controls and security has the end result of improving the service level to each user. Enabling users to have the portability, mobility and flexibility of moving from location to location on a collection of devices with a consistent user experience optimizes the effectiveness of the support personnel.

With increased productivity for the college's workforce, this alludes to reductions in end-user downtime, automated backup and recovery and a simplified desktop presentation for customers. The scalability of the model has encouraged the college to adopt a virtual desktop capability wherever possible. From a desktop support viewpoint the more the virtualized desktops the more manageable the continuation spiral becomes. The thin or zero clients provide long-term accessibility to these applications without replacement in the order of two to three times longer than a regular personal computer. Naturally cost savings in power consumption also come from having a pass through device that has no moving parts and virtually nothing to repair. If one were to stop working, simply unplug it, plug in a new client and the user is back in business.

4.7 Improved Data Security

One facet of desktop virtualization that is an added bonus is the ability to increase the security of information collected and used at the college. Because every connection is secure and individually-designed for the user in mind, issues which existed with the use and sharing of personally identifiable information have been reduced. The concern was always what was being stored on hard drives and laptops that might be an issue if stolen or lost. Virtual desktops help to reduce the data leak possibilities by encouraging use of secure network file shares stored in the central data center but completely accessible to users whenever they sue their virtual desktops.

Through this availability at any time, from anywhere, users have been encouraged to move their files to a secure file share designed for them and those with whom they want to share. Giving them control of the permissions of these file stores reassures them that they determine who gets to see data and information that is private and potentially harmful if compromised. With the need to be portable, mobile and accessible increasingly desirable, the security aspect of desktop virtualization enables IT to guarantee the safekeeping of files using all the safeguards of the data center.

Truly the benefit becomes the fact that the data is secure in the data center, the centralized location of most campus-based analysis and reporting tools and utilities. Fully integrating with various anti-virus, anti-malware products, endpoint security comes into a central management facility where everyone can be protected in a standard and easily monitored fashion.

4.8 Secure Remote Access

Another promise of the desktop virtualization effort is the ability to offer a secure remote access window for every user. Using the security tools available for virtual private networking, any user can be assured that their connection is encrypted and securely locked down. Once again this feature is extremely important for faculty when working on sensitive information that should not be made available outside the campus walls.

4.9 Fewer Application Compatibility Problems

Last but not least, the time to deploy has been greatly enhanced by the fact that through application virtualization, compatibility issues have been eliminated. New applications can be added to those offered on a campus or to a course without fear of their impact on other courses or to other software offered to that particular course. Introducing new software at the last minute, while in the past a very scary proposition, does not endanger the content of the coursework or campus. When textbook publishers would come late with a new version of their applications to be used in the instruction process, it would create havoc because it would have to be tested for compatibility with every other package. That no longer requires the time-consuming and untimely delays to bring required materials into the classroom.

Through the application virtualization process, each new software offering is introduced in its own personal virtual environment.

5. Virtual Desktop Futures

While CCRI has reaped several benefits from the desktop virtualization effort, the future of this endeavor looks even brighter. The evolution of the consumerization of IT and the population of tablet and smart phones coming to campus creates new challenges and opportunities. Virtual desktop plays nicely into the utilization of all of these devices and the number of possibilities they offer.

Certainly one obvious advantage of the newer technology is the availability of added communication and connectedness for our students and faculty. Brining their desktop with them from class to class, campus to campus and at home enables them to use campus-licensed software through the network to complete assignments and participate in classroom activities in the event they cannot attend. The ubiquitous natures of wireless connections provide multiple locations for them to study, complete and store projects and coursework and share those same files with classmates and faculty. No longer needing to come to campus and work in the Academic Computing Labs to get access to required software, their schedule becomes more user-friendly and adaptable to them when they want to get work done.

The endpoint flexibility possibilities through re-purposed personal computers to thin or zero clients to mobile devices become only a challenge for the technology and not the support personnel. Enabling a virtual desktop does not require knowing what a user has in their possession or what they choose to use. Additionally the virtual desktop supports multimedia and USB redirection, print optimization, multi-monitor capabilities and flash content and graphics without being a bandwidth overload.

5.1 Software Purchase Efficiencies

Exploring the possibility of increasing the efficiency with which software is licensed for courses, programs, departments and campuses is one long-term aspect of desktop virtualization. If the college can take advantage of the virtual desktop environment to maximize software acquisition and only license required numbers of copies, they might create a new model of efficiency and cost savings. Buying the correct number of licenses to guarantee accessibility for all students while not over purchasing potentially unused copies is the key goal.

A really wonderful feature of the program is the capability to lock down a certain number of copies of software for classroom consumption and then when the class is no longer in session, release the copies to students trying to do homework. Working out the individual magic number of what is required and what is being purchased will involve several inputs but is something that could have an impact on how software is delivered to the classrooms and individual.

5.2 Granular Role Assignment

One other area that requires further study but has enormous possibilities is the capability of applying several granular elements to software delivery that will allow certain applications to be offered to students in a particular program or course. This ability to be very detailed could guarantee that software purchase for an individual course would only get to those students for which it was acquired. Additionally as students enroll or drop out of courses that could immediately take effect on software use.

There are several other possibilities surrounding guest usage of software and the ability to limit populations and times based upon the Academic Calendar. This level of granularity is in the future but certainly something that has been discussed.

6. REFERENCES

[1] Brodkin, Jon March 9, 2011. "VMware unleashes virtual desktops for Apple iPad" http://www.networkworld.com/2011/030911-vmware-virtual-desktops.html .

[2] Citrix Staff august 29, 2011. "Top 10 reasons to strengthen information security with desktop virtualization" White paper from http://www.citrix.com

[3] Dubie, Denise June 18, 2009. "weighing the pros and cons of desktop virtualization" http://www.networkworld.com/news/2009/061809-desktop-virtualization.html

[4] Goldworm, barb June 2010. "Desktop Virtualization; why It's Real at Last and Why One Size Does Not Fit All" http://www.focusonsystems.com.

[5] Madden, Brian April 7, 2009. "Desktop and application Virtualization; What is it, what it's not, why IT managers should care" http://eventd.techtarget.com/virtualdesktop

[6] McLeod, Jack, Chris Gebhardt, Abhinav Joshi February 2010. "VMware View on NetApp Deployment Guide" Technical Report on http://www.vmware.com/files/pdf/partners/netapp/netapp-2000-seat-vmware-view-TR-3770.pdf

[7] Network World staff November 24, 2009. "Desktop virtualization cheat sheet" http://www.networkworld.com/news/2009/114209-vdi-desktop-virtualizartion-cheat-sheet.html

[8] Oley, Michael February 1, 2012. "Virtualization Trends in 2012"

http://www.windowsitpro.com/article/virtualization2/virtualization-trends-2012-142011

[9] VMware Team May 20, 2011. "Desktop Modernization; A guide to addressing end-User requirements and IT challenges using VMware desktop virtualization" E-book downloadable from http://moreover.tradepub.com/free/w_vmwa54

[10] Warren, Steven February 5, 2009. "What are the benefits of VDI?" http://www.techrepublic.com/blog/datacenter/what-are-the-benefits-of vdi/579

Helping Student Employees Become Members of Your Organization

Wesley Marks

Operations Manager

University of Florida

PO Box 118461, Gainesville, FL 32611

352-392-5573

wesmarks@ufl.edu

ABSTRACT

One of the challenges with using student employees is for them to have invested interest in the success of the organization. While handling customer support issues are the primary focus of all Help Desks, student employees need to feel that they are a part of that process. This can be accomplished by setting up a structure that involves them in both the daily and long term success of the organization. At the University of Florida, our student supervisors are responsible for the support provided to our clients. This includes monitoring phone and walk-in traffic as well as dealing with system outages. During the term, our senior student staff is responsible for interviewing prospective employees and making hiring recommendations. They also work with the help desk staff to determine effective changes to both our policies and procedures, which are essential to continuing success of the organization. Other employees take on the role of trainers for our new hires as well as updating their technical skills. Finally, ongoing projects allow all employees to make their contributions to the organization. By employing these techniques, the student employees become a part of the success of the organization.

Categories and Subject Descriptors

K.6.1 [**Project and People Management**]: Management Techniques, Staffing, Planning, Training

General Terms

General Literature, General.

Keywords

Help Desk, Student Workers, Customer Support.

1. INTRODUCTION

The University of Florida consists of 52,271 students including 6,300 international students and over 330,000 alumni. These numbers do not include the over 29,000 individuals that apply for admission to the university. The university has 5,434 faculty members and 12,633 full and part-time staff. The result

is that over 420,000 individuals are supported by the University of Florida Computing Help Desk.

The Help Desk consists of 13 full-time staff members and 65 student staff. The structure for the UF Computing Help Desk begins with the front line employees who are known as Account Specialist. Our Account Specialists also work in the Application Support Center (ASC) providing assistance for graduate students completing the electronic version of their theses and dissertations. Some student employees undergo additional training to become consultants. This is a second level of support for more advanced support. This includes helping clients with browser settings, email setup, wireless setup and other laptop issues. Finally, we have three supervisors that manage client support. They are also student employees. The first position is the ASC supervisor who manages the traffic in the ASC location. The second position is the Consultant Backup who manages consultant traffic and helps with technical issues. The third position is the Supervisor who manages all operations. The primary focus for the Supervisor is to make sure that all clients are being assisted. They also make sure that all of the University and Help Desk policies are being followed.

The UF Computing Help Desk supports phone, walk-in and e-mail clients. During the past year, we answered 89,603 phone calls, assisted 14,568 walk-ins, and responded to 27,358 emails. We have an average answer rate of 97% for all the calls that we received. The Help desk is open Monday through Thursday from 7:30 am to 10:00 pm, Friday from 7:30 am to 5:00 pm and on the weekends from 12:00 noon till 6:00 pm, except on noted holidays.

The UF Computing Help Desk is the tier-1 support center for the University of Florida community. Within the Help Desk, there are three tiers of support. To avoid any confusion with the existing UF support tiers, these will be referred to as levels. When the front line is not able to resolve the issue, it is escalated within the Help Desk. When it is a technical issue, it is escalated to one of our level two student consultants. Should they be unable to resolve the issue, it is escalated to our full-time technical staff. This is our third level of support. Other issues concerning E-learning, video conferencing and staff issues are escalated within the help desk directly to the level three help desk staff. Should the full-time staff is not able to resolve the issue; the issue is escalated to tier-2 support that is outside of the help desk.

2. Problem

To be able to provide excellent support to our clients, we need a team of committed, dedicated employees. To provide support, we use pay as our major incentive for our student employees. Unfortunately, the pay that we can provide is limited so we needed more creative ways to encourage student employees to become contributing members of the organization.

3. The On-going Solution

From the very beginning of the UF Computing Help Desk, we have utilized techniques to manage the daily operations of the organization. While the use of these techniques did not originate with our help desk, we have embraced them as a means to help the student employees to become members of our organization. These ideas include:

1) Positive work reports
2) Working on projects
3) Training
4) Promotion to Supervisor positions
5) Promotion to Senior Supervisor positions

4. Positive Work Reports

The UF Computing Help Desk uses a home grown reporting system for documenting attendance, work, project and progress reports. Attendance reports are used to record when an employee is late or misses a work shift. Work reports are used to document either good or negative employee events. The areas for these reports include work performance, team work and client interactions. Project reports are used to document the work that the employees does on their projects. Finally, we use progress reports to document training and to address employee issues. The attendance, work and project reports are then used for our evaluations done at the end of each term. These evaluations are used to determine the pay raise that the student employee will receive for the next term.

Over a period of time, we found that our reporting system was mostly being used to document negative events rather than positive events. The result was that employees became upset each time they were notified that they had received a report. This was causing them to detach from the organization. We also found that this was a problem for our supervisors because they would finish the term with few or no work reports.

To counteract the negative reports and to increase the number of reports for our supervisors, we made it possible for any of our employees to create a report. At first, we only saw a small increase in the number of positive reports because our non-supervisors were not used to writing reports. It is considered a part of the supervisor job to write reports so we needed an incentive that would encourage non-supervisors to write reports. The solution was to recognize when a non-supervisor wrote a positive report. By doing this, we found that they have started to write more reports, even about staff. We feel this has gotten them more involved with our organization.

5. Working on Projects

From experience, we knew that there were many tasks that do not directly support the clients but were needed to indirectly support them. Training is an excellent example, as our employees need to have knowledge before they can assist our clients. We have created projects for our student employees to accomplish these tasks.

The list of our projects include:

- Account Specialist Training
- Application Development
- Application Support Consultant Training
- Canned Emails
- Consultant Tools Maintenance
- Consultant Training
- Continuing education
- E-Learning
- Employee of the Month
- Employee Relations
- Help Desk Cleaning
- Lost and Found
- Marketing & Client services
- Meeting Minutes
- New Services Testing
- Operations
- Personnel Files
- Reference Sheet Updates
- Senior Supervisors
- SharePoint
- Supervisor/Tech Backup Training
- Temporary (used for one time projects)
- Wiki Content Management.

We found that the projects also brought benefits for our student employees. By working on a project, the student employee receives an increase in pay and improves their chances for future promotions. It also gives them something to work on during slow traffic times. Some projects are one-time events or easy projects while other projects are highly technical and take a significant amount of time to complete. Because we value the work they do on their projects, student employees can be given project hours to work on their projects.

Projects provide our employees the satisfaction of making a contribution to the success of the UF Computing Help Desk. In other words, they become more involved with the organization.

6. Training

As with all jobs, a new employee needs to be trained to perform their job. When an employee first begins working for us, they receive training to perform as a front line employee. The training that they receive is from more experience student employees. Once they have completed their training, they are able to assist clients with basic problems. To move up in the organization, the employee must complete additional training.

6.1 Consultant Training

As describe in the introduction, our student consultants provide the next level of support within the UF Computing Help Desk. To become a consultant, the employee must interview with the consultant trainer and technical staff member. Once they have completed training, they help the clients that have more technical issues. Once they have gained some experience as a consultant, they can receive additional training to become a Consultant II. Once they have completed training, they can directly work on a client's mobile device or laptop computer.

6.2 Trainers

Most of the UF Computing Help Desk training is provided by our student employees. In some situation, the training is provided by our full-time staff. The training that our student employees provide includes Account Specialist (new hires) training, Consultant training and Consultant II training. As with becoming a consultant, all student employees who would like to train others must interview for the position. There are two types of training used at the UF Computing Help Desk. Each week, the employees have classroom training with a training coordinator. Training coordinators are the more experience trainers that lead the classroom training and decide when the employee has completed training. The second type of training is the on-the-job training. By working one on one with the person being trained, the trainer works with the employee as they assist our clients. The trainee will first observe the trainer. Once basic skills are learned, the trainee works directly with the client with the trainer's help.

We have found that there are many benefits of using student employees as our trainers. The first is that they can relate well to the individual being trained. This is because they went through the same process. A second benefit is that the student employee tends to be more up to date as they are working directly with our clients. The third benefit is that they become more involved in our organization.

7. Supervisors

The UF Computing Help Desk has three positions that give the student employee management skills. These positions are Application Support Center (ASC) supervisor, Consultant Backup and Supervisor. To work in one of these positions, the employee must interview with staff members.

Supervisors have a monthly meeting with a member of staff. This meeting serves two functions. The first function is to address any issues that the staff might be concerned about. It is a good opportunity to make sure that everyone is on the same page. The second function and perhaps the more important function is to give the supervisors an opportunity to discuss issues and concerns that they have. By allowing them to have a voice, they increase their involvement in our organization.

7.1 ASC Supervisor

The ASC Supervisor manages our Application Support Center. While the ASC provides assistance with Word, Excel and Photoshop, the main support area is with assisting graduate students with the formatting of their Electronic Thesis and Dissertation. The supervisor's tasks are to make sure that everyone is being assisted and to answer incoming ASC emails.

7.2 Consultant Supervisor

The Consultant Supervisor provided technical assist to both the Consultant I and Consultant II employees. In addition, they manage the walk-in consultant help and schedule laptop appointments. They also respond to technical emails, which are escalated to outside tier two support.

7.3 Supervisor

The Supervisor is the controller for the entire UF Computing Help Desk. Their primary responsibility is ensuring that our clients are being assisted in a timely manner. They monitor the phone traffic and walk-in traffic and are expected to move resource (employees) around to handle the incoming traffic. They also watch to be sure that the employees are here and on task. If a system issue should occur, they must notify the appropriate support group. It is also their responsibility to answer incoming emails.

8. Senior Supervisors

Our Senior Supervisors are the highest position that a student employee can occupy at the UF Computing Help Desk. Supervisors with two terms of experience may interview with the staff for this position. Each Senior Supervisor has an area that they manage. The current areas are Account Specialist training, Consultant training, Technical Support, Projects and Operations. Each term they must find employees to work in their area. This is done by selecting the employees that are interested in helping with the project. During the term, they monitor the progress of each project and then pass the information to the staff. In addition, all Senior Supervisors are involved in hiring of new employees, evaluating students and meeting with staff once a week.

8.1 Hiring

The UF Computing Help Desk has had a tradition that our Senior Supervisors perform the hiring process. This way they have a strong desire to hire the individuals that they will be working with in the future. While a staff member oversees the process, the bulk of the work is performed by the Senior Supervisors.

The process begins with advertising that we have openings. The Senior Supervisor evaluates each application to be sure that they meet our requirements. If so, they conduct a phone interview the applicant. The reason for the phone interview is that 95% of our traffic is phone traffic. We need to be sure that they can be understood over the phone. If they do well on the phone interview, the applicant is schedule for a walk-in interview. The interview is with two different Senior Supervisors so that three different Senior Supervisors have talked to the applicant. Once the interviews are completed, the Senior Supervisors meet with the operations manager. During the meeting, they determine which of the applicants we are going to hire. To complete the process, the Senior Supervisors make the arrangements to sign the new hires up with our human resources staff. They also have to notify the individuals who were not selected.

8.2 Evaluations

At the end of each term, the UF Computing Help Desk evaluates all of our student employees. The reason why we evaluate our employees is to document the work performed during the term and to determine their pay rate. Each Senior

Supervisor and staff member has four or five employees to evaluate. At the beginning of the term, each Senior Supervisor and staff member is notified who they will be evaluating. During the term, they act as a mentor for each of their employees. This includes discussing with them their trouble tickets and their work reports. The final evaluation is completed using our reporting system.

8.3 Weekly meetings

Senior Supervisors meet weekly with a member of staff. The primary reason for the weekly meeting is to brief the full-time staff about the area which they oversee. The meeting also serves to update the full-time staff about the status of the projects. We also use the meeting time to discuss upcoming events that will impact the student staff. Often these discussions include the Senior Supervisor's recommendations on how to effective respond to the upcoming event. The final reason and maybe the most important reason is to give the Senior Supervisors time to discuss issues that they are seeing

from their perspective. We feel that the organization benefits when they are able to express their thoughts about the organization.

9. Conclusion

The UF Computing Help Desk has always strived to have an excellent working relationship with our student employees. By using these techniques, we try to make each employee feel that they are more than just being paid to do a job. By making them a member of the organization, they take ownership of the organizations. As a result, the student employees provide the level of support that our clients appreciate.

10. ACKNOWLEDGMENTS

Special thanks the Information Technology department at the University of Florida and the University of Florida Help Desk for allowing me to share our system.

Capturing Malicious Bots Using a Beneficial Bot and Wiki

Takashi Yamanoue
Kagoshima University
Korimoto, Kagoshima
890-0065, Japan
+81-99-285-7187

yamanoue@cc.kagoshima-u.ac.jp

Kentaro Oda
Kagoshima University
Korimoto, Kagoshima
890-0065, Japan
+81-99-285-7474

odaken@cc.kagoshima-u.ac.jp

Koichi Shimozono
Kagoshima University
Korimoto, Kagoshima
890-0065, Japan
+81-99-285-7474

simozono@cc.kagoshima-u.ac.jp

ABSTRACT

Locating malicious bots in a large network is problematic because its internal firewalls and NAT routers unintentionally contribute to hiding bots' host address and malicious packets. However, eliminating firewalls and NAT routers for merely locating bots is generally not acceptable. In this paper, we propose an easy to deploy, easy to manage network security controlling system for locating a malicious host behind the internal secure gateways. This network security controlling system consists of a remote security device and a command server. Each of the remote security devices is installed as a transparent link (implemented as a L2 switch), between the subnet and its gateway, to detect a host which is compromised with a malicious bot in a target subnet, while minimizing impact of deployment. The security devices are remote controlled by 'polling' the command server in order to eliminating NAT traversal problem and to be firewall friendly. Since the remote security device lives in transparent, remote controlled and robust to security gateways, we regard it as a beneficial bot. We adopt a web server with wiki software as the command server in order to take advantage of its power of customization, easy to use and easy to deployment of the server.

Categories and Subject Descriptors

C.2.0 [**Security and protection**]: Installation Management – *Benchmarks*.

General Terms

Management, Security.

Keywords

Network security, Security Monitor, Security Control, Bot, Wiki, Java, API

1. INTRODUCTION

A bot is a software application that runs automated tasks over the Internet. It is usually a malicious application controlled by a malicious herder who is the master of the bot. Many resent viruses are used for recruiting a host into a botnet which is a collection of malicious bots. Once malicious bots have intruded a campus LAN, Important information such as private information of students and research secrets in the campus may be leaked. Furthermore, the

bots may spam other people and attack other web sites via distributed denial of service(DDos). A campus with malicious bots may be considered to be engaging in criminal activity. The manager of the campus LAN has to be careful about malicious bots and remove the bot quickly when found.

A fire-wall and a Network Address Translation (NAT) are powerful tools to enhance network security of a LAN. They may defend the LAN against intrusion of a malicious bot. A LAN protected by these tools is like a house protected by a door with a key. Only permitted IP packets may pass through the fire-wall or the NAT much like only people who have the key may pass through the door of the house. However, when a host in the LAN is compromized by a malicous bot, it is hard to identify the compromized host from the outside of the LAN, much like it is hard to find a robber who is hidden in the house or the building. DHCP and IPv6 with privacy address extension (RFC 3041) also make it difficult to identify a compromized host because the IP address of a suspicious host, which uses them, is changed dynamically.

A campus's LAN usually consists of a central network infrastructure and sub-LANs. Some sub-LANs may be protected by a fire-wall or a NAT. Network managers sometimes have to find out bots which are hidden in such protected sub-LANs. One way to realize this is to prohibit use of a fire-wall or a NAT for a sub-LAN. It is easy to define the rule,but unrealistic because broadband routers with fire-wall or NAT function are so common.

When malicious communication between a bot in a protected sub-LAN and another host on the outsideis discovered by the manager of the central network infrastructure (or the central manager), the central manager usually directs the manager of the sub-LAN (or the sub-manager) to disconnect the sub-LAN from the central network infrastructure immediately. The sub-manager inspects all PCs in the sub-LAN using anti-virus software. However this process cannot always find the bot because anti-virus software can not find 0-day attacks, which is a computer threat that tries to exploit computer application vulnerabilities that are *unknown* to others or the software developer, and the central manager can not observe the malicious communication.

Sometimes, the central manager would like to monitor sub-LANs in order to find the compromized host. The compromized host should be found as quickly as possible. The central manager can monitor the sub-LAN by re-configuring the LAN (for example - connect the sub-LAN directry to the central network infrastructure). However such re-configuration without care may cause serious trouble. Such re-configuration usually takes a long time. The manager should have an easy and fast way to monitor and control sub-LANs.

We have made a network security controlling system which uses a remote security device and a web site with wiki software. The device can be deployed fast and easily because it is portable. The central manager can monitor and control the sub-LAN behind a fire-wall or a NAT easily from a web site with common wiki software, using the remote security device. The remote security device is a kind of bot which is controlled by the central manager. The device can do the following:

- Monitor traffic between hosts in the sub-LAN and outside hosts.
- Filter out malicious packets of the traffic.
- Intercept DNS query packets from the suspicious host and return the IP address of the fake host which pretends the herder's host.
- Pretend the herder's host such like returning the fake syn-ack packet to the syn packet from the suspicious host.

The remote security device is connected to a sub-LAN which may have a malicious bot between the switch of the sub-LAN and its NAT. The device is remote controlled and communication in the sub-LAN can be monitored by the central manager using wiki software. This paper discusses the implementation, usages and related work of the security controlling system.

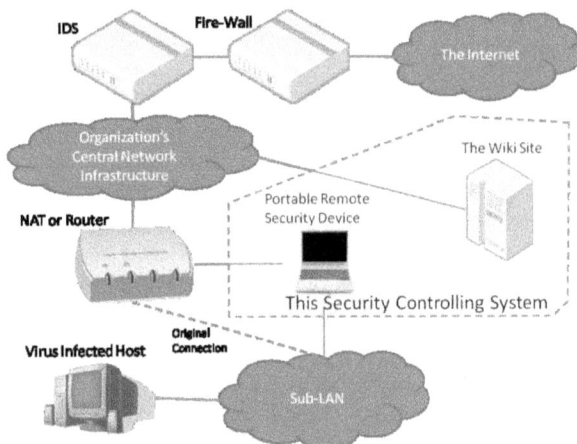

Figure 1. Outline of this system

The rest of this paper is organized as follows: In section 2, a summary of the monitoring system is shown. In section 3, usage example is presented. In section 4, related works are shown. Finally in section 5, we summarize this paper and present some possible future works.

2. IMPLEMENTATION

The security controlling system consists of a portable remote security device and a web site with Wiki(PukiWiki) software. The security device consists of a laptop computer and auxiliary network interface. The sensor device is controlled by commands which are written on the wiki page of the site. Results of command execution are written on the same page. The security device is connected between a sub-LAN side port of a NAT(or router) and the switch of the sub-LAN(Figure 1).

An auxiliary switch is used if PCs were connected to LAN ports of the NAT(or router) directly. An auxiliary Wi-fi access point is also connected to the auxiliary switch if the wi-fi access point

function of the NAT was used. The wi-fi access point function of the NAT should be disabled. The web site with wiki software is connected to the place of the network where both of the sensor device and the web site are able to access.

Figure 2 shows the structure of the remote security device. The hardware of the device is a laptop PC with two Network Interface Cards (NICs), which is realized by adding an auxiliary NIC to the PC. One NIC is the WAN side NIC and it is connected to the NAT or router. Another NIC is the LAN side NIC and it is connected to the sub-LAN. A linux virtual machine is implemented in the PC. The virtual machine has two network bridges and the control program. The control program has two DAQs(data acquisition library) and the "filter/controller". Two DAQs are conntected by the filter/controller. The filter/controller monitors and controles traffic between two DAQs. Each of the DAQs is connected to one of the bridge and each of the bridges is connected to one of the NICs. All communication between hosts (except the NAT) in the sub-LAN and hosts outside the sub-LAN passes through the filter/contoller. The communication can be observed and can be controlled by the filter/controller. The filter/controller is controlled by receiving commands from the "wiki access engine" and it does followings for each packet of the communication.

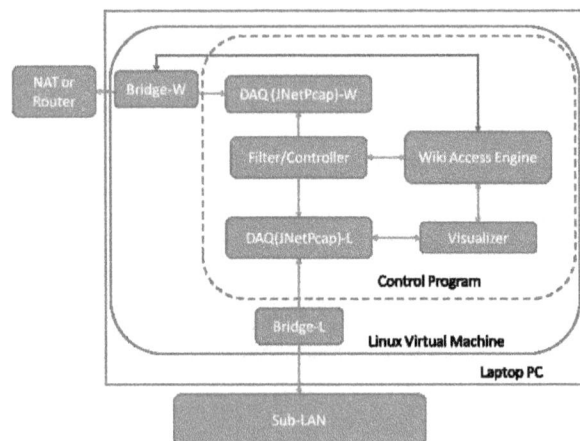

Figure 2. Structure of the remote security device

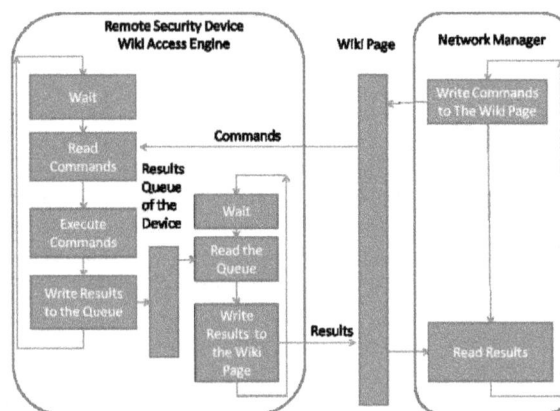

Figure 3. Control flow outline of this system.

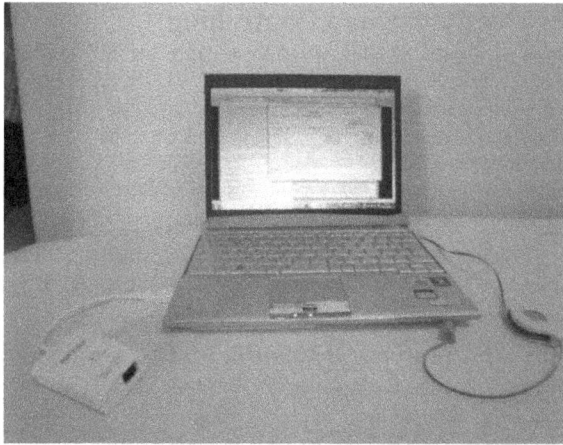

Figure 4. A picture of the remote security device.

- If the packet matches up to a "select pattern", pass through the packet (from one DAQ to another DAQ) and send the information of the frame of the packet to the wiki access engine with the status.

- If the packet matches up to a "drop pattern", do not pass through the packet and send the information of the frame of the packet to the wiki access engin with the status.

- If the packet matches up to a "forward pattern", replace the destination IP address and destination port with the IP address and port of a pseudo application of a pseudo host, and pass the replaced packet to another DAQ. Send the information of the frame of the original packet to the wiki acces engine with the status.

Iit also does the following.

- Sends a packet to one of the bridges from one of the DAQs. The sending packet is one of the following.

  ➢ The pseudo syn-ack packet to a syn packet of dropped packets.

  ➢ The pseudo DNS answer packet to a DNS query packet.

The wiki access engine sends information of frames, which includes the packet of selected, dropped or forwarded, to the wiki page of the web site. This means that the central manager can obtain the MAC address of the suspicious host and can identify the host from outside of the sub-LAN. The central manager can also control the traffic of the suspicious host directry from the wiki.

All observed communication at the DAQ of the sub-LAN side is visualized by the "visualizer"[2][7].

JNetPcap is used as the DAQ. JNetPcap is able to not only capture frames but also generate and send frames. Commands for the filter/controller are setted by the wiki access engine by executing commands which are written on the wiki page. The wiki access engine is implemented by converting the "Pukiwiki-Java Connector"[4][5][6].

Figure 3 shows the control flows of the wiki access. Figure 4 shows a picture of the sensor device.

3. USAGE EXAMPLE

This section shows an example of usage.

3.1 Booting and Setting

After the security device was connected to the sub-LAN, the program of the sensor device is booted by executing the command "trafficController" in the linux virtual machine of the sensor device. The window in figure 5 will be shown afterwards.

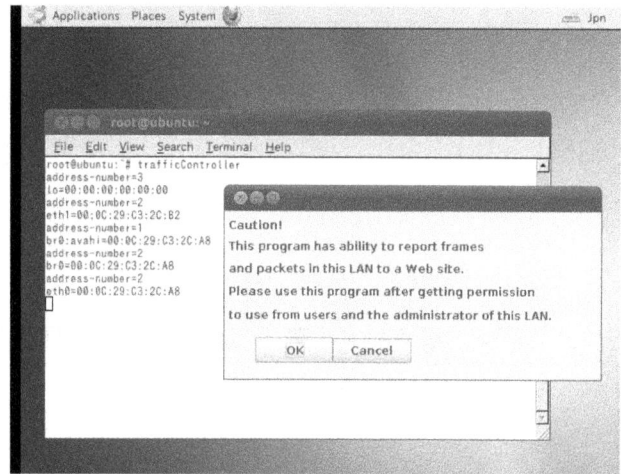

Figure 5. Notification window after booting the software.

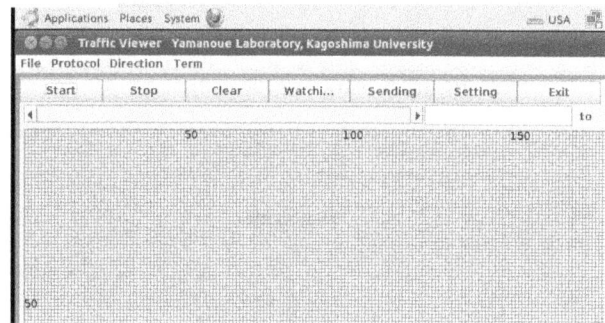

Figure 6. Traffic Viwer

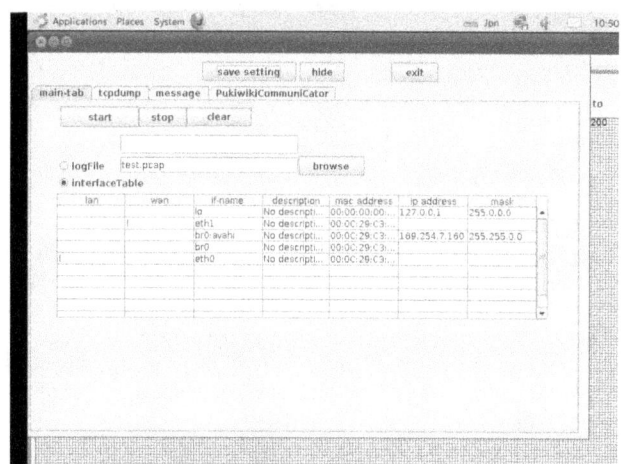

Figure 7. Network interface setting page.

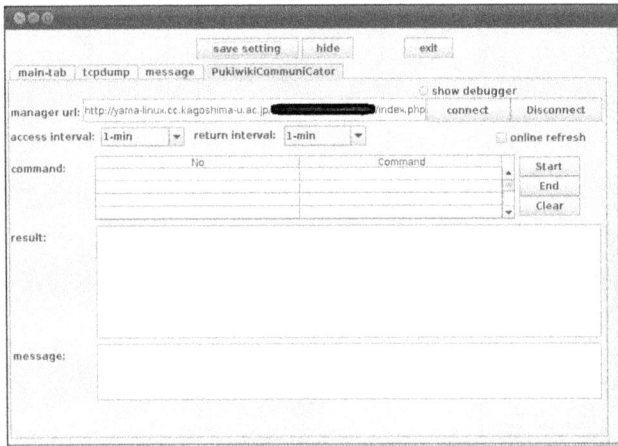

Figure 8. Wiki page setting page

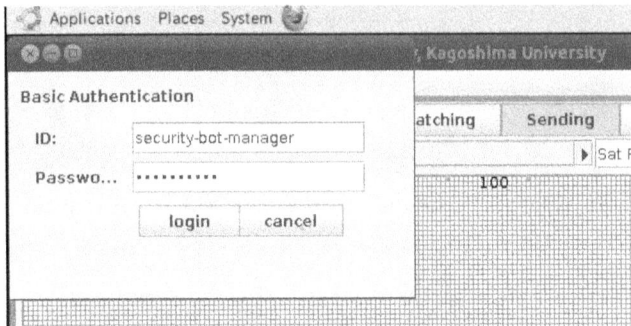

Figure 9. Authentification Dialog

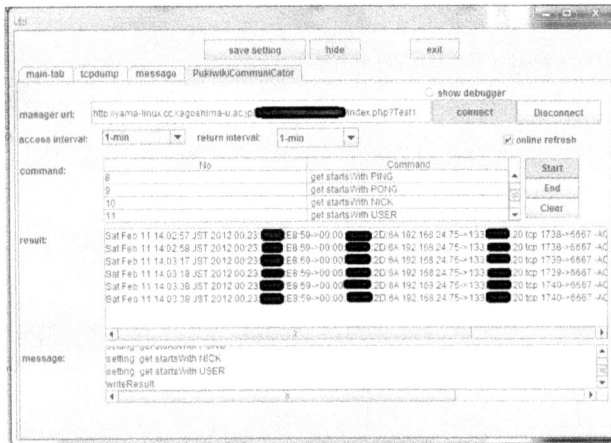

Figure 10. Commands and results at the sensor device.

After clicking the "OK" button of figure 5, the "Traffic Viewer" window(Figure 6) is shown. The setting window (Figure 7) is shown when the "Setting" button of the window of figure 6 is clicked. The user of this system chooses the network interface for the DAQ in the page of "main-tab" of the window. Figure 8 shows the setting page of the "PukiwikiCommunicator" tab of the setting window.

The url of the wiki page of the web site is written in the text field at the right hand side of the "manager url:" label. "Access interval" and "return interval" are also seton this page. Settings are saved when the "Save settings" button is clicked. The setting window is hidden when the "hide" button is clicked.

3.2 Monitoring and Controlling

Frames of communication are aquired from the DAQ after the "Start" button of the figure 6 is clicked. Accessing to the wiki page will be started after the "Sending" button in figure 6 is cliked. If authentification is required to access the page, the authentification dialog in figure 9 is shown. Reading and executing commands, and writing results on the wiki page are started when the "Watching" button in figure 6 is clicked.

When commands were read normally and information of filtered frames were aquired nomally, the commands and results in figure 10 are shown at the sensor device.

3.3 Commands and Results on the Wiki page

There are following commands for controlling the remote security device.

get ip=<IP address>

This command selects the IP packet, which has the <IP address> of the source address or the destination address, in the packets which are captured. One of the two DAQs passes through the packet to another DAQ, and writes the frame information of the packet to the wiki page.

get startsWith <String constant>

This command selects the IP packet, whose payload starts with the <String constant>, in the packets which are captured. One of the two DAQs passes through the packet to another DAQ and writes the frame information of the packet to the wiki page. For example, if "PING", "PONG", "NIC" and "USER" are replaced with the <String constant>, the communication(which may be IRC) can be detected.

lan2wan drop ip=<IP address>

This command drops the packet from the LAN-side if the source or the destination IP address matched up to the <IP address> and writes the frame information of the packet to the wiki page. The packet is not forward to the WAN-side.

wan2lan drop ip=<IP address>

This command drops the packet from the WAN-side if the source or the destination IP address matched up to the <IP address> and writes the frame information of the packet to the wiki page. The packet is not forward to the LAN-side.

lan2wan return-syn-ack ip=<IP address>

This command returns the syn-ack packet to the syn packet with the destination <IP address> from the LAN side, and it does not pass the packet to WAN side. This command can be used for capturing packets from the malicious bot without passing through the packets to the herder's site when the central manager knows the herder's IP address.

lan2wan forward ip=<IP address 1> to <IP address2>:<Port>

This command forwards the packet with the destination IP address of <IP address 1> from the LAN side to the application of the <Port> at the host of <IP address 2> and saves the source address and the destination port in the security device. When a packet whose destination address is the saved IP address comes from the WAN side NIC, the source IP address of the packet is replaced by <IP address 1> and the source port is replaced by the saved port.

This command is used for mimicing the herder's site behaviour by the central manager using the application like a telnet server.

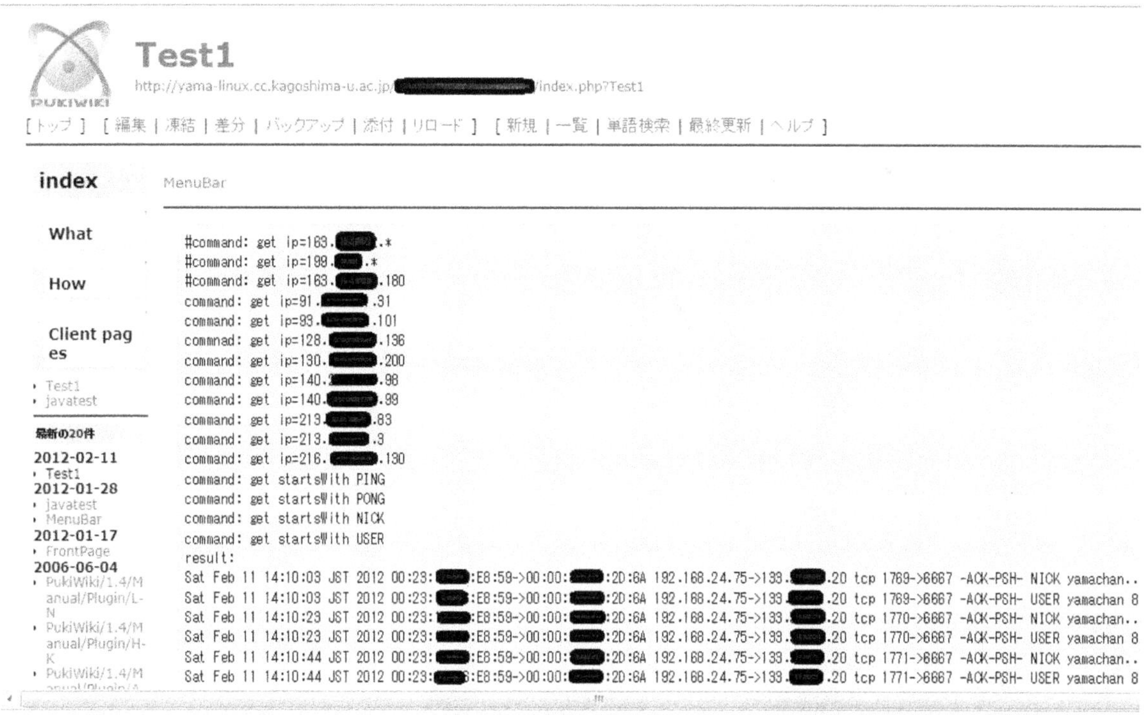

Figure 11. Commands and results on the wiki page.

lan2wan dns-intercept ip=<IP address 1> to <IP address 2>

This command intercepts the DNS query whose answer is <IP address 1> and returns the answer as <IP address 2>.

This command is also used for mimicing a herder's site behaviour by the central manager using the application lika a telnet server.

Figure 11 shows an example of commands and results of the monitoring system. Commands and results are written in the pre-formatted area of the wiki page. A command is written after the label "command:" in a line of the pre-formatted area. Results are written after the line with "result:" label. The label should be followed by the last command.

In this figure, the line which starts with the letter "#" means that this line is a comment. In this example, commands in this page direct the sensor device to capture IP packets with IP addresses of commands in the page and packets for IRC communication with their frames. Each line of the results shows the time, source MAC address, destination MAC address, source IP address, destination IP address, protocol of the IP packet, source port, destination port, flags of TCP if the IP packet is TCP and pay-load from the left side.

3.4 Responding to Infection

The following procedure shows an example of a response to a malicious bot infection after the central manager notices suspicious communication.

1. The central manager identifies the suspicious sub-LAN by using an IDS or a firewall.

2. The central manager asks the sub-manager of the sub-LAN to disconnect the NAT or router of the sub-LAN from the central network infrastructure.

3. The central manager writes commands on the wiki page to capture and filter out the suspicious packets. The manager configures the remote security device to connect the device to the wiki page.

4. The central manager sends the portable sensor device to the sub-manager after the sub-manager agrees with the need for identifying the suspicious host. The sub-manager connects the remote security device to the sub-LAN and starts it.

5. The remote security device reads the commands on the wiki page periodically. When the device detects suspicious packets, the device drop the packets and writes information of the packets with the MAC address of the suspicious host in the sub-LAN on the wiki page.

6. The central manager confirms the information of the suspicious packets on the wiki page, and if the manager judges the packets to be malicious, the central manager asks the sub-manager to disconnect the host from that sub-LAN. If the central manager feels more deep analysis on the traffic, the manager can prepare a telnet server and s/he can write commands for forwarding the packets from the suspicious host to the telnet server on the wiki page. When a suspicious packet is forwarded to the telnet server, the central manager can see the contents of the packet and can response to the packet on the telnet server. When the sub-manager cannot identify the suspicious host, the central manager writes the command, which transfers packets from the host to a notification web server, on the wiki page. The notification web server notifies the user of the suspicious host that the host is suspicious and asks the user of the host to call the sub-manager.

7. The sub-manager disconnects the suspicious host, which has the source MAC address of the suspicious host, from the sub-LAN and removes the viruses from the host.

4. RELATED RESEARCH

4.1 Security Monitoring System

We have developed a security monitoring system using a remote sensor device and wiki software similar to this system[8]. This monitoring system can also monitor traffic of the sub-LAN behind a NAT. It can not control the traffic. The security controlling system of this paper is developed by extending the security monitoring system.

4.2 Snort

Snort [10] is a common open source IDS. Snort has the function of automatically updating signatures. The manager can see the results from Snort at a web site using ACID and has the option to see remote Snort alerts by e-mail. It is not possible to change the settings of Snort at the NAT-protected sub-LAN from the outside. Snort cannot control the traffic, while our system can control the traffic.

4.3 Observing MAC address at the WAN side

Yamai et al. show a technique to observe MAC addresses of hosts in a NAT-protected sub-LAN from the outside [3]. This technique is effective when replacing the NAT with a new, less expensive device. In addition, their system does not need to add a new monitoring infrastructure such as a web server. Their system can effectively make use of the existing monitoring infrastructure. In contrast, our system needs a new web server for controlling the sensor device and monitoring the sub-LAN. However, our system does not need to replace the NAT and our system can observe the MAC address, even if another NAT is placed between the sub-LAN and the monitoring location.

4.4 Unix device with two NICs

Ishida et al. show a way to manage devices (target devices) with a networking function without SNMP [1]. Their technique uses a Unix device with two NICs. A target device is connected to one of the NICs of the Unix device and another NIC of the Unix device is used to manage the target device. The Unix device replies with management messages delegating the target device. Other messages for the target device pass through the Unix device to the target device. This technique can also use the existing management infrastructure effectively. Both their devices and our sensor device use a Unix machine with two NICs. Their technique is used for management and our system is used for monitoring, even though both share a similar mechanism. A combination of all these devices would be a more effective tool.

4.5 KASEYA and UNIFAS

The PC management system of KASEYA [9] and the wi-fi access point management system of Furuno Systems (UNIFAS) [11] consist of agent programs at the devices, such as PCs or wi-fi access points, and a web site to manage them, as in our security monitoring system. Their devices can also communicate with the web site over a NAT. However, they use a specialized web server, whereas our monitoring system uses a web site with common wiki software.

5. CONCLUDING REMARKS

A network security controlling system for capturing malicious bots is shown. This realizes an easy way of capturing malicious bots using a portable security device and a web site with common wiki software. This system can be used for easy and fast identification of a virus infected host behind a NAT from central network infrastructure of an organization.

This system can be regard as a bot system. If the system is used by malicious people, it can be malware because this system can get and control internal information from the outside. We are going to improve this system to remove this aspect of the system.

6. REFERENCES

[1] Ishida, M. Nakano, N. and Masuda, H. 2011. Implementation and Evaluation of Transeparent Proxy System of Addable Network Functions. *IOTS2011-02*, pp.1-7, (Tokyo, Japan, December 01-02, 2011) (In Japanese).

[2] Shinkawa, T., and Yamanoue, T. 2006. A Visualization of Network Traffic by a 2D Plane of IP address and Port. *IPSJ Technical Report*, 2006-DSM-043,pp.31-36 (In Japanese).

[3] Yamai, N. Murakami, R. Okayama, and K. Nakamura, M. 2011. A MAC-address Relaying NAT Router for Host Identificaton from Outside of Internal Networ, *IPSJ Journal*, Vol.52, No.3, pp.1348-1356 (In Japanese).

[4] Yamanoue, T. 2010. A Draw Plug-in for a Wiki Software, In *Proceedings of the Saint, 10th IEEE/IPSJ International Symposium on Applications and the Internet*(Seoul, Korea, July 19-23, 2010) pp.229-232. DOI= http://doi.ieeecomputersociety.org/10.1109/SAINT.2010.102.

[5] Yamanoue, T. Oda, K. and Shimozono, K. 2011. PukiWiki-Java Connector, a Simple API for Saving Data of Java Programs on a Wiki, In *Proceedings of the 7th international symposium on Wikis and Open Collaboration*(Mountain View, CA, USA, Octobar 3-5, 2011). DOI=http://doi.acm.org/10.1145/2038558.2038606.

[6] Yamanoue, T. Oda, K. and Shimozono, K. 2012. A Simple Application Program Interface for Saving Java Program Data on a Wiki , Advances in Software Engineering, Vol. 2012, Article ID 981783, Hindawi Publishing Corporation, 2012 . DOI=10.1155/2012/981783.

[7] Yamanoue, T. Oda, and K. Shimozono, K. 2012. A LAN Traffic Visualization System which can Show Changes of Traffic between Past and Now, *IPSJ Technical Report, 2012-IOT-16* (In Japanese).

[8] Yamanoue, T. Oda, and K. Shimozono, K. 2012. A Casual Network Security Using a Portable Sensor Device and Wiki Software, In *Proceedings of the 12th IEEE/IPSJ International Symposium on Applications and the Internet*.

[9] KASEYA: http://www.kaseya.com/

[10] SNORT: http://www.snort.org/

[11] UNIFAS: http://www.furunosystems.co.jp/product/unifas.html#unifas01

Building a Call Center in Two Days: How a World Class Support Center Responds to Crisis

Thom Mattauch
VCU helpIT Center Manager
901 Park Ave Room B-30
Richmond, VA 23284
804-827-0532

mattauchtj@vcu.edu

Rami Hatoum
VCU helpIT Center Supervisor
901 Park Ave Room B-30
Richmond, VA 23284
804-828-2471

rhatoum@vcu.edu

Hannah Pettit
VCU helpIT Center Supervisor
901 Park Ave Room B-30
Richmond, VA 23284
804-828-4727

pettith@vcu.edu

ABSTRACT

In the Fall of 2011, VCU was faced with a crisis. During routine monitoring of servers at the VCU Computing Center, suspicious activity was found on one of the servers. The server was taken offline and an investigation was put into motion, which determined that a hacker had access to the server for a period of 56 minutes. This server stored 10 files that contained information on 176,567 individuals, including VCU students, employees, and VCU Health System employees. Data items included social security numbers and either individual names or eID usernames; and, in some cases, date of birth, contact information and various programmatic or departmental information. The investigation indicated a low likelihood of the data actually being compromised. The university began preparing for a response to this incident. Letters were both emailed and sent via the US Postal Service to all 176,567 individuals. What was needed to support this mass mailing was a call center to respond to the incident. The VCU helpIT Center was contacted by VCU TS Administrators to create such a call center on Tuesday, November 8 at 4:55pm. The issue at hand was that the call center had to be online and operational by Friday, November 11th at 7:30am. This presentation will discuss what was done to create such a call center in such a short time frame, the lessons learned along the way, and how VCU turned this experience into an ongoing Emergency Communications Plan.

Categories and Subject Descriptors

K.6.1 [**Management of Computing and Information Systems**]:

Project and People Management — *staffing, training.*

General Terms

Management, Measurement, Documentation, Performance, Reliability, Experimentation

Keywords

Management, Support, Staffing, Training, Call Center, Crisis Communication, Security Incident

1. INSTITUTIONAL CHARACTERISTICS

Virginia Commonwealth University (known to the locals as VCU) sits in the heart of Richmond, Virginia, enrolling more than 32,000 students and employing close to 18,000 faculty and staff members. Since its establishment in 1968, VCU has expanded to include two downtown campuses in Richmond, as well as 6 satellite locations throughout the state of Virginia as well as Doha, Qatar. Offering 216 degree and certification programs through 13 separate schools and one college, VCU has been able to provide students with a full range of courses, from sculpture to microbiology, engineering to foreign language, business to philosophy, and many others.

The helpIT Center (Image 1) is the central computing support office for the VCU community. Supporting an estimated user base of over 120,000 people, the helpIT Center provides "over the phone" tech support in addition to two walk-up support locations on our main downtown campuses. It is currently staffed by eight full-time employees, as well as an additional 12-15 part-time students and hourly workers.

Image 1. Walk-up counter at the main office on the VCU Monroe Park Campus.

2. WHAT HAPPENED TO REQUIRE A NEW CALL CENTER ON SHORT NOTICE?

On October 18th 2011, an internet worm infected one of VCU's Banner servers. The next day hackers accessed that server to create accounts to access other servers within the Banner cluster. The hackers then accessed a separate server for 16 minutes. This server contained personal data on 176,567 individuals. The data that was accessed included personally identifiable information such as Social Security Numbers, birthdate, eID (the VCU Electronic ID), and contact information, in addition to various other programmatic or departmental information. On October 29th, University Computing Center technicians detected that two unauthorized accounts were created on the Banner server. On that same day a forensic investigation began on the Banner Servers and access to the Banner servers was revoked.

2.1 Notification to the VCU helpIT Center and the VCU Community

On November 8th at 4:55pm, the VCU helpIT Center management was notified of the security incident and was alerted that a response was forthcoming. This response would be directed in the form of a mass email, and follow up USPS mailing that would begin at 1:00am on Friday November 11th. Subsequently, the VCU helpIT Center would have to staff a new and separate call center to respond to this incident. Early projections put the call volume between 1700 and 9000 potential calls regarding this incident. However, this number was only based on hypothesis. In reality the call center had a user base of 176,567 users and there was the possibility that the call volume could be much greater than projected.

2.1 Scope of the Call Center

The Security Incident Response Team call center was to begin operations at 7:30 a.m. on November 11th. Technology Services administration mandated that the call center be manned Monday through Friday from 7:30 a.m. until 8:00 p.m., on Saturday from 10:00 a.m. until 6:00 p.m., and on Sundays from 12:00 p.m. until 8:00 p.m. for the first two weeks. After those two weeks, the schedule would be modified based on the metrics discovered over the previous two weeks. The call center was to stay open until March 2012 to give ample time for response by those impacted by the incident.

3. CHALLENGES

Many challenges presented themselves in the two days leading up to the opening of the incident line. First was staffing. Second was the scripting of the responses the staff could give to users. Third was the creation of the technology behind the scenes. Fourth was training. The final challenge was internal communication regarding the incident and the incident response.

3.1 Staffing

Given the sensitive nature of the incident, it was determined by VCU Technology Services administration that the Security Incident Response Line was to be staffed by classified full-time employees only. This presented a challenge to the management of the VCU helpIT Center, who was managing the new call center. Due to the fact that 8 full-time employees and 12 – 15 part-time employees staff the VCU helpIT Center, providing ample coverage for the Security Incident Response Line proved difficult. VCU helpIT Center management reached out to various other departments within Technology Services to request assistance. The VCU TS Telecommunications Team had experience with working a call center and offered up four of their employees to assist. Also, the VCU TS Information Security Office and the Administrative Support team offered up staff to augment the VCU helpIT staff.

3.2 Scripting

Critical to the success of the Security Incident Response Line was presenting a clear and consistent message to the users calling in. As a result, scripting was needed. Immediately following the first meeting regarding the Security Incident, VCU helpIT management began working on such scripts. One thing that the scripting needed to insure was that the statements the Security Incident Response Team gave to the end users would not incite them further. Phrases like "data breach," "data loss" and "compromised information" were to be avoided at all cost. Furthermore, the staff were to be instructed not to offer up suggestions such as "you should contact your bank immediately," since there was no forensic evidence that a data breach actually occurred. The investigation had concluded that the amount of time the hackers spent on the servers indicated a low likelihood of any data actually being accessed.

3.3 Creation of the Back-End Technology

To operate the call center, first we needed a call-in number. While it would have been simple to piggy back on the existing VCU helpIT Center phone number, that would not allow for a separation of duties between the classified full-time employees and the part-time employees. Furthermore, a distinction between the VCU helpIT Center and the Security Incident Response Line was necessary. Additionally, many of the affected users would be contacting the Security Incident Response Line from outside of the local calling area, thus a toll free number needed to be established.

Keep in mind as well that while the Security Incident Response Line was being manned, many of the same employees staffing that line also had to cover the normal VCU helpIT Call Center line. To accommodate this, the VCU TS Telecommunications Team programmed the phone system to allow the classified full-time employees to be listed as primary on the Security Incident Response Line and secondary on the VCU helpIT Center Call Center. What this allowed for was that if a call came in simultaneously on the Security Incident Response Line and the VCU helpIT Center Call Center lines, the Security Incident Line would ring on the classified full-time employee's phone, and the part-time employees would only receive the VCU helpIT Center calls. If all of the part-time employees were on calls, and another call came into the VCU helpIT Center and a classified full-time employee was available, then the call would be directed to the full-time employee.

The next step in the back-end technology implementation was to create a view for the heads-up displays at each agent's workstation. The VCU helpIT Center has a monitor in each cube to show current call statistics at the call center. A new view to display both the VCU helpIT Center statistics as well as the Security Incident Response Line statistics was needed.

3.4 Training

Once the scripting was created, staffing was established and the back-end technology was ready, it was time to train the staff that would be answering the phones. Because many of the staff that would be augmenting the VCU helpIT Center staff had never worked in a call center environment, the VCU helpIT Center management developed a "Call Center 101" crash course. This training would provide the new staff with a quick overview on how to answer the phone and how to distinguish between calls coming into their local phones vs. calls coming into the Security Incident Response Line. Next, training was needed to instruct the employees on how to use the script that was created and the need to stick to the script.

3.5 Internal Communications

Because this was a completely new call center and there were only two days to create it, a methodology for internal communications needed to be developed. VCU uses Blackboard as a collaboration tool. As a result, a Blackboard organization was created for the Security Incident Response Team. This would house the documentation for the team, such as the scripting documents, the staffing schedule, and any other pertinent documents. It would also allow discussion boards to be created to foster ongoing communications regarding lessons learned as they arose. Furthermore, given the size of the new staff for the Security Incident Response Line, an email list was created for quick and easy communication to all staff members.

4. GONE LIVE!

On November 11, 2011, an email was sent out to the 176,567 users impacted by the security incident. At 7:30 a.m. that morning, the Security Incident Response Line was live and ready to answer questions.

4.1 The Email

Below is a copy of the email that was sent out to the individuals impacted by the security incident. It was also sent out via registered mail to the same user base.

*I am writing to inform you of a security incident that resulted in unauthorized access to a Virginia Commonwealth University computer server containing files with personal information on current and former VCU and VCU Health System faculty, staff, students and affiliates. **We believe the likelihood is very low that any personal data on the individuals in the files was compromised, but it is impossible to be completely certain**, so we are notifying all involved via email and first-class mail.*

On October 24, routine monitoring of servers supporting a VCU system uncovered suspicious files on one of the devices. The server was taken offline and a forensic investigation was launched to identify what unauthorized activities had taken place and the vulnerabilities that led to the compromise. The vulnerabilities have been corrected, and it has been determined that this server contained no personal data.

Five days later, VCU's continuing investigation revealed two unauthorized accounts had been created on a second server, which also was taken offline. Subsequent analysis showed the intruders had compromised this device through the first server. The intruders were on the server for a short period of time and appeared to do nothing other than create the two accounts.

Files on this second server contained data on 176,567 individuals, which included your information. Data items included your name or eID, Social Security Number and, in some cases, date of birth, contact information, and various programmatic or departmental information.

*Our investigation was unable to determine with 100 percent certainty that the intruders did not access or copy the files in question. **We believe the likelihood that they did is very low.** However, because this data was potentially exposed, we are proactively informing you of this event and subsequent actions you may wish to take to monitor your personal information. The following website contains more detailed information about this incident, as well as resources on how to monitor your personal information, including credit monitoring or acquiring identity protection services: http://go.vcu.edu/securityincidentresponse .*

VCU continues its investigation and is working with local and federal law enforcement agencies. If you have any questions or concerns, please contact the Security Incident Information Center we have established to handle your inquiries: (855) 886-2931 or responseteam@vcu.edu. Over the next two weeks, this Center will be staffed from Monday to Friday 7:30 am – 8:00 pm, Saturday from 10:00 am – 6:00 pm and Sunday from 12:00 pm – 8:00 pm to answer your questions.

VCU is reviewing its information technology security measures and procedures and will make improvements to prevent this type of incident from happening again. We regret this incident, and I apologize for any inconvenience or worry this may have caused you.

Sincerely,

Mark D. Willis
Chief Information Officer

4.2 Customer Response

Over the course of the first two weeks, the Security Incident Response Line received over 1000 calls. In week one, there were 783 calls answered by the Security Incident Response team. The average call time for those calls was 4 minutes and 16 seconds. The Security Incident Response Line had a call answer rate of 92%. The VCU helpIT Call Center Line had a call answer rate of 91%. In week two, there were 258 calls answered by the Security Incident Response Team. The average call time for those calls was 3 minutes and 57 seconds. The Security Incident Response Line had a call answer rate of 92%. The VCU helpIT Center Call Center Line had a call answer rate of 97%. Week two was a short week due to the Thanksgiving holiday, which resulted in the lower call volume.

4.2.1 Customer Issues Raised

Given the nature of the security incident and the lead-time given to create a response team, there were many lessons learned in the early stages of the Security Incident Response. First, many customers complained that VCU was not offering Identity Theft Insurance. While this was true at the start, it was something that was quickly rectified. By the time the Security Incident Response Line was closed on the first day, Identity Theft Insurance became an option. This allowed for a smoother transaction on the phone with users, for when they called in and asked about it, it was now something the Security Incident Response Team could offer. Second, many people complained about their personal information still being stored by VCU. For many, their affiliation with VCU had ended years ago, yet their personal information was still being stored on the Banner Servers. As a result of these complaints, an audit of all systems began to determine what data should be retained and what data could be purged from the system. This is an ongoing project.

4.3 Other Communications

In addition to the Security Incident Response Line being established, and the email and letters that were sent to the VCU Community, there were other communication methods that VCU Technology Services employed to address the Security Incident. First, an email account was created to allow people to email their questions and concerns into the staff. This email account was monitored during normal business hours to provide a prompt response to those who chose to email their questions. Also, a website was created to openly address questions and concerns in a more proactive way (Image 2). This website contained information about the incident, commonly asked questions, and a video of the VCU CIO discussing the incident. As a result of this communications effort, information was provided in a timely manner, which led to the reduction of calls that could have come into the Security Incident Response Line.

5. LESSONS LEARNED AND ONGOING CRISIS COMMUNICATION PLAN

As a result of the security incident, VCU underwent a university-wide security policy and system assessment. From that, many subcommittees were created to address various systematic issues. It was also apparent from this incident that VCU needs to have a standing crisis response plan. As such, there is a need for prompt communications with the user base. The Crisis Communications Team developed a plan that placed every system at the university in a matrix. The matrix quantifies the urgency and impact that each system has in the event that it is unavailable or compromised. From this matrix, a calculation of the urgency each system has was created which displays the impact it has on the users of the system if it is taken offline. Action plans were created to determine what action to take when those systems are offline and or compromised. The action taken ranges from a simple blog post which alerts the community that a system is experiencing issues, all the way up to a broadcast email and/or text message being sent out to alert the user base of a crisis. Furthermore, the plan establishes a timeline for follow up communication for each type of crisis.

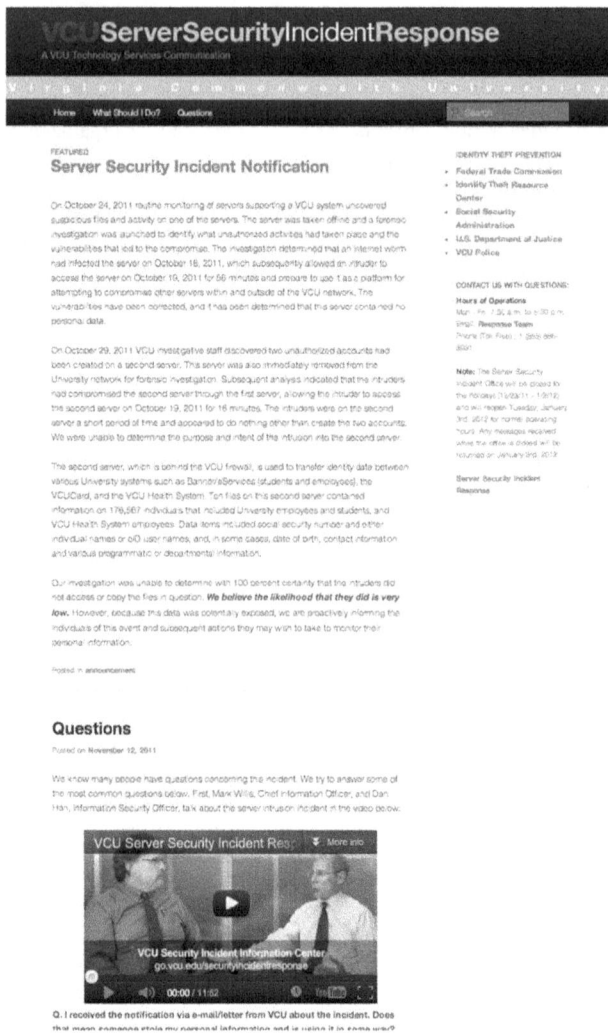

Image 2. Screenshot of the VCU Server Security Incident Response Webpage

Making the SIGUCCS Experience Last Year-Long: How a Regional Conference Became a Local Chapter

Lisa Brown
University of Rochester
Rush Rhees Library
Rochester, NY 14627
1 585-275-9162

lisa.brown@rochester.edu

Mat Felthousen
University of Rochester
Lower Hoyt Hall
Rochester, NY 14627
1 585-275-9015

mat.felthousen@rochester.edu

ABSTRACT

In 1997, as a result of conversations that started during a SIGUCCS conference, several NY state schools formed a regional conference called NYCHES (New York Computing in Higher Education Symposium). SIGUCCS attendees from these schools wanted to continue the 'SIGUCCS dialogs' throughout the year, so NYCHES has met a few times a year since 1997, with participation increasing to include dozens of schools across central and western NY state.

Schools would volunteer to host the day-long meeting, and provide food for the attendees. There was no membership fee to be involved in NYCHES, so costs to attendees were minimized to travel expenses. Cost containment, particularly in the face of constricting travel budgets for many schools, made a regional conference an attractive option for schools that could not afford to send many people to national conferences. Even so, based on their experiences in NYCHES many members became active SIGUCCS attendees, and conversations started during SIGUCCS would continue on in NYCHES meetings through the year.

On March 19 2012, NYCHES became the first local chapter for SIGUCCS. SIG Chapters, and their membership, receive considerable benefits from the Association of Computing Machinery (ACM) including website hosting, membership tools, mailing list hosting, recruitment tools, ACM email addresses, subscriptions to ACM publications, and access to the ACM Distinguished Speakers Program. Chapter members are not required to pay for membership, unless they wish to serve on the Board of the Chapter, so despite the substantial benefits, costs to their respective institutions are still minimized.

This paper will discuss how NYCHES was successful as a regional conference, and how this format could be duplicated in other parts of the country. It will also discuss how the members of a regional conference would benefit from a formal association with both ACM and SIGUCCS.

Categories and Subject Descriptors

K.3.1 [Computers and Education]: Computer Uses in Education

K.6.1 [Management of Computing and Information Systems]: Project and People Management

K.7.2 [The Computing Profession]: Organizations

General Terms

Management, Standardization

Keywords

Regional conference, Helpdesk

1. INTRODUCTION

On March 19 2012 the first local chapter of SIGUCCS, called 'NYCHES Chapter of ACM SIGUCCS', was established, with a Board comprised of Lisa Brown from the University of Rochester (Chair), Laurie Fox from SUNY Geneseo (Vice Chair), and Mike Allington from St. John Fisher College (Secretary/Treasurer).

The origin of this chapter can be traced back more than 15 years to a SIGUCCS conference, when several attendees discussed how to continue the SIGUCCS experience and networking opportunities throughout the year. From that conversation, a regional group called NYCHES- New York Computing in Higher Education Symposium- was formed. NYCHES representatives have typically been from four-year higher education institutions in western and central New York.

NYCHES has met three to four times a year since 1997, with a school hosting a day-long meeting based on topics proposed in advance by attendees. There are no fees for membership. Schools would volunteer to host the meeting, including providing food, so that the responsibility and costs involved in the meeting would be minimized and equitably distributed. The meetings usually concluded with a tour of the host's facilities so that each school has an opportunity to showcase their accomplishments. NYCHES participants have included dozens of institutions and more than a hundred participants, many of whom became active in SIGUCCS as a result of NYCHES.

In addition to SIGUCCS, NYCHES participants have also attended conferences such as EDUCAUSE, NERCOMP (a regional extension of EDUCAUSE), ResNet, LabMan, Infocomm, and HDI. NYCHES meetings benefitted from this wide range of experiences as the information would be shared back to the group. A frequent comment at NYCHES meetings over the years was that in terms of opportunities to network with peers, SIGUCCS is a unique resource.

It was a logical progression therefore for NYCHES to become a Local Chapter for SIGUCCS. The sole requirements for establishing a chapter are to have three Board members who are members of both ACM and SIGUCCS, and to have ten members who would be willing to carry out the mission of the chapter. Nearly 40 NYCHES members voted unanimously to establish a SIGUCCS Chapter.

Chapter members are not required to pay for membership, unless they wish to serve on the Board of the Chapter. Board members must be members of both SIGUCCS and ACM. Despite the substantial benefits of being associated with both ACM and SIGUCCS, costs to chapter members and their respective institutions are still minimized. SIG Chapters, and their members, receive considerable benefits from the Association of Computing Machinery (ACM) including website hosting, membership tools, listserv hosting, membership recruitment tools, '@acm.org' email addresses, subscriptions to ACM publications, and access to the ACM Distinguished Speakers Program.

2. WHAT / WHO IS NYCHES?

NYCHES was formally established in 1997 based on efforts of IT professionals from Syracuse University and Cornell University. These two individuals made contact with IT professionals from four other schools to pull together the first ever meeting. That small group decided that a forum was needed to provide an ongoing idea exchange. More information about the early NYCHES years can be found in the 1999 SIGUCCS conference proceedings.[1]

Much has changed since 1999. People have changed jobs and left the group, but word about the group has spread. We now have participation from over twenty schools in the central and western NY region and over eighty active members subscribed to our listserv.

We meet annually at least twice a year at participating host schools and model our meetings around the SIGUCCS experience. Sometimes a host school will present about a new technology that they are in the process of implementing and discussion/questions will follow. Other times, the topic will be an open forum for discussion of a specific topic so participants can get an understanding of how that service is being provided at other schools. In addition, we always leave time for a round robin of quick questions that have recently come up at the schools.

3. WHAT / WHO IS ACM?

The Association of Computing Machinery (ACM) is the largest educational and scientific computing society in the world, with more than 96,000 members. ACM publishes more than 40 publications, organizes more than 150 conferences annually, and has 34 Special Interest Groups, including SIGUCCS. ACM is also home of the premier Digital Library[2] for the computing industry, which includes 50+ years of content.

Individuals can become members of ACM for $99/$198 yearly, with lifetime memberships being available. Membership benefits include:

- Email digests, 50+ journals
- Learning Center, aimed at lifelong learning
  - 4500+ online courses
  - Online books (Safari ® and Books24x7®)
- ACM Career & Job Center
- Email forwarding/filtering (you get an @acm.org mailing address)

- Discounts, such as on insurance, shopping, subscriptions, car rental, credit cards
- Access to ACM Digital Library, at the higher price level

4. WHAT / WHO IS SIGUCCS

SIGUCCS is the Special Interest Group on University and College Computing Services. With a membership of several hundred people, SIGUCCS' content includes the annual conference, webinars, listservs, Facebook, and LinkedIn sites.

For more information on SIGUCCS, please visit http://www.siguccs.org/

5. SIGUCCS MEMBERSHIP

For $25 per year SIGUCCS members receive the following benefits:

- Access to ACM Digital Library for SIGUCCS content
- Access to a members-only listserv and webinars
- Discounted registration fees for conference ($110 for the combined conference this year)

For more information on SIGUCCS membership, please visit http://www.siguccs.org/involve/join.html

6. BENEFITS OF BEING A LOCAL CHAPTER OF SIGUCCS

Local chapters of ACM are entitled to a number of administrative tools, including the management of membership rosters and an ACM-hosted website. Additionally, events offered by the chapter can be posted on the ACM Activities calendar[3] to broaden the exposure of the organization.

If your local chapter has less than ten members, ACM will help recruit members from your area. They can also provide ACM promotional materials[4] for chapter events and offer access to a list of distinguished speakers[5] for your events with over 250 lectures from nearly 100 different speakers.

For more information on Special Interest Group Chapters, please visit http://www.acm.org/chapters/sig

7. INDIVIDUAL BENEFITS OF CHAPTER MEMBERSHIP

Aside from the benefits a chapter enjoys from being associated with ACM, individuals who are members of a chapter receive:

- A complimentary three-month electronic subscription to ACM's publication *Communications of the ACM*
- Eligible for an "acm.org" email forwarding address with Google Postini filtering
- E-Newsletters: *TechNews* 3 times weekly, *CareerNews* bi-monthly, *MemberNet* monthly

8. FORMING A LOCAL CHAPTER

Becoming a local chapter is easy. A group needs ten members and a Board comprised of a Chair, Vice Chair, and a Secretary / Treasurer. The three Board members must hold membership in

---

[1] http://dl.acm.org/citation.cfm?id=337125&dl=ACM&coll=DL& CFID=102793126&CFTOKEN=11014398

[2] http://dl.acm.org/dl.cfm

[3] http://campus.acm.org/public/chapters_conf_cal/index.cfm

[4] http://campus.acm.org/public/profqj/promotional_materials.cfm

[5] http://www.dsp.acm.org/

both ACM and SIGUCCS. Every year the chapter must submit an annual report consisting of information about meetings, as well as a financial report (if necessary).

For NYCHES, we already had over 10 members participating on a regular basis at our meetings. We also had eight people willing to participate as board members, so we scheduled a vote. We do not collect dues or have any financial standing, so an annual report will simply be a recounting of our meetings and planning for the future.

9. OUR DECISION
In November of 2011, we decided to bring information on being a local chapter to the group and make a decision. There were various factors that were weighed when we made our decision.

PROS
Since NYCHES grew out of the SIGUCCS conference and meetings are modeled after SIGUCCS, a relationship with both ACM and SIGUCCS would be a good thing. It would provide a level of professional association to the group, and it would bring broader exposure to the group.

Chapters are offered a number of services through ACM, including a listserv and website. While NYCHES had always been fortunate to have a stable listserv presence through one of the participating schools, we had not been so lucky with a website presence. The opportunity to have both of these hosted in one location that allowed shared maintenance was a bonus.

Being affiliated with both ACM and SIGUCCS offers professional development opportunities beyond what was possible with remaining a separate regional conference, in terms of networking with a broader audience. This networking would also benefit SIGUCCS with recruitment of attendees for the annual conference.

Finally, we considered the many ACM and SIGUCCS membership benefits, including access to the Digital Library.

CONS
One of the drawbacks of becoming a local chapter was a fear of losing our branding. We had been NYCHES for so long that we had hoped to keep this name recognition. This ended up not being an issue as we learned after our vote that we were able to keep NYCHES in our chapter name.

A second potential drawback is the expenses for the three board members. Each is required to have individual membership in both the ACM and SIGUCCS organizations. For most people willing to participate on the board, this was not an issue.

Third, expansion of membership may make it more difficult to identify host locations for meetings, or force us to choose central locations for the main meetings.

Despite these concerns, NYCHES voted unanimously in favor of becoming a Local Chapter.

10. FUTURE PLANS
At our first official chapter meeting in April 2012, we talked about how to make the best use of our new organization.

Volunteers from various schools stepped up to take charge of different identified gaps, specifically membership management, hosting challenges, and our website. We also talked about continuing to meet twice annually (spring and fall) for general topics, but added that we should identify more specific topics to engage smaller groups between meetings.

General, large group meetings would consist of NYCHES business, as well as broad topic discussions. Smaller meetings would focus on a specific topic, possibly things that drew a lot of discussion or interest during a general meeting, such as desktop virtualization, as was the case from our inaugural meeting as a chapter. Future small meetings may also address areas like learning management systems, audio/visual support, and staff/team management issues.

We have also received interest from a number of schools about hosting future events, while identifying problems that have come up in organizing past meetings. Previous hosts are planning to put together a checklist for future hosts so that we can help overcome these issues.

The group also discussed vendor support and decided that they did not want to lose touch with the spirit of NYCHES. They did however indicate that they wanted individuals from the group to share opportunities with the rest of the chapter for meeting with vendors of specific technologies, so that multiple schools could attend.

Membership was discussed, and we determined that anyone from the NY region willing to travel to our host location should be allowed to attend. We will continue to recruit members from area schools and encourage them to join us. We will also encourage hosting in all locales, with the expectation that the host school provides information on low-cost accommodations for those traveling long distances.

11. CONCLUSION
As travel and conference budgets shrink due to economic pressures, regional conferences are very cost-effective ways to achieve some of the benefits of attending the SIGUCCS conference. The time commitment is minimal- just a day in most cases- and the travel costs are typically limited to mileage reimbursements. In exchange, chapter members develop the same types of long-lasting connections with peers at other institutions that they do at SIGUCCS, and the conversations can continue throughout the year.

ACM and SIGUCCS both benefit from increased awareness and potential increases in membership, as institutions who could not otherwise afford to send personnel to the annual SIGUCCS conference will still learn from the experiences shared by other chapter members.

For more information on NYCHES ACM SIGUCCS, please visit http://nyches.acm.org/

What Is It With These Kids? – A Generational Insight into Student Workers and Customers

Sean L McLane
Information Technology at Purdue
Purdue University
150 N. University Street
West Lafayette, IN 47907
1-765-494-1597
mclane@purdue.edu

ABSTRACT

While supporting the advancement of technology in the educational environment is a common concern these days, we also need to keep in mind the targets of this technology. They are the Millennial Generation (those born between 1982 and 1997[1], approximately), a body of people who are as numerous as the Baby Boomers from two generations previous. They have been brought up in a world of ubiquitous technology and instantaneous information. How do their expectations as employees and customers differ from those who are running the show? Is their work ethic compatible with established norms? How difficult will it be to communicate with them?

This paper looks at all these questions and more, to address challenges with Millennial Generation students using educational information technology. Attitudes and behaviors have been studied to produce an image of the current student generation, which lets us see how we can best serve them.

Categories and Subject Descriptors

K.4.2 [Computers and Society]: Social Issues – *employment*

K.6.1 [Management of Computing and Information Systems]: Project and People management – *staffing, training*

General Terms

Management, Human Factors

Keywords

Generations, Millennials, Digital Natives

1. INTRODUCTION

One of the challenges faced in the university environment is addressing the difference in attitudes between members of other generations. Often, a conflict between the work styles of two generations is seen as an "attitude problem", or a "poor work ethic". Is there a way to get the student workers to fall in line with the "right way" to do their jobs? What is the best way to motivate them? Working to understand and appreciate these differences can enhance their value as employees.

2. WHO ARE THE MILLENIALS?

The Millennial Generation (also known as Generation Y, Echo Boomers, or 24/7s) were born between 1982 and 1995. Unlike the previous generation of latchkey kids, the Millennials were coddled and protected. They experienced the greatest advancements in child-protection technology ever. They were rewarded for participating, and given trophies for finishing in eighth place. They were told that they could do anything, and they believe it. As a result, they are a generation of achievers that doesn't know the meaning of failure.

The participatory encouragement has given them a strong collaborative mind set. They function well as a team, and embrace group projects. They have learned from an early age how to think outside the box and come up with creative solutions to their problems.

The Millennials do not just embrace diversity, they celebrate it. They have grown up in a world where they can see the other side of the planet, and have had the events from around the world streamed at them continuously. To the Millennial, someone from another country is just a fellow resident of Earth.

3. TECHNOLOGY

The Millennial Generation cannot be evaluated without taking technology into account. In their lifetimes, the world has transformed from analog to digital. Vinyl records, audio cassettes, and video tapes have all disappeared to be replaced with CDs, DVDs, and MP3s. The World Wide Web sprang into being. The telephone became portable, then became ubiquitous, then became smart. Their phones let them access the Internet, send text messages, listen to music, watch movies, get directions via GPS, and on rare occasion, make phone calls.

The Internet is a key part of the life of a Millennial. They keep up on email, continuously exchange text messages, follow their favorite stars on Twitter, and religiously maintain their Facebook statuses. When they want to find out about something, they only have to check on the Web with their smart phone. Many Millennials do not understand why Wikipedia is not a good source of information for a report. Information is available at the touch of a finger, so why not use it?

4. REWARDS

Previous generations recognized different means of being rewarded. The Baby Boomers (1946-1964) valued public recognition from their superiors, and token rewards, such as plaques and certificates. Generation X (1965-1981) does not care as much for public praise. They would rather get extra time off or a salary increase. What motivates the Millenial? They not only want praise, but have come to expect it. Not only do they wish to be praised for doing well, but the way they have been raised has made them expect and appreciate praise for simply doing their job adequately.

The Millennials do expect to work, and when they are given more meaningful work to do, they see that as a form of reward. They are eager to please their superiors, and want to contribute to the group success.

Millennials also value communication of all kinds. Email updates, voice mail progress reports, or simple face time tells them that their efforts are being monitored and appreciated.

5. WORK ETHIC

The way Millennials view the work place is different than their elders, and this can be misconstrued as a poor work ethic. Baby Boomers and Generation X supervisors need to realize this difference. They can try to force the Millennials to conform to their standards, but this will produce unhappy employees, and when unhappy, the Millennial will quickly leave to find other work. Alternately, supervisors can take into account different attitudes, and make adjustments to policies where they do not significantly impact job performance.

What does the Millennial employee want from work? In addition to a pay check, they want to have flexibility in scheduling, so they can fit their many other activities in among their work hours. They want a friendly, encouraging work environment. They want ethical leaders and mentors. They want to be told what expectations are being held for them, so that those expectations can be met and exceeded.

5.1 Getting the Job Done

It would be easy to paint Millennials as a slackesr who can't focus on the tasks in front of them. This is far from the truth, however. Millennials do want to work, and they want to be challenged by their work. They want to learn new skills and apply them to the job. Give them this challenge and let them make a difference, and their loyalty will be earned.

5.2 Attention Span and Working Long Shifts

A common perception of the typical Millennial is that he or she does not have a long attention span and has trouble staying focused on a single task. Actually, Millennials tend to multi-task, doing several things at once. If they are given the opportunity, they will do a job in addition to other task.

Some Millennials are quite eager to work long shifts as well. In Spring 2011, Purdue University changed its overtime policy such that it was no longer overtime to work more than 8 hours in a day. Some student workers for ITaP took this opportunity to work 10 hours in a day, with a couple opting to work as many as 13. In short, if they have work to do, Millennials will do the job.

5.3 Interaction with Each Other

Millennials are excellent at interrelations with their peers. Their minds are geared toward group work, and they will put needs of their work group first. To a Millennial, group success is personal success. Since their peers use the same means of communication, a Millennial group will get a lot of work done with very little direct face time. Because they are expert at that communication, the work does not suffer, and deadlines are met.

5.4 Interaction with Other Generations

Working with older coworkers and supervisors poses a challenge for Millennials. They may find lengthy face-to-face meetings to be boring, particularly if they are expected to refrain from consulting their smart phones. Focusing on just one task is a drudge for the Millennial. Compromise should be sought, with some of the communication done less by meetings, and more by electronic means. Members of Generation X can help facilitate this, as their technological knowhow is closer to the Millennials than any other older Generation.

6. COMMUNICATION

Communication is a strength of the Millennial generation. Text messages, email, voice mail, and social networking all garner quick responses. In fact, the Millennial may become impatient if they do not receive an instantaneous response to a message they have sent. Their communications will be polite, and upbeat.

When communicating with a Millennial, be respectful, and don't talk down to them. They know they are intelligent, and wish to be seen as intellectual peers. While they may not know as much as their elders, they are eager to learn.

Use direct speech, and positive action verbs when talking. Millennials are doers, and connect with that type of speech. Using language that portrays vivid imagery also works well. Talking to a group of Millennials is more productive than each in turn, as they will interact and build knowledge off each other.

7. MILLENNIAL CUSTOMERS

What about your customers of the Millennial generation? Interacting with them is a necessity, and know how best to do so will enhance the customer service they receive.

The points mentioned above related to communication apply here as well. The customers want rapid response, and they want as many details as possible. Talking to them via text or electronic forums is just as good as communicating on the phone. Help centers should consider using electronic means of communication with their customers. Self-help pages should also be kept up to date. Obsolete information will be noticed by the tech-savvy Millennial generation, though they may make a suggestion to correct the error.

Millennials want to be respected, and they don't want to spend a lot of time getting things fixed. They have a dozen things they want to do, and waiting for tech support is not high on the list.

8. WHO IS NEXT

The Millennial generation has been in college for some time now, and the next generation is already waiting in the wings. Who will be the next ones, and how can we prepare for them?

Known as Generation Z, Generation I, or Digital Natives, this next generation has had many of the same influences as the Millennials, but to a greater degree. Their parents have been even more protective, and have pushed them to achieve more and more. This next generation is likely to be more self-entitled, and will expect direct response to their needs.

There are a lot of factors that have yet to be determined about this generation, though. One thing is certain: they are even more immersed in information technology than any other group. They have never known a world without the Web. Many learned how to text as toddlers, and have their own cell phones by the time they are in elementary school. Using the Internet is the de facto means of answering a question.

Whatever differences this next generation has, it's best to recognize them early, and find a way to work that is compatible with both the older generations and the newer.

9. ACKNOWLEDGMENTS

I wish to thank Professor Beverly Davis for introducing me to the concept of generational studies and helping me learn all the ways they can be applied.

10. REFERENCES

[1] Peters, Marilee. 2008. Generation Y: Challenging Employers to Provide Balance. *Family Connections.* 12, 2 (Summer, 2008)

[2] Generational Differences Chart. *Everett Community College.* Retrieved from: http://www.everettcc.edu/uploadedfiles/Faculty_Staff/TLC/Bridges_Across_Generations_Teaching_Lab/GenerationalDifferencesChart.pdf

[3] Strauss, W., Howe, N. (2007). *Millennials Go to College: Strategies for a New Generation on Campus.* Washington, DC. American Association of College Registrars

[4] Hawkins, P., Schmidt, L. (2008). GenZ: Digital Natives. *Essential Kids.* Retrieved from: http://www.essentialkids.com.au/entertaining-kids/games-and-technology/gen-z-digital-natives-20080716-3g5p.html?page=-1

Building an Effective Software Deployment Process

John B. Tyndall
Information Technology Services
The Pennsylvania State University
University Park, PA 16802
(814) 865-2886
jbt8@psu.edu

ABSTRACT

Software defines the functionality and availability of computer systems, particularly those in higher education. Often, though, installing the appropriate applications in a multi-platform environment can be time-consuming, unorganized, and altogether onerous. A common approach to this problem is to create a thick image with all of the software pre-installed; especially with computer labs, however, these images can quickly become large and difficult to maintain and update.

This paper presents best practices for building a phased-installation software deployment paradigm. When combined with thin imaging techniques, software installations on both academic and administrative machines become more organized, flexible, and discreet. While examples are implemented using IBM Tivoli Endpoint Manager and Active Directory/Group Policy, IT professionals can easily extend these core concepts into their own environments regardless of infrastructure.

Categories and Subject Descriptors

C.5.3 [**Computer System Implementation**]: Microcomputers—*personal computers, portable devices, workstations*; D.0 [**Software**]: General

General Terms

Design, Documentation, Performance, Standardization, Theory

Keywords

baseline, best practice, installation, process, software, software deployment, thin imaging

1. INTRODUCTION

The Pennsylvania State University is a public research institution with 19 campus locations in addition to University

Park, as well as several special-mission campuses throughout the state. While Information Technology Services (ITS) provides core technology, IT is mainly decentralized. As a result, each campus and college has its own IT staff and infrastructure and may or may not utilize all of the University's recommended or offered services.

Provisioning computers in these types of environments can be complex since there are staff, faculty, research, student lab, and other types of computers. Many times applications are pre-installed onto images; however, maintaining these is cumbersome as well. Often the classification of a machine is simply the kind of software that is installed; a deployment-based model can theoretically allow systems administrators to use one minimal image for all machines and then deploy bundles of applications based on the type of machine, thereby making the deployment process easier to maintain, update, and execute.

2. IMAGING CONCEPTS

Disk imaging is a popular industry-standard method used by systems administrators to clone a system's hard drive, i.e., take an *image* of it, and then deploy that image to another system. Imaging is useful for various computing scenarios, such as provisioning new computers with a standard operating system, software suite, and configuration; performing a comprehensive backup of the exact state of a machine; upgrading hard drives to larger disks without re-installing everything; recovering from system failures; and more.

2.1 Thick Image

A *thick image* is a disk image that contains all of the anticipated applications, drivers, files, and configurations. Traditionally, a systems administrator builds a reference machine, installing the operating system, drivers, software, updates, etc., and making any other changes. This "golden image" can then be cloned to other computers in the organization. The primary advantage of a thick image is guaranteed consistency: subsequent machines will be built exactly as constructed in the golden image. Thick images work well for homogenous environments, where all users require the same software and where machines are configured the same way.

Maintaining and updating these types of images can sometimes be complex and cumbersome. Lab images—which could have hundreds of applications installed— can become quite large; furthermore, each image is typically comprised of two images: one before Sysprep (for editing) and one after Sysprep (for deployment) [9]. If a small update is required (e.g., operating system patches, software updates, a change to a file, etc.), the entire image needs to be modified, captured, sealed, re-captured, and deployed. Since these images are commonly destructive in nature (i.e., they overwrite the existing disk image), updates usually do not occur on production systems unless mechanisms such as WSUS or automatic software updates allow this or unless administrators manually install them.

2.2 Thin Image

A *thin image* is a disk image that contains a minimum amount of customization, typically just the operating system. Software is then deployed after the operating system has completed its initial setup. Systems administrators can build a reference machine; however, the golden image-approach can be avoided using modern, built-in Windows tools for an automated process, such as in [11].

A thin image lends itself well to the heterogenous environments found in higher education. For instance, thick imaging usually requires at least one image per machine type (e.g., general lab image, faculty/staff image, research cluster image, departmental lab image, etc.); furthermore, an additional image is required per hardware abstraction layer, as well as per architecture. Since the thin image merely installs the operating system (which typically works with most hardware), systems administrators need only to maintain a 32- and a 64-bit "image."

2.3 Hybrid Image

A *hybrid image* is a disk image that combines a thin image (operating system, drivers) with a subset of a thick image (i.e., instead of all possible applications, only the core software, e.g., Office, anti-virus, etc.). As described in [11], a hybrid image can be used to quickly deploy a machine with the out-of-box readiness of a thick image and the customization and low maintenance of a thin image.

3. SOFTWARE INSTALLATIONS

Basically, the difference between a public lab computer and a faculty/staff computer is the software installed on the system. Both computers typically have the same operating system, drivers, and fundamental authentication. A public lab computer may have hundreds of applications, perhaps a modified and categorized Start Menu, and maybe even roaming profiles. Faculty/staff machines, however, may only have a small subset of the lab applications installed, local profiles instead of roaming profiles, etc.

There is no need to create separate images for different classifications of machines if the only disparity is the software suite or policy-based settings. Deploying software after the OS has been installed (as opposed to pre-installing on a thick image) not only reduces duplication of effort but allows for easier troubleshooting and organization.

The following section describes how to manipulate software installations so that they can work in a deployment-based scenario.

3.1 Silent and Unattended Installations

A *silent* installation is one that does not display any windows or messages to the user during the installation. An *unattended* installation is one that requires no user interaction, but it may not necessarily be silent (e.g., a progress bar may show the status of the installation, a macro may simulate keystrokes and mouse-clicks to automatically enter information on setup screens, etc.). A silent installation, however, generally is also unattended.

Although most applications are typically meant to be installed by running the installer and answering questions (as is normally the case with thick images), many applications can be configured to run noninteractively, i.e., silently and unattended when executed from the command line. These modifications allow the installations to occur in the background with minimal interruption of users' sessions.

3.2 Common Windows Installers

The following describes common installers for Windows systems as well as the command-line switches and syntax to make installations silent and unattended.

3.2.1 Windows Installer

Windows Installers[8] are identified with the **.msi** extension and are executed using `msiexec.exe`, a utility included with Windows. An **.msi** is installed as follows:

msiexec.exe /i filename.**msi** [other switches]

Common switches and properties include the following:

- **/qn** - perform a silent installation.

- **/log** filename.**log** - create an installation log at the specified location.

- **REBOOT=ReallySuppress** - do not restart after the installation is complete.

For example, to execute a silent **.msi** installation that does not reboot and generates a log file:

msiexec.exe /i setup.msi **/qn /log** setup.**log**
REBOOT=ReallySuppress

3.2.2 InstallShield

InstallShield[6] installers are normally named `setup.exe`. A response file, `setup.iss`, may also be included; if not, it can typically be generated to store custom responses to setup dialogs. An InstallShield installer is installed as follows:

setup.exe [switches]

Common switches include the following:

- **/s** - perform a silent installation with the default settings.

- **/sms** - pause until the installation is complete. Not all InstallShield installers seem to support this switch.

- **/r** - generate a response file to store customized information and options. This is generally created in `C:\Windows` unless specified elsewhere with a **/f1** parameter. If the vendor included custom dialogs, they may not be supported by the response file.

- **/f1**filename.**iss** - specify a fully qualified path to a different response file. There is no space between the parameter and the path.

- **/f2**filename.**log** - create an installation log at the specified location. There is no space between the parameter and the path.

For example, to execute a silent InstallShield installation that generates a log file:

setup.exe /s /f1C:\Installers\setup.iss /f2C:\Windows\Temp\setup.log

3.2.3 InstallShield with MSI

Some vendors wrap **.msi**'s inside of InstallShield installers. In this case, parameters can be passed to both the `setup.exe` and **.msi**. An InstallShield installer is installed as follows:

setup.exe /s /v"[MSI switches or properties]"

Notice that the **/s** switch is the same as a normal InstallShield installer. Typically, a **/qn** switch is not required for the accompanying **.msi**; however, it can be included just in case. The **/v** switch passes the supplied parameters and/or switches to the **.msi**.

For example, to execute a silent installation that does not reboot:

setup.exe /s /v"/qn REBOOT=ReallySuppress"

3.2.4 Inno Setup

Inno Setup[7] is a popular open source installer system, typically of the form, `filename.exe`.

Common switches include the following:

- **/verysilent** - perform a completely silent installation. If a reboot is required when the installation is complete, the machine will automatically restart without asking unless the **/norestart** switch is specified.

- **/norestart** - do not restart after the installation is complete.

- **/sp-** - disable any startup prompts.

- **/saveinf="filename"** - generate a response file to store installation settings (similar to an InstallShield response file).

- **/loadinf="filename"** - specify a path to a response file.

- **/log="filename"** - create an installation log at the specified location.

For example, to execute a silent installation that does not reboot and generates a log file:

filename.exe /sp- /verysilent /norestart /log="C:\Windows\Temp\setup.log"

3.2.5 Nullsoft Scriptable Install System

NSIS[10] is another popular open source installer system, also of the form, `filename.exe`.

Common switches include the following:

- **/S** - perform a silent installation (if the vendor scripted the installer that way).

- **/NCRC** - disable the cyclic redundancy check verification (unless the vendor scripted the installer to force it).

- **/D=path** - set the default installation directory. This must be the last switch used, and it must not contain any quotes, even if the path contains spaces.

For example, to execute a silent installation that disables the CRC and installs to a custom location:

filename.exe /S /NCRC /D=C:\Program Files\PSU

3.2.6 Other Installers

Some installers have silent and/or unattended mechanisms that are different from the above (e.g., Mozilla, Adobe, AuotDesk, etc.). Consult the software's documentation, website, or forums for details on how to silently deploy these applications. A popular software deployment community is ITNinja[5] (formerly `AppDeploy.com`), which provides details on creating silent installations for thousands of software titles.

If an installer is not one of the above types, it may still have silent capabilities. Try using a **/S**, **/silent**, or **/quiet** switch even if it is not documented; sometimes it will work.

If no silent mechanism exists, it may be possible to create a macro to simulate keystrokes and mouse-clicks; one such scripting utility is AutoIt[4]. Although the installation may not be silent, it will at least be unattended.

3.3 Common Mac Installers

The following describes common installers for Apple systems as well as the command-line switches and syntax to make installations silent and unattended.

3.3.1 Application Bundles

An application bundle is a self-contained file that is run by executing it. It is identified by the **.app** extension and is typically installed by copying the application to the /**Applications** folder using **cp**[1], a utility included with Mac OS, as follows:

cp -Rfp "filename.app" "/Applications"

Three switches are used to ensure a clean copy: **-R** recursively copies all of the bundle's components; **-f** overwrites any existing files; **-p** preserves the bundle's attributes.

3.3.2 Installer Packages

A package, identified by the **.pkg** or **.mpkg** extension, is a compressed installer that allows the user to customize the installation. A package can be executed using `Installer`[2], a utility included with Mac OS, as follows:

installer -package "filename.pkg" -target /

The **-package** switch tells `Installer` the type of bundle being installed, i.e., **.pkg** or .mpkg. **-target** tells `Installer` which volume to install to; typically, this is **/**, i.e., the **root** volume.

3.3.3 Disk Images

Many installer packages and application bundles are wrapped inside of disk images (**.dmg**) or other types of images (e.g., .iso) to allow for easy distribution. Disk images must first be mounted; afterwards, the application bundle can be copied or the installer package can be installed using the commands above; finally, the disk image can be unmounted. Mounting and unmounting is executed with `hdiutil`[3], a utility included with Mac OS. For example, to mount a **.dmg**:

hdiutil attach -quiet -nobrowse -private -mountpoint "/tmp/folder" "filename.dmg"

The **attach** verb tells `hdiutil` to attach the specified image as a volume. The **-quiet**, **-nobrowse**, and **-silent** switches make the mount silent and invisible to Finder. **-mountpoint**

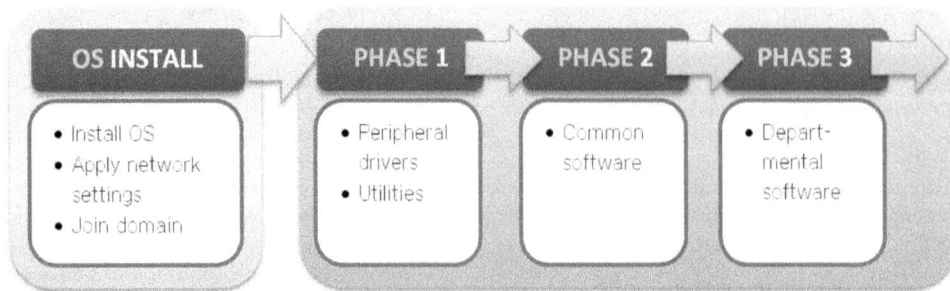

Figure 1: Phased Software Deployment

specifies where to mount the volume; a temporary location is recommended.

At this point, if the image contains an application bundle, it can be copied using the command described in Section 3.3.1; similarly, if the image contains an installer package, it can be installed using the command described in Section 3.3.2.

After the installation, the image can be unmounted with `hdiutil` as follows:

hdiutil detach -force "/tmp/folder"

This forces an unmount of the specified volume.

4. PHASED SOFTWARE DEPLOYMENT

When using a thin imaging scheme, typically only the operating system is installed and configured; software must be installed afterwards to make the system functional. Instead of manually installing software, systems administrators can use the silent and unattended capabilities of most applications to remotely install software. While commercial systems management software can streamline this process, group policy can also be used to deploy *.msi*'s, and startup scripts can be used to install other types of installers.

While deployment-based installations do have an added wait after the OS installation, the advantages of such a model include easier maintenance (it is easier to make updates to packages since only the installer source needs to be modified, not an entire image); focused troubleshooting (if something goes wrong after an application is deployed, it is easier to remove the package instead of re-imaging an entire machine); as well as better organization (it is easier to see which applications are being deployed to systems as opposed to opening an image and looking at the software).

4.1 Baseline Organization

To ensure that prerequisites are fulfilled and executed in order, installers can be organized into baselines. A *baseline* is a collection of software installers, typically grouped according to function. A *phase* is a particular stage, or baseline, in the deployment process.

Figure 1 shows an example of a deployment process with three baselines.

Phase 1 includes required software packages that must be installed to ensure that the machine works correctly, such as peripheral drivers (e.g., scanners, printers, or other devices) or other utilities (e.g., registry settings, runtime redistributables, antivirus software, etc.).

Phase 2 includes common software typically installed onto thick images: office suites, web browsers, media players, etc. In a lab setting, Phase 2 might contain all freeware and/or site-licensed applications that would be available to all students.

Phase 3 includes software that is more departmental in nature. A Phase 3 baseline may exist for Engineering applications (e.g., Matlab, Mathematica), while another Phase 3 baseline exists for Humanities applications (e.g., Creative Suite).

More baselines can exist depending on how granular the environment is. In the example above, MathType and Mathematica may be common to all Engineering labs; however, a Phase 4 baseline may differentiate between them (e.g., a Phase 4 Civil Engineering has AutoCAD, while a Phase 4 Electrical Engineering has LabVIEW and Matlab).

Essentially, the baseline deployment replaces what would normally be a separate image.

4.2 Automation

Baseline deployments can be automated, and order can be enforced, by using control files. A *control file* is simply a text file written to a common location on all machines. The last component of a baseline should be to write the control file; the first component of the next baseline should wait until that control file is present before executing.

For example, in Figure 1, the last component of Phase 1 is to write a control file to the machine, e.g., C:\Windows\PSU \Phase1BaselineComplete.txt. Phase 2 would not execute until it sees that the Phase 1 control file is present, and Phase 2 would write its own `Phase2BaselineComplete.txt` control file so that Phase 3 could execute.

Control files help not only to automate the deployment process (e.g., baselines can be left open as policies and applied to machines as they check-in to the environment), but also to ensure that software is deployed in a specific order and that installer dependencies are fulfilled (e.g., by putting prerequisites in earlier baselines).

4.3 Wallpapers

Using software deployment baselines allows systems administrators to communicate the install process with users. Particularly with lab machines, where deployments could take many hours, logon wallpapers are easy to incorporate into the build process and are useful for relaying the current system status.

Figure 2 is an example of a custom wallpaper configured immediately after Windows is installed. At this point in the

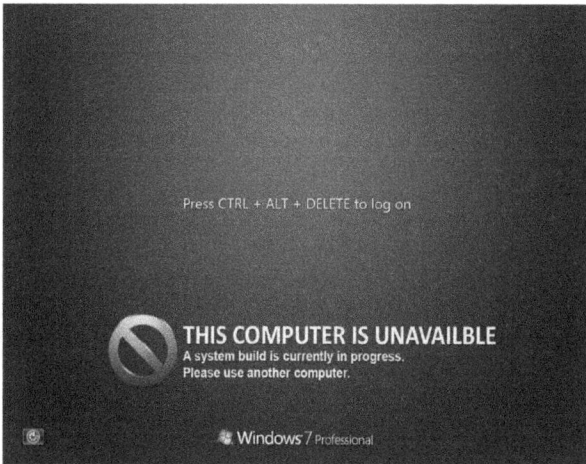

Figure 2: Custom Logon Wallpaper During Build Process—Initial Build

Figure 3: Custom Logon Wallpaper During Build Process—Installation Phase

deployment, no software or utilities are installed; perhaps the computer is not yet joined to the domain or authentication is not yet possible. Without a custom logon wallpaper, a user may try to login to the computer, receive an error, and submit an unnecessary help desk ticket.

Figure 3 shows a custom wallpaper configured during a later baseline, perhaps Phase 2. At this point, users can log in to the computer; however, software is currently installing. A helpful message warns users that the build is not yet finished but is in the process of completing. At the end of the final baseline, the wallpaper can be set back to the default or to a custom logon wallpaper.

4.3.1 Modifying the Windows Logon Wallpaper

In current builds of Windows, a custom logon wallpaper can be used instead of the default logon wallpaper. Two settings are required to configure this:

- **Enable OEMBackground**

  In the registry, set (or create) OEMBackground to the DWORD value of 1. This value is located at the following key:

  HKEY_LOCAL_MACHINE\SOFTWARE\Microsoft\Windows \CurrentVersion\Authentication\LogonUI\ Background

- **Copy the Wallpaper to the System**

  The logon wallpaper must be named backgroundDefault.jpg and have a size less than 256KB; if possible, it should also match the resolution of the screen. Place the file in the following location (note: some folders may need to be created first):

  C:\Windows\System32\oobe\info\backgrounds

To restore the default logon wallpaper, simply set OEMBackground to 0 or delete backgroundDefault.jpg.

5. TESTING

Testing is an integral component of the deployment process. Often, the computing environment (whether it is a public lab, podium computer, or office workstation) is the most visible aspect of an IT organization, and proper testing ensures that software installations and deployments work correctly in a small-scale environment.

5.1 Test Environment

While it is generally best practice to have a consistent environment (particularly in public labs), this is not always feasible, and multi-platform environments are inevitable. Because not all software works between different versions of operating systems, a dedicated machine (virtual or physical) should be used for each environment in which software will be installed.

Each test operating system environment should have the following:

- All up-to-date drivers, patches, service packs, and software updates.

- The same general software suite as production systems.

- A working network connection, ideally matching that of the production environment.

- At least one password-protected local Administrator user account as well as at least one password-protected local Standard User user account.

The test environment should match the production environment as close as possible.

5.2 Test Installation

Although not necessary, it is helpful to perform a test installation in a clean environment (separate from the testing environment) to see how the software interacts with the operating system. This test installation can occur using the normal, interactive method. Performing such a test yields two things:

- What a normal, successful installation looks like.

- How to tell if the application has successfully been installed.

It is useful to know what a successful installation looks like; otherwise, it is difficult to determine what an abnormal one looks like.

Typically, once software has been installed, it writes details about its installation (including application name and version) to the operating system. In Windows, the following registry key can be used to check whether or not an application has been installed onto a system:

```
HKEY_LOCAL_MACHINE\SOFTWARE\Microsoft\Windows
        \CurrentVersion\Uninstall
```

Similarly, on a Mac OS system, each application usually has a .plist, typically found at:

/Applications/filename.app/Contents/Info.plist

While this may not always be the case, such testing in a small environment makes it easier to gather this data.

5.3 Test Procedure

Once an application has been tested interactively, its silent installation can be tested from the command line. This test should be performed in the testing environment that matches the production environment. A general procedure is as follows:

- Log in with a local Administrator account.

- Copy all of the installer files to a known location (or, if installing from a network location, mount the share).

- Open Task Manager (Windows) or Activity Monitor (Mac OS). These tools show all of the currently running processes on the machine and are useful for checking to see if the installer's processes have executed and terminated.

- Open a Command Prompt (Windows) or Terminal (Mac OS).

- Run the appropriate commands to execute a silent installation.

- Once the installer's processes have terminated, log in with a local Standard User account.

- Start the application and verify that it works as it did when performing a clean, interactive installation.

It is helpful to enable logging when performing silent, command-line installations. Typically, installations exit with a code of 0 if they are successful; if the application did not install correctly, the log can sometimes provide a clue as to where things went wrong.

6. CONCLUSION

In higher education institutions, computers are typically classified based on the software suite installed on the computers (this may include other policy-based settings as well). Instead of pre-installing these applications onto thick images (and often duplicating effort), systems administrators can use thin images to install a base installation of an operating system onto all machines. The benefit of this is that one image can be used for all machines.

Software can be deployed to each machine after the operating system is installed. In order to do this so that the installations do not interfere with users' sessions, systems administrators can perform silent and unattended installations by using command-line switches and parameters.

By categorizing software packages into baselines, systems administrators can organize installers so that, when deployed, they mimic the same effect of a thick image without the typical hassle of thick-image maintenance. The phased deployment approach allows software installations to be more organized and updatable.

7. REFERENCES

[1] Apple Inc. Mac os x manual page: Installer, February 2005. https://developer.apple.com/library/mac/ #documentation/Darwin/Reference/ ManPages/man1/cp.1.html.

[2] Apple Inc. Mac os x manual page: Installer, April 2007. https://developer.apple.com/library/mac/ #documentation/Darwin/Reference/ ManPages/man8/installer.8.html.

[3] Apple Inc. Mac os x manual page: Installer, March 2011. https://developer.apple.com/library/mac/ #documentation/Darwin/Reference/ ManPages/man1/hdiutil.1.html.

[4] Bennett, Jonathan and AutoIT Consulting Ltd. Autoit. http://www.autoitscript.com/site/autoit.

[5] Dell Inc. It ninja. http://www.itninja.com.

[6] Flexera Software LLC. Command-line switches for the microsoft windows installer tool, June 2006. http://kb.flexerasoftware.com/doc/Helpnet/ installshield12helplib/IHelpSetup_EXECmdLine.htm.

[7] Jordan Russell Software. Inno setup, 2010. http://www.jrsoftware.org/isinfo.php.

[8] Microsoft Corporation. Command-line switches for the microsoft windows installer tool, February 2007. http://support.microsoft.com/kb/227091.

[9] Microsoft Corporation. How sysprep works, October 2010. http://technet.microsoft.com/en-us/library/dd744512%28v=ws.10%29.aspx.

[10] NSIS Project. Nullsoft scriptable install system, February 2011. http://nsis.sourceforge.net.

[11] J. B. Tyndall. The windows 7 build key: redesigning and automating image deployment. In *Proceedings of the 39th ACM annual conference on SIGUCCS*, SIGUCCS '11, pages 111–118, New York, NY, USA, 2011. ACM.

Continuous Change: A Help Desk Motto

Joyce Davidson
University of Idaho
PO Box 442440
Moscow, Idaho 83844
1-208-885-2119

joyced@uidaho.edu

Darren Kearney
University of Idaho
PO Box 442440
Moscow, Idaho 83844
1-208-885-4053

darrenk@uidaho.edu

ABSTRACT
The University of Idaho Help Desk started in October 1992 in a basement room with one full-time employee, two part-time student workers, and a Manager, Joyce Davidson. Their task was to provide staff, faculty, and students with assistance using email, connecting to the new Banner system, using the modem pool, and acquiring how-to documents for common lab applications.

Jump forward 20 years and the UI Help Desk mission has grown and changed in ways that were unimagined in the beginning. New products and technologies create an ever changing support landscape, and customer needs and expectations continue to outstrip the resources we can provide. Challenges such as new facilities and locations, increasing customer base, wireless and wired networks, mobile devices, VPN, print servers, Exchange support, shared-drive permissions, student computer lab assistance, best-effort assistance on unsupported applications, and web technology assistance, as well as staff development and recruiting, are all part of everyday business.

In this paper, Joyce Davidson, the original Help Desk manager, and Darren Kearney, the current manager, will review the history of the Help Desk and illustrate how far this critical service has come and where it may go. While we don't believe it is possible to clearly predict where emerging trends will take us, we will discuss how we approach these trends to help chart a course for the Help Desk going forward.

Categories and Subject Descriptors
K.6.1 [**Project and People Management**]: Staffing

General Terms
Management, Documentation, Economics, Standardization.

Keywords
Staffing, technical support, customer service.

1. INTRODUCTION
In the fall of 1991 new leadership at the University of Idaho determined that a customer support group needed to be created to support new services coming on line within the next year. The first of the new services, Banner, would be the first time a distributed computing environment would be available across campus without the need to have a 'batch' run on the mainframe systems. Banner decentralized a service by assigning access across campus empowering individual departments to manage their own accounts and work directly on student records. A new era of computing required the computer service group to invest in a new way of supporting services. This was the start of the ITS Help Desk.

From its humble four-person beginnings through the last 20 years the Help Desk has continued to change to meet ever evolving challenges and requests. Economic realities have challenged us, technology caused us to evolve, staffing levels have fluctuated, departmental missions have changed, but still our core value of providing the best possible customer support remains our guiding principle for everything we do.

So what has changed and what will change as we move forward? Staffing, technology, training, facilities and mission have all been modified over time to meet new expectations. By understanding that change is one of the few constants in the Help Desk environment we have embraced it and made it part of our core culture.

Born from a long-awaited re-organization of ITS was an implementation of a new service to the campus community entitled "Help Desk" in 1992. The Help Desk had limited funding yet faced strong demand for support, so a decision was made to utilize our most valued resource, our students. As we began it was quickly noted we had mountains of requests/demands of our technical support service. The old adage of 'the more you give the more they want' was very apparent in the Help Desk's rapid growth from two full-time employees and two part-time student staff members to four full-time employees and twenty-two student employees within six years.

2. THE FIRST YEARS
Meeting the technical demands from campus had quickly become over-bearing. We needed to work smarter while satisfying the customer. No longer were telephone support and office walk-in visits fulfilling all of the contact avenues of our customers. We added new services such as: in-office hardware repair, software application training, and technical support in our student labs. Utilizing the new world wide web, we designed help sheets with frequently asked questions, developed an "ask us" email process, and created a monthly on-line newsletter with tips and tricks from the Help Desk staff. Time passed and we were implementing on-line services for changing your password and adding more print pages to your account. All the while, as the front-line service of the Help Desk was maturing, so were the end users and we needed to have expertise and in-depth consulting. Starting in 1998 and over a period of 2 years, we added 6 full-time analysts to a

new level of service called Secondary Support. Then almost as natural as time itself, we were totally saturated in a purchase-to-own laptop business for all students. The sky was the limit – we were soaring!! What started as an incident "help" service had spread to a full new division of Customer Support within ITS.

3. THE CURRENT HELP DESK

The ITS Help Desk is currently made up of 1 full-time employee engaged as the Help Desk Manager and one 40-hr. per week TH (temporary help) staff member as the Lead Technical Support Representative with 16 part-time Technical Support Representatives (TSRs). Our current staffing is now lower than in recent years due to the recent economic conditions. With this staff the Help Desk is open 8:00 a.m. through 5:00 p.m., Monday through Friday, year round, as well as providing 204 hours of staffing between our Library and Student Union Building labs each week.

The Help Desk has aligned itself with the Service Desk model from ITIL. We are the front door for all ITS services and are tasked with documenting issues, providing first-level support, and routing tickets to the appropriate groups. Our customer base consists of all students, staff, faculty, retirees, alumni, and vendors working with the University. This constituency numbers approximately 17,000 not counting the alumni and is spread throughout the state and beyond. During the last year the Help Desk closed 27,008 tickets within our queue representing over 90% of the customer contacts to ITS. We pride ourselves on providing the best customer service possible and on treating each of our customers with respect.

The Help Desk has recently worked to overcome some challenges. The personnel budget has been cut each year for the last 3 years while we have been asked to take on more responsibilities. Campus departments have reduced their own internal support personnel and asked staff members to turn to us for direct assistance, adding to our work load. We have done our best to absorb these workloads after an approximate 20% reduction in funding but our ticket resolution times have suffered.

4. HOW WE CHANGED

The years between the first year and now have seen dramatic changes not only in how we support users but in what type of support they expect from a Help Desk.

4.1 Staffing

The initial staff of four was quickly expanded to meet the evolving mission. At first they were required to be student staff. Within the first six years 28 staff members were actively working at the Help Desk. These staff became specialized based on the newly discovered needs, and new groups were made to flesh out their offerings. Two new groups were spun off the Help Desk, Secondary Support group and an OnSite Services group. Even with the new service offerings in a supporting role, the responsibilities of the Help Desk continued to grow. Ten years into its existence a new Supervisor was on board, and the Help Desk staff was merged with the Lab monitors. This allowed us to provide Help-Desk-level assistance across campus by requiring lab monitors to become proficient with the tools and procedures from the Help Desk. This merger expanded the staffing to around 40 people at its peak. The merger did have some growing pains and came at the same time as a financial lean time at the University. TSRs who were unable to adapt to their new roles left

the Help Desk and smaller labs were designated as unstaffed labs. This brought the Help Desk staffing numbers down to around 24. The supervisor plus five to six TSRs worked at the Help Desk while two more TSRs served in the lab locations. During this time we were open at the Help Desk from 7:00 a.m. to 6:00 p.m., Monday through Friday, and staffing two lab locations from 7:00 a.m. to 3:00 a.m. every day. The current supervisor joined the team seven years ago and has overseen the recent staffing reduction. This reduction has reduced our active staffing during the day to the supervisor plus three to four TSRs at the Help Desk, and two more TSRs at the two lab locations.

4.2 Facilities and Tools

During the first few years the Help Desk consisted of 3 desks in a small office in the basement of the UI Administration building equipped with computers that ran a simple tracking system and the few supported applications. Most support was done by phone and by walk-in if the customers were able to find the location. As the service grew, staff and customers quickly noted that the space did not meet the needs. A review by ITS administration identified a larger office on the first floor as the new location for the Help Desk.

Moving upstairs also solidified the modern organization of the Help Desk which had already developed service outgrowths. The OnSite services group worked outside the Help Desk to provide in-office support, and the Secondary Support group provided direct assistance to the Help Desk by full-time technicians. A Customer Support manager position was created to oversee all these groups and to keep them working efficiently together.

With the organization getting larger and more specialized the new groups were provided separate offices so we needed to improve our tracking system. Since we now had employees comfortable with handing large projects we opted for an in-house solution that worked well with our email system. We configured this custom application to provide most of the functionality needed at the time for interoffice communication.

By 2001 the Help Desk had matured into a fully integrated department supporting all of campus. The campus labs system was moved under the Customer Support umbrella and the integration of the Lab monitors with the TSRs had started. Feedback from customers had identified that even our newest location had some issues. Being at the periphery of campus the Administration building required most customers to walk quite a distance to see us. The Administration building was equipped with noisy window-mounted air conditioners making quiet conversation almost impossible. The volume of customer visits during peak times created safety concerns due to the crowded hallways. Since one of the primary classroom buildings on campus was getting ready to undergo a full renovation and it was situated almost exactly at the center of campus, planning started on creating a dedicated suite of offices that would be configured to our specifications. From the start of this project until we were ready to move in took over five years of planning, saving, and waiting but in 2007 we finally moved into our new digs. We now have a centralized location that is more convenient for most of our customer base. We also enjoy a modern office that does not need window-mounted air conditioners. And within a year we replaced our in-house tracking system for an ITIL-based one. An auto-transcription service was recently added to our tool chest which allows us to process our voice mail quickly and accurately to record every voicemail into our tracking system. This allows us to make sure every customer contact is managed and frees up time that we can use to help our customers.

4.3 Technology

The support topography of 1992 was undergoing major changes. Personal computer ownership was still not the norm, and many students were just experiencing networked computers for the first time as the campus wired network was expanded. Faculty and staff were in the process of transitioning away from paper-based documentation, and toward a computer-based administration system. Voicemail was still a new feature available to campus and the phone system was still the primary method of communication. As campus quickly adopted new technology the Help Desk was expected to provide 'service with a smile' for everything new.

Moving forward to 1998 and changes were easily spotted on campus. More labs had sprung up due to increased demand. The internet was rapidly expanding and network access was becoming a priority in the daily lives of everyone on campus. Computer accounts and email were being required for classes and all of this required visiting with the Help Desk in person. At the Help Desk a new internally created tracking system was being used as the prior one had not met the needs of the department. The phone tree had been removed as too many customers assumed it was just a voicemail message and hung up. The new phone setup rang the Help Desk first then went to voicemail if unanswered. A modem pool on campus increased the support range to the local community as the Help Desk was asked to provide assistance to off-campus customers. On campus, ITS was providing email, web and file services to its customers, our core services had changed rapidly and the rate of that change was not showing any signs of slowing down.

By 2005 changes had again swept through as personal computing was mainstream and email communication with students, faculty and staff was considered the standard. All areas of campus were experimenting with uses of technology where it had not existed before. Digitized timesheets, online testing services, WebCT for course management, electronic reserve in the library, PDAs synced to the campus-wide calendaring system, departmental networked printers, and many more changes were introduced. Online services were changing and we were starting to see the effects of "Web 2.0." Everyone Googled, wikis were the place to go for research, and many student social activities had also moved online. Much to the joy of every ITS support team member, the modem pool was decommissioned. Customers were connecting to our services from their own broadband connections in increasing numbers.

Now we find ourselves in the mobile device era. Customers are using multiple devices accessing information stored online within cloud-based services. Customers may need to access services on every device as each fills a particular niche in their work-life space. Rather than provide files to each other, more and more we see connections to new services passed between customers. Helping customers navigate these services can be a challenge that is complicated when something as mundane as a print copy is needed from a service being accessed on an iPod.

5. IDENTIFYING CHANGE

It is very easy to see the amount of change that occurs in any technology organization over a relatively short period of time. As a Help Desk we are expected to be able to take these changes in stride and be able to support them from day one with a high degree of confidence. How can this be done? At our Help Desk we strive to keep ourselves ready for change by engaging a few simple low- or no-cost methods.

5.1 Watch for Disruptions

Disruptions are hard to plan for but very noticeable when they occur. The iPhone was a classic example of a technology disruption that changed the mobile game when it was released. Be aware of something that does not fit into the normal operations for the Help Desk. If you find yourself asking "How would we connect this to our services?" you may be talking about a disruption.

5.2 Participate in Open Discussions

Like canaries in a coal mine, your staff discussions can quickly alert you to new needs and upcoming changes that will affect your customers. We frequently have informal discussions on new technology and how it may be used across campus or in our day-to-day lives. Most IT staffs have those few employees that revel in using the newest technology in their own day-to-day lives. Giving them an avenue to discuss what they have found not only provides you with firsthand information but grants them a stage to talk about their interests.

5.3 Ask Your Customers

Yearly surveys have frequently opened our eyes to new concerns and directions our customers are taking. When given a sufficiently simple way of providing information, we have found our customers able to provide insightful information about what they need and why. To keep costs low, use freely available online surveying applications. These surveys can be modified quickly to get at the answers you need. Participation in national survey initiatives such as TechQual+ allows you to compare your data with peer institutions.

Don't forget the power of the informal discussion with units outside your department. Visit them in their offices or off-site locations to keep the customers comfortable and at ease. Ask them about what ideas they have not only for your department but for their own. What you can discover can be eye opening.

5.4 Industry Sources & Networking

Don't forget to keep up on what your peers are doing at other institutions. Make sure your Administration understands the value of attending conferences and events like SIGUCCS. These events do a good job of keeping you up to date on new trends as well as provide you with access to other institutions' experiences and an opportunity to directly discuss directions they are taking. By consuming this informed data you are able to avoid the pitfalls that others have encountered ultimately making you available to provide superior support at a lower cost to the institution.

6. THE CRYSTAL BALL

We know things have changed and are changing still. How do you prepare for the coming years? We watch trends and then push them out two to three years mentally and play the modern-day witch doctor reading bones to determine the future. From these readings we try to determine how to provide support for changes that have not been fully realized. Let's examine some trends pulled from reputable sources and apply some techniques which may guide us toward strategies for preparing for the future.

6.1 Cloud Services

Arthur C. Clarke once said, "Any sufficiently advanced technology is indistinguishable from magic." Cloud computing may meet this standard for many users in the near future as it continues to offload data and functionality from the local workstation, allowing any connected device to access resources and processing power previously available to only a few. Instant access to data, communications, processing power, and applications are just the start of this new technology shift. Microsoft, Apple, Google, Amazon, and many other major players in the technology industry have already invested heavily in the paradigm. Services leveraging this new technology are already being used by our customers who may not even know they are using the "Cloud." At the UI we utilize Microsoft's Live@Edu product and plan to move to the Office365 offering soon. Once a collection of loosely associated tools, Microsoft's Cloud service infrastructure is quickly maturing and will soon be an integrated part of the new Windows 8 operating system. Apple is already deeply integrated in its ecosystem with the iCloud service.

So what do our customer expect from us? Everything. The one downside to true cloud services is they require a robust network connection. To avoid outage issues bothering customers, many services are adopting hybrid models that still retain functionality when a network is not available, then syncing data and state information once a connection is restored. This requires that as an institution we must make sure network services are dependable and have the growth capacity to meet demand. We also must recognize that customers now expect that all our services will soon be accessible online while hiding the traditional barriers IT services have erected in the name of security.

6.2 BYOD

The Bring Your Own Device trend seen in industry is starting to trickle into the academic environment. We have been dealing with customers that access our services on their own computers for quite a while but the implications to IT need to be addressed.

The first change is the type of devices that are being used to consume services and how we provide the support needed to make them successful. Smart phones, tablets, and laptops are considered standard fare when dealing with media streamers, network-enabled TVs, portable game devices, and other devices that customers expect to consume services from. Faculty frequently bring their own devices into the classroom, expecting them to work as well as devices provided or supported by the university. These devices may be perceived as necessary to the business of learning regardless of who owns them or what they are. We must be aware of new devices and how they fit within the infrastructure as well as how they access services.

Second, since these devices are purchased outside the standard purchasing procedures they do not fit into the normal service processes that institutionally purchased devices do. Currently the University of Idaho does not support personal devices within our normal procedures so this may need to change rapidly as the lines between personal equipment and devices owned by the university continue to blur. It will be impossible to avoid impeding the day-to-day operations of the University without creating methods of security and support when dealing with personally owned devices.

6.3 Virtualization of Everything

While toes have been dipped into virtual spaces such as Second Life with mixed results, the virtualization of everything will continue to take place. At an infrastructure level we have already virtualized many servers and services but the biggest changes may take place in regards to teaching, experimentation, and other historically face-to-face services. Campus tours may take place utilizing augmented reality on mobile devices. Offsite tours may integrate live information to help prospective students get a better feel for the campus. Expensive applications once only accessible through specialized labs are now being run in virtual spaces available to students across the globe. Even the devices or operating systems used to run the virtualized services can be virtualized inside other devices, making support of these systems feel like you're playing a part in the movie *Inception 2*.

Virtualization of physical objects, software, and spaces will continue to accelerate, making impossible situations possible and possible situations cheaper.

6.4 Touchy Systems

Just a few short years ago we were trying our best to get people to stop touching monitors with their hands or, worse, an absentmindedly pointed pen. The screen was something that you just looked at with an occasional wipe-down to remove dust. We are moving quickly into a new computing interface realm where the sense of touch is being integrated into what we see. No longer are the keyboard and mouse considered the only ways to manipulate objects on screen. While touch is the primary input mechanism for iOS and Android operating systems, with Windows 8 it is expected to move onto the desktop in a major way. We are still asking ourselves what the impact will be. Some early interactions involve standardizing how to document 'swiping' instructions for customers, how to identify touch-based vs. non-touch-based systems to reduce customer irritation, and how to do remote support for touch-based devices that may not have traditional input mechanisms.

6.5 The Support Guru

Staff training no longer can just be confined to narrow University hardware and software standards. New employees must quickly prove themselves efficient at dealing with issues in a mobile multiplatform environment that changes from month to month. Very few institutions are able to afford enough employees to have experts in every operating system, application, or hardware device. We must focus on developing Help Desk skills that enable our employees to find and absorb relevant information very quickly to be able to provide the speedy and accurate support our customers demand. With great frequency we are finding new employees with engineering backgrounds are not always equipped with the communication skills or flexibility required to provide rapid assessments or interpret customer concerns into actionable communications. This changes the ideal employee from someone who has a technical background to one who has strong communication skills and is able to learn technology.

7. CONCLUSION

Only three things have been constants at the University of Idaho Help Desk over the last 20 years. One, we remain a vital strategic resource to the day-to-day activities on campus. Two, our greatest asset is still the dedicated staff members who work hard to provide ongoing support. Every other aspect of the Help Desk has changed and is hardly recognizable from the humble beginnings of four staff located in a non-descript office hidden in an office building basement.

And three? Continuous change. We must continue to provide top-notch support for technology in all its various forms. Any attempt to paint a detailed view of the future would take much hubris and include much folly, but not trying to watch new trends and do our best to prepare for the future would be disastrous. We need to keep thinking flexibly and be ready to change directions as the new takes form.

8. REFERENCES

[1] Grajek, Susan & Pirani, Judith (May/June 2012) *Top-Ten IT Issues, 2012*. EDUCAUSE Review, vol. 47, no. 3 (May/June 2012). Retrieved from http://www.educause.edu/ero/article/top-ten-it-issues-2012

[2] Davidson, Joyce. (1998). Proceedings from ACM SIGUCCS: User Services Conference 98. 87.

Building Collaborative Technology Learning Environments

Kenneth Janz
Winona State University
Somsen Hall 111i
Winona, MN 55987
1-507-457-2299
kjanz@winona.edu

Ken Graetz
Winona State University
Maxwell Hall 130
Winona, MN 55987
1-507-457-2339
kgraetz@winona.edu

Chad Kjorlien
Winona State University
Maxwell Hall 130
Winona, MN 55987
1-507-457-5167
ckjorlien@winona.edu

ABSTRACT

The rapid advance of technology has enabled students to use powerful technology both inside and outside of the classroom. A major issue facing higher education is whether students truly know how to use this technology, can our learning spaces support it, and can it be integrated with other technologies to extend students' capabilities?

This paper focuses on the how Winona State University went about improving learning spaces on campus. It includes six major sections. First, the development of the e-Warrior: Digital Life and Learning Program and Technology Master Plan provided the foundation. Second, quantifying the quality of classroom spaces on campus through the development of an online database and a campus report card provided a common point of reference. Third, faculty members engaged in the design of new learning spaces on campus to align design with pedagogy. Fourth, new technologies supported the online delivery of what used to be classroom lecture, paving the way for classroom flipping. Fifth, the intersection between formal and informal learning spaces played a role in instruction. Sixth, WSU developed two new flipped classrooms; the Math Achievement Center and Visual Media Studio. The Math Achievement Center and Visual Media Studio are collaborative classrooms designed by faculty that demonstrate the potential of mobile computing integration. Finally, recommendations for improving learning spaces found on any campus are offered.

This paper provides a replicable roadmap for developing collaborative technology learning environments and highlights the many successes and challenges you may experience along the way.

Categories and Subject Descriptors

K.3.1 [Computers and Education]: Computer Uses in Education

General Terms

Management, Measurement, Documentation, Performance, Design, Economics, Human Factors, Standardization, Theory.

Keywords

Learning Spaces, Classrooms, Flipped Classrooms, Digital Life and Learning, Classroom Report Card, Assessment, Visual Media, Math Achievement Center, Class Capture.

1. INTRODUCTION

Classroom learning spaces support faculty and student interactions. Literature on some core learning spaces design principles to facilitate student learning has been published [6]. A new method of teaching called the flipped classroom is turning the traditional classroom on its head [3]. How one plans for this change is almost as important as the actual execution of the change in the classroom [4]. Important questions need to be asked before a teacher takes on flipping their classroom into a more collaborative learning environment [2, 5]. These questions lead the authors of this paper to ask the question: do the students know how to truly use this technology, can our learning spaces support it, and can it be integrated with other technologies to extend students' capabilities?

This paper focuses on how Winona State University built collaborative technology learning environments on its campus. This paper will discuss:

- The development of the e-Warrior: Digital Life and Learning Program and Technology Master Plan providing the foundation that drove planning and decision making around learning spaces on campus.

- The quantifying the quality of classroom spaces on campus through the development of an online database and a campus report card.

- A discussion of how faculty members were engaged in the process of the design of new learning spaces on campus.

- The changing role learning spaces play in instruction.

- The presentation of two newly developed flipped classrooms on campus, the Math Achievement Center and the Visual Media Studio. The Math Achievement Center and Visual Media Studio are collaborative classrooms designed by faculty that demonstrate the potential of mobile computing integration.

- Recommendations for improving learning spaces found on any campus.

This paper will provide a replicable roadmap for developing collaborative technology learning environments and highlights the many successes and challenges you may experience along the way.

2. BACKGROUND

Three important foundation items impacted the development of learning spaces on the campus of Winona State University. The first was the support structure on campus for learning spaces, the second was the e-Warrior: Digital Life and Learning Program. Finally, third was the Technology Master Plan.

2.1 Information Technology Support

Winona State University (a mid-sized university located in southeast Minnesota of 9,000 students) IT support is provided by Information Technology Services (ITS) which is organized into four units: User Services, Development and Web Support Services, Infrastructure Services, and Teaching, Learning, and Technology Services. The ITS leadership team consists of the Chief Information Officer and the Directors of User Services, Development and Web Support Services, Infrastructure Service, and Teaching, Learning, and Technology Services. At Winona State University the Teaching, Learning, and Technology (TLT) Services unit is responsible for the design, development, and maintenance of learning spaces on campus.

2.2 e-Warrior: Digital Life and Learning Program

The e-Warrior: Digital Life and Learning Program provides every student with a laptop computer to enhance his/her studies on the Winona campus. The conceptual model of the e-Warrior: Digital Life and Learning Program appears in figure 1. The program has been woven into the fabric of the institution. The program has had a direct impact on the development and design of learning spaces on campus. This program integrates communication and information technology into a student's social and learning experience at Winona State University. The program provides students with a powerful set of tools (e.g., a laptop, updated software) and services (e.g., help desk) to support all facets of their academic work and residential life at Winona State. More than just a laptop, the e-Warrior: Digital Life and Learning Program ensures secure, reliable, and supportable technology 24x7. Unlike other institutions within the Minnesota State Colleges and Universities (MnSCU) system or many other campuses, there are no traditional computer labs on the Winona campus. These specialized rooms for working with technology have given way to anytime, anywhere learning. The entire campus is a learning space with access to worldwide information resources. Innovative pedagogies are in practice on campus with current action research projects looking at e-books and enhanced communications with students. Winona State's experiment with e-books is possible and facilitated by the Digital Life and Learning Program.

Conceptual Model

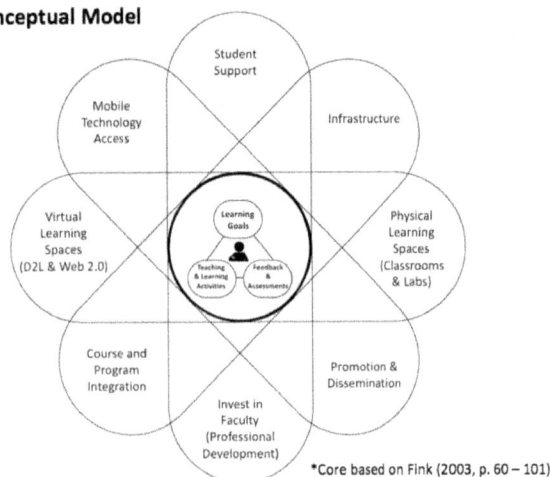

*Core based on Fink (2003, p. 60 – 101)

Figure 1. Conceptual Model - e-Warrior: Digital Life and Learning Program

Winona State's new buildings on campus (i.e., science building, library, Maxwell renovation) were designed around a mobile computing environment. All the building spaces and equipment, including science labs, are built with the assumption that students have mobile computing devices. This mobile computing environment has allowed Winona State to create more efficient teaching and learning spaces that allow connecting to high-tech science equipment. The design of the new Wellness Center also incorporates the realities of mobile computing. An outcome of this environment is the Winona campus has one of the largest wireless network installations in the state of Minnesota and was named one of the top 25 wireless college campuses in the United States in a survey conducted by the Center for Digital Education and Intel Corporation.

2.3 Technology Master Plan

As part of the Technology Master Planning Process 5 cornerstones emerged from conversations with the campus community. One of the cornerstones "Engaging Student Learning Environments" directly aligned to enhancing learning spaces on campus. It was determined that this cornerstone was to develop, support, and foster technology enriched student-learning environments, which inspire and teach learners to acquire, apply, and extend knowledge; to think critically; and to solve challenges imaginatively. The technology master plan can be found online at: http://www.winona.edu/it (click on about). The technology master plan lays out all of the initiatives related to learning spaces that follow.

3. QUANTIFYING THE QUALITY OF CLASSROOM SPACE ON CAMPUS

The Technology Master Plan provided a roadmap to improving learning spaces on campus. The first step improving learning spaces was to inventory the spaces on campus. This process can be broken into three phases.

3.1 First Online Database

There has been an interest in quantifying the quality of classroom space for last three years on the Winona State University campus. The first effort was building a database of the 162 centrally assignable spaces on campus. At the request of the CIO: Teaching, Learning, and Technology (TLT) Services, worked with key members of facilities and the registers office to collect relevant data concerning classrooms across campus. This database was completed in the spring 2009. This database contains the type of classroom, picture of each classroom, room capacity, fixed or flexible seating, type network data, and technology located in the room. This database is located online and can be used by any member of the campus community:

http://edutech.tlt.winona.edu/LearningSpaces/locations/

3.2 Classroom Report Card

In the fall of 2011 at the president's request, Kenneth Janz (CIO) and Kurt Lohide (Vice President of Finance) were instructed to collect additional information about classroom space on campus with the intent of brining classroom spaces up to a level more aligned with our peer institutions. The second step involved measuring the quality of classroom conditions. A measurement tool called the Classroom Report Card was developed. See figure 2 for an example question from the Classroom Report Card. The first draft was completed in November 2011 by TLT. It was reviewed and revised by the CIO, CFO, and the Director of ITS Infrastructure Services and approved for use during winter break of 2011-2012.

Figure 2. Classroom Report Card

3.2.1 Methodology

The Classroom Report Card is an online survey created in Qualtrics and used jointly by Facilities Services and TLT staff to assess the general physical and environmental conditions of campus classrooms. Two versions, one for Facilities Services and one for TLT, are used. Equipped with a laptop, an individual staff member visits a classroom to complete the assessment. Multiple raters can visit a single classroom and repeated assessments of the same room are saved separately for later reliability analysis.

3.2.2 Conditions

The Classroom Report Card focuses on the following 16 physical and environmental conditions:

- Ambient environment: light, noise, HVAC (temperature)

- Electrical, networking (wired and wireless), and phone services

- Room surfaces: Floor, walls, and ceiling

- Student and instructor furniture

- Installed instructional tools: marking surfaces, projection, audio, instructor controls

3.2.3 Condition Grades

A 5-point scale, with values represented by familiar "grades" of A, B, C, D, or F, is used. Each grade value is explained on the survey. For example, grades for ceilings, walls, and floors are described as follows:

- A (far exceeds) = In exceptional condition, recently remodeled, distinctive

- B (exceeds) = In good condition, no immediate need for repair or update

- C (adequate) = In fair condition, minor damage, spot cleaning or repair needed, moderately outdated

- D (inadequate) = In poor condition, major damage, major repair or refinishing required, very outdated

- F (unusable) = In unacceptable/unsafe condition, room should not be used until addressed

3.2.4 Overall Grade

Currently, the overall classroom grade is the unweighted average of the 16 condition grades. A formula for weighting the individual conditions to generate a more valid overall grade is forthcoming.

3.2.5 Comprehensive Approach to Facilities Assessment

The Classroom Report Card does not replace other methods of assessing building systems (e.g., HVAC) and is intended to complement data gathered through other means, including from students and faculty, to help:

- Identify classrooms with potentially deficient physical or environmental conditions

- Maintain "dashboard" awareness of the current state of all campus classrooms

- Facilitate planning and responsiveness to changes in instructional goals and strategies

3.2.6 A Work in Progress

Following this first trial run of the Classroom Report Card during the semester break, ITS and Facilities Services are working together to improve the process by:

- Reassessing several room conditions (e.g., HVAC) with greater input from Facilities Services

- Reassessing wireless networking in all classrooms using heat maps provided by ITS Infrastructure Services

- Assessing the reliability of the rating system and adjusting the instrument accordingly

- Developing a usable "dashboard" of the results that can be used by stakeholders

- Combining the Classroom Report Card data, the WSU Classroom Database information, and self-help documentation for faculty and students.

3.3 Combined Database

The combined database summarizes room condition and is available online for browsing teaching and learning spaces. Figure 3 provides a sample webpage view of the combined database.

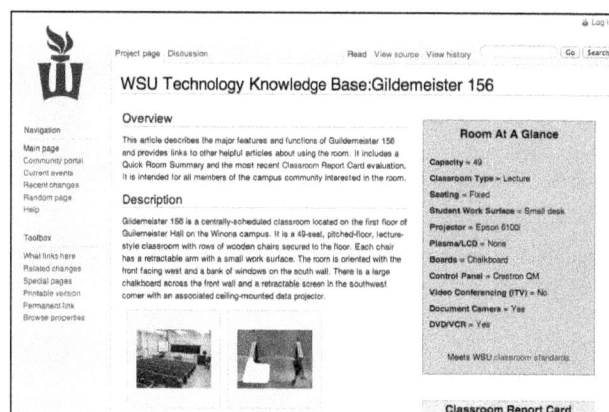

Figure 3. Combined Learning Space Database and Classroom Report Card

4. Faculty Engagement in Process

Like most universities, WSU has a Facilities and Finance advisory committee that makes resource allocation decisions, but does not address classroom design details. Historically, classroom design decisions are made at the time an entire building is constructed or significantly remodeled. Facilities Services and TLT develop an initial predesign and instructors were asked to react to it.

This is problematic when it comes to making quick changes based on new, emerging instructional strategies. The traditional method is well suited for implementing standard features across many classrooms, but what is needed today is a method that focuses on individual learning spaces and engages faculty to develop a design that meets specific instructional needs.

4.1 Faculty Feedback in Development of the Technology Master Plan

Learning space improvement is a cornerstone of our ITS Technology Master Plan and faculty are involved in all phases of its development, review, and ratification. Instructors have the opportunity to provide informal feedback throughout the year. Formal feedback opportunities are also available through our annual Faculty Technology Survey, Faculty Focus Groups, and Chair and Dean Survey. Finally, the All University Technology Committee plays an integral role in the revision of the plan and insures the participation of faculty bargaining units.

4.2 Faculty Involvement in Design

WSU is finding more and better ways of involving faculty in the remodeling and redesign of learning spaces. Each year, TLT and Facilities Services work with Deans, Chairs, and instructors to identify three to five significant learning space redesign projects, typically one from each college. Instructors are engaged in every phase of the project, from the initial design to the faculty training in the finished room. Both of the projects covered in this paper, the Math Achievement Center and the Visual Media Studio, were managed in this way. Once through this process, faculty join a learning community dedicated to further exploring their own learning spaces and providing ideas and support to other faculty just starting the process.

The other change in classroom planning underway at WSU involves the Classroom Report Card. These data are motivating faculty and academic leadership to engage in regular discussions about learning space improvement. Members of TLT and Facilities services are typically invited to these meetings, which can go on for several weeks. This spring, a group of faculty teaching humanities courses met once a week for a month to develop a plan for improving classrooms in Minné Hall, creating spaces that will support collaboration and group work more effectively. This new model, wherein the impetus for change comes from the faculty and they present their "predesign" to Facilities Services and TLT is certainly a "flipped" method with great potential.

4.3 Faculty Training and Support

Traditional workshops and documentation via our Technology Knowledge Base Wiki have been shared with the faculty along with a robust use of synchronous desktop conferencing, asynchronous video, and class capture strategies.

Our support of faculty in their use of our class capturing systems, Tegrity, Camtasia, and Adobe Presenter, is almost entirely conducted using the same technologies to show faculty their capabilities and appropriateness for specific instructional situations. These are complemented by the use of interviews with WSU faculty where they speak to their experiences with specific hardware, software, and classroom designs.

5. Learning Spaces

Although teaching and learning have never been confined to classrooms, the lecture hall has long been the gold standard for defining campus-learning spaces. This is changing, largely due to advances in technology. First, as content normally presented in lecture is migrated online in engaging, multimedia formats, instructors are feeling more comfortable spending class time on other, more collaborative activities. Freed from the burden of "getting through the content," instructors are looking to engage students in discussion, guided hands-on work, and group activities during class meetings. Second, as wireless networking and mobile computing devices continue to pervade college campuses, students can easily access the information and tools they need to learn from virtually any location on campus. Coffee bars, cafeterias, hallways, and alcoves with comfortable couches all become potential learning spaces for individuals and groups and the line between formal and informal space continues to blur. Finally, the explosion in popularity of such applications as Facebook is extending the definition of learning space to include virtual places that are just as real and meaningful as brick-and-mortar classrooms.

The vast majority of college classrooms are designed around one instructional strategy: lecture. Most traditional classrooms do not just support this strategy, they perpetuate it. National trends and WSU data indicate that this strategy and these classrooms are already failing to meet student and faculty needs and are headed for obsolescence. In 2012 focus group interviews, WSU faculty described the ideal classroom space as a "lab" where application, experimentation, and discovery of new ways of thinking would take place. They found that classrooms designed to promote healthy group discussions are far and few between and yet such interaction is core to the curriculum in many courses and disciplines. They reported feeling frustrated that that a chemistry instructor would never be assigned to a physics lab, but there is little concern assigning a communications studies instructor who relies heavily on active and collaborative methods to a traditional lecture hall with seats bolted to the floor. See figure 4 for a conceptual overview of the issues involved.

Formal vs. Informal Spaces

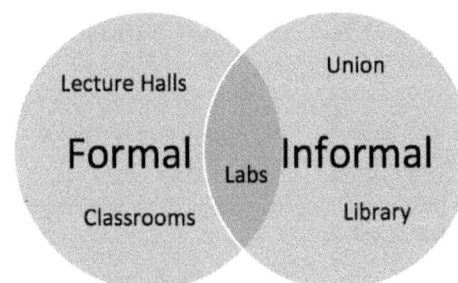

Figure 4. Formal vs. Informal Learning Spaces

A new approach is needed to redesign existing classrooms and prepare new construction to support new teaching methods and faculty must be deeply engaged in the process. WSU is developing such an approach and has applied over the past two years to create two "flipped classrooms," the Math Achievement Center and the Visual Media Studio. See figure 5 to see how new classroom designs can combine elements of both formal and information classroom spaces.

Formal vs. Informal Spaces

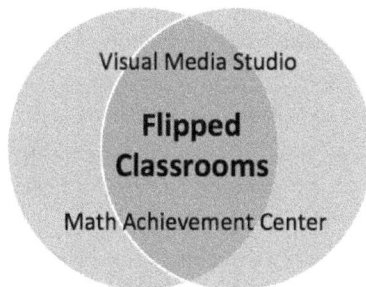

Figure 5. Flipped Classroom

6. NEW FLIPPED CLASSROOMS

The Math Achievement Center and Visual Media Studio are collaborative learning spaces designed by faculty that demonstrate the potential of mobile computing integration. These are the first of many learning spaces designed to support the concept of the flipped classroom. Each of these learning spaces will be described in detail in the space below.

6.1 Math Achievement Center

In the fall 2010 TLT Services started to engaged the Math Department about creating a Math Emporium similar to others across the country (for example Virginia Tech.). It was decided to create a hybrid design of the Math Emporium model and the SCALE-UP [1]. As you can see in figure 6, round tables for collaborative group work and technology enabled breakout tables were built added to the room to create differentiated instructional opportunities for faculty.

Figure 6. Math Achievement Center

In figure 7 you will see close-up of the technology enabled breakout table. At these tables students can connect their laptop to a 46 inch LCD through a Crestron control system. Microphones at the tables facilitate communication in the large space. LCD supports screen sharing and allows the instructors to display their screens to the students.

Figure 7. Breakout Table

6.2 Visual Media Studio

In the spring of 2011 members of the Art, Mass Communication, Marketing, and Computer Science departments came together to create more effective interdisciplinary student engagement, leveraging the many tools of the eWarrior: Digital Life and Learning program. In figure 8 we see the general layout of the classroom with two of the five tables each with its own 46 inch monitor.

Figure 8. Visual Media Studio

In figure 9 we see the faculty 70 inch Smartboard on which faculty can draw on the screen. The Smartboard is touch sensitive allowing instructors to annotate content and save annotations to share with students after class.

Figure 9. Smartboard in Visual Media Studio

In figure 10 you will see the laptop sharing information through the Tidebreak ClassSpot software. Students can share display their screens to the larger LCD, share files, take control of the MacPro workstation located at each desk.

Figure 10. Tidebreak ClassSpot in Action

7. Recommendations

From our experiences with constructing flipped classrooms, we can make several recommendations regarding classrooms, tools, and faculty development. In terms of classrooms:

- It is important to assess your learning spaces to find the best opportunities for spaces that can be flipped. Working from a common set of data allows for effective decision-making and communication among all stakeholders.

- Start with a small project that can be completed in a short timeframe and yields visible results quickly. This helps stakeholders visualize the concept and generalize it to other spaces.

- Plan for untethered, small groups of users. Flipped classrooms must support collaboration and mobility. Students and instructors will need to move around the space easily, bringing their devices with them. Both furniture and technology can be used to promote this level of flexibility.

- Work closely with faculty and students during the design, construction, and implementation process.

- Pick a room used by a specific discipline or limited set of disciplines that are working together effectively to gain consensus on design features quickly. Pedagogical alignment among faculty who will use the room can facilitate the process.

With respect to the tools involved in flipped class instruction:

- Plan for the storage and management of online lecture content. Policies and procedures may need to be established for purging or archiving content from your class capture system in order to meet licensing requirements.

- Use a high quality microphone for recording lectures and classroom activity. In addition, establish a process for getting this equipment into the hands of faculty and students.

- The classroom will probably be used to support projects and assignments that cannot be completed in one sitting. Infrastructure and policies may be needed to create project-based storage for students.

Regarding the faculty development and training involved in preparing instructors to deliver flipped classes:

- Faculty must be comfortable with collaborative instructional strategies that can be applied in a flipped classroom.

- Bring faculty who are considering flipped classes together for training as much as possible. Working together with peers is not only more engaging but it models effect collaborative learning.

- It is very important to training instructors in the actual room and with the tools that will be used for the flipped class. Direct, hands-on experience is the best way to learn how to manage a flipped classroom.

- If possible, a faculty development professional should be present in the classroom the first day the instructor uses the room.

- Faculty should be instructed to prepare their online lectures prior to the term they intend to teach in a flipped classroom. They will need to make decisions about the best tool to use and they will need to learn how to use it effectively. This will also allow more time to learn how to use the collaborative features of the room more effectively.

8. REFERENCES

[1] Beichner, R. 2006. North Carolina State University: SCALE-UP. In Oblinger, D. (Ed.), *Learning Spaces*, Educause: Boulder, CO.

[2] EDUCAUSE Learning Initiative. 2012. *7 Things You Should Know About....Flipped Classrooms.* http://net.educause.edu/ir/library/pdf/ELI7081.pdf

[3] Knewton. 2012. *The Flipped Classroom Infographic.* http://www.knewton.com/flipped-classroom/

[4] Miller, A. 2012. *Five Best Practices for the Flipped Classroom.* Edutopia. http://www.edutopia.org/blog/flipped-classroom-best-practices-andrew-miller

[5] Musallam, R. 2011. *Should You Flip Your Classroom?* Edutopia. http://www.edutopia.org/blog/flipped-classroom-ramsey-musallam www.esd

[6] Oblinger, D. G. 2006. *Learning Spaces: An EDUCAUSE e-Book.* EDUCAUSE. http://www.educause.edu/LearningSpaces

Self-Service Portal Solves
the Forgotten Password Dilemma

Christopher Wiggins
University of Colorado Colorado Springs (UCCS)
1420 Austin Bluffs Parkway
Colorado Springs, CO 80918
+1 719-255-3826

cwiggins@uccs.edu

ABSTRACT

The number of online students at the University of Colorado Colorado Springs (UCCS) was growing rapidly, and the university's policy of requiring on campus, in person only password resets was no longer feasible. Not only did the policy need to be updated, the tools utilized by the Help Desk also required a refresh. The demand for Help Desk support was growing faster than current procedures could handle, topping off at 2,000 reset requests each month. Additionally, a state/system-wide policy change mandated password resets every 90 days, causing requests to skyrocket and demand to grow faster than current processes could accommodate.

UCCS wanted to begin exploring and adopting some basic ITIL best practices, as well as an automated password recovery system. The Help Desk needed to become more than just password resets and common break fix issues. The goal was to offer services that would minimize technology related downtime across the campus. Through the implementation of service management software, including a self-service password recovery function, from Cherwell Software, the university's password reset requests dramatically decreased by 63 percent within several weeks.

Categories and Subject Descriptors

K.6.3 [**Management of Computing and Information Systems**]: Software Management – *Help Desk, password protection, service management, authentication, unauthorized access*

General Terms

Management, Measurement, Performance, Security.

Keywords

Exception Accounts, Help Desk, Password Reset, Self-Service Password Recovery, Service and Support.

1. Overview

At the University of Colorado Colorado Springs, the cost of resetting passwords for students and faculty was adding an extra burden to already tightened budgets. The Information Technology Help Desk was tasked with devising a new method of handling password reset requests, which would make the Help Desk more

efficient and reduce overall costs per incident. A Help Desk Institute (HDI) report backed up these assertions—the report noted that the average fully-burdened cost per incident at $30 for each walk-up and $20 for each phone request compared to just $7 for each self-help password reset. While 79 percent of supports centers agree that self-help is critical, slightly more than 41 percent utilize self-service password reset. Average costs per incident to replace passwords can cost organizations tens of thousands of dollars each year. By implementing an account maintenance portal, UCCS dramatically reduced its password resets—the number one incident reported—by 63 percent. This paper will explore the UCCS challenge, solution and quick wins. This paper will also discuss integration, migration and security considerations. Finally, this paper will discuss the ways in which the university was able to boost efficiency and lighten the workload.

1.1 The UCCS Challenge

The number of online students at UCCS was growing rapidly, and the current policy of requiring password resets to be done on campus and in person was no longer feasible. Not only did the policy need to be updated, the tools utilized by the Help Desk needed a refresh as well.

The demand for Help Desk support was growing faster than current procedures could handle, topping off at 2,000 reset requests each month. Additionally, a state/system-wide policy change mandated password resets every 90 days, causing requests to skyrocket and demand to grow faster than current processes could accommodate. UCCS wanted to begin exploring and adopting some basic ITIL best practices, as well as an automated password recovery system. The Help Desk needed to become more than just password resets and common break fix issues. The goal was to offer services that would minimize technology related downtime across the campus.

1.2 The Solution

By implementing Cherwell Service Management software, including a self-service password recovery, UCCS dramatically reduced the university's password reset requests—the number one incident reported. Implementation wasn't enough: the utility had to integrate with an existing account maintenance portal and pass information to both UNIX and Windows servers so end-users did not have to learn yet another new system.

By providing a solution that enhanced the existing account maintenance portal, end-user registration reached 94%. Once password changes and recovery could be automated, the Help Desk could begin focusing on offering new services such as remote assistance and mobile device support.

1.3 Quick Wins for UCCS

The impact was immediate, long lines for walk up support and excessive hold times disappeared. Those end-users who had technical issues could now properly be assisted.

Password related incidents decreased by 50% within the first week. With the implementation of a Self-Service portal, overall service requests were reduced by 63% within the first semester. These implementations boosted Help Desk efficiency, now, only 20%-25% of all incidents and service requests are password-related

2. THE UCCS CATALYST FOR CHANGE

In Fall 2011, enrollment at UCCS exceeded 9,400 students—an increase of 5.4%. The IT Department needed to quickly address the growth of the campus as staffing levels were not increasing. The Help Desk received 2,000 walk-up or call-in password reset requests every month. Upwards of 70% of all work was password related and end-users often had to call the Help Desk multiple times before non-password related incidents were resolved. Processes used were informal, and demand for support was growing more quickly than these processes were equipped to handle. Furthermore, the Help Desk software at UCCS was multiple student employees checking a single e-mail address and, unfortunately, sometimes end-users never received a response.

To complicate matters, a state/system-wide requirement mandated password resets every 90 days, causing password-related requests to skyrocket. Additionally, the CU system implemented a new student portal requiring the local Colorado Springs Active Directory to control all account authentication. Students could no longer register for classes, access financial aid information, or pay their bill if they didn't know their password. Combined with the rapid growth of online student enrollment at UCCS, it was no longer practical to ask them to come on campus for password resets, especially since online students can be located anywhere.

Simply stated, UCCS quickly surmised that there had to be a better way of handling password reset requests and making the Help Desk organization more efficient, not to mention, reduce overall costs per incident. The 2011 HDI Practices and Salary Report confirmed our assertions. In the report, HDI notes that the average fully-burdened cost per incident at $21 for each walk-up and $20 for each phone request compared to just $6 for each self-help password reset.

With approval from UCCS administration, the Help Desk, System Administrators and Security Principal teamed up to develop the business case for upgrading the system tools and embarked on finding a vendor who could help take the UCCS Help Desk to the next level. Specific criteria that needed to be met included:

- Implementation of a tool that automated repetitive tasks.
- Self-service password recovery functionality, eliminating the number of incidents and the need to spend the majority of time resetting passwords for end-users.
- A portal that would allow UCCS to combine all IT service requests and forms into one location, eliminating the myriad web forms scattered over multiple websites and PDF files that had to be faxed or hand delivered.
- A codeless program in which to develop applications and tools; the program also had to be easy to learn, scalable and flexible.

- A program that allowed for customization; watching to not over-customize the solution, but conversely, did not want to be constrained with an inflexible solution.

Essentially, the IT Help Desk department needed a product that allowed the team to literally hit the ground running.

3. DECISION TIME AND A NEW SOLUTION

The team evaluated systems from Cherwell Software, Numara, ServiceNow and TechExcel before making a decision. The password recovery requirement quickly eliminated several vendors including Cherwell. Upon informing the vendors of this requirement, Cherwell was the only vendor to respond and let the UCCS team know they could easily deliver the password recovery requirement within a matter of days. Less than a week later, the team vetted the solution provided and was impressed with the system's flexibility and ease-of-use, in concert with the speed in which the solution was developed and the commitment Cherwell was willing to make to UCCS; the team reached a decision and was ready to move forward.

3.1 IMPLEMENTATION YIELDS SPEEDY RESULTS

With Cherwell software, UCCS acquired more than just IT service management software—they obtained a powerful Platform as a Service (PaaS) that provides a WYSIWYG development environment for creating additional fully-integrated business applications. Since the Help Desk team did not have to write a single line of code or script, implementation went quickly, and the team was able to put into practice more streamlined processes and efficiencies. This has allowed the team to shift focus and begin offering new services such as mobile device support and remote assistance..

The implementation was very smooth and UCCS saw immediate results. Since the previous Help Desk software at the university was Microsoft Access and escalations were e-mail only, there were times when end-users never received a response. Now, every transaction is recorded and tracked until the request is resolved. End-users no longer have to call the Help Desk multiple times. Cherwell software also allows UCCS to provide consistent and much more efficient support, so if a user calls three times about the same problem, he/she should receive the same answer all three times. That is a huge issue for UCCS because the Help Desk front line is comprised entirely of student employees, and the level of turnover is quite high.

The new solution was implemented in December 2009 and went live with Incident and Service Request tracking in January 2010 to coincide with the start of the spring semester. More than 400 self-service requests were placed before the "go live" date. Self-service was being used even before the Help Desk began tracking requests. When IT needed to redistribute 500 lab computers to faculty and staff offices, they used a self-service approach, requiring end-users to complete a request form for a computer. In turn, this created a service request the Help Desk used to track imaging, configuration and distribution of all 500 computers. This all was completed in one-third of the time it previously took to distribute computers. The password recovery utility was not implemented until the fall 2010 semester. This was planned to coordinate with the start of the new school year.

The Help Desk organization achieved several "quick wins," including:

- Service requests were reduced by 50% within the first week.
- Overall service requests have been reduced by 65%, mostly due to the elimination of multiple phone calls and emails regarding status updates.
- Password-related requests now average only 20% to 25% of all weekly incidents and service requests.

Needless to say, students are thrilled not to have to be on campus to reset a forgotten password. In addition to password reset successes, improving tools and processes at UCCS yielded more efficiency. Prior to the implementation of the new student portal, there was no single sign-on and IT accounts were not tied to student registrations. Now, if students are unable to access their account on the student portal, they cannot register for classes, check the status of classes, check grades and their financial aid, or pay bills.

4. INTEGRATIONS AND CULTURAL CHALLENGES

To achieve a successful implementation, Cherwell had to integrate and communicate with both UNIX and Windows servers. The team had to work closely with the System Administrators to ensure communication between systems provided the necessary information to work together, regardless if it was a text file or direct access to an SQL table.

Other systems and student/faculty tools which have been integrated and automated include:

- Several internal systems to help streamline IT processes.
- Wireless Guest Account Creation—Aruba Networks.
- Active Directory for tracking, monitoring and expiring generic department/club account management.
- Human Resources employee separation process.
- Course shell creation with Blackboard and iTunesU (currently implementing a process).
- Tracking of requests and communications within several other departments outside of Information Technology.

5. THE UCCS ACCOUNT MAINTENANCE MENU

Since UCCS launched its account maintenance portal in July 2010 to coincide with the start of the fall semester, the timing guaranteed a greater number of student registrations. Since the system was new, communication to the students was a critical component and followed a multifaceted approach. Returning students and existing faculty and staff received multiple e-mail communications alerting them to the new system. The Admissions office also included information on the new account portal in its registration letters to students. During new student orientation, the Student Success office included an overview and explained the process. Finally, during phone-in password requests, our Help Desk technicians guided end-users to the site and trained them on how to use the account portal.

The account maintenance portal (accounts.uccs.edu) is both comprehensive and easy to navigate; the menu options are listed below:

- **Claim Your Account:** New UCCS students use this service to lookup their username and set their password.

- **Account Status:** Test UCCS username and password, and list all systems your account can access.
- **Password Change:** Change password for UCCS username.
- **Self Service Password Reset:** Recover a lost or forgotten password for UCCS username.
- **Who is Who:** Faculty and staff identify their UCCS username.
- **Additional Assistance:** Contact the UCCS IT Help Desk.

6. VERIFY IDENTITY AND PROTECT PRIVACY

Within the UCCS system, 94% of all accounts utilize registered security questions. In retrospect, there should have been more thought put into security questions as the system needed to support a higher level of questions. Initially, questions were somewhat generic and could be answered easily by friends or by doing a bit of snooping on social media websites. So a security question such as "Where were you born?" is an easy answer others could figure out. To remedy any potential security breaches, UCCS has implemented a feature which allows students to change security questions and establish new ones any time the change or reset their password—students will no longer be locked into the same security questions.

When a new student claims their account, they are prompted to register security questions, which are then passed to Cherwell. If an existing student, faculty or staff member does not have their security questions completed they will be prompted when logging on to any machine on the UCCS domain. The popup will appear every time they log on until security questions are answered.

An area that was overlooked was the amount of time allotted to end-users when trying to recover their password or someone else's. Initially, end-users had an unlimited amount of time which raised some security concerns. In less than 2 hours, a timed lockout feature was fully tested and implemented; end-users now can only attempt recoveries 3 times in a 10-minute period. This also generates an incident to the Help Desk so technicians can proactively follow up with the end-user and assist as needed.

The system allows for more than one e-mail address, so students, faculty and staff can forward their e-mail, such as 90-day password reset reminders or an alert that someone tried to reset their password, to a Gmail, Yahoo or other account. UCCS found that many long-time employees did not have alternate e-mail addresses, which caused some problems when the system first went live, as it would not allow a UCCS email address to be registered as an alternate e-mail. The primary target was students, and overlooked the needs of UCCS staff and faculty. While there was some resistance to change, most staff and faculty were receptive once they understood the changes and why they were made. Additional modifications to the form were made to allow end-users to provide an alternate UCCS e-mail address, such as a co-worker or supervisor address, however, they could not enter the same address twice.

7. TAKE NO EXCEPTION TO EXCEPTION ACCOUNTS OR CUSTOMIZATION

In addition to the thousands of personal e-mail accounts at UCCS, the university maintains over 400 Exception Accounts—generic accounts for school clubs or departmental accounts (e.g., helpdesk@uccs.edu). UCCS needed to be able to track the owner, or sponsor, for each of these accounts so they do not become "orphaned."

In order for UCCS to comply with CU System Security Guidelines, IT is required to expire (or renew) these accounts on a yearly basis. Bryan Carey, Work-Study Student/Team Lead, has spent the last two years working at the Help Desk, developing new business processes and forms with Cherwell.

To make exception account renewals easier, Bryan created a customized form and process to monitor these accounts. One month, one week and one day prior to expiration, the "account owner" and the account receives a renewal e-mail reminder asking them to log into the system to complete an IT account renewal request. Within the e-mail reminder is a key which the account owner enters into the form; they can then either renew or transfer ownership of the exception account. It took Bryan under two hours to create the form and the Help Desk saw immediate results—within 1.5 hours! Prior to this implementation, the accounts would simply expire and stop functioning, this resulted in a loss of productivity and upset customers. In addition, Bryan was also able to take other university forms that had to be completed by hand and convert them to electronic forms that could be completed online through the self-service portal.

8. MEASURING SUCCESS

Before implementing the Cherwell solution, UCCS relied on information from the system administrator to obtain metrics, including the number of password resets in a particular timeframe. Now with Cherwell Service Management in place, the dashboard number clearly displays for the team the number of requests diverted from Help Desk—this functionality alone saves more than 350 student hours per semester, allowing us to provide several new services, such as remote assistance to faculty and staff. The team is now also able to troubleshoot on the spot. Previously requests went to the Help Desk and could take the staff up to 24 hours to provide tech support. UCCS administration is very pleased with results.

9. HINTS, TIPS AND LESSONS LEARNED

Chris Wiggins' advice to service and support teams, based on his lessons learned when implementing a new solution, would be to take baby steps when making major changes and don't try to change everything at once. It is critical to ensure people have enough time to learn new processes and adjust, and training is essential in ensuring a successful implementation.

Additionally, you must also make sure your plan is aligned with the organizational needs, and it is critical to be aware of the existing culture within your organization. No one wants to adapt to a system—they want the system to adapt to them. Finally, communication is key in any successful implementation and communication needs to occur every step of the way. This experience has shown, it is better to over-communicate with end-users—case in point: the students, faculty and staff at UCCS have never once told the IT Help Desk organization to stop e-mailing and communicating changes, hints and tips.

10. FUTURE STEPS

Since it's all about providing a positive experience and consistent support for both students, faculty and staff, I'm always thinking of ways to continue to enhance those experiences, while also conserving UCCS financial resources. Besides keeping up with the university's growth and providing exceptional customer service, Chris Wiggins' long-term plans focus on moving from a traditional Help Desk environment to an ITIL-based process service desk.

11. REFERENCES

HDI. (2011). *Support center practices & salary report 2011*. Colorado Springs, CO: United Business Media.

Cherwell Software. www.cherwellsoftware.com

Service Now. www.service-now.com

Numara Software. www.numarasoftware.com

TechExcel. www.techexcel.com

An Evaluation of Private Cloud System
for Desktop Environments

Mikifumi Shikida
shikida@jaist.ac.jp

Kanae Miyashita
k-miya@jaist.ac.jp

Mototsugu Ueno
mototugu@jaist.ac.jp

Satoshi Uda
zin@jaist.ac.jp

Research Center for Advanced Computing Infrastructure
Japan Advanced Institute of Science and Technology, JAIST
1-1 Asahidai, Nomi, Ishikawa, Japan

ABSTRACT

We design our computing environment as a centralized system since our university's foundation. By our system, users can connect with their desktop environment on a server at anywhere in the campus. Two years ago, we have built up a new private cloud system. For our system we adopted a combination of three virtualization products: VMware vSphere, Citrix XenApp, and Microsoft Application Virtualization. Our users consist of graduate student, faculty, and staff in the whole university. We can increase efficiency of resource use because they have a different use pattern, respectively. Our other goals are increase of usability and decrease of operation costs. In this paper, we describe the analysis of statistics. Although we have increased average CPU utilization of each server, it is not adversely affected the user experience. We realize that only several tens of servers are enough for use in the whole university. Finally, we discuss the effects of private cloud system in university.

Categories and Subject Descriptors

K.6.4 [**Computing Milieux**]: Management of Computing and Information Systems System Management [Centralization/decentralization]; C.5.5 [**Computer Systems Organization**]: Computer System Implementation Servers; H.4 [**Information Systems Applications**]: Miscellaneous

General Terms

Measurement, Performance

Keywords

Private Cloud System

1. INTRODUCTION

Recently, cloud computing is widely spread for large-scale services. Our university was established in 1990. We designed our computing environment as a centralized system since the

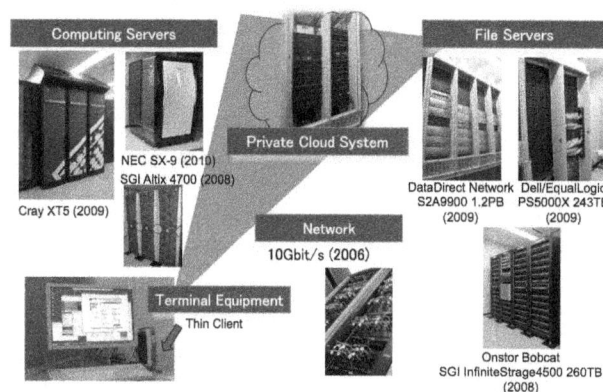

Figure 1. The overview of our information system

foundation. By our system, users can connect with their desktop environment on a server at anywhere in the campus.

But our previous system cannot manage computing resources effectively. The quality of services and usability are not enough. Two years ago, we have built up a new private cloud system. For our system we adopted a combination of three virtualization products: VMware vSphere, Citrix XenApp, and Microsoft Application Virtualization.

Our users consist of graduate student, faculty, and staff in the whole university. We can increase efficiency of resource use because they have a different use pattern, respectively. Our other goals are increase of usability and decrease of operation costs.

In this paper, we describe the design of our system and the analysis of statistics. Although we have increased average CPU utilization of each server, it is not adversely affected the user experience. We realize that only several tens of servers are enough for use in the whole university. Finally, we discuss the effects of private cloud system in university.

2. PREVIOUS SYSTEM FOR DESKTOP SERVICES

In this section, we describe our previous system.

2.1 JAIST Information Environment

Figure 1 shows the overview of our information system.

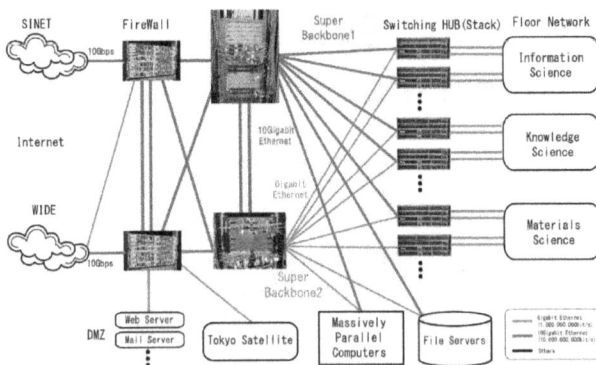

Figure 2. The network in our campus

We designed our computing environment as a centralized system [1] since the foundation. Each user has a thin client as terminal equipment on his/her desk. Users can connect with desktop environment on high-speed application servers. We provide both UNIX and Windows servers for the application servers. All of users' data are stored in file servers. And we provide several types of high-performance parallel computing servers. All of them are connected by high-speed and reliable duplicated network system[2] as shown in Figure 2.

2.2 Hardware for Desktop Services
We introduced more than 130 servers of Fujitsu PRIMERGY RX200 S2 and BX620 S2.

2.3 Problems
Users can log into any server. But then do not have a method to know which server is available. We allocated physical servers for each laboratory and division in order to balance loads of servers. They always log into initially allocated server. There is not enough resource for laboratories in computation fields. They always thought the resources are insufficient. But nobody uses a server for some laboratories. The average of CPU load is extremely low.

3. DESKTOP SERVICE ON OUR PRIVATE CLOUD SYSTEM

3.1 Purpose
The goals of our new system are the following.

1. Efficient resource management
2. Cost down, energy save
3. Better performance
4. Usability

3.2 Physical Machines
We have introduced 51 servers of Fujitsu PRIMERGY BX920 S1. The number of servers is less than half of previous servers. We saved 48% of power supply and 70% of room space. We got an award by Ministry of the Environments in Japan.

3.3 Virtualization Mechanisms
We installed the following three different virtualization mechanisms.

1. VMware vSphere[3]

2. Citrix XenApp[4, 5]

3. Microsoft Application Virtualization[6] (Softgrid)

3.3.1 Host Virtualization
We use VMware vSphere for host virtualization. We place several virtual hosts on a single physical server. Each physical server has two quad-core CPUs and 48GB memory. But we place more than five 4CPU hosts on a server. Administrative staff use a group of hosts different from students' hosts because they work in secure network area. But their hosts and students' hosts run on same physical servers.

3.3.2 Session Virtualization
We use Citrix XenApp for session virtualization. Users can log in by a page on Web Gateway as shown in Figure 3. They select the type of environment and favorite language. They never choose hostname of virtual hosts. The load balancing is performed because they can log on a lowest-load host automatically. When there are some hosts, which require maintenance, we remove their names from a list of available hosts.

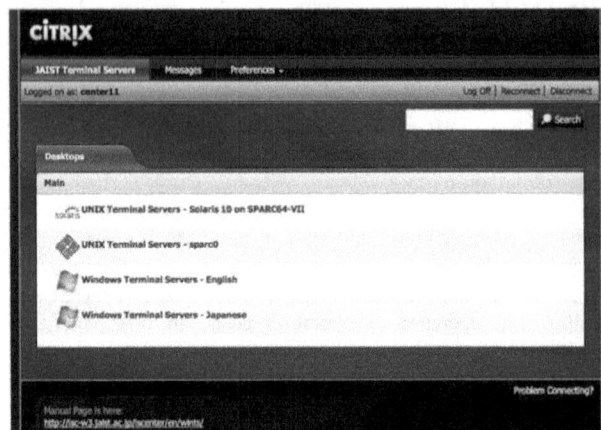

Figure 3. The login window of Citrix XenApp

3.3.3 Application Virtualization
We use Microsoft Application Virtualization for application virtualization. This mechanism controls distributions of images for already installed applications. We can provide applications for all hosts by only one type of installation. Each application runs on a virtual environment. It allows simultaneous use of multiple languages and multiple versions of same application. We can provide a new version of some application, even when the user is using the application. This system can control licenses. We can provide Adobe Photoshop for 1,500 users by only 50 volume licenses.

4. EVALUATION
In this section, we describe evaluation of our private cloud system.

4.1 Resource Management
We show CPU utilization rates of some virtual hosts in Figure 4 and Figure 5. Hosts in Figure 4 are for students. Hosts in Figure 5 are for administrative staff. The averages are normally from 5 to 7% in case of students' hosts. The averages are almost 3% in case of staff hosts. Students' hosts are higher because some users use computation applications such as MATLAB. In the other hand, the averages of CPU utilization rates of physical hosts are 10 to 25%. Figure 6 shows one of physical servers. We saved 48% of power supply and 70% of room space. But we could save more.

We have a plan to provide computation service on same physical servers in order to use available CPU resources.

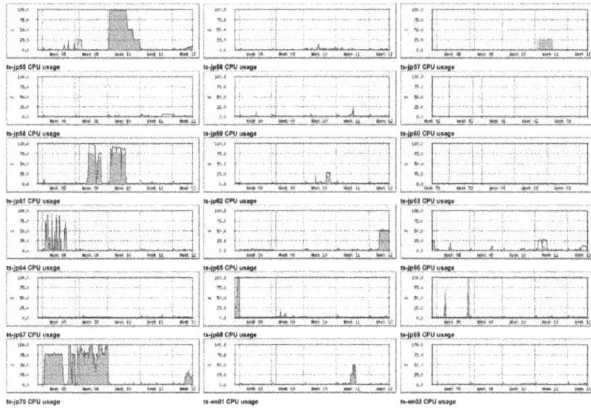

Figure 4. CPU utilization of some virtual hosts for students

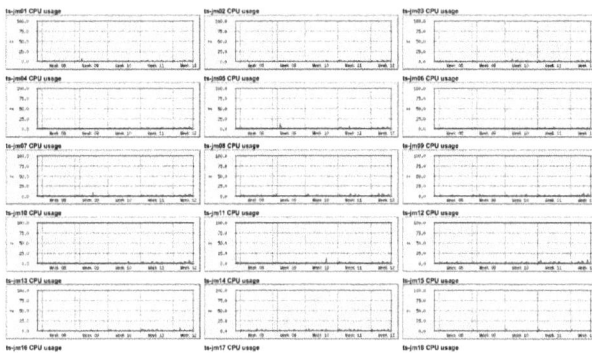

Figure 5. CPU utilization of some virtual hosts for administrative staff

4.2 Maintenance

We can maintain our system without suspend of services.

We can use VMware vMotion for live migration of virtual hosts. We can repair hardware failures in the daytime on weekdays without suspend of services. In the last year, we did largest scale of maintenance. We moved the location of main server chassis in the daytime without suspend of important services. We migrated all of important virtual hosts on subsidiary small system.

The update of Windows is more often than hardware failure. There is no mechanism to migrate Windows session. We can also maintain without suspend of services using session virtualization. When there are some hosts, which require update of Windows and basic software, we remove their names from a list of available hosts. Users have to logon every week because we scheduled automatic reboot at Sunday midnight. We double number of hosts and remove half of them in the list of available hosts. We can maintain all of hosts within two weeks.

The total cost of maintenance is not only for technical operations. We have to notify detail of maintenance and we have to describe influence for each user. Some users missed the notification and they make a complaint to us on the day of maintenance. It takes much effort to respond them. That is the reason we think this is the most important advantage of our system.

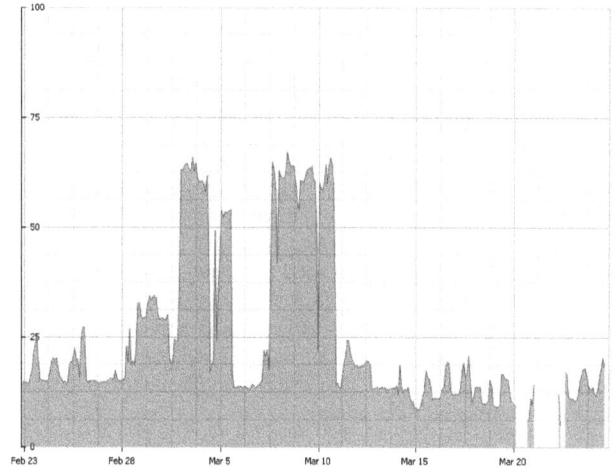

Figure 6. CPU utilization of a physical host

4.3 Advantages for Users

4.3.1 Improvement of services

The specification of hardware was not changed by the replacement of our system. But most users think improvement of hardware, because users can see larger resource by efficient resource management mechanism.

Almost of administrative staff logon at 8:30 A.M. and try to read e-mails. The performance degradation at this time is one of our big problems for our previous system. But there are only few users on students' hosts at that time. There are no degradation on our new system because staff can use the whole of resources.

4.3.2 Improvement of usability

Users can select OS and language on the unified interface. They do not need to search a lower load machine. They do not have to install applications by themselves. It is important to use both of English and Japanese version of application because 30% of students are foreign.

4.3.3 Improvement of availability

Our system can provide high available services because we can maintain in the daytime without suspend of services. But the system is complex and has a lot of bugs. When a single point failure has occurred at any part in entire system and failover mechanism does not work well, users feel entire system down. We need to introduce more safety mechanisms in several different ways.

4.4 Disadvantage of Our Cloud System

4.4.1 Inconsistency among software

We started to serve Windows Server 2008 at 2010 and we can provide service of Windows Server 2008 R2 in this year. There were many inconsistencies among software such as Windows, App-V and XenApp because this combination is rare. We have to wait for release of fixed version.

4.4.2 Complex failures

Our system is large-scale and complex. We introduce virtualization mechanisms in several layers. A system failure is appeared at different place of the source of the failure. The analysis of failure is very hard.

133

4.4.3 Expensive license fees

We installed three different virtualization products. The total amount of license fees becomes higher. The fee would be decreased if one of products would provide all of features.

5. CONCLUSION

In this paper, we describe the design of our private cloud system and the evaluation of statistics in these two years. For our system we adopted a combination of three virtualization products: VMware vSphere, Citrix XenApp, and Microsoft Application Virtualization. This system is used for many kinds of services. The most important and large service is Windows desktop environment for all of students and all of administrative staff in this university. Our system has many advantages for both of users and technical staffs. We could provide better quality of services and we could save energy.

6. REFERENCES

[1] M. Shikida, Y. Inoguchi, Y. Tan, and T. Matsuzawa. Efficient Management Techniques for Large-scale Distributed Systems (in Japanese). In Proceedings of Symposium on Distributed Systems, Internet and Operation Technology, 75-80. Information Processing Society of Japan, (1999).

[2] M. Shikida, Y. Inoguchi, S. Miwa, Y. Tan, and T. Matsuzawa. The Design Method of Large-scale High Availability Servers (in Japanese). In Proceedings of Symposium on Distributed Systems, Internet and Operation Technology, 57-62. Information Processing Society of Japan, (2001).

[3] VMware, Inc. VMware vSphere, http://www.vmware.com/jp/products/vsphere/, (2010).

[4] Citrix Systems, Inc. Citrix XenApp, http://www.citrix.com/ApplicationVirtualization, (2010).

[5] Citrix Systems, Inc. Citrix XenServer, http://www.xensource.com/, (2010).

[6] Microsoft Corporation. Microsoft Application Virtualization, http://www.microsoft.com/systemcenter/appv/default.mspx, (2010).

Ink, Paper, Scissors: Experiments in Cutting Campus Printing Costs

Malinda Lingwall Husk
Indiana University
2709 E 10th Street
Bloomington, IN 47408
812-855-9982
mlingwal@iu.edu

ABSTRACT

Universities are always looking for ways to economize, both because of rising costs and because of growing awareness of ecological issues. Printing is a common target. Indiana University's Pervasive Technology Institute (PTI) compared several typefaces, looking at ink usage, paper usage, and readability. PTI chose to standardize on 11-point Times New Roman for printed documentation such as internal reports and white papers. PowerPoint presentations and other items with relatively small blocks of text are done in Century Gothic. Reports for external audiences will include a mix of fonts with deliberate mindfulness toward ink and paper usage. In short, if a message is rendered ineffective by its presentation, any ink or paper used can be considered wasted.

Categories and Subject Descriptors

I.7.0 [**Computing Methodologies**]: Document and Text Processing—*General*

General Terms

Documentation, Human Factors, Measurement

Keywords

Typography, readability, printing, on-demand publishing

1. INTRODUCTION

In 2010, one Midwestern university decided to cut costs by changing the default font of its e-mail system from Arial to Century Gothic and by encouraging everyone at the university to switch to Century Gothic for word processing documents and spreadsheets [15]. The rationale behind this decision is that Century Gothic uses approximately 30% less ink than Arial. University officials estimated that they spent $100,000 a year on toner [13].

Permission to make digital or hard copies of all or part of this work for personal or classroom use is granted without fee provided that copies are not made or distributed for profit or commercial advantage and that copies bear this notice and the full citation on the first page. To copy otherwise, to republish, to post on servers or to redistribute to lists, requires prior specific permission and/or a fee.
SIGUCCS'12, October 15–19, 2012, Memphis, Tennessee, USA.
Copyright 2012 ACM 978-1-4503-1494-7/12/10 ...$15.00.

In theory, a savings of $30,000 per year on toner sounds great. The reality, however, may look different on paper. On a typical college campus, the amount of e-mail printed by today's tech-savvy students is likely to be far surpassed by longer documents such as term papers, dissertations, and administrative reports. Does "going green" via typography really help the environment? This question led one Indiana University department to examine what it would take to produce all of its printed documentation in Century Gothic.

2. SAVE THE INK, SAVE THE WORLD?

The Indiana University Pervasive Technology Institute produces several lengthy reports and other electronic documents each year. Most are made widely available, and we have no way to know how many times each is printed on campus. Nevertheless, at first blush it is certainly reasonable to think that we could help reduce the university's printing costs by using a font that requires less ink.

To determine the validity of this idea, we created documents filled with the same amount of *lorem ipsum*, traditional incomprehensible Latin placeholder text [1], in a variety of fonts and sizes (one font at one size per document). We initially chose to compare two common serif fonts (Times New Roman and Garamond) and two sans-serif fonts (Century Gothic and Arial). Results are in Table 1.

In 2009, Printer.com tested several commonly used fonts to determine which used the least ink. They ranked 10-point Century Gothic, 10-point Ecofont, and 11-point Times New Roman highest, followed by 11-point Calibri, 10-point Verdana, 11-point Arial, and 11-point Sans Serif. Coming last on the list were 11-point Trebuchet, 11-point Tahoma, and 11-point Franklin Gothic Medium. Their findings show that the cost difference between 10-point Century Gothic and 11-point Times New Roman is negligible [2]. We thus chose to focus our comparison on these two typefaces. (While it is true that 11-point Garamond yields a slightly better result than 11-point Times New Roman, we decided to drop it in the comparison due to perceived readability issues.)

Our experiment clearly shows that while Century Gothic may use 30% less ink than Arial, at 10 points it uses approximately 10% more paper than 11-point Times New Roman. If a user is printing a one-page e-mail, this isn't an issue. However, if a user is printing a 100-page report, the tradeoff becomes clear. Fifty users printing a 100-page document in 10-point Century Gothic on a non-duplex printer will use an entire ream of paper more than the same users printing the same document in 11-point Times New Roman.

Table 1: Comparison of fonts and sizes using blocks of *lorem ipsum.*

Font	Size	Number of lines	Approx. number of pages	Approx. number of characters per full page
Century Gothic	12	275	6.5	3,110
Century Gothic	11	242	5.5	3,702
Times New Roman	12	242	5.5	3,702
Arial	12	242	5.5	3,702
Arial	11	242	5.25	4,086
Century Gothic	10	242	5	4,093
Garamond	12	209	5	4,197
Times New Roman	11	209	4.5	4,623
Garamond	11	198	4.25	4,886

This raises certain questions: At what point does the cost savings on toner balance the extra expenditure on paper? Will the additional wear on the printer cause it to require more maintenance or have a shorter life? At what point will the extra paper we use noticeably increase our negative impact on the environment? A preliminary study done by Indiana University in 2009 concluded that duplex printing on recycled paper certainly decreases environmental impact; however, the amount of carbon dioxide produced during the paper manufacturing process is significantly higher than the impact of printing itself [12].

Using our data from Table 1, we extrapolated to page counts of 100, 200, and 300 using 11-point Times New Roman as our baseline typeface. The results, shown graphically in Figure 1, indicate that 111 pages of 10-point Century Gothic roughly equals 100 pages of 11-point Times New Roman. This scales linearly as the number of pages in the document increases.

What about documents that *don't* comprise solid blocks of text with no headings or graphics? We next looked at three papers previously published by Indiana University. To compare them, we used Microsoft Word's Word Count feature to count pages and lines in the font in which each was originally published, and then chose one page of text from which to estimate a character count.[1] We then substituted our chosen fonts for the body text of each. For two of the three papers, 11-point Times New Roman still came out ahead of 10-point Century Gothic (Table 2). However, we noted that for documents with lists, headings, and other non-body text, the difference between the two fonts was much less striking. (Additionally, the fonts in which papers 1 and 2 were originally published yielded fewer pages than either of our chosen fonts.)

3. CAN YOU READ ME NOW?

We looked next at readability. Allan Haley, director of "words and letters" at the firm which developed Century Gothic, has stated that the font is suitable for small blocks of text such as headlines. He does not recommend its use for longer documents, instead promoting Times New Roman or Arial [3].

For presentations, Microsoft recommends avoiding serif fonts [11]. When it comes to the printed page, however,

---

[1]Paper 3 was converted from PDF. This caused breaks between paragraphs to be counted as very narrow lines, yielding an unusually large line count for the number of pages. This may also explain why the page and character counts were equal, while the line count differed.

according to Merriam-Webster's Manual for Writers & Editors, "...serif faces are somewhat easier to read in blocks or paragraphs of text than sans-serif..." [10].

Readability is, of course, subjective. It's based not only on personal preference, but also on the context in which a typeface is used; e.g., a tabloid-sized concert poster printed in a 10-point typeface isn't likely to get the point across. Not only is it important to choose a readable typeface, but it is also important to choose one that conveys the correct tone. Figure 2 is a reimagining of Arnold Skolnick's iconic 1969 Woodstock poster. It deliberately flaunts standard rules of design, using typefaces that are either unreadable, inappropriate, or both. This illustrative revision makes the dates of the concert indecipherable from the rest of the text – even at full size – and expresses the main message in a typeface more evocative of a horror movie than of the peace and love symbolized by the concert.

In a perhaps more relevant example, the National Science Foundation's (NSF) Grant Proposal Guide says: "The guidelines [for formatting grant proposals] ... establish the minimum type size requirements; however, ... readability is of paramount importance and should take precedence in selection of an appropriate font for use in the proposal. Small type size makes it difficult for reviewers to read the proposal; consequently, the use of small type not in compliance with the above guidelines may be grounds for NSF to return the proposal without review." [14] (It should be noted that 11-point Times New Roman is, as of this writing, one of the typefaces allowed by the NSF. Century Gothic, however, is not listed as an acceptable choice at any point size.)

4. THE DEPARTMENTAL MONEY SINK

The wide variety of print jobs on a typical college campus makes it difficult to control ink and paper usage in campus computer labs. Print quotas currently in place at Indiana University are an effective mechanism toward controlling overall student printing costs [6]. It would be difficult, if not impossible, to institute a mechanism that limits students' print jobs to certain fonts at certain sizes. Doing so would most certainly cause an uproar from the student body. It would be fairly simple, however, to educate those using shared printers about the effect font choice can have on their print quota. There is already information online about conserving paper in the Student Technology Centers (STCs) [7]. A bullet item on this page would reach hundreds of students. (Ironically, hanging eye-catching posters that graphically demonstrate how to manage conservation

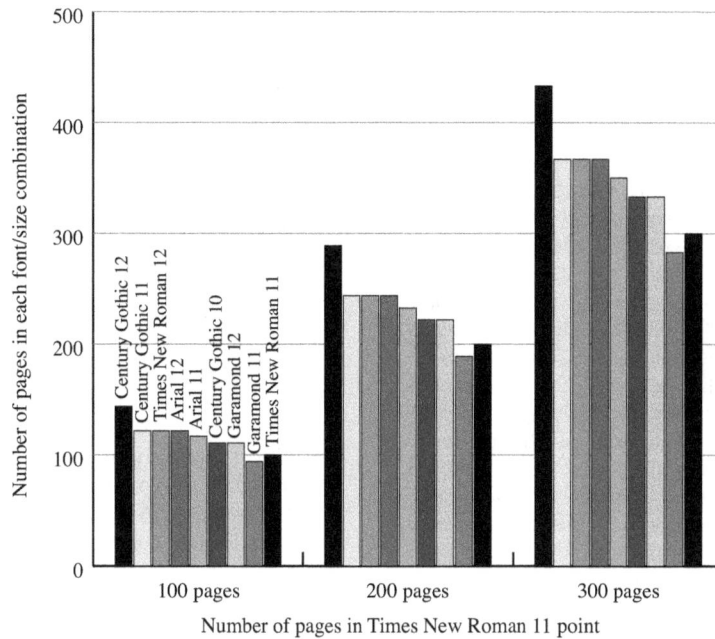

Figure 1: Pages used for the same amount of text in various typefaces.

Table 2: Comparison of fonts and sizes of actual documents.

		As published			Century Gothic 10 points			Times New Roman 11 points		
Paper	Original font	Pages	Lines	Characters per page	Pages	Lines	Characters per page	Pages	Lines	Characters per page
1	Calibri 12	106	5,883	2,899	108	6,415	3,370	107	6,165	3,491
2	Garamond 11	59	2,289	4,178	65	2,548	3,765	63	2,361	3,983
3	Times New Roman 12	104	13,302	2,719	103	12,488	2,719	103	12,577	2,719

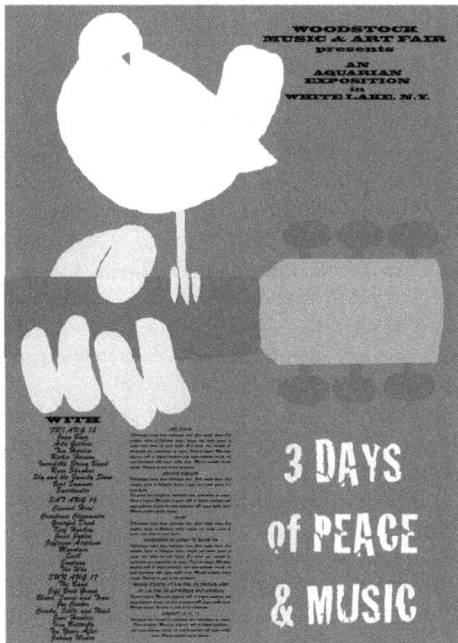

Figure 2: Woodstock reimagined – poorly. (Figure based on original artwork ©1969, Arnold Skolnick.)

through font choice would probably be the most effective way to educate students.)

Departmental printing costs, however, may be somewhat easier to mitigate. Among the reports produced each year by the Indiana University Pervasive Technology Institute are several that must be high-quality, bound copies. In late 2009, printing costs for a perfect-bound, full-color, 152-page report were quoted at approximately $31 each for 160 copies, and approximately $21 each for 260 copies. We quickly determined that printing costs for this particular project would far outstrip the remaining budget. Not only that, but a quick tour of our document storage indicated that we sometimes overestimate our needs, producing more documents than we actually use. With shrinking storage space, a desire to be environmentally friendly, and continued higher education budget cuts, it was time to seek a new solution. We examined several print-on-demand options. Indiana University is a staunch supporter of open source systems, and so our first candidate was Rice University's Connexions [16]. Unfortunately, our ability to design the finished product was too limited by the system. We began to compare commercial options.

All commercial print-on-demand options have pros and cons that will vary depending on one's needs. We found CreateSpace [4] to be the best option for the report in question [8]. Using a print-on-demand service allows us to print only as many copies as needed, with the option to order more at any time without additional setup costs. In this particular instance, we printed only two copies for our records. While our per-unit cost was slightly higher than the price quoted for 260 copies by our local printer, we are not required to purchase a minimum number of copies. What would have been a $5000 print job was instead just over $50.

With the print-on-demand model, the entire cost may be passed to the consumer. While this model saves the university money, the message will tend to reach a narrower audience – only those willing to pay for the printed document. We've alleviated this by offering the same document electronically for free [9]. We also have made every attempt to keep the cost to the consumer as low as possible by offering the report at "publish-at price" – i.e., the cost to CreateSpace for the actual printing and binding. Although self-publishing options are designed to allow the author to set a price in order to receive royalty payments, we did not take advantage of this. The legal, ethical, and public relations issues that would likely stem from a university profiting from a report such as this were easily avoidable. Finally, we are able to purchase copies of our own documents for a lower price than that offered to the general public, so we could certainly use departmental money to purchase copies for others if necessary.

5. CONCLUSIONS: A FONT OF WISDOM

Typography is a surprisingly popular subject (e.g., the documentary *Helvetica* [5]) and a sometimes controversial one (e.g., the online movement to ban Comic Sans [17]). Even mainstream comic strips such as Dilbert, FoxTrot, and Doonesbury have at one time or another poked fun at font choices. No longer solely a tool of printers and graphic designers, fonts can get our message across, save money, and help save the environment – all at the same time.

Following this study, the Indiana University Pervasive Technology Institute chose to standardize on 11-point Times New Roman for printed (or likely to be printed) documentation consisting mainly of blocks of text, such as internal reports and white papers. For items with a high design-to-text ratio, such as glossy brochures and posters, Century Gothic is certainly a feasible choice. Additionally, PowerPoint presentations and other items with relatively small blocks of text may be done in Century Gothic, although presentations are by nature less likely to be printed. Documents destined for professional design and printing, such as reports for external audiences, will continue to include a mix of fonts deemed appropriate by the designer with deliberate mindfulness toward ink and paper usage. And finally, employees are encouraged to avoid printing whenever possible. The bottom line is this: Choosing a font based solely on how much ink or paper it uses is dangerous. If your message is rendered ineffective by its presentation, any ink or paper used can be considered wasted.

6. ACKNOWLEDGMENTS

The author wishes to thank her Indiana University colleagues Craig Stewart, Dennis Cromwell, Kim Milford, Stacy Morrone, Susan Coleman Morse, and Sue Workman for their valuable comments on the first draft of this paper.

7. REFERENCES

[1] C. Adams. What does the filler text "lorem ipsum" mean? *The Straight Dope*, http://www.straightdope.com/columns/read/2290/what-does-the-filler-text-lorem-ipsum-mean, 16 Feb 2001.

[2] bob. Printing costs: Does font choice make a difference? *Printer.com Blog*, http://blog.printer.com/2009/04/printing-costs-does-font-choice-make-a-difference/, 13 Apr 2009.

[3] CBSNews Tech. Are smaller fonts go-green money savers? *CBSNews*, http://www.cbsnews.com/stories/2010/04/07/tech/main6370415.shtml, 7 Apr 2010.

[4] CreateSpace. Home page. https://www.createspace.com/.

[5] Helvetica: A documentary film by Gary Hustwit. http://www.helveticafilm.com/

[6] Indiana University Knowledge Base. About STC printing allotments at IUB. http://kb.iu.edu/data/aouh.html, 16 Dec 2011.

[7] Indiana University Knowledge Base. At IU, how can I conserve paper in the STCs? http://kb.iu.edu/data/aqez.html, 2 Feb 2011.

[8] Indiana University Pervasive Technology Institute. Cyberinfrastructure software sustainability and reusability: Report from an NSF-funded workshop held 27 & 28 March 2009. https://www.createspace.com/3506064.

[9] Indiana University Pervasive Technology Institute. Cyberinfrastructure software sustainability and reusability: Report from an NSF-funded workshop held 27 & 28 March 2009. http://hdl.handle.net/2022/6701.

[10] *Merriam Webster's Manual for Writers & Editors*. Merriam-Webster, Inc., p. 329. 1998.

[11] Microsoft Corp. Fonts, text, and readability. http://msdn.microsoft.com/en-us/library/bb189125.aspx.

[12] S. C. Morse and K. Hanks. An exploration into the environmental impact of duplex versus simplex printing. http://www.indiana.edu/~sustain/docs/Coleman%20Morse%20Duplex%20Summary.pdf, 2009.

[13] P. Murray. Changing font to save ink. *National Public Radio*, http://www.npr.org/templates/story/story.php?storyId=125639616, 6 Apr 2010.

[14] National Science Foundation. Grant proposal guide. http://www.nsf.gov/pubs/policydocs/pappguide/nsf11001/gpg_2.jsp#IIB, Jan. 2011.

[15] U. of Wisconsin Green Bay. Going green with century gothic. http://www.uwgb.edu/compserv/topics/CenturyGothicGreen.htm.

[16] Rice University. Connexions. http://cnx.org/.

[17] E. Steel. Typeface inspired by comic books has become a font of ill will. *The Wall Street Journal*, http://online.wsj.com/article/SB123992364819927171.html, 17 Apr 2009.

Putting iPads in the Hands of Faculty

Kelly Wainwright
Lewis & Clark College
0615 SW Palatine Hill Road
Portland, Oregon 97219
1-503-768-7020

kelly@lclark.edu

ABSTRACT

The Apple iPad has the potential to change how faculty teach using technology. With the small size and touch screen, iPads can be more flexible in a classroom setting than a laptop. With the plethora of apps (short for applications) being created for the iPad, there is tremendous potential for how this new technology can be used to enhance the teaching and learning process.

At Lewis & Clark College, IT and the Library were funded to explore this potential by putting iPads in the hands of faculty across all three campuses (Law, Graduate, and Undergraduate) and then partnering with those faculty to explore innovative ways they can incorporate the iPads into their teaching and learning process.

One semester into the program, this paper will discuss the logistics of the program How about: as well as ways our faculty have found for using their iPads for teaching, learning, and research.

Categories and Subject Descriptors

H.5.2 [**Information Interfaces and Presentation**]: User Interfaces – *input devices and strategies.*

General Terms

Documentation, Experimentation, Human Factors.

Keywords

Faculty Development, iPads, Blogging, Teaching.

1. INTRODUCTION

Will Apple iPads change the way that faculty teach and conduct research? Will they impact a student's experience in the classroom? What other applications do iPads have in the higher education environment? These were only a few of questions that we were hoping to answer by putting iPads in the hands of faculty at Lewis & Clark College. We decided to take an approach of exploration—simply give a faculty member an iPad and let them experiment with it and tell us how it would be useful. Below is a detailed description of how we structured the program, how we

chose our iPad recipients and the results of their first semester of using the iPads in their teaching and research.

Lewis & Clark (L&C) College is a small liberal arts college located approximately six miles outside of downtown Portland, Oregon. Our student body consists of close to 2000 undergraduates, 800 law students, and nearly 900 other graduate students primarily in education and counseling. These students represent 48 states and 69 countries. Serving these students, we have approximately 375 full- and part-time faculty. The Information Technology consists of twenty-five individuals, five of us with iPads and charged with supporting the faculty in this endeavor.

2. PROGRAM STRUCTURE

2.1 Funding

Each year at Lewis & Clark College, our President sets aside funding for strategic initiatives. "The President's Strategic Initiatives Fund provides support for projects that help Lewis & Clark advance key initiatives. In order to be considered for funding projects must serve a strategic interest, must represent a one-time expense, and must be sponsored by at least one Executive Council member. Projects that involve collaboration between the three schools receive strong preference."

We had been looking for ways to explore the use of iPads in an educational environment and were encouraged to apply for funding. In our application, we requested a total of $12,483.00. This budget would allow for the participation of 15 faculty. They would be provided with a 16GB WiFi iPad. Any upgrades would be the responsibility of the participants. They would also be provided with an Apple Dock to VGA adapter for use when connecting to the classroom projection systems and a $50 iTunes gift card for initial app purchases. Additional app purchases beyond this amount would be the responsibility of the participant. The budget also reflected the purchase of three iPads for use by the Information Technology Consultants and Watzek Librarians to allow them to better partner with and support the faculty. Additional iPads were purchased by the IT department and by the library for staff that were not covered by this proposal.

We learned in November of 2011 that our proposal had been funded.

2.2 Faculty Expectations

The expectations for faculty were made very clear in the proposal process and on our iPads in Education web page (http://www.lclark.edu/information_technology/client_services/ipads_in_education/). Faculty who received an iPad through the iPads in Education initiative should expect to participate in the program in the following ways:

- They would agree to use the iPad in at least one class, overseas program, or sabbatical project for three consecutive semesters (excluding summer).

- They would agree to post to a blog at least once a month to provide feedback on their experiences with the iPad. This can include both applications that were tried and situations in which the iPad was used. Both positive and negative feedback was welcomed. This blog is publicly available for the L&C community and those outside the L&C community at http://lcipad.blogspot.com/.

- Participants would agree to complete a survey at the end of each of their three semesters providing formal feedback of their experience using the iPad.

Once all the expectations are met, including the participation in the program for three semesters, the iPad would be given to the faculty member. While some individuals on campus questioned this, I believe that an iPad is a personal device that needs to be customized to the needs of the owner. I also knew that after a year and a half, the technology would be starting to get old. Finally, I knew that the various faculty would be potentially purchasing apps and accessories with their own funds that would be useless without an iPad in hand.

2.3 Selection Process

With funds in hand and the expectations and rewards agreed upon, it was time to award the iPads. We decided to award only ten iPads as a first phase of the program and 5 iPads in the second phase. The idea was that this would allow the program to last an extra semester. It would also allow us to award the 3rd generation iPad in the second phase so that we could see how it compared to the 2nd generation iPads.

The timeline for awarding the first round of iPads was necessarily aggressive since we wanted to give the faculty winter break to begin exploring their iPad before they would need to begin using it for the spring semester. Since we were on a tight deadline, I decided to keep the application process fairly simple. Both on the program's web page and in an email sent to the faculty listservs for all three schools, interested faculty from the CAS, Graduate School, and Law School were instructed to submit a proposal detailing the following:

- The courses in which they anticipated using an iPad.

- How they believed an iPad could add value in these courses.

- The type of Apps they were interested in trying.

- Their agreement to meet the expectations outlined above.

Faculty were asked to keep their applications to no more than two pages and submit them by email. The initial email was sent to the faculty listservs on all three Lewis & Clark campuses on December 15, 2011 with the deadline of December 16, 2011. In that time, we received 35 individual applications.

With this high number of applicants, I decided to use funds traditionally used to purchase instructional software for faculty to purchase an additional five iPads, brining our initial pool to fifteen.

The selection committee was comprised of two faculty members representing the Computer Science Department and the Psychology Department, a library staff member, the instructional technologist from the Graduate School, and myself. We discussed the desire to spread the iPads across all schools, giving two each to the Law and Graduate Schools and the remaining iPads to

College of Arts and Sciences faculty. We also wanted to spread the iPads across disciplines, making sure not to favor the Sciences and Social Sciences where the use of the iPad was more obvious, but also include faculty from the Arts & Humanities. We also looked at proposed uses with an eye to faculty who wanted to use the iPad in a manner that cannot be duplicated by using a classroom computer and/or laptop. Finally, we looked at technology skill levels wanting both those comfortable with technology and technology neophytes to have a chance to share their experiences. With this in mind, we quickly identified the initial group of iPad recipients.

3. THE FIRST SEMESTER

While the faculty received their iPads prior to winter break, they were not responsible for meeting any of the expectations of the iPads in Education program until the beginning of the spring semester, 2012. Faculty used the break to familiarize themselves with their iPads and to begin purchasing iPad apps using their iTunes gift cards.

3.1 *iPads in Education* Blog

The purpose of the blog was to have a way for the faculty to share their experiences both with each other as well as with others exploring the use of iPads in education. Blogger was chosen as our blog platform because we were in the process of converting the campus to Google—since all faculty would soon be required to have a Google account in the Lewis & Clark domain, it seemed a good fit and a good motivation to get this small group of faculty converted.

In January, I sent an email to all the iPad recipients with instructions on how to begin blogging and to reiterate the blogging expectations. Beyond that, there was little structure provided.

For the initial posts, faculty identified what they were hoping to accomplish with their iPads. In the very first faculty blog post, appropriately titled "Getting Started..." one Biology faculty member identified some of his iPad plans stating, "With the iPad's ability to record and play back video and sound, I look forward to being able to share and review observations with students while in the field... something I've never been able to do before." Another faculty member who took his iPad on an overseas program in New Zealand stated, "The major focus of my work with the iPad over the first few weeks of the program has been using it to help create and manage the program "digital journal" that the students have been creating." A professor in our Rhetoric and Media Studies department outlined her plan, "I plan to use the iPad to support my Interpersonal Media course. It is an introductory course in our department that is organized around the question: Do basic interpersonal communication processes change when we do them through electronically mediated channels instead of face-to-face?" And finally, one of the art professors articulated his plans saying, "My goal for using the iPad in the classroom was to find an immediate way of sharing images to an individual student or to a small group of students in the studio rather than moving the class to a smart room."

As the semester continued, the blog posts seemed to focus around two themes. The first was apps that the faculty were using with their iPads. They discussed what apps they had used and found useful or not. One Economics faculty member stated "Air Sketch is a phenomenal app for use in the classroom if you lecture with power point slides. It allows you to freely walk around the classroom with only your iPad in tow, while still having full control over what the students see projected." A physics professor stated, "If you don't already have Star Walk, go get it now! It's summer and the skies are clear, just do it! This app allows you to hold your iPad up to the sky and it will display what stars and planets are immediately behind the iPad, as if it is giving you a window on the heavens."

In addition to calling out specific apps, the faculty identified categories of apps that they were exploring. For example, a Spanish instructor posted that "My second idea is to find the "perfect" attendance/grade keeping app … well, I'm learning the hard way there's nothing perfect!"

The other theme that seemed to permeate the blog posts was a discussion of challenges and obstacles that the faculty encountered in using the iPad. These obstacles included the learning curve for faculty to increase their comfort level in using the iPad. Posts examples included comments like "I haven't yet conquered my fears. Replacing time-tested paper-and-pencil techniques for a digital 'drawing pad' is taking WAY more training time - and there are more dead ends - than I anticipated.". Feeling overwhelmed by the sheer number of apps available to them I browsed the App Store for something I could actually USE, but rather than encouraging me, the SHEER number of applications actually made me give up looking for a solution after less than an hour.. Another post contained issues with the device itself "About the only problem I had with the iPad was how to carry it. It is too big to fit in a pocket, and in the field, I need my hands free to use my binoculars, etc." or "The difficulty about having the iPad version which I have, minus 3G, is that I don't have a consistent Internet connection."

Challenges that I encountered with the blogging process were finding a way to get several reluctant faculty members to participate. There were three faculty members who had not yet posted as the end of the semester approached. It required threatening to reassign their iPads to other applicants to get them to publish their first posts. Part of the issue was that faculty felt that each of their posts needed to be polished essays and they needed to have identified something groundbreaking to be worthy of making it public. Blogging is an interesting medium for which many faculty had difficulty in adapting their writing styles.

3.2 iPad Gathering

Upon receiving their iPad, several of the faculty suggested a gathering of all the iPad recipients. I arranged such a gathering several weeks into the semester. This was a great opportunity not only for the faculty to meet each other but also as a time to discuss some common issues and questions. While we only had about a third of the faculty able to participate, those that were there were able to use their collective experience to quickly identify some of their favorite apps, help each other with some iPad basics, and to commiserate over difficulties that they were encountering in iPad use.

This gathering also proved as an excellent time for the IT staff and the librarians to remind the faculty that we were available to assist them with their iPad explorations.

3.3 Faculty Technology Institute

An even more successful gathering of iPad users was our annual Faculty Technology Institute. This is a week each spring when we offer conference style tracks of workshops specifically geared toward the faculty. Our full session title iPad Tips and Tricks had many attendees from the iPads in Education program as well as faculty who had personally purchased iPads.

We also offered two mini-sessions: one on connecting remotely using the iPad and one on iPad projection. Both of these sessions were popular as well.

Finally, for one of our general afternoon sessions, we offered an iPads in Education update. Four faculty members from the iPads in Education group shared their experiences and answered questions for those in attendance. This developed into a great discussion about the various uses of an iPad in the classroom as well as some suggestions for IT on what services would make the use of various apps more streamlined for faculty.

4. SPRING 2012 IPAD SURVEY

One of the expectations for the iPad in Education iPad recipients was that they would complete a survey at the end of each semester for which they are required to use their iPad. The first survey, therefore, was to be done at the end of Spring Semester, 2012.

The purpose of the survey was to in a more formal and structured format, gather information about how the faculty were using their iPads. Again, with some cajoling of reluctant faculty, we had 18 participants in the survey. This included a couple of librarians who had received iPads and Law faculty who, when they did not receive an iPad through the iPads in Education program, had iPads purchased for them by the Law School.

4.1 iPad Use

One of the initial questions on the iPad survey was attempting to categorize how faculty were using their iPads. The categories that were presented to faculty and their responses are below.

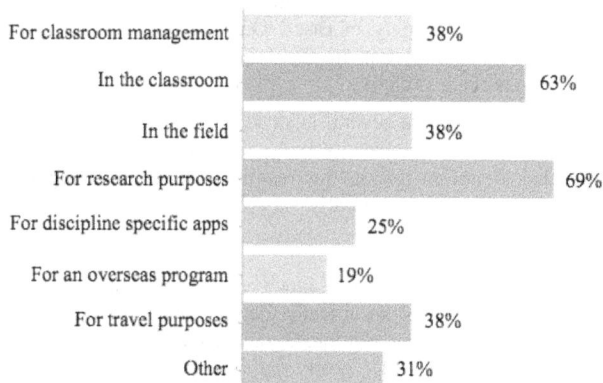

Figure 1. Chart of iPad use distribution.

I'm happy to see that the two largest categories here are for classroom and research purposes, since this was the initial goal of the program. Note that there is definitely overlap in some of the categories—a faculty could use the iPad for a discipline specific app in the classroom, for example. I was also pleased with the diversity in the other categories that faculty selected. This demonstrated to me that we had succeeded during our selection process in identifying faculty with varied applications.

4.2 iPad Apps

As part of the survey we inquired about what apps they had used that they would recommend and what apps they used that they would not recommend. The list of popular apps for this group of faculty included:

- GoodReader
- Air Sketch
- Dropbox
- CloudOn
- Evernote
- Currency
- Genius Scan +
- JotNot Pro
- Pocketcloud
- Papercamera Sibley e-guide to North American Birds
- HeinOnline
- Calculator HD
- GradeBook Pro
- Errands

From this list the most popular apps identified by numerous faculty were GoodReader for PDFs, CloudOn for Microsoft Office functionality, and DropBox for sharing documents between multiple devices.

The list of less popular apps was not as easy to come by. It seems that many faculty simply deleted the apps that they didn't find useful and quickly put them out of their mind. So, when it came time for the survey, they couldn't even remember the titles.

4.3 Accessories

The accessories that we had provided to each iPad recipient were an iTunes card for app purchases, and an iPad to VGA adapter for classroom display purposes. Beyond that, including cases and accessories were the responsibility of the individual. We wanted to see what accessories they deemed to be important.

Of course, the majority of individuals purchased a case. Some purchased name brand cases from Belkin or Apple. Others purchased a wide variety of cases. One individual purchased a Zagg keyboard case, but in the end felt that its Bluetooth connection was a bit "clunky."

Another accessory that several folks identified as important both in the survey and at the Faculty Technology Institute was a stylus. They also identified that in this realm, there are advantages in purchasing one of higher quality.

4.4 Obstacles

Due to the obstacles we saw faculty identify in the blog, we decided to ask them to specifically identify their obstacles in the survey. Many of them reinforced the obstacles that they had identified in their blog posts that were discussed earlier. Additionally, they identified a lack of time in the midst of the semester to be learning and integrating a new technology. As stated by one faculty member, "I found it to slow down my teaching in ways that are unwelcome. But on reflection that has more to do with my own technical skills (lack of) and cumbersome way with something more than a dry erase marker."

The survey was also a better avenue for identifying the technical limits of the iPad. Three that were specifically identified in the survey were the difficulty with the on-screen keyboard, the lack of a USB port, and the lack of Flash for video. While most individuals found workarounds for these issues, it required both time and frustration to do so.

In the end, all but one faculty member answered affirmatively to the question "Overall, was having the iPad of value to you in your teaching and research." In the additional comments section, one Theater professor offered, "It's a great thing to have, and as I said - I'm now considering it the essential tool for me both as a 'private citizen' and a college professor and an artist."

5. IPADS IN EDUCATION–PHASE II

In April, 2012, it was time to give away the remaining five iPads funded by the President's Strategic Initiatives fund. This needed to happen prior to the end of the fiscal year which ended May 31st. By waiting this extra time, it allowed us to provide faculty with the third generation of iPads with improved screen resolution.

We again sent out an email soliciting applications and I was again amazed that we received 17 applications for the five iPads. The same selection committee met to evaluate the applications, having decided to give one to a Law faculty member, one to a Grad faculty member, and three to College of Arts & Sciences faculty. Using the same criteria that we had developed for the first round, we quickly identified four recipients. However, when we couldn't decide between two faculty members for the remaining iPad, I offered to use my departmental budget to purchase one more iPad, allowing us to award a total of six.

One of the faculty members in this round of awards decided that he was interested in both more memory and the 4G option for his iPad. This would provide him with additional flexibility during his environmental studies fieldwork. He was able to supplement the budget for his iPad to add these features.

The iPads were distributed at the beginning of the summer break, again with the idea of giving faculty the extra time to familiarize themselves with their iPad. However, some have already expressed interest in beginning the process of blogging.

6. LESSONS LEARNED

With a semester of the iPads in Education program behind me, there are a couple of items that I would consider doing differently in the future, or that you should consider if you wish to do a similar program.

6.1 Training

I believe that a training session on iPad basics would have been beneficial to help jumpstart faculty use of the iPads. Many of them struggled with basics of navigating the iPad such as learning the hand gestures and organizing apps into groups. One faculty member identified this need on the survey when she explained, "I know IT gave us the iPads in a hurry before the winter break so we could use them and take them with us on trips or overseas programs, so this is NO criticism,,but I think a mini training session or workshop would be very beneficial. I never had used and iPad before, so I feel it's a big learning curve. I'm still trying to learn about its capabilities and try apps at the same time, what makes me feel I'm not using it to its potential. Maybe this is exactly what I'm supposed to be doing." So, an initial 60 minute session that would elevate everyone's ability level would probably eliminate a large amount of frustration.

One area that I totally ignored with the iPads that would have benefitted a little training is security. Establishing some guidelines to help faculty to understand mobile device security would have been very appropriate.

6.2 Contracts

In their application, we asked each individual to express their willingness to meet the expectations of the survey, which most folks did to one degree or another. However, even with that, I still spent too much time persuading the faculty that they *really* did need to post to the blog or complete the survey. It was very unpleasant having to remind faculty multiple times and to threaten the removal of their iPad, sometimes more than once, to entice them to participate fully in the program.

I believe that having faculty sign a contract when they were claiming their iPads explicitly identifying the requirements of the program and identified the consequences if they didn't meet them would have been helpful in assuring those expectations are met. I fear the day that my coaxing doesn't work and I will be forced to actually reclaim an iPad from a faculty member.

6.3 Apps

While I really wanted the faculty to explore apps on their own, and to learn from their experiences, I think that having a base set of apps to recommend to faculty would have helped them get started. For the discipline specific apps, faculty really need to be the experts. However for general productivity apps, I believe having IT take the lead on that research would have allowed the faculty to jump into the more significant software exploration more quickly.

Additionally, there are now easier methods for subsidizing the purchase of apps. While an iTunes card allows the faculty a great start on their apps purchases, Lewis & Clark College is now exploring a volume purchasing agreement license with Apple that would potentially be easier for the faculty and allow IT to see what apps faculty are purchasing.

7. CONCLUSION

Overall I believe that the iPads in Education program is accomplishing its goals. It is both encouraging faculty to explore a new piece of technology and allowing them to learn from the experiences of their peers. It has been rewarding to watch the faculty as they increase their confidence in using this new tool and as they discover what role it will fill in their classrooms, their research and their lives.

One Law faculty in a blog post expressed, "I found that the iPad facilitated a level of interaction and engagement with the students that I would not have been able to achieve otherwise." And another Theater professor said it all when he stated, "It is almost the end of the spring Semester and my iPad and I have become inseparable friends. I simply cannot imagine my life without that little tablet of mine, and I truly "Don't Leave Home (or the Office) Without It."

Blending Military Chain of Command with the Typical IT Support Model to Support the Largest Dormitory in the World

David Tyler
United States Naval Academy
290 Buchanan Road, Annapolis, MD 21601
410-293-7143

tyler@usna.edu

ABSTRACT

The Commandant & Staff IT zone within the Information Technology Services Division (ITSD) at the United States Naval Academy in Annapolis, MD provides IT support to a student body of over 4400 individuals (The Brigade of Midshipmen), the Commandant and his staff, and the company officers and senior enlisted leaders responsible for governing their respective Midshipmen companies. The entire Brigade resides in Bancroft Hall, the largest dormitory in the world, which also houses the office space for the support staff and officers. A dormitory of this size presents its own particular challenges technologically as well as logistically. The IT issues presented by the Brigade of Midshipmen are resolved by a support model which includes the use of government employees, contractors, and students who are referred to as Midshipmen Information Systems Liaison Officers (MISLOs) and have been appointed by their senior officers. Using a combination of the military chain of command and ITSD's information technology support model, the Brigade of Midshipmen have all of their IT needs addressed in a timely manner. In addition to this support model, USNA began using the 3rd party application Web Help Desk™ in October of 2010. The transition from the existing Remedy™ ticketing system to a system using approvals and escalations has ensured trouble tickets don't "fall through the cracks," and are addressed in a timely manner. The use of MISLOs and Web Help Desk has greatly improved the IT process in supporting the Brigade of Midshipmen.

Categories and Subject Descriptors

A.2 [Reference]

General Terms

Management, Documentation, Design, Reliability

Keywords

Midshipmen Information Systems Liaison Officer (MISLO), Midshipmen Computer Repair Center (MCRC), Commandant & Staff IT Zone, Zone, Commandant, Contractor, Dormitory, Midshipman, Midshipmen, USNA, Deck, Web HelpDesk™, Remedy™

1. INTRODUCTION

Bancroft Hall, the only dormitory at the United States Naval Academy, houses every student who attends the institution. A dormitory of 4400 students presents its fair share of information technology challenges. Each room has two to four Midshipmen living within. Each Midshipman has either a personal computer, a netbook, or both, and each Midshipman has an active Ethernet port at his/her desk. Networking requests/issues are resolved by the ITSD networking team, hardware requests/issues are resolved by the Midshipmen Computer Repair Center (MCRC), and software/application requests/issues and active directory/email password issues are resolved by the Commandant & Staff IT zone. All of these requests are received and disbursed to the respective area by the IT zone leader or the company MISLO via the Web Help Desk™ application.

2. BANCROFT HALL

Bancroft Hall is one of the most unique dormitories in the world. "Among the largest residential halls in the world, Bancroft Hall comprises eight wings spread over thirty-three acres, with 4.8 miles of corridors and more than 1,800 dorm rooms, a 55,000 square foot department store, a barber shop, a tailor shop, a cobbler shop, a pistol range, and post office (Bancroft Hall has its own zip code!), a radio station, a credit union and an after-hours snack shop."[1] While there is a certain mystique and sense of history associated with Bancroft Hall, the size and age of the building, as well as the sheer number of students all living in one building, present many issues from an IT perspective.

2.1 Hardware used by the Brigade

One thing that separates USNA from other colleges and universities is the hardware used. Upon arriving at USNA, every incoming Midshipman purchases their computer system (desktop PC, laptop PC, and/or netbook). All purchased systems for the respective Midshipmen class years are identical, meaning there are only six different systems used by USNA Midshipmen at any given time (two classes purchased a desktop PC and a netbook.)

2.2 Structure of the Brigade within Bancroft Hall

The Brigade of Midshipmen is divided into six battalions. Each battalion consists of five companies and each company contains approximately 150 Midshipmen.

3. THE PREVIOUS METHOD

In October of 2010, the process in which IT issues were handled within the Commandant & Staff IT zone at the United States Naval

Academy clearly needed improvement. Specifically, when a Midshipman had an IT related issue, there was no clear and concise method of reporting said issue. A Midshipman could stop by one of the IT representatives' offices, send them an email, or call them. Once the request was received, there was no way of determining when an issue would be resolved or who would resolve it. The aforementioned factors all contributed to the unrest throughout the Brigade regarding the reporting and tracking of IT issues.

3.1 Remedy™ Ticketing System

For many years, ITSD used the Remedy™ ticketing system to manage trouble tickets. While the system was adequate, the policies and procedures for documenting and tracking work were not defined and/or enforced. Some IT representatives created tickets religiously for each task, while others never created tickets at all. The Commandant & Staff IT zone was no different. When a Midshipman had an IT issue, they would "drop-by" one of the IT offices, send an email, and/or call one of the IT representatives in the Commandant & Staff IT zone or the Information Resource Center Help Desk (the latter of which resides in a different building). Occasionally, a Remedy™ ticket was created and tracked by whoever received the reported issue. Often, no ticket was created, and the Midshipmen had no way of knowing if/when their issues would be resolved. There are several reasons the Remedy™ ticketing system didn't fit the Naval Academy's needs, including the confusing design of the interface, the unreliable backend database, and the difficulty tracking tickets. However, the biggest reason Remedy™ wasn't working was the inadequate policy and procedure regarding its use at the Naval Academy.

3.2 Lack of Structure

While the IT representatives within the Commandant & Staff IT zone did their best to resolve the IT issues of the Brigade of Midshipmen in a timely and efficient manner, a lack of instruction led to many Midshipmen not knowing how to report their IT issues. Guidance for reporting IT issues seemed to be spread through word of mouth from upperclassmen. Some "heard" they should report issues to the IRC help desk. Others "heard" their issues should be documented in an email to various members of the Commandant & Staff IT zone. Still others were told they should "drop-by" the Commandant & Staff IT zone offices. Even the IT representatives within the zone had varying ideas of what they were required to support. Some IT representatives believed they were supposed to send all Midshipmen IT issues to the MCRC (Midshipmen Computer Resource Center), while others believed they should attempt to resolve all Midshipmen IT issues. The lack of structure with Midshipmen reporting and tracking Midshipmen computing issues were major reasons IT issues went unresolved.

4. SOLVING THE ISSUE

Several things needed to happen in order for the Midshipmen computing support issue to be resolved. First and foremost, there needed to be some structure. At an institution where structure is a key component to the Academy's success, the lack of structure with regards to Midshipmen computing support within Bancroft Hall was very evident. Furthermore, either a new ticketing system needed to be adopted, or the use of Remedy™ needed to be enforced and improved. Finally, guidance needed to be established which would inform the Brigade of Midshipmen of how to report their IT issues.

4.1 Using the Military Chain of Command

The Midshipmen Information Systems Liaison Officer program was established to help provide IT support to the Brigade of Midshipmen by the Brigade of Midshipmen, with guidance, management, and oversight by the Midshipmen Information Systems (MIS) Officer. The MISLOs "execute duties as assigned by the Midshipmen Information Systems (MIS) Officer."[3] The MIS Officer is also the zone leader for the Commandant & Staff IT zone. Prior to each academic year, the MIS Officer nominates two Midshipmen whom they believe are qualified for the role of Brigade MISLOs. Once the head of the Brigade (the Commandant of Midshipmen) approves the nominations and the Brigade MISLOs take over, the Brigade MISLOs appoint six battalion MISLOs. Each battalion MISLO then appoints a company MISLO for each of the five companies within their respective battalion.

While the MISLO program was established many years prior, several of the MISLOs were not proactive in assisting the Brigade of Midshipmen with computing issues. Figure A. shows the chain of command/organizational chart of the MISLO program.

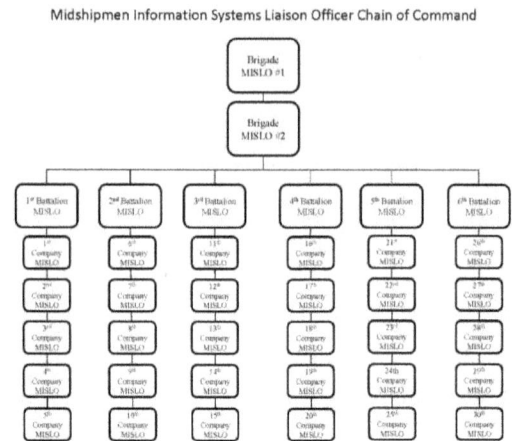

Figure 1. MISLO Chain of Command

Upon being inducted into the USNA, Midshipmen are taught to obey their chain of command at all times. Each Midshipman in the Brigade must answer to a superior. The highest ranking Midshipmen answers to the Commandant of Midshipmen. Using this chain of command to help support the IT issues of the Brigade seemed a natural fit.

Beginning in June of 2011, the Brigade MISLOs adopted a much more proactive approach towards resolving the IT issues of the Brigade. The Brigade MISLOs and the battalion MISLOs now attend monthly meetings with various members of upper-management within ITSD. These meetings are designed to pass along information on any new IT initiatives in the pipeline. In the past, large-scale initiatives (email server migrations, domain changes etc.) were passed only to the Brigade MISLOs under the assumption the Brigade MISLOs would disseminate this information down the chain. However, quite often, the Brigade MISLOs would not inform the Brigade of Midshipmen properly of these upcoming events, leading to many Midshipmen never being notified of an impending IT initiative. With the new approach of monthly meetings with Brigade and battalion MISLOs, information on large IT initiatives is disseminated to all Midshipmen in the Brigade. These meetings are also designed to give the MISLOs an avenue to express outstanding issues with regards to Midshipmen computing and serve as a "checks and balances" to ensure all IT issues are handled in a timely manner. Furthermore, the Brigade MISLOs routinely interface with the MIS officer to resolve all IT issues within Bancroft Hall. The increased interactions between ITSD and the MISLOs coupled with the incorporation of the military's chain of command strategy to leadership have improved the relationship between ITSD and the Brigade tremendously.

4.2 Integrating Web HelpDesk™

In October of 2010, USNA began the migration from the Remedy™ ticketing system to a separate third party application called Web Help Desk™ (WHD.) The shortcomings of Remedy™ were immediately seen to be nonexistent in WHD. Creating tickets was no longer a mystery and a burden. Tracking tickets became a two click process rather than "10 clicks and a prayer." Most importantly, ticketing through WHD was enforced and monitored by upper-management within ITSD. The ticket escalation feature within WHD helped create a checks and balances where if a ticket went untouched for a set period of time, the ticket would be escalated to the IT representative's superior. Requiring all members of the Commandant & Staff IT zone to "buy in" to the new ticketing system was a major factor in improving the IT support provided by the zone. Guidance was given to all members of ITSD regarding the use of WHD, and the requirement to document all trouble tickets was strictly enforced by ITSD upper-management. Since the main issue with Remedy™ was related more to the lack of guidance on its proper use than a lack of desirability to use the ticketing system by the IT representatives, ITSD welcomed the new web-based system with open arms. Furthermore, ITSD embraced a system that was much more user-friendly and efficient. Additionally, WHD allowed for the storage and simple searching of previous tickets for historical reference. The ticketing system has gone from a bone of contention to an embraced tool.

Specifically, within the Commandant & Staff IT zone, WHD helped track Midshipmen computing issues better than ever. Tickets for trouble calls are created immediately (upon receiving the request) and the client (Midshipman) is able to track the status of the ticket. No longer are Midshipmen left to wonder when their issue will be resolved. With WHD, anyone can track the ticket and see the work that's been completed on it. Integrating WHD into the Commandant & Staff IT zone, and strictly enforcing its use, improved IT support for the Brigade of Midshipmen immensely.

4.3 Structure and Guidance

While the new ticketing system helped provide the checks and balances needed within the Commandant & Staff IT zone, the IT representatives within the zone still had varying views on how they supported Midshipmen computing issues. The integration of WHD helped establish a baseline for IT support. Establishing and enforcing some guidelines on supporting the Midshipmen was another key factor. Figure 2 shows the structure adopted by the Commandant & Staff IT zone.

Once this troubleshooting guideline was established, members of the Commandant & Staff IT zone no longer wondered which issues they were required to support. Furthermore, each potential issue resolved by USNA ITSD was to be documented in a WHD ticket for tracking (note: as of April 2012, the Midshipmen Computer Repair Center (MCRC) continues to use Remedy™ as their ticketing software because of migration issues from Remedy™ to WHD.)

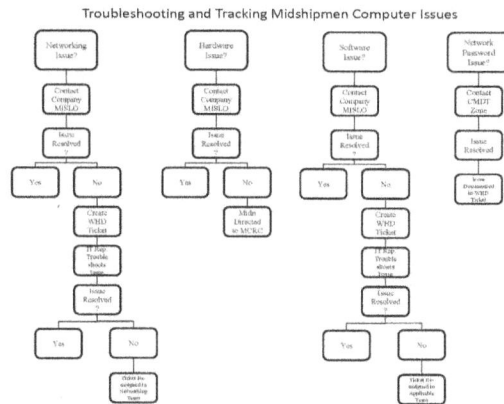

Figure 2. Flow Diagram for Midshipmen IT Trouble Tickets

Finally, the Brigade MISLOs disseminated, down through their chain of command, the support structure. All Midshipmen were reminded they should initially contact their company MISLO for any IT related issues. The company MISLOs are efficient in first level troubleshooting and often resolve issues without the need for escalation. At the beginning of each semester, the Brigade MISLOs remind the Brigade of the ITSD support structure, which includes initially using their respective company MISLOs rather than the Commandant & Staff IT zone. While the Commandant & Staff IT zone is ready and willing to assist with IT issues, the use of MISLOs and the knowledge that the Company MISLOs are there to help has greatly improved the IT support the Brigade receives.

5. CONCLUSION

Several factors have contributed to the improvement and continued success of IT support in Bancroft Hall. Establishing and enforcing the use of Web Help Desk™ helps create a culture of documenting everything. Using the military chain of command to allow the MISLOs the power and authority to help resolve IT issues is vital. Combining technology with military structure proved to be a difficult but largely successful venture which has helped allow the Brigade of Midshipmen the best opportunity to fulfill the mission of the United States Naval Academy.

6. REFERENCES

[1] Kiland, Taylor, and Howren, Jamie. 2007. *A Walk in the Yard: A Self-Guided Tour of the U.S. Naval Academy*. Annapolis: Naval Institute Press.

[2] Mack, William, and Seymour, Harry, and McComas, Lesa. 1998. *The Naval Officer's Guide*. Annapolis: U.S. Naval Institute.

[3] United States Naval Academy. Office of the Commandant of Midshipmen. 2011. *Commandant of Midshipmen Instruction 1601.12C: Brigade Striper Organization and Selection Procedures*.

An Introduction to the Special Interest Group on Internet and Operation Technology (SIG-IOT) of Information Processing Society of Japan

Takashi Yamanoue
Kagoshima University
Korimoto, Kagoshima 890-0034, Japan
+81-99-285-7187
yamanoue@cc.kagoshima-u.ac.jp

Naomi Fujimura
Kyushu University
4-9-1, Shiobaru, Minami-ku, Fukuoka Japan
+81 92 553 4434
fujimura.naomi.274@m.kyushu-u.ac.jp

Hideo Masuda
Kyoto Institute of Technology
Matsugasaki, Sakyo-ku, Kyoto 606-8585, Japan
+81-75-724-7128
h-masuda@kit.ac.jp

Motonori Nakamura
National Institute of Informatics
2-1-2 Hitotsubashi, Chiyoda-ku, Tokyo 101-8430, Japan
+81 3 4212 2541
motonori@nii.ac.jp

ABSTRACT

This paper introduces the Special Interest Group on the Internet and Operation Technology (SIG-IOT) of the Information Processing Society of Japan (IPSJ). IPSJ SIG-IOT is a similar association to ACM SIGUCCS in Japan. It retains about four hundred members who are mainly managers and operators of ICT infrastructures in universities and colleges, and staff members of companies. The activity of IPSJ SIG-IOT focuses on the technologies for the Internet in general and the techniques for the construction, operation, and administration of the distributed computer/network systems.

IPSJ SIG-IOT organizes regularly four workshops and one symposium once a year, and also issues a special section in the IPSJ journal every year. All papers submitted for the symposiums and journals are reviewed. IPSJ SIG-IOT participates in the Multimedia, Distributed, Cooperative, and Mobile Symposium (DICOMO) every year, as one of the organizing SIGs. It also hosts the Workshop on Company, Campus and Community Networking (C3NET) every year. C3NET is a workshop of the International Symposium on Applications and the Internet (SAINT), which is co-sponsored by IPSJ and IEEE CS.

The fields of operational technologies may look modest and tend to be shunned, especially by young people. However, it must be an important portion of the fundamentals of the ICT (Information and Communication Technology) infrastructures that continue to grow. We are encouraging the research activities and preparing academic papers for young people and hope the activities of IPSJ SIG-IOT help to convey the importance of the field.

Categories and Subject Descriptors

A.1 [**INTRODUCTORY AND SURVEY**]

General Terms

Management, Experimentation

Keywords

Association, special interest group, the Internet, operation technology, management, administration

1. INTRODUCTION

The Special Interest Group on the Internet and Operation Technology (SIG-IOT) of Information Processing Society of Japan (IPSJ)[2] is a similar association to ACM SIGUCCS in Japan. It retains about four hundred members who are mainly managers and operators of ICT (Information and Communication Technology) infrastructures in universities, colleges, and staff members of companies. The activity of IPSJ SIG-IOT focuses on the technologies for the Internet in general and the techniques for the construction, operation, and administration of the distributed computer/network systems.

The target research area of IPSJ SIG-IOT is the technologies for the Internet in general and the techniques for the construction, operation, and administration of large-scale distributed systems, including the Internet including the followings:

- Architecture and communication methodologies for the Internet,

- Technologies for the construction of network systems with/without support for user authentication/authorization,

- Techniques for the improvement and evaluation of network performance, methods for system monitoring and managing, and technologies for the construction, operation, and administration of large-scale distributed systems.

In particular, this group will be very useful for people who are working as system administrators or who are developing products to support such systems to obtain information that may not be obtained anywhere else since specific cases on practical systems have also been and will be reported on.

The fields of operational technologies may look modest and tend to be shunned, especially by young people. However, it must be an important portion of the fundamentals of the information and communication infrastructures that continue to grow. We are encouraging young people to work on the research activities and to submit academic papers and hope the activities of IPSJ SIG-IOT help to convey the importance of the field.

2. HISTORY

Founded in April 1960, the IPSJ, Information Processing Society of Japan[1], has been a leading authority in technical areas of information processing and computer science for professionals and students in Japan. IPSJ will provide a leadership for sound evolution of the computer science, and technology in an increasingly computerized society and will contribute to creation of new ideas to cope with the accountability for evolving information technology. Through its authoritative publications, conferences, and other activities, IPSJ will play a critical role in the world for the global prosperity.

IPSJ promotes development of the arts, sciences, industry, and humanity through conducting various activities about information processing with computers and communications and providing resources for discipline and opportunities of cooperation with sister societies to members.

IPSJ has 38 special interest groups which issue technical reports, hold conferences, and edit transactions.

The Special Interest Group on Internet and Operation Technology (SIG-IOT) of IPSJ was organized in April 2008 through the integration of the Distributed System and internet Management technology (SIG-DSM) and the Quality Aware Internet (SIG-QAI). Approximately 500 people are enrolled in this group in total.

SIG-DSM was initially established in 1996 to discuss the technologies for developing and operating large-scale distributed systems at universities or companies. As the Internet explosively grew, the topics were shifted to technical issues that many organizations had about the construction or administration of network systems, and also to the wide variety of applications that not only administrators but also users are deeply concerned with.

Meanwhile, SIG-QAI was established in 2001 to discuss various issues for the improvement of the quality of communication services over the Internet and research topics for the construction of high-quality next generation Internet. Since the quality of communication over the Internet was very poor at that time, various research proposals, mainly how to smoothly pass along voice and video streams, were actively discussed. As the bandwidth of the Internet improved, the research topics widely spread into technologies such as the reliability and stability of various communications and techniques for the construction and operation of networks systems.

Each SIG, SIG-DSM and SIG-QAI, had different origins although their situations in regards to the information and communication fields in social environments has been changed. The research areas of these SIGs have overlapped, and it has been difficult to see a difference between the research fields of the two SIGs from the point of view of the participants. Moreover, even if the names of both SIGs have the keyword "Internet", there was a tendency for the targeted research field to be only the Internet. However, there is a wide range of research fields related to the Internet, such as communication methods, construction techniques, management practices, and their applications. Therefore, it seemed to be important to share information between the two SIGs.

So, the two SIGs were integrated and named the Internet and Operation Technology (IOT) to clarify the target areas as the technologies of the Internet in general, and the technologies for the construction, operation, and administration of large-scale distributed systems, including the Internet, and to make it possible to involve more people.

The first memorable IOT workshop was held in Kagoshima City in May 2008, and was co-hosted by the technical committee on the Information and Communication Management (ICM) of the Institute of Electronics, Information, and Communication Engineers (IEICE).

3. STRUCTURE

SIG-IOT consists of the executive members, the board members, regular members and student members. The executive committee consists of six members including the chair and the treasurer. The board members consist of 33 members recently. Some of them are in charge of local arrangement and program committee chairs of workshops and symposiums. There also are chairs of awards committee in the board members. Five board meetings are held each year. Table 1 shows the number of regular members of IPSJ SIG-IOT.

4. WORKSHOPS AND SYMPOSIUMS

IPSJ SIG-IOT organizes regularly four workshops and one symposium every year as shown in Table 2 and Table 3. Some of workshops are accompanied with data center or computer center tours. IPSJ SIG-IOT participates in the Multimedia, Distributed, Cooperative, and Mobile Symposium (DICOMO) every year, as one of the organizing SIGs. IPSJ SIG-IOT co-operates with other SIGs in locally and internationally.

Table 1. IPSJ SIG-IOT Members

Year	# of Members
2008	468
2009	405
2010	404
2011	385

Table 2. IPSJ SIG-IOT Activity

Year	# of Workshops	# of Presentations	Average participants
2008	4	99	67
2009	4	48	63
2010	4	49	63
2011	4	71	53

Table 3. IOT-Symposium

Year	Theme	Submitted	Accepted	Inviting	Panels	Participants
2008	Towards Unifying and Association of Various Network Services.	23	18	2	1	115
2009	Internet and Operation Technology in the Virtual Age	18	15	3	1	77
2010	Aiming construction of dependable systems	17	16	3	1	84
2011	Considering Operation Technology from the viewpoint of emergency management	14	12	2	1	50

5. JOURNAL

"Publish or perish" is also applicable to many of the IPSJ SIG-IOT members. It was hard to write academic papers on operation, management, and administration of ICT infrastructures in Japan because such kinds of activities are considered less valuable in Japan. They must be important to maintain ICT environment smoothly. To improve the situation, IPSJ SIG-IOT has been to issue a special section in the IPSJ journal every year since SIG-DSM started the activity. The members of IPSJ including IPSJ SIG-IOT review all papers submitted for the journals. In order to help authors to write and improve their papers, the reviewers of the special issues are required to play the role of a mentor. We have applied the reviewing process of the ACM SIGUCCS conference[5][6] to the reviewing process of this journal. We also welcome English papers. Some of accepted papers are in English.

Table 4 shows our activities in the IPSJ journal. The followings are titles of the latest issue[3].

Table 4. Special section in the IPSJ Journal

Year	Theme	Submitted	Accepted
2008	Internet Technology and Distributed System Management Technology for Supporting Soft Services.	40	11
2009	Internet and Operation Technology for Unifying and Association of Various Network Services.	27	9
2010	Internet and Operation Technology in the Virtual Age.	19	7
2011	"Development, Operation and Management of Dependable Systems	19	8

- Self-contained Binary and De-duplication to Mitigate Problems caused by Dynamic Link

- Action of Saving Energy for Air Conditioners in Server Room

- Implementation and Evaluation of Single Sign-On Function for Switch based Authentication Network

- A High Performance Discovery Method of Configuration Data of System for Large-scale Data Center

- A Method for User-oriented Notifications Using Part Dependence in Large-scale Servers

- Development of a Monitoring System of Digital Signage to Improve Dependability of Displaying Contents

- A Study of Development in Information and Communication Technologies for the University-wide Education and Information System at Kyoto Women's University

- An Adaptive Route Selection Mechanism Per Connection Based on Multipath DNS Round Trip Time on Multihomed Networks

6. INTERNATIONAL ACTIVITY

IPSJ SIG-IOT also hosts the Workshop on Company, Campus and Community Networking (C3NET) every year. C3NET is a workshop of the International Symposium on Applications and the Internet (SAINT), which is co-sponsored by IPSJ and IEEE CS. From 2004, some of IPSJ SIG-IOT members are participating ACM SIGUCCS conferences every year.

The following is the program of the latest C3NET workshop[7].

The Third Workshop on Company, Campus and Community Networking - Technology, Management and Ethics - (C3NET 2012)

Welcome Note by Workshop Organizer: Nariyoshi Yamai

Session 1: Mobility and Traffic Engineering

Chair: Ikuo Nakagawa

Vertical Handover Control Considering End-to-End Communication Quality in IP Mobility
Takuya Hourai, Kaori Maeda, Hayato Morihiro, Yasuhiro Ohishi and Tomoki Harase

Design and Evaluation of Global Live Migration with Mobility Support for IP Multicast
Keisuke Kamada, Tohru Kondo, Kouji Nishimura and Reiji Aibara

An Adaptive Approach for Network Traffic Load Balancing by Using One-Way Delay
Hiroki Kashiwazaki, Satoshi Kobayashi, Shugo Kawai, Norikatsu Ohishi and Yoshiaki Takai

Multihoming Method Using Routing Header in IPv6 Environment
Takuya Yamaguchi, Yong Jin, Ryoichi Tokumoto, Nariyoshi Yamai, Kiyohiko Okayama and Motonori Nakamura

Session 2: Network and Distributed System Management

Chair: Kaori Maeda

A Location Free Network System Applicable to Geographical Terms of the Electronic Journal Site License
Yoshihiro Ohsumi, Kiyohiko Okayama, Nariyoshi Yamai, Takaoki Fujiwara and Takashi Hieda

Koshien-Cloud: Operations of Distributed Cloud as A Large Scale Web Contents Distribution Platform
Yoshihiro Okamoto, Satoru Noguchi, Satoshi Matsuura, Atsuo Inomata and Kazutoshi Fujikawa

An Account Provision and Management Architecture for Messaging Services in Emergency
Kazuyuki Tasaka, Yasutaka Nishimura and Kiyohito Yoshihara

An Execution Control System for Application Software Reducing Administrative Burden of Educational PCs Masanori Fujiwara, Keita Kawano and Nariyoshi Yamai

Session 3: Network Security

Chair: Hiroki Kashiwazaki

Spam Mail Discrimination System Based on Behavior of DNS Servers Associated with URLs
Shuji Suwa, Nariyoshi Yamai, Kiyohiko Okayama, Motonori Nakamura, Gada and Keita Kawano

A Casual Network Security Monitoring System using a Portable Sensor Device and Wiki Software
Takashi Yamanoue, Kentaro Oda and Koichi Shimozono

Session 4: Workshop Keynote

Chair: Motonori Nakamura

Trustworthiness in Next Generation Networks
Serap ŞAHİN

Concluding Remarks by Workshop Organizer: Nariyoshi Yamai

7. AWARDS AND PRIZES

IPSJ SIG-IOT prepares some kind of awards such as IPSJ Yamashita SIG Research awards[4] to encourage persons working in the Internet.

IPSJ SIG-IOT also arranges the Prize for students' presentations, Discounting of Member's fee to attend IPSJ SIG-IOT conferences and symposiums.

8. CONCLUDING REMARKS

An introduction to IPSJ SIG-IOT is presented. IPSJ SIG-IOT is one of the most important academic forums for operators, administrators and managers of the Internet and ICT infrastructures in Japan. As members of similar group to ACM SIGUCCS, we would like to enhance the relationship with ACM SIGUCCS.

9. REFERENCES

[1] IPSJ http://www.ipsj.or.jp

[2] IOT http:// iot.ipsj.or.jp/

[3] IPSJ Journal 53(3), 937, 2012-03-15

[4] IPSJ Yamashita SIG Research Award
http://www.ipsj.or.jp/english/organization/aboutipsj/
award/yamashita.html

[5] Deits, G. 2008. Developing a Content Management System for SIGUCCS. In *the SIGUCCS '08 Proceedings of the 36th annual ACM SIGUCCS fall conference*,(Portland, OR, October 19-22, 2008). DOI=
http://doi.acm.org/10.1145/1449956.1450000

[6] Murphy, T. Read, write, and present for ACM SIGUCCS conference. In *the SIGUCCS '11 Proceedings of the 39th ACM annual conference on SIGUCCS*(San Diego, CA, November 12-17, 2011). DOI=
http://doi.acm.org/10.1145/2070364.2070394.

[7] SAINT http://www.saintconference.org

Extending the Centralized Helpdesk Functionality to Improve Decentralized Support

Rachael Cottam
University of Memphis
001 Wilder Tower
Memphis, TN 38152
901-678-8027

rcottam@memphis.edu

Jeff Goff
University of Memphis
001 Wilder Tower
Memphis, TN 38152
901-678-3986

jeffgoff@memphis.edu

Peter Nguyen
University of Memphis
001 Wilder Tower
Memphis, TN 38152
901-678-5782

pnugyen2@memphis.edu

ABSTRACT

Academic Affairs Technology (AATECH) provides support for 500+ computers on the University of Memphis (UofM) campus and remote sites. As part of our ongoing commitment to provide excellent customer service, we utilize the centralized helpdesk system. However, we have created additional tools to extend the functionality of that system. These tools allow technical professionals to monitor open helpdesk tickets for critical issues that arise throughout the day. We plan to demonstrate how we use the existing infrastructure and newly created tools throughout our support footprint in a helpdesk ticket's lifecycle. Topics to be covered include the helpdesk ticket lifecycle at our university, the centralized helpdesk system, and the newly created tools. Through this poster session we hope to encourage an exchange of information that will benefit us and others who are seeking innovative approaches to monitoring and improving customer service.

Categories and Subject Descriptors

K.6.4 [System Management]: Centralization/decentralization.

General Terms: Management, Documentation, Performance, Reliability, Human Factors.

Keywords: Helpdesk, monitoring, support, customer service.

1. INTRODUCTION

Academic Affairs Technology (AATECH) is a non-centralized support unit at the University of Memphis (UofM) that provides support to 500+ customers and computers on the main campus as well as five remote sites. AATECH consists of nine local technical support providers (LSPs), one web specialist, and one director. AATECH processed 3360 and 4043 tickets in 2010 and 2011, respectively. A major goal for AATECH is to respond as quickly as possible when help is requested. Therefore, a need for additional tools was recognized.

AATECH extended the use of the university's enterprise helpdesk system by creating additional tools to help improve AATECH's response time and resolution of issues for our customers. Having these tools at our disposal allows us to prioritize requests and follow through with customers to ensure we respond in a timely manner. We have consistently received high marks from customers regarding our quick response times.

This paper will provide an overview of the helpdesk ticket lifecycle at UofM, the centralized helpdesk system, and the newly created tools.

2. HELPDESK TICKET LIFECYCLE

A ticket can be submitted by various means. A client has the option of calling the helpdesk, walking into the helpdesk office, or submitting a ticket via the web site (helpdesk.memphis.edu). In an emergency situation the customer can also call an LSP and the LSP can submit the helpdesk ticket on the customer's behalf. Customers contact the helpdesk for a wide range of issues. The helpdesk triages incoming request and escalates the issues to LSP units throughout campus if additional help is needed (Figure 1). When tickets are assigned to LSP units, LSPs receive notification via enterprise helpdesk system.

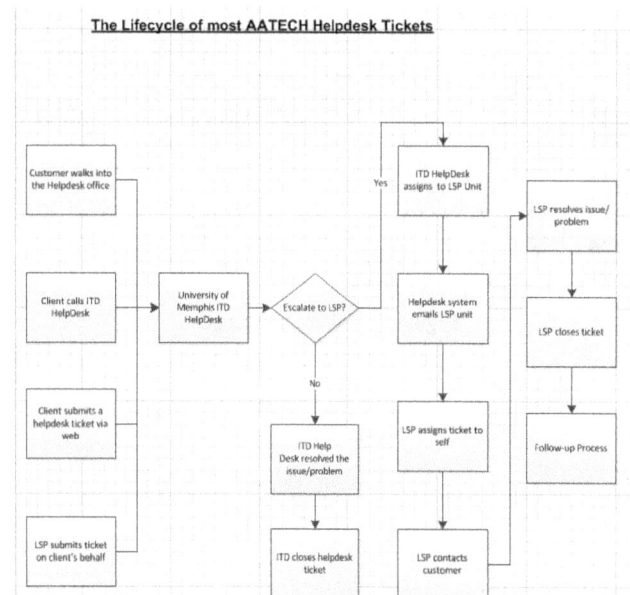

Figure 1. Lifecycle of most AATECH Helpdesk Tickets

3. AATECH TOOLS

AATECH has developed three tools that enhance our customer service: a dashboard, an email reminder script, and a follow-up process.

3.1 Dashboard

The dashboard provides an overview of outstanding helpdesk tickets. "Outstanding" is defined as any helpdesk ticket assigned to AATECH that does not have a status of "closed." This dashboard utilized symbols and colors to help AATECH identify the severity and current disposition of helpdesk tickets.

Figure 2 depicts the symbols used by the dashboard. The symbols designate the priority of the ticket: low, medium, high, or critical.

◯	Non-critical - low, medium, high
🔥	Critical

Figure 2. Symbols indicating Priority

Figure 3 depicts the colors used by the dashboard. The colors designate the current disposition of the ticket: green, yellow, red, and purple represent a ticket less than three days old, a ticket less than 14 days old, a ticket more than 14 days old, and a ticket with a status of "pending," respectively.

🔥	A green flame means the ticket's priority is critical and the ticket was submitted less than 3 days ago
🟢	A green circle means the ticket's priority is low to high and the ticket was submitted less than 3 days ago
🔥	A yellow flame means the ticket's priority is critical and the ticket was submitted 4 to 14 days ago
⚪	A yellow circle means the ticket's priority is low to high and the ticket was submitted 4 to 14 days ago
🔥	A red flame means the ticket's priority is critical and the ticket was submitted over 14 days ago
🔴	A red circle means the ticket's priority is low to high and the ticket was submitted over 14 days ago
🔥	A purple flame means the ticket's priority is critical and status is pending
🟣	A purple circle means the ticket's priority is low to high and status is pending

Figure 3. Dashboard Legend

A combination of these symbols and colors on the dashboard

provides LSPs a graphical representation of tickets currently assigned to them. The dashboard also provides the director with an overview of all tickets currently assigned to the department. Figure 4 depicts the dashboard.

Figure 4. AATECH Dashboard

3.2 Email Reminder Script

The helpdesk system generates emails when tickets are assigned to the LSP unit. However, sometimes the emails are not consistently formatted. In addition, AATECH had some instances where tickets "fell through the cracks" and customer service suffered. To address these issues, AATECH created an email reminder script.

The script runs every 15 minutes and emails a list of all AATECH tickets that have yet to be assigned to an LSP. The email contains ticket details and any notes added to the ticket (Figure 5 and Figure 6). This email enables AATECH to quickly take action on unassigned tickets and also provides consistent formatting of ticket contents. These "nag" emails also constantly remind AATECH staff of tickets that are waiting to be addressed.

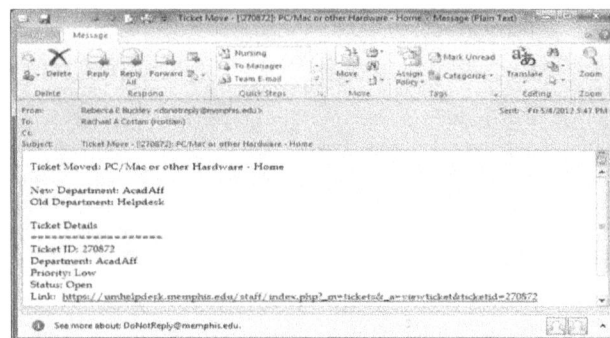

Figure 5. Helpdesk system email

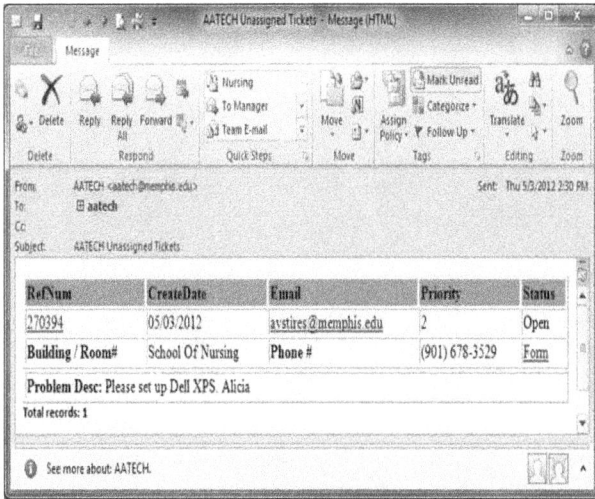

Figure 6. Email Script

3.3 Follow-up Procedure

Several years ago AATECH implemented a follow-up process for helpdesk tickets. On a regular basis, AATECH student workers review tickets closed more than seven days ago. The student worker follows up with the customer to confirm the issue is resolved. If the issue is not resolved, the student worker re-opens the ticket and notifies the director for follow-up with the LSP. Customers have consistently expressed their appreciation for our follow-up procedure.

4. SUMMARY

This paper demonstrated the tools created by AATECH, a decentralized support unit, to expand the functionality of the centralized helpdesk system at the University of Memphis. These tools assist with AATECH's goal of providing excellent customer service to a broad array of customers including students, faculty, researchers, and staff.

Effective Zero-Cost Help Desk Software

Dan R. Herrick
Colorado State University
Engineering Network Services
Fort Collins, CO 80523-1301
970-491-3131

Dan.Herrick@Colostate.edu

Lisa Metz
Colorado State University
Engineering Network Services
Fort Collins, CO 80523-1301
970-491-3465

Lisa.Metz@Colostate.edu

Andrew Crane
Colorado State University
Engineering Network Services
Fort Collins, CO 80523-1301
970-491-2465

Andrew.Crane@Colostate.edu

ABSTRACT

The College of Engineering at Colorado State University provides computing support for a growing population with a shrinking budget. Help desk communications with our clients, such as problem reports and resolutions, was inconsistent. We had difficulty tracking trouble tickets, our staff collaboration tools were insufficient, and our response times were poor due to the lack of proper software tools. In an effort to provide quality customer service and support, we had to find a solid help desk software solution at no cost.

We implemented Trellis Desk in August 2008 to replace our limited-capability open source help desk system. Since that time, we have achieved positive results. Response times to our clients have decreased, employee collaboration has grown, and client satisfaction has increased. We have better management tools including reporting capability, an overhead view of issues, and logical grouping of tickets. We will explain how an effective help desk software tool gives us the ability to better manage support for our clients by using the "right tool for the job".

Categories and Subject Descriptors

H.3.4 [**Information Storage and Retrieval**]: Systems and Software – *Performance evaluation (efficiency and effectiveness), Question-answering (fact retrieval) systems.*

H.4.1. [**Information Systems Applications**]: Office Automation – *Workflow management.*

H.5.2. [**Information Interfaces and Presentation (e.g., HCI)**]: User Interfaces – *Graphical user interfaces (GUI), Training, help, and documentation.*

H.5.3. [**Information Interfaces and Presentation (e.g., HCI)**]: Group and Organization Interfaces – *Computer-supported cooperative work.*

General Terms

Management, Documentation, Human Factors, Standardization.

Keywords

Client Service, Desktop Support, Help Desk, Software

1. INTRODUCTION

Colorado State University (CSU) has a highly decentralized IT environment. CSU has a central IT group, which provides basic infrastructure for all administrative and academic units, including internet backbone, basic email and calendar support and course management software. Each college and department must provide additional support based on the needs of its faculty, staff and students. Desktop computing support most often falls to the individual college or department.

The Engineering Network Services (ENS) group provides computing support for the College of Engineering (COE). The COE has 2,474 students and 498 faculty and staff and occupies three main campus and eight off-campus buildings. ENS employs eight permanent, full-time staff and 25-30 temporary, part-time student employees.

2. BACKGROUND
2.1 History

Historically, ENS employee roles were divided into about half client services (including labs and desktop support), and half network and systems infrastructure. Each department of the college was assigned one Support Analyst who was their primary point of contact and who primarily performed all the required work. Eventually, restructuring and budget cuts reduced the number of Support Analysts to below the number of departments, which necessitated a change in our (ENS') service strategy. Work was divided among the pool of Support Analysts, although individual Support Analysts were still the primary point of contact for departments.

2.2 Centralization and Consolidation

In 2007, we saw that we would need a better way to manage our help requests. Our one-analyst-per-area model was becoming increasingly cumbersome and, as a result, internal and external (client) communication was less than ideal. At the same time that our college grew in faculty lines, our student enrollment increased. Support became more costly from a time and resource perspective. One of our full-time Support Analysts departed, after which we lost one FTE completely. We knew at that point that we would need a different, more cohesive way to support the College without extra cost.

We developed two approaches to changing our service strategy: We would centralize all desktop support work and create one central point of contact for our entire IT group.

2.3 Centralizing Desktop Support Work

To support the first approach, we ceased our practice of assigning one Support Analyst to one or more departments, and instead gave all desktop support work to a pool of available Support Analysts. After we lost one FTE, we were able to use some of our budget to increase our student labor force, which in turn required even more coordination of tasks and facilitation of information sharing. The current help desk, established in November 2006 to serve the needs of the student computer labs, was expanded into a full help desk in November 2007 that served all of the college's users (students, faculty and staff). Overall responsibility for and staffing of the help desk formally transitioned from the labs team to the analyst team.

The second approach required even more information sharing among multiple sub-groups within our IT group: The analysts group, the labs group (which supports the computer labs), and the systems group (which supports network and systems infrastructure at the college level).

Our first tactic to support this strategic change was to find a Help Desk software suite that would not only help us manage workflow, but improve communication with our clients and staff. Our hope was to implement Help Desk software, which would allow us to communicate internally (staff only) through a specific trouble ticket and allow the client to ask questions of our staff without the need to call a specific staff member. We also thought that a new system would allow for more sharing of information amongst our group that would help expedite problem solving.

3. GENERAL NEED FOR A HELP DESK TOOL

In general, help desk software allows IT organizations to improve customer support, become more efficient at handling customer requests, prioritize customer requests, and generate reports. It has long been recognized that help desks, and in particular help desk software, add value to an organization.[1]

A help desk software tool provides a standard, central communications method between staff and clients (internal or external), and among staff. For example, staff may need to collaborate to solve a problem, and they may communicate within the help "ticket" about the problem. That way, troubleshooting steps and eventual resolution are documented within the same ticket where the original problem is noted. The ticket provides a way for staff to ask clarifying questions and to communicate the status of an issue, and allows clients to provide further information about a problem. It also allows a client to query for the status of an open issue without involving staff.

Organizations further gain efficiency by being able to assign a priority to tickets and respond to tickets in a centrally defined prioritized order. Clients appreciate having a central point of contact, which takes the guesswork out of who to call.

4. OUR SPECIFIC NEEDS

Our existing help desk tool worked well for internal communications, and tracking systems or labs-related issues. However, it was not an ideal candidate for tracking desktop support issues and it was certainly not a tool that we could transition to a fully functional, client-friendly help desk system.

Losing one FTE forced us to take a good look at our existing model and find a way to more easily handle help requests.

Our next step was to determine what was most desirable in a Help Desk solution. We created a list of important components: cost, ability to assign tickets, staff-only notes, searchability, and customization.

4.1 Cost

Given our budgetary issues, cost was clearly the number one factor in helping us to determine which solutions we could look at. Our IT Director gave us a budget of "a few hundred dollars," which was to include technical support. This seemed to limit us to free, open-source software tools.

4.2 Assignation

Because we have several different functional groups, whose area a ticket needs to be directed to, we required the ability to assign a ticket to an entire group or to an individual.

4.3 Staff-Only Notes

At times we may need to discuss the technical issues of a ticket internally to the IT group, without the client hearing the "chatter" of the work-in-progress of the support issue. We desired a mechanism to attach technical or staff notes to a ticket that the client did not see.

4.4 Searchability

As part of an increasingly complex knowledge base of support information, we needed to be able to quickly and efficiently search through solved and unsolved tickets for keywords, client or computer names, and similar information to help more quickly resolve repeat support issues.

4.5 Customization

Our group has always been inclined to use open source software because we are comfortable modifying existing software, and often see the need to enhance the performance of the software and tune it to our specific needs. The "free" price tag certainly helps.

We also have developed our own software tools to query databases of software tools like a help desk tool to extract relevant data and generate our own reports. It is often easier to manipulate data directly than to go through a software tool's built-in reporting features.

5. THE FIRST ATTEMPT WAS A "WREQ"

Prior to this season of change, we had been using a web-based tool called wreq as our help desk software.[2] According to the wreq web site, "Wreq is designed to be a distributed request/problem tracking system with builtin [sic] knowledge database to help systems personnel to stay on top of requests and to prompt knowledge sharing among all local support groups."

The wreq tool is highly customizable using Perl, and has very minimal system requirements, but only runs on UNIX-based web servers. It is offered as free open source software.

Although the wreq tool can be adapted to serve the IT department's clients, as we did, it was primarily developed as an internal tool for IT staff. Thus, it does not have a "user friendly" interface and few of the options for users that other help desk software tools offer.

We used wreq from November 2003 to August 2008. We re-evaluated our use of the wreq tool in March 2004. At that time, we determined that the need for enhancements was not worth the time, effort and cost to change tools. Although we acknowledged that it was not a very robust tool, it was sufficient for our needs. Active development of this tool seems to have ceased, as the last update was March 2005.

Several usability flaws were encountered with the tool. For example, wreq was unable to quote text in replies to tickets by default (so users did not have the context of an issue). When responding to a ticket, options exist both to quote the original ticket submission, and to include the "action log", which is the entire conversation thread. Unfortunately, both options must be checked in order to include all data, and neither can be selected by default. This demonstrates one fundamental flaw of the tool: It is sometimes too configurable, allowing many options without a cohesive strategy to logically bundle menus of options.

The promise of an internal knowledge base gleaned from wreq tickets failed to materialize. The interface was deemed too arcane by our staff, and the internal search features inefficient.

6. SELECTING NEW HELP DESK SOFTWARE

After exploring several options, we selected three software tools to review in detail: Best Practical RT: Request Tracker (RT)[3], OTRS (Open Technology Real Services)[4] and ACCORD5 Trellis Desk (Trellis)[5]. We established a test server to allow our group to test features, create tickets and evaluate the pros and cons of each program. Once we felt primary testing was complete we held a meeting and addressed all possible concerns regarding each piece of software.

In this process, it was helpful to us to acknowledge that the final solution would not have to be a perfect one -- just better than the rest. We documented the limitations of each and asked ourselves: "Will this limitation prevent us from using the product effectively?"

6.1 Costs and Support

All three software tools had no cost to download and use the software. Best Practical provides custom support for RT for a monthly fee. OTRS provides value-enhanced customized versions of the software and custom support for a fee. All three had a variety of community support options. RT and OTRS are open source software. Trellis is not open source, but the license agreement allows for full access to and customization of the code.

6.2 Formally Evaluated Components

All three tools fulfilled our requirements for assigning tickets. Trellis gives the ability to assign a ticket to a group separately from an individual, so that tickets may be assigned to a group and not to an individual, thus allowing greater flexibility.

All three tools allow for some type of staff-only note or comment. Trellis allows for two types: A general "Notes" section for each ticket, which is not incorporated into the timeline of the ticket; and a "staff-only reply", which logs a reply within the timeline, which only staff can see.

All three tools had built-in search functions. RT seemed the most complex and robust, allowing a SQL-like syntax for searching tickets. Trellis provides search by predefined fields, and filters for viewing tickets.

Each of the three tools provided some ability for customization, either through the provided interfaces or administrative tools, or direct modification of the code. Trellis uses PHP for its operations and interface, and MySQL for the backend database, both of which we are familiar and comfortable with. RT and OTRS both use Perl and support MySQL, PostgreSQL and Oracle database options. (In addition, OTRS supports Microsoft SQL Server.)

In general, we found RT to be complex in setup, configuration and customization. OTRS seemed to be more straightforward in setup, partially because it provided less customization capability.

Trellis seemed to outperform the others in the flexibility of components, speed of operation, and ease of use.

6.3 Other Factors Affecting the Evaluation

Although we did not initially decide to elect usability as a specific evaluation point, we had to acknowledge its effect on the final outcome. We had to look at usability from a client standpoint, and a staff standpoint.

For clients, the usability had to be very simple: a web-based and an email interface that provided the same information. Clients can email a central email address to create a ticket, and create a ticket from the web-based tool. We also added a custom form to our web site, which allowed users to create a ticket without entering the Trellis web interface. Later, we also added functionality so that email replies to a ticket appended to that ticket rather than creating a new ticket.

For staff, we acknowledged that some staff are not as technical as others. A senior level UNIX systems administrator is not going to approach a user interface the same way as a student lab consultant. Also, the typical help desk worker is going to work within the tool much more often than a systems administrator, but the tool needs to accommodate both.

In appearance and operation, RT was too reminiscent of the "barebones", text-oriented wreq tool for our liking. OTRS, while much more streamlined and modern, had a too-high level of complexity in everyday operation, requiring, for example, several clicks to accomplish a simple task like viewing all responses to a ticket.

7. IMPLEMENTATION

We tested Trellis for only two months (concurrent with our old help desk software) before we were satisfied enough to go ahead with a full implementation, in August 2008.

Trellis implementation was relatively straightforward as it is built on PHP and uses MySQL for the database. One of our systems administrators was able to easily install the software and get the basics running for us with no issues. We defined our departmental headings and added our staff members to the Staff Group with appropriate permissions. Trellis Desk is very customizable so we created fields for Academic/Administrative Department, Building, Room Number, Operating System and Computer Type.

Trellis allows us to define a group (department), which a ticket can be assigned to, as well as individual assignments. We selected the following departments: Systems, Analysts, Labs, and Help Desk. Later, we added an Admin group to cover general questions like chargebacks for accounts and software licensing. All tickets are initially assigned to a generic "ENS" group, which prompts us to manually assign it to the correct group. Our help desk workers are tasked with answering common questions, and asking clarifying questions before moving the ticket to the appropriate group.

8. FEATURES OF TRELLIS

Trellis Desk allows us to group tickets logically. We can view them by internal department, user or owner (who has been assigned a ticket). When our employees arrive for their shifts, their first task is to check tickets assigned to them for follow up. They will then go through the remainder of all tickets in their department to ensure nothing gets missed. Trellis Desk makes this easy and we're able to use the Internal "Staff Only" replies to communicate with each other on issues without the client being aware of what we're doing. We also make use of "canned replies" to easily enter frequently used text into a ticket.

Because the Trellis database is hosted on our MySQL server, we can manipulate the data directly for fixing data issues, and export the data for reporting purposes.

Trellis provides a "System Overview" dashboard view, which shows a customizable snapshot of items like tickets awaiting action, last few actions, and system status. The Ticket Control view allows for fast sorting and filtering of tickets by priority, department, last reply and other criteria. A staff member can quickly see what tickets are assigned to them personally or to their department. Tickets can be bulk-managed (for example, sorted into a department or closed.)

Email integration is excellent. When a user sends an email to our help desk email address, a new ticket is automatically created and a confirmation response sent to the user. A direct link to the user's ticket is included in the email so that they may refer to it for updates. Future responses to the ticket are also sent to the user's email address. A user may click on the provided link and respond to the ticket through our Trellis web site, or reply to the email to update the ticket.

9. LIMITATIONS OF TRELLIS

Every piece of software comes with pros and cons and Trellis was no exception. We noticed that the initial version didn't handle attachments well and there was no asset management component. These issues were not enough to deter us from using Trellis; however, and the attachment issue was addressed in a more recent revision.

Reporting capability is minimal but it wasn't high on our list of priorities. While we can look at some statistics through the Trellis management portal, we find it most beneficial to export relevant data and use our own tracking and reporting methods.

We recently re-evaluated our help desk software tool, with the intention of finding one that incorporated asset management. We decided to stay with Trellis as our help desk software and implement a separate asset management tool, because we could not find one within our price range that performed noticeably better.

10. BENEFITS

We are able to tell that over half of our help tickets have been help desk or desktop support related so we are certainly taking advantage of this resource. The other groups, like the systems and lab groups, have benefitted from a centralized ticket tracking system, since they do not have to handle many of the "frequently asked questions", as well as try to determine what staff member is the best equipped to handle a problem.

This software tool has certainly improved staff collaboration, as we are able to easily converse with each other within the context of the ticket about the issue at hand, without resorting to email. When the staff-only response is used, rather than two staff members emailing each other, other staff are informed of the issue and frequently (and voluntarily!) add their own helpful responses.

Response times have increased due to the efficiency of the tool. Our internal policy is to respond to every ticket within 24 hours, but in practice, we usually respond to each ticket within minutes during business hours. The web-based tool is easily accessible and some staff members choose to respond after hours (a practice we do not encourage but also do not forbid, because it indicates high involvement with work).

Most of all, our customers are happier. We do not formally track customer satisfaction, but in surveys and informal feedback, our users very much appreciate having a clear, concise route to asking for help. Our clients now have four methods of contacting our help desk: An email to our help address, a web form, a telephone number and a visit in person to our help desk. Each contact opens a help ticket in the same place, so they can check the status of their issue at any time.

Looking ahead, Trellis is preparing to come out with a new major version and will convert to a GNU General Public (open source) license. Community involvement with the software is at an all-time high, and we are excited to see what other developments will result from this new energy.

11. REFERENCES

[1] Middleton, I. "Key Factors in HelpDesk Success (An analysis of areas critical to helpdesk development and functionality.)" British Library R&D Report 6247, The British Library 1996.

[2] http://www.math.duke.edu/~yu/wreq/. WREQ – a distributed request/problem tracking system.

[3] http://bestpractical.com/rt/. RT: Request Tracker – Best Practical.

[4] http://www.otrs.com/en/. IT Service Management Software – Free Open Source Help Desk – Problem Management System – Customer Interaction Software – OTRS.

[5] http://www.accord5.com/trellis. ACCORD5 – Trellis Desk.

Food and Drink in Computer Labs: Why Not?

Dan R. Herrick
Colorado State University
Engineering Network Services
Fort Collins, CO 80523-1301
970-491-3131

Dan.Herrick@Colostate.edu

ABSTRACT

Traditionally, computer labs have a number of logical policies, one of which is to ban or highly restrict food and drink consumption. Evolving usage patterns of computer labs point to the desire by users to make computer labs more "lounge-like" and less "cave-like". Managers of these spaces are accommodating this desire, and some managers have begun to relax these restrictions and allow some food or drink consumption under limited circumstances. Most are still uncomfortable with the idea of unlimited food and drink.

Two years ago, the College of Engineering at Colorado State University removed a 30-year ban on food and drink in its computer labs. The results are far from the increase in filthiness and equipment damage that are generally feared from consumables near computing equipment. In fact, the insignificant cost increases are far outweighed by the savings in staff time spent enforcing this unenforceable policy, and by the dividends of goodwill that our organization receives from its users. We explain why computer lab managers should reconsider their policies toward food and drink, and the potential benefits they can derive from relaxing or removing these policies.

Categories and Subject Descriptors

K.4.1 [**Computers and Society**]: Public Policy Issues – *Computer-related health issues*

K.4.3. [**Computers and Society**]: Organizational Impacts – *Computer-supported collaborative work*

K.6.0. [**Management of Computing and Information Systems**]: General – *Economics*

K.6.2. [**Management of Computing and Information Systems**]: Installation Management – *Computing equipment management, pricing and resource allocation*

General Terms

Management, Human Factors.

Keywords

Computer Labs, Food, Drinks, Policies, Management

1. BACKGROUND

The College of Engineering (CoE) at Colorado State University (CSU) serves about 2,500 students with about 400 computer seats in 15 computer labs and computer classrooms. The CoE employs one FTE Computer Lab Manager and about 8 part-time student employees in the computer labs. The funding for all computing equipment, plus wages for the student employees, is provided by an Engineering-specific Charge For Technology (CFT), aka "technology fee". This CFT is managed by the Engineering Student Technology Committee (ESTC), which is comprised of students and faculty.

2. INTRODUCTION

The ubiquitous "no food or drink allowed" sign at the computer lab entrance is a part of the computer lab's cultural history and the restriction is part of routine computer lab management. From elementary school to graduate school, we teach students to leave the snack packs inside the backpack – or outside the room entirely. With good reason: Sugary water plays havoc with circuit boards, and keyboards already contribute enough to the dark side of germ warfare without adding greasy organic particles to the mix.

But many students spend more of their lives in these labs, particularly in disciplines like Engineering and Computer Science which require specialized computing and software resources to complete routine class work. An oft-repeated rule of thumb is that students should expect to spend 2-3 hours outside of class working on course materials or homework for every hour spent in the classroom [1]. This means that students will frequently spend multiple hours, often spanning mealtimes, in computer labs.

A computer lab is no longer necessarily rows of humming terminals under a sterile bank of fluorescent lights. Recent trends in computer labs also show that students use these areas as flexible, social, multi-use spaces, and the managers of these areas sometimes even encourage this use [2].

Computer lab managers are becoming pressured to allow food or drink in these spaces as the use of these spaces evolves. Tension and conflict occur between student users and lab managers and their assistants. Rather than perpetuate this conflict, it may be simpler to adapt to the situation and change food- and drink-related policies.

2.1 Survey

In March and April 2012, we conducted a survey of college computer lab managers regarding their organizations' policies surrounding food and drink in computer labs. The most common concerns are to prevent damage to the equipment (67%), keep the area clean (67%), and prevent sticky keyboards or mice (58%).

Other concerns are confrontations with users, germ and sickness spreading, and preventing rodent/insect activity. Some seem concerned that students already do not take care of their work area or clean up after themselves, even with restrictions on food and drink in place.

Some organizations do allow food and/or drink in their computer labs to some extent. A majority (58%) allow water and other drinks in a closed container in any computer lab. 53% allow open drink containers only in certain areas. 56% allow food to be consumed in certain areas, while 44% allow it anywhere.

3. RATIONALE

The CoE had banned food and drink from its computer labs since its first lab of mainframe terminals was brought online 30 years ago. The reasons for the original ban are not recorded, but it can be assumed that the common wisdom of computer lab management prevailed. When computer terminals cost several thousand dollars, it made sense to keep hazards like drinks and food away from them to avoid potential mishaps.

In more recent years, however, the cost of common computer components such as keyboards and mice has gone down dramatically. These are now commodity items and often tracked in a separate maintenance budget rather than tracked as capital equipment.

At the same time, computer lab usage has risen significantly in the CoE. Higher enrollment and a changing culture have led to more students spending more and longer blocks of time in the computer labs. The CoE IT staff found that most staff contact with users in the labs was a result of enforcing the ban on food and drink, which resulted in a more negative perception of IT staff.

4. ENFORCEMENT

According to those surveyed, most (58%) enforcement of food/drink policies is done by lab managers or assistants, while instructors do 20%. It is generally agreed that instructors can make better use of their instruction time than enforcing lab policies. 33% of respondents don't enforce policies at all.

In most cases, the worst users get is a verbal warning or lecture (45%). Other common consequences include the user leaving the lab and returning without the offending food/drink item (30%), and IT removing or throwing away the item (18%). Respondents report that 39% of the time, there are no consequences to a violation of this policy.

The CoE's enforcement consisted of a verbal warning on the first offense, followed by closing the user's network account until the user spoke in person to a manager. Subsequent violations resulted in closing the user's account for a progressively higher amount of time (24 hours to start), and a mandatory meeting with a higher level manager or Associate Dean. When a user's network account was closed, they could not log in to lab computers, or access computing resources, potentially causing grade penalties if they could not complete electronic homework assignments. Only twice in ten years did a user's account reach the fourth level, which consisted of closing the user's account for a week and a meeting with the Associate Dean of Academic Affairs.

One of the problems we faced is that although most of our computer labs were open 24/7 with swipe card access, we only staffed the labs during business hours. Thus, the policies were not enforced during evening and nighttime. With budget reductions, we only had enough staff to populate three of 15 lab areas even during business hours. Thus, it was impossible to enforce this policy consistently and fairly, which became a noted complaint.

5. CHANGE IN POLICY

5.1 Rationale

22% of computer lab managers surveyed have designed, built or remodeled a computer lab space specifically to address food or drink issues. We are no exception. In 2001, a new CoE computer lab called the Internet Cafe was created and populated with thin clients. The cost of an individual thin client unit was less than $300, which dramatically lessened the impact of equipment damage to the replacement budget. As part of the room's theme, and responding to student requests, food and drink were specifically allowed in that one lab.

In three general IT and computer lab surveys between 2001 and 2008, students consistently rated a policy of allowing food and drink in the computer labs as one of their top priorities. One more lab of thin clients was exempted from the food/drink ban in 2008. Around that time, we provided a "food allowed" zone on one of the study tables in the most popular computer lab. Although students appreciated the extra food-consumption spaces, lab users had difficulty keeping track of which lab spaces allowed food (despite appropriate signage). Disallowed food consumption went up because of the inconsistency of the policy.

In March 2010, the Computer Lab Manager asked the ESTC to reconsider the ban and the ESTC agreed. Any food and drink was then allowed in any CoE computer lab and computer classroom space. This follows the larger trend: 33% of respondents to the survey have changed their policies from disallowing to allowing in the last two years.

Before the ban was lifted, other interested parties were consulted, including the other IT staff, college administration staff and the college student council. All agreed that the model of the labs that did allow food and drink could be consistently applied to the other labs and classrooms.

The Computer Lab Manager presented a plan that involved a minimal increase in cost for the change in policy. He anticipated a slight increase in equipment replacement, recommended additional cleaning tools and supplies including a commercial vacuum cleaner, and asked to add another student position to help clean the labs. Total estimated cost would be $750 one-time and $3,760 annually.

5.2 The Switch

After the policy was changed, the many signs in the labs were changed from forbidding food and drink to notices that these activities were allowed. The signs read: "Food and Drink Allowed Here: Please be respectful of your lab environment and clean up after yourself."

Along with signage change, the website was updated, and the lab computer background images reflected the change in policy. The annual "what's changed" email sent to students and faculty noted this change.

We provide sanitizing materials (disinfectant wipes and hand sanitizer) and cleaning materials (paper towels and disinfectant spray) for student use in the computer labs.

5.3 Repercussions

We did not see an immediate rise in cleanliness problems, broken equipment, or any other issues surrounding food and drink. In fact, the change in policy passed by quietly. Our lab assistants already incorporated keyboard, mouse and surface cleaning into their everyday tasks, and adding another student position (for a total of four lab assistants) helped distribute the work. Our lab assistants report spending about 5-10 minutes per hour dealing with food- and drink-related spills and cleanup, both before and after our change in policy.

Over time, we saw a much reduced cost impact than we originally estimated. Keyboard, mouse and mouse pad replacements amounted to only about $200 per year for approximately 400 computers, or an extra cost of $0.50 per computer. This was less than half of the estimated cost. The additional cost of student labor and cleaning supplies went toward making the labs cleaner and more efficiently operated as a whole, so the exact cost impact was difficult to measure. However, there have been no complaints surrounding cleanliness.

6. BENEFITS

6.1 Cost

25 survey respondents answered the question about cost recovery. The average annual amount per year to recover from food/drink mishaps or damages (from those who responded) is $428, or $1.52 per computer seat.

Assuming a computer station (PC plus monitor) costs $1000 and is on a 4-year replacement cycle, the annual cost for PC equipment is $250. That $1.52 results in a 0.6 percent added cost.

According to the survey, staff spends about 3 hours per week, on average, enforcing food/drink policies. Assuming a $10/hour wage, that is about $1,560 per year of staff time. The average number of computer seats from the survey is about 450, so that is about $3.47 per computer seat annually.

This shows that it is over 200% more cost efficient to allow food and drink, and purchase replacement equipment, than to enforce a ban on food and drink.

6.2 Public Relations

This goes beyond mere cost impact, however. The goodwill from our policy toward allowing food and drink has benefited our IT organization intangibly. Complaints against the IT organization and its policies, in general, have been significantly reduced. (Sometimes the only measure we can use, lacking adequate tracking or reporting features, is the number of complaints.)

In the past, our staff reported at least one verbal or physical confrontation with a computer lab user over the food and drink policy each week. These confrontations have entirely disappeared, creating a healthier workplace environment for our staff and a better rapport with our users.

6.3 Staff Impact

The impact on staff productivity needs to be considered. Without another difficult-to-enforce policy, staff is allowed to focus their limited resources on other things. Confrontations surrounding this policy create personal stress for the staff, and policies of this nature may create a hostile environment and intentional abuse.

(We once witnessed a faculty meeting in the computer lab space that involved a full dining experience. When asked why, the faculty responded that they thought the policy a bad one.)

6.4 Other Intangibles

As part of a welcoming lab environment with modern, comfortable spaces, allowing food and drink consumption helps keep the students happier and more productive. It encourages student camaraderie and collaboration.

Because we place a stress on our new signs ("YOUR lab environment"), and encourage responsible activity ("please clean up after yourself"), it drives the point home that the students need to be responsible for their actions and their environment, and helps teach a stewardship model to students. Indeed, it is far more the norm to see students cleaning up their area of food-related trash than leaving it. They seem happy to do so. Students even aid in identifying spills when they happen, because a student knows they will not be punished.

7. SOLUTIONS

If an organization is still considering a change in policy toward allowing food or drink consumption in the computer labs, consider the following.

Equipment is more respected if the environment is a social one, such as with comfortable seating, tabletops, cup holders, and more frequent trash containers. The CoE's Internet Cafe was designed this way. After our policy change, we partnered with custodial services to provide larger and more frequent trash containers, and to allow our student employees to access custodial resources (trash bags and cleaning materials) as necessary. This allowed us to provide a more rapid response to problems, and custodial services appreciated a reduced workload.

Remove the computer or monitor from the "danger zone". Install small form factor PCs that mount behind the monitor. In some cases, lab managers have installed both computer and monitor above the table. In the CoE's Internet Cafe, we have glass tabletops with fully recessed monitors, and the thin clients are mounted underneath the table, so the only equipment students physically encounter is the keyboard and mouse.

Consider a compromise. Allow students to eat and drink in designated spaces, such as tables that are three feet behind each computer station. This may require more diligent supervision, however.

Whatever the policy, consider having a higher authority, such as a Dean's council, set the policy. This can make a big difference in the success of the policy. For the CoE, our Computer Lab Manager specifically asked the ESTC (the student computing funding body) to form a partnership for the new policy.

8. REFERENCES

[1] Williamson, E.G. 1935. The relationship of number of hours of study to scholarship. Journal of Education Psychology, Vol. 26(9), pp. 682-688.

[2] Herrick, Dan R., (November 2011). This Isn't Your Father's Computer Lab: Computer Labs Redefined. Proceedings of the 39th ACM annual conference on SIGUCCS; Association for Computing Machinery, New York, NY, pp. 65-72.

The USC School of Social Work Faculty Technology Workshop

Terris B. Wolff
University of Southern California
School of Social Work
669 W. 34th St
Los Angeles, CA 90089-0411
1-213-821-2316

twolff@usc.edu

ABSTRACT

The USC School of Social Work runs an annual, week long training for faculty. This intensive workshop has become known as the school's "Boot Camp" or "Tech Camp". The faculty are expected to attend 9am to 4pm, Monday thru Friday. We feed them lunch and snacks every day to keep them on-site and on schedule. At the end of the workshop each faculty member is expected to give a five to ten minute lecture or guide an activity that will demonstrate what they have learned.

Categories and Subject Descriptors

K.3.m [**Computing Milieux**]: Computers and Education – *miscellaneous.*

General Terms

Documentation.

Keywords

Training.

1. INTRODUCTION

The University of Southern California School of Social Work is one of 18 Graduate and Professional Schools at the University, located in downtown Los Angeles. The faculty in the campus based program (versus our virtual program) consists of approximately 180 full-time faculty and approximately 80 part-time or adjunct faculty. The actual numbers vary from semester to semester as the number of courses and topics vary, and faculty are hired.

The faculty members of the school have a wide range of technology oriented skills. Most all use a computer for web browsing, email and word processing. But first and foremost, they are Social Workers. They typical classroom technology used is the DVD, which has been a major advance from VHS tape, although there is still a significant amount of frequently used resources to be found in this

latter format. Hence, all our classrooms have DVD/VHS combo players along with data display equipment.

This does not mean that the faculty as a whole make no use of technology for the delivery of instruction. There are several who have significant knowledge of PowerPoint and routinely "wow" other faculty. But they are in the minority. We have one, very popular instructor who teaches documentary film making! These are the rare examples.

With this in mind, I initiated the Faculty Technology Workshop to encourage the use of technology for teaching and instruction. The workshop is open to all Social Work faculty – full-time, part-time – although enrollment is limited to 15, the capacity of the training lab.

The timing of the workshop has shifted over the years. Initially it took place the week after graduation in mid-May. This conflicted with an activity centered around the internship program, which meant approximately a third of the faculty could not attend. After a couple years the workshop was shifted to early June to accommodate this group of faculty. Two years ago, the workshop week was moved to early August. This time frame brought in recent hires – people new to USC.

After the first year of the workshop it was being called "Boot Camp" by some, but is now generally known as "Tech Camp."

2. TECH CAMP FORMAT

Tech Camp is an intensive, week long workshop. We start each day at 9:00am, which gives all the participants the opportunity to get another cup of coffee, check their morning email or take care of any other of their typical daily communication needs. The camp day officially ends at 4:00pm. This gives everyone a chance to check email or return phone calls before the close of business.

Like any event involving faculty, food is always a major attraction. Lunches and afternoon snacks are catered! Providing the participants with lunch does two things – most important, it keeps everyone in the vicinity and minimizes the opportunity for them to go to their office and get involved in other work. Additionally, by keeping the participants together, they get to know one another better, and share in their teaching experiences. In the past couple of years, this has proved to be particularly valuable to the recent faculty hires.

The expectation is that everyone will attend all five days of the workshop from 9:00am to the end of the day. The activities build on one another. Missing a day, or half a day, puts the attendee behind. In advertising the workshop it is made clear that attendance all five days is required. I remind people of their irritation when a student, having missed class, asks "did I miss anything important?"

Unfortunately, expectations and reality are not always the same. I have let people attend the first two or three days and then quit. I do not, however, let them miss the first two days and then join. Too much has been introduced, and having someone join in the middle has always been disruptive.

Tech Camp meets in the School's computer lab. While the lab has 20 computers, class size is limited to 15. This allows me to keep the lab open for the occasional student who is trying to do their own work. Having random students at random times has proven to be beneficial. The students invariably find the camp interesting (yes, they can learn things, too), and are more than willing to talk about some of their classroom experiences. They are happy to tell the faculty what they do or do not like.

Talking for a full day can be very tiring. Doing so for five days straight is exhausting. To give myself a break, and to give my attendees a break from listening to me, I bring in a series of guest instructors. I ask these people to present their materials prior to lunch. They are then encouraged to stay for lunch and to interact more with the faculty. The workshop is also highly interactive – hands-on. The participants spend as much, or more, time testing their understanding and trying things out as listening to an instructor.

3. WORKSHOP CONTENT

The content of Tech Camp has varied over the years, although there are some parts that are constant, the main focus of the workshop.

3.1 The Constants

The overriding purpose of Tech Camp is to bring immediately practical skills to the faculty member. Hence there are two major topics covered – Blackboard and PowerPoint.

The University currently supports the Blackboard Learning Management System. Blackboard is, in fact, a part of the University's Disaster Recovery Plan – if the campus is destroyed through natural causes (a large earthquake being the most likely event), the Provost expects classes to continue through Blackboard (USC has a high speed link to a disaster recovery site in Arizona. All central systems are continually being mirrored – the site is about 2 seconds behind real-time).

Between the University's disaster recovery plans, and pressure from the School to use Blackboard as a means to distribute information and for communication, at a minimum, it has become important for our faculty to have a good knowledge of Blackboard. We want our faculty to know how to post materials, use it for communication, discussion tasks, paper assignments and grading. To facilitate the disaster recovery aspects, the University Blackboard group creates a section for every class in the University (undergraduate and graduate) that is taught. In Social Work a student affairs staff members posts a syllabus into every class section. The rest is up to the faculty member. This is where Tech Camp comes in. Giving our faculty the knowledge and skills needed to use Blackboard.

We spend one and a half days learning Blackboard. Faculty learn how to post announcements, post/upload documents, use discussion boards, create writing assignments, use Turnitin assignments (USC licenses Turnitin – plagiarism checking – as a Blackboard plug-in), use adaptive release, and the Blackboard grade center. They are exposed to group tools, content management tools, and are engaged in a discussion of how to take advantage of the various reporting and statistical tools available to faculty. I am able to bring in people from the University Blackboard support team to give some of this instruction.

This is a large amount of information to absorb in a day and a half. I don't expect them to use it all. At a minimum they know how to post documents for their classes, and they have some ideas centered on effective use of discussion boards. Otherwise, I do expect that, having been exposed to a wide variety of topics and features, some faculty will, given time, want to put a reasonable amount of it into use. At that time, they know who to turn to for refresher information and further instruction.

The second major component of Tech Camp is PowerPoint. We spend a full day delving deeply into this tool. Not only do we spend time creating slides, but we spend time learning about animations, how to insert images/graphics, use the built-in chart engine, insert video clips and audio clips. A key feature that the novice PowerPoint user doesn't understand is how video and audio files relate to the PowerPoint file. To enhance this understanding we spend time using the "Package for CD" feature, and demonstrating the disastrous effect of simply copying one's PowerPoint file to their flash disk when there are video or audio files involved.

Just as important as technical competence with PowerPoint is the theory of what makes good PowerPoint. We center the discussion around Seth Godin's "*Really Bad PowerPoint*" (www.sethgodin.com/freeprize/reallybad-1.pdf) and several books, such as Cliff Atkinson's *Beyond Bullet Points* and Garr Reynolds' *Presentation Zen*. To help people planning research presentations, some time is spent with Edward Tufte's *"The Visual Display of Quantitative Information."* And of course, it is always worth a quick look at Peter Norvig's interpretation of the Gettysburg Address (http://norvig.com/Gettysburg/). These discussions have been opportunities for guest speakers – former Camp participants and faculty from other parts of the campus have made valuable contributions.

These discussions help change how people view their typical PowerPoint slide deck, and how they display information. After Tech Camp, participants have moved away from the slides dense with text and numbers toward slides that contain a few ideas or images that encourage discussion.

3.2 Related Constants

To be successful with this new vision of how to use PowerPoint, faculty are also taught how to locate images, video and audio files on the internet that they can embed into presentations, or post directly into Blackboard.

It shouldn't be surprising that many resources are found using tools such as Google's and Yahoo!'s image search, and searching YouTube. Faculty learn how to capture these items for use in their instruction.

A major discussion, with the help of our librarian, focuses on Intellectual Property Rights and Copyright. What is "Fair Use" and what do you have to license or otherwise purchase. Nobody claims to be a copyright attorney, and we all encourage erring on the side of the owner of the materials.

3.3 Other Content

Manipulating images, audio and video is important. The faculty are exposed to the Microsoft Office Picture Manager which is installed on their computers when we install Office for fairly simple image modifications. For more complex image work we spend some time with GIMP. Simple video editing is learned with Windows Moviemaker. Tools for capturing YouTube video are discussed and played with, giving everyone a chance to manipulate some video.

At all times, questions are encouraged. If people want to delve into the mysteries of the Windows 7 Operating System, then time is devoted to that. Features of Acrobat Pro and creating fillable forms are a frequent question.

Because everyone has access to a digital camera or phone with a camera, time is taken to explore how to capture these digital resources so that they can be imbedded in PowerPoint or even Word files. (The first year I had people bring in their digital cameras I was surprised by the number of people who had no idea how to get the images from the camera to a computer! Even fewer people know how to get images or movies off their smart phones.) A past participant has told groups that she now always carries a small camera that shoots both stills and video and has frequently captured images that she uses in class.

I find it a surprise that the majority of our faculty don't know how to burn a CD, hence this is a topic every year.

3.4 Things That Come and Go

Because questions are encouraged, there are many topics that appear at random times during the week, but may not appear every year. They include:

- Using Word's track changes feature and commenting feature
- Podcasting
- Blogs and wikis
- Clickers (or Audience Response systems) (http://www.polleverywhere.com/ is lots of fun)
- Using the University's web mail system

- iPad email configuration
- Scanning photos
- Prezi

4. PROBLEMS

There are two problems with my approach. The biggest is the five day commitment I ask of faculty. A significant number of the School's faculty have told me that I need to modify the time allocation because they are not willing to give up a solid week. They are willing to give up one day a week for a few weeks, though.

The second problem is my attempt to cover a broad range of topics. The faculty who complain about the five day commitment also want two or three hour individual workshops on specific topics. And of course, they want them when they are available, which doesn't take into account when the teaching space can be used, or when I might be available.

None the less, there is continuing interest and the camp is always full.

5. CAN YOU EMULATE TECH CAMP?

No reason not to! You need to figure out several things: subjects you want to teach that will benefit your faculty, find a time period that will work for you and for your faculty, get a budget for food, and think about other possible incentives.

Like any good camp, everyone gets a camp T-Shirt. I also have bags of goodies that I've collected from vendors that I use to encourage people to be on time (show up before 9:00am, pick something from the bag, return from lunch on time, pick something from the bag). The goodie bag is sort of like the treasure chest that elementary school teachers have in their classrooms – good student performance, get a prize! The faculty, like those elementary age kids, love it.

In summary, if you have the time and energy, you can put on your own workshop, and the faculty will come.

Customer Service 101: A Refresher For Us All

Kelly Wainwright
Lewis & Clark College
0615 SW Palatine Hill Road
Portland, Oregon 97219
1-503-768-7020

kelly@lclark.edu

ABSTRACT

While we all work in the field of technology, at the heart of what're do is customer service. However this is a skill that we seldom take the time to reflect on or improve. While many consider customer service to be common sense, it still warrants a regular review of the basics. Using the book DELIVERING KNOCK YOUR SOCKS OFF SERVICE by Ron Zemke, this paper will review the basics of customer service to help us all ensure that we are on the correct path.

Categories and Subject Descriptors

K.m [**Computing Milieux**]: miscellaneous.

General Terms

Management, Human Factors.

Keywords

Customer Service, Client Services, User Support Services, Help Desk

1. INTRODUCTION

Think about a time when you came away from a bad situation in dealing with a company feeling great. What made that interaction end on a positive note? What did the person representing the company say or do that helped you connect with them and helped them find a mutually satisfactory outcome? Did they go beyond the basics to really "WOW" you?

Customer service skills are something that all of us, from programmers to user support specialists, from the help desk to the CIO, must use every day in Information Technology. While we may think that we have a captive audience, that there is no other game in town if our clients are unhappy, but that is not true. When we damage our customer service reputation, while our clients can't turn to another IT organization for support, they can damage our relationships with other clients, turn to their colleagues or students where they might receive incorrect information or advice, or they can just wallow in their discontent, becoming more and more ineffective in their jobs.

Since our relationships with our clients are so important, it is important to review occasionally the basics of good customer service in order to cultivate and strengthen these relations. It is

also important to check in and make sure that everyone in your organization is on the same page in understanding good customer service. For this, I like to use a book called DELIVERING KNOCK YOUR SOCKS OFF SERVICE[1], by Kristin Anderson and Ron Zemeke. If we offer our clients good customer service, then strong relationships of trust and respect will follow.

Lewis & Clark (L&C) College is a small, liberal arts college located approximately six miles outside of downtown Portland, Oregon. Our student body consists of close to 2000 undergraduates, 800 law students and nearly 900 other graduate students, 375 full- and part-time faculty, and approximately 750 staff members. Our IT staff consists of twenty-five professionals divided into four departments, including Client Services, the department for which I am the director. My staff of seven and I work to help the campus community to effectively use technology in their teaching, learning and work. We do this through our help desk, our training program and simply working with individuals in a more customized environment to find solutions to their needs.

2. DEFINING CUSTOMER SERVICE

Before we can have a discussion about how to achieve good customer service, we have to understand what good customer service is, what it looks like. This is especially difficult because it really depends on many different variables.

There is an old adage that "the customer is always right" and many believe this to be the basis of good customer service. I think that we have all had experiences where this is simply not the case and that the customer is flat out wrong. There are times when what our clients tell us happened simply could not have happened in the way that they describe it. They're not maliciously getting it wrong but simply misinterpreting what the technology is doing or telling them. Anderson and Zemke however state that *"Customers are not always right, but they are always our customers."* (Anderson and Zemke, p. 39) Therefore, we must work to build a relationship of mutual and trust and respect with our clients in order to achieve good customer service.

For our purposes, I'm going in with the understanding that the "business" is higher education Information Technology (IT) organizations and that our clients are those that we serve.

2.1 Who Are Our Clients

Of course this varies depending on what our role is in our organization, but we in IT have many customers, or clients, some obvious and some less so. On the obvious side, we have the students, staff and faculty on campus. However we also must help the parents of our students to feel that their student is receiving what they need, the alumni, the board of trustees, and sometimes even visitors to campus—all with different needs and expectations.

Another group that often gets overlooked as clients is our fellow employees in IT. We are on both ends of customer service with these folks—both the providers and receivers. These are, at times, our most important clients because our ability to serve all other clients depends on the relationship that we have built with them and by the service that we have provided to them in the past. According to Jan Carlzon, former CEO of Scandinavian Airlines said: *"If you're not serving the customer, your job is to be serving someone who is."* I believe that this is definitely the case in IT.

2.2 The Three Questions

According to Anderson and Zemke, there are three questions that you should ask in attempts to ascertain what your clients are looking for. They are:

1. *What do my customers want from me and my company?*

2. *How do the different areas in IT work together to serve the company?*

3. *What are the details—little things—that make a big difference in my customer's satisfaction? (Anderson and Zemke, p. 6)*

By knowing the answers to these three questions, you can have at least a general understanding of what your customers expect from you and IT.

2.3 RATER

The RATER system, developed by Dr. Leonard Berry at Texas A&M University provides a measuring stick to which we can evaluate and quantify customer service. The RATER system is based on Reliability, Assurance, Tangibles, Empathy and Responsiveness.

2.3.1 Reliability

Reliability consists of setting reasonable expectations and then meeting or exceeding these expectations. It is far better to say that you will do little, and then achieve more than to promise the moon and not even come close in being able to deliver.

At Lewis & Clark College, we have these expectations built directly into our call tracking system. From a priority of one for issues that are urgent and need immediate attention, to a priority of seven, which is for items that we will get to when we can. However, our default priority is a four, which sets the expectation that we will call the client within 24 hours. Mind you, that is to call them, not that their issue will be fixed in that time frame. By setting these expectations for all of IT, it allows anyone that the client initially deals with to consistently be able to set reasonable expectations.

However, setting reasonable expectations is one of the most difficult items for our help desk students to grasp. When a customer comes in with pre-conceived expectations, many of our help desk students don't feel as though they have the knowledge or the power to reshape these ideas. If is difficult for them to understand that every client can't be handled immediately, and by setting those unattainable expectations, everyone ends up unsatisfied.

Reliability is all about setting and managing expectations. *"You are in a position to shape your customers' expectations to match what you actually can and will do for them. When you do that well, customers perceive that your services are reliable."* (Anderson and Zemke, p. 12)

2.3.2 Assurance

However, not only must we be competent, we must also be courteous and professional so that our clients will trust what we are telling them.

Being reassuring is especially difficult for those of us in IT with less personal skills. Some of our programmers and technicians, while they are brilliantly skilled, have difficulty in speaking with the customer. This is an area where most Client/User Services professionals excel, in knowing how to speak with the clients so they understand what is happening.

I believe that the language we use plays and important part in this and that this is especially difficult in dealing with technological questions and issues. We are constantly walking a tightrope in not talking down to a client and yet talking at a level that they can understand and helps them feel good about the interaction.

2.3.3 Tangibles

Not only is what we say important in conveying to the customer that they are important, but the environment that we say it in is also important.

I remember vividly a debate that I had with a past lab manager about dress code for our student employees. I wasn't asking for anything radical, simply that our students not wear ripped clothing, wear nothing with inappropriate slogans, and wear shoes. It was this last item that he had the most difficulty understanding. In his mind, if our students are competent and were able to answer questions and help the client, then how they were dressed and if they had shoes on shouldn't matter. I, on the other hand, felt that shoes displayed a small sense of professionalism that I wasn't willing to sacrifice.

First impressions, no matter how fair or not, are important. If I walk into a restaurant that is clearly not clean, that matters. If I walk into an office, that is clearly disorganized, I quickly assume that my request will become lost in that shuffle.

Beyond the first impression, how we treat the customer beyond that point is also important. Making them feel heard by writing down important pieces of information, giving them related handouts when appropriate, turning off your computer monitor when you are talking with someone are all tangible ways to tell the customer, what you say is important and I'm listening.

2.3.4 Empathy

Empathy goes hand in hand with reassurance. Empathy is the piece where you try to understand where your customers are coming from. Empathy revolves around being able to read the cues that your customer is giving you to let you know where they are coming from and what their level of understanding is.

I've often told people that my background in foreign languages is actually very helpful to my career in client services. Obviously computers are a foreign language to many, but in studying foreign languages I developed the ability to read if those I was speaking to were understanding what I was saying, and if not, to try a different way. We must constantly listen to our clients, both what they are saying and their emotional state. While again there are clues as to someone's emotional state, you often don't know what brought them to that point, making the interaction a potential mine field.

While it is important to understand someone's emotional state, it is even more important that you don't get sucked into it. When someone comes to you frustrated about the day they've had to that point, it is important not to take on their frustration, but be the calm that they are looking for.

2.3.5 Responsiveness

When most people think responsiveness, they think that people want everything instantly. This is a myth that has been perpetuated by our fast food culture. Really they want to be able to negotiate that timeline with you and then have you live up to your commitment. It is not how quickly that you can achieve something, it is achieving it in a reasonable amount of time and then communicating through the process.

I recently had an interaction with a well-known shoe manufacturer. A pair of their boots that I had purchased both cracked across the bottom prematurely. I sent them an email to see if they could do anything for me, and they told me to mail them in and they would send me a new pair of shoes. This was exactly what I was hoping for. The expectation that they set on their form was that after they received the return, it would take up to two weeks to process. However, the customer service experience fell apart for me as I waited for four weeks with no response. It was only when I contacted them that I received any feedback on where the process stood. I knew that the process would take a little time, but when that timeline was not met, there should have been communication.

I always maintain that most of our customers don't need instant gratification. They simply need to know what the timeline is and then be notified when that changes.

2.4 Baber's Rules of Customer Service

Michael Baber, in his book **INTEGRATED BUSINESS LEADERSHIP THROUGH CROSS MARKETING**[2] gives us another method for understanding how the customer defines a positive customer service experience. Known as Baber's Rules, these state:

- *Make the customers feel heard.*
- *Make the customers feel understood.*
- *Make the customers feel liked.*
- *Make the customers feel respected.*
- *Make the customers feel helped.*
- *Make the customers feel appreciated.*

I believe that if all of these can be achieved, then you are well on your way to building that relationship of trust and respect with your customer. I believe that the best way to achieve this is through clear and consistent communication.

3. COMMUNICATION

I believe that communication skills are the most important for anyone working with customers to develop. It is through communication that we must negotiate expectations, and then keep them informed when there are changes to those expectations.

Of course the most important element of initial communications with the client is listening. We must listen to the customer, ask clarifying questions, write down important facts, and then confirm that you correctly heard them. It is so easy to have potential troubleshooting ideas running through our head and to begin solving the problem while our clients are talking with us. However, this is in direct conflict with the first two Baber's Rules. We must listen to our customers.

It is not only the words that we must listen to, but 70-80% of what we say is non-verbal. This includes proximity, eye contact, silence, body language, gestures, posture, facial expressions, physical contact, smell, and overall appearance. Closely related to these are the vocal qualities such as tone and volume. In face to face interactions, we have the ability to use all these clues when listening and communicating with a client. When we are communication over the phone or via email, listening is much more difficult.

There will be times when we find that our methods of communication simply don't work with another individuals. There have been times when I'm convinced that we are both speaking English, but the client simply does not understand what I'm saying. In these instances, it is a good idea to pass them off to a colleague. Simply stating, "I'm not being very clear about this, maybe my colleague can explain it better," gives you a graceful exit before the entire interaction ends poorly.

In IT, we deal with our customers generally in three ways: in-person, by telephone or through email.

3.1 In-person Communication

In-person communication can be the most satisfying as well as the most demanding. When you are dealing with a person standing in front of you, as we often do at our help desk, you have the full benefit of both verbal and non-verbal communication cues. You can see if they feel comfortable with the information often by what they are saying corroborates the non-verbal cues they are giving you.

However, this also means that they are receiving these same cues from you. We have to again think about the tangibles that our clients are getting from us that tells them they are heard and their issues are important. Sometimes, writing down pertinent facts can convey this. And of course, asking clarifying questions is essential.

Technology, while it is the focus of our profession, can be a major distraction. It is very easy to hide behind our monitor, be doing a search for a solution before the client has even finished explaining the issue or checking an email that has come in while you are talking taking your attention away from the client. If you find that you can't tune these things out, try turning off your monitor while you are talking with someone, or at very least, remove your hands from the keyboard.

3.2 Telephone Communication

Customer service on the telephone is a whole different animal. First, you don't have the non-verbal clues to help you see if they are understanding and having a satisfactory interaction. This is all done with tone of voice. Second, in today's age of voicemail and phone trees, it is much easier to get lost in the black hole of the telephone system so that by the time they get to you, the frustration level of the client might be high.

Here are some recommendations to help make telephone interactions pleasant for everyone. Most importantly, get the callers name and phone number immediately. If you don't know who it is, and they don't identify themselves, ASK. Simply having their name will help you not only make the phone call more personal, but it will give you back ground information as to their skill level. It also helps if you need to transfer the call to someone else. Second, get their phone number. My desk phone has caller ID so when someone calls, I immediately jot down their name and phone number in a notebook that constantly sits by my phone. Then, if we become disconnected, I have a way to reconnect. This notebook also provides me with a place to write down pertinent details.

If you do need to transfer a call, wait for the person on the other end to pick up the phone and give them the name of the caller and basics of their issue before you connect the caller. This allows the person receiving the call to not require the caller to rehash everything they just said so that the conversation can start from their, instead of starting again with the preliminaries.

Technology can also be a major distraction while you are on the phone. Without someone standing in front of you, it is very easy to think that you can quickly respond to an email, only to realize that you missed a pertinent piece of information from the client. I sometimes resort to closing my eyes when I'm on the phone to simply tune out my computer and other such distractions.

3.3 Email Communication

Email presents its own set of difficulties in communication. Not only do you lose the visual non-verbal cues, but you lose the audible non-verbal cues such as tone and volume as well. The only thing that you have to go on is the written text. This makes email valuable in some situations, but not all. It is important to judge when sending email will be more problematic and frustrating than beneficial.

I find that the best times for an email are an initial introduction of a topic or of yourself. An email is less intrusive than a phone call and can be read at the receiver's discretion. Emails are also invaluable as a vehicle for follow-up. Sending an email after a conversation to confirm the understanding reached or to say thank you is perfect. It is also a good way to send status updates, if they aren't too contentious.

That being said, making a telephone call can often times be much more efficient and productive than trying to solve a problem through email. I sometimes get caught up in an email exchange that lasts for a while as I as one clarifying question after another in email in trying to get to the real issue. Doing this with a quick phone call can be much more expeditious and satisfying for both parties.

It is also difficult to try to solve issues via email without the clues mentioned above to give you insight as to either the frustration or knowledge level of the individual with whom you are dealing.

4. DIFFICULT CLIENTS

No matter how hard we try to do it all right, inevitably we will at one time or another fall short of the expectations of a client. Sometimes it is our fault personally when we simply miss something. Other times, those on whom we were relying may not be able to achieve their commitments. Whatever the cause, the result is that we have broken a promise, stated or not, to our customer.

In this situation, it is best to immediately apologize. Make it a sincere apology and, if you don't feel comfortable apologizing for what went wrong (maybe it wasn't your fault or you don't feel comfortable accepting blame), at very least apologize that the client has been inconvenienced. Beware that the apology phase might involve some venting on the part of the client. It is difficult to not become defensive, but instead to allow the customer to express their frustration, and then find a place to begin the process of moving forward. It is helpful to remember that "*Angry customers are almost never angry at you personally. They are mad at a situation they don't like.*" (Anderson and Zemke, p. 120)

After the apology, then the negotiating begins of what will make this right for the customer. Sometime, this is as simple as establishing a new set of expectations such as, "Let me look right into this and give you a call with an update within the hour." If the client lets you off this easily, then it is imperative that you don't miss the next deadline.

Another approach is to let the client begin the negotiations. A simple, "What do you need right now?" can allow the client to identify a starting point for the re-negotiation of expectations. This allows them to be part of the solution, which helps with the adoption of the new agreement.

When you are dealing with a difficult or upset client, it is important to remember that you are trying to salvage and rebuild your relationship with the client.

5. TAKING CARE OF YOURSELF

When you work in a service field as we do, it is important to remember that there are two people in every interaction. Up to this point, we have discussed the client and how to manage your relationship with them. However, just as important is taking care of yourself so that you have the energy and the attitude to work with your clients.

5.1 Celebrating Successes

It is very important to congratulate yourself on a job well done. It is also very important to let your co-workers know when you've been successful. Often times, those around you may not know when you've accomplished something unless you tell them. Then they can join in the celebration with you.

It is equally important to let your employees and co-workers know when they have done a good job. Feeling acknowledged and appreciated by those around us in what we do plays an important role in our job satisfaction. I actually keep an email folder titled kudos where I save emailed compliments. When I'm feeling especially dejected, I can read through these emails for a boost. A simple thank you to those who go out of their way for you will help them in wanting to do so again.

5.2 Dealing with Stress

One question that I often ask in interviews is two-part. First I ask the interviewee how they deal with stress. The second part that I ask is how they deal with those around them being stressed. Stress in our profession is inevitable. Based on numerous variables including time of year, staffing levels, and major projects, there will be times in our professional life when stress will enter in.

So first, it is important to know how stress manifests itself in your life. Do you become short-tempered? Do you become ultra-focused? Do you become disorganized? Knowing that you are stressed is the first step. The next is to have a plan in place to diffuse your stress. Personally, I find taking a walk either by myself or with a co-worker to whom I can vent. Less healthy, I also know that I seek chocolate when I'm stressed.

The question about dealing with others around you who are stressed is also important. If you cannot take on their stress but find ways to help your co-workers diffuse the stress, that is especially helpful. Knowing when to offer assistance, knowing when and when not to bring out the humor, and keeping a desk stocked with chocolate (in my instance) can help a situation.

5.3 Keep Learning

Probably the best way to keep your job interesting and keeping yourself satisfied and engaged is to create and maintain a professional development plan for yourself. I often tell people that I love working in higher education because it is an environment that encourages learning new things. Take advantage of this environment. Know what skills you would like to develop to move you along your desired career path and make sure that you make the time to pursue these interests, both at work and away.

6. CONCLUSION

If customer service is such an easy concept, then why do we all have so many disappointing customer service experiences? It is because customer service is a skill that, unless practiced regularly cannot grow and develop. We must first understand what our customers want, which is in my opinion the ability for us to meet the expectations that we have negotiated with our clients and then clear and consistent communication about the status of their request. If we develop the skills necessary for making and keeping promises with our clients, then they will learn to trust that well work in their best interest and respect our skills and knowledge. Developing and honing your customer service skills is beneficial to everyone involved.

7. REFERENCES

[1] Anderson, K., and Zemke, R. 1998. *Delivering Knock Your Socks off Service.* Performance Research Associates, Inc. United States.

[2] Baber, M. 1986. *Integrated Business Leadership Through Cross Marketing.* Warren H. Green.

Security Challenges in IT infrastructure for Cybersecurity Curriculum Support

Vijay Anand

Industrial Engineering and technology,
Southeast Missouri State University,
Cape Girardeau, USA 63701
vanand@semo.edu

ABSTRACT

With the evolving challenges in cyberspace there is a need for curriculum development in cybersecurity. Students in a cybersecurity curriculum need to access and learn about topics in cybersecurity such that they have a clear understanding of the sophistication of threats such that they can implement mitigation response. Development of hands on curriculum in cybersecurity therefore poses significant challenges to the information technology infrastructure in an instructional environment. Among the various challenges one of the significant challenges involves attack simulations of a cyber-attack requiring the creation of a walled infrastructure to accommodate the equipment where computing services are hosted. The challenges of containing malicious software which can be released by accident are also significant to the IT infrastructure. In this paper we show how the walled infrastructure with computing service can be created such that cybersecurity curriculum can be institutionalized where students locally and remotely can access this infrastructure. The walled IT infrastructure is based on risk escalation wherein connectivity and access to computing resources is contained as risk to computing infrastructure increases. We also show IT challenges in curriculum development on topics of hardware, software and networking for cybersecurity and how virtualization is a means for solving the challenges in those respective topics.

Categories and Subject Descriptors

K.6.5 [**Management of Computing and Information Systems**]: Security and Protection – Access controls, Authentication, Cryptographic controls, Information flow controls, Verification.

General Terms

Management, Performance, Reliability, Security, Verification.

Keywords

Attacks, Virtualized, NETLAB+, VLAN, Honeypot, Honeynet, Sanitization

1. INTRODUCTION

The range of attacks [1] on a cyber-infrastructure has increased many times in the last few years requiring the creation of a curriculum with aspects of security to addressing hardware, software and networking aspects of security curriculum [2]. The infrastructure required to stage an educational setting for students may run in direct contravention with those of information technology (IT) requirements in an educational setup [3]. To accommodate different nuances in cybersecurity education the IT framework for setting up cyber-security education has to adapt such that it forms an experimental and learning platform. An attack on the cyber-infrastructure requires a. Cybersecurity encompasses protection of digital assets, preserving user privacy and counteracting threats to digital assets in an ethical and legal way. Digital Assets in this context refers to:

- Digital personal data(Email, Facebook content etc..),
- Computing Systems(Server, PC, Tablets, Smartphones),
- Networking Infrastructure(Wireless(802.11, 3G, LTE), Wired)

The primary objectives of cybersecurity education encompass [2], [3]:

- Comprehensive program over all aspects of digital assets
- Foster understanding of ethical issues in cyber security
- Foster understanding on legal issues
- Understanding of threat modeling on digital assets and security policy generation
- Development process of risk based security architecture
- Auditing of cyber framework under various compliance requirements
- Understanding of issues with evolution of the cyber infrastructure

To accomplish these objectives of a cybersecurity education an infrastructure to support networking concepts, software development framework, a staging area to understand attacks in a computing system and hardware. Classification of different types attack scenarios are required to chalk up the IT based education for a cyber-infrastructure.

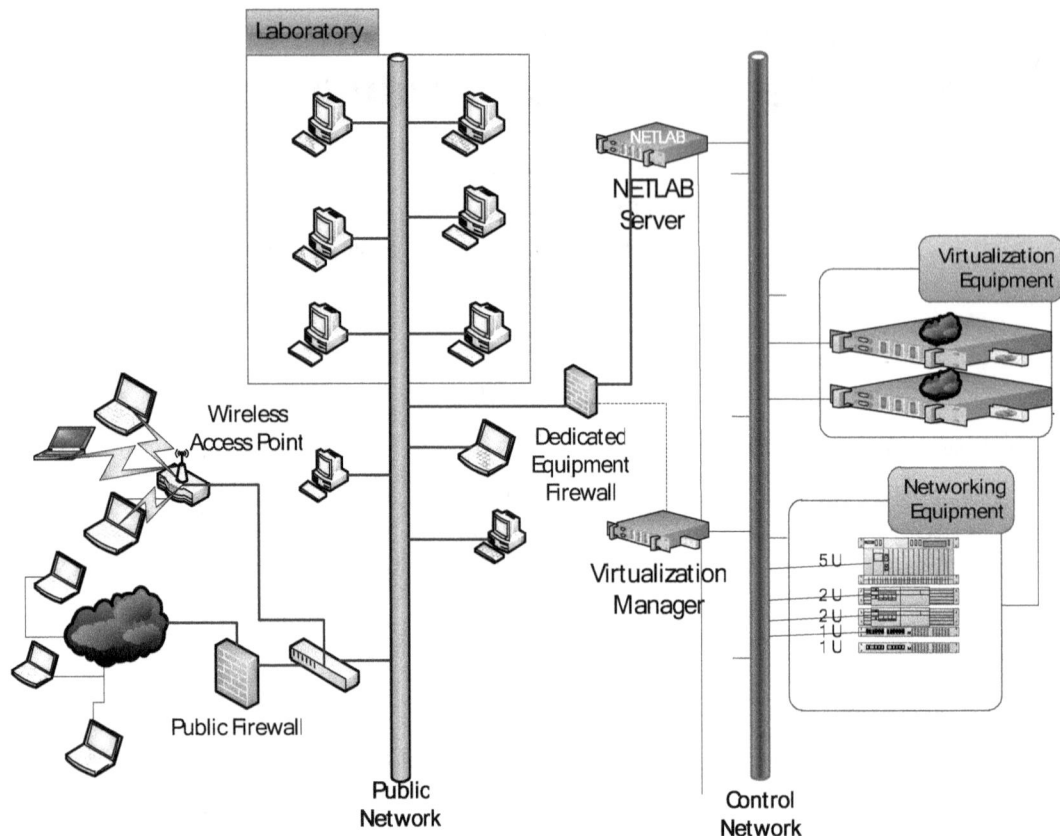

Figure 1. Networking Infrastructure for Cybersecurity Education

In section II we show the impact of security by creating a virtualized networking infrastructure for educational purpose. In Section III we show various aspects of a malware based attack and how to create a framework to contain an attack within the premise of a laboratory infrastructure. Section IV deals with the setup for a directed attack and how a framework be created to address educational requirements of such an attack.

2. Networking IT

A comprehensive education framework for secure networking concepts requires goals to prevent[4], [5]:

- Shared Media Attacks: These kinds of attacks are based on the premise that data traffic passes through all the computing elements in a network. This is true for a bus topology, star or hub topology which is commonly used in a networked computing laboratory. To prevent these kinds of attacks the most commonly used technology is by encrypting the traffic of the communicating entities accomplished by creating SSL communication.

- Remote Attacks: These kinds of attacks are based on the premise that the adversary launches an attack from outside of the local communication framework. The attacker exploits vulnerability on the communicating entity by misrepresenting or intercepting messages. To prevent these kinds of attacks the most commonly used framework is to create an encrypted communications outside the local or logical networking framework accomplished by using the virtual private networking principles using IPSEC based communications.

- Monitoring traffic accomplished by intrusion detection techniques for active as well as automated attacks.

A practical setup for education in these attacks requires the setting up of routers, switches firewalls with appropriate protocols. To accomplish this NETLAB+ [6]infrastructure provides a perfect educational framework. The only drawback of this setup is the education platform is based on CISCO devices and can portray a CISCO specific concept. But fundamental concepts in network design for securing the network can be used for education with this setup. A typical NETLAB+ setup is divided into two network zones one of which is the public network and the other which provides connectivity to all devices is the control network as shown in Figure 1. The NETLAB device provides basic connectivity and management to all networking elements.

2.1 NETLAB Administration

The NETLAB+ framework allows users to schedule configure and interact with networking lab equipment in a safe and sandboxed virtual environment. The networking lab equipment and devices supporting this equipment are zoned behind a NETLAB+ server in a safe way such that they are not directly exposed to the public network. A set of networking equipment along with its support devices in the NETLAB+ framework constitutes an equipment bundle whose access management is done via the calendar interface. This automation allows minimal human intervention thereby making it scalable and accessible remotely.

The management feature of the NETLAB+ software include loading and saving of device configuration for experiments, scrubbing of equipment, preparation of the equipment into a state of factory reset for future reservation and password recovery in case of lost passwords.

As a consequence of pedagogy to review and assess a students work after a lab session on real equipment this framework provides an excellent interface. The moderator console can be shared with students by the moderator in real time using this framework which is a very important pedagogical instructional requirement.

Another important aspect of this framework is power consumption management. This framework allows switching off power if there are no scheduled reservations. Depending on reservation schedules the NETLAB+ framework would switch the equipment on and preload all equipment configurations. The two important hardware pieces apart from the NETLAB+ hardware are the equipment pods and remote PC.

2.1.1 Equipment Pods

A pod in the NETLAB+ framework refers to a singular and unique networking device topology which constitutes a set of lab equipment whose interaction during an instructional session of students and instructors is managed by the NETLAB+ [6]system. Thus an equipment pod represents a logical group of networking equipment which is physically interconnected. The reservation of such a pod as a singular resource for experimentation can be done via the scheduler in the NETLAB+ framework. Another aspect of this logical framework is physical isolation of equipment during normal operation. What this means is that two different experimenters cannot reserve a pod concurrently.

2.1.2 Remote PCs

For distance education the NETLAB+'s remote PC[6][7] technology provides a framework to add PCs to existing lab pods. This Remote PCs technology includes the following features:

- Access to PCs is controlled by the scheduler.
- Share a session between instructors and students fostering collaboration.
- The access to PC is similar to access to any other lab device hence simplistic.
- All remote access sessions over the TCP port(s) that are selected by the administrator are proxied by the NETLAB thereby not requiring opening multiple IP address or ports on the firewall. This also eliminates the exposure of computing devices to the public network.
- PCs can be restored to a clean state after a lab reservation.

2.2 IT Challenges

The most significant IT challenge is to not put misconfigured networking elements [7] on the live network. The NETLAB+ interface accomplishes this aspect since access to routers; switches and all other networking lab equipment participating in NETLAB+ framework do not have direct access to the network but are routed through the NETLAB+ interface. One downside of this is that of a single point of failure to access all the networked equipment in case the NETLAB+ interface is non-functional or the equipment malfunctions. To overcome this there is a possibility of creating a hardwired terminal interface to a network appliance apart from the NETLAB interface. This provides a channel to recover in case of some catastrophic incidence on to the networking hardware which cannot be accessed through the NETLAB interface. This secondary control management system

can be secured by further creating an encrypted connection anytime that is accessed.

The other challenge of keeping the equipment in an approved configuration is accomplished by the NETLAB+ frameworks scrubbing and configuration features. The scrubbing feature allows NETLAB+ to remove any persistence of data and the configuration feature allows the equipment to boot-up in the approved configuration mode.

3. Software Vulnerabilities Simulation

Software is the key glue to utilize hardware and networking resources in transforming a barebones computing system to a service providing computing platform [8]. Software is the primary location for expressing algorithms which can be modified and changed depending on the need for a computing service. Most Operating Systems, applications constituting a computing service are built as software that is malleable and adaptable to the computing needs. This malleability and adaptability [8][9] of software in meeting computing needs, becomes a source of vulnerabilities in the computing framework. To address such vulnerabilities, there is a need to train software engineers in the concepts of secure software development. There are three kinds of software vulnerabilities that need to be addressed in a cyber-security course work. They are:

- Active attack[9] based curriculum where the adversary is make intelligent choices based on the system behavior.
- Defending against automated attacks [9][10] where malicious software exploits system vulnerabilities.
- The objectives of secure software development such that tools for secure software development are incorporated with secure software development guidelines.

Based on these requirements there is a need to create a cyber-infrastructure to foster such an educational environment. The IT infrastructure in an educational setting needs to address the following for such an educational framework:

1) Sanitization of computing resources utilized in a cybersecurity education
2) Network Isolation of computing resources participating in the cybersecurity education
3) Protection of the rest of the IT infrastructure from the attacks and simulations in the cybersecurity laboratory
4) Proper decommissioning procedures of computing equipment used in the cybersecurity laboratory infrastructure

3.1 Isolated Laboratory Infrastructure

The need for network isolation is required to provide a wholesome education to students without violating any aspect of the IT infrastructure in an educational institution. It also allows drawing up novel systems where malicious behavior can be studied and contained fostering research in malicious behavior of software. A computing system attack is comprised of three parts, the creation of malicious software, and the transmission of malicious software and the execution of malicious software. By restricting just the transmission aspect of malicious software the risk is limited to the hardware which is used to study the behavior and development of protection schemes for the malicious software. To accomplish this isolation from communication from the rest of the communication framework the concept of virtual LAN's[11] provides the necessary framework.

A classical LAN is defined as a broadcast networking of computing elements with no routing between themselves. Routing is required when data has to move from one LAN to another. A virtual LAN on the other hand arranges computing elements that accomplish a logical or organizational task together. Within the virtual LAN the digital broadcast reaches only members of this logical association and physical colocation is not important. There are many significant advantages in using virtual LAN's[12][13] but in case of a cybersecurity curriculum IT support the most significant aspect this allows is grouping together of computing resources participating in the cybersecurity education and the isolation that can be created for these communicating entities. Depending on the layer of the protocol stack the VLAN functionality can be either based of Layer 1 that is based on physical ports, the layer 2 based out of the MAC address and layer 3 based out of the IP address[11].

Choices in any layer in the protocol stack would allow an isolated network. To eliminate any software based protocol implementation vulnerabilities it's less risky to use the layer 1 VLAN approach also referred to as port switching. It does come with the requirement of having a VLAN enabled switch and the ability to configure it. The downside of layer 1 VLAN is that it does not allow user mobility which is not required in the laboratory framework. Once a VLAN enabled system is created, the concept of tagging has to be addressed in the VLAN for packet routing. Tagging in VLAN[11] done as:

- Initial switch adds tag containing VLAN id to all incoming packets.

- Intermediate switches do not re-compute the VLAN id.
- Final switch removes tags from all outgoing packets.
- Tag is not swapped at every hop.

A port in a VLAN[11] [12][13]with Layer 1 switching can be configured for any of the following modes:

- 1Q Trunk: Transmission of all data frames in this mode includes a tag header. Port transmission in this mode is set to another device that is 802.1Q aware. All untagged frames received by the switch on the 1Q trunk port are dropped in this mode. All VLANs are included in the port's egress list.

- 1d Trunk: Transmission of all data frames in this mode is untagged. The switch in this configuration; through the 1d trunk port receives only untagged data frames. Ports in this mode allow transmission to legacy 802.1d switch fabric as well as device sharing in multiple. The Egress List in this mode for a port is updated such that it is eligible for all VLANs.

- Hybrid: Transmission of data frames in this mode at the port can be both tagged and untagged. In this mode a port is assigned to a VLAN id along with the forwarding list of the default VLAN. In the event of a change in the port VLAN id, a modification to the Egress list is done by the replacing the new port VLAN id to the existing (older) VLAN id. The exception to this modification is in the case where the switch configuration forwards the default VLAN on all ports which in effect requires the default port VLAN id on the list. The untagged frame format in this configuration is always matched with port VLAN id in the forwarding list entry thereby allowing the port to receive tagged and untagged frames.

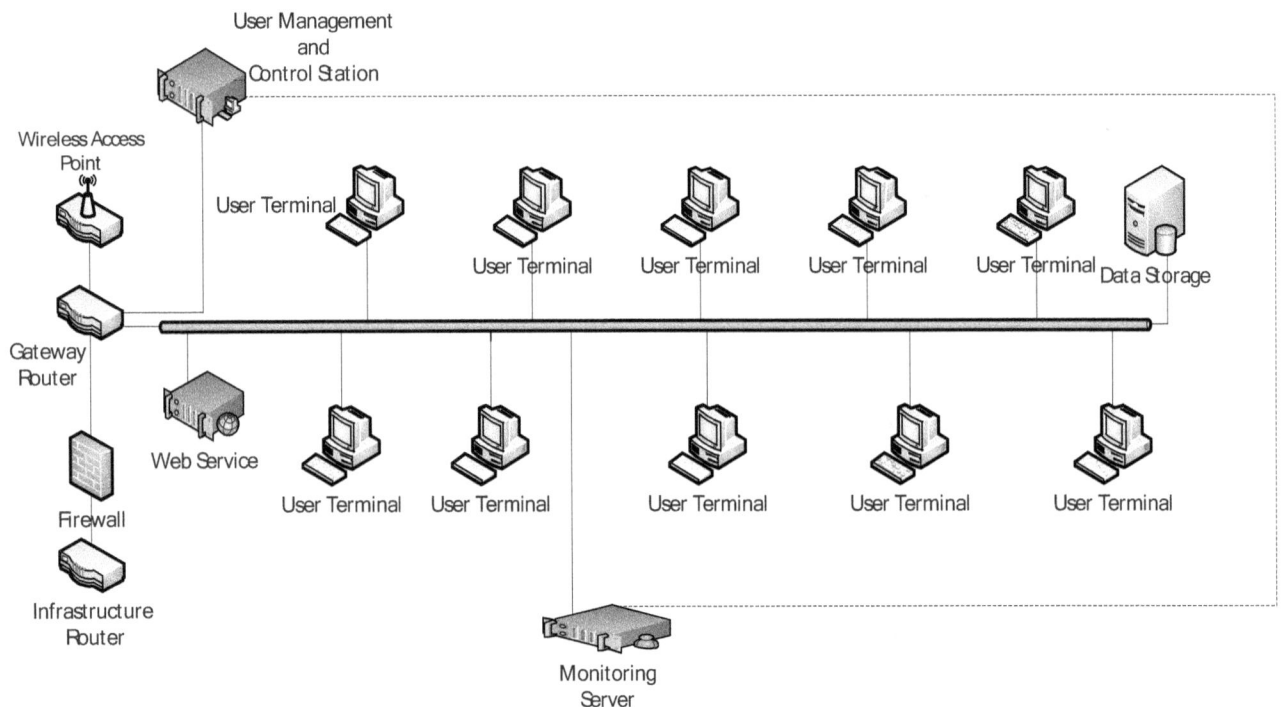

Figure 2. Computing Infrastructure for Cybersecurity Education

In typical educational infrastructure devices with VLAN capability and non VLAN capability coexist. Hence the Hybrid mode offers the best possible framework for data routing. A typical laboratory framework is shown in the Figure 2.

Once VLAN type is decided there is a need to set up the control and management structure for such a VLAN. To control traffic movement from inside and outside of the LAN there needs to a soft switch approach to turn off and turn on external network access to such a laboratory infrastructure. As shown in the figure the management module is controlled by the instructor. To enable this structure there needs to secure communication channel between the management module and the switch. To establish such a management module a local certificate is used for creating encrypted communications between the management module and the switch. The public certificate is stored on the switch and the private key is stored on the management module. The secure communications allows the control structure not to be compromised. The additional setup in this case is the storage of this certificate in the switch.

3.2 Monitoring

One of the important things to analyze is to monitor attack simulations and detect anomalies in the attack scenarios. The intrusion detection system[14] is one of the most important inside the laboratory framework. Typically an intrusion detection system is used to monitor suspicious activity on a networked computing service by utilizing intrusion signatures. This can be created by creation of honey nets and honeypots[15] inside the network during an attack simulation. In this setup the services are all virtually hosted inside a private cloud where these honeypots are instantiated.

Honeypot is a computing construct made up of special software applications that can be easily compromised by a cyber-attack.
Honeynet is a networking construct whose purpose is to attack attackers and can be easily compromised.
Any traffic that enters and exits through the honeynet/honeypot constructs is deemed as suspicious and needs to be carefully monitored. If a successful attack is constructed further attacks on the computing resources can be launched.
The monitoring server in this setup formulates the instantiation of honeypots and intrusion detection system which allows behavior monitoring for risk analysis. By integrating intrusion detection system the aspect of intrusion prevention by triggering certain firewall configurations can be affected and research onto behavior is also fostered.

3.3 Sanitization
Computing elements participating the in the study of automated attacks and live attacks can pose risk to the rest of the computing resources once networking connectivity is restored. To avoid any malicious attack on computing resources outside of the cybersecurity laboratory infrastructure there is a need to sanitize computing resources before restoring network connectivity. One way to affect this is by utilizing memory only system boots [16]. Memory only system boots for operating systems allows the execution of the operating environment[17] without any permanent storage functionality. All the attack simulation is done on virtualized resources hence the core operating elements are never affected after the simulation is complete. User management policies also need to put in place to delete all files that are not part

of the core operating system. User privileges on the computing resource needs to be kept at minimum privilege level. Since the virtualized aspect of the operating system can have varieties of privileges it provides good enough platforms for education without affecting any infrastructure privilege constructs.

4. CONCLUSIONS
In this paper the need for IT requirements for cybersecurity education is highlighted. To foster cybersecurity education for networking the case for NETLAB framework is shown. To foster cybersecurity education for software based vulnerabilities a computing framework with VLAN's is shown. To foster educational goals of computing service interaction the effectiveness of the usage of monitoring by honeypots/honeynets, and sanitization by memory only virtualized boot of operating systems in an IT infrastructure is shown.

5. REFERENCES
[1] Stefano Zanero. 2009. Wireless Malware Propagation: A Reality Check. *IEEE Security and Privacy* 7, 5 (September 2009), 70-74. DOI=10.1109/MSP.2009.142 http://dx.doi.org/10.1109/MSP.2009.142

[2] Ernest McDuffie. 2011. NICE: National Initiative for Cybersecurity Education. In *Proceedings of the Seventh Annual Workshop on Cyber Security and Information Intelligence Research* (CSIIRW '11), Frederick T. Sheldon, Robert Abercrombie, and Axel Krings (Eds.). ACM, New York, NY, USA, Article 12 , 1 pages. DOI=10.1145/2179298.2179311 http://doi.acm.org/10.1145/2179298.2179311

[3] Victor Piotrowski. 2011. NSF investments in cybersecurity research and education. In *Proceedings of the Seventh Annual Workshop on Cyber Security and Information Intelligence Research* (CSIIRW '11), Frederick T. Sheldon, Robert Abercrombie, and Axel Krings (Eds.). ACM, New York, NY, USA, Article 13 , 1 pages. DOI=10.1145/2179298.2179312 http://doi.acm.org/10.1145/2179298.2179312

[4] Sylvain P. Leblanc, Andrew Partington, Ian Chapman, and Mélanie Bernier. 2011. An overview of cyber attack and computer network operations simulation. In *Proceedings of the 2011 Military Modeling & Simulation Symposium* (MMS '11). Society for Computer Simulation International, San Diego, CA, USA, 92-100.

[5] W. Victor Maconachy, Corey D. Schou, Daniel Ragsdale and Don Welch "A Model for Information Assurance: An Integrated Approach" Proceedings of the 2001 IEEE Workshop on Information Assurance and Security United States Military Academy, West Point, NY

[6] Nicky Moss and Andrew Smith. 2010. Large Scale Delivery of Cisco Networking Academy Program by Blended Distance Learning. In *Proceedings of the 2010 Sixth International Conference on Networking and Services* (ICNS '10). IEEE Computer Society, Washington, DC, USA, 329-334. DOI=10.1109/ICNS.2010.52 http://dx.doi.org/10.1109/ICNS.2010.52

[7] Weiqing Sun, Varun Katta, Kumar Krishna, and R. Sekar. 2008. V-NetLab: an approach for realizing logically isolated networks for security experiments. In *Proceedings of the conference on Cyber security experimentation and test*

(CSET'08). USENIX Association, Berkeley, CA, USA, , Article 5 , 6 pages.

[8] Anthony D. Wood, John A. Stankovic "Security of Distributed, Ubiquitous, and Embedded Computing Platforms" Wiley Handbook of Science and Technology for Homeland Security

[9] Shari Lawrence Pfleeger "Anatomy of an Intrusion" IT Pro, 2010

[10] Raheem A. Beyah, *Michael C. Holloway, and John A. Copeland "Invisible Trojan: An Architecture, Implementation and Detection Method"

[11] IEEE Standard for Localand metropolitan area networks Virtual Bridged Local Area Networks, IEEE Std 802.1Q™- 2005

[12] Mario Ernesto Gomez-Romero, Mario Reyes-Ayala, Edgar Alejandro Andrade-Gonz\&\#225;lez, and Jose Alfredo Tirado-Mendez. 2010. Design and implementation of a VLAN. In *Proceedings of the 2010 international conference on Applied computing conference* (ACC'10), Petru Andea and Stefan Kilyeni (Eds.). World Scientific and Engineering Academy and Society (WSEAS), Stevens Point, Wisconsin, USA, 87-90.

[13] Julia Allen, "Governing for Enterprise Security" Technical Note CMU/SEI-2005-TN-023

[14] Salah Alabady "Design and Implementation of a Network Security Model for Cooperative Network "International Arab Journal of e-Technology, Vol. 1, No. 2, June 2009

[15] Gurdip Kaur, Meenu Khurana, and Monika Sethi. 2011. Intrusion detection system using honeypots and swarm intelligence. In *Proceedings of the International Conference on Advances in Computing and Artificial Intelligence* (ACAI '11). ACM, New York, NY, USA, 34-38. DOI=10.1145/2007052.2007060 http://doi.acm.org/10.1145/2007052.2007060

[16] Ed Crowley. 2006. Open source, live CD based, security lab design: tutorial presentation. *J. Comput. Small Coll.* 21, 4 (April 2006), 278-279.

[17] Megumi Nakamura and Seiji Munetoh. 2007. Designing a trust chain for a thin client on a live Linux cd. In *Proceedings of the 2007 ACM symposium on Applied computing* (SAC '07). ACM, New York, NY, USA, 1605- 1606. DOI=10.1145/1244002.1244343 http://doi.acm.org/10.1145/1244002.1244343

Shakin' Up Your Management Style

Karen McRitchie
Grinnell College
1119 Sixth Avenue
Grinnell, Iowa 50112
1-641-269-4531

mcritchi@grinnell.edu

ABSTRACT

There are thousands of management books out there in the world, guiding us to lead, follow, create a great team, coach your team, team collaboration, lead from above, lead from the middle, motivate the team, reward the team, reward yourself, manage change, manage performance, manage your time, think inside the box, think outside the box, manage without thinking…whew!

Regardless of the book, article, webinar, or seminar that we learn from, it centers on the positive aspects of managing and most find a way to align themselves with the message, often not recognizing their own management styles may actually conflict with the message. What about the negative aspects of managing? Very few I.T managers are given proper training or mentoring before being assigned human beings to "manage" and many of them fall short of the managers outlined in all of the great advice given by authors and facilitators.

Whether you work for someone with bad management habits or you identify with some of the undesirable qualities, yourself, it is helpful to be able to recognize the qualities of these styles and either work to rid the world of the not-so-great management habits or learn some creative techniques in dealing with those traits and the people you cannot change.

Categories and Subject Descriptors

K.6.1 [**Management of Computing and Information Systems**]: Project and People Management – *staffing, training.*

General Terms

Management, Measurement, Performance, Human Factors

Keywords

Management, Student Staff, Teams, Leadership

1. INTRODUCTION

All managers and team leaders want to think that they are good in their roles, and it is important for all managers to evaluate their own management and leadership skills to confirm that they are succeeding. One thing that most managers have in common is that they are not consciously aware that they have some bad management traits or lack of supervisory skills. Managers are not

seen wearing a sign that states "poor communication skills" or "unapproachable." If a manager is aware of his/her deficiencies, are they willing to obtain the necessary skills or seek advice on their own professional development?

Amazon's website lists approximately 705,833 books on the topic of management. Everything from a One Minute Manager to 21 Things To Know To Hit The Ground Running can be found in hardcover, paperback or electronic formats. There are 48 laws, 7 principles, 5 essential elements, 7 secrets, 4 keys, 7 habits, no, 8 habits and 12 absolutes. Then, after all of the principles, habits and secrets, there is First, Break All The Rules. It is a complicated topic and it's easy to align with the habits, rules and secrets.

It is also important to understand the relationship of poor management and the effects on staff. An effect may not be obvious as it is often emotional or indirect. Years of poor management can create loss of credibility, trust, poor morale and an unwillingness to engage in projects. The difficult task is to identify those habits, principles or secrets that need to be developed so bad management becomes history.

2. REACTIVE STYLE

One of the undesirable characteristics of a manager is the reactive management style. This is a person who believes everything is going well because they have not had any complaints from constituents or colleagues. This type of style deals in crisis management or "putting out fires" because they do not take an active management role in daily operations. They simply react to the problem, often in an inconsistent and decisive manner, without gather sufficient information about the problem.

One example of this type of style is the IT manager who received a complaint that a faculty member requested some software to be installed over two months ago and complained that it hadn't been completed. The manager's response was to apologize to the faculty member, telling them that the team had "dropped the ball" and he would make sure that someone would get right over there and get the software installed.

When the manager checked with the team, he wanted this done immediately regardless of other scheduled tasks. When the team member assigned to the task visited the faculty office, it turned out that the software was installed as requested within 24 hours of the original request; so he informed the faculty. The problem was that the list of programs on the computer was not alphabetical, and so the program was not listed where it was expected, but at the end of the program listing. The task had been accomplished completely and without error at the time of the request from the faculty.

There are several concerns about this example. The IT manager's quick response was one that hurt the team's credibility with that faculty member. It created an initial impression that the staff was not performing, even though it turned out that this was false. Other tasks were postponed while the staff member went immediately to the faculty office, which may have inconvenienced others waiting on tasks to be completed. Unnecessary time was spent by several people checking, visiting and discussing this issue. Most of all, it hurt the morale of the team because they were accused of not doing their jobs and did not receive any support from their manager.

The best way to have handled the complaint was to listen to the complaint, tell the faculty member that someone would investigate this matter today and contact them. The manager could then address the team member who had the task, inform them of the complaint and ask them to investigate and/or install the software if necessary. The manager would then be able to follow up with the team member and the faculty later that day, in this case, to remind the faculty that we did the job as requested.

Every problem or question does not need an immediate answer. Sometimes more information needs to be collected and it is acceptable to communicate that the solution is being investigated. A reactive style just escalates the problem and emotions unnecessarily. This type of style can often stifle creativity and innovation as staff members do not feel supported.

3. MICROMANAGING

Those who micromanage do not realize that this is counterproductive and creates fear among the team members. Micromanaging is communicating a lack of trust and a level of incompetence to the team. A functioning team is created from several people who have varied skills, personalities, and strengths. This is what makes the team successful; working together to complete tasks and projects. Their contributions are creativity, innovation, process improvement and a general engagement with their work.

The message sent by micromanaging is "you are not competent enough to be trusted with that task alone or that decision alone," "my way of performing the task is the right way" and "I do not trust you." Micromanaging creates a lot of unproductive time because of repetition, unnecessary emails/communications and an unwillingness to volunteer for projects by team members.

Another message sent by micromanaging is that failure is not acceptable. Often those managers who find themselves involved in every little task are those who are perfectionists. They feel if they can control everything, then mistakes will not occur. When a team is not allowed to make mistakes, then they become afraid to do anything without permission and it lowers morale.

It is the job of the manager to create superstar team members. Provide resources and support so that they excel and the manager will excel. When people are valued for their skills and knowledge, they engage with their work. Mistakes need to be supported as learning moments and projects/tasks evaluated by asking "what can we have done better?" The more the team members are involved in decisions, planning and evaluation, the more successful they will be as a team. Micromanagement does not fit in a true team environment.

There seem to always be complaints that there are too many meetings. Unnecessary meetings are a sign of micromanaging. A traditional meeting is often in a micromanager's "comfort zone" and so meetings are scheduled for all communication. A manager who has a recurring daily or weekly meeting needs to evaluate the purpose and effectiveness of such things. Meetings should happen when different groups need to communicate, such as a project team or the stakeholders in a project. Meetings need to happen to communicate a new process or discuss a new procedure. Meetings need to have a specific agenda, time limit and time for assignment of tasks to participants. Daily communication should be occurring with each team member, then status of tasks and questions can be discussed at that time, otherwise only step in when asked or if deadlines look like they are not going to be met. A manager needs to be the one who supports and provides necessary resources so that the team excels at their work.

4. INCONSISTENCY AND DECISIONS

Another negative characteristic of a manager is being inconsistent, especially in decision-making opportunities. This could be a manager who establishes policies, yet continually allows "exceptions" to those policies. The team will question the policies and the policies will become invalid. This destroys the credibility of the manager as well as those who are adhering to policies, and will be very frustrating to all involved.

Inconsistency also is found in attendance. Where is the manager? Are they accessible to staff? Is their calendar accessible? Managers who are always in meetings or disappear become a frustration to the staff, who eventually gives up communication.

IT staff are often those with analytical personalities. They are problem solvers and logical in their planning and execution of tasks. Communication of the "what" and "why" is important to maintain productivity. It is hard for one of these workers to be involved in something that does not make sense to them. It is the job of the manager to be able to communicate these things so that all of the staff sees the big picture and understand how things relate. When decisions or projects are not perceived as being logically planned, it is extremely frustrating to the team members.

5. AVOIDANCE

Avoidance is a very common trait for those in management. As humans, we have a comfort zone and when we need to step out of that comfort zone to perform a task or make a decision, it is very stressful, and often just avoided.

For example, let's say a team member is not performing a task properly, but since everyone dislikes confrontation, there is no conversation with the team member about his performance. It is not fair to the other team members or the one doing his job improperly to avoid having a difficult conversation.

Managers need to step up and practice the skills that they need for effective communication when they need to confront a team member on their performance. It is permissible to have notes in a meeting, say to the employee, "this is an important conversation and I need to make sure that I don't forget anything so I will be using my notes as reference."

It is important to make sure that it is the behavior of the team member that is discussed, and not the person. For example, if you think that a team member is lazy, it would not be acceptable to say, "hey, you are really lazy?" Instead, list behaviors that relate to "lazy" such as lack of initiative when it comes to taking support tickets or letting others take the difficult tasks. Explain the performance behavior, explain how it affects the team and the job, then state how the behavior should change for the future.

5.1 Excuses! Excuses!

Here are some common excuses given by managers who are practicing avoidance:

- Not enough time
- I manage too many people
- I have people in remote locations
- I manage people who work in areas where I don't have experience
- I don't have authority over certain projects
- I am afraid of micromanaging
- People might think I am unfair
- I am not a natural leader
- I have persistent problems with some people that just don't go away
- The staff has a bad attitude
- How do I hold people accountable if the work is not easily measured?
- Too many conflicts within team
- It's too hard to fire people in my company
- It's too hard to get rewards for high performers.
- My boss doesn't back me up
- Conservative corporate culture—don't rock the boat!
- We are understaffed and everyone is overworked
- Language barriers
- Priorities shift and change…how can I manage clear expectations?
- I have been accepting mediocrity for too long
- I have inherited staff whose managers accepted their level of performance in the past
- They are my friends
- I want people to like me
- My employee is a relative or friend of the boss
- Corporate politics make it difficult
- I don't have discipline skills [1]

There is a solution to every excuse, and the best management practice is to address the performance issue when it happens and not avoid the issue.

6. EMOTIONAL INTELLIGENCE

Hundreds of studies link human emotions with quantitative outcomes. If employees feel they are treated fairly, the organization will be successful. Organizations have a better chance of succeeding when their people are committed, energized and engaged, instead of fearful, exhausted and overwhelmed. If people feel valued, they are much more likely to make a commitment to the organization, take on grater responsibilities and initiate positive changes. Good managers know that the feelings of the team members do matter and affect performance.

"When people are anxious about work, they're afraid that no amount of effort is good enough. To make themselves safe, they work very hard at everything. They don't feel secure enough and are not courageous enough to differentiate among tasks and set priorities. When all work seems enormous, there is not closure—satisfaction—it results in overload." [2] It is the manager's job to provide the resources and support to create superstar employees. Job satisfaction is a large part of employee performance. Unhappy people are not always productive and one of the top reasons that employees leave their jobs is a result of their manager, not the company or the work.

A manager must realize that equal is not always fair. Each employee is an individual, find out what motivates them and provide those things. For example, in most employee surveys, salary seems to rank in the middle of motivators, with flexible time, autonomy, and being a part of decision making ranking higher. For instance, a team member who has sleep issues and trouble being productive in the mornings was assigned a later shift which took him beyond the "normal" hours of ending the day at 5:00pm. By doing this, the team had a person after hours, which allowed many tasks that were difficult to schedule during the daytime to be completed easily and emergencies could be responded to quickly if after the regular work day. This doesn't mean that everyone wants to work at this time or would it benefit the team. A good manager will consider benefits to the employee and the team when making decisions.

7. UNDERMANAGMENT

Many managers in I.T. got their job because they performed well as a team member or on projects. They are given the responsibility of a team without any mentoring or management skills training. They don't want to micromanage, but they have to guide their team and its resources. In the 90s employees should be empowered, in the 80s, it was teams…there is not one management philosophy that works for everyone. More importantly is to make sure that management occurs every day. Undermanaging staff is as serious a problem as having a micromanager or bully for a boss. There are just as many performance issues from not paying attention or letting staff become too autonomous as there is from micromanaging. How many times has a manager addressed a performance problem in a yearly review, rather than speaking with the employee directly when the problem occurred? What benefit does it have, other than punishment, when an employee finds out that 7 months ago, they did not complete the project on time and that caused delays in the other areas?

Undermanagers do not know what their team members are doing, do not know the status of projects and are not very educated when a decision is necessary. It is as important for a manager to schedule time for team management and daily communication as scheduling their own projects. The team operations is their job and letting the team falter without clear expectations and direction will only result in failures and problems. Most employee performance problems are a direct result of poor management; either lack of direction or unclear expectations. It is the manager's responsibility to provide these things EVERY day.

8. BULLIES AND OTHER CREATURES

There are some general characteristics of bad managers that need to be acknowledged and these types of behaviors need counseling from a human resources expert or counselor to overcome as they are often personality related. Do the team members avoid communication with the manager? Do they lack initiative on accepting new projects or tasks? Is the culture within the team different when the manager is present? Do the team members look forward to the times when the manager is out of the office?

A manager can read their own style and effectiveness by knowing their team. The team or lack of team participation is a great management indicator.

8.1 Bully

This type of manger is always right, wants things done his/her way only and may reprimand employees publicly or say things that are derogatory to make the employee feel bad for their mistake. This type of manager should be avoided if possible as the team will never function well, always afraid to make mistakes or say things that will cause the bully to react negatively.

8.2 Chameleon

This is the manager whose demeanor and decisions change based on the level of others in the room. For example, status reports to the President of the college will be different from those given to subordinates. Requests are approved based on status so a faculty member may be granted something that a staff person is not allowed.

8.3 Managing from the Past

Some managers only know what they learned as an employee and will pass that on to their current team. In the 1960s and 70s, the baby boomers were primarily in the workforce and the management style was "do what you are told and don't question." Often older managers use this same philosophy and haven't had experience with a more modern approach to managing their staff. In today's work environment, we have new generations of team members who are not going to be managed in that "old-fashioned" way. There has been a lot of research and information that supports a more modern approach to managing people.

8.4 By The Book Managers

Have you saved every policy ever communicated? Do you refer to a manual for decisions? Managers may have the characteristic of doing everything "by the book" and not allowing room for human personality styles or exceptions to the rules. These managers quote policy and rules and the team members must follow the rules without exception. It is a lack of confidence or just not wanting to be responsible for a decision that makes these managers adhere to the rules only. As long as the rules are followed, someone else is responsible.

8.5 "I only know what I do wrong."

Many employees do not get any gratitude or acknowledgement for tasks and projects that are done well, and are only told when they make a mistake. Managers who do not allow the team members to treat mistakes as learning opportunities will create teams that are afraid of making mistakes and also those who are afraid to communicate when a mistake occurs.

9. LISTENING SKILLS

One of the most important skills that a manager can have is to have good listening skills. Not only does this benefit the people who are part of the team, but also allows the manager to hear the meanings behind the words.

A manager with poor listening skills will only focus on the parts of the conversation that challenge the rules or policies, not the "big picture" of the problem. When this occurs, the team gets frustrated because they are not being understood and a solution usually does not present itself easily. This can cause teams to circumvent processes or policies that might interfere and cause future problems or resolve problems in their own without manager input.

10. CONCLUSION

Management ideas and concepts have evolved over the past decades and it is the job of the manager to have the right skills and experience to lead a superstar team. There are many ways to improve skills or experiences so that a manager is an asset to the team rather than a liability.

Find someone that is a great manager and ask them to be your mentor, learn from others who have had great ideas succeed and those who have tried things and failed. Read books, articles and take classes that will strengthen skills. Most of all, leave the comfort zone. Our comfort zone prevents us from change and challenging ourselves with new ideas. Step out of the management comfort zone and improve the bad management habits that are found in your organization. It is the job of the manager to provide resources and support to create superstar employees and in doing this the manager will be a superstar!

11. REFERENCES

[1] Tulgan, Bruce, Rainmaker Thinking Inc., http://www.rainmakerthinking.com/

[2] Bardwick, Judith M. Ph.D., One Foot Out The Door: How to Combat the Psychological recession That's Alienating Employees and Hurting American Business. (2007) p.13 AMACOM, a division of American Management Association, 1601 Broadway, NY, NY 10019.

A Video Support Model for Liberal Arts Colleges

Trevor Murphy
Williams College
22 Lab Campus Drive
Williamstown, MA 01267
011.413.597.2231

Trevor.M.Murphy@williams.edu

ABSTRACT

Supporting video in the liberal arts college context is a broad topic including training and instruction, production, event support, simulcasting, film festivals, college courses on video, media lab support, internships for students, software and hardware access, and loaner pools of equipment. Williams College has been working to develop a support model to handle the wide ranging video support needs of the college. The evolving model makes use of existing course support programs, a well defined training path for student employees, and project based initiatives. Developing our understanding of video production, support and training, has increased our capacity at Williams College to support video based scholarship on campus.

Categories and Subject Descriptors

H.5.1 [**Information Interfaces and Presentation**]: Multimedia Information Systems – *Video*.

General Terms

Management, Human Factors, Standardization.

Keywords

Video, Liberal Arts, Support, Film, Training, Production, Employees, Teaching, College.

1 WILLIAMS COLLEGE

Williams College is a residential liberal arts college located in the northwestern corner of Massachusetts in the town of Williamstown. The college has about 2,000 students and 300 faculty. The Office for Information Technology (OIT) at Williams College consists of four groups including Networks and Systems, Desktop Systems, Administrative Information Systems, and Instructional Technology (ITech). The ITech group is the focus of this paper.

The ITech group is the largest subgroup in OIT consisting of 12 staff members and a manager. ITech can be further divided into three subgroups consisting of the Instructional Technology Specialists, the project group, and Media Services. ITech provides a variety of services with a focus on supporting faculty in their use of technology in teaching and research.

When it comes to video, there is an Equipment Loan Center Coordinator, Computer Labs and Software Administrator, and a Media Studios and Technologies Coordinator who maintain the equipment and video editing stations. The broader support group consists of approximately nine staff members who support video use on campus as part of their responsibilities. There are no full time staff that are solely dedicated to the support of video at Williams College.

There is no film studies program at Williams College. Several faculty representing the English, Art, German and Russian, and Asian Studies departments have worked with video as a teaching tool or taught video as a creative medium.

2 HISTORY OF VIDEO AT WILLIAMS

The history of video support at Williams College reflects changes in video editing hardware and software, student expectations, faculty perception of digital scholarship, and efforts by OIT to shape technology use on campus. The movement from analog to digital video editing and recording, the rise of Youtube.com and other video distribution services, and the affordability of the technology influenced the design of media lab facilities at Williams. Not covered in this paper are the uses of video by the Athletics Department, Alumni Relations and Development, and the Office of Communications which have independently worked with video with a combination of outsourcing and in house expertise.

2.1 It's an Analog World.

In 2001 the support of video at Williams College was completely an analog process using a massive editing station where the output was on VHS tape. One staff member was confortable with the analog editing station. Training was a one on one affair simply because there was only one station to work at. If production work was required, the resident expert worked on the project and others could observe from afar. Analog camcorders were available from the Williams College equipment loan center.

2.2 Enter Digital Video Editing

At that same time, the introduction of digital video editing was quickly making the analog editing station obsolete. File storage and video distribution changed from tape to DVD. Whole computer labs had video editing software installed. Hands on video editing classes for up to 8 students started to be offered. The Williams College equipment loan center started carrying small portable video cameras that used mini dv tapes. The college brought in outside consultants to teach digital video editing using Final Cut Pro. Attendees would spend a day or several days learning about video editing concepts and put together a cereal commercial using stock footage and sound effects.

2.3 Digital Storytelling Changes Video Training

In 2002, the Director of ITech at Williams College was introduced to Digital Storytelling [4] at a New Media Consortium conference, http://www.nmc.org/. The digital storytelling model of teaching where class participants create and craft their own story from still images and an audio narration over a period of three days in groups of eight students changed video training in important ways. The classes were still taught by outside consultants, in this case the Center for Digital Storytelling, http://www.storycenter.org/. The difference was that students found working on their own materials motivating. Even though students had to commit to a three-day training, there was often a waiting list for the next workshop.

2.4 Lecture Capture and the Flash Streaming Server

A lecture capture solution was tried at Williams. It was installed in specific rooms on campus and the solution was not portable. An advantage of the system was that it automatically linked in to the course management system the college supported. The system was in use for perhaps a year and a half. Many workshops were recorded, but few were watched. Faculty who had expressed initial interest in lecture capture didn't actually follow through and use it for their courses.

The Flash streaming server serves as the college's video distribution service. Videos can be imbedded in web pages with some effort and coding.

2.5 Training and Hiring Students to do Video Work

Starting in 1997, ITech started a ten-week summer program using hired 12 students to work on faculty proposed curricular projects. Initially funded by the Andrew W. Mellon Foundation grant, http://www.mellon.org/, the program became a regular part of the ITech budget until 2010 when the funds were cut. The program was called Williams Instructional Technology or WIT [3].

Faculty proposed projects could involve any number of technologies including but not limited to web development, 3d modeling, mapping, programming, database design, video, and animation. Video and animation projects were not common, but they came up from time to time. Even so, two and a half days of the two-week training of students included digital storytelling. Not only did students learn the video editing process, and project and time management, but as a bonus, students were able to get to know each other through sharing their stories using video. Some students did create videos and animations for faculty.

2.6 The Video Intern Program and Williams Thinking

After the demise of the WIT program, a much smaller nine-week summer internship program was created in 2011 with only three or four students focusing exclusively on video and animation. This program was called the Video Intern Program or VIP. A series of 20-minute faculty talks called Williams Thinking created in an effort to generate demand for video production services over the summer. The students filmed the faculty speakers and followed up by editing a three-camera shoot into videos that would end up being distributed on the Williams College Youtube channel at http://www.youtube.com/user/WilliamsCollege. Other projects in the first year addressed advertising Williams College IT services.

Though initially the Williams Thinking video series was imagined just as an annual summer event connected to the VIP program, it was successful enough that the Communications Office of Williams College took an interest in having Williams Thinking events throughout the year. Supporting video production during the academic year without a dedicated video production staff involved sometimes heroic staff efforts to fit in 40 to 80 hours of video editing along with the other regular daily ITech staff member duties and responsibilities.

While the summer edition of Williams Thinking is still handled by the VIP interns, faculty have begun to propose curricular video projects for the interns to tackle.

2.7 Winter Study Courses, Workshops/Training, and the Film Festival

Winter study, or January term as it is sometimes called, is an opportunity for students to take only one course for a month from faculty and adjunct faculty in between the fall and spring semesters. The past couple years, the author has co-taught a course on video and animation. Students have weekly projects that result in video pieces to share with the class.

From December to January a series of workshops on video topics are offered that help attendees learn to put together short video pieces. In addition, several ip-based Lynda.com stations are available for online tutorials in how to use video editing software.

This culminates in February with the film festival with categories including video (5 minute maximum), animation, mockumentary/parody/spoof, long-short (15 minutes maximum), and Williams College theme. Prizes have included iPads and other similar devices as well as a trophy. The final showing of the prize winners is held in an auditorium where attendees only learn who the winners are as they are announced and the pieces are played. The first film festival was in 2011 though there was a similar contest in 2010.

2.8 Students Become Employees and Spread Video Awareness on Campus

Students who have completed a winter study course on film and animation, have submitted entries to the film festival, or who have served as summer interns are often hired to work for ITech during the academic year as a Student Media Consultant or SMC. SMCs staff media labs and assist patrons with video development or other media based projects.

SMC workers can also serve as media mentors for regular Williams College courses that include a multimedia project as part of the regular course assignments through the Integrating Digital Literacies Initiative or IDeaL Initiative. The IDeal Initiative supports faculty using multimedia-based assignments by providing a student employee who will support the technical needs of the students in the class as they complete the assignment. The faculty member can then be free to work on course content, rather than learning how to support the assignment technology.

Students who have video editing experiences have had some success in convincing faculty that a video project may in some cases replace a traditional paper writing assignment. In this way faculty learn from the students about the potential for multimedia scholarship.

2.9 OIT Restructures and is Relieved of Web Support

In the past, the ITech group supported web development for the campus in an unofficial capacity. The ITech mission is to support faculty in using technology in instruction, yet the college's website is maintained by many staff members with no clear support model. ITech members who taught web development workshops for the campus became the favored contact for web issues.

This changed when the college created a new group in the Office of Communications that manages the college web presence. While

ITech still cares for and maintains the college's course management system and the Networks and Systems group maintains the servers, OIT has been relieved of supporting client level web development.

3 CURRENT VIDEO SUPPORT AT WILLIAMS COLLEGE

Video initiatives that have survived at Williams College include the equipment loan center, the media labs and availability of video editing software, the flash streaming server, the VIP summer intern program, VIP production support of faculty proposed curricular video projects, video workshops on particular software titles, winter study video and animation courses, employment opportunities for students, the film festival, and the IDeaL initiative.

The Williams Thinking series continues to exist, but it is shared now between ITech and the Office of Communications.

Video initiatives that have been retired at Williams College include the WIT program, digital storytelling workshops, workshops offered by outside consultants, analog video editing support, and lecture capture.

The change of the summer intern program to focus exclusively on video has improved the body of knowledge and the level of support offered by ITech staff. There is more familiarity with animation and video software, hardware, and techniques on campus.

3.1 Content of Winter Study Course

The winter study course has enrolled up to 14 students. The duration of the course is limited to the month of January. There are generally 6 hours of class and 6 hours of lab a week. The first week starts with storytelling. Students tell each other stories in small groups. Technical terms and examples are explored. Script writing and storyboarding is covered using Celtex software. Students create a comic using Comic Life and Adobe Photoshop.

The second week starts with workshops on iMovie, advanced Photoshop, videography, Soundtrack Pro, and copyright. The students create a short film. The third week covers animation using Adobe Flash, and motion. The students create a short animation.

The last week gives students the freedom of creating a final project of their own design.

Each week there are showings of short films and animations that thematically cover topics in the course. Students are encouraged to submit their final projects to the film festival.

3.2 Content of VIP Internship Training

The content of the VIP internship training depends on the faculty projects submitted to the program. Typically, each workshop is followed by an assignment where students apply what they learned in the workshop to achieve some task. The workshops are every day and last 8 hours a day and lasted for two and a half weeks. In 2012, the training started with videography, learning to use the camera, Adobe Photoshop using a Wacom drawing tablet, Final Cut Pro, media management and storage, Motion, color correction, storyboarding, Adobe Flash, recording audio, Soundtrack Pro, project management, lighting, stop motion animation, and a final project.

4 A VIDEO SUPPORT MODEL

4.1 Support Paths for Faculty, Staff, and Students

It is helpful to consider the how the various facets of video support and the stakeholders fit together in creating a support model for video on campus. Focusing on what students, faculty, and staff will be doing to develop their skills and also how they will implement their ideas can help define services and facilities.

At Williams College, the video support model is influenced by the historical use of the technology as well as a vision of the future. The support for students is largely geared toward creating a pool of trained potential workers. Faculty support is focused on the curricular use of video in instruction. Staff support is more incidental, as an OIT driven staff technology training curriculum does not exist. Staff may take advantage of video instruction and video editing facilities as time allows.

Students engage in video editing as learners and as workers. We support student learning through the IDeal Initiative in their classes, winter study courses in video and animation, workshops, the film festival, regular semester courses in video, Lynda.com, SMC staffed media studios, and on the job training. As workers, students serve the campus as SMCs staffing the media labs, as media mentors supporting media rich courses, and as summer interns creating faculty proposed curricular video.

Staff learners use Lynda.com and attend video workshops as they are available. They also can request one-on-one assistance for projects related to the mission of Williams College.

Faculty learners can request one-on-one assistance, attend workshops, and make use of Lynda.com. Faculty can make use of the IDeal Initiative and have a media mentor help with video intensive assignments in their courses. There is also the VIP summer intern program that provides student production for video to be used in instruction.

Faculty, staff, and students take advantage of infrastructure that includes the video editing station equipped media studios, the equipment loan center, and the trained students and staff.

4.2 Support Paths by Function

The project plan for a video entails coming up with a story to tell, storyboarding/scriptwriting the idea, borrowing necessary equipment, capturing footage, editing the piece, and sharing/publishing the final piece. Considering the available support for each phase of a video project can reveal opportunities for additional support.

The story development phase, which may include storyboarding and scriptwriting, is supported through workshops, one-on-one support consultations, VIP internship training, and the winter study video and animation course. Faculty may encounter support in the story development phase in one-on-one consultations particularly if they proposed a VIP project. This area of support is critical for creating a clear direction and purpose for the video.

Making equipment available including still and video cameras, tripods, microphones, lighting kits, green/blue screens, and other accessory items makes projects possible. If workshops on video production recommend the use of a tripod, then tripods should be accessible. The Equipment Loan Center Coordinator knows the available equipment well and has experience with video production. When college affiliated faculty, staff, and students go to borrow equipment they may ask questions about particular technical needs and receive hardware specific advice so that they borrow the most appropriate tools for the job.

Advice on capturing video is covered in workshops, one-on-one support consultations, VIP internship training, and the winter study video and animation course. Faculty participating in the VIP program may not learn about capturing video as that task is delegated to the student interns.

Editing footage can happen in media labs or on the personal machines of faculty, staff, or students. Video editing software is widely available. Larger projects benefit from newer and faster machines equipped with large quantities of RAM and multiple processors. Such machines are maintained in the media studios. The media studios also happen to be staffed during regular hours by trained and experienced student media consultants. Video editors may have had training from workshops, one-on-one support consultations, VIP internship training, and the winter study video and animation course, but they also may have learned to use the software on their own or from a source such as Lynda.com. Video editing support can be specific and context dependent. An editor may need specific help on a topic such as working with multiple layers of video or topics not covered in workshops. Such situations justify the presence of trained staff to assist as needed in the media studios.

The publishing/sharing phase of a video project is supported in multiple ways. Videos can be hosted on the college flash streaming server, the college YouTube channel, or on other video hosting services. The film festival may be an avenue for sharing and celebrating video scholarship, but press releases may publicize work as well. VIP projects are promoted through all campus daily message systems and shared with various departments and programs. Faculty lectures may be promoted by the Office of Communication or Alumni Development who have a variety of means of sharing college related news. Videos may also be embedded in course pages of the course management system on campus or on a blog. How final projects are shared depends on the context of the work.

The VIP program acknowledges the challenges for faculty in terms of time intensive nature of video production by offering trained student labor and instructional technology support for their projects. The IDeal program assists faculty in creating media rich assignments for their courses. Some support offerings guide faculty, staff, and students through the entire process while others focus just on one aspect of production. It is useful to think about how each phase of video production will be supported when considering a prospective video project.

5   THE FUTURE OF VIDEO AT WILLIAMS COLLEGE

Williams College is in the process of building a new library with a technology facility called the Center for Media Initiatives or CMI. The focus of the new facility will be to promote and provide support for multimedia production for teaching and learning. The CMI will have a recording studio, video editing project rooms, and a music composition room. The equipment loan center will be in this new space as well. The centralized combination of facilities, equipment, and support and training will provide an opportunity to promote video as an instructional tool.

Also in development is a college institutional repository which may serve to house, organize, archive, or distribute video. A video distribution service or appliance that may work together with the institutional repository is also being investigated.

Lecture capture has been tried as a pilot before at Williams College, but it was not used. The technology has progressed in many years in the past 5 years. A new lecture capture pilot is also in the works.

There are discussions about hiring a staff position that would focus on video production. It is unclear yet if the position will be funded and what department on campus would be the best home for such a position.

Video is a growing medium for scholarship on campus. As video use changes, so will the college's support model.

6   ACKNOWLEDGEMENTS

Thanks to Dinny Taylor, Chief Technology Officer of OIT, and Jonathan Morgan-Leamon, Director of Instructional Technology, who support the author's professional development.

7   . REFERENCES

[1] Murphy, Trevor and Hirai, Mika. 2003. Teaching with technology, setting an example. In *Proceedings of the 31st annual ACM SIGUCCS fall conference* (SIGUCCS '03). ACM, New York, NY, USA, 208-212. DOI=10.1145/947469.947523 http://doi.acm.org/10.1145/947469.947523

[2] Murphy, Trevor. 2004. Research based methods for using powerpoint, animation, and video for instruction. In Proceedings of the 32nd annual ACM SIGUCCS fall conference (SIGUCCS '04). ACM, New York, NY, USA, 372-374. DOI=10.1145/1027802.1027892 http://doi.acm.org/10.1145/1027802.1027892

[3] Murphy, Trevor. 2007. Williams instructional technology: summer students working on faculty projects. In *Proceedings of the 35th annual ACM SIGUCCS fall conference* (SIGUCCS '07). ACM, New York, NY, USA, 272-276. DOI=10.1145/1294046.1294110 http://doi.acm.org/10.1145/1294046.1294110

[4] Murphy, Trevor. 2007. A tale of 101 digital stories. In *Proceedings of the 35th annual ACM SIGUCCS fall conference* (SIGUCCS '07). ACM, New York, NY, USA, 269-271. DOI=10.1145/1294046.1294109 http://doi.acm.org/10.1145/1294046.1294109

ULearn More: Transitioning to a Learning Management System for Staff at American University

Jacqueline Palumbo
Office of Information Technology
American University
4400 Massachusetts Ave. NW
Washington, DC 20016

(202) 885-2243

jpalum@american.edu

Matteo Becchi
Office of Information Technology
American University
4400 Massachusetts Ave. NW
Washington, DC 20016

(202) 885-3027

becchi@american.edu

Sheila Way
Workplace Learning and Development
American University
4400 Massachusetts Ave. NW
Washington, DC 20016

(202) 885-3586

way@american.edu

ABSTRACT

American University's Office of Information Technology (OIT) training unit provides classroom-based and online training to over 1,800 staff, students, and faculty attendees annually. This group develops, schedules, markets, and delivers the training. The training unit also evaluates the effectiveness of the training and provides detailed reporting for the university's staff performance management program.

In 2011, the OIT training unit was invited to partner with the University's Human Resources department and other campus trainers to select a vendor and implement an online Learning Management System for full-time university staff, and faculty with supervisory responsibilities.

The training partners went through a lengthy assessment process, chose a vendor, assigned system roles, attended extensive administrator training, and then the hard work began!

Although some of the training partners shared similar technological tools and processes, generally each group had a distinct, and well-established, method for managing the administration, marketing, and assessment of their training program. Combining these methods, while maintaining each group's autonomy proved challenging.

This presentation will discuss how the team leveraged the learning management technology to meet our shared goals, culminating in a successful system launch in February, 2012. We will explore how we selected the technical components we would utilize, and how we developed a common language and unified processes. We will also discuss the process of branding our new system as "ULearn," how we created a ULearn portal, and how

we marketed the system. Lastly, we will explore how we are fostering a "ULearn More" environment by empowering our customers to navigate their own learning path.

Categories and Subject Descriptors
K.8.3 [**Personal Computing**]: Management/Maintenance

General Terms
Performance, Design, Documentation, Management.

Keywords
Learning management system, Training, Registration, Assessment, American University.

1. INTRODUCTION
The decision to implement a learning management system can generate seismic shifts in an organization's established technologies and processes. Within an organization, specific groups need to be identified that have responsibility for providing workplace learning opportunities for their function. When considering the scope of learning on an institutional level, it quickly becomes evident that responsibility for managing learning is stratified throughout the organization.

In 2011, American University began the process to implement an online Learning Management System for full-time university staff, and faculty with supervisory responsibilities in support of our Strategic Goal # 9 "**Encourage Innovation and High Performance:**

We will build a culture of innovation and high performance. To respond to the needs of the twenty-first century and the requirements of the university and its students, we will encourage innovation and high performance in learning, scholarship, technology, financial management, and organizational processes.

We will create effective IT governance that broadly manages Information Technology and computational operations across all pillars of the university. Motivating and rewarding high performance and providing opportunities for professional development and advancement, we will train, inform, and empower staff, faculty, and administrators to make those decisions for which they are best qualified."

The university searched for and selected a Talent Management / Human Capital Management System for full-time university staff and faculty supervisors with the LMS being the first component to implement. The vendor needed to be able to provide a learning management platform that would support the effort to manage, develop, and deploy online and instructor-led training in the near-term. The university was also looking for a vendor that would have the capacity to provide a platform for an online performance management system, and a compensation system for future deployment.

A request for proposals was distributed to qualified vendors. After a thorough vetting process, American University selected the SuccessFactors Learning Management system. Seven months were allotted from the project launch to the go-live date. The implementation team immediately convened and, an aggressive project timeline was created. The team would need to determine which technical components to include, develop a common language, and agree on unified procedures. The team would also need to promote a self-service culture to enable our customers to navigate and manage their own learning path.

2. THE STAKEHOLDERS

The primary project owner for the learning management system was American University's Office of Workplace Learning and Development, which is a unit of the University's Human Resources department. Other key stakeholders included representatives from the Office of Information Technology's training unit, the University Library, the Office of Risk Management and Safety Services, the Office of Campus Life, and the Training and Development office of the Washington College of Law. Although some of the training partners shared similar technological tools and processes, generally each group had a distinct and well-established method for managing the administration, marketing, and assessment of their training program.

Some training partners, such as the Office of Information Technology and Human Resources, used long-established Lotus Notes databases to manage training registration, attendance, and survey results. Other departments utilized Microsoft Office programs, such as Excel or Access, to manage attendance and create reports. Some partners had online self-registration systems, while others did not. Most partners had responsibility for assigning and tracking some mandatory, compliance-based internal and external training.

2.1 Shared Needs – Different Customers

The training partners served multiple constituencies. Included in these constituencies are full-time and part-time staff members, full-time and part-time students, and full-time and adjunct faculty members. Each of these populations shared similar needs: the ability to access the training course catalog with detailed course descriptions; register for training; access information on completed training for performance-based or compliance reporting; and the ability to request training on an-as needed basis.

The learning management system was implemented and made available only to full-time staff and faculty with supervisory responsibilities, due to licensing costs. Therefore, some partners were required to maintain dual tracking and registration systems, since they serve other constituencies. This necessity influenced the selection of the technical components utilized for learning management roll-out. Partners needed to maintain or enhance current levels of functionality and customer accountability, which resulted in a requisite duplication of efforts by some groups.

2.2 Shared Gain – Enhanced Functionality

From the beginning of this project, the team focused on the advantages of the enhanced functionality of the Success Factors system. Enhanced functionality for our customers included a customized learning plan, learning history for individual end users, and a view of direct reports' learning history for managers.

Customers can make training requests through the system. Training administrators can push out required training to end users as needed. This functionality empowers our customers to take responsibility for their own learning path.

Although online training was not part of the program at the initial go live date in February, it was incorporated a few months later.

3. THE PLAN

The project plan incorporated specific deliverables throughout the implementation process. The kick-off began with a project team orientation for the identified training partner administrators. This was followed by a configuration workshop facilitated by Success Factors.

Groups offering training to staff and faculty supervisors were invited to participate in the selection and configuration of the system to obtain maximum value and to provide a central resource for staff learning activity

Next came several months of guided user testing, and an extensive administrator training six weeks before the go-live date.

3.1 Branding and Transition

An inclusive strategy was needed to encompass the entire three phases of the project. A naming process was developed by using "Creative Problem Solving" techniques of idea generation and focusing exercises, with a variety of staff. The name was determined as "AsuccessfulU" with "ULearn" as the name for the learning management system component.

"UPerform" and "UEarn" have been proposed for the performance and compensation components. The name integrates all components under one family of branding using the "U" to stress the focus on the individual and reference the abbreviated name of the institution.

A web portal page was developed and built to promote the overall branding and roll out of "ASuccessfulU" and "ULearn". A single-sign-on solution was developed, so users can log on directly from the portal without any additional password challenges.

The colors and logo were developed to synchronize with the current university portal page design for a seamless look and feel to the application. The portal page serves as a central resource of access to the system and future components, Help Desk information, user guides, FAQ's, and externally hosted online training resources available to staff.

3.2 End User Training

Training for end users was offered concurrently with the system launch in February 2012. Multiple training modalities were offered to the user community, including on-line and instructor led training, job aids, and targeted departmental training on request.

Table 1. The Training Plan

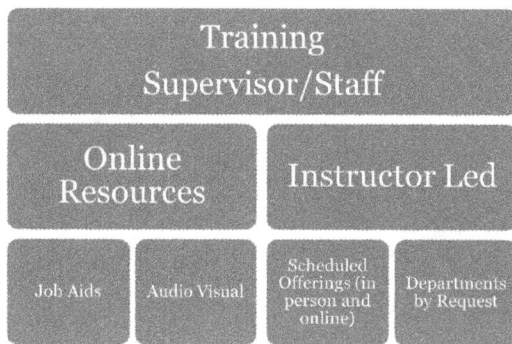

3.3 The Launch

The launch date was determined by the project team and was dependent on data readiness. Various marketing sources including direct e-mail and campus announcements were used to promote the launch.

Once launched, system utilization was tracked via analysis of traffic to the portal page through SharePoint administration tools. Questions about the system were tracked and monitored using the university's incident management system (iSupport); and, a dedicated email address (ulearn@american.edu) was established to serve as a single access point for requesting assistance.

Customer questions about ULearn were directed first to the Workplace Learning and Development team. This team created an incident management ticket to track each customer contact. If needed, they escalated issues to other training partners or to the vendor's Customer Success Organization (support center) to achieve an appropriate resolution.

4. THE PROJECT OWNER'S PERSPECTIVE (WORKPLACE LEARNING AND DEVELOPMENT)

The primary driver for the learning management system was the strategic initiative for Human Resources to support high performance throughout the university and automate high volume processes. To support the learning plan component of the human capital product, a system was desired to house campus training activity that could be linked to a new set of competencies for staff.

Due to the percentage of students and faculty who would use the learning management system, it was determined not to be cost effective to include these populations in the per-person licensing for this product for the initial implementation.

The roll out of ULearn marks the end of Phase I of a three-year phased implementation. The successful launch of the ULearn system has established a foundation for online, automated, real-time reportable data to show the cost value of goal progress, competency development, and to support a clear link of pay to performance to help managers develop staff, create succession pathways, and support knowledge transfer and sustainability.

Phase II of this project, the performance management module, will be implemented during the 2012-2013 academic year. This system will replace a cumbersome, internally-developed Lotus Notes database. The performance module will provide an online

service, individual accounts for staff, learning plans, as well as tracking and reporting features.

Phase III, the compensation module, will follow and a succession planning module will be considered for future deployment.

5. THE IT PROJECT MANAGER'S PERSPECTIVE

There was a change in Project Managers as the project shifted from tool search and selection to tool implementation. This transition meant that the new PM had to learn the LMS concepts and terminology (both industry and tool specific), and the tool search and selection contextual information as well as develop tool implementation project goals and expected outcomes all at the same time, during the implementation project kick off period.

An early challenge for the project team was scope definition, as we started the implementation project without much of a chance to perform due diligence around requirements analysis and definition from all Stakeholders of this system (we basically took the vendor's implementation plan and went with it); this produced a few surprises along the way:

- Online Content – we had to exclude online content from initial scope of this project as we did not have the necessary resources (we added the production and delivery of online content as an additional phase 1-A of the project, which is going live beginning in June, 2012)

- Sunsetting of the legacy Lotus Notes Database tracking system – since we only licensed the LMS for staff and faculty supervisors this presented the project team with the challenge of determining how to shut down the legacy system for staff only, while keeping it available for Students and Faculty

- Project Staffing Challenges – we had to identify the system administrators and system owners during the course of the system implementation project; this carried on through to post-production-delivery, as the implementation of such a sophisticated LMS meant additional staffing was needed in order to maintain and grow the system and the learning program at AU (still working on defining said resources)

- Vendor Integration - the LMS system has been constantly changing since Plateau Systems (the original producer of this LMS) has recently been purchased by SuccessFactors; as we implemented we had to account / adjust for changes to the system stemming from the SF / Plateau Integration Roadmap – this proved to be very challenging as it presented a moving target for the project team (and this continues as we proceed with our Performance Module Implementation now)

- Single-sign-on (SSO) development was a challenge, as the vendor had to account for the legacy LMS platform architecture, as well as for the incoming Performance Management system platform architecture as we defined the final solution

Throughout this LMS implementation project, the project team had the benefit of having 2 Co-Project Managers: like having two captains of one team, one might think this would have caused more confusion than good; however, one PM was more fluent in the program and system content, while the other was more versed in IT; both PMs stretched their skills, and their duties, to become subject matter experts of the LMS system itself. This provided constant clarity around how the system should be configured (how it should work) in order to accomplish the project's goals and expected outcomes (to deliver the requirements).

6. THE IT TRAINING PERSPECTIVE

American University's Office of Information Technology training unit provides classroom-based and online training to over 1,800 staff, students, and faculty attendees annually. While our primary customers are full-time university staff, we also have an active and growing community of students, part-time staff, and faculty who attend our courses.

The transition to the learning management system has required our unit to maintain dual training registration and management systems for the time being; however, future iterations of the learning management system may include access for faculty and part-time staff. Students are not targeted for inclusion with the current licensing model, so we expect to maintain dual systems indefinitely. However, our administrators continue to lobby the Success Factors executives to adopt a licensing model based on concurrent users, rather than named users or Full Time Equivalents, to make their products more attractive to American University and other peer universities.

Surprisingly, the biggest challenge for OIT has not been the maintenance of the two systems, but managing the expectations of our customers. Academic offices that may be staffed by a variety of faculty, full and part time staff members, and students now have to register for training, and evaluate training in separate systems. Since OIT often rolls out new software applications with close collaboration with individual offices, we have needed to coach our customers through this altered process.

To support this transition, we have updated our web presence to identify where various constituencies can register for training. We have also provided, ad-hoc training sessions at the end of our classroom courses. In addition, we are working on a brief online video on using the two systems.

7. LESSONS LEARNED

This project had several challenging aspects during implementation. For example, the vendor relationship was complicated due to the fact that Success Factors had just acquired the vendor that developed the Learning Management System, Plateau. Both organizations were still trying to identify the appropriate support teams and models to ensure a successful

implementation of the LMS, as well as seamless integration with Success Factors existing industry leading performance management and compensation products.

Within AU, there was a great deal of coordination and collaboration necessary to work with the various cross-departmental partners. There were different levels of engagement and involvement from executives within each of the offices. We had a dedicated administrator designated for the configuration process which was advantageous. Technical issues that arose included: challenges with developing the single-sign-on process, questions about configuring online content, and complications with customizing reports using the report builder tool.

American University still has a long way to go to fully implement AsuccessfulU, but this first phase has been very positive. Effective team leads were identified from each of the primary stakeholder groups, who led with vision. The branding strategy was successful. Comprehensive administrator training was offered to acquaint the technical leads with the inner workings of the system. Finally, the initiative was fully supported by campus leadership.

The implementation of ULearn has enabled staff and staff supervisors to easily view the entire university staff learning catalog online. Staff can register for any course in the catalog, request training and run learning reports. This functionally has empowered staff to assume responsibility for charting their own learning course, and has also freed training staff to spend more time developing content, rather than managing training administration.

8. MOVING FORWARD

This Project continues with the performance management and compensation phases, which are scheduled to be completed by 2014. If authorized, the succession planning module will follow. Support for ongoing administration of the system is provided through the established Administrative Partners group, which continues to meet on a regular basis.

The implementation of online training modules is on track. Ongoing training and introduction to the ULearn system continues through webinars, instructor led sessions, and new hire orientation sessions.

Human Resources is leading the roll out of the next level of functionality to end users, which include the assignment of required training by job, and additional reporting capability.

Crafting Great User Experiences

Nic Bertino
Santa Clara University Law School
Santa Clara Law Webmaster
500 El Camino Real
Santa Clara, CA 95053
1 (408) 551-3000 x6137
nbertino@scu.edu

Andrew Corrales
Santa Clara University Law School
Santa Clara Law Support
Consultant
500 El Camino Real
Santa Clara, CA 95053
1 (408) 554-5135
aamadorcorrales@scu.edu

Allan Chen
Santa Clara University Law School
Assistant Dean of Law Technology
and Academic Computing
500 El Camino Real
Santa Clara, CA 95053
1 (408) 210-6274
abchen@scu.edu

ABSTRACT

As a user of products and technology, one often experiences a wide range of emotions: happiness, frustration, gratitude, irritation, excitement, and apathy amongst others. Yet, as designers and deliverers of these tools and services, the human factor is often neglected with dire consequences. Deadlines and budgets become more important than analyzing the needs and behaviors of the user, unlinking the resource from its consumer. This degrades the perception of the offering and can be irreversible (and potentially fatal) to the reputation of software companies, IT departments, and hardware manufacturers. Despite the failings of many companies that have neglected the human element - companies that lacked empathy for their users - products continue to be delivered that are unintuitive, over designed, or inefficient.

A great product or offering considers the user's experience (UX) when interacting with the service. The product is efficient and intuitive, while being transparent in presentation. UX is generally associated with software, but experiences are designed outside of computing as well. An often-polarizing example is customer service; customers remember great customer service experiences as much as they remember poor experiences. Technology often enhances the user experience, but the experience itself is not confined to interactions with specific tools. Training IT help desk staff on how to interact with customers may not be something traditionally thought of as a UX initiative, but this is one small part of the experience that is designed for individuals having issues with their devices.

At Santa Clara Law, the Law Technology and Academic Computing (LTAC) group has improved efficiency, customer satisfaction, and saved time by considering UX principles early and often. Decisions once made with dangerous assumptions on the user's behalf are now considered with comprehensive data collected from a variety of different sources. Listening to what users are saying also helps LTAC adapt to the users' changing needs and continually enhance offerings.

Categories and Subject Descriptors

H.1.2 [**Information Systems**]: User/Machine Systems – *human factors.* D.2.2 [**Software Engineering**]: Design Tools and Techniques – *user interfaces.*

General Terms

Human Factors

Keywords

User Experience, User Interface, Human Computer Interaction

1. INTRODUCTION

The Law Technology & Academic Computing (LTAC) department at the Santa Clara University Law School has been in existence in various forms since 2001. Currently numbering 7 members, the team is separate from but works closely with University Central IT and other related departments. LTAC is the only other full-service "IT shop" at Santa Clara University. The school has a student population of roughly 1000 students, including those in our part-time program, and is known nationally for many of its programs, including those in intellectual property, social justice, and clinics such as the Northern California Innocence Project. Roughly 50 tenure-track faculty, a few dozen adjuncts, and nearly 125 staff make up the rest of the community.

LTAC specifically works in a hybrid mode - providing everyday support and services ranging from fixing computer issues to web development to data center management, as well as focusing on its core values of customer service, agility and innovation to quickly evaluate, pilot, and potentially deploy solutions to the community. To support this, while each team member has a relatively distinct area of supervision (desktop support vs. media production vs. systems management, etc), LTAC utilizes what has become known as "The Polygon" organizational structure to leverage our strengths individually and as a team. The model recognizes and actually reinforces the heavy interdependency each team member has on another and on the department as a whole. In order for any one person or any one sub-team to succeed, others must contribute. Sometimes this is along obvious organizational roles - the Project Manager works with the Help Desk Manager to test out new solutions for trouble ticket management. Other times, specific strengths of an individual - perhaps expertise outside of one's role on the team - come into play and can be major contributors to success. The dependency goes both ways - a project is successful only if everyone contributes to the best of each person's abilities, but also only if the project is designed to minimize overhead on what is already a small team covering a wide scope of responsibilities.

The Polygon is referenced and the concept is utilized on a daily basis - regular 15-minute "scrum" meetings frequently lead to multiple separate meetings to discuss points of intersection on projects and other ways that team members can contribute to each other to improve operations.

A holistic view of the support and services we provide as an "experience" by customers (faculty, staff, and students) is one that emerges naturally from this interdependence model. In the same way that none of our projects or daily activities exist in a vacuum, the connection between our operations and customer service are also part of a larger eco-system. As LTAC examines work done in web development and considers the fundamental principles of UX, it is a logical extension to consider the experience of the user at the Help Desk, or when we visit one's office for a consultation, or how we design our classroom recording systems.

2. DEFINING USER EXPERIENCE

Nielsen Norman Group defines user experience as *"encompass[ing] all aspects of the end-user's interaction with the company, its services, and its products. The first requirement for an exemplary user experience is to meet the exact needs of the customer, without fuss or bother. Next comes simplicity and elegance that produce products that are a joy to own, a joy to use. True user experience goes far beyond giving customers what they say they want, or providing checklist features. In order to achieve high-quality user experience in a company's offerings there must be a seamless merging of the services of multiple disciplines, including engineering, marketing, graphical and industrial design, and interface design."* [1]

UX has recently gained prominence in the mobile device market. Mobile phones have seen exponential adoption across all segments [see Figure 1]; this mainstream adoption requires service providers to design experiences for a wide range of users, explaining the need for user experience design at the earliest stage of a product's lifecycle. Great UX is the key to adoption in the mobile atmosphere, while poor experiences generally lead to rejection. As investments into UX are providing both hard and soft returns [2], the application of concepts is moving from an idea traditionally associated with user interfaces to the entire experience as a whole.

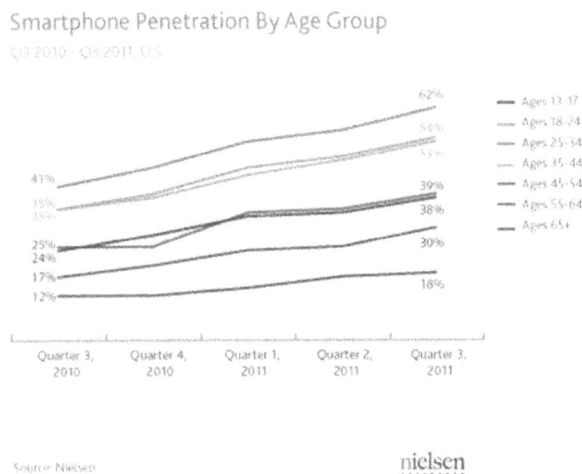

Figure 1 – Year over year smartphone adoption by age group, Q3 2010-Q3 2011.

2.1 User Interfaces

User interface (UI) is commonly confused with user experience. Where user experience generally refers to the end-to-end interaction with a product including non-technological processes, the user interface specifically refers to the visual or auditory information presented to the user and how the user controls the program. For example, consider a consumer that would like to order a new pair of shoes online through their favorite retailer, Zappos.com. A user interacts with Zappos.com's UI by visiting their homepage and controlling their experience through a series of mouse clicks and keyboard input. UX is the analysis of the entire process, from the order, to delivery, and if needed, customer support – the entire interaction with the company, service, and products.

A website's UI is considered a graphical user interface (GUI). Other types of user interfaces include touchscreens and command line interfaces (CLI). Evaluating different methods of interaction is critical, particularly in consideration of accessibility, which often relies on specialized input methods for users with disabilities. An example of a non-computing UI would be elevator controls or a button that activates a crosswalk.

2.2 Everyday UX

User experience goes far beyond interaction with computer or machine interfaces. Product packaging is a wonderful example of real-world user experience and usability. It is, after all, the first interaction a user has with a product, and the perception of the product can be instantly degraded by a poor first impression. Scissors, for example, often ship with plastic ties holding them together [see Figure 2]. This approach certainly solves a problem; if the scissors were not secured together, there is a possibility that the user could be injured. But there is one inherent, glaring issue. Scissors are needed to remove this plastic tie.

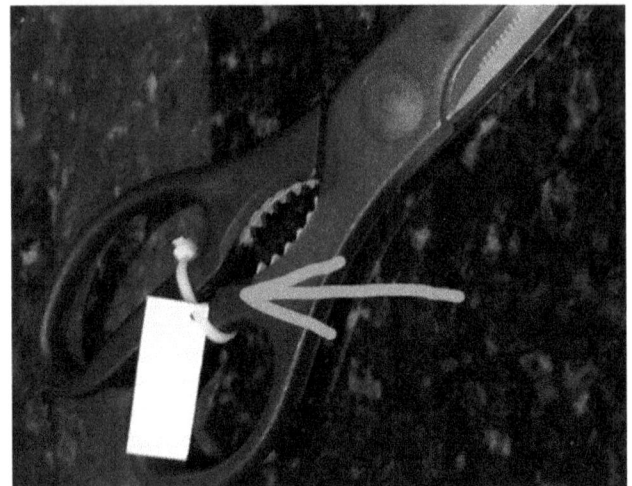

Figure 2. Scissors secured by a plastic zip tie for safety.

There is a legitimate need for this feature, and again, it is for the safety of the user. Assuming the user already has means of removing the tie, however, is an oversight by the product team. The purchase itself indicates that the user may not possess cutting apparatus. Testing this product would have sent the packaging team back to the drawing board to explore using a different mechanism, such as a snap mechanism that offers the same benefits [see Figure 3].

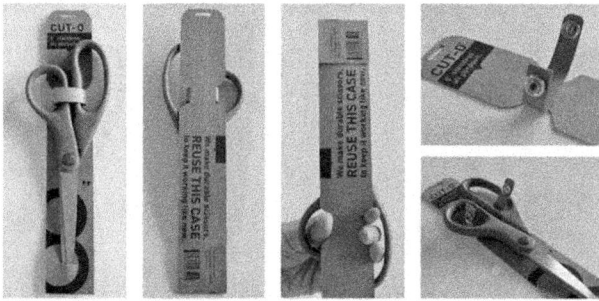

Figure 3. Scissors secured with a snapping mechanism that does not require a cutting tool.

3. TOOLS USED BY UX ARCHITECTS

UX developers use a variety of techniques to plan, monitor, and improve offerings. These tools and techniques often borrow from other disciplines such as marketing or project management. For example, "swim lane" diagrams (or functional bands) are generally used to visualize business processes and potentially identify inefficiencies. In UX, swim lane diagrams incorporate the user and the potential touch points they may encounter during task flow. Other tools include card sorting, personas, flow charts, web analytics, wireframing, A/B testing, and heuristic evaluation.

3.1 Early Design

The use of these tools comes early and often. Fictional profiles of groups of users sharing common traits, or personas, are used to consider the user's point of view when approaching new features or offerings. Flow charts are used to model user stories, which identify tasks that the product will assist with. Wireframes or paper prototypes are used to quickly model the experience before being handed off to designers to create working prototypes. Working prototypes are tested, and further revisions are made.

3.2 Usability Testing

The fastest way to realize issues with the user experience is to conduct usability testing. In its most sophisticated form, this includes the user test-driving a prototype or production system, monitored by video and audio, as users should be encouraged to voice their emotions while completing tasks. Eye tracking software is used to follow the user's gaze as well. A moderator issues tasks and notates responses without leading the user.

User testing takes many different forms, though. Implementation here at Law Technology and Academic Computing at Santa Clara Law School is described below in section 5.3.

3.3 Incremental Improvements Post Launch

After a product has been deployed, it is necessary to continually monitor and evaluate the user experience. This can be accomplished through a variety of methods, including the solicitation of feedback, analysis of web logs, or just having conversations with users.

4. UX IN WEB DEVELOPMENT

Many organizations can immediately benefit from UX research on their corporate websites. In content-driven systems, a balance is necessary between content that serves business objectives and content that is relevant to the user. Decisions to deliver content without regard to the user often demotes information that may be important (and sometimes critical) to the visitor, making the browsing process frustrating. Modeling content to serve the user and interjecting or promoting business objectives makes the process of information acquisition more efficient.

4.1 Approach to Improving Web UX

To organizations that are trying to analyze their user experiences, capturing data about their users can be daunting at first. Finding the user's expectation when interacting with the product is critical to understanding how they use it. One approach is to identify the audience and build personas. For example, a university website may have personas for prospective students, current students, faculty, and staff. Once the audience has been identified, random sampling of the user base is a great way to find out how users interact with products. Similar to hall tests, opening conversations with users will reveal their goals and what is important to them. Some segments, like prospective students in the above example, may be harder to reach than others. In these cases, incentivizing their participation may be warranted. Once this information is gathered, web analytics can help bridge the data together.

4.2 Web Analytics

When referring to web analytics, marketing departments may come to mind. Conversion rates, funnels, return on investment, and outside source referrals serve as key concepts for web marketing professionals. Analytics can also tell organizations a lot about the user's experience. For example, Google Analytics has the ability to track search terms that are being used on a website. Analyzing commonly used search terms may indicate that users are having a difficult time finding the information they need, signaling that there was a failure at some point during the experience. It may also suggest user tasks that were not previously considered or voiced by users.

Analytics can help make design decisions as well. If data logged by analytics software indicates that 96 percent of visitors use Mozilla Firefox or Google Chrome, interface enhancements can be made that are not possible with other software such as earlier versions of Internet Explorer. LTAC's analysis of server logs revealed that mobile usage was rising, leading to the evaluation of its website on various mobile devices and future design implications. Visitor Flow, a recent feature in Google Analytics, provides extensive navigation information by segment [see Figure 5], making it an extremely powerful tool.

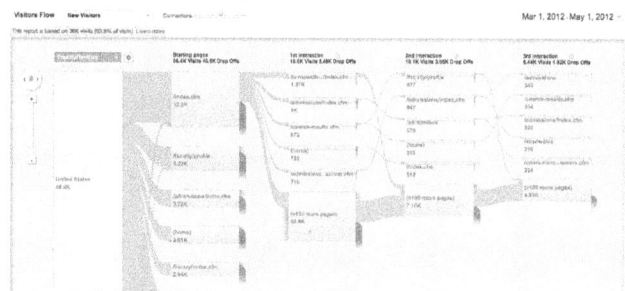

Figure 5. Visitor Flow screen from Google Analytics showing user navigation by segment.

4.3 Accessibility and Internationalization

Accessibility (colloquially known as a11y) and Internationalization (known as i18n) are UX considerations for serving webpages to users with disabilities and users from the international community. Accessibility focuses on designing experiences that are consistent for all users, including those with impairments or disabilities. Testing on screen readers, alternative browsers, and with Javascript disabled are a few ways to follow progressive enhancement, or the concept that a page's content should be available for anyone regardless of connection or browser type. Internationalization focuses on delivering content consistent to the user's locale. Because of the scope of internationalization, it is best implemented at the core level and should be considered for future projects.

5. APPLICATION

UX principles are applied within the LTAC organizational environment in a number of ways. There are obvious and traditional applications to web experience design. The way one experiences the "front-facing online presence" of an organization (UX) vs. the web design itself (UI). The Zappos.com scenario referenced above is an example. Our Webmaster utilizes UX as a fundamental tenet of his approach to changes to our site, be it in the form of recommendations or actual implementation.

However, when one considers our operations from a holistic view and as under one large umbrella of guiding principles and core values, UX becomes highly relevant to human interactions at our Help Desk, field support, and even project management/consulting levels. Models based on traditional values such as "customer service" have become less and less useful in shaping our operations. There are so many ways of interpreting these values that it becomes harder and harder to effectively shape and change our service catalog to improve customer satisfaction. It is always important to examine problems and situations from multiple perspectives, and UX provides this needed viewpiont in a formal, established and easily-translated form.

The examples below include the application of UX principles not only in web site development and management but also in the human interactions that make up the many other operations at LTAC.

5.1 Human Interactions

5.1.1 Help Desk (Passive)

The LTAC Help Desk is a small, 10' long surface attached to a wall in the "mailroom" next to the student lounge [see Figure 6]. Students working at the Help Desk actually face away from "customers" (law school students). Because of common fluctuations in support request frequency and then the onslaught of requests during exams, this arrangement poses a number of logistical issues above and beyond challenges common to other institutions - quality of trouble ticket systems, efficiency of workflow, etc. We do not see ourselves as unique, but many of the approaches that have worked at other schools have proven ineffective at SCU Law and we have struggled for years to improve our methods. Again, the basic value of "high quality customer service" does not lend itself to meaningful operational changes. Application of UX principles, however, sheds a new light on the situation, and allows us to manifest this core value into business practices that are more effective in achieving our goals.

As described above, it is important to separate the User Interface (UI) from the User Experience (UX). The UI consists of the entrance to the mailroom, the way that customers are noticed/get attention (especially relevant considering our support students actually face away from the entrance), the Help Desk space itself,

Figure 6. LTAC Help Desk

the location of the computer used to create trouble tickets, and the general flow of people from place to place within this confined area. The end-to-end UX starts from when we first inform students of our services and location to when they recieve back their (hopefully) fully-functioning computer. In between are experience elements such as the interactions with the support staff, time to escalation to tier 2 (usually full time staff), overall expediency and time to resolution (and the effects of not having a computer), and then how we return the computer to the student.

Keeping all of this in mind, we have made a number of changes to our Help Desk.

5.1.1.1 Signage

We have utilized both general digital signage to help inform customers (students) of our hours and location (in ability to actually locate the Help Desk is certainly part of the user experience) and use physical signage to help students navigate the already-crowded mailroom area. We also have utilized an existing large whiteboard as a simple, low-cost method for providing updates to customers on turnaround times, existing workload (and therefore potential delays in support). At first we attempted to put up formal signs on the board but eventually found that the best way of conveying information to customers was to simply write things out - sometimes good user experience is achieved through simpler means, even if less elegant.

5.1.1.2 Flow

The mailroom consists mostly of a large set of file folders in the middle of the room, where students are able to pick up documents and papers distributed and/or returned by groups and faculty [see Figure 7]. This poses a significant problem in terms of actual flow in the room and to the Help Desk. If everyone enters the room and goes to the right, a significant "traffic jam" can occur which adversely affects customer access and potentially prevents law students from getting the attention they need. Via simple arrows we now navigate students around the other end of the mailboxes, creating a circular flow.

Figure 7. LTAC Help Desk situated in mail room

This has two effects. The obvious one is that there is now a "beginning" and an "end" to the Help Desk and we can locate resources accordingly. The computer used to log trouble tickets (a ticket is created for all customer requests, small or big) seems to be at the far end of the Help Desk when one enters the mailroom, but is at the "beginning" of the Help Desk if one flows around the mailboxes as the arrows indicate. We can take care of administrative tasks - such as liability waivers - before passing the actual hardware onto student techs that handle repairs. The second benefit is that the room feels less crowded. If students jam up along the "wrong" side of the mailboxes, the line can extend out of the room and into the lounge with just 3-4 students in line. This gives a very negative feeling and causes a greater sense of frustration. By routing students along the other end of the mailboxes more students feel that they are "in" the Help Desk area and will be seen soon.

5.1.1.3 Off-site Activities

The Help Desk is simply too small to handle significant workload increases such as those during exams, or intensive work needed for computers with significant problems. For the former, we have "exam prep sessions" in various classrooms in the building in the weeks leading up to exams. We advertise these on digital signage and all over the Help Desk area. We also send out messages via our "Official Announcements," which tends to get more notice than our other mailing lists. For laptops needing more intensive support, we actually transport them to another building - the law library - where we have a small but private work room. Only one or two students work in this area but are able to get more done due to seclusion and ability to more easily concentrate on the problems at hand. Taking that laptop away from the small Help Desk surface while running diagnostics, which can take hours, also mitigates the space issue and therefore allows us to see more customers.

5.2 Field Support (Active)

LTAC also support faculty and staff, specifically, directly in their offices and other locations through our field support efforts. Via one dedicated staff and the occasional intervention of others during busier times, we provide a very high-touch level of end-to-end support, from consultation to diagnostics to testing to warranty repair. All work is followed up afterwards before closing service request tickets to ensure that all needs have been met. This process is already heavily customer-oriented but still benefits from application of UX principles.

The UI, in this case, is the actual person that answers the phone, shows up at one's office, and works on the computer. Obviously, that person is tasked with providing quality customer service, which would yield a positive user experience. This does not mean that the UX principles are not applicable. How does one modify communication and interaction patterns to continually improve the customer experience? How can examining things from the customer's point of view - and an end-to-end experience point of view - affect our practices? How do we keep our core values consistent with our business methods? UX provides many of the tools that help shape our progressions.

The scissor example of UX works well. In that case, one must already own scissors (or at least something similar to them) in order to use the newly-purchased pair of scissors. If, in fact, you do not have those first pair of scissors then the experience is very frustrating. Similarly, if there is not a strong tie between how a customer submits a request for support and the communication that ensues when someone knocks on the customer's door for interpersonal interaction, a disconnect occurs and the experience is degraded. Why provide information about the problem only to have to repeat it when field support arrives? How can we, therefore, tighten this connection and create a self-reinforcing loop that keeps this connection strong and reliable? How do we integrate new sources of information? How do we make sure that others can access this information - and the interactions that result from it - so that it is not merely one field support individual that is aware of the entire situation? From this one issue - the experience of a user that has already reported a problem in detail - multiple questions arise.

5.3 Web Site Testing

Law Technology, in conjunction with the Marketing and External Affairs department at the school, conducts user experience testing of the school's website. These tests are based on core UX principles. As with the above examples, realities of budget and other constraints require modification to and deviation from ideal scenarios and testing methods.

Limited resources pose a challenge for LTAC. Coordinating formal usability tests interferes with the ability of staff involved to complete other tasks, "informal" tests are often conducted in various forms. This begins early in the design phase with random persons chosen for fast and informal testing consisting of one or two tasks, also known as a "hallway test." While not offering the comprehensive data that a formal test provides, testing non-designers or engineers early can remove potential design issues. Feedback from hallway tests are implemented and retested accordingly. This creates an ongoing development, feedback and redesign loop that continuously improves the user experience without requiring a one-time investment in a large-scale site update. It does not, however, obviate the need for significant redesigns in general. It very likely does keep the site "current" between major redesigns.

For major issues or potential changes, moderated testing with three or more defined tasks and a minimum of five users is conducted. These tests are mostly conducted on LTAC's projects, but may evaluate other websites or offerings to offer insight on how interfaces and experiences developed by other entities resonate with users. Results from user tests are compiled [see Figure 4], analyzed, and incorporated. Testing resumes on the modified product, and further changes (and as a result, more testing) may be necessary.

As seen in Figure 4, only 3 participants provided feedback in this particular test. However, even this seemingly-small sample size provides valuable feedback. As with UX testing in general, the key is the design of the test. Provided that the right aspect of the user experience is being tested (e.g finding total cost of attendance specifically, rather than simply locating the financial aid office), even 3 users can provide meaningful feedback.

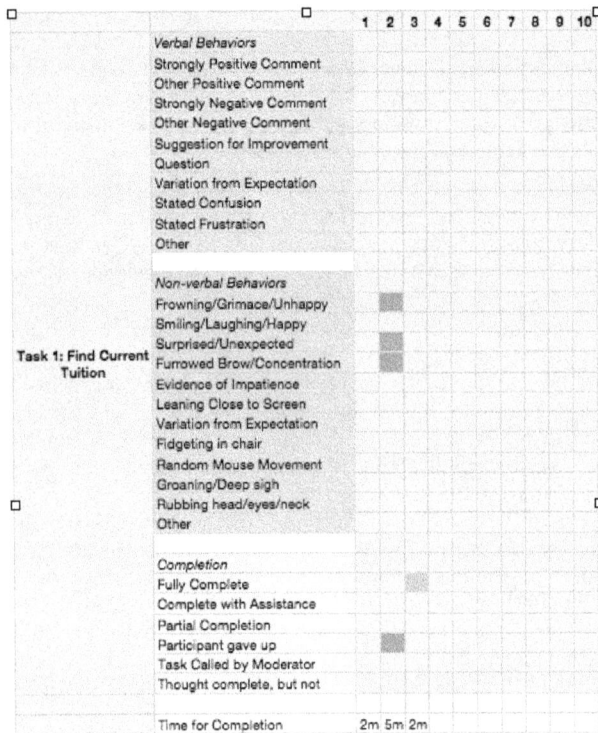

		1	2	3	4	5	6	7	8	9	10
	Verbal Behaviors										
	Strongly Positive Comment										
	Other Positive Comment										
	Strongly Negative Comment										
	Other Negative Comment										
	Suggestion for Improvement										
	Question										
	Variation from Expectation										
	Stated Confusion										
	Stated Frustration										
	Other										
	Non-verbal Behaviors										
	Frowning/Grimace/Unhappy		▨								
	Smiling/Laughing/Happy										
	Surprised/Unexpected		▨								
Task 1: Find Current Tuition	Furrowed Brow/Concentration		▨								
	Evidence of Impatience										
	Leaning Close to Screen										
	Variation from Expectation										
	Fidgeting in chair										
	Random Mouse Movement										
	Groaning/Deep sigh										
	Rubbing head/eyes/neck										
	Other										
	Completion										
	Fully Complete		▨								
	Complete with Assistance										
	Partial Completion										
	Participant gave up		▨								
	Task Called by Moderator										
	Thought complete, but not										
	Time for Completion	2m	5m	2m							

Figure 4. Moderator's Notes from User Testing

6. CONCLUSION

User experience (UX) principles are used throughout various industries. It is commonly used by web designers and developers as tools for creating a web site that is a product above and beyond simply where to place links or the size of a banner photo. Viewing the journey of a user navigating through a site is extremely powerful in choosing various options and making changes. Continuous testing based on these same UX principles – whether via sophisticated systems involving tracking cameras and recording devices or simple "hallway tests" – are tried and true methods for gathering feedback that lead to better web site design.

UX principles are grounded in looking at the product from the perspective of the user, and the experience from start to finish. Therefore, UX is very applicable to other products and/or services. At Law Technology and Academic Computing, we use these same principles to make changes to our Help Desk and Field Support methods and policies. In adopting this broader view of the overall implementation of our services, we are able to not only address physical and communication limitations or obstacles, but to also continuously adopt or test changes. By staying focused on how a change affects a user's experience, we can then make more changes (or revert back to an earlier methodology). It is easy to make presumptions about how a Help Desk of "X" size and located in a specific spot is "better" than the alternative. But if these basic beliefs are not tested against user experiences, then we may find ourselves providing an inferior product.

UX has proven to be a powerful tool for all Law Tech services, and continues to be used on a regular basis throughout the organization.

7. REFERENCES

[1] NIELSEN NORMAN GROUP. 2012. User Experience: Our Definition
http://www.nngroup.com/about/userexperience.html

[2] WATSON, BEN. 2011. The ROI of User Experience
http://socialmediatoday.com/bitpakkit/267487/roi-ux

Reducing Costs, Improving Service, and Extending the Life of Computers with Solid-State Drives

Mat Felthousen
University of Rochester
Lower Hoyt Hall
Rochester, NY 14627
1 585-275-9015

mat.felthousen@rochester.edu

ABSTRACT

Due to compliance concerns, during the summer of 2011 the University of Rochester began requiring that all individuals authenticate in order to use the network. Benchmarking with other institutions indicated that Windows 7 took two to three minutes from the time someone logged on to the point the machine was fully responsive and a browser could be used. We had optimized the machines such that the time had been reduced to about a minute and a half, but students complained about how long the logon process took.

At the same time, budget constraints forced extending the three-year replacement cycle for computers, and the older machines were both slower and less reliable, usually due to hard drive failures.

Student leaders indicated that they needed strategically placed computers, referred to as 'kiosks', to be optimized for logon time so that students could have immediate access to email and the web between classes. They would also accept a reduced suite of applications on kiosks if it meant faster logon times.

There are less than twenty kiosks across campus, compared to more than 550 public machines total. Kiosks are ideal for evaluating experimental software or hardware, as changes made on them would not affect classes or other production uses. We installed solid state drives in kiosks with a minimal suite of applications. The time from logon to having a fully functional browser dropped to fifteen seconds, and the performance of our oldest PCs exceeded a new PC with a regular hard drive. The lifespan of the PCs could potentially be extended by years.

Feedback has been so positive that we are now evaluating switching all machines to solid state technology. This paper will discuss the results of our performance testing of solid state drives, including the performance gains in all types of applications, and the costs involved; both in implementing solid state drives on already deployed PCs, and avoided due to not having to replace PCs as often.

Categories and Subject Descriptors

K.6.1 [**Management of Computing and Information Systems**]: Project and People Management

K.6.2 [**Management of Computing and Information Systems**]: Installation Management

K.8.2 [**Hardware**]

K.8.3 [**Management/Maintenance**]

General Terms

Life cycle, Benchmarks, Computing Equipment Management, Performance and Usage Measurement

Keywords

Solid State Drive, Life cycle management

1. INTRODUCTION

The University of Rochester, located in Rochester, New York, is a private, tier-one research university with 5400 undergraduate and 3200 graduate students.[1] The University is comprised of a teaching hospital and six academic divisions located across three main campuses. The primary academic divisions responsible for undergraduate instruction, with more than 4700[2] undergraduates, are the schools of Arts & Sciences, and the Hajim School of Engineering and Applied Sciences, which combined are most commonly known as "The College." Classroom Technology ("ClassTech") is part of a central University Information Technology organization, and is primarily charged with providing technology support to College undergraduates and academic departments.

"Technology support" currently includes public computing facilities, "smart" rooms, pay-for-printing, and streaming. The number of public computers has grown from 195 in 2002 to nearly 600 by the end of the summer of 2012. The hours during which these machines have to be available have also increased, with more facilities open until midnight or later, including on weekends. In some cases facilities are considered to be 24/7 environments, leaving little opportunity for routine maintenance or updates.

Despite this expansion ClassTech's employee count and budgets have remained essentially static since 2003. ClassTech has had to investigate ways to stretch resources to cover the old and new technology requirements, increased demand for support, and a broader geographic distribution of computing. This has included both reducing the cost spent per computer and extending the replacement cycle for the computer beyond the warranty period.

During the summer of 2011 we began requiring the use of a network credential for anyone who uses public computing.

---

[1] http://www.rochester.edu/aboutus/

[2] http://www.rochester.edu/college/aboutus/facts.html

Previously, all public computers automatically logged into a generic account when a computer was powered up. We began to receive complaints from the community about the length of time involved in the logon process, which could take up to three minutes from the time credentials were entered and when the computer was actually usable, due primarily to the length of time involved in creating a default profile. Even after we improved the logon time to just over a minute, students indicated that the logon time was still excessive, and identified the time involved in logging into the walk up "email kiosks" as being particularly problematic.

During the fall of 2011 we were also told that due to economic constraints the IT budget would need to be reduced. We would know how much the reduction would be until several months later, but we did know that we would need to extend the lifespan of our computers beyond the normal 3 year cycle, even while we were experiencing significant hard drive failure rates while these machines were still under warranty.

This paper will describe the process by which we evaluated and deployed solid-state drives in place of traditional hard drives in our public labs, and how this technology had an immediate effect on public perception of our services.

2. SYSTEM OPTIMIZATION

We knew from our peers that the typical logon time for a Windows 7 machine to having a usable web browser (by far the most prevalent use of a public machine) could take 2-3 minutes, as measured from the time someone types in their password to the time the browser was responsive. When we first received complaints about the amount of time it took the computers to log on, we began making modifications to improve the logon time, which involved iterative testing to ensure that the PC remained stable. As we have several dozen applications on our public PCs, the default profile had grown to 1.5 gigabytes in size.

Some applications contributed a disproportionate amount of data to the default profile. Google Earth alone accounted for 500 megabytes (33%) of the size of the profile. Since Google Earth was used infrequently, we removed all associated data from the profile, and did the same for other less-used applications, eventually getting the default profile down to 200 megabytes. We also changed the timing of startup processes, such that they would start minutes after logon, rather than during logon. One example would be checking for antivirus updates. Through these efforts we were able to reduce the logon time to a little over a minute, but we still heard from the community that this time was excessive. The campus newspaper ran articles and Op-ed pieces about degraded service.

3. KIOSKS, AND DIFFERENT EXPECTATIONS

Taking into consideration that the gap between classes is only 10-15 minutes, students still felt that a minute was too long to wait for a usable browser, particularly for the 20 'kiosks' distributed across campus. We had placed PCs in high traffic areas on campus at the request of students, so that they could have immediate access to email and view documents between classes. These PCs had all of the same software as the PCs in the computing labs, with several dozen applications in all. Most of these kiosks were intentionally placed at standing height without chairs, so as to discourage long-term usage and keep the kiosks available for quick usage.

We met with the Student Government to discuss their concerns during the fall of 2011. They indicated that having fewer applications on kiosks would be an acceptable compromise if it meant measurable improvements in logon times. We built a new image for our PCs that consisted of Microsoft Office, web browsers, our printing software, and all optimizations that we had applied to the regular machines. These steps got the logon time down to 45 seconds.

4. SOLID STATE TECHNOLOGY

While we optimized the kiosks for maximum speed, we began evaluating solid state drives. A solid state drive (SSD) is essentially flash memory that plugs into the same cable as a regular hard drive. The technology has been popular for a few years in netbooks and other ultra-light laptops that require extended battery life, and are becoming more popular in desktop and server computing.

SSDs do not have the capacity of traditional hard drives, and are more expensive per gigabyte. However, they are significantly faster, consume less power, generate less heat, and are less prone to failure as they have no moving parts.

A typical hard drive can read data at 100MB/s. We selected SSDs with 500MB/s read times, and a Mean Time Between Failure (MTBF) rating of 1.2M hours (136 years). Since these computers can be on for 24 hours a day, we often experience heat-related failures of hard drives, so durability is a concern. The power draw for an active SSD is less than that of an idle hard drive, the operating temperature range is greater, and the shock resistance is more than 5 times better.

5. PILOT

Our kiosks were Dell Optiplex 960 machines, with 4GB of RAM. With everything else being the same, a PC would log on in 15 seconds with the SSD, compared to 45 seconds with a hard drive. We initially deployed five SSD-equipped kiosks across campus locations that had more than one kiosk, so that side-by-side comparisons could be made in an uncontrolled environment. The feedback was immediately positive, which prompted us to replace all 20 kiosk hard drives with SSD technology within a month.

Once kiosk performance was improved, complaints about logon times dwindled overall. In their "cheers / jeers" column at the end of the year, the campus newspaper commended our efforts, and it is very difficult to earn a 'cheer' from them. For a quick and reasonably inexpensive solution the twenty drives were a sound investment.

6. ADOPTION

Based on the success of the kiosks, the Libraries approached us with a request to convert all 120 of their public computers, which we manage, to use SSDs. This posed a few challenges. First, we had to estimate the costs involved in the undertaking, beyond the costs for the drives themselves. We had to determine how to most efficiently install our software image onto this many drives, and how to install the drives while still minimizing downtime for the facilities. We had to determine how long the entire process would take.

The most daunting issue however was how to maintain a consistent experience across all computing facilities, and there were more than 300 other PCs that would not have the benefit of the faster technology.

At the same time, the IT budget was being reduced due to economic factors, and we were looking at the ramifications of having machines be in service for 4 or more years. In labs that had high performance video cards, we were seeing hard drives fail in less than two years, so we were concerned about how support costs would increase as a result of a decrease in our renewal/replacement budget, when in actuality the funds available for support were also reduced. We were also concerned about feedback from the community, indicating that some of the labs with older PCs were already not meeting their performance expectations. We had to look into ways to improve performance and extend the life of our labs, so we decided to test whether SSDs would be a cost-effective way of upgrading the labs without purchasing new PCs.

7. TESTING PARAMETERS

In order to evaluate performance of SSD technology and determining the practical limits of what could be done with existing hardware, we purchased three SSDs each from three different manufacturers (9 in total). We wanted to see if there was any measurable difference between manufacturers. We then set up a test lab with 1 to 3 year old representative samples from all of our facilities, plus some even older hardware to emulate the results of extending PC lifespan beyond 4 years.

We use Dell Optiplex PCs in our labs all with Windows 7 32-bit. We tested SSD technology in 620, 755, 960, 980, and 990 chassis. Our baseline was an Optiplex 980 with a mechanical hard drive, with 4GB of RAM, and a 32-bit installation of Windows with some of standard applications. We also tested the effects of upgrading to 8GB of RAM where possible, and also tested performance of 32-bit vs. 64-bit installations. The 620 chassis was limited to 1GB, and the 755 chassis was limited to 2GB, but these are no longer used in any production sense in our labs. All other models were tested in 4GB and 8GB configurations.

For each configuration, we timed how long the computer would take to perform a specific task. These tasks included disk-intensive and processor-intensive tasks so that we could determine whether it was cost effective to maximize the RAM in some or all of the PCs, as long as we were already opening them up to replace the drives.

Tests included launching ProEngineer, opening large (50MB) Excel files, logon times, resampling video files, and 'vectorizing' a TIFF file in Illustrator.

8. PERFORMANCE RESULTS

Our labs currently use Windows 7 32-bit, in order to support legacy applications. As of this summer we will no longer support those legacy applications, so we wanted to test what performance increases we could expect from upgrading the labs to Windows 7 64-bit.

Our Windows 7 image is currently 120GB. We tested drives from OCZ, Intel, and Corsair, each with equal specifications. As the measured differences between the drives were minimal, the final selection was based on cost per drive, including the bracket necessary for installation. We chose the Corsair Force Series GT 2.5 inch 180GB SATA3 drive.

Our tests showed conclusively that just the addition of a SSD improved the performance of a 5 year old Optiplex 755 with 2GB of RAM to the point where it often exceeded the performance of a one year old Optiplex 980 with 4GB and a regular hard drive. Table 1 shows the time in seconds it took each sample PC to run a task. The lower the number is, the better the performance. The machine used as a control, an Optiplex 980 with a mechanical hard drive, 64-bit Windows, and 4GB of RAM, appears in the second column.

Table 1: Speed, in Seconds

	Optiplex 980 MHDD - 32bit 4Gb RAM local	Optiplex 980 MHDD - 64bit 4Gb RAM local	Optiplex 620 SSD - 64bit 1Gb RAM	Optiplex 755 SSD - 64bit 2Gb RAM	Optiplex 960 SSD - 64bit 4Gb RAM	Optiplex 980 SSD - 64bit 4Gb RAM	Optiplex 990 SSD - 64bit 4Gb RAM
ProE Launch	60	20	12.3	9.8	8.1	7.6	7.1
Open TIFF in Photoshop	22	15	14	8.5	7.4	8	7
Handbrake video resample	43	32	136	44	38	27	16
Vectorize TIFF in Illustrator	15.5	15	42	17	18	14	11.5
Import AI file to ProE	22	32	86	37	35	34	28
Excel Query & Raw					10	10	8
Excel monster 50Mb file					33	29	22
Domain User login and IE			66	27	25	24	23

With just a SSD, a seven year-old Optiplex 620 outperformed a one year-old Optiplex 980 on tasks that did not require much memory or processing power. This finding supports the trend towards using older PCs as thin clients, or in situations where limited processing is needed.

What was more surprising was the performance improvements gained from updating the operating system from Windows 7 32-bit to Windows 7 64-bit. As Table 2 illustrates, in many tests a machine with Windows 7 64-bit and a mechanical drive outperformed Windows 7 32-bit on a SSD.

Table 2: Speed, in Seconds, 32 / 64 Bit

	Optiplex 980 MHDD - 32bit 4Gb RAM local	Optiplex 980 SSD - 32 bit 4Gb RAM local	Optiplex 980 MHDD - 64bit 4Gb RAM local	Optiplex 980 SSD - 64bit 4Gb RAM	Optiplex 980 SSD - 64bit 8Gb RAM
ProE Launch	60	45	20	7.6	6.5
Open TIFF in Photoshop	22	8.5	15	8	8.2
Handbrake video resample	43	40	32	27	31
Vectorize TIFF in Illustrator	15.5	15	15	14	14.5
Import AI file to ProE	22	21	32	34	30
Excel Query & Raw		14		10	10
Excel monster 50Mb file		31		29	30
Domain User login and IE		30		24	25

As 32-bit operating systems cannot address more than 3.5GB of RAM, we reserved testing of 8GB of RAM for Windows 7 64-bit only. As shown in Table 3, tests revealed that in most cases performance remained the same or degraded slightly with the additional memory. This result is surprising, and bears further testing, perhaps on systems that are used for editing large videos or other memory-intensive tasks. For most PCs however our conclusion is that 4GB of RAM is sufficient.

Table 3: 4GB Versus 8GB Performance

	Optiplex 960 SSD - 64bit 4Gb RAM	Optiplex 960 SSD - 64bit 8Gb RAM	Optiplex 980 SSD - 64bit 4Gb RAM	Optiplex 980 SSD - 64bit 8Gb RAM	Optiplex 990 SSD - 64bit 4Gb RAM	Optiplex 990 SSD - 64bit 8Gb RAM
ProE Launch	8.1	6.4	7.6	6.5	7.1	6
Open TIFF in Photoshop	7.4	6.5	8	8.2	7	6.5
Handbrake video resample	38	42	27	31	16	19
Vectorize TIFF in Illustrator	18	16	14	14.5	11.5	12
Import AI file to ProE	35	38	34	30	28	27
Excel Query & Raw	10	13	10	10	8	7
Excel monster 50Mb file	33	31	29	30	22	24
Domain User login and IE	25	26	24	25	23	23

9. CLONING COSTS, IMPLEMENTATION

In a typical year we will replace about a third of our public computers, or 180 PCs. At an average cost of $1200 per PC, that is $216,000. The cost for 550 180GB SSDs, to upgrade all computers in one year, will be $114,000, or nearly half what we would otherwise pay to upgrade just a portion of the computers.

The cost of the drives is just one consideration for this project. As we did not have funds for hiring additional staff for the summer to undertake this project, we had to determine the average amount of time it would take to clone the drives, and the average time it would take to install them. It is estimated that it will take 150 hours, at 20 minutes per PC, to replace the drives. While some practice will reduce this average, there is little that can be done to make this process more efficient. It involves the removal of security cabling, the removal/installation of drives, and reinstallation of security cabling- all of which is time-consuming.

What could be made efficient is the cloning process. We investigated drive cloning services and commercially available drive cloning devices, all of which involved high costs or limited flexibility. We built our own drive cloning devices from Atom-processor based PCs running Ubuntu, with the capability of cloning up to 7 drives per hour. Each system costs less than $260, and has a script that will automate the cloning of the drives from a simple command.

Using three such systems, we will be able to clone more than 450 drives in 27 hours, while minimizing the costs involved with labor and building additional cloning stations. The total costs for cloning are estimated at less than $900. Costs will be further minimized by having the cloning process handled by helpdesk personnel, as the process does not need to be closely monitored.

Once the drives are cloned, they will be installed in the computing facilities incrementally so as to minimize downtime. No more than half of a facility will be offline at any time. This same approach has been used with success in the past, when we reimage the labs during breaks, but the disruption in this case will be less as the time required for swapping drives is less than the time it takes to reimage the machine using Ghost.

This entire process has been designed so that it can be done with student labor, thus minimizing the labor costs, even if work after hours is necessary. This approach also eliminates the need for any system administrator support during the roll-out of the drives.

By extending the lifespan of the PCs, ongoing yearly replacement costs are also reduced. If our current budget reduction were to become permanent, this lifespan adjustment becomes critical. Table 4 shows the costs involved for a fleet of 550 computers, at an average cost of $1200 per computer, and the annual savings achieved by extending the lifespan beyond 3 years.

Table 4: Deferment 'credit'

Years of service	3	4	5	6
Machines/year	183	138	110	92
Cost per year	$220,000	$165,000	$132,000	$110,000
Difference from baseline	$0	$55,000	$88,000	$110,000

10. CONCLUSION

Considering the cost of a new PC, replacing hard drives with solid state technology presents an attractive alternative in the face of budget reductions. The performance gains are impressive, and there are 'green' benefits to extending the life of PCs and reducing power consumption. We cannot predict how long these PCs will last in public computing environments beyond their current 3-year warranty period, but even a single year means an annual savings of $55,000 in hardware. There are savings in labor, as fewer machines are being replaced annually. There are also 'green' considerations stemming from reduced waste, and reduced energy consumption.

Beyond cost considerations, community perception of service is an important, but not easily quantified, measure of success. It was significant that improving just 20 kiosks with SSD technology addressed the majority of community perception on the performance of public labs. While circumstances in our case are dictating that we consider a wholesale replacement of drives, some schools would do well to consider an incremental approach to adopting SSD, as they may find that having these drives strategically placed in facilities would have a substantial positive impact on services.

Google Apps for Education:
Valparaiso University's Migration Experience:

Rebecca Klein
Valparaiso University
1410 Chapel Drive
Valparaiso, IN 46383
(219) 464-5986
Becky.Klein@valpo.edu

Richard Orelup
Valparaiso University
1700 Chapel Drive
Valparaiso, IN 46383
(219) 464-5024
Richard.Orelup@valpo.edu

Matt Smith
Valparaiso University
1410 Chapel Drive
Valparaiso, IN 46383
(219) 464-5773
Matt.Smith@valpo.edu

ABSTRACT

Many campuses are investigating cloud-based or hosted email solutions. This paper will cover Valparaiso University's decision to move to the Google Apps for Education platform and our campus migration strategy. Google Apps offers significant savings in both cost of service and cost of support / maintenance while simultaneously offering functionality improvements to the campus experience over our previous system. Valparaiso University was using the GroupWise email and calendaring system and began the process of migrating all of campus to the Google Apps for Education platform in early 2011. Our process began with a student led evaluation team to select the new platform and started rolling out to new students beginning summer of 2011 with migration of existing students conducted from July 2011 through October 2011. Faculty / Staff migration began in December 2011 and were rolled out on a department by department basis throughout the spring 2012 Semester. Heavy promotion and utilization of multiple "Meet Google Apps" presentations greatly enhanced communication about the process and reduced migration anxiety. Apps were limited during migration process to those that reproduced existing system functionality to avoid over-taxing IT support resources. Valparaiso University's migration process has been refined several times and overall feedback from students, faculty, and staff has been very positive throughout the process.

Categories and Subject Descriptors

H.4.0 [**Information Systems Applications**]: General

General Terms

Documentation, Human Factors, Management.

Keywords

Electronic Mail, Google Apps, Migration.

1. INTRODUCTION
1.1 Valparaiso Overview

Valparaiso University is an independent Lutheran institution located in Valparaiso, Indiana, a city of 31,000 people, in Northwest Indiana just an hour east of Chicago. Valpo hosts more than 4,000

students from most states and 50 countries enrolled in more than 70 programs in five colleges: Arts and Sciences, Business Administration, Engineering, Nursing, and Christ College (the honors college). Valpo employs around 1,400 faculty and support staff.

1.2 Why We Needed to Leave Novell GroupWise®

Balancing the delivery of services against escalating costs (capital, maintenance, and support) in a budget constricting economy is an ongoing challenge for all IT departments. Novell GroupWise® was a cost-effective decision when packaged alongside other Novell products but with our intention to transition the university onto an Active Directory infrastructure, it made sense to find an alternative to GroupWise for the university's email and calendaring needs.

The student population is increasingly tech savvy and adept at mastering web-based applications. The increased demand for mobile device support with email and calendaring is also a strong motivating factor for looking at web-based applications.

In addition to reduced maintenance costs, we estimate that we are going to save 10-20 hours a week of System Administrator time that was necessary to support our older and limited GroupWise installation.

1.3 Choosing Google Apps

A student focus group was allowed to make the decision between Google Apps for Education and Microsoft Live@Edu. During the 2011 spring semester, the student focus group used each platform as their primary email system for a period of 4 weeks. An anonymous survey was used to collect feedback and the results showed an overwhelming majority preference for Google Apps; only one student selected the Microsoft option.

2. MIGRATION CONSIDERATIONS
2.1 In-House vs. Cloud-Based

Student use of GroupWise was limited to the web access client and virtually no students used the calendar functionality. Faculty and Staff, however, had different needs and demands than the student population. This led to an internal discussion on whether we should run our own Microsoft Exchange servers for faculty / staff while the students used Google Apps. There was a perception of greater control and trust in maintaining our own internal system. The arguments against running two separate systems were: reduced savings on server maintenance contracts, limiting the savings to system administrator time, continuing the need to maintain use of our Sophos PureMessage spam and virus filtering systems, and complications in managing dual email services, especially for those individuals who have employee and student status.

2.2 Technical Considerations

Any service that we chose needed to have a robust API to allow for integration with our current processes for the automatic creation of accounts. We also needed our next platform to integrate with our current authentication systems so users would continue to have one password for everything. Google's provisioning web service fit the bill perfectly and handled all of our needs with regards to these issues.

2.3 Mobile Support

Moving to Google Apps allowed for better support of mobile devices and integration into with a variety of other outside services. Because of the more standards compliant nature of Google (especially compared to Novell) and Google's constant development of the product, any future tech trends will be easier to address by our internal developers or may not need to be addressed at all.

3. STUDENT MIGRATION PROCESS

3.1 Online Presence

One very useful tool we used in communicating with campus was the IT department's website. We created a whole section of the website with FAQ's, tip sheets, schedules, statistics, training information, and much more. We also created an easy URL (valpo.edu/googleapps) for the website so that we could easily direct users to the site. This was in place for the student migration and grew throughout the process as additional information and documentation was available. Google's help pages covered the majority of the information we needed to disseminate so the focus of our website was facilitation and redirecting people to the appropriate help pages. We also posted a live migration stats page on the website that allowed campus to see exactly how many had gone through the migration process already.

3.2 Freshmen Bypass

Valpo sees the majority of incoming freshmen during the FOCUS orientation program for new students each June. The students who were registered for the FOCUS sessions were separated from the automatic account process so they could be created in Google Apps initially. Documentation was added to our incoming students section of the IT website and distributed to the freshmen class during their orientation process. By timing the roll-out for students to begin during the orientation we were able to remove roughly 25% of the student body from the pool of students needing migration.

3.3 Upperclassmen Migration

Upperclassmen had only been able to access the web client for GroupWise, thus their use was considerably less than faculty / staff. Our initial migration utilities only copied mail; most students didn't use the address book or calendar functionality of GroupWise. We opened the migration process in late July 2011 to all students at once, and then sent occasional reminders to those who had not yet migrated. Migration was complete in early October 2011; there were a couple hundred students who hadn't yet opted in to migration at that point, so we forced their migration at that time.

We experienced a large rush of students who started the migration process shortly after it was announced. During this rush we discovered that both Google and GroupWise have limits on the number of accounts that can go through the process at once. To address this issue, we created a wait queue that would start the next user once another person's migration was completed and limited the number of concurrent syncs to 20.

Once a student opted into the migration process, our utilities copied over mail at a rate of one message per second. Depending on the amount of mail in a student's account, this could take anywhere from a few minutes to many hours. They also were provided a login link to the new Gmail@Valpo account once they had begun the process, so they could immediately access their new account. During the time that messages were being copied from one system to another, students were able to login to both the GroupWise and Gmail@Valpo systems. This led to quite a bit of confusion, because students received mail in both accounts.

The migration process also required adjustments to our routing tables. The opt-in for migration was completed via an internal website, and this website was programmed to update routing and begin the message copying process at the same time. We learned that in the GroupWise system, when a person addressed a message, it would first look for a matching internal user and deliver the message to that account. Our routing tables properly updated to indicate that new incoming messages should be delivered to the Gmail@Valpo account, but this only applied to messages that did not originate from GroupWise. To address this we wrote additional scripts that would check address books throughout the GroupWise system and replace any user objects with the student's email address. We received many complaints from faculty, both officially and anecdotally, that their messages to students were never received during the migration. In 100% of the cases reported to us, the students did receive the messages but they were usually buried in a conversation that the students had not seen. Gmail by default turns on a feature called "conversation view," which threads all messages with matching subject lines together.

After the student's mail was migrated, they received an email at their new account indicating that all messages had been copied, and that they had 24 hours to notify the IT Help Desk of any problems. After the 24 hour period (which usually ended up being 48-72 hours), we deleted the student's GroupWise account. This then resolved the message delivery issue, because once a GroupWise account was deleted, all mail addressed to the student was correctly sent through the routing tables. We did receive some complaints from students claiming that they were not getting mail or that messages had not transferred but in each reported case they were either still in the migration process or were still using GroupWise and not checking Gmail for their new mail.

We did not provide any training to students on the new mail system, and did not receive any complaints. In our experience, students don't usually attend training classes and seem to be content with clicking around a service to learn it on their own. Many students were already familiar with Gmail because of pre-existing personal accounts. The students therefore were up and running on the new system quickly. Even if students weren't familiar with Gmail specifically, most of them were familiar with web-based email systems such as Hotmail, Yahoo, or other services. The functions across many of these different systems are very similar; it's mainly the look & feel that is different between them.

3.4 Student Aides

Since students were migrated to Gmail before faculty and staff, they had no accounts left to use for accessing shared resources that remained in GroupWise. To solve this problem, we created generic accounts in GroupWise and provided the usernames and passwords to supervisors in the departments. They then provided the login information to their student aide employees so that they could login and access the shared resources. Faculty Advisors for student organizations were also given a temporary account to share with the student leadership until the resources could be migrated to Gmail.

4. PREPARATION FOR FACULTY / STAFF MIGRATION

4.1 Functionality Comparison

When comparing GroupWise to Gmail, there are far more similarities between their functionalities than differences however the differences are the only thing likely to be noticed by the end-user. The main functionality differences that we identified as cause for concern were:

- In GroupWise, you could open a message, view the properties, and see who had received/opened/deleted a message. In Gmail, you cannot view this type of information; the only option is to request a read receipt and be notified when a recipient opens a message.

- In GroupWise, you could share a folder within your account with other users. Gmail uses a label system instead of folders, so messages are in one repository and not separated out; therefore the only way to share messages is to share your entire account of messages with another user.

- In GroupWise, you could share a contact list with other users. Gmail does not have contact list sharing; they do offer the option to export a contact list, send to another user, and that user can import into his/her contact list.

- Google calendar functions and sharing are far superior to GroupWise as the Google system is more intuitive and easier to manage. Compatibility on mobile devices was more stable and user friendly with Google.

4.2 Meet & Greet Sessions

To communicate the upcoming transition period and address campus concerns IT hosted several "Meet & Greet" sessions to introduce the new Gmail@Valpo system to faculty and staff. In these sessions we outlined the migration process, addressed common concerns, and answered any questions they had. Four sessions were initially planned during the two weeks before semester break. The response to these sessions was overwhelmingly high and six more open sessions were scheduled in the first two weeks of the spring semester. At the request of the Athletics department, we also scheduled two Meet & Greet sessions for them specifically later in the semester so the information was given closer to their actual migration. The first two sessions were advertised as being administratively focused and we personally invited every Administrative Assistant on campus to attend; the theory is that excited Administrative Assistants would be advocates for the change within their respective departments.

The fear of change was by far the biggest obstacle we faced in working with the faculty and staff. In this regard, the Meet & Greet sessions we held were the most valuable part of the entire process. Faculty and staff were able to come to a brief presentation where we provided a general overview of Google Apps, described the migration process, and answered questions they had. Those sessions felt more like counseling sessions, because we worked very hard to soothe people's fears and concerns. We know the Meet & Greet sessions didn't completely eliminate all fears, because we heard from many people after their migration who said, "Wow, that was a lot easier and less painful than I expected it to be!"

4.3 Meet & Greet Sessions – Major Topics

Many faculty and staff were initially worried about privacy of data and the security once their email was in "the cloud". Our contract with Google very explicitly states that they are required to abide by all laws protecting the privacy of student data, including FERPA and others. Google is not allowed to mine our data for the purpose of advertising.

One common issue we saw during the faculty and staff migration process was related to distribution lists in the GroupWise system. As individuals migrated over to Gmail@Valpo and their GroupWise accounts were deleted, their names also disappeared from internal GroupWise address books and distribution lists because these lists pointed to user objects instead of email addresses. This caused a few problems and complaints because faculty and staff were often unclear about which departments were migrating at different times. We created scripts to run within the GroupWise system so that when a user account was deleted, references to that user object in distribution lists and address books would be replaced with email address listings instead. We sent out campus-wide messages educating people on this issue and instructed them on what to do on their end to minimize the disruption. We also posted a Google calendar on our website showing when each department was migrating so that users could refer to the schedule and see when various users on their lists may be affected.

We used a pre-migration process which copied the majority of their mail to Gmail the week before their scheduled migration to limit the transition time; when the end-user "started" the migration process, the were already most of the way finished. The student process of 1-3 days and risking mail delivery at two separate systems was not an acceptable process for staff and faculty. Minimizing the loss of productivity due to down time was a major goal in adapting the process for faculty and staff.

We do assume that some productivity was lost due to this conversion, but how much is difficult to gauge. We designed the migration process for staff and faculty to enable them to immediately switch from one email system to another. The actual time on the day of migration averaged about five to ten minutes from the end-user perspective. Beyond that point, any lost time depended largely on how skilled the user was in Google Apps and whether they had attended training sessions prior to migration. Quite a few users already had personal Gmail accounts, and had some level of familiarity with the service. This helped them to get up and running on their new Valpo account quickly, with confidence that they knew what they were doing. Other individuals didn't have any experience at all with Gmail, and had a steeper learning curve on the new system. Throughout the process we routinely heard that the training in advance of migration made everyone less apprehensive and allowed them to begin utilizing the new system quickly.

Within about a week of a user's migration date, they were technically able to login and access their account. If they attended one of our training sessions during that period they were able to login to their account. This allowed them to choose settings and preferences, start to feel comfortable navigating the service, and build their confidence. When the user actually migrated they had often been able to setup delegation, create their filters, and customize their account before they needed to use it. After their migration, these folks told us how much easier it was to adjust to using the new system because they were already familiar with it before they were forced to use it.

4.4 Department Meetings / IT Liaison

Each department had a specific member of the Google Project Team assigned as their primary liaison to help schedule and prepare the department for migration. We were able to meet with most departments as a whole shortly before their migration to remind them of the process and coordinate the timing of the migration day(s). Many departments were scheduled on a specific day and everyone migrated together whereas some of the larger departments (Dining Services, Facilities Management, Athletics, etc.) were migrated in smaller groups over the course of a week. The IT Help Desk was informed of the migration process and had been trained to assist with general questions, training, and migration assistance but adding a personal contact helped with communication and concerns specific to that particular department.

5. TECHNICAL PROCESS
5.1 Archives

Archives within GroupWise are stored locally on a machine, thus we were unable to transfer archives to their new Google account for end users automatically. There is a field set in eDirectory that will only have a value if a user has setup archives on their own as it is not setup by default. This gave us a list of the specific users that we needed to talk to about their archives. When asking if they used archives, we found many end-users believing that moving a message to a sub-folder was archiving the message. A large number of staff had clicked on archives at one point or another but never actually archived any messages. For those users with archives, we removed their quota within GroupWise and had them un-archive the messages so they were back on the server and could migrate through our process.

5.2 Pre-Migration

To help make the "migration" process look smoother to end users we added a "pre-migration" step to the process. Counting on the size of a user's mailbox and any other issues with an account that we would run into, the synchronization of an account could take over 24 hours. By "pre-migrating" users a few days before their official migration we could make the migration process look almost instantaneous as there was significantly less mail to move.

During this process we also cleaned up any malformed or large emails in the user's account that could not migrate. We moved them into one of two folders within each user's GroupWise account: vuTooBig and vuMalformed. These folders were not included in the migration so the users could manually forward the messages, save the attachments, or opt to delete them. This greatly reduced productivity issues where individuals were waiting on their new account to finish migrating and reduced confusion about what account they should be using. We were also able to run several tests on their accounts during the pre-migration step to locate potential problems such as missing inboxes before the migration. The Google Team was alerted of the issue and that department's Liaison was able to address the issue with the end-user before it became a problem during the migration process.

5.3 Migration Process

On the designated day, each user was sent an email containing a link to an internal web form where they would verify the pre-migration folders, opt in/out of calendar and contact migration, and click to "start" the migration. Once the form was submitted their mail routing was set their gmail1.valpo.edu destination. Routing tables were set to refresh every 15 minutes during the migration process to begin sending messages to the Gmail accounts quickly. We then migrated any new email that came in since the last pre-migration was run and migrated the user's calendar and contact information if they opted to have this done.

Once that was complete we sent an email to the user to verify everything was there and giving them a link to a second form to "finalize" the migration. Once the end-user had completed this step we deleted the GroupWise account. GroupWise account deletions were a manual process so our programmers kept watch during the days people were scheduled to migrate and deleted these as soon as they were approved for deletion by the end-user. As a precautionary measure, a final sync was performed before each deletion to ensure that the window of possibility between a GroupWise generated message being sent to their old account before it was deleted was reduced to under a minute.

5.4 Shared Resources

In GroupWise, shared resources were objects assigned to the ownership of users. Because of this setup, the shared resources couldn't be migrated using our back-end tools. Our first attempts to create rules in GroupWise to forward all messages from the resource to its Gmail location were very unsuccessful. In most instances, the rule would fail without indicating on which message. We could manually compare the messages in both accounts and then manually forward or print out the messages that didn't forward already, but that was exceptionally time consuming.

Our solution was to use Mozilla Thunderbird as an IMAP bridge in order to migrate the contents of these resources. We had several dummy GroupWise accounts, which could be set as the owner of the specific shared resource(s) we were trying to migrate. We could share folders from the dummy account to the resource and then move the messages into the shared folders, thus back into an account which could utilize IMAP. The dummy GroupWise account and the Google User Account were each connected via IMAP to Thunderbird where we could copy the messages from folder to folder. This process is admittedly convoluted so IT staff handled this for the end users to reduce the potential for mistakes or confusion.

6. FACULTY / STAFF MIGRATION PROCESS
6.1 Department Recon

An important aspect of the migration process as a whole was to find out how users on campus were using GroupWise and the various features. We referred to this as reconnaissance (or "recon"). We didn't want to "break" any departmental processes or workflows because of migration. We identified key contacts in each department on campus and focused our communication efforts with these people. In some departments, these contacts acted as an intermediary to pass information back and forth between the department staff and the IT staff. In other departments, these contacts were coordinators and communication happened via department-wide emails or meetings. The method utilized largely depended on the size of the department, since larger departments are harder to coordinate in the sense of scheduling face-to-face meetings.

We also created a Google Form to aid in collecting information about departments' and individuals' usage of GroupWise. The form asked which functions and features each person used, and was sent a week or two before migration. The form was most useful in larger departments so that we could reach more people in a shorter period of time. We were able to follow up with individuals who completed the form and ask for more information about the features they used. This helped us identify any unexpected uses as well as sharing between accounts and resources. The support on the day of migration was better tailored from the form responses since we knew who had a smartphone, who wanted mac documentation, who needed help sharing calendars, etc.

As part of this process, we were able to help provide users with instructions on how to use similar functionality in Gmail as well as advise them on which functions would not be available in Gmail. This applied mainly to shared folders, shared address books, and mobile device usage. We explained how sharing worked differently in Gmail versus GroupWise, and pointed them to tip sheets, help pages, and online instructions for accomplishing the same tasks in Gmail.

6.2 Pre-Migration
During the week prior to their official migration date, the pre-migration process ran behind the scenes. Most end-users were unaware of this process occurring unless something was identified that required the IT Liaison to follow up with an individual. One unexpected issue was a missing inbox. GroupWise allows the user to move their inbox folder into their cabinet, address book, calendar, etc. but still manages to deliver messages. Our migration utilities could not see the inbox once it was moved; the solution was simply to move it back and restart the pre-migration process.

6.3 Day of Migration Email
Each user was scheduled for a specific date to complete their migration. This date was determined through communication with contact person(s) in their department; in most cases, a single date was chosen for each department. On a department's migration day, an email was automatically generated by our migration tools that would send a message to the user with a link to the online website to proceed with the migration process. The website had four pages which provided instructions on each step. Each email was sent from Migration.Team@valpo.edu which was a Google group that informed the entire project team of any issues or replies.

6.4 Day of Migration Support
For most departments, IT staff was available on site at their location to assist with questions and issues as they arose while users were migrating. Many users were comfortable navigating through the process on their own, but for those who were less confident, we were able to provide support as they went through the steps.

Help Desk staff had all been trained in Google Apps and the migration process and were available for support through our regular channels (walk-ups, phone calls, emails, web tickets). Most Help Desk staff are students and had been using Gmail accounts for several months already as well, which gave them valuable experience and insight into using the system. They were well-equipped to provide support on the new email system.

For users unable to migrate the same day as their department, they could move forward with the process at any time they were ready. Once they had received the automated migration email, they could start when it was convenient for them. This was reassuring to users who were out of the office on their specified migration day.

For two departments, migration was scheduled differently due to the nature of their departments. Both Dining Services and Facilities Management are large groups of staff where they share computers among users, and the nature of their duties is not computer-based. For these groups, we scheduled specific migration sessions during two week timeframes chosen by their departments. The sessions were held in a computer classroom of the Library, and users signed up in advance for a session so that the number of users at any time was not more than the number of seats in the classroom. IT staff were available in the room at these sessions and assisted users with logging in and navigating through the migration process, as well as providing some basic training as they first logged into their accounts. We worked closely with each department to select session times that fit in with their departmental work schedules. This way we didn't have sessions during their busiest times of day.

6.5 Shared Resources
Migration of messages within shared resources was mostly completed by IT staff, and therefore didn't require much from the end user. We worked with users of shared resources to determine whether a Google Group or a full user account would be a better solution for their shared email needs. In the majority of cases, a full user account was preferable because of the ability to label messages, archive messages and grant delegated access to other users in the department. In a few cases, a Google Group was preferable because the department didn't need the ability to manage messages, and only needed the ability for multiple users to receive messages. Temporary accounts were setup as was done with student access to shared resources previously until the resource could be manually moved by IT for the department. This allowed more flexibility in timing the moves with only a minimal amount of inconvenience during the transition.

6.6 Training
IT provided multiple training opportunities to make it more convenient for end users to take advantage. Users were strongly encouraged to participate in some sort of training to ease their transition to the session. Many users did take advantage of the opportunity, and noted that training helped make it easier to switch from one system to another. Some users didn't take advantage of any training, and then complained about the transition being too difficult or confusing.

One method we used was traditional classroom-based training, where users were invited to attend a class with an IT trainer. This class covered the basic functions and uses of Google Apps including Gmail basics, the contact list, Calendar basics, and a brief overview of Docs. These classes were offered four times per week beginning in mid-January and going through mid-May. For at least two departments, training sessions were scheduled at a time of their choosing instead of our default scheduled times. If departments asked us, we did everything we could to accommodate their requests.

Another training class we offered biweekly was an open Q&A session, called "I've migrated to Gmail...now what do I do?" This session had no specified agenda, and was open to any person to bring any Google Apps questions at all. IT staff were available to assist them in solving their problem. These sessions were useful for individuals who may have spent time already in Gmail and needed answers to more advanced questions.

A third option available was the use of the lynda.com Online Training Library®. Valpo has a lyndaCampus site license, which allowed us to promote use of their existing Gmail courses as an option for our users. The lynda.com option was attractive to people who found it more difficult to carve out time for a 90 minute dedicated session, since the courses are all online and divided into smaller videos of between 2-7 minutes each. A user could go online anytime, whether on campus or off, and access the videos when it was convenient for them. They could also choose whether to view an entire course, or just the few segments that were most relevant to their needs.

6.7 Emeritus / Retired Staff

The deadline for finishing migrations as set by the CIO was April 15th for campus departments. We arranged to handle the migration of emeritus faculty and retired staff with computer access privileges and accounts after this date to enable more hands on assistance with these groups. We scheduled two open evening sessions for any emeritus / retired staff in the area and communicated the plans for migrating through ReVU, the retired faculty / staff social group. This was the first major system transition where the retired and emeritus staff were addressed as a user group specifically; the feedback from these end users was overwhelmingly positive.

6.8 Forced Migrations / GroupWise Shut Off

Despite our best efforts to get everyone to migrate, there were a couple hundred who did not start the migration or finalize the migration. We were able to schedule forced migrations for many of these stragglers and ran the process on a specific day without any interaction from them. The drawback to the force migration is that we didn't have any user authorization to delete the GroupWise account. Fortunately, we have not heard of any issues from this as most of the stragglers were adjunct faculty who infrequently used their Valpo accounts. Authentication to the GroupWise system was shut off on June 30th. IT staff retained access to finish moving a small amount of shared resources that had not yet been addressed.

7. CONCLUSIONS
7.1 Survey

We conducted a post migration survey among all faculty and staff that had gone through the process voluntarily. When asked how well would they would rate their Gmail migration experience 36% indicated Good and 48% indicated Excellent. 82% of respondents agreed that Gmail was an improvement over GroupWise and 81% indicated they were either satisfied or very satisfied with Gmail as their email client.

We posed several open ended questions in the survey and learned that people felt we had provided more communication during this transition than with others. We also learned that people appreciated the variety of ways we used to communicate information about the changes. The Meet & Greet sessions were considered very helpful, as well as the regular email updates we sent to campus. We learned that in the future, we should do more individual meetings with departments to review how these changes affect their areas, since not everyone was able to attend a Meet & Greet.

7.2 General Conclusions

At the conclusion of the migration process the Google Project Team came to several conclusions as to the main items that made this migration such a resounding success.

- Pro-active communication prior to the migration is exceptionally useful in mitigating concerns and alleviating campus anxiety.

- A balance between continuously offered training and on the spot training is necessary.

- Liaisons enhance communication and set better expectations for the process. Departments know they have a specific person they can contact who is aware of their specific situations and needs.

- Scheduling departments instead of allowing them to go all at once was necessary to provide the on-site support on the day of migration.

Valparaiso University's experience migrating to the Google Apps for Education platform is one that any campus could replicate.

8. ACKNOWLEDGEMENTS

Special thanks to Tara Teeple, Director of Technology and Data Services in Enrollment Management, and William Klein, Associate Director of Technology for the Valparaiso School of Law, for their assistance in beta-testing and coordinating their department migrations. Special thanks to Library Services, Integrated Marketing and Communications, and the Office of the President for being the first to undergo the migration process.

Transitioning to Universal Print Queue and Remote Campus Distribution of Printing and Copying Services

Leonard M. Williams
University of Texas at San Antonio
One UTSA Circle
San Antonio, TX 78249
(210) 458-7699

Leonard.Williams@utsa.edu

Roxann Koch
University of Texas at San Antonio
One UTSA Circle
San Antonio, TX 78249
(210) 458-7699

Roxann.Koch@utsa.edu

ABSTRACT

Our paper demonstrates how University of Texas at San Antonio's Office of Information Technology (OIT), Student Computing Services revolutionized student printing and copying at the University of Texas at San Antonio with "Print-Spot". Students were limited to three physical locations on two campuses with a total of 15 printers to obtain their printouts. Through our Pint-Spot printing program we are able to provide students the capability to print from anywhere to anywhere including from home to campus. During this time of austere budgets and finances we are able to lower the costs of student printing on campus for the colleges, the students and OIT, as-well-as remove the burden of providing copy capability from UTSA's Auxiliary Business Services, while improving the capabilities and the management of student printing and copying campus wide.

Categories and Subject Descriptors

H.4.1 [Information Systems Applications]: Office Automation – *equipment.*

General Terms

Management, Performance, Economics, Human Factors.

Keywords

Print-Spot (PS); Remote Print-Spot (RPS); Multi-Function Device (MFD); Pharos; Computer Labs (Labs); Colleges/Departments (X-Labs); Library Information Common (LIC)

1. INTRODUCTION

Two of the Universalities Tri-Campuses are serviced by the Print-Spot Program Office, the Main campus and Downtown campus. The Institute of Texan Culture Museum campus does not offer traditional student support so it is not included in the Print-Spot program. The OIT department has approximately 189 IT and Customer Service Support personnel which includes the Manager for the Print-Spot Program Office, who is backed up by 10 full time staff members and 20 hourly staff members spread across seven work days from the Student Computing Services Laboratories,. There is one Systems Analyst III assigned to OIT/Support Services who provides ancillary server and analytical support to Print-Spot.

Prior to the implementation of Print-Spot OIT provided students with printing in three Student Computer Lab facilities. We provided a total of 12 black and white and 3 color printers within the three labs located at the 1604 campus Business Building (BB), Multi-Disciplinary Studies building (MS), and the Downtown Campus Frio Street Building (FS). The cost to lease those 15 printers was $9,555.00 per month. Our software provider is Pharos and the software licenses for pharos print management utilized to charge the students, track their allowances, and release their print jobs, were obtained through a third party called TracSystems at a separate cost of $300.00 for each new license and 125.00 per license for renewal. We had to have a license for each computer release station used to release jobs from the printers. We had to have separate release stations for each printer as well as for wireless printing from laptops. Each lab had 5 printer release stations which meant that 15 desktop systems were being used exclusively to release print jobs.

1.1 Previous Student Printing Resources

Preceding the Print-Spot program implementation students were limited to visiting the Student Computing Services Labs and using the desktop workstations provided to submit their print jobs. For work done off campus they had to print from either a USB memory stick or from attachments opened from the internet or email and queued to the printers in one of the three locations.

The Business Auxiliary Services Office provided copying services for the campuses. However, they were unable to maintain and stock the copier devices consistently, resulting in lost revenue opportunities for the University and inconvenience to the students who needed copying services.

1.2 Enrollment Statistics

(http://utsa.edu/registrar/enrollment.cfm)

Fall 2009 – 28,955	Spring 2010 – 27,183
Fall 2010 – 30,258	Spring 2011 – 28,296
Fall 2011 – 30,968	Spring 2012 – 28,806

2. PROJECT EXPECTATIONS

We established a printing project to revamp student printing and entered the project with the following expectations:

1. Enlarge the printing footprint on Campus providing students the ability to release their prints in areas other than the computer labs enabling them to print from anywhere to anywhere.

2. We would lower the cost of printing to the students.

3. We would involve as many of the colleges in student printing as possible in order to maximize efficiencies.

4. OIT would remove the burden of paper and toner acquisition, printer purchase and maintenance, as-well-as storage of supplies from the participating colleges.

5. The university would have a central Point of Contact for all matters related to student printing.

Students would eventually be able to print from home and release the print jobs after arriving on campus.

2.1 Project Implementation

The University Chief Information Officer, Kenneth 'Ken' Pierce, was the project owner and commissioned the Steering Committee. Chief Operations Officer, Lee Gildon, SCS Assistant Director, Almond 'A.D.' Dillard, former   , Annette Evans, Executive Director for Enterprise Systems, Bryan Wilson, Assistant Director of Information Technology, Edward 'Brant' League, Senior System Analyst, Alexander 'Alex' Ward, comprised the project Steering Committee. Other University stakeholders who were involved in establishing the project's remote printer locations were Campus Police Department, Physical Plant - Facilities Services, and the Environmental Health, Safety and Risk Management Office.

After the Vendor selection process was completed the External stakeholders were RICOH's Major Account Executive, Wayne Parker, Consultant, Jacob P. Tezak, and dozens of RICOH technical support personnel, and Pharos Regional Sales Representative, Ron Carson.

2.2 Print-Spot Program Implementation

It took a little over a year and half from conception to current evolution of the Print-Spot program. We had to work through a project management process that lead to some interesting learning curves. First it involved taking our concept and research and coordinating a project strategy with project milestones tied to various stages of completion and metrics for success measures. After soliciting for bids from potential vendors and making a selection based upon their proposals, we had to coordinate efforts with the OIT Infrastructure and resource personnel, program budgeting for contracted services through the selected vendor ICON who is now RICOH. The services included Pharos packages and software as Pharos is a RICOH partner.

We staffed the Print Management Office by taking a Customer Support analyst position within SCS and converting it to a Print Systems Manager. The initial salary for this position was set at 40K. The Student Print Systems Manager is the central point of contact for all matters related to student printing.

Pharos related print drivers were provided to laptop and notebook users via the SCS web site that would permit them to send print jobs from those devices to the SCS Labs without needing to occupy a workstation in the lab itself. Using a universal print queue allowed us to expand our offering of printer devices to all of our academic buildings, permitting students to obtain their print jobs in a timely fashion and closer to the buildings where their classes are held. This reduced over-crowding and freed up computing resources in the SCS Labs for those students who do not have laptop or notebook devices.

3. PROGRAM ACCOMPLISHMENTS

After implementation of the Print-Spot Program students are now able to print from anywhere to anywhere. They can send print jobs from any networked computer on campus or their laptops over the wireless network. We now have a total of 49 multi- function printing devices (MFDs) located throughout the 1604 and downtown campuses. Because the MFDs have built in user interface we no longer have to provide separate release stations. Print jobs are released at the device via card swipe or touch screen input. Students can download the Print-Spot package to their home computers and print from home to campus releasing their print job upon arrival at any MFD. Students are also able to go to the Print Spot Web site and find convenient printing locations. There are six Colleges and departments participating in the Print-Spot program with OIT.

We reduced the basic price per copy to the student from eight cents per page to six cents per page for black and white copies and from 48 Cents per page to 24 Cents per page for color Copies. We also made odd sized paper available in 81/2 X 14 and 11x17 in various locations. All-in-all the Print-Spot program has met or exceeded all expectations.

Our initial focus was providing only printing to students; however, with the MFDs in our inventory, we were able to take over the copy service from Business Auxiliary Services who were losing money and having issues keeping their equipment functioning to meet the student copying demand. The price per copy is the same as for printing.

3.1 Remote Campus Support

Student Computing Services (OIT-SCS) Computer Laboratory staff members assist in the daily support for public remote printers and external lab partners with the Print-Spot Program Office. On a daily basis the staff team leaders and/or lab supervisor can monitor the digital readings for all Print-Spot printers currently located at the downtown campus and when lab staffing coverage is in place visit in person and refill paper and toner supplies at remote printer locations. The daily routine involves cleaning the digital display panels and glass copier surfaces, checking for any physical damage or tampering with the Print-Spot printers, reporting any findings that are out of the ordinary to the Print-Spot Program Manager, refilling paper trays and initiating vendor trouble ticketing.

4. PROGRAM SETBACKS AND FAILURES

We attempted to work with on campus student housing to place printers in the dormitories; however, the Campus Housing department chose to continue providing free printing to the student's with the caveat that they must provide their own paper.

We negotiated with the Food Contractor (Aramark) and the Campus Business Development office in an attempt to place a printer at the Campus Dining Facility, but that was unsuccessful because, they did not want the students to camp out in the Dining facility to do homework. They preferred that they come in, eat, and depart making room for other students.

We had to disable the copy function on the printing devices located in the University Center (UC), due to the University Center's copy agreement with the UPS store.

The Business College chose not to place any printers in their areas, but did allow us to place printers in the first and second floor hallways. They then downloaded the Print-Spot printing packages from our web-site and loaded them on their classroom computers. Students are now able to print to the Print-Spot printers from the classrooms in the Business College and pick up their prints at any of the hallway printers.

5. FIRST YEAR PRINT-SPOT/COPY TOTALS

The Program was started with the lease of 47 printers and increased to 49 to accommodate the increased printing demands within the Library Information Commons (LIC). Printing in that area and the Business Building (BB) Lab increased after the closure of the computer lab in the Multi-Disciplinary Studies (MS) building. The initial cost of the lease included toner, maintenance, 47 Multi Function Devices and six million total copies, with 495,000 black and white and 5,000 color prints per month, totaling 5,940,000 black & white and 60,000 color copies per year. The end-of-year total for pages printed was within 97% of the initial estimate of 6,000,000 at 6,137,739 (Figure 1). We have since increased to 7,000,000 copies per year.

The John Peace (JP) LIC is the highest printing area of all of our printing locations. We began the project with four printers in the JPLIC (3 black & white and 1 color), but soon had to increase the number of printers available to six (5 black & white and 1 color). The current configuration is 3 B/W printers in the main LIC and 1 Color printer in the XLIC or East Information Commons. There are two printers Located near the stairwell in the library with their primary function being to serve as copiers. There were a total of 2,258,799 prints made in the Library through August of 2011.

The BB Lab has three black and white printers and one color printer inside, with one additional black and white device located just outside of the computer lab in the entrance. There are printers located in every Academic building on the 1604 campus as well as downtown. There were 1,111,490 prints made in the BB Lab through August of 2011 which is almost half of what was printed in the Library.

5.1 Year to Date Print-Spot Print/Copy Totals

Our student population has increased over the past year and there are presently 27,000 unique student logins utilizing Print-Spot and at the end of our spring semester, there have been approximately 6,833,134 total prints of which 903,952 are for copies, see Figure 1. Total Printing Impressions.

6. PLANNED AND ACTUAL INCOME AND EXPENSES

The original pay-for-print program at UTSA was called Print-Smart. Taking the very limited historical information from printing in the three lab facilities under the Print Smart program, we estimated the income from printing and the expenses for the first year. Income was estimated to come in at $63,064 and the actual income received for the year was 71,567.00 which is an $8,503.00 difference. We were within 88% of our prediction on the income.

Our expenses for the program were estimated to come in at $251,879.00 for the year. The actual expenses came in at $254,105.00 for a $2,226.00 difference which is within 1% of our estimate for the year, (See Figure 2. Planned/Actual Income and Figure 3. Planned/Actual Expense).

7. VENDOR ASSESSMENT

We concluded the 2nd year of a 3 year contract. The vendor who is now RICOH has provided outstanding support. They have responded to service calls within the scope of the contract. They are averaging approximately 17 hours turnaround time from contact to resolution where outages have occurred. They have also been very helpful in resolving issues related to software performance. RICOH currently uses our Print-Spot program as a model to demonstrate capabilities to other colleges and universities. We have provided tours of our program to UT Austin and Texas A&M San Antonio, as well as other local colleges and Universities.

Pharos is the software vendor; although not local they have also been very helpful in resolving software related issues through e-mail and conference calls with our Print-Spot management and support team. Our current contract is renewable without going back out for bid and at this point we would recommend renewing and continuing with the existing Vendor.

8. PRINT-SPOT (SMART DEVICE MONITORING SYSTEM)

We are able to monitor each device from the desktop. This system allows real-time access to each device as to device status/errors, paper and toner levels, and total device count. There is a capability to setup device alerts for low/out of paper/toner, trays not connected, device door opened and many others (See Figure 4. Smart Device Monitor for Admin).devices directly to the printers. These are some of the exciting technology possibilities we are exploring in 2011/2012.

9. SUMMARY

In summary the Print-Spot program can be classified as a highly successful project. The benefits gleaned from student satisfaction are remarkable. We provided a cost savings for other colleges and departments on campus with the program as-well-as greatly improved student access to printing and copying. We have become the benchmark for other colleges and universities while we continue to innovate and provide improvements to our program. We are looking forward this year to the possibility of integrating printing from mobile devices such as iPhones, iPads, androids, etc...We are also exploring the possibility of adding scanning to our student offering as a free service, where they would be able to scan to their USB devises. They would also be able to download and print from USB devices directly to the printers. These are some of the exciting technology possibilities we are exploring in 2011/2012.

We would also recommend looking at some type of printing solution for Faculty and Staff that would mirror the student printing program. A Faculty/Staff solution would save the campus a great deal of money.

Print / Copy Totals		
Total Copying for FY2010-2011	Total Printing for FY2010-2011	Device Totals Count for FY2010-2011
313,771	5,823,968	6,137,739

Print / Copy Totals Downtown Campus		
Total Copying for FY2010-2011	Total Printing for FY2010-2011	Device Totals Count for FY2010-2011
64,681	1,131,236	1,195,917

Figure 1: Total Print Impressions

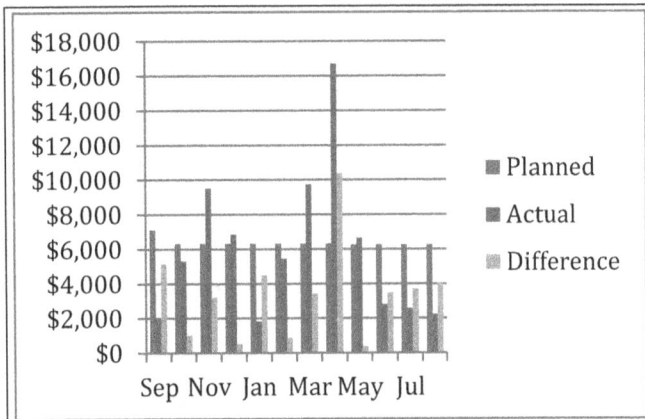

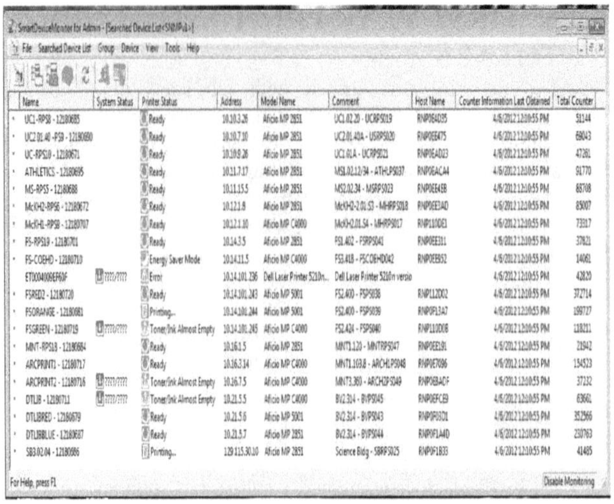

Figure 4: Smart Device Monitoring Interface

Figure 2: Planned / Actual Income

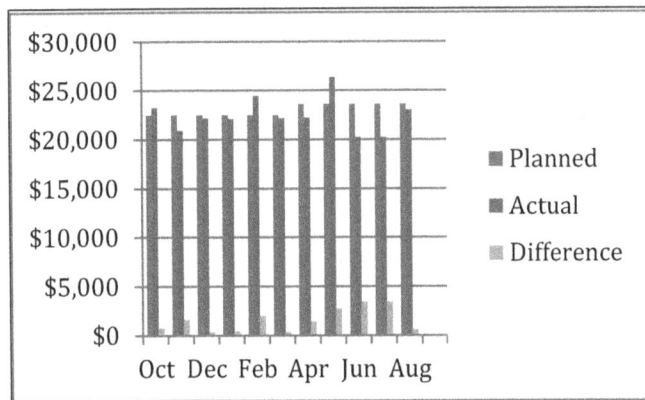

Figure 3: Planned / Actual Expenses

Getting the Most Out of Your Help Desk Software

Miranda Carney-Morris
Lewis & Clark College
0615 SW Palatine Hill Road
Portland, Oregon 97219
(503) 768-7220
mccm@lclark.edu

Elizabeth Young
Lewis & Clark College
0615 SW Palatine Hill Road
Portland, Oregon 97219
(503) 768-7220
eayoung@lclark.edu

ABSTRACT

Many of us have a love - hate relationship with our Help Desk software. Often seen as a necessary evil, it can be a great source of frustration for IT staff as well as our clients. When we look for a way to eliminate our frustrations, we often look first for a software solution, confident that all we need is a program with the "right" feature set. Less attention is paid to how our management team, Help Desk staff, and clients are using the systems we already have in place. In this paper, we'll discuss how a disconnect between implementation and procedures and an institution's culture can be the root cause of Help Desk software failures and frustrations and share strategies for improving overall satisfaction with your current Help Desk system.

Categories and Subject Descriptors

K.6.1 [MANAGEMENT OF COMPUTING AND INFORMATION SYSTEMS]: Project and People Management – *management techniques, staffing, training*

General Terms

Management, Documentation, Performance, Human Factors

Keywords

Management, Help Desk Software

1. INTRODUCTION

Lewis & Clark College (L&C) is a liberal arts college located approximately six miles outside of downtown Portland, Oregon. Our student body consists of close to 2000 undergraduates, 800 law students and nearly 1000 other graduate students, primarily in education and counseling. We support a staff and faculty of approximately 1000.

Our Help Desk software is Numara Track-It![1] We have a central Help Desk that is our designated entry point for phone and drop-in requests for assistance for students, staff and faculty. The reception desk in the nearby Main IT Office also fields drop-in requests and is often the first point of contact for those new to L&C. General email inquires are fielded by second tier technicians.

Our Help Desk is staffed by student workers and is open during business hours year round. During the academic year, the Help Desk is open evenings and weekends. Other assistance is provided by professional staff and is available during normal business hours only.

Programs like Numara Track-It! are designed to help manage the business of tracking and responding to client requests for technical assistance and are considered a necessary evil by Information Technology support organizations. Staff is expected to utilize technology to be more effective and efficient in their positions, however, standard guidelines for successful help desk software deployment are often created with enterprise corporate organizations in mind, organizations that have cultures quite different from those found in most academic institutions.

At L&C, we have come to believe that several of our frustrations with Track-It! are the result of a mismatch between organizational culture factors and criteria we used to configure the software. In cases like ours, simply moving to a different Help Desk package won't fix the problem. In this paper, we'll review some of the most common frustrations expressed by IT staff and management about Help Desk software, discuss how to look for solutions with your local context and priorities in mind, and propose some solutions.

2. HELP DESK SOFTWARE PROMISES

There are numerous resources available to help us evaluate and select Help Desk software from Professional Organizations such as the Help Desk Institute.[2] When configured correctly, Help Desk software has great potential to make our services more accessible, accountable, and efficient. These systems can improve customer satisfaction, make our workers more efficient and accountable, make IT more transparent to our institutions, and give management the data necessary to justify budgets and make strategic decisions about allocating resources. With all of this promise, we can feel justified in the large price tag that often accompanies full-featured Help Desk systems. This was the situation at L&C when we decided to replace our home-grown call tracking and inventory system with Numara Track-It! about 10 years ago.

Much of our original Track-It! configuration was based on recommendations from a consultant provided by the company. Generally speaking, we were dazzled by the feature set, followed the recommendations of our consultant, and focused on ensuring calls could be entered in a systematic way for reporting purposes. Looking back, we realize we focused on what our Help Desk software *could do* rather than L&C specific goals and priorities for what Help Desk software *should do* at Lewis & Clark.

Track-It!, like many other Help Desk software programs, is geared towards non-academic environments. Professional organizations and standards such as the Help Desk Institute and Information Technology Infrastructure Library (ITIL) also have a business rather than academic/non-profit focus. Help Desk software is often designed and implemented to meet these corporate standards. Since we followed these types of guidelines when implementing Track-It!, it is not surprising that we ended up with a system that did not easily "fit" how we work at L&C.

Over the years, we discovered that we had as many complaints and problems with Track-It! as we did with our home grown system. Several of the complaints were repeats. New employees found the system unintuitive, cumbersome, and avoided using it if possible.

As good technologists, we looked first for a technology solution. We traded notes on different Help Desk software solutions with colleagues at other institutions. We compared feature sets and discussed options with various Help Desk software vendors. We discovered that our system shared many of the features as others and that our peers voiced many of the same Help Desk software complaints we did. We started to wonder if maybe our particular complaints had more to do with human factors at L&C rather than the feature set and capabilities of our particular Help Desk software package.

3. ORGANIZATIONAL CULTURE

Numerous studies on organizational effectiveness have shown that organizational culture is an important factor in the success or failure of specific initiatives. An organization's culture resists standardization as it is defined in Schein's book Organizational Culture and Leadership (p. 18) as "a pattern of shared basic assumptions learned by a group as it solved its problems of external adaptation and internal integration, which has worked well enough to be considered valid and, therefore, to be taught to new members as the correct way to perceive, think, and feel in relation to those problems."[3] Unique experiences result in organizational differences, and studies show that academic organizations tend to have quite distinct differences from their corporate counterparts and have an overall more complex organizational culture. [4]

3.1 Overall Cultural Factors

Here are some factors that may influence your organization's culture[3]:

- Physical environment (size, furnishings, buildings, geographic location, etc.)
- Policy and mission statements, Codes of behavior (dress, etc.), nature of the organization
- Technology used
- Language used
- Patterns of behavior – what people say and do, what is rewarded, how conflict is resolved, how mistakes are treated
- Moral and ethical codes, organization world view or other values that constrain behavior and formulate basic assumptions
- Underlying sense of purpose that links individuals to organization
- Basic underlying assumptions of individuals – (beliefs, values, and perceptions that impact thinking, behavior and feelings)

Most Help Desk software is designed with the larger and more lucrative corporate market in mind and related industry recommended standards, protocols or business strategies such as the Information Technology Infrastructure Library (ITIL) or Six Sigma target these organizations as well. Not all will be suited for our more complex cultural environments. We must pick and choose those elements that will be effective at addressing what is valued by our organization.

3.2 IT Specific Factors

The values and management style of IT at your institution also impacts what strategies will work best. Consider:

- How is return on IT investment measured?
- Are metrics and statistics an important tool in the budgeting and planning process?
- Attitudes towards risk and early adoption of technology
- How and how often does IT management communicate and promote its agenda?
- Is IT centralized or decentralized? Do you work in teams?
- Level of control over institutional hardware & software purchases
- Level of specialization within the department
- Is IT seen as an integral part of the teaching and learning process?

4. COMMON FRUSTRATIONS & PRACTICAL SOLUTIONS

4.1 Entering Tickets is Cumbersome

One of the most common complaints we hear about Help Desk software is that entering and processing tickets is cumbersome and takes too much time. Clients who have trouble entering their own tickets (commonly called self-service) will simply bypass the system and opt to call, email, or drop by to ask for assistance from IT staff. IT staff may start to see entering and documenting tickets as meaningless busy work that gets in the way of "real" work. The path of least resistance for staff is to only input tickets that must be routed to others and spend as little time as possible updating tickets and documenting resolutions. Open tickets are rarely updated. Tickets are often closed long after the problem is actually solved with little or no description of the ticket resolution.

This situation undermines any chance of your Help Desk software to generate useful information for a knowledge base or training, the effectiveness of any self-service or 24x7 support features, and the ability to collect accurate information on type and quantity of calls, time spent on tickets, ticket volumes, etc. Leaving this situation unaddressed will limit the potential effectiveness (return-on-investment) of your Help Desk software. Moreover, staff forced to rely on the system will resent those who do not use it. This can lead to conflicts and misunderstanding within IT and poor communication and service for our clients.

At its core, this issue is a people and process management issue that will inevitably be voiced, no matter the Help Desk software. Entering accurate and detailed trouble tickets takes time, especially for those who have no need to refer issues to others and will be simply documenting work already completed. Those responsible for the Help Desk software need to team up with management to ensure that time spent entering and processing tickets corresponds with how management values and uses data mined from the ticket system.

As you analyze your workflow, consider the process for entering tickets, updating tickets, and closing tickets, as these are all places where ticket processing can break down. Software design factors such as the ease of navigating screens, finding tickets, integration with email and a knowledge base of known solutions greatly influences the amount of time it takes to update and document tickets; however, management decisions such as how to catalog tickets, required fields, escalation policies, and what information is made available to clients also impacts time spent. Keep in mind, it doesn't matter how much information your system can collect and catalog, what matters is whether management uses that information in setting departmental policies and procedures and assessing staff performance. Once you have a handle on what information management values, the next step is to fine tune ticket management in your system to make meeting these data collection needs as efficient as possible.

As you fine-tune your system consider:

- What can you do to make initial ticket entry easier?
- How much information can you realistically expect a client to enter on a self-service ticket before the ticket is abandoned?
- If you collect statistics, should cataloging happen at call creation, close, both?
- How will reporting be accomplished?
- How important is automatic ticket assignment versus manual intervention to ensure accuracy?
- Is there data you don't need to collect? Don't waste time on ticket data entry for information already tracked elsewhere.

You may discover, as we did at L&C, that staff complaining about the complexity of entering tickets had a valid point. In our case, we designed an extremely detailed call classification system designed to provide detailed reports and maximize the automatic routing of tickets. In practice, our management team rarely views reports or analyzes data from the Help Desk system. We have also discovered that our overly complicated classification scheme inhibits use of the system for both self-service and IT staff. For those who do not need to use the system to route tickets, it's often easier to resort to face-to-face communication in lieu of entering or updating tickets.

In our case, simplifying our classification system and requiring fewer fields to enter a call is an easy way to mitigate this complaint. On a campus where there is often a long-term personal relationship between IT staff and our clients, IT staff can often fill in the blanks if a call is entered with incomplete information. If at some future point our management team wishes to collect statistics, tickets can be cataloged when closed.

4.2 Initial Ticket Description Inadequate
Many of us have experienced the frustration and extra work associated with receiving an overly vague ticket that simply states, "Email doesn't work." These tickets can be frustrating for both clients and technicians as often the technician must contact the client for additional information before work on the ticket can begin. Help Desk software features such as call templates, required fields, pull down lists to guide data entry, and so on can go a long way towards resolving this problem

4.2.1 Self Service
Self Service tickets entered directly by often non-technical end users are a special case. Software techniques that help ensure accurate ticket entry such as requiring fields such as platform, operating system, software, connection type, service needed, and so on, in addition to a description make the system overly cumbersome (see section 4.1) and can scare clients away from self service ticket entry. On the flip side, if you make ticket entry too easy you may not collect the information necessary to appropriately route and triage tickets.

At L&C, it makes sense for us to err on the side of ease-of-use as we limit our self-service to staff and faculty. Staff responsible for triage are familiar with the computing environment of those entering tickets – this makes it easy to fill in blanks and interpret incomplete tickets. In addition, our support culture places a high value on cultivating and building personal relationships. Calling or dropping by to follow up on a ticket comes naturally.

Look to the culture and Help Desk workflow of your institution to find a balance between ease-of-use and accuracy. Consider the following:

- How well do you know clients using self service?
- What is the cost of tickets that are incorrectly assigned due to cataloging errors?
- Volume of tickets vs. staff available to triage
- Create templates/forms for most common questions
- Set a different standard of service for Help Desk technicians when responding to client entered tickets
- Clear instructions on self service entry pages
- What doesn't belong in the ticket system and possible alternatives (chat, web forms, email)

4.2.2 Help Desk / Front Line Staff
When it is first tier support entering vague tickets, it is much more problematic. Not only is this frustrating to those actually working to solve a ticket, but it also creates a perception with both the client and the non-Help Desk technician that bypassing the Help Desk (and possibly the Help Desk software) might be a more efficient way to resolve future problems. In this case, the customer would have received better service by directly contacting the technician rather than the Help Desk.

Historically at L&C student workers at our Help Desk and our receptionist enter the majority of tickets. This is something we expect to continue given that our clients prefer to report problems to a person rather than communicate electronically. These workers are the lowest paid, least knowledgeable and, in the case of our student workers, least familiar with internal policies and procedures in our department. Given who we have entering tickets, it is not a surprise that incomplete and inaccurate ticket is an issue we experience frequently.

Ticket accuracy is a measure used by our Help Desk manager in evaluating our student workers, but is prioritized below criteria such as dependability and working on tickets assigned to the Help Desk. Other IT managers do not factor ticket accuracy into performance evaluations for full-time staff and mostly look to the system in response to questions or complaints about unresolved tickets.

Two cultural factors we encourage you keep in mind as you consider how to improve initial ticket descriptions:

(1) Who fields initial trouble reports and enters tickets

(2) How important is ticket accuracy to management?

Technical solutions can catch some problems, but not all. Examples include work order templates for common problems and required fields (can create problems – see section 4.1). However, as more of our clients look to self help resources to answer common questions and report routine problems, an increasing number of issues reported to the Help Desk are complicated and cannot be easily funneled into a template.

Ensuring quality ticket entry has become primarily a management issue. Establishing and enforcing clear expectations for what information to collect during a call and providing consistent reinforcement and feedback when these expectations are not met is key. The quality of the calls entered into the system will be a direct result of the message other users of the system send every time they don't address a poorly entered call. At L&C in addition to direct management feedback via performance evaluations, we use a combination of having tickets auto-assign to support teams rather than individuals, peer pressure, and periodic venting at staff meetings.

We have also addressed this issue at L&C by reclassifying our receptionist position. This position is now responsible for initial troubleshooting and more knowledgeable on what type of information needs to be collected when calls are entered. Peers also hold this position to a higher standard and are more willing to provide direct feedback when mistakes are made.

4.3 Automation Doesn't Work Right

Most major Help Desk programs can automate ticket logging, routing, escalation, and query/reporting. Less popular options include automated response/resolution and knowledge base integration. When configured correctly and maintained, these features can save time and greatly improve the effectiveness of your Help Desk software. However, poor implementation or implementing features that don't really add value at your institution can backfire and result in frustrating experiences for technicians and clients.

4.3.1 Create a Strong Foundation

Successful automation requires accurate data entry, well maintained lookup databases, and the ability to predict and program for patterns of behavior. Setting up and maintaining this support structure takes time and resources, and the cost involved may or may not be worth it to your institution.

The general rule of thumb is to automate as much of ticket entry as possible. Automatic entry of client details from telephone or other campus directories is a huge time saver and should be made a priority. If possible, make sure that the database used to auto complete client information is refreshed and kept as up-to-date as possible. At L&C new technicians quickly come to rely on this feature and all system users become frustrated when the database is incomplete or has old information.

Look for and capitalize on patterns for how calls are entered. For example, computer moves are usually initiated using Help Desk software self-service. Students report problems face-to-face or by email. Faculty report problems face-to-face or by phone. For the best success, identify who enters the most tickets in your system and then automate data entry with them in mind.

Automatic routing and escalation requires more careful planning. Automation is usually linked to categorization of incoming tickets or pre-populated templates for common ticket types. As we discussed in Section 4.1, overly complicated categorization schemes make tickets cumbersome to enter. Clients and entry-level staff will likely make mistakes when entering tickets that can lead to unexpected routing in an automated workflow. This can certainly lead to delays in resolving tickets and inefficient use of skilled third tier technician time. Pre-populated templates can mitigate this problem, but are time consuming to set up and only work for routine and predictable tickets.

4.3.2 The Human Factor

What works for us at L&C is to err on the side of caution with automatic call routing. We are gradually shifting to using broad categories for client-entered tickets that automatically route to second-tier support who know our client base well enough to accurately route tickets in a timely fashion. For routine and high volume requests, we use a combination of web forms and ticket templates, however, these make up very few of our overall tickets. In practice, we've found that we are willing to pay the cost of extra human intervention to ensure that the majority of tickets that reach third tier support are complete and have been routed correctly.

Another potential promise of automation is to use ticket resolutions as a knowledge base of common answers that clients can use to search for potential solutions in lieu of entering a ticket. Some systems even have built-in intelligence that will scan incoming emails for key words and auto-reply with canned responses. However, we argue that this level of automation has limited promise for higher education, especially for smaller institutions for several reasons.

The primary problem with this promise is that a knowledge base that simply consists of ticket resolutions isn't particularly easy to use or understand. Ticket resolutions are usually tailored to a specific circumstance. Simply searching through ticket resolutions for an answer to a problem often takes more effort and requires more technical know-how for a client than simply reporting a new problem directly. Identifying and then consolidating resolutions into easy to find generic solutions takes human curating. Small institutions like L&C with a strong cultural preference for face-to-face interaction need to think carefully about whether our clients will value an IT investment of time and money in self-service automation.

4.3.3 Wild West Computing Environment

When you have little or no control over the computing environment you must support it is hard to predict and program for patterns of client behavior. Unlike an internal corporate Help Desk, most of us do not support a single standard configuration, but several. Also, we must solve problems that occur both at the institution and at home. This complexity limits automations such as the ability to automatically resolve tickets with canned responses.

4.3.4 Complex Customer Relationships

The nature of our relationship to our customers is different in higher education. Consider a company like Hewlett Packard. They want happy customers, but want to supply this support as cheaply as possible. When customers know that the printer or other product in question cost less than $100, they are more likely to be forgiving of support options that are cumbersome or difficult to use. Also, if knowledgeable telephone support isn't available, clients are more likely to put in the extra time to wade through a ticket resolution populated knowledge base or other automated support option.

The stakes are quite different in higher education. Consider our students. Students have more money and time invested in their education than they do in a $100 printer and take computer problems they view as hampering their ability to get a good grade and ultimately a good job down the road, seriously. Many of our institutions not only wish to create a welcoming environment to retain students, but want a positive long-term relationship with future alumni. Finally, many of our IT departments consider education an important part of our mission, and we have an incentive to resolve tickets in a way that helps students avoid the problem in the future. All of these factors can make resources such as a knowledge base or automated ticket resolution intelligence less desirable. This is even more the case when you consider the relationship between IT departments and staff and faculty.

4.4 Unrealized Promises of Efficiency

One of the prominent selling points of any Help Desk software package is a promise of efficiency. The current brochure for Track-It! has a sidebar item entitled "Decrease IT inefficiencies" and goes on to promise to eliminate "disorganized handling of operations" and helping to "operate more efficiently by supporting ITIL best practices."[5]

As outlined in section 4.3, automation requires far more set-up and maintenance than is necessarily fruitful in a smaller population of requests than are typically found in larger organizations or corporate environments. Processes can only increase efficiency if they are both consistently re-evaluated and updated, and if the goals and expectations of the process is communicated well to the front-line staff.

4.4.1 Communicate Goals & Expectations

Training for our student workers at L&C is immersive in nature, and usually takes place during the busiest weeks of the semester, resulting in an often over-whelming barrage of information for new employees to take in. We recently deployed a home-grown knowledge base in order to more effectively communicate the standards of ticket entry for the most frequently received calls and incidents. We have discovered that the culture of face-to-face communication extends to our student workers, who have found it easier to ask second tier staff for assistance than to reference the knowledge base. Our staff has been inconsistent with reminding students to use the knowledge base as a first resource, and so the expectation has not been properly set that would lead to greater efficiency and consistency in ticket entry. Departmentally, management has not set the expectation or goal that entry and resolution of calls is of a high priority, so the desired standards of efficiency have not been met.

To improve efficiency, there are three different phases in the lifecycle of a ticket for which expectations should be clearly set, as well as subsets of those phases that give guidance to the technicians and support staff:

1) Entry
a. Complete contact information
b. Complete issue description
c. Complete hardware/software/network information
d. Initial troubleshooting steps taken

2) Updates
a. Additional information from end user
b. Attempts to contact end user
c. Further troubleshooting steps taken
d. Plan of action

3) Closure
a. Timely closure of completed tickets
b. Complete information as to resolution

These expectations should be tied to overarching goals in order to provide concrete motivation regarding the priority of entering, updating and closing tickets. Defining goals prior to implementing new software would be the ideal, but even post-implementation, management can do a great deal to improve utilization of the software. Goals should be clear, concise, and measurable. Vague goals such as "improve customer service" do not allow for measurement, nor is it easy to define what such goals entail.

Aligning processes with the end goals, and then communicating those goals and the expectation of their implementation to the staff can only improve efficiency. If entering tickets gives the technicians or clients the feeling that the software hampers efficiency, the goals and expectations to staff have not been communicated well.

4.4.2 Unrealistic Expectations

Be realistic about what you can expect from your system. Human error, especially with data entry, is inevitable. Accept that you will still need some human intervention and error checking procedures.

Change doesn't happen overnight and efficiencies that require a change in how clients interact with your department may take years rather than months. Just because you build a self-service system doesn't mean clients will default to using it. Successful implementations of self service options such as a online knowledge base, service catalog, FAQ systems, etc. usually require promotion and are often adopted first by incoming students and new hires. It may take years (or graduation) to change behavior of existing staff and students.

Don't fight battles you can't win. Keep in mind your peers will spend time on tasks valued by clients and supervisors. If certain features of your system are under utilized or procedures are not followed, it's usually a clue that staff doesn't see them as a high priority compared with other responsibilities. If you can't explain how the system benefits day-to-day work or benefits the overall mission of your department, maybe you need to rethink how you use your system. Otherwise, work with management to ensure you have the training, regular communication, accountability, and feedback mechanisms in place to get and keep IT staff on board.

4.5 Grass is Greener

One of the most common complaints about Help Desk software comes from people who have used a different system either elsewhere or at the institution in a different context. The perception is that the aforementioned issues with the software could be solved through implementation of another product, or even a homegrown solution rather than evaluating the processes and procedures within the organization. At L&C we went from a homegrown to a pre-packaged solution, and experienced many of the same issues with the latter that we had with the former. As discussed, many of our issues relate to areas where L&C organizational values create "mismatch" situations with more traditional Help Desk software implementation recommendations.

If you are in this situation, look below the surface when considering a switch or discussing experiences with others. How much do you have in common with the organization using a 'better' product? When you find areas where you match up well, then it's time to look at revamping your current practices or moving in a different direction.

4.6 Inadequate and Inflexible Reporting

Getting data in to a ticketing system is important for individual reference, but to discern overall trends and goal achievements, reporting needs to be a part of the system. Evaluating a reporting module prior to purchasing and implementing software should be a high priority. Often the reports that come pre-packaged with software are inadequate to the individual needs of the department, and generating personalized reports requires specialized additional software, such as Crystal Reports. According to a white paper about Help Desk ROI from SMA Management Systems[6], the most common reports that are pre-built into Help Desk software systems include:

- How many calls have I received this week, month, year?
- How many open tickets do I have that are open for more than "x" hours, days, or weeks?
- What are the most typical types of issues and how long does it take to resolve them?
- How many issues are assigned to particular support technicians?
- Am I meeting my service commitments (SLA's)?

Many of the complexities of the higher education support environment described in Section 4.3, make these types of canned reports not terribly valuable to many higher education institutions. Often qualitative rather than quantitative measures are considered a more important indicator of success. When planning for reports, focus on capturing what's important to your institution and plan to spend time determining the best way to capture and report this information. Even if you are a smaller institution that does not rely on SLAs, regularly reviewing reports on common call types will help you discover patterns and can be invaluable for guiding automation efforts.

Don't discount the importance regular review of reports can have on ensuring your system is used consistently. Updating tickets takes time, and for many technical staff, taking time away from solving a problem to document seems counterproductive. The type and frequency of reports viewed by management has a significant impact on how staff will prioritize using the system. If management never mentions reports or discusses Help Desk metrics in staff meetings or performance evaluations, using the Help Desk system will become a low priority as staff realize they are more likely to be rewarded or punished for how they perform on other tasks. This creates a situation where there is little incentive for technicians to quickly close and catalog tickets. It is also be tempting to enter no or a very concise resolution

If this sounds like the culture at your college, then it's probably best to accept that most tickets won't be updated regularly and trust that close working relationships between colleagues will ensure client needs are met most of the time. The occasional poor customer experience due to a Help Desk system break down may be reasonable given the overall time saved on entering regular ticket updates that are never viewed or accessed.

5. CONCLUSION

After 10 years of experience with our Help Desk software at L&C, we have realized that the source of many of our frustrations are due to issues that are independent of a particular software package's feature set. No matter the solution, it is by focusing on what our department and greater community view as critical and useful functions in Help Desk software that will determine success or failure. This focus on our needs has let us let go of frustrations that result from "failures" that are really attempts to implement features that don't make sense for us. This has also allowed us to hone in on improvements we can make to improve how our system is used in practice rather than how it could be used if we had infinite time and resources.

As you start to search for a new system, look to retool and improve your current system, or vent your frustrations at the water cooler, we encourage you to take a step back from the software and consider the following first:

- What care and feeding do you give your current system? If you don't periodically re-evaluate and update, and revamp goals and expectations, they will get outdated.
- What level of automation makes sense at your institution?
- How do you measure return on investment?
- What data will help you effectively focus your planning efforts? How will you gather that information?
- Who are your customers? How do they like to communicate with you? How has it changed in the last year? Five years?
- How important are Help Desk tickets and Help Desk metrics to your management team?

6. REFERENCES

[1] http://www.numarasoftware.com/track-it/help-desk/

[2] http://www.thinkhdi.com/

[3] Schein, Edgar H. 2010. *Organizational culture and leadership*. San Francisco: Jossey-Bass. http://public.eblib.com/EBLPublic/PublicView.do?ptiID=588878

[4] Bergquist, W. H., and K. Pawlak. Engaging the Six Cultures of the Academy: Revised and Expanded Edition of the Four Cultures of the Academy. Jossey-Bass Inc Pub, 2008.

[5] http://www.numarasoftware.com/resources/track-it/brochures/track-it-helpdesk.pdf

[6] SMA Management Systems, inc, "Help Desk ROI: Improving the Return on Your Help Desk Investment", January 2002.

Modern Version Control: Creating an Efficient Development Ecosystem

Nic Bertino
Santa Clara Law Webmaster
500 El Camino Real
Santa Clara, CA 95050
1 (408) 551-3000 Ext 6137

nbertino@scu.edu

ABSTRACT

In 2011, Santa Clara University School of Law Technology and Academic Computing (LTAC) identified that its version control system could greatly benefit from the use of modern source control management software. Source code for high value projects such as the Santa Clara Law website, were previously held in a Subversion (SVN) repository in a client-server model, providing version control and redundancy. Because of the resource footprint associated with SVN, only projects with high importance could be setup with version control. As more web-based applications were introduced, the need for a more efficient revision control system arose.

Git, a highly efficient decentralized version control system (DVCS), was selected after evaluating similar technologies. This change transformed the entire development process, making the development cycle more streamlined and with greater flexibility. In the early use of Git, LTAC also discovered its use as a deployment tool, increasing redundancy on servers and reducing overhead usually associated with revision control. It also serves as the vital link between LTAC's issue tracking system, Redmine, and the development team. The introduction of Redmine has helped LTAC monitor website issues, manage projects, and continually review changes to the code base.

LTAC has created a development ecosystem that provides redundancy and accountability using open source products that carry no cost. Git has significant performance gains over SVN, making its integration and use less frustrating and distracting for developers. Redmine gives developers and customers the opportunity to organize, track, and resolve issues. The flexibility of the technology used means that any project, from a content management system to a one-off script, can benefit from source control without large costs or long deployment times.

Categories and Subject Descriptors

D.2.7 [Software Engineering]: Distribution, Maintenance, and Enhancement – *Version control*

I.7.1 [Document and Text Processing]: Document and Text Editing – *Version control*

General Terms

Management

Keywords

Git, Redmine, Issue Tracking, Source Control, Decentralized Version Control, Automated Deployment

1. INTRODUCTION

The Santa Clara University Law School' Law Technology and Academic Computing (LTAC) department supports Law faculty, staff, and students through a variety of means. One area of responsibility is the deployment of web applications and appliances, with the main Law website being the high value application that serves as Santa Clara Law's front-facing identity on the internet.

Deployed applications often require customization or modification of source code. These enhancements may introduce issues, and source control management allows the development team to quickly locate changes to the source that may have introduced the bug. In other uses, a new developer working on an application may need to become familiar with the development history. This change history is crucial to quickly understanding the life of an application.

The "safety net" that source control management software provides should not impede on the workflow of the developer; it should also allow anyone working on the code to quickly acquire, view, and contribute to its history. LTAC's legacy SVN system served as a source control management solution, but its centralized nature and sheer size made it a candidate for replacement. In moving to Git, LTAC realized workflow efficiency improvements coupled with fewer systems resources.

It should be noted that version control is not a replacement for backup systems. It is best used as in addition to disaster recovery initiatives. Version control should not be used on non-project or system files under any circumstances. Backups of these files should be made using rsync or similar.

2. REVISION CONTROL CONCEPTS

Revision control operates on the premise that files are watched for changes. These changes are stored in a repository. Exact changes, additions, and subtractions (deltas) are captured and stored in the repository, documenting the history of the project. Multiple file modifications are grouped by commits, which are generally associated with a bug or feature. In team situations with two or more developers working on the same code, revision control can become a powerful tool by assisting with the merging of two persons' work. Developers can branch off of working states of the code and easily merge their changes if successful or delete them if needed.

Similar to a ghost image of a computer or a snapshot for a virtual machine, revision control allows a developer the ability to restore a file or group of files to a previous state easily. This redundancy allows developers to experiment with code and easily revert to a working state in the event that their code creates more issues.

2.1 Centralized Version Control

Centralized version control focuses on a client-server approach to revisions. All actions are generally performed against the server, meaning a checkout, check-in, or history review would be downloaded from a server hosting the repository. This approach, used by SVN and CVS, taxes network resources, along with creating a major point of failure in the event that there is an issue with the central server.

2.2 Decentralized Version Control Systems

DVCS operate on the principle that all developers have a full and complete local copy of the repository, and changes are transmitted via incremental patches. This methodology creates natural redundancy, as every person that clones the repository has full access to the project files and their history. Version control operations, such as commits, viewing file history or differences, are significantly faster as the repository is kept locally.

DVCS methodology isn't just for programmers; Apple OSX Lion introduced Versions[1], which automatically creates and stores snapshots of files as a user is working. The need for version control originated from software development, but the fundamental benefits can be used by anyone creating and modifying files on a computer system.

2.3 SCM Evolution

Currently, many free and proprietary options exist for version control. Local-only options such as Source Code Control System (SCCS)[2] and its successor Revision Control System (RCS)[3] were the first distributions of source code management software. Concurrent Versions System (CVS) was introduced in 1990[4] as the first client-server technology, allowing developers to collaborate on common source code by checking out a codebase, making changes, and checking the changes back in.

SVN was created in 2000[5] as another client-server application with the intent of drastically improving upon CVS. In the proprietary realm, BitKeeper[6] was launched in 1998 as a distributed version control software (DVCS) marketed toward medium and large businesses.

In 2002, BitKeeper was controversially selected for the development of the Linux kernel[7]. Due to issues with the licensing model of BitKeeper[8], Git was created in 2005 to provide an open source, distributed option for work on the Linux kernel. Two other open source applications also emerged that year, with Mercurial and Bazaar seeing initial releases.

3. CONVERSION TO GIT AND DVCS

The qualification of a new source control management tool consisted of an evaluation of the available DVCS programs. LTAC elected Git for its widespread use, update cycle, documentation, ease of use, and flexibility. Git is used by many high profile open source projects, including the Linux kernel, Ruby on Rails, Perl, and Android. Resources for the conversion from SVN to Git were also abundant. The objective of the transition was to migrate the Santa Clara Law website, and to specifically reduce the repository size and integrate production, development, and staging servers into the DVCS environment.

3.1 Planning

Planning the conversion to Git required careful consideration of the migration of previous data, setting up a branching model, and managing repository permissions. Due to the centralized nature of

SVN, migrating the existing revision history proved difficult. Ultimately, it was decided that the last stable version would be checked in as the "master" branch. The legacy SVN codebase would remain in place for additional reference as needed.

LTAC designed a branching model that worked off of the master branch. Each server in the environment had its own branch; the production server had a "prod" branch, development had "dev", and the local "alpha" environments had local branches. The servers would sync only with their branch, meaning a change made on the developer's workstation could be merged with the development branch and synced to the server for testing prior to a rollout to production. Changes to the website were now handled by Git without the use of FTP (see Figure 1).

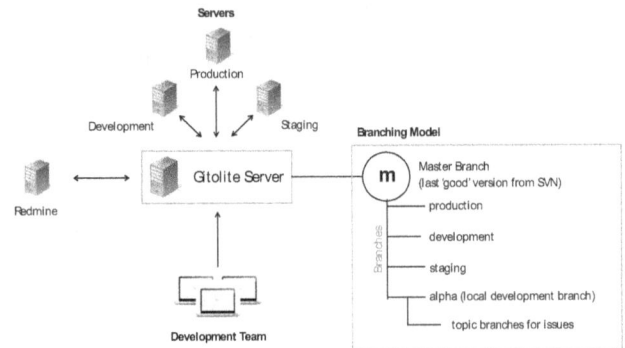

Figure 1 Branch model and deployment planning

The "trunk" from SVN was exported into Git, and had an initial size of 4.06 gigabytes (GB). Ignoring non-codebase related files, particularly binary files, such as MP3, PDF, and FLV files that had been generated by users, reduced the repository size significantly. After finalizing the files that should not be indexed by version control, the repository size was 334 megabytes (MB). With only the most critical code files and all user-generated files ignored, the repository size was further reduced to 9.8 megabytes (MB) (see Figure 2).

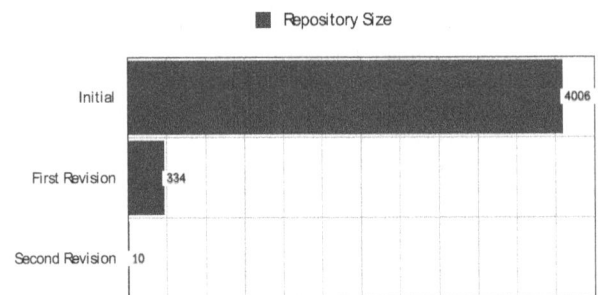

Figure 2 Repository size in megabytes after adjustments to Git ignore file.

3.2 Performance Gains

The smaller repository size resulted in faster implementation and deployment of the website. Setting up a clone of the development server now just required using Git to synchronize the "dev" branch. The total size of the SVN server at the time of retirement was approximately 14 gigabytes (GB); as of writing, the remote Git server is 409 megabytes (MB). Reliance on the local network is also minimized.

The nature of the application also allowed further performance gains with regards to version control. Because LTAC uses a content management system that publishes static pages daily, those published files did not need to be indexed. Instead, a "hook" was created that published the files when the repository was first cloned to the server or workstation. Redundancy on those files is handled by a database, so tracking revisions proved to be superfluous.

A perceived disadvantage to distributed systems is repository size on the initial clone of the repository. Because the entire commit history is copied, the repository size can grow quickly and eventually eclipse the size of the working directory. Taking actions early to eliminate files that do not need to be tracked or utilizing submodules can reduce the overhead of the repository. Some application frameworks, such as Ruby on Rails, have premade ignore files that automatically disregard unnecessary files from the Git repository.

3.3 Access Control Using Gitolite

While the setup of remote repositories is trivial, there is no inherent access control to restrict groups or teams from accessing or committing to those repositories. To secure and manage LTAC's repositories, the open source software Gitolite was elected. Gitolite uses SSH and scripts to securely manage access to repositories. Combined with CentOS, a fully secured remote repository was deployed.

The remote repository serves as a router for code changes, and a finalization of a patch or bug fix. Code changes should be tested on the developer's local machine before pushing to the remote repository; doing so keeps experimental or non-tested code from entering the permanent project history. Once code is pushed to the remote repository, amending or changing it can cause issues for servers and team members.

Because interactions with Gitolite are done through SSH, an intimate understanding of the technology is necessary. Authentication is handled through the use of public keys, which are a pair of unique files. One file resides on the developer's machine, while the other is transmitted to the Gitolite server. Developers and servers that interact with Gitolite need to generate these keys in order to access remote repositories. LTAC has identified public keys as a much more secure method of access than password-based authentication, so while there may be an initial learning curve with SSH and public keys, the security of this method definitely warrants the time it may take to learn the protocol.

3.4 Git as a Web Deployment Tool

The automation of branch synchronization has made Git a web deployment tool. Using shell scripts called on repository events such as new commits, servers are synchronized with the latest commits automatically, with the exception of the production server. Due to the sensitivity of automatically pushing new code in a production environment, synchronization on the production server is handled manually. The flexibility of Git allows multiple approaches to web deployment.

Gitolite acts on new code and triggers actions accordingly. Using very simple scripts and SSH, servers are updated and relevant participants are notified of changes via email. Other external services that use the source history are updated with the new changes as well. These triggers, known as hooks, can be executed from any copy of the repository.

3.5 Revisions and Lessons Learned

Because Git was developed for Linux, the integration for Windows/Windows Server is not as seamless as it is on Linux/UNIX based systems. A BASH command line emulator is used, creating a more setup steps for automation and some performance loss. Windows Server is being phased out of LTAC's server environment, so these hurdles will be lessened in the future.

The Git ignore file was revised multiple times as unnecessary files were identified. Tracking only the most critical development files and providing a build step or submodule is the key to keeping repository sizes low and deployment times fast. Transactions against the repository, both remote and local, benefit from lower overhead as well. For instance, Git scans each file in the working directory for changes. If the working directory has tens of thousands of files, this operation can be delayed significantly, even with modern technology such as solid state disks.

Initially, a nightly automated commit was in place to take periodic snapshots of LTAC's content management system. After approximately six months of deployment, the development history was inundated with daily commits that did not provide additional redundancy. Furthermore, attempts to consolidate the commits and tidy up the development history created more issues. Once commits are pushed to the remote server, they cannot be modified without consequences for the development team. This practice was discontinued after six months of deployment.

4. ECOSYSTEM ENHANCEMENT

With Git in place, LTAC analyzed the overall process of handling issues that required codebase changes. These issues would often originate from users, who would experience a bug or need functionality added, and email these issues to the Webmaster. The Webmaster would then create a fix, commit it to the codebase, and push it to the live server, followed by an email to the user informing them that the issue had been addressed. As more issues were submitted, the need for tracking software specifically for bugs and issues was realized.

4.1 Issue Tracking Software

Issue tracking software allows developers, managers, and users to create, fix, and monitor software. Much like ticket systems for help desks, issue trackers allow management, accountability, and detailed history of interactions. With issue tracking software, requests are reported to a central location where all interested stakeholders can easily manage them with detailed information about progress. A user of the software can submit an issue and follow its progress. A developer can easily see all of the issues that are assigned to them. Managers can see the workload or time spent by their staff on issues related to the software, along with the ability to change priority of issues.

4.2 Redmine Deployment

After a careful review process, the open source software Redmine was selected for issue management. Redmine is an open source Ruby on Rails-based web application with comprehensive version control integration and extensibility via plugins. Native support for LDAP authentication was another key consideration when selecting Redmine. A turnkey image of Redmine is also available, making deployment into LTAC's virtual environment simple.

After electing Redmine, LTAC was able to offer enterprise-level issue tracking. Because of Redmine's strong integration with version control, issues were now associated with commits, allowing developers to close issues without ever logging in to Redmine. Email notifications are another feature of the software, allowing all involved parties to stay informed during the life of the ticket.

4.3 The Life of an Issue

With Redmine deployed and configured with internal email services, LTAC had the opportunity to revisit the issue creation process. Redmine has the ability to create issues by email; to take advantage of this feature, the Law website's error logging object was modified to submit errors to Redmine via email and create a new ticket. Before, these emails would be emailed directly to the Webmaster, who would have to create a new issue manually. With the issue tracker in place, the Webmaster receives an email that from Redmine indicating that a new issue was created.

Users can also email issues directly to the issue tracking software to take advantage of the automatic issue creation. Once their issue is created, the developer can address the issue by creating a hotfix on their local machine. These changes are tested thoroughly on the local machine before being committed with a reference to the ticket such as "Fixes #34" to the remote repository. Gitolite, recognizing a new commit, synchronizes its development history with Redmine by issuing a command over SSH. Redmine then reads the repository history and scans for certain keywords such as "fixes" or "references" and associates those commits with their parent issues. In the case of the commit having the "fixes" keyword, the issue is closed automatically and an email is dispatched to the user and developer.

Because the code revision is associated with the issue, Redmine complements the version control system by providing context, and if needed, extensive documentation of the problem. The exact changes, including the precise deltas of each file modified, exist forever with the issue. If the change causes a new bug or issue, the code can be referenced quickly and refactored.

5. MOVING FORWARD

5.1 Project Management with Redmine

In addition to its ability to track issues, Redmine also contains extensive project management tools to assist with the lifecycle of projects. In pre-project development, tasks can be setup with timelines that can be easily visualized in the form of a calendar or Gantt chart. Versions and milestone releases can also be used for products or deployments that adhere to strict lifecycle expectations. Time entry is also available to monitor cost and investment.

Redmine also has collaborative features, like a wiki and file uploads. As a front-facing application, the publication of issues and documentation in the form of a wiki can help users self-serve if they are experiencing an issue that has been documented previously. Redmine also offers granular control over access to its modules; internal tickets and features can require explicit access rights, restricting public access.

5.2 Use of Git on Open Source Projects

Git has proved to be extremely useful in the customization of open source projects. Traditionally, customizations to core elements in open source projects have caused issues with future upgrades. With version control, the effects of customization on the ability to upgrade in the future can be significantly lowered. For example, the blogging platform WordPress can be setup and deployed as an unmodified installation. By committing this untouched and working base to the repository, the plain state of the install is preserved. Customizations can then be made on branches of the working installation. In the event of an upgrade, the project can be temporarily reverted to its original state and the upgrade or patch applied. The customizations can then be merged on top of the upgraded base and tested for issues. Should the customizations create issues with the upgrade, "line by line" merges can be made to quickly identify the offending code.

6. ACKNOWLEDGMENTS

The author sends his thanks to Ed Mananquil, Systems Administrator at Santa Clara Law, for his wisdom and assistance in realizing this project.

7. REFERENCES

[1] APPLE, INC. 2012. Apple - Auto Save and Versions - Every edit and rewrite. Saved.
http://www.apple.com/macosx/whats-new/auto-save.html

[2] berliOS. 2012. SCCS - The POSIX standard Source Code Control System.
http://sccs.berlios.de/

[3] GNU. 2012. GNU RCS - GNU Project - Free Software Foundation (FSF).
http://www.gnu.org/software/rcs/

[4] GNU. 1995. CCVS Revision Log
http://cvs.savannah.gnu.org/viewvc/ccvs/NEWS?revision=1.1&root=cvs&view=markup

[5] Collins-Sussman, Ben; Brian W. Fitzpatrick; C. Michael Pilato. 2011. *Version Control with Subversion (for Subversion 1.7)*.
http://svnbook.red-bean.com/en/1.7/svn.intro.whatis.html#svn.intro.history

[6] LKML. 1998. LKML: (Larry McVoy): A solution for growing pains.
https://lkml.org/lkml/1998/9/30/122

[7] Jeremy Andrews. 2005. Feature: No More Free BitKeeper.
http://kerneltrap.org/node/4966

[8] Linus Torvalds. 2005. 'Re: Kernel SCM saga..' – MARC
http://marc.info/?l=linux-kernel&m=111288700902396

We're Going Google! Making the Most of Marketing

Julio G. Appling
Lewis & Clark College
Portland, OR
(503) 768-7221
jappling@lclark.edu

ABSTRACT

In the 2011-2012 academic year, Lewis & Clark College migrated its email system to Google Apps for Education. To support this project, a Marketing and Branding Committee planned how to best keep our community informed and updated before and during the migration period. This project brought new opportunities to forge relationships with our users over the short and long term, as they relied heavily on the IT department for support during the transition. Integrating our marketing with our existing services improved attendance in our training and information sessions, and provided a key point of contact with our users in both providing project updates and receiving feedback

This paper explores the challenges of marketing and branding our campus email migration to Google Apps for Education, which included publicizing large-scale changes, reaching traditionally non-responsive groups such as students and adjunct faculty, and coordinating marketing on multiple campuses. Benefits that come with a strong, integrated marketing campaign will be addressed as well, which include leveraging the increased face time to build and maintain a social media presence and using the excitement of new products and services to bolster existing services and programs.

Categories and Subject Descriptors

K.6.1 [**Management of Computing and Information Systems**] Project and People Management

General Terms

Management, Documentation, Human Factors

Keywords

Google, Apps, Branding, Marketing, Training, Support, Social Media, Collaboration, Transition, Client Services

1. INTRODUCTION

Small liberal-arts colleges rely upon face-to-face interactions not only within classrooms, but also develop a face-to-face culture within staff and administrative interactions. In Lewis & Clark Information Technology we leveraged face time during the transition to Google Apps, but in reasonable and efficient ways given staff numbers and hours.

Focused and clear communication in conjunction with accessible, on-demand resources allowed our relatively small numbers (four IT Client Services consultants and twenty-one total IT staff) to reach our large and widespread community.

2. GOOGLE PROJECT SCOPE

2.1 Project timeline overview

The Google Migration Project for Lewis and Clark College included five phases. Phase I began in June of 2011 as IT began initial planning and preparation for the Google Project. This phase concluded with the initial "Going Google" announcement which went out to the Lewis & Clark on November 4th, 2011.

Phase II of the transition, began with the launching of the Google Information page which contained detailed project information, Google Apps helpsheets, the training calendar, and eventually the account migration page. Phase II also included a pilot period where accounts within the IT department were migrated, followed by the migration of a small pilot group of users.

Phase III marked the beginning of the fourteen-week open mail migration period lasting from January 9th, 2012 through May 7th, 2012. To complete mail migration, users navigated the Lewis and Clark migration page, entered their username and password, and opted to either click & drag their email from the old server (Webmail) to the new server (LCmail) using a desktop client, or migrate mail automatically. This process could take anywhere from ten minutes to twenty-four hours depending on the amount of mail to be migrated. Users who did not migrate by the May 7th deadline would have account passwords reset and their mail auto-migrated to LCmail.

Following completion of the open mail migration period, Phase IV transitioned our Meeting Maker calendar users to LCcalendar powered by Google. This single-day transition occurred on May 22nd. IT is currently in Phase V of the Google Migration Project which involves the migration of hosted faculty, staff, and organization websites.

2.2 Committees

For the initial phases, the Google Project team consisted of three committees—Marketing, Training, and Technical—with smaller individual teams for Google Calendar, Google Sites, and an overall Project Meeting for committee chairs. Each of our four IT Consultants chaired a Google Subcommittee and sat on the other committees as well. While this may have led to some cluttered schedules, it ensured that our primary client support staff remained up-to-date on most aspects of the project. For the later phases of the Google Migration project (after mail and calendar migration) we condensed individual committee meetings to a single meeting with all committee members present and others present as deemed necessary.

The purpose of the Google Marketing Committee was to keep the campus informed of the Google Migration process and important milestones along the way. Sitting on the marketing committee were the project lead, the director of IT Client Services, the Google Training Committee lead, a Graduate school staff representative, a Law School IT representative, and two additional members of IT who specialized in graphic design. Meetings were bi-monthly through the Gmail transition, moving to monthly during the Calendar transition, and merging with Training and project meetings following the Calendar migration.

3. MARKETING GOOGLE

3.1 Branding Google

One of the first steps recommended by Google when setting up the Google Apps for Education is establishing customized branding. While Google has strict guidelines in regarding the use of its logo, Google encourages Business and Organizations to establish unique branding for Google Apps within the organization. The marketing committee decided on "LCmail," and adapted the "LC" branding to other services in the apps suite (LCapps, LCcalendar, etc.).

Integrating the branding consistently proved to be a challenge. Many users already familiar with the Google Apps Suite—IT staff included—often found it difficult to consistently use the organization-specific branding in publications and conversation. Immediately following the announcement that Lewis & Clark was "Going Google," it was difficult to make "LCmail" initially stick. By Google's suggestion, most mentions of our LC-branded Google Apps would be immediately followed by "Powered by Google" to avoid confusion.

The branding issue largely worked itself out with the official launch of the mail migration period. The email landing page "lcmail.lclark.edu" helped establish the familiarity of our domain-specific branding. Additionally, the LCmail identifier distinguished users' institutional Gmail account from their personal Gmail account. In retrospect, coinciding the branding launch with the beginning of the open migration period may have alleviated some confusion.

3.2 Google Ambassadors

Rather than initially pushing for the *entire* campus to migrate at once, IT enlisted the help of a control group of users to migrate early and provide feedback before the general campus migration began. These "Google Ambassadors," comprised mainly of departmental secretaries and resident assistants, served as the initial pilot group for the new Google new services as well as our training workshops and handouts. IT required Google Ambassadors to provide early feedback that we then used to polish and revise our documentation in preparation for the open migration period.

Google Ambassadors were not only essential as a pilot group for Google services, but also as support satellites during the open migration period. Google Ambassadors were encouraged to be available to their colleagues as an information resource. Throughout the Google Project, our outreach method for the campus followed a general pattern:

1. Establish talking points within the Google Project Committee.
2. Share talking points within IT Department as a whole.
3. Share talking points with Google Ambassadors.

While general Google information was made available to the entire campus via our IT Google Information page, users often lacked the time and/or patience to sift through our information resources—hence the term "TLDR" or "Too Long, Didn't Read." To be prepared for user questions, all members of IT staff were provided with general talking points regarding the transition, as well as information on how and where to seek help. This information was also provided to Google Ambassadors. Such a system reduced the support load on IT, and could be scalable to larger institutions.

3.3 Social Media Integration

Even with Google Ambassadors acting as satellites to the campus, other avenues were necessary to publicize Google updates. During this transition, our IT department launched pages on both Facebook and Twitter. To do both successfully required integration with our existing services. We placed Facebook and Twitter buttons on our IT and Google home pages, included the addresses in our official documentation, and encouraged users to follow us on Twitter and Facebook for up-to-date information at the opening and closing of our training sessions.

The Fall 2011 announcement of the impending Google migration coincided with our social media launch and as of June, 2012 Lewis & Clark Information Technology has 43 Facebook likes and 22 Twitter followers. Members of our Marketing and Communications department followed on Twitter, while several administrative assistants were among our Facebook "likes." These individuals responded well to our updates, frequently registering for sessions or passing along news to others who may have asked them. While the numbers were few, reaching these individuals regularly is an important enough goal that we continued to dedicate our time toward publicizing through social media.

To both strengthen our social media presence and create additional technology training opportunities, we integrated our social media outlets into our professional development bootcamps. We publicized the hashtag #SDD2012 for our winter Staff Development Days. At the recent spring Faculty Technology Institute, a monitor in the primary meeting room displayed a feed of Tweets which included the hashtag #2012FTI. We individually reached out to those already using social media to make generous use of the hashtag, and this activity encouraged others "on the fence" about Twitter—as well as Twitter "lurkers"—to get involved.

The Faculty Technology Institute also included a Social Media Quest activity, in which participants completed seven Social Media-related activities over the course of the three-day event. These included sharing a tech-related link on Twitter, sharing a link on Google+ (included in the Google Apps for education Suite), liking IT on Facebook, Following IT on Twitter, and commenting on our iPads in Education blog. While participation was sparse—we had only a few participants complete the activity—those who completed continue to follow us via social media and receive our updates.

3.4 Google SWAG

Google provides a generous amount of promotional materials to help promote the transition to Google Apps. The items included 8.5x11 and 11x17 signs, a small banner, index cards with pre-printed Google tips, t-shirts (all perplexingly medium-sized), bookmarks, stickers, and pin-on buttons. Most of these items included the message "We're Going Google," though other messages included:

- "_____ has gone Google."

- Leave a project file at home? Chill. We're going Google."
- [Insert happy trumpet sound], we're going Google.

While initially unsure of how to leverage the posters, an open space between the text and the brand at the bottom left room to print a more institution-specific message.

Our-custom bookmark-sized printouts were the most effective handout. These bookmarks included the web address of our Lewis & Clark Google information and account migration page (go.lclark.edu/google) on one side, and selected frequently-asked questions on the opposite side. We provided stacks of these to our Helpdesk and front desk to distribute to visitors, but also made them available to administrative assistants and others who wished to distribute within departments.

While faculty and staff were less interested in "Google Swag," the giveaways proved popular at Google information tables, which were also the most effective way to reach students. On two occasions—once in the first week of the migration period and once in the penultimate week—IT set up Google information tables outside the main cafeteria and in the library lobby to directly reach students. Students who migrated were encouraged to take an item of their choice from the table, while students who had not migrated were given a bookmark with the account migration page address.

4. RECEPTION
4.1 "TLDR"
Spreading the word "Google" around the campus is easy. Disseminating correct and accurate information on the transition is more difficult. IT regularly received questions that had been addressed explicitly in our documentation as well as within our FAQ. While some users appreciate detailed documentation, it invites the possibility of TLDR, which contributes to the spread of misinformation if users rely on word-of-mouth only rather than IT news and announcements.

To alleviate this phenomenon, IT staff and Google Ambassadors were encouraged to provide some brief answers to user questions, but ultimately direct users to our online information resources. This not only encouraged our users to leverage existing resources, but created continued opportunities for us to receive feedback from our end-users regarding the quality and clarity of our documentation.

4.2 Squeaky wheels
Inevitably, errors happen. For various reasons, the migration process was less smooth for some users than others. Users were typically patient with minor hiccups in the process, but some users who were unhappy either with the migration process or Google services (or both) were more vocal about their dissatisfaction than those who experienced a smooth transition. These "squeaky wheels" often played a role in reinforcing misconceptions about the migration process with other users who had yet to migrate, amplifying existing anxieties.

Most common myths regarding the migration process involved "losing mail" or "having no email for days," but the source of this had less to do with the user experience, and more to do with users hesitant to begin the process on their own without assistance. In response, IT provided a face-to-face Migration Assistance request form, finding that many users were more willing to migrate provided that they would not feel responsible for possible errors

or pitfalls in the process. A rotation of six IT staff members responded to Migration Assistance requests, completing them on-site with the users. Users appreciated this individualized attention, and it created an additional opportunity to get project feedback.

While not originally conceived as a method of addressing user complaints, our bi-weekly Google Mornings were also an effective means for hearing and responding to user questions and concerns. Originally aimed internally at IT staff and eventually our Google Ambassadors, Google Mornings were informal, one-hour information sessions where IT presented specific Google-related topics such as email management, mobile device programming, and overviews of Google Calendar and Groups. These sessions rotated between our Graduate, Law, and Undergraduate campuses, and allowed more time for open questions regarding both the topic as well as the Google Migration process. The sessions were not hands on, and included light breakfast (coffee, fruit, doughnuts) for those in attendance.

4.3 By the numbers
While we did not always have direct quotes and testimonials, we did have numbers and statistics. The open migration period saw the highest numbers of users make the switch to Google in its first and final weeks. Predictably, the highest frequency of migrations took place in the final few days of the migration period, while migration seemed to slow during the middle of the period from late-February to early-March. Generally, users were either eagerly anticipating the transition, and migrated early, or putting off (or dreading) the switch and migrated late.

Internally, migration numbers provided a measurable sense of progression during the process. Reporting numbers at the outset of marketing and training committee meetings became commonplace, serving as a point of departure for planning. Additionally, these numbers served as a regular morale boost which served as a continuing reminder to our staff that we were, indeed, making process with a this rather large-scale transition ("We had 21 migrations yesterday!").

To our end-users, the migration numbers were a way of demonstrating both the continuing progress of our migration, and for those holding out until the last possible minute to begin account migration, the inevitability of the transition. Important milestones, such as the 500th, 1000th, and 2000th individuals to migrate would be publicly acknowledged through Facebook and Twitter.

4.4 Misconceptions
A question that came up *less* than we expected was the nature of the Google privacy agreement. During February of the mail migration phase of our Google Project, Google made a highly-publicized change to their privacy agreement. This announcement set off alarm-bells for some of our faculty and staff concerned about the ownership of the information being handled on Google's servers. Outside of a few incidents where grumblings about Google privacy surfaced during grumblings about the migration process in general, concerns about Google privacy were relatively uncommon. Whether this is due to general faculty understanding of the privacy agreement, or perhaps a larger social trend of desensitization to privacy concerns, was unclear.

Another common misconception of the Google Transition was that IT intended to "replace" our supported desktop email client Mozilla Thunderbird with Gmail. While correcting this misconception took a few moments, this misconception alerted our training and support staff to the larger issue of a general lack of understanding by our users regarding the email servers. To correct this misconception, we released news items via our website informing our users that Thunderbird could still be used with Gmail, and demonstrated that Thunderbird users could *also* check their mail using the web client when they were away from their primary computer.

Most students believed that Google migration was either optional or would happen automatically. This information came in through email inquiries, but primarily through interactions with students at Google Information Tables. To address this misconception, IT generated targeted emails to all users forwarding their email which contained specific instructions on how to remove forwarding, migrate accounts, and re-enable forwarding within LCmail. While mostly students using their personal email fell into this group, it also included a large number of adjunct and overseas faculty members.

4.5 Outreach Challenges

Individuals not present on campus presented the greatest challenge for outreach. These included emeriti faculty, overseas students and faculty, and faculty on sabbatical. Emeriti faculty and faculty on sabbatical were most likely to take advantage of migration assistance requests, which would typically be resolved over the phone. Detailed instructions would be provided for overseas users, and those who had difficulty with this process could be migrated by IT, though this involved a password reset.

Among active users, those forwarding their email to a personal address had the lowest numbers for conversion. Graduate students and adjuncts made up a large portion of this group, with their migration percentage lying below 20% by the conclusion of the open migration period. In retrospect, a combination of early outreach to these groups, tangible flyers in campus locations, and increased face-to-face outreach may have been more effective means of outreach to these groups.

5. CONCLUSION

Beyond face-time, the most important interactions with our users were those that not only answered a question, but also provided an opportunity for instruction and generated feedback to our support staff. While some information delivered via Social Media included links and general tips, the most effective messages advertised the availability of IT for assistance either through on-site migration assistance or through training workshops. In most cases, the mere knowledge that *someone* was available and willing to help with assistance made the difference between a positive and negative migration experience.

6. ACKNOWLEDGMENTS

My thanks to the incredibly hard-working Lewis & Clark Google Project Team, IT Staff, and Google Ambassadors who helped make for a successful Google Migration on our campus.

7. REFERENCE

[1] "Google Logo and landing page policies" http://support.google.com/a/bin/answer.py?hl=en&answer=36726.

Fine Tuning Online Faculty Development Workshops

Kathryn Fletcher
West Virginia University
Office of Information Technology
Application Support and Training, PO Box 6501
Morgantown, WV 26506-6501
(304) 293-8769
kathy.fletcher@mail.wvu.edu

ABSTRACT

At West Virginia University (WVU), the Office of Information Technology and the Instructional Technology Resource Center (ITRC) have been teaching a variety of online faculty development workshops since the spring of 2008. We currently use Blackboard Vista and Wimba Classroom as our platforms to deliver self-paced workshops and synchronous live webinars. This paper summarizes refinements we have made over the past four years based on lessons learned while developing our current program. Issues include managing enrollment and providing follow-up support in addition to workshop design and delivery. Future challenges face our online workshop development efforts as WVU prepares to migrate to Blackboard Learn 9 and Blackboard Collaborate products over the next two years.

Categories and Subject Descriptors

K.3.1 [**Computers and Education**]: Computer Uses in Education – *Computer-assisted Instruction, Distance Learning.*

K.6.1 [**Management of Computing and Information Systems**]: Project and People Management – *Training.*

General Terms

Documentation, Experimentation, Human Factors.

Keywords

online course development, e-learning, faculty development, Blackboard Learn 9, Blackboard Vista, Wimba Classroom.

1. INTRODUCTION

In the spring of 2010, I developed a large online workshop, *WVU eCampus: from Soup to Nuts*, and wrote about my instructional design and online teaching experiences for the annual ACM SIGUCCS Fall User Services Conference [2]. This paper will describe some of the advantages and disadvantages of using this model along with my future plans for this workshop as we prepare to upgrade to Blackboard Learn 9.

One of my concerns as I finished my first semester with the *Soup to Nuts* online workshop was faculty enrollment and participation in online workshops. I will summarize data gleaned from tracking data for all of our online faculty development sessions to see if there are any patterns to predict faculty participation.

In the spring of 2012, I developed two new online workshops for the faculty development program on Wimba Classroom and Turnitin, topics related to our course management system since we have PowerLinks from Blackboard Vista to those products. I will discuss how I applied what I learned from my first online workshop when creating these two new offerings.

I have attended most of the face to face faculty development workshops offered by our Instructional Technology Resource Center and have reviewed the online sessions they have offered. I will discuss refinements made by the other faculty development trainers to their online workshops.

1.1 About West Virginia University and OIT

West Virginia University is the state's public land-grant institution with over 29,600 students on its main campus. It has seventeen colleges and schools, including an Honors College and four off-campus divisions in other regions of the state. The Office of Information Technology (OIT) provides both systems and end-user support for all WVU campuses.

1.1.1 Instructional Technology Resource Center

OIT and WVU's Office of Extended Learning jointly fund and manage an Instructional Technology Resource Center (ITRC) [5]. Five instructional designers and two media designers develop and present faculty development workshops and provide technical assistance with online course development projects for faculty members. I interviewed four of the staff members to learn more about their experiences with developing and teaching online workshops for faculty.

1.1.2 Application Support and Training

Application Support and Training [6] has seven employees including its director. Responsibilities include specialized software application administration, IT standards, third-tier help desk support, technical training for WVU students and employees, and information technology projects.

1.2 Terminology

In this paper, I use the term *online workshop* for self-paced training sessions conducted using WVU eCampus. *WVU eCampus* is WVU's name for our installation of Blackboard Vista.

I use the term *webinar* to describe a web conference session held in Wimba Classroom. I link to recordings of webinars in my online workshops and conduct both online group meetings and online office hours during the period of time an online workshop is open. Although OIT occasionally offers faculty development sessions as short real-time webinars [1], this paper focuses on the longer self-paced online workshops presented in eCampus.

2. ONLINE WORKSHOP STRUCTURE

The following is a list of resources that one or more of the workshop instructors incorporate in the online workshops.

2.1 Content

2.1.1 Audio and Transcripts

Some of the instructors record audio lectures and provide a text transcript. These mini-lectures are incorporated into the learning modules.

2.1.2 Software Demonstrations

Some of the instructors use a screen recording tool such as Adobe Captivate to create a demonstration of how to complete a task. A PDF version of each demonstration movie is also posted.

2.1.3 Workshop Handouts

In addition to audio transcripts and PDF versions of screen demonstrations, we provide links to downloadable documents.

2.1.4 Learning Modules

All of the instructional designers and I use the Learning Modules tool and html documents as a way to organize and present the workshop content. The learning modules often include links to discussion topics, learning activities, and online resources in addition to the text content.

2.1.5 Web Links

We all provide links to outside online resources, either via the Web Links tool or by providing links from within content pages in the learning modules.

2.1.6 Webinar Archives

Since I offer one or two webinars via Wimba Classroom during my online workshops, I provide links to the webinar recordings for those unable to attend the live sessions. I also link to recorded webinar archives on relevant topics from previous terms, especially in the *WVU eCampus Soup to Nuts* workshop.

2.2 Learning Activities

2.2.1 Assessments and Self-tests

Currently I am the only instructor using the Assessments tool to create quizzes on workshop content; however, several of the other instructors indicated that they plan to add more types of assessment to their online workshops. Some of the instructors created self-tests using Flash or some other tool. Some of the instructors use the Assessments tool to conduct the workshop evaluation survey for the Provost's Office.

2.2.2 Assignments

I am the only instructor who used the Assignments tool to create and manage learning tasks for my faculty participants. The other instructors used other tools or directives in their learning module content pages to present learning activities.

2.2.3 Discussions

We all include at least one discussion topic in our online workshops. An "Introduce Yourself" topic tends to get the most postings. Another discussion topic included in almost all of the online workshops is one designed to handle questions from the faculty participants. Some instructors also include a discussion topic for each learning module.

2.2.4 Notes

Several of the ITRC instructors included the Notes tool which is intended to allow a student in a course take notes on what they are viewing in the course. At least one instructor asked the faculty participants to use the Note tool record their reflections on the content and how they would use what they learned in their teaching.

2.2.5 Practice Courses

Since I have group manager access, I create empty course shells for my faculty participants to use for learning activities. For the Wimba Classroom and Turnitin workshops, I enroll all workshop participants as instructor/designers in a single practice course and use page folders to organize their work.

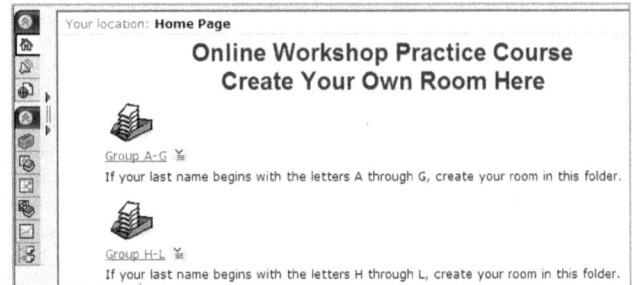

Figure 1: Sample Practice Course for Multiple Participants

After conducting discussions with my ITRC colleagues, some of them were interested in requesting practice course access for one or more of their own online workshops. Faculty participants would be able to practice new skills that require access to WVU eCampus without risk of damage to an actual course in development or production.

2.2.6 Webinars

I have been presenting faculty development sessions as live synchronous webinars since 2007 [1]. As part of the eCampus Soup to Nuts workshop, I offered a few webinars on eCampus topics and related software such as Respondus during each semester. For the Wimba Classroom and Turnitin workshops that I offered in Spring 2012, I included two webinars as part of the agenda for each workshop. I included these webinars on my regular workshop schedule and enrolled a few WVU faculty and staff who were not participating in the faculty development workshop.

2.3 Communications with Participants

We provide personal support via email to the participants during and after the online workshop. Most of the online workshops include a discussion topic for posting questions; an instructor responds to postings within one working day. A couple of the instructors use the Announcements tool. I include the My Grades tool as an additional way to communicate since my workshops include assignments with feedback and a quiz.

2.4 Workshop Evaluation Form

We all use the same evaluation form as requested by the Provost's Office. Some workshop instructors provide a web link to the online form from within the eCampus course; some instructors recreate the form as an eCampus survey then forward the results to the Provost's Office.

3. MANAGING ONLINE WORKSHOPS

As the Manager of IT Training, I am the Group Manager for OIT Training in the WVU eCampus Learning Academy institution. I manage enrollment and content copying for all of our online faculty development workshops.

3.1 New Sections

One week before a new offering of an online workshop is scheduled to begin, I create an empty course section and copy the most recent workshop's content into it. For a new workshop, the instructor must put in a formal request to have content copied by our eCampus administrators from our development system as I only have group manager access and cannot copy content across institutions.

3.2 Enrollment

I manually enroll the workshop instructors in the copied workshop as soon as I complete the content copy. A few days before the first day of an online workshop, the faculty development administrator or the workshop instructor emails me a list of the registrants. Although the deadline for registration is three days before the session begins, all instructors allow individuals to be added to an online workshop after it has started. I manually enroll individuals from the initial list and those who register late.

The enrollment process doesn't take long but I have encountered a few minor issues. If I enroll the participants as soon as I get the list, they immediately gain access to the content if they login to our eCampus Learning Academy for a different online workshop; at that time, the workshop might not be ready if the instructors is still making final refinements. If I enroll them early and set them to "denied access", I usually forget to return to the administrative tool to allow access at the right time. Sometimes I overlook a name on the list and fail to enroll them; I quickly fix this as soon as that person tries unsuccessfully to login and emails the instructor. I often forget to remove access to an online workshop when its term is complete; this can confuse those participants who enroll for several workshops.

3.3 Tracking Participation

To summarize participation for all of our faculty development online workshops, I used the Blackboard Vista Tracking tool. I reviewed the login dates and the amount of time spent in each session. I exported this data to Excel and calculated median time spent in each online workshop. I calculated a participation rate by dividing the number of registrants by the number of active participants.

For my Turnitin, Wimba Classroom, and eCampus Soup to Nuts workshops, I also summarized tracking data available for the Wimba Classroom webinar rooms and archived recordings. I reviewed the participants' practice course sections to see if they customized the sections' appearance, uploaded content, created online quizzes, created webinar rooms, or created and graded Turnitin assignments. Refer to sections 4 and 5 in this paper for more information on workshop participation statistics .

4. FINE TUNING

4.1 Modifying Current Online Workshops

Each online workshop is designed and updated by the instructor assigned to teach that session. Some online workshops have additional instructors who assist with online communications or content creation but they do not modify the design. This section summarizes some of the modifications I and the instructor designers made over the past few years for those online workshops presented more than once.

4.1.1 Basic Flash for Faculty

The major change between the first offering of the online workshop to the most recent session in April 2012 was to the content: one lesson on creating a quiz using Flash was deleted and two lessons were added on "click to reveal" and "drag and drop". This workshop content modification was probably related to changes in templates included in more recent versions of Adobe Flash.

4.1.2 Keeping it Legal: Copyright Crash Course

One obvious enhancement to this online workshop was the addition of a discussion topic set up as a journal. The instructor posed a thought provoking question on the workshop content and each participant responded individually. Since the discussion was set up as a journal, only the workshop instructors could view the responses.

4.1.3 Creating Text that Begs to be Read

This workshop has been presented online six times now, starting in the spring of 2009. The first three offerings were unchanged other than instructor responses to discussion postings. In spring of 2011, the instructor added a link to video about the effective use of white space in a discussion board post and added the Who's Online tool so faculty participants who were in the course at the same time could send messages to each other.

For this particular online workshop, all of the content is in a single learning module. The icon for the learning module is made out of text and text appears as part of the background image. The first time I entered this online workshop, it took me a couple of seconds to click on the "So you expect them to read that?" icon in the middle of the page. Some of the faculty participants needed more guidance to know to click on the text blob to gain access to the content. In the fall of 2011, the instructor added an arrow pointer graphic, directing the participants to click here to enter the workshop content.

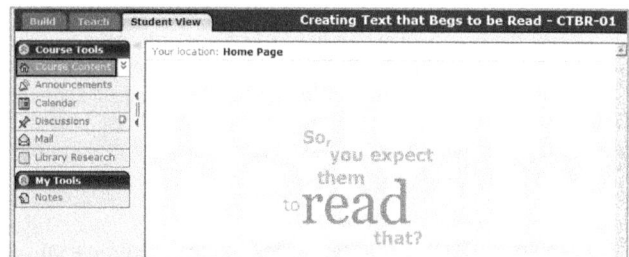

Figure 2: Course Home Page Link to Learning Module

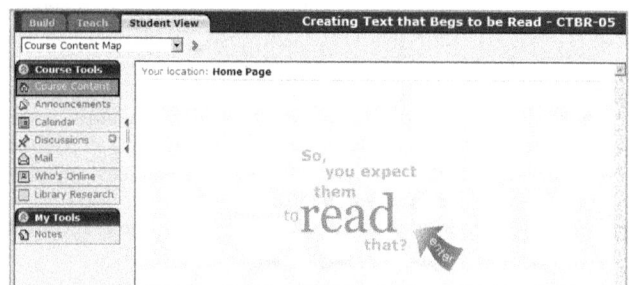

Figure 3: Course Home Page after Adding Pointer Graphic

4.1.4 Online Video for Educators

In subsequent offerings of this online workshop, the instructor added informative text at beginning of the first two learning modules: "Please Note: All links in this workshop, unless otherwise noted, will open in a new browser window or tab." Some of our faculty attendees benefit from the extra guidance, especially those new to attending online workshops.

Figure 4: Added Text to Top of Learning Modules

4.1.5 Podcasting

One example of fine tuning that I discovered in this online workshop was a demonstration movie that was embedded in a content page instead of in a new window from a page hyperlink.

4.1.6 WVU eCampus From Soup to Nuts

After my first round of offering a semester-long online workshop in spring 2010, I had planned to break it into smaller workshops and offer the shorter sessions as part of the official faculty development program. Instead, due to a shortage of resources, I have continued to enroll faculty and technical support staff into the same section of the Soup to Nuts workshop, assigning each term's cohort to its own group and allowing some participants to remain in the workshop for multiple terms.

The *Soup to Nuts* workshop has had reasonable enrollment but very little active participation since the beginning. My theory is that the amount of content is overwhelming as I included content about almost every feature in Blackboard Vista 8 plus the PowerLink products we have installed (Turnitin, Studymate Class, and a little on Wimba Classroom). I always keep the workshop open for an entire semester; this long period of time might encourage the faculty members to procrastinate or forget about the workshop. Since we are preparing to upgrade to Blackboard Learn 9, I will not bother with rehabilitating this particular online workshop. Instead I will create smaller workshops that are designed to last two weeks or less as I had intended to do during the fall of 2010.

4.1.7 Wimba Classroom

In February 2012, I developed a new online workshop on an introduction to Wimba Classroom, a web conference tool that we have integrated into our eCampus system via a Blackboard PowerLink. The workshop creation was a bit hasty and I didn't complete my vision of what it could have been but the actual delivery of the workshop was a resounding success. Most of the enrolled faculty logged in and spent at least 30 minutes in the course. Six of the participants completed most or all of the optional assignments. Several of the faculty members attended webinars, viewed archive recordings, created their own rooms in the practice course shell, uploaded content, and recorded themselves delivering mini-presentations.

Since this workshop went so well, I offered this workshop again in mid-May as part of our annual Faculty Academy to a smaller group of faculty, most of whom worked in the same department. Although I think they met their own minimal goals to learn more about what Wimba Classroom could be used for, the session was not as much fun to teach. The participants did not create rooms or practice recording presentations; most of them never entered a Wimba Classroom room or viewed an archive recording. Repeating this workshop led me to the insight that an online workshop is more than just a lot of well organized content and learning activities attractively arranged—any workshop or course,

whether online or in a classroom, also depends on the participants' background skills, motivation, and available time.

4.1.8 Turnitin

In April 2012, I tried to duplicate my first success with the Wimba Classroom online workshop by offering an online session on Turnitin. I followed the same course structure for content and assessment and offered live webinars and office hours. I created Turnitin paper assignments that the participants could have submitted as students; this would have been a great learning opportunity because in real life, an instructor does not see the same interface for Turnitin as the students do (in Blackboard Vista, the Teach tab and Student View tab present the same interface for instructors). I also created follow-up peer review Turnitin PeerMark assignments and had my student employee submit a couple of papers for peer review in case only one participant wanted to do this. I provided access to a practice course where the participants were enrolled as instructors; in that course, they could practice creating and grading Turnitin assignments.

A few of the participants attended the live webinars or viewed the recordings. However only one faculty member created a Turnitin assignment in the practice course; she then submitted a paper via the instructor interface. None of the participants submitted a sample paper or a peer review as a student.

4.2 INSTRUCTOR DISCUSSIONS

I interviewed three of the ITRC instructional designers and one of the media designers who develop and teach most of our online faculty development workshops in order to learn more about their current processes, their future plans, and to compare our online teaching methods and experiences.

4.2.1 Attendance

"How do you decide if a particular faculty member has attended your online workshop? Do you report the actual attendance to the Provost's Office?"

All of the instructors including myself look at the tracking data and any available evidence of participation such as posts to the discussion board, questions asked via email, and completion of learning activities. However, I learned during these interviews that some of the instructors do not report the actual faculty participation to the Provost's Office since the faculty development administrator does not ask them to. Instead they just keep track of the total number of faculty members who attended for their internal record keeping.

4.2.2 Technical Issues

"Do you or your students ever encounter technical issues that interfere with online teaching and learning experiences?"

Some of us have had more issues dealing with audio and the lack of required plug-ins in our hands-on workshops on campus than in online workshops. Some of the online workshops require downloading and installing software and plug-ins which sometimes requires a few email messages or discussion postings to provide extra assistance.

4.2.3 Office Hours

"Do you hold scheduled online office hours? Do you meet with your workshop participants online? Do you answer questions via phone or email?"

I am the only faculty development instructor who scheduled formal online office hours during online workshops; however, due to lack of participation, I will switch to offering to meet online by appointment. All of us have been responding to email from the faculty members, often after the workshops have concluded.

4.2.4 Contact Frequency
"How often do you email your workshop participants?"

All of us email the registrants a welcome message that also provides login instructions to the online workshop. Some will send an email reminder halfway through the session that the course is still open, especially to those faculty participants who have not logged in yet. Sometimes a workshop instructor will alert the faculty registrants that the workshop is closing soon, along with a reminder to complete the online evaluation form. I also email a follow-up email message to those who participated with links to online resources they can access to review some of the content without logging into the workshop.

4.2.5 Discussions
"Do your faculty attendees participate in the online discussion topics?"

The consensus seems to be that participation in the threaded discussion boards varies by topic and enrolled group. Discussion postings can be sparse or non-existent. It appears that the workshop on copyright and legal issues generated the most discussion, mostly questions answered by workshop instructors.

In most of the online workshops, the faculty participants rarely discuss concepts and do not respond to others' postings. Several of the participants, especially those who are not the first ones to login, will read the others' introductions but they do not comment on them.

4.2.6 Assessment
"Do you provide assignments? Do you offer quizzes on the content?"

Most of the other instructors offer a variety of learning activities or practice exercises but do not use the Assignment tool to do so. Activities might consist of a set of instructions to complete outside of the workshop, a self-test, worksheets, group discussion questions, or a private journal discussion where only the instructors can read the faculty responses.

The instructors from the ITRC have completed *Quality Matters* training [3] as part of our participation in peer reviewed quality control process for online courses. Based on what they learned, they plan to enhance their training by incorporating more outcome-related assessments related to learning objectives when they revise their online workshops or create new ones.

In my own online workshops, I use the Assignment tool where each optional assignment has one or more tasks for the faculty participant to complete. Instead of numeric or letter grades, I enter "Completed" where applicable and provide individualized feedback. I provide an optional quiz and allow immediate review of submissions. Since a numeric score is recorded for the quiz, I allow multiple attempts and report only the highest score.

4.2.7 Evaluation
"Do you send a link to the evaluation form to all registrants or only the ones who have met your criteria for attendance?"

The other instructors provide the link to the evaluation form or to an eCampus survey version of the evaluation form in the online workshop. For my online workshops, I email the evaluation form link only to those who have logged into the course and spent more than 10 minutes there. The link is also available on the Faculty Development open web site [4] – a faculty member could choose to complete the evaluation form without prompting from one of us (and without actually attending the online workshop).

4.2.8 Updating Online Workshops
"For those online workshops you have taught more than once, what modifications do you make before you teach it the next time? What influences you to make changes (if any) to your workshop?"

Common modifications include checking web links to outside resources and online videos to make sure they still work, adding new content or clarifying content in response to faculty questions, updating content due to new versions of software, removing outdated content, and updating learning activities. In addition to faculty questions, software updates, and dead links, a workshop will be modified as needed to reflect growth in the instructor's own knowledge of the topic and online teaching.

4.2.9 Upgrade Concerns
"What issues are you concerned about in updating your online eCampus-based workshops for Learn 9?"

We all need more hands on experience with Learn 9 to truly be prepared for this upgrade. Based on what we have learned so far, we fear that a lot of the learning modules will have to be rebuilt due to how Learn 9 handles web page content with style sheets, images and other integrated media. We also have concerns about whether Flash-based interactive objects and demonstrations will still work. Another concern about Learn 9 is possible changes in file management.

It appears that the Learn 9 environment does not support the customized icon graphics that we like to create for our course pages. This aesthetic change might not seem important but it is a shock after we have had years of creating custom appearances for our online workshops and online courses for credit.

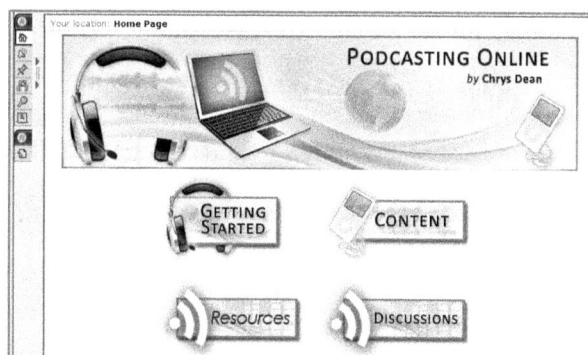

Figure 5: Podcasting Workshop in Blackboard Vista 8

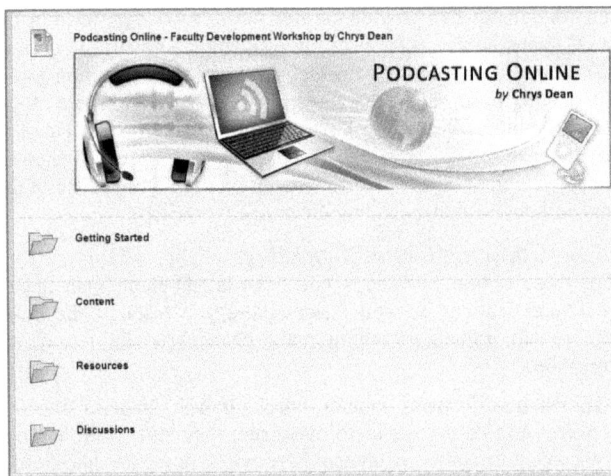

Figure 6: Podcasting Workshop in Blackboard Learn 9

5. SUMMARY

5.1 Participation Statistics

Tracking data provided by Blackboard Vista is not a perfect tool for truly summarizing workshop participation. A person can remain logged in for long periods of time and not actually be doing anything. Others can login, print content, and review material while not being logged in. My perception of a lack of participation in some of my online workshops is not supported by the raw tracking data. However, the participants are not asking questions, not posting in the online discussions, nor completing learning activities where I can review their work. I cannot assess their learning so it feels as if they are not doing anything.

It is difficult to discern a pattern in workshop participation from reviewing tracking data. It didn't seem to matter if the workshop were offered for the first time or repeated from a previous semester. Sometimes enrollment is higher for first time offerings but actual participation numbers are not significantly different.

While comparing Spring 2011 workshops with Spring 2012 workshops, I noticed that some workshops had an increase in active participation while others plunged. In 2012, the "Keeping It Legal: Online Copyright Crash Course" workshop was offered during the last week of class and finals week; in 2011, it was offered during the last 2 weeks of class (1 week earlier in term).

Table 1: Reported Attendance Spring 2011 & Spring 2012

Online Workshop	Spring 2011	Spring 2012	Percent change
Blocks Instructional Design	13	16	23%
Creating Text	10	11	10%
Customizing Courses	3	11	267%
Flash for Faculty	6	4	-33%
Keep it Legal - Copyright	15	2	-87%
Podcasting	7	2	-71%
Soup To Nuts eCampus	12	10	-17%
Video For Educators	4	5	25%
Wimba Classroom	--	22	--

5.1.1 Webinar Participation

I offered three online workshops through Faculty Development in Spring 2012: "Intro to Wimba Classroom" (WC) in February and repeated in May and "Intro to Turnitin" in April. Below is the summary of how many participants took advantage of the Wimba Classroom resources I offered. Two of the online workshop included two synchronous online group webinars. The numbers in each column indicate how many unique participants attended each online event. In the second column, "entered" refers to the number of faculty members who logged into the online workshop even for a few minutes and "enrolled" refers to the number who had registered.

Table 2: Webinar Participation in Online Workshops

	Entered / Enrolled	Webinar 1	Webinar 2	Viewed Archive	Office Hours
Turnitin	5 / 7	1	1	0	0
WC Feb	26 / 30	2	4	10	2
WC May	7 / 8	n/a	n/a	2	1

5.1.2 Workshop Descriptions Online

Additional statistics for our online faculty development workshops and workshop descriptions are available online at http://oit.wvu.edu/training/online-facdev/ .

5.2 Lessons Learned

5.2.1 Focus Content

I have learned that an online workshop needs to be focused on a reasonable list of topics similar to the amount of content covered in a half-day face to face workshop. Attempting a complete survey of a topic that would take more than two full days in a classroom is overwhelming for both the participants and the workshop designer.

5.2.2 Finish Before You Begin

The instructional designers and media designers from the ITRC complete their online workshops' development before their sessions start. However, for my own online workshops, I ran out of time before each new offering and decided that what I had developed by the first day of the workshop was "good enough". I started the online sessions while adding and refining content. I had envisioned including a few more interactive learning activities and content modules that I still have not had time to develop. During the workshops, I needed to focus on the participants without the stress of worrying about workshop deficiencies. Be sure to allow yourself enough time to properly design and develop an online workshop; you need to allow sufficient time so you can still perform your other job duties and deal with unexpected crises and new projects.

5.2.3 Shorten or Lengthen Workshops

As I learned from my eCampus Soup to Nuts online workshop, a semester is too long to keep an online workshop open. The participants can easily let their participation drop to the bottom of their to-do lists; online discussions fall by the wayside when each faculty participant logs in during different months. As an instructor, it was extremely difficult for me to remember to check on the online workshop and to regularly remind the participants that they were enrolled.

We started our program by making all of the official faculty development online workshops open for one week; we always had to extend the workshop access for another week. We now schedule online workshops to go for two full weeks and extend limited access for another week upon request.

5.2.4 Offer in Faculty Development Series

I have offered online workshops and webinars as part of my regular OIT workshop schedule and on the official faculty development schedule published by the Provost's Office. I definitely get higher enrollment and participation when the workshop is publicized by the Provost's Office. The direct posting of the faculty development and faculty academy schedules to the faculty mailing list improves publicity; however, I am not allowed to announce my OIT workshops to that list, only to a general daily e-news announcement list for all faculty and staff (that frequently goes unread) where it is easy to overlook the link to my schedule. I also feel that faculty members take instructional technology workshops more seriously when they are associated with Academic Affairs.

5.2.5 Create Separate Sections

For a couple of the faculty development online workshops, I have re-used the same section of an online workshop for a new cohort after denying access to the first group of faculty participants. The workshop delivery itself went okay using this technique—the problem was when I went back to calculate participation statistics. I had to find the original lists of enrollees to determine which no shows belonged to which cohort as I had already denied access to all participants by that time.

5.2.6 Offer Earlier in Semester

I could not find a statistically significant relationship between when a workshop is offered and its participation rate. However, it did seem to be a problem for faculty to participate in online workshops during the last week of the semester or finals week.

5.2.7 Email Reminders

Emailing a reminder to the participants seems to spur some of them to login and review at least some of the content and to ask questions or to cancel their registration in the session. In my experience, if a faculty member does not login during the first week a workshop is open, he or she is less likely to complete the content or attempt the learning activities.

5.3 Future Plans

I plan to work with the ITRC instructional designers to create a uniform attendance reporting plan for online workshops. I will also work with them to create practice course shells for their participants to use for learning activities where appropriate, at least for the next year as we continue using Blackboard Vista 8.

All of the online workshops will have to be migrated and modified for Blackboard Learn 9. The eCampus workshop will be broken into smaller modules and recreated from scratch as its content will completely change due to the upgrade. After we finish the upgrade to Blackboard Learn 9, we plan to upgrade Wimba Classroom to Blackboard Collaborate. The Wimba Classroom online workshop will be rebuilt from scratch at that time.

I would also like to compare attendance statistics from face-to-face faculty development workshops with statistics from the corresponding online workshops.

6. ACKNOWLEDGMENTS

I'd like to express many thanks to Chrys Amy Dean, Lydia Mong, Erin Kelley, and Carla Corsetti from the WVU Instructional Technology Resource Center for sharing their teaching and workshop design experiences and for allowing me to review their online workshops and tracking data.

7. REFERENCES

[1] Fletcher, Kathryn. 2008. Blazing training trails with Wimba Classroom to Avoid travelling 'round the mountain. *Proceedings of the 36th Annual ACM SIGUCCS Conference on User Services Conference.* (Portland, OR, USA, October 19-22, 2008). SIGUCCS '08. ACM, New York, NY, 181-186. DOI=http://doi.acm.org/10.1145/1449956.1450011

[2] Fletcher, Kathryn. 2010. Diary of a Trainer: Learning to Create Online Learning Experience, *Proceedings of the 38th Annual ACM SIGUCCS Conference on User Services Conference.* (Norfolk, VA, USA, October 19-22, 2010). SIGUCCS '108. ACM, New York, NY, 257-264. DOI= 10.1145/1878335.1878399

[3] Quality Matters Program. http://www.qmprogram.org/

[4] WVU Faculty Development. http://wvufaculty.wvu.edu/development/

[5] WVU Instructional Technology Resource Center. http://oit.wvu.edu/itrc/

[6] WVU Office of Information Technology: Application Support and Training. http://oit.wvu.edu/ast/

Every Day is Like Survival: Here, There and Everywhere

Mo Nishiyama
Oregon Health & Science University
3505 SW Veterans Hospital Road, Rm 420
Portland, OR 97239
1-503-494-1406

nishiyam@ohsu.edu

Lucas Friedrichsen
Oregon State University
121 The Valley Library
Corvallis, OR 97331
1-541-737-8244

Lucas.friedrichsen@oregonstate.edu

ABSTRACT

Satisfying the expectations of both the IT organization and the department, while maintaining the momentum of our own professional development, is often tricky. We strive to align our work with the goals of the organization, but are interrupted by the immediate needs of our department. We work to strategize long-term but are asked to put out fires at a moment's notice. We struggle to reconcile the disparities between following the goals of upper management and the, sometimes-conflicting, edicts of direct management. We wonder if it is possible to provide superb customer service, apply innovation in our work, and simply produce, in spite of often conflicting goals. Pursuing institutional goals often gets interpreted by our immediate peers and management as us not being team players. Our commitment to the team is then called into question. We are caught between a rock and hard place. And what does this mean for our own professional growth and learning opportunities?

It is possible to both rock and roll even while being pulled in many directions. Even when we are urged to spend more time embracing the foxhole, we can shine while contributing beyond the silo. Reaching the area of optimal production is a never-ending experiment where the target moves daily. However, it can be done by increasing self-awareness, aligning our activities with our truth, and a applying a bit of political savvy.

Categories and Subject Descriptors

K.7.2 [**The Computing Profession**]: Organizations.

General Terms

Management, Performance, Experimentation, Human Factors, and Standardization.

Keywords

Juggling priorities, politics, project management, work demands, professional development.

1. INTRODUCTION

Employees, and in particular IT support employees, are concurrently pulled in various directions. Simultaneously juggling customer service requests, cross-functional project team membership, professional development and growth and fostering

a team environment can be difficult. This can occur for people at all levels of the organization, from CIOs to student employees. To help address the growing juggling act, our author team, which formed at the SIGUCCS Fall 2011 combined conference, seeks to provide thought provoking ideas to help you navigate the various demands of your workplace.

2. SURVIVING AND THRIVING IN AN ENVIRONMENT WITH MANY DEMANDS

2.1 Being pulled in many directions: who do you work for, and what do they want?

Working as an IT support professional in an academic setting involves more than showing up to work, putting in the hours, and collecting a paycheck fortnightly. Your skills, labor, and presence are wanted by several entities, who are all interested in your time and attention. They can include:

1) The institution: they often have long-range strategic plans for maintaining IT services, and are focused on containing costs.
2) The department: they often have immediate issues which require prompt resolution, and perpetually have needs which relate to training, monitoring performance, and managing workload.
3) Cross-functional teams: these collaborative teams typically exist for the sole purpose of accomplishing time-sensitive tasks, and the siren call of these teams often echo louder as deadlines loom.
4) Professional, technical, and personal growth opportunities: we are all motivated to learn and grow in our jobs.

2.2 How can I meet the demands of these entities?

Different entities have different needs, and often times, it helps to analyze what they are motivated by.

1) Find out the long-term IT plans for the institution. Often, these IT plans are driven by economic, geographic, or strategic necessities. Then learn the skills that will help the organization meet their vision. For example, if an institution has a long-term plan in place to reduce costs associated with desktop support, and is looking for virtualization technologies; it would be a good idea to start learning about VDI. If an IT department has been mandated to provide support for end-users' tablet devices, it would help to become familiar with Android OS and iOS.
2) Learn the pain points of your department's management. What annoyances or issues are they experiencing in their day-to-day operations? It's not

necessary to solve all of their problems, but it is a good idea to ask them how you could be of assistance. Offer to assist with repetitive administrative tasks that no one else wants to do, and figure out how to make the process better. Offering assistance can sometimes lead to new growth or leadership opportunities.

3) Gain a cursory knowledge about the different areas that comprise the cross-functional teams that you are involved in, and why they are important to the team's success. Understanding how these pieces fit together can bring new insights to teams' successes, and can help break down silos.

4) Set aside time each day to learn skills that will help advance your career. These skills can include visiting technical and industry news sites, reading leadership blogs, learning "soft skills," or leveraging online training. Setting a daily goal of reading 3 to 5 articles that relate to professional, technical, or personal growth is an effective strategy.

2.3 What do you do when the worlds collide?

From time to time, the demands of these different entities can conflict, or at least vie for your time and attention. In modern IT organizations that share the "do more with less" mantra, it is essential to do what is important for you, first and foremost.

1) Learn to say "No."
2) Delegate or postpone tasks and responsibilities.
3) Prioritize tasks.
4) Embrace what you value most. Ask yourself what is more important--working extra hours for a bigger paycheck, or leaving work on time so you can spend the evening with your family?
5) Set aside protected time for focusing on important, intensive tasks.
6) If you have to multitask, "combine active-thinking tasks only with automatic, embedded routines." [1]
7) If you know that there is an important deadline coming up, proactively apprise others who may be impacted by your reduced availability.

The work of an IT support professional can be exciting, fast-paced, and full of opportunities. It can also be a land mine full of conflicting expectations, time management issues, and other forms of frustration. Once you gain an understanding of what entities you work for, and take steps to optimize your interactions with these entities, work can be rewarding.

3. HOW CAN I GET IT ALL DONE?

Schedule your time during the day to enhance your effectiveness. Focus on specific tasks or projects in at least 20-minute blocks of time or larger. The human brain does not effectively multi-task and studies have been performed that indicate focusing on a single task provides the most benefit. [2]

Work with your manager/supervisor to allocate a certain amount of hours per week for professional development and training opportunities.

If you are not able to set a regimented schedule, try to set aside specific times for the high priority tasks and focus only on those items. The following table provides a quick illustration of a potential regimented work day schedule.

Table 1. Example 8-hour work day (manager)

Time	Task
8:00-8:30am	E-mail
8:30-9:30am	Highest priority tasks/priorities
9:30am - 9:45am	Break (leave desk)
9:45 - 10am	E-mail
10 - 11am	Meeting
11am - 12pm	Customer service/task time
12 - 1pm	Lunch
1 - 2pm	Check in with staff
2 - 3pm	Focused project time
3 - 3:30pm	E-mail
3:30 - 3:45pm	Break (leave desk)
3:45 - 4:30pm	E-mail
4:30 - 5pm	Professional development

4. HOW CAN I MAINTAIN MOMENTUM FOR PROFESSIONAL DEVELOPMENT ITEMS?

Treat your professional development like an on-going project. Select your end goal, such as acquiring a Project Management Professional (PMP) certificate in one calendar year. Work backwards from that goal and develop achievable milestones to help you succeed. Imagine the following project outline:

Milestones -

1) Each week - Study for 3 hours.
2) 3 months - Complete one practice test.
3) 6 months - Complete second practice test, find colleagues or others attempting the PMP and connect with them.
4) 9 months - Complete third practice test; develop a full project plan from start to finish.
5) 1 year - Complete the PMP certification. Celebrate!

Track your progress each week to illustrate what you have accomplished, which will help propel you forward. Repeat for each additional professional development accomplishment and you will be well on your way to strengthening your career.

5. WHAT ABOUT MOMENTUM WITH OTHER TASKS?

Setting goals is an invaluable way to move tasks forward and maintain positive energy. First, establish goals and direction for yourself with regards to your career. Second, use the same process to set goals and milestones for tasks and projects at work.

Reaching those smaller milestones will help you keep positive momentum for the task and project.

Following the goal setting process will also enable you to better understand your personal resource constraints and outlays. Using that information will empower you to accept and maintain the amount of work that will not overwhelm you. Instead of just saying "yes" or "no" to a project, your goal information will provide data to support your response and allow you to defer the project or task to a later time. Knowing and understanding your limits will reduce the anxiety and stress from over-committing yourself to tasks and projects.

6. WHAT IS ONE WAY I CAN UNDERSTAND MYSELF AND MY COLLEAGUES BETTER?

Do you know how you approach situations or what topics make you feel most alive? The keynote speaker at SIGUCCS Fall 2011 discussed the importance of a personality assessment and understanding yourself. One recommended method involved using the Myers Briggs assessment. [3] The evaluation could also raise your awareness to the personality traits of others and what topics empower and encourage them. For example, as an introvert that person might be quiet and introspective but might have invaluable ideas. Don't assume they are withdrawn and uninterested; instead, try to understand their personality and capitalize on their strengths. As a manager, learning how people process information and work best are some of the most helpful skills in the management toolbox.

7. WHAT IF I NEED A SUPPORT STRUCTURE?

IT workers tend to work in silos, either individually or at a department level. While the silo can help someone advance in specific tasks or a career area, it might also drain your energy and hinder career development. To help drive solutions forward and provide encouragement, find a kindred spirit from your workplace environment. In an ideal situation, find someone from a different section of your department that you don't interact with often. Meet for coffee/beer/wine/food and grow a relationship based on honesty, respect and trust. Building that informal bridge will spark conversations about projects and the direction of the organization. The informal relationship will also help when you or another member of your team needs to interact with that department.

Another option involves starting a community of practice in your geographical area to learn and share ideas. The community of practice is a group of people from different organizations performing the same work. The group can provide many good ideas and even lead to resource sharing information amongst group members. [4]

If you are not comfortable connecting with someone in your department or organization, consider forming a MasterMind group instead. [5] MasterMind groups are small peer groups who meet regularly to discuss topics of common interest and to encourage each other. These groups are comprised of people with similar interests, determination and goals. Members provide experience and ideas that others in the group can leverage. Peers in the group naturally support each other through tumultuous times and also provide fresh perspective. The group can be as dynamic as the membership. Find people in the same geographical area or people from around the world, meet over chat, use e-mail, etc. The concept is the same as connecting with someone at work. Talk to the MasterMind group about whatever topic you desire, use the group to help motivate you, springboard your career or help overcome a current hurdle. Both authors of this paper are currently members of a MasterMind group and have found a lot of value in the connections amongst the group. The encouragement, ideas and momentum gained within the group is incredibly helpful.

8. ACKNOWLEDGMENTS

Thanks to Mo for working with me on this paper! (Lucas) Many thanks to all the hardworking people that make SIGUCCS work throughout the year and at each conference. Your efforts are VERY much appreciated.

9. REFERENCES

[1] Rock, David. 2009. Your Brain at Work: Strategies for Overcoming Distraction, Regaining Focus, and Working Smarter All Day Long. *HarperCollins*.

[2] Whitson, Gordon. SEP 13, 2011 8:00 AM. How to Reclaim Your Time in Seven Days for a More Productive and Stress-Free Workday. *Lifehacker.com* http://lifehacker.com/5839691/how-to-reclaim-your-time-in-seven-days-with-rescuetime

[3] Myers Briggs Foundation. 2011. The MBTI instrument for life. *The Myers Briggs Foundation*. http://www.myersbriggs.org/

[4] Mojta, Debbie. 2004. Communities of practice: dare to share the knowledge. *Proceeding SIGUCCS '04 Proceedings of the 32nd annual ACM SIGUCCS fall conference*.

[5] Karyn Greenstreet, K. 2004. How to Create and Run a Mastermind Group. *Passion for Business*. http://www.passionforbusiness.com/articles/mastermind-group.htm

Operational Experiences from the Viewpoint of University IT System Administrators in the Metropolitan Area on East Japan Great Earthquake

Kohichi Ogawa
Saitama University
Information Technology Center
255 Shimoookubo, Sakura-ku, Saitama, 180-8570 Japan.
+81-48-858-3674
kogawa@mail.saitama-u.ac.jp

Noriaki Yoshiura
Saitama University
Information Technology Center
255 Shimoookubo, Sakura-ku, Saitama, 180-8570 Japan.
+81-48-858-3674
yoshiura@fmx.ics.saitama-u.ac.jp

ABSTRACT

Saitama University is located in the metropolitan area of Japan. In March 2011 on the East Japan Great Earthquake occurred. The university is about 200 km from the epicenter of the earthquake. While the earthquake did not have a direct impact on the university, it did result in multiple indirect damages. The earthquake influenced operations of the university's information infrastructure, whose system administrators had to take several operations in order to keep the infrastructure service functioning. One of the damages of the earthquake was a rolling blackout. The earthquake caused damages to various electric power plants, including Fukushima Daiichi Nuclear Power Plant. The area in and around Tokyo, the Metropolitan Area in Japan, was short of electric power, and rolling blackouts were unavoidable. Some important servers, such as web servers and e-mail, could not run because the rolling blackouts frequently caused hardware troubles. As a result, it was difficult for the people of the university to use communication tools such as e-mail, web and so on. This paper explains operational experiences and lessons based on the experiences from the viewpoint of system administrators in Saitama University; the article also discusses operation and management of information systems in disasters.

Categories and Subject Descriptors

[K.6.4 System Management]: Centralization/decentralization

General Terms

Human Factors, Management

Keywords

Data Center, Information System Management, Virtual Private Server

1. INTRODUCTION

This paper reports the operational experience of the Saitama University Information Infrastructure after the East Japan Great

Earthquake on March 11th 2011. The earthquake compromised the operation of the university's information infrastructure, whose technical staff had to undertake several countermeasures in order to keep the infrastructure in service. This operational experience offers valuable insight regarding to information infrastructure administration regarding how best to prepare for future disasters.

2. University Information Infrastructure

The Saitama University Information Technology Center (to which the authors of this paper belong) manages the Saitama University Information Infrastructure. The information infrastructure includes educational information facilities, research computing facilities, campus network, DNS service, e-mail system, web server, e-mail hosting service, web server hosting and other services. The duty of this center is to maintain the information infrastructure services. The earthquake made it difficult to run all functions of the said infrastructure. Thus, after the earthquake, the following infrastructure functions were deemed essential, and their operation had to be assured:

1.   Campus Network,

2.   DNS Services,

3.   E-mail Service and E-mail Hosting Service and

4.   Web Server and Web Hosting Service

2.1 Network Topology

Figure 1 illustrates the university network topology. About 1800 rooms, which comprise the majority of the university's rooms, are connected to one server room by single mode optical

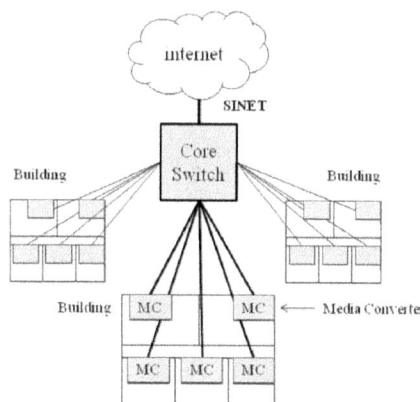

Figure. 1 Network Topology of Saitama University

fibers [1]. Each room has a media converter of 100Base-T or 1000Base-T, and the server room has about 1800 media converters. The server room has all information infrastructure equipment, such as network backbone switches, several servers, etc. There is no network switch between each room and the server room, making it easy to check network connectivity between each room and the server room after the earthquake. However, this network topology does not provide sufficient defense against disasters.

2.2 Situation immediately after the Earthquake

The university is located in Saitama City in Japan, about 200 km from the epicenter of the earthquake. The university had an intensity of a lower five on the Japanese seismic scale of seven. The server room of the university has several servers and network equipment of information infrastructure fixed in 19-inch racks. Despite the earthquake, the servers and network equipment did not move significantly and suffer serious damage. The server room also terminates about 1800 optical fibers and none of them were damaged.

3. Situation after the Earthquake

This section describes the administration of the university information infrastructure under the influence of the earthquake. The most important influence of this earthquake is the shortage of electricity. The administrators of the information infrastructure planned to use Data Center and Virtual Private Server to deal with the shortage of electricity.

This earthquake damaged several electric power plants, notably two nuclear power plants of Tokyo Electric Power Company (TEPCO) in Fukushima Prefecture and the supply of electricity was weakened. This fact influenced ongoing operations of the information infrastructure because the Government of Japan announced a rolling power outage. In order to execute this rolling power outage, the area of TEPCO was divided in four groups and the power outage was executed in each area in a different time. Table.1 is a timetable of rolling blackouts of Saitama University. This rolling blackout continued for a week and the technical staff of the information infrastructure of the university had to cope with this rolling blackout. Fortunately, the university could rent an electric generator (Figure.2 left). However it was arguable that the university used this electric generator because electric generators with fuel are less necessary in the university than in the Tohoku region, which is near epicenter of the earthquake. The university decided to use the electric generator because it was very difficult to move the generator with fuel and to

transfer the right of renting the generator to Tohoku region. This generator made it possible to operate the campus network and servers for several hours of rolling blackouts.

3.1 Operation for rolling power outage

The university has a facility (Figure.2 right) to connect a temporary electric generator used in the legal inspection of electric equipment. In the legal inspection, electric power supply is stopped in the university and the temporary emergency power supply enables the university to operate the campus network and servers at requisite minimum. When the blackout of the legal inspection of electric equipment starts, the technical staff has to perform operations such as starting a temporary emergency power supply, changing a power supply switch and stopping several servers and network equipment. When the blackout finishes, the technical staff has to perform the operations in reverse order. After these operations, the technical staff has to check all servers and network equipment. The operations related with blackout are heavy work because of the following reasons; in the operation related with blackout, the administrators have to check whether several servers and network equipment stop and start safely. If one of them cannot stop or start safely, the administrators have to check its availability and recover it. If this recovery takes much time, from the viewpoint of users the down time of services becomes long because the down time includes blackout time and recovery time. This fact imposes mental burden on the administrators. Moreover, turning on and off of servers and network equipment is likely to bring breakdown.

During a rolling blackout, the technical staff is in charge of operations from beginning to end. It is necessary to plan the schedule of the technical staff accordingly because there are only three technical staff members and some blackouts are planned outside of working hours (Table.1). If the rolling blackout continues for a long duration, there would be several problems including management and health administration of the technical staff, transportation of the staff from and to the university, and securing fuel for the temporary power supply. Table.1 shows that on March 16th, the rolling blackout started at 6:20 a.m., this was challenging for some of staff members as there is no public transportation to the university at that time.

Figure. 2 Temporary Power Generator and Changing Switch

3.2 Influence of rolling power outage

The rolling blackouts are bad for the servers and network equipment because frequent turning on and off of the server and network equipment can be the cause of failures of the server or network equipment. During this rolling blackout, we had several problems with hardware: on 22nd March there was a trouble with two servers and three uninterruptible power supplies (UPS) because the frequency of the electric power of temporary electric power supply had some inconsistency with the frequency of servers and because surge electricity occurred in switching between usual electric power and temporary electric

Day	14 Mon	15 Tue	16 Wed	17 Thu	18 Fri	19 Sat	20 Sun	21 Mon	22 Tue	23 Wed
0:00										
6:00		9:20 ~ 12:30	6:20 ~ 10:00 ※							
12:00	13:50 ~ 17:30				15:20 ~ 18:40	Wait	Wait	Wait		15:50 ~ 18:45
18:00				18:50 ~ 21:45					18:20 ~ 21:00	

Table. 1 Rolling Blackouts in Saitama University on March 2011

power. Moreover, the batteries of UPSs were old and some of UPSs could not provide enough electric power to keep the servers running for the duration of switching electric power supplies. On March 23rd the university experienced the breakdown of a Layer 3 network switch because frequent powering on and off the network switch caused software and hardware troubles. Because of this trouble, some network segments of the campus network were unavailable and unreachable for about three days. This unavailability of the network adversely influenced university services and researches.

3.3 Usage of Data Center and VPS

One week after the rolling blackout started, the supply of power generator fuel had been stopped. Because of the troubles described in the previous section, the administrators of the information infrastructure of the university judged that it would be difficult to keep the availability of the information infrastructure and planned to use a data center and relocate the important servers(important or with sensitive data) to a data center. Before the relocation, the president of the university approved the usage of data center.

In early March 2011, before the earthquake, some staff of the Information Technology Center of the university visited a data center and learned how to use a data center in detail. Visiting the data center made it easy to relocate the servers to the data center and to operate the servers in data center. The administrators decided on the following policy of using data center:

· The data center must be easy to access from the university,

· the data center should provide electric power to the servers even if there are some problems regarding power supply,

· the data center must have sufficient security,

· the data center must have sufficient earthquake resistance? and,

· the cost of the data center must be proportionate.

Based on this policy, the administrators took the following two approaches: 1.) using a data center and 2.) using a virtual private server. All servers for e-mail, mailing list, authentication, DNS and Web services were located in the university. The first plan (using a data center) was to move all servers to the data center, but there were too many servers to move. Therefore, the administrators decided to use a virtual private server (VPS) to move web services. The mail services of the university use hardware equipment for spam mail filter, and it is difficult to move mail services to VPS. Thus, the administrators decided to move mail services to the data center and web services to VPS. The web servers were not relocated to the data center to mitigate the risk of installing too many servers at the same place or near the university.

Authentication servers were also moved to data center because mail services require authentication servers. DNS servers for the university name domains are necessary to provide mail services and web services; a new DNS server for the university zone is created on a VPS to host mail and web services.

3.3.1 Usage of data center

The administrators found a data center within a 20-minute drive from the university. They decided to use this data center and to relocate important servers to the data center. Visiting the data center before the earthquake enabled the team to use the data center within two weeks. Moreover one of the technical staff had the experience of constructing IT systems in data centers. This experience also enabled the university to relocate the servers to the data center smoothly. The bandwidth of the data center is 100Mbps without band warranty. The administrators would like to use network with band warranty. However, the administrators use this data center because they would like to relocate servers to date centers as soon as possible and because it would take much time to search another data center with a good network quality. The servers related with the following servers and systems were relocated to the data center:

1. Mail System

2. Mailing List Server

3. Authentication Server

4. DNS Hosting Server

5. Mail Hosting Server

3.3.2 Usage of Virtual Private Server

Web servers are important because they can give information during an earthquake. Continuing web service is an important issue in rolling blackouts. The administrators decided to use Virtual Private Server (VPS), provided by Sakura Internet Corporation [2]. Sakura Internet Corporation supports hardware maintenance of VPS, which does not have to be near the university. VPS could be used a week after the application of VPS. This VPS is used as DNS server of the university domain name. Moreover, this VPS works as the secondary mail spool server for mail redundancy. The VPS used by the university has high volume disk space and several servers are virtualized there. The following systems were relocated to the VPS:

1. Secondary Mail Spool Server

2. DNS Server (slave server)

3. University Web Server

4. Web Hosting Server

3.4 Effectiveness of Data Center and VPS

Using the data center and VPS obtains stable bust costly service of information infrastructure. It costs about 3,000,000 yen per a year to use data center and it costs about 360,000 yen per a year to use VPS. These costs were unnecessary before relocation of the servers, but using the data center saved about 2,000,000 yen of electricity per year. As a result, it costs about 1,360,000 yen per a year to use a data center and VPS. The saved electricity price was unexpected and demonstrates that servers occupy large electricity. Using the data center and VPS omits operations for power outages and maintains stable web services and e-mail services. Before using data center, the administrators wondered if the network quality of the Internet access from the data center was enough, but there has been not trouble with the network quality. Moreover, the electricity rate will be high. From these facts, using a data center has proved to be good choice.

3.5 Importance of Communication in Disasters

After the earthquake, it was important to communicate among faculty, staff and students of the university. Transportation trouble that was caused by electricity outage and fuel shortage made it difficult for faculty and staff of the university to go to the university. Thus, communication among faculty and staff of the university was important for university routine works. Confirmation of the safety of students was also important, but web services of the university were unstable and there was no preparation for confirmation of the safety of students. As a result, the university sent an e-mail to all students to confirmation of the safety. Fortunately, no students sustained large damage from the earthquake, but it was difficult to confirm the safety only by e-mail.

In disasters, information exchange and gathering is important and communication among staff of universities is also important. Information technology development provides many methods of communication, but to use them efficiently requires the good way of using communication methods. This paper calls this good way "Communication flow". The way of communication method is necessary to prepare for disaster and should be well-established.

4. Lessons Learned from the Earthquake

The administrators of information infrastructure of Saitama University learned several lessons from the earthquake. This section discusses these lessons.

4.1 Balance between Centralization and Distribution

In Saitama University, many servers and network equipment are centralized; the network topology enables this centralization. Centralization makes it easy to administrate or maintain the servers and network equipment. Moreover, the administrators of the university information infrastructure recommended using web hosting service or mail hosting service to the administrators of the servers of departments or laboratories in the university. These administrators are not experts of IT and some of them do not have ability enough to operate servers securely. Decreasing servers can decrease the administrators, and therefore using web hosting service and mail hosting service can decrease the cost of administration of servers in the university. The centralization and these hosting services shorten the total downtime of all the servers in the university. However, there are several problems and one of them is as follows; each room in the university is connected to the Layer 3 network switches of the campus network backbone and these network switches are classified by the rooms connected to the switches but not by the role of the switches. Thus, it is difficult to classify important Layer 3 network switches.

Another problem is power supply of media converters. Each room is connected to the backbone network switches by media converters, which use electric power. Even if several servers and network equipment work in a blackout by temporary power supply, the users cannot use the campus network because the media converters cannot obtain electric power.

4.2 Temporary Power Supply Equipment

Following an earthquake, the university could rent temporary power supply equipment, but this earthquake showed clearly that the information infrastructure of the university had to been stopped without temporary power supply. The administrators realized that Constant-Voltage Constant-Frequency system and temporary power supply whose fuel can be easy to obtain are

very important. Moreover, wireless LAN access points cannot be used in blackout because access points need electric power. Power over Ethernet (PoE) should be installed to keep connectivity of the Internet from the personal computer and so on. Usual temporary power supplies use oil as fuel, but earthquakes may make it difficult to obtain fuel. After the earthquake, large capacity batteries were provided from several companies. These kinds of batteries can be a candidate of temporary power supply because the batteries do not need transportation of fuel.

4.3 Communication Flow

After the earthquake, communication among university members was important, but there was no communication flow and information announcement for faculty, staff and students of the university. Phone based communication flow for faculty and staff of the university had been established, but it is difficult to use phone at the time of earthquake. Thus, web based communication flow is necessary. Shizuoka University has already installed a safety confirmation system on a cloud system [3]. After this earthquake, Saitama University also developed and installed the safety confirmation system on a VPS. This system is for faculty and staff of the university. This system will be extended for the students of the university.

4.4 Usage of Data Center and VPS

Use of data center requires new administrations and operations of information infrastructure. One of them is to keep security. The servers in the data center have many user data such as ID, password, etc. These data are transmitted between the data center and the university campus via the Internet, and thus this transmission must keep safety of the user data. In particular the data center has an authentication server to check mail account. The similar authentication servers are in the campus network and data synchronization is necessary. The users in the campus network access the mail server to read mail. Thus, the connection between data center and the campus network should be constructed by VPS.

Another new operation is the data center backup. This usage of the data center was not well-planned and the backup system could not be prepared for the data center. Since the bandwidth of the data center is not so wide, it is possible but difficult to backup the data of the data center to the storage of the campus network.

4.5 DNS Trouble

In changing IP addresses of servers, DNS configuration is an important point. The relocation of the servers to the data center requires a change of IP addresses of the servers. After changing IP addresses, some users cannot access the mail servers because of DNS cache. To prevent such a trouble, there are several techniques of DNS configuration such as shortening Time to Live (TTL) of DNS. However, the relocation of the servers occurred suddenly due to the earthquake, there was no time to prevent troubles of changing IP addresses. Moreover, some local DNS servers (used only in stub network segments in the campus network) hold DNS cache data for a long time and the users cannot access mail until the addresses are resolved. In order to resolve this accessibility trouble, the local DNS servers were rebooted or restarted. This trouble suggests that all DNS servers in the campus network should be restarted when important servers in the campus network change IP addresses.

5. Future Plan

This section discusses a future plan for the university information infrastructure to prepare disaster. The lesson learned from the East Japan Great Earthquake affects the future plan.

5.1 Design of Next Information Infrastructure

Saitama University information infrastructure was replaced in March 2012. The staff of Information Technology Center of the university started discussing the specification of the new information infrastructure at August 2010. When the earthquake happened, the specification was almost completed. However, the earthquake influenced the specification and the specification changed for disaster preparation; the new information infrastructure uses a data center and the specification includes the equipment of a data center. Virtualization technology is used in the new infrastructure more than expected before the earthquake in order to save electric power and prepare against disasters. The new infrastructure also includes electric power measuring equipment in order to save electric power and duplexes much of network equipment in order to prepare against disasters.

5.2 Cooperation among Organizations

There are some attempts of cooperation among universities against disasters. These attempts are to backup data among several organizations and to set backup web servers for each other among several organizations; however it is difficult to backup web servers and e-mail servers for each among several organizations because of difference of the systems of the organizations and because of security. Some of the authors plan to create a backup system for continuity of communication method [4]. This backup system does not backup data, but provides e-mail service and web service in the case that the primary servers stop. This backup system will be designed from the viewpoint of hardware security because the backup site system administrators should not view inside of the backup system.

5.3 Contribution for Areas near the University

After an earthquake, communication method is important not only for the university members but also for members of the community. The university will become an evacuation area for people near the university and for commuters unable to get home. Therefore, the university has to help the people near the university at disasters. From the viewpoint of information infrastructure, we plan to provide university campus network for the people near the university at disasters. Wireless LAN, wired LAN, temporally mail address, PC and so on will be provided to the people, but there are several problems: keeping network security under many users, setting up many kinds of PCs or smart phones of the people to use LANs, traffic control and so on. We are trying to solve these problems.

6. Concluding Remarks

This paper reported the operational experience in Saitama University Information Infrastructure on East Japan Great Earthquake. This operational experience gives the future plan against disasters. We will execute this future plan to prepare for disasters.

7. ACKNOWLEGEMENTS

We wish to express our thanks to the staff of Information Technology in Saitama University and those who read our paper and made helpful suggestions for the paper.

8. REFERENCES

[1] Toshiharu Tanabe, Kohichi Ogawa, Kazuhito Ito, Noriaki Yoshiura, "Administration and Operation of Campus Network based on Fiber to the Laboratory," Internet Technology Workshop (in Japanese) No9, p1-8, 2008

[2] Copyright 1996-2011 SAKURA Internet Inc, "VPS of Sakura," http://vps.sakura.ad.jp/ (in Japanese), accessed Nov. 4. 2011

[3] Takahiro Hasegawa, Haruki Inoue, Naokazu Yamaki, "Development of a low running cost and user friendly safety information system.," Journal for Academic Computing and Networking (in Japanese) No.13, p91-98, 2009

[4] Kohichi Ogawa and Noriaki Yoshiura, "A framework for communication infrastructure against disasters," In the Proceedings of World Telecommunication Congress 2012.

Implementing an Online Registration Process for the IT Short Course Training Program

Kathy Garramone
The University of Montana
IT-Client Support Services
Missoula, MT 59812
406-243-5392
kathy.garramone@umontana.edu

ABSTRACT

Information Technology at The University of Montana provides free technology training to faculty, staff and students through the IT Short Course Training Program. Each semester, courses are offered on a variety of topics including: accessibility, Banner, Moodle, MS Office, general computer maintenance, and web technologies.

Course registration was available through the program website and worked well for both registrants and administrators. However, new technologies prompted us to redesign and update the process.

Beginning in fall 2011 we rolled out a new online registration process. Registrants log in to a Short Course Manager using their NetID, the login credential for UM centrally accessed services and applications. Once in the system, they create a user profile and can register, view, and cancel their current courses. Additionally, transcripts are available for all courses completed.

This new system has been well received by campus. For administrators, system improvements include: online registrant record-keeping, a permanent library of course offerings editable and available for future semesters, more flexible mid-semester course additions and changes, and automated course confirmation and cancellation notices. New features for program instructors include online roster availability and access to instructor policies and procedures necessary for lab preparation and shut-down.

What went well? What still needs improvement? As we move forward with this new system, we will continue to assess its functionality ensuring that the process allows convenient and smooth course registration for University members and efficient, easy management for administrators.

Categories and Subject Descriptors

H.5.2 [Information Interfaces and Presentation (I.7)]: User Interfaces (D.2.2, H.1.2, I.3.6) – *training, help, and documentation; user interface management systems.*

General Terms

Design, Human Factors, Performance, Assessment

Keywords

Registration system, training, course management

1. INTRODUCTION

The University of Montana, located in Missoula, Montana, has a student population of approximately 15,000 and about 900 faculty and 1300 staff.

Information Technology at The University of Montana provides free technology training to faculty, staff and students through the IT Short Course Training Program. Each semester courses are offered on a variety of topics including: accessibility, Banner, Moodle, MS Office, general computer maintenance, and web technologies.

IT Short Course offerings, including details for each course, are available for viewing and registration on the IT website. In the fall of 2011, IT-Client Support Services (CSS) rolled out a new IT Short Course management system. This move was made primarily for two reasons: first, the campus web hosting environment was moving from a Visual Basic .NET environment to a new PHP environment, and secondly, the current system was difficult for the non-technical administrators to manage from the back-end. It functioned well, but most updates and changes were only available through contacting the IT database administrator.

2. THE ORIGINAL SYSTEM

Short course registration through our website began in the late 1990s. The system was created internally and was very successful during its tenure, offering an online tool for both the campus community and the short course administrators.

2.1 How the System Worked

The original short course registration system was created using ASP and morphed into ASP.NET in 2004 with MS Access as the primary data source.

2.2 Features for Users

Registrants viewed course descriptions and registered for courses by clicking on a link that routed them to a registration page where they entered their campus information and selected the specific course(s) they wished to attend. An email process was set up to send a confirmation message to the registrants moments after they registered. A waitlist process was also available when courses became full, providing email notification to registrants when they were placed on a waiting list, and that they would be contacted regarding their status prior to the course date and time.

2.3 Features for Administrators

On the administrative side of the process, the system generated a roster for each course through MS Access and in conjunction with MS Word, the system also created certificates for course attendees. The waitlist process placed registrants from the waitlist to the roster appropriately. This was a manual process managed by the course administrators.

2.4 Other Processes

All other processes were handled manually. Confirmation phone calls were placed to all registrants at least 24 hours in advance of a course. Registrants were required to call a specific short course cancellation phone number to report a cancellation. System cancellations were initiated through the IT training coordinator by accessing the database and changing registration status from an "A" to a "C." Hard copy "office" rosters were generated to record registration information. Course evaluation forms created in MS Excel were printed and provided to instructors prior to their courses. Instructors distributed the evaluation forms to attendees at course conclusions, collected them, reviewed them, and then returned them to the training program office.

3. DESIGNING A NEW SYSTEM

During summer 2011, CSS worked closely with an IT web programmer to plan, create, and implement a new management system for the training program, to be rolled out in conjunction with a new IT website rollout during fall 2011. This was also our opportunity to revise and add new content to our IT training web pages including: a program overview, policies and procedures, course catalog, registration and registration help, resources, a feedback button, and other training opportunities outside of IT.

An evaluation of the current system and a brainstorming session of new features resulted in an ambitious but attainable project.

3.1 Registrant Options

We wanted to retain some features of the original online process and add to that base. UM is moving towards single sign-on with a Central Authentication Service (CAS) to University services and applications. We discussed the feasibility of using the service for our online training program registration process. The original registration process based identity on email addresses. Occasionally some registrants would have two or more identities because they would register for courses using different email addresses.

As with the current system, we wanted the registrant to set up a profile including: name, affiliation, email, phone, department, and an index code. The purpose of providing an index code was to charge penalty fees to those who register for short courses but fail to attend.

Additionally we wanted more than a registration process; we wanted a system allowing campus members the ability to self-manage their registrations. We wanted them to be able to register for courses, unregister from courses, view current course registrations, and view courses completed, always having access to their course history.

3.2 Administrative Options for Registration Management

For the administrators, which included the training coordinator and student assistant, we wanted online registration record-keeping to be able to quickly view registrant course history, track course enrollments, track communication with registrants, and communicate via email to all course attendees.

We wanted an online process for tracking registration status. With the original system, we would contact all registrants to verify attendance prior to a course and record the information on paper. We still needed to track responses and changes and add additional notes.

It was also important to have the option of updating past courses with attendance information, since there were occasions when registrants were absent from a course or they attended a course without registering.

3.3 Administrative Options for Course Management

The administrators wanted to add brand new courses or use old course data as templates for new courses. This feature was available in the original system, but the process needed simplification. In addition, we wanted the ability to edit a current course by adding a new section or updating instructor information, dates, times, and locations.

Courses are sub-categorized under major categories. We needed the ability to edit, update and add new categories. Sometimes a course would be added in the middle of a semester and the course did not fall under any of the current categories.

3.4 Instructor Capabilities

The original system allowed instructors to view their current courses and rosters. We needed this feature built into the new system. We also wanted an email function that provided instructors the ability to email their registrants if they so desired.

IT Short Course instructor policies and procedures for the original system were sent via email to all instructors at the beginning of each semester. In addition, instructors attended a hands-on lab overview prior to their first course. We have learned that one email at the beginning of a semester and one brief lab overview are not adequate training. Unintentionally, some instructors forget the policies and procedures and lab protocol, which cause problems such as failure to return materials to the administrators and failure to shut down the lab completely. This information needs to be placed in an accessible web location for review at any time, especially prior to teaching a course and includes the user registration process, roster access, course evaluations, IT training lab setup and close down, class cancellations, roster handling, and student assistant responsibilities.

We also desired an automatic process for notifying instructors once they have been added as an instructor of a course.

3.5 Evaluation Process

Up until now, paper evaluations were distributed to course attendees at the end of each course by the instructor. We decided it was time to move this process online, so we explored available online options.

4. THE IMPLEMENTATON

The rollout of the new system during fall semester 2011 went much better than we anticipated, even with a larger than normal number of course offerings resulting in more registrants than usual for a semester. Changes and additions to the system were minor.

4.1 What Went Well

For registrants, the process of registering for courses begins with logging into CAS with their NetID. Once logged in, they select the IT Short Course Training Program icon from a list of NetID-based services. They are routed to a Profile page where they enter contact and departmental information, and then the course listing page displays on the next screen for course viewing and registration. For each course registered, an auto-generated email confirmation sends to the email address registrants entered in their profiles. Registrants also see an online course confirmation immediately upon registering. We expected questions from registrants, mostly because the process was new. However, we were pleased when very few registrants actually contacted us with questions about this process.

Two days prior to a course, short course administrators contact all course registrants to confirm attendance. This new online process allows administrators to record online when they contact registrants, how they contact registrants (phone, voice mail, or email), and whether or not the registrants will be attending the course. At that point, if registrants indicate that they cannot attend the course, they are asked to login to the system and remove themselves from the roster. With minimal assistance, registrants are able to perform the cancellation steps. Short course administrators have the ability to remove registrants, but registrants are encouraged to self-cancel to become familiar with this process.

In the event that a course is full, a wait list process is in place and functions similarly to the process in the original system. Confirmation emails are sent to the registrants indicating that they are on a waiting list and that they will be contacted prior to the course with their registration status. This is still a manual process. However, since registrants can self-cancel from courses, sometimes waitlisted registrants automatically move to registrant status when this happens, which may occur many days before a scheduled course date. This is a positive change. The more notice we can provide about registration status changes, the more likely the registrant will be able to attend the course.

The process of automatically adding an instructor to a course is now in place. If there are any questions about whether a course has been added to the schedule, instructors can now check their email for messages from IT short courses confirming they are on the training schedule and their course is available for registration.

As with the original system, instructors have the ability to view their rosters. Once logged in to the system, they click on an "Instructor" link which lists the course(s) and includes links to view rosters for each. A new feature provides the ability to ability to email course registrants.

The "Instructor" link also includes a statement at the top of the web page advising them to read IT short course instructor policies and procedures prior to teaching their first course. This statement links to an instructor policies and procedures web page.

4.2 What Needs Improvement

The following list of items has recently been improved and completed or is still pending with the goal of completion prior to the start of fall 2012.

4.2.1 Non-registered Course Attendees

An issue we discovered early on was that if university members arrived at short courses without prior registration, we had no way of registering them after the course was completed. We approached our programmer about this issue and this capability is now available. We manually enter walk-in attendees into the completed course roster by NetID and they are added as registrants. If they have not previously created profiles in the system, no other information about them is available. In these circumstances, we contact these specific attendees and ask them to log in to the system and complete their profile.

4.2.2 Accessibility Indicator

The original system provided a check box for registrants to indicate a disability or special need requiring additional or different lab accommodations. We neglected to incorporate this indicator in the new system. It is a priority will be added prior to fall 2012.

4.2.3 NetID Unavailable

Occasionally situations arise when a registrant does not have a NetID, either because they are not yet in the University's Banner system or they are located at a different UM campus. We cannot enter them in the system manually at this time. This is an issue that has yet to be resolved.

4.2.4 New Section Numbering

The new system easily allows the addition of new courses and course sections throughout the semester. However, the numbering sequence doesn't renumber sections. For example, if a new section is added in April, but a May section is already on the schedule, the April section is assigned a section number that is out of date sequence. Currently correcting this issue is a manual process by our programmer. This issue is on this list to be corrected prior to fall 2012.

4.2.5 Waitlist Process

The waitlist process is improved in that waitlisted registrants are automatically moved to registrant status when registrants self-cancel from courses. However, waitlisted individuals are not automatically notified via email when their status changes. We notify them as soon as we are able to do so, but we still need to improve the timeliness of notification.

4.2.6 Course Evaluation Process

At UM a survey tool called Select Survey is available for survey creation, distribution, and management. This tool also works well as a feedback form and an evaluation form. We chose Select Survey for our short course evaluation process. We created a short course evaluation web page listing all courses. For each course, a survey is created and is appropriately linked to the course name. At the end of each course, the instructor guides the attendees to a desktop shortcut that directs them to the evaluation web page. The attendees select the correct course, which routes them to the online evaluation form. They complete the evaluation form, and once finished, the data is saved to a database. Next, a summary of the evaluation data is forwarded to the course instructor. This last step is a manual process.

If an instructor neglects to ask their course attendees to complete the online course evaluation form during their course, the administrators email a course evaluation link to the course attendees. We've discovered that the response rate is very poor in this type of circumstance.

The current process of using Select Survey as the course evaluation tool works okay, but is not ideal. The process is partially manual in that the instructor has to invite the attendees to complete the online evaluation form and the administrator has to provide course evaluation summaries to the instructor. If the instructors and the administrators fail to complete these tasks, evaluations won't be completed in a timely manner. It's critical to seek evaluation input from course attendees as quickly as possible or they will not provide it. Also, evaluation data from completed courses must be manually removed from the survey tool for newly offered courses or evaluation data will be inaccurate. We are exploring other evaluation tool possibilities to better meet our needs.

4.3 What Our Users Tell Us

We completed a self-assessment process but we also felt we needed campus input. Following are results of a survey distributed to university members who completed training through our IT Short Course Training Program and used the course management system to register for and manage their course enrollments. The registrant survey was distributed to 633 registrants and the instructor survey was distributed to 24 instructors.

4.3.1 Registrant survey results

We received 106 responses to the registrant survey. Respondents included staff (90%), faculty (6%) and students (4%). Overall satisfaction with the course management system results are as follows: very satisfied – 56%, satisfied – 43%, neutral – 1%.

We asked the respondents to indicate which short course manager tools they use. Most use the system for course registration as indicated in the chart below:

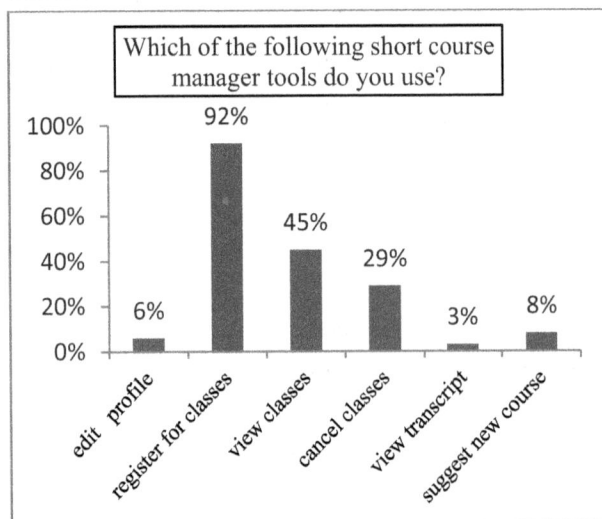

We asked one open-ended question: Do you have any additional comments or suggestions for improving the IT Short Course Training Program online registration and course management process? 35 respondents provided positive and helpful feedback. Some comments include:

- "I appreciate how easy the system is to use and I like the reminders."
- "I really think the registration process is convenient, and I also like being able to see all the courses and sections offered at once."
- "Cancelling online is convenient, as sometimes unforeseen things come up in my schedule."
- "I did not notice the *Suggest a new course* link until completing this survey. Perhaps that link could be more visible."
- "The confirmation process still leaves a little to be desired. I always put it right on my calendar, and am sometimes called more than once to confirm."

Several respondents commented that integration with their Outlook calendars would be helpful.

4.3.2 Instructor survey results

We received 10 instructor survey responses. Overall satisfaction with the course management system from an instructor point of view results are as follows: very satisfied – 33%, satisfied – 67%. We asked instructors to indicate which short course manager tools they use. All 10 respondents indicated that they use the system for viewing their rosters; 5 respondents use the system to view instructor policies and procedures; and one respondent uses the email feature to email their course registrants.

As with the registrant survey, we asked instructors one open-ended question: Do you have comments or suggestions for improving the IT Short Course Training Program online process from an instructor perspective? Some comments include:

- "It was extremely useful. I'd have no hesitation about using it again next fall."
- "I appreciate the advertisement and coordination efforts provided by the training program."
- "I think this works very well."
- "The less I have to do to administer the class, the better."
- "Printing the rosters could be made easier."
- "It would be nice to receive some feedback so sessions can be improved (instructor did not receive evaluation feedback)."

4.3.3 Addressing the comments

The feedback we received confirmed our initial thoughts that the system works well and is easy to navigate. Areas of improvement from the registrant perspective will be addressed in the next version of the system, including Outlook calendar integration, relocating information so it is easier to find, and improving the confirmation process to avoid duplication.

Instructor improvements include reviewing the roster printing process and exploring other printing options for the instructors. The evaluation process needs to be streamlined and automated to avoid human error.

5. ADDITIONAL FEATURES

We are pleased with the outcome of the rollout of our new IT Short Course Training Program management system. We continue to discuss new processes to improve and fine tune the system.

5.1.1 Documentation

Our short course system is an in-house system. We are concerned about development and management. What if our developer leaves his position? What if our management team is unavailable when questions arise? What will Client Support Services do then? One of our goals for the summer is to document all processes both for back-end programming and for front-end administration and management.

5.1.2 Outlook Calendar

In the development stage we discussed the feasibility of adding a calendar function that would add course information to a registrant's Outlook calendar upon registration. We still desire this function, as do our survey respondents, and we will continue to explore the possibility.

5.1.3 University Calendar

The University uses a calendaring system for placement of items on the UM home page events calendar and departmental-specific calendars. IT has a departmental calendar on the UM home page which includes IT-specific events, training, and meetings. Currently we are duplicating our efforts with training course information. We must manually enter all courses into the calendaring system each semester. We are exploring ways of pulling the information from our training management system into the calendaring system.

5.1.4 Departmental Interest

If a department is interested in offering campus technical training through our program, our current procedure requires the department to contact the IT training coordinator to discuss their training needs and obtain policy and procedure information about our program. This information is not available online but we plan to make it available very soon securely on our website.

6. THE FUTURE

When we decided to implement a new IT Short Course Training Program web presence and management system, we embarked on a journey. We are delighted with the progress that has been made. Our programmer is very open-minded and knowledgeable, which helped us to explore options we didn't know were possible. We've shared a "thinking outside the box" attitude. As the need for technology training at The University of Montana continues, we will work towards expanding and improving our IT Short Course Training Program and management system.

7. ACKNOWLEDGEMENTS

Special thanks to Nick Shontz, IT-Web Technology Services, for his invaluable programming and web design experience that led to the development and implementation of the IT Short Course Training Program management system. I'd like to thank my student assistant, Stephanie Lubrecht, for her input on this project from start to finish. She added valuable feedback and insight throughout the process, critical to the success of the system. In addition, I thank Tom Battaglia, Interim CIO, IT-Technology Support Services, and Lorrie DeYott, Manager, IT-Client Support Services, for their encouragement of this joint project effort.

Author Index

www.ingramcontent.com/pod-product-compliance
Lightning Source LLC
Chambersburg PA
CBHW061359210326
41598CB00035B/6038